Blackstone's

Police Operational Handbook

Blackstone's

Police Operational Handbook 2025

Police National Legal Database

Editor: Dr Mark Hartley

Consultant Editor: Paul Ozin KC

OXFORD
UNIVERSITY PRESS

OXFORD
UNIVERSITY PRESS

Great Clarendon Street, Oxford, OX2 6DP,
United Kingdom

Oxford University Press is a department of the University of Oxford. It furthers the University's objective of excellence in research, scholarship, and education by publishing worldwide. Oxford is a registered trade mark of Oxford University Press in the UK and in certain other countries

First Edition published in 2006
Eighteenth Edition published in 2024

Published in the United States of America by Oxford University Press
198 Madison Avenue, New York, NY 10016, United States of America

British Library Cataloguing in Publication Data
Data available

Library of Congress Control Number: 2024945311

ISBN 978–0–19–892956–7

DOI: 10.1093/law/9780198929567.001.0001

Printed in the UK by
Bell & Bain Ltd., Glasgow

FSC www.fsc.org MIX Paper | Supporting responsible forestry FSC® C007785

Foreword

In 2019, I had the honour of being asked to write a Foreword for the 2020 edition of this publication. Since that time, I have been appointed as its Consulting Editor and I have, in that capacity, made my own modest contribution to parts of subsequent editions.

What I said in 2019 and the subsequent editions of this book seems to me still to be apposite, although I am no longer the entirely impartial onlooker that I then was. So, without much modification, I repeat what I said then.

The Police Operational Handbook is now into its eighteenth annual edition. In that time, it has established itself as the pre-eminent pocket publication for police officers on the beat. In the era of the smartphone, that has involved fitting into the pocket in both hard and electronic form. Either way, it maintains a tried and trusted formula. It is broken up into sections with supplemental appendices that tell the busy police professional the essentials about a generous range of policing situations that they will, or might, encounter. The strength of the book is that it tells the reader just enough to understand the important essentials of the topic under discussion without burdening them with unnecessary detail; and it does so in a format that is easy to follow, highlighting with shading and icons the key sub-topics and summarising the key considerations in bullet points. That way, a reader familiar with its style can find what they want in an instant.

Of course, it is essential in a publication of this sort that the content is well-researched, up-to-date, and correct. That task becomes more exacting each year as the pace of change becomes ever faster. Dr Mark Hartley, the editor responsible for the past eight editions, is to be commended for his work, as are the legal advisers at the PNLD. It is no small achievement to digest and condense the relevant legislation, case law, and practical considerations into a usable, reliable, and user-friendly text; but in this small book he manages to do just that. Practitioners and police professionals alike know that at any one time there are a few priceless reference sources that will be sure to give a mercifully clear and quick answer to the questions that come up about the things that one does not know and the things that one forgets. The new edition of this book maintains its place in that select league. I am sure that it will continue to enjoy the well-deserved success of its predecessors.

Paul Ozin KC
June 2024

Preface

This is the eighteenth edition of the *Blackstone's Police Operational Handbook*, which has been specifically designed as a useful 'tool kit' to meet the needs of operational police officers, community support officers, community support volunteers, special constables, and other practitioners who have to interpret and apply the criminal law within our communities.

Formulated and written by qualified staff from the Police National Legal Database (PNLD) (<http://www.pnld.co.uk>), the book covers a wide range of offences, and clearly explains and interprets the relevant legislation. It follows the style of the PNLD database by providing the wording of the offences with database references, points to prove, meanings, explanatory notes, relevant cases, and practical considerations. To assist further, the law/guidance notes are all presented in a 'bullet point', easy-to-understand format; thus, at a glance, a quick and informed decision can be made in a host of everyday policing situations.

Although every effort has been made to include as many 'commonly dealt with offences' as possible, the size of the handbook dictates how many offences can be included. However, the number and variety of offences given within the areas of crime and road traffic, including a sample of PACE powers and procedures, and useful appendices, provides sufficient information for most eventualities.

Officers are required to know what offences are indictable or either way for their search or arrest powers—the mode of trial icons (within each offence) provided in the book give this important information.

This edition of the handbook replaces the previous edition of 2024 and includes several updates regarding existing, new, or amended legislation and guidelines. These include, but are not limited to, revised provisions in PACE Codes of Practice; updates to s 1 of PACE; Public Order Act 2023 relating to offences of obstruction etc of major transport works, interference with the use or operation of key national infrastructure and new powers to stop and search without suspicion for offences under the Act, and for wilful obstruction under s 137 of the Highways Act 1980 and intentionally or recklessly causing public nuisance under s 78 of the Police, Crime, Sentencing and Courts Act 2022; s 1 of the Malicious Communications Act 1988; new offences under the Online Safety Act 2023; changes to s 127 of the Communications Act 2003 for offences of sending a false communication with intent to cause harm, sending a communication threatening death or serious harm, sending or showing flashing images electronically, and the offence of encouraging or assisting serious self-harm; the Criminal Justice and Courts Act 2015; s 66A of the Sexual Offences Act 2003 for the offence of sending etc a photograph or film of genitals and s 66B for sharing or threatening to share an intimate photograph or film; updates to the common law offence of outraging public decency; and s 31 of the Domestic Abuse Act 2021 which now allows the county court to issue a domestic violence protection order against an individual involved in any relevant proceedings, and updates to s 1 of the Dangerous Dogs Act 1991 and the classification of XL Bully dogs. Additionally, several recent cases have been added throughout the handbook providing informative court judgments on the practical application and interpretation of the law.

Whilst every care has been taken to ensure that the contents of this handbook are accurate, neither the publisher nor the authors can accept any responsibility for any action taken, or not taken, based on the information contained within this handbook.

Please email <police@oup.com> with any comments or queries.

Dr Mark Hartley, Editor
July 2024

Acknowledgements

The Police National Legal Database (PNLD) (<http://www.pnld.co.uk>) is well known by all police forces in England and Wales, the Crown Prosecution Service, and other recognised organisations from within the criminal justice system.

Special thanks are extended to all the PNLD legal advisers and other staff who, over the years, have contributed to the production of the *Blackstone's Police Operational Handbook*.

Contents

Table of Cases xxv
Table of Legislation xxxv
Table of Conventions lvii
List of Abbreviations lix
Icons List lxiii

1 Introduction 1
1.1 Powers of Arrest 1
1.1.1 Arrest without warrant: constables 1
1.1.2 Information to be given on arrest 4
1.1.3 Arrest procedures 8
1.1.4 Release a person prior to arrival at a police station 10
1.1.5 Arrest without warrant: other persons 12
1.2 Lawful Authorities—Use of Force 15
1.3 Stop and Search Powers 22
1.3.1 Stop and search 22
1.3.2 Search and detain 22
1.3.3 Conduct of a search 27
1.3.4 Terrorism stop and search powers 28
1.3.5 Written records of stop and search 29
1.4 Entry, Search, and Seizure Powers 32
1.4.1 Search upon arrest 32
1.4.2 Power of entry to arrest, save life, or prevent damage 34
1.4.3 Searching of premises after arrest 37
1.4.4 Powers of seizure from premises 39
1.5 Enter and Search Warrants 43
1.5.1 Premises search warrant 43
1.5.2 Application procedures for a search warrant 46
1.5.3 Execution of search warrants 48
1.5.4 Access to excluded and special procedure material 50

2 Assaults and Violence 53
2.1 Assault (Common/Actual Bodily Harm) 53
2.1.1 Common assault—battery 53

2.1.2	Assault occasioning actual bodily harm (AOABH)/Defences to assaults	56
2.1.3	Maliciously administering poison, etc, with intent	60
2.2	**Assault/Resist/Impersonate and Obstruct—Police or Designated/Accredited Person or Emergency Workers**	**63**
2.2.1	Assault with intent to resist or prevent lawful arrest	63
2.2.2	Assault constable in execution of duty	65
2.2.3	Resist/obstruct constable in execution of duty	67
2.2.4	Impersonate constable or wear/possess article of police uniform	68
2.2.5	Assault/resist/obstruct designated or accredited person in execution of duty	70
2.2.6	Assaults on emergency workers	72
2.2.7	Obstruct/hinder emergency workers and persons assisting	75
2.3	**Wounding/Grievous Bodily Harm**	**79**
2.3.1	Wounding or inflicting grievous bodily harm	79
2.3.2	Wounding or grievous bodily harm—with intent	82
2.3.3	Use gunpowder and corrosive substances with intent to cause grievous bodily harm	86
2.3.4	Non-fatal strangulation and non-fatal suffocation	87
2.4	**Child Cruelty and Taking a Child into Police Protection**	**91**
2.4.1	Child cruelty	91
2.4.2	Taking a child at risk into police protection	93
2.5	**Threats to Kill**	**97**
2.6	**False Imprisonment, Kidnapping, and Child Abduction**	**100**
2.6.1	False imprisonment	100
2.6.2	Kidnapping	102
2.6.3	Child abduction	103
2.7	**Sudden and Unexplained Deaths**	**109**
2.7.1	Murder	109
2.7.2	Manslaughter	113
2.7.3	Corporate manslaughter	116
2.7.4	Death or serious physical harm to a child/vulnerable adult	118
2.7.5	Overlaying/suffocation of infant under 3	120
2.7.6	Infanticide/child destruction/concealment of birth	122
2.8	**Domestic Abuse**	**125**

3	**Crime: Dishonesty**	**130**
3.1	**Theft**	**130**
3.1.1	Theft (general)/theft of scrap metal	130
3.1.2	Removal of articles from places open to the public	137
3.2	**Robbery**	**140**
3.2.1	Robbery	140
3.2.2	Blackmail	142
3.3	**Burglary/Aggravated Burglary**	**145**
3.3.1	Burglary	145
3.3.2	Aggravated burglary	147
3.4	**Dishonestly Abstracting Electricity**	**150**
3.5	**Handling Stolen Goods**	**152**
3.6	**Going Equipped**	**156**
3.7	**Making off without Payment**	**158**
3.8	**Fraud Offences**	**160**
3.8.1	Fraud offence	160
3.8.2	Meaning of fraud by false representation	162
3.8.3	Meaning of fraud by failing to disclose information	163
3.8.4	Meaning of fraud by abuse of position	164
3.8.5	Admissible evidence	165
3.8.6	Possess or control article for use in fraud	167
3.8.7	Making or supplying article for use in fraud	169
3.9	**Obtaining Services Dishonestly**	**171**
4	**Crime: General**	**173**
4.1	**Criminal Attempts/Meaning of Intent/ Meaning of Aid, Abet, Counsel, and Procure/ Encourage or Assist Crime**	**173**
4.1.1	Criminal attempts	173
4.1.2	Meaning of intent	175
4.1.3	Meaning of aid, abet, counsel, and procure	177
4.1.4	Encourage, assist, or accessory to commit crime	178
4.2	**Vehicle Interference and Tampering with a Motor Vehicle**	**182**
4.2.1	Vehicle interference	182
4.2.2	Tampering with motor vehicles	183
4.3	**Taking a Conveyance without Owner's Consent**	**185**
4.3.1	Taking a conveyance without owner's consent	185

4.3.2	Aggravated vehicle-taking	188
4.3.3	Take pedal cycle without owner's consent	191
4.4	**Criminal Damage**	**193**
4.5	**Damage with Intent to Endanger Life and Arson**	**198**
4.5.1	Damage with intent to endanger life	198
4.5.2	Arson	200
4.6	**Threats to Destroy or Damage Property**	**203**
4.7	**Custody/Control of Articles with Intent to Damage and Sale of Paint Aerosols to Persons under 16**	**206**
4.7.1	Custody/control of articles with intent to damage	206
4.7.2	Sale of aerosol paints to children	208
4.8	**Intimidation of a Witness/Juror and Perverting the Course of Justice**	**210**
4.8.1	Intimidation of a witness/juror	210
4.8.2	Perverting the course of justice	214
4.9	**Slavery and Human Trafficking**	**217**
4.9.1	The Modern Slavery Act 2015	217
4.9.2	Slavery, servitude, and forced or compulsory labour	218
4.9.3	Human trafficking	219
4.9.4	Slavery and trafficking prevention orders on sentencing	222
4.9.5	Defence for victims of slavery or trafficking	223
4.9.6	Duty to notify the Home Office of suspected victims of slavery or human trafficking	225
4.10	**Ill-treatment or Neglect by a Care Worker**	**227**
4.11	**Forced Marriages**	**230**
4.11.1	Forced marriage offences	230
4.11.2	Forced marriage: protection orders	232
4.12	**Computer Misuse**	**235**
4.12.1	Unauthorised access to computer material	235
4.12.2	Unauthorised access with intent to commit further offence	236
5	**Controlled Drugs**	**239**
5.1	**Produce/Supply a Controlled Drug and Supply of Articles**	**239**
5.1.1	Produce/supply a controlled drug	239
5.1.2	Supply articles to administer or prepare drugs/drug-cutting agents	245

5.2	**Possession of/with Intent to Supply a Controlled Drug**	**248**
5.2.1	Possessing a controlled drug	248
5.2.2	Possession with intent to supply	252
5.3	**Cultivate Cannabis, Possess Khat, and Psychoactive Substances**	**254**
5.3.1	Cultivate cannabis	254
5.3.2	Possess khat	256
5.3.3	Psychoactive substances	257
5.3.4	Producing a psychoactive substance	257
5.3.5	Supply of a psychoactive substance and offering to supply a psychoactive substance	258
5.3.6	Possession with intent to supply psychoactive substances	260
5.4	**Search Powers for Controlled Drugs/Permit Use of Controlled Drugs on Premises**	**263**
5.4.1	Power to search, detain, and seize drugs	263
5.4.2	Occupier/manager permits drug use on premises	266
5.5	**Proceeds of Crime**	**270**
6	**Sexual Offences and Assaults**	**275**
6.1	**Rape Offences**	**275**
6.1.1	Rape	275
6.1.2	Rape of a child under 13	281
6.2	**Sexual Assault by Penetration**	**284**
6.2.1	Assault by penetration of a person aged 13 or over	284
6.2.2	Assault by penetration of a child under 13	287
6.3	**Sexual Assault by Touching**	**289**
6.3.1	Sexual assault by touching a person aged 13 or over	289
6.3.2	Sexual assault by touching a child under 13	291
6.4	**Sexual Activity with a Child**	**294**
6.5	**Child Sexual Exploitation Offences**	**297**
6.5.1	Cause/incite child under 16 to engage in sexual activity	297
6.5.2	Paying for sexual services of a child	300
6.5.3	Cause/incite child under 13 to engage in sexual activity	302
6.5.4	Arrange/facilitate commission of a child sex offence	304
6.5.5	Meeting a child following sexual grooming	307
6.5.6	Sexual communication with a child	310

6.6	**Indecent Photographs/Images: Persons under 18/Disclose with Intent to Cause Distress**	**313**
6.6.1	Take, make, distribute, publish indecent photographs of person under 18	313
6.6.2	Possession of indecent photograph(s) of person under 18	318
6.7	**Indecent Exposure, Images, Public Decency, and Voyeurism**	**322**
6.7.1	Indecent exposure	322
6.7.2	Sending etc photograph or film of genitals	323
6.7.3	Sharing or threatening to share intimate photograph or film	325
6.7.4	Outraging public decency	328
6.7.5	Voyeurism	330
6.7.6	Voyeurism offences: operating equipment and recording images	333
6.8	**Sexual Harm Prevention Orders and Sexual Risk Orders**	**337**
6.8.1	Sexual Harm Prevention Orders	337
6.8.2	Sexual Risk Orders	339
6.9	**Sexual Activity in a Public Lavatory**	**342**
6.10	**Administer Substance Intending to Commit a Sexual Offence**	**344**
6.11	**Prostitution: Soliciting and Paying for Services of Prostitute (Subject Exploitation)**	**346**
6.11.1	Persistently loitering/soliciting in street/public place for prostitution	346
6.11.2	Soliciting to obtain services of a prostitute	348
6.11.3	Paying for sexual services of a prostitute subject to exploitation	349
7	**Public Disorder/Nuisance**	**351**
7.1	**Penalty Notices for Disorder**	**351**
7.1.1	Penalty notices for disorder offences	351
7.1.2	Police operational guidance for issuing PNDs	353
7.2	**Drunkenness in Public Places**	**358**
7.2.1	Drunk and disorderly	358
7.2.2	Drunk on a highway	359
7.3	**Breach of the Peace**	**362**
7.4	**Riot and Violent Disorder**	**365**

7.4.1 Riot 365
7.4.2 Violent disorder 367

7.5 Affray 370

7.6 Fear or Provocation of Violence 373

7.7 Intentional Harassment, Alarm, or Distress 376

7.8 Threatening/Abusive Words/Behaviour 380

7.9 Racial, Religious, or Sexual Orientation Hatred Offences 384

7.9.1 Use of words/behaviour or display of written material (racial) 384
7.9.2 Publishing/distributing written material (racial) 386
7.9.3 Religious or sexual orientation hatred offences 387

7.10 Racially/Religiously Aggravated Offences 390

7.10.1 Meaning of 'racially or religiously aggravated' 390
7.10.2 Racially or religiously aggravated assaults 391
7.10.3 Racially or religiously aggravated criminal damage 393
7.10.4 Racially or religiously aggravated public order offences 394
7.10.5 Racially or religiously aggravated harassment/stalking 396

7.11 Harassment/Stalking 398

7.11.1 Harassment—no violence 398
7.11.2 Harassment (fear of violence) 401
7.11.3 Stalking 403
7.11.4 Stalking (fear of violence/serious alarm or distress) 405
7.11.5 Stalking Protection Orders 408
7.11.6 Restraining orders 409
7.11.7 Civil remedies 411
7.11.8 Harassment of person in their home 413

7.12 Communications Causing Distress, Anxiety, or Serious Harm 418

7.12.1 Sending letters etc with intent to cause distress or anxiety 418
7.12.2 Improper use of electronic public communications network 421
7.12.3 Send false communication with intent to cause harm 424
7.12.4 Send communication threatening death or serious harm 426
7.12.5 Sending or showing flashing images electronically 427
7.12.6 Offence of encouraging or assisting serious self-harm 430

7.12.7	Gives/causes to be given false alarm of fire	433
7.13	**Anti-Social Behaviour**	**435**
7.13.1	Injunctions—application/breach	435
7.13.2	Act in anti-social manner—fail to give name/address	438
7.13.3	Intentionally or recklessly causing a public nuisance	439
7.13.4	Closure of premises (nuisance/disorder)	441
7.13.5	Causing nuisance/disturbance on NHS premises	447
7.14	**Vehicles Causing Annoyance**	**451**
7.14.1	Vehicles used in a manner causing alarm, distress, or annoyance	451
7.14.2	Retention/disposal of seized motor vehicle	454
7.15	**Dispersal Powers/Public Spaces Protection Orders**	**456**
7.15.1	Dispersal powers	456
7.15.2	Public spaces protection orders (PSPOs)	460
7.16	**Community/Environmental Protection**	**465**
7.16.1	Community protection notices (CPN)	465
7.16.2	Leaving litter/removing or interfering with litter bins	469
7.16.3	Unauthorised dumping/abandoned vehicles/fly tipping	471
7.17	**Trespassing on Premises/Land**	**474**
7.17.1	Trespassers (squatting) in residential building/residing on land (failing to leave)	474
7.17.2	Violent entry to premises	479
7.17.3	Adverse occupation of residential premises	481
7.17.4	Aggravated trespass on land	483
7.17.5	Causing serious disruption by locking-on	485
7.17.6	Causing serious disruption by tunnelling or being present in a tunnel	488
7.17.7	Obstruction etc of major transport works	490
7.17.8	Interference with national infrastructure	493
7.17.9	Powers to stop and search without suspicion	495
7.18	**Football/Sporting Event Offences/Banning Orders**	**498**
7.18.1	Possess alcohol/article or drunk at sporting event	498
7.18.2	Throw object—designated football match/football banning orders	502
8	**Firearms, Fireworks, and Weapons**	**507**
8.1	**'Section 1 Firearms' Offences**	**507**
8.1.1	Possessing s 1 firearm/ammunition without certificate	507
8.1.2	Aggravated s 1 offences/registered firearms dealers	512

8.1.3	Restrictions on s 1 firearms/ammunition to under 14 years	514
8.1.4	Imitation/replica firearm—convertible to s 1 firearm	516
8.1.5	Failing to comply with firearm certificate conditions	518
8.2	**Shotgun Offences**	**520**
8.2.1	Shotgun without a certificate	520
8.2.2	Shotgun restrictions to under 15 years	522
8.2.3	Fail to comply with shotgun certificate conditions	523
8.3	**Criminal Use of Firearms**	**525**
8.3.1	Ban on possession by convicted person	525
8.3.2	Possession with intent to endanger life	527
8.3.3	Possession with intent to cause fear of violence	529
8.3.4	Using a firearm to resist or prevent a lawful arrest	530
8.3.5	Possession at time of committing/being arrested	531
8.3.6	Carrying firearm—criminal intent/resist arrest	533
8.3.7	Using person to mind a firearm/weapon	535
8.4	**Trespassing with Firearms**	**537**
8.4.1	Trespass with any firearm in a building	537
8.4.2	Trespass with firearm on land	538
8.5	**Possess Firearm or Imitation Firearm in a Public Place**	**541**
8.6	**Police Powers—Firearms**	**545**
8.6.1	Requirement to hand over firearm/ammunition	545
8.6.2	Police powers—firearms/shotgun certificates	547
8.6.3	Premises search warrant	548
8.7	**Firearms, Air Weapons, Imitation Firearms—Age Restrictions**	**551**
8.7.1	Purchase/hire or supply by/to under 18	551
8.7.2	Air weapons—further offences (others)/under 18 restrictions	552
8.7.3	Air weapons deemed prohibited weapons	557
8.7.4	'BB guns'	558
8.7.5	Under 18—sell/buy an imitation firearm	559
8.8	**Fireworks**	**561**
8.8.1	Categories of fireworks	561
8.8.2	Under 18 years—possessing 'adult' fireworks	562
8.8.3	Ban on possession of Category 4 fireworks	563
8.8.4	Use firework after 11 p.m.	564
8.8.5	Supply of fireworks and pyrotechnic article offences	566
8.8.6	Throwing fireworks	567
8.8.7	Causing danger in the highway	568

8.8.8	Discharging firearm/missile or throwing fireworks	569
8.8.9	Possession of pyrotechnic articles at musical events	570
8.9	**Offensive Weapons and Crossbows**	**572**
8.9.1	Offensive weapons in public place—possess/threaten	572
8.9.2	Offensive weapons—threaten in private	576
8.9.3	Offensive weapons—provide/trade/ manufacture/possess in private	577
8.9.4	The Criminal Justice Act 1988 (Offensive Weapons) Order 1988	579
8.9.5	Trespassing with weapon of offence	581
8.9.6	Crossbows	582
8.10	**Bladed Articles/Knives Offences**	**586**
8.10.1	Possession of bladed/pointed article in public place	586
8.10.2	Sale of knives/blades to persons under 18	589
8.10.3	Deliver bladed product to residential premises/locker	591
8.10.4	Deliver bladed product/article to under 18	593
8.10.5	Possess, manufacture, sell, hire, or lend dangerous weapons	595
8.10.6	Threaten with article in public place/school/ further education premises	597
8.10.7	Possess weapon/blade/sharp point on school/ further education premises	599
8.10.8	Nuisance/disturbance/powers at school premises	601
8.11	**Corrosives**	**605**
8.11.1	Sell/deliver corrosive products to under 18	605
8.11.2	Deliver/arrange delivery to residential premises/locker	607
8.11.3	Possess a corrosive substance in a public place	608
8.12	**Stop and Search Powers—Knives and Weapons**	**609**
8.12.1	Search warrant for premises	609
8.12.2	Powers for article/weapon on school/further education premises	610
8.12.3	Stop and search—serious violence/offensive weapon	611
8.13	**Serious Violence Reduction Orders**	**615**
9	**Alcohol and Licensing**	**619**
9.1	**Alcohol Restrictions on Persons under 16/18**	**619**
9.1.1	Unaccompanied children prohibited from certain premises	619
9.1.2	Sale of alcohol to person under 18	622
9.1.3	Allowing the sale of alcohol to children	623

9.1.4	Purchase of alcohol by or on behalf of person under 18	625
9.1.5	Consumption of alcohol by person under 18	627
9.1.6	Delivering alcohol to person under 18	628
9.1.7	Sending person under 18 to obtain alcohol	630
9.2	**Drunkenness on Licensed Premises**	**633**
9.2.1	Sale of alcohol to person who is drunk	633
9.2.2	Failure to leave licensed premises	634
9.2.3	Allowing disorderly conduct on licensed premises	636
9.3	**Powers to Enter/Close Licensed Premises and Test Purchases**	**638**
9.3.1	Test purchases	638
9.3.2	Powers to enter licensed premises and clubs	639
9.3.3	Police powers—closure notice	640
9.4	**Public Spaces Protection Order—Alcohol Restrictions**	**643**
9.4.1	Power to require person to cease drinking alcohol	643
9.4.2	Failure to comply with alcohol requirements	644
9.5	**Alcohol in Public Place (under 18)—Offences/Confiscation**	**646**
9.5.1	Offences/confiscation of alcohol (under 18)	646
9.5.2	Persistently possess alcohol in public (under 18)	648
10	**Road Traffic**	**651**
10.1	**Meanings: Roads, Public Places, Vehicles, and Drives**	**651**
10.1.1	Roads	651
10.1.2	Public place	652
10.1.3	Vehicles/motor vehicles/mechanically propelled vehicles	653
10.1.4	Drives/driving	655
10.2	**Powers to Stop/Direct Vehicles and Pedestrians**	**658**
10.2.1	Drivers to comply with traffic directions	658
10.2.2	Directions to pedestrians	660
10.2.3	Police powers to stop a vehicle on a road	661
10.3	**Fail to Comply with Traffic Signs**	**663**
10.4	**Traffic Fixed Penalty Notices**	**666**
10.4.1	Traffic fixed penalty notices	666
10.4.2	Control of vehicle and use of hand-held device	671
10.4.3	Graduated fixed penalties, penalty deposits, and immobilisation	674

10.5	**Notice of Intended Prosecution**	**678**
10.6	**Driving without Due Care and Attention**	**680**
10.6.1	Driving without due care and attention	680
10.6.2	Request details after reckless, careless, or inconsiderate driving or cycling	683
10.7	**Dangerous Driving/Cause Serious Injury**	**685**
10.7.1	Dangerous driving	685
10.7.2	Cause serious injury by dangerous driving	687
10.7.3	Causing serious injury by careless, or inconsiderate, driving	688
10.7.4	Wanton or furious driving	689
10.8	**Fatal Road Traffic Collision Incidents**	**691**
10.8.1	Causing death by dangerous driving	691
10.8.2	Causing death by careless driving when under influence	693
10.8.3	Causing death by driving: disqualified driver	695
10.8.4	Causing death by careless, or inconsiderate, driving	697
10.8.5	Causing death by driving: no insurance or licence	698
10.9	**Road Traffic Collisions**	**700**
10.9.1	Incidents to which applicable	700
10.9.2	Duties of driver after accident	701
10.9.3	Duty of driver to report the incident	702
10.10	**Drive/Attempt to Drive/in Charge of Vehicle While Unfit through Drink/Drugs**	**705**
10.10.1	Drive while unfit drink/drugs	705
10.10.2	Preliminary test powers	707
10.11	**Drive/Attempt to Drive/in Charge While Over the Prescribed/Specified Limit**	**712**
10.11.1	Drive motor vehicle while over the prescribed (alcohol) limit	712
10.11.2	Drive motor vehicle while over the specified (drugs) limit	715
10.11.3	Provision of specimens for analysis	719
10.12	**Pedal Cycle Offences**	**723**
10.12.1	Dangerous cycling	723
10.12.2	Careless, and inconsiderate, cycling	724
10.12.3	Cycling when under the influence of drink or drugs	725
10.12.4	Riding or driving on the footpath	726
10.13	**Driving While Disqualified/Cause Serious Injury**	**728**
10.13.1	Obtain licence/drive on a road—while disqualified	728

10.13.2	Causing serious injury by driving: disqualified driver	730
10.14	**Driving Not in Accordance with a Driving Licence**	**732**
10.14.1	Drive motor vehicle of a class not authorised	732
10.15	**Drive with Defective Eyesight**	**735**
10.16	**Vehicle Document Offences and Seizure of Vehicles**	**737**
10.16.1	No insurance (use, cause, or permit)	737
10.16.2	No insurance (registered keeper)	740
10.16.3	No test certificate	742
10.16.4	Fail to produce driving licence	744
10.16.5	Fail to provide details or produce vehicle documents	747
10.16.6	Seize and remove motor vehicle (no insurance/ driving licence)	749
10.17	**Seat Belts**	**751**
10.17.1	Seat belts—adults	751
10.17.2	Seat belts—children	753
10.18	**Motorcycle—No Crash Helmet/Eye Protectors**	**758**
10.19	**Improper Use of Trade Plates**	**760**
10.20	**Vehicle Excise/Trade Licences and Registration Marks/Documents**	**763**
10.20.1	Using/keeping unlicensed vehicle	763
10.20.2	No registration mark on vehicle/fail to produce registration document	765
10.20.3	Obscured/misrepresented registration marks	767
10.21	**Obstruction of the Road/Footpath**	**769**
10.21.1	Wilful obstruction of the highway	769
10.21.2	Builders' skips on the highway	771
10.21.3	Cause injury/danger/annoyance on the highway	774
10.21.4	Unnecessary obstruction	775
10.22	**Off-Road Driving**	**778**
11	**General: Patrol**	**781**
11.1	**Police Powers for Civilian Staff and Volunteers**	**781**
11.1.1	Schedule 3B—designations under s 38	782
11.1.2	Powers to issue fixed penalty notices etc	784
11.1.3	Powers to require the names and addresses	785
11.1.4	Powers to search for and seize alcohol and tobacco	787
11.1.5	Powers to seize and detain—controlled drugs	788

11.1.6	Powers to seize and detain—psychoactive substances	789
11.1.7	Powers to detain pending arrival of a constable etc	790
11.1.8	Powers to search etc—individuals detained	791
11.1.9	Persons detained for park trading offences	792
11.1.10	Road traffic powers	792
11.1.11	Power to use reasonable force	792
11.2	**Mental Health Act—Removal etc of Mentally Disordered Persons without a Warrant**	**796**
11.3	**Illegal Entry into the UK/Identity Documents/Illegal Entry by Deception**	**802**
11.3.1	Illegal entry into the UK	802
11.3.2	Identity documents	805
11.3.3	Illegal entry by deception	808
11.4	**Wasting Police Time**	**810**
11.4.1	Wasting police time	810
11.4.2	Bomb and terrorist-type hoaxes	811
11.5	**Supplying Tobacco**	**815**
11.5.1	Supplying butane lighter refills and tobacco	815
11.6	**Animal Welfare and Control of Dogs**	**817**
11.6.1	Unnecessary suffering	817
11.6.2	Offences involving animals fighting	819
11.6.3	Dangerous dogs not under control	822
11.6.4	Dog control orders	826
11.6.5	Restrictions on dangerous dog breeds	827
11.6.6	Guard dogs	830
11.7	**Unmanned Aircraft (Drones)**	**833**
11.7.1	Unmanned aircraft—permission for certain flights	833
11.8	**Shining or Directing a Laser Beam Towards a Vehicle or Aircraft**	**837**

APPENDICES 839

1 Human Rights 839
2 Useful Contacts and Links 845
3 Traffic Data—Vehicle Categories and Minimum Ages 853
4 Firearms Offences Relating to Age 857
5 Religious Dates/Events 859

Index 865

Table of Cases

United Kingdom

Abdul and others v DPP [2011] EWHC 247 (Admin) 7.8
Adams v DPP [2002] EWHC 438 (Admin) 5.2.1
Alger v Commissioner of Police of the Metropolis [2023] EWHC 1582 (KB) 1.1.1
Atkin v DPP [1989] Crim LR 581, QBD 7.6
Atkins v DPP and Goodland v DPP [2000] 2 All ER 425 .... 6.6.2
Attorney-General's Reference (No 1 of 1991) [1993] QB 94 .... 4.12.1–4.12.2
Attorney-General's Reference (No 2 of 1992) [1993] 4 All ER 683, CA 10.3
Attorney-General's Reference (No 1 of 1999) [2000] QB 365 .... 4.8.1
Attorney-General's Reference (No 1 of 2002) [2002] EWCA Crim 2392 .... 4.8.2
Attorney-General's Reference (No 2 of 2004) [2005] EWCA Crim 1415 .... 5.3.1
Attorney-General's Reference (No 1 of 2020) [2020] EWCA Crim 1665 .... 6.3.1
Attorney-General's Reference (No 1 of 2022) [2022] EWCA Crim 1259 .... 4.4
Avery v CPS [2011] EWHC 2388 (Admin) 10.1.4
Aznanag v CPS [2015] EWHC 3017 (Admin) 2.2.3

B v DPP [2008] EWHC 1655 (Admin) 1.3.5
Baker v CPS [2009] EWHC 299 (Admin) 1.4.2
Bates v DPP (1993) 157 JP 1004, QBD 11.6.5
Bendt v CPS [2022] EWHC 502 (Admin) 10.4.2
Bentley v Dickinson [1983] RTR 356 .... 10.5
Blench v DPP [2004] EWHC 2717 (Admin) 1.1.2
Briscoe v Shattock [1999] 1 WLR 432, QBD 11.6.4
Brock v DPP [1993] 4 All ER 491, QBD 11.6.5
Brutus v Cozens [1972] 2 All ER 1297, HL 7.6
Burgoyne v Phillips [1983] RTR 49, QBD 10.1.4
Burns v Currell [1963] 2 All ER 297, QBD 10.1.3

Campbell v CPS [2020] EWHC 3868 (Admin) 2.2.6
Candlish v DPP [2022] EWHC 842 (Admin) 3.1.1
Capon and others v DPP [1998] All ER QBD 7.17.4
Carey v CC of Avon and Somerset [1995] RTR 405, CA 10.21.4
Cawthorn v DPP [2000] RTR 45, QBD 10.1.4
CC of Avon and Somerset v Fleming [1987] RTR 378 .... 10.1.3
CC of Cleveland Police v McGrogan [2002] EWCA Civ 86 .... 7.3
CC of North Yorkshire Police v Saddington [2001] Crim LR 41, QBD 10.1.3
CC of Thames Valley v Hepburn [2002] EWCA Civ 1841 .... 5.4.1
Chamberlain v Lindon [1998] 2 All ER 538, QBD 4.4
Chambers v DPP [2012] EWHC 2157 (Admin) 7.12.2
Clarke v Kato and others [1998] 4 All ER 417, HL 10.1.1
Coates v CPS [2011] EWHC 2032 (Admin) 10.12.4
Connolly v DPP [2007] EWHC 237 (Admin) 7.12.1
Cooke v DPP [2015] EWHC 3312 (Admin) 2.2.4
Coombes v DPP [2006] EWHC 3263 (Admin) 10.3
Cowan v Commissioner of the Metropolitan Police [2000] 1 WLR 254, CA 1.4.3–1.4.4
Cowan v DPP [2013] EWHC 192 (Admin) 10.1.2

CPS v Chalupa [2009] EWHC 3082 (Admin).. 10.11.3
CPS v Thompson [2007] EWHC 1841 (Admin).. 10.11.1
Croitoru v CPS [2016] EWHC 1645 (Admin) 10.11.1
Cumberbatch v CPS; Ali v DPP [2009] EWHC 3353 (Admin)......................... 2.2.2
Cutter v Eagle Star Insurance Company Ltd [1998] 4 All ER 417, HL 10.1.1

D'Souza v DPP [1992] 4 All ER 545, HL.. 1.4.2
Darroux v The Crown [2018] EWCA Crim 1009... 3.8.1
Davey v Lee (1967) 51 Cr App R 423.. 4.1.1
Dawes v DPP [1995] 1 Cr App R 65, QBD.. 4.3.2
DE v Chief Constable of West Midlands [2023] EWHC 146 (KB) 1.1.1
Dhesi v CC of West Midlands Police [2000] All ER (D) 1172, CA.................. 1.3.2
Dixon (Corey) v CPS [2018] EWHC 3154 (Admin).. 2.2.2
DPP v Ahmed [2021] EWHC 2122 (Admin).. 2.2.6
DPP v Armstrong-Braun (1999) 163 JP 271, CA.. 2.1.2
DPP v Baker [2004] EWHC 2782 (Admin)... 7.11.1
DPP v Bailey and others [2022] EWHC 3302 (Admin)................................... 7.17.4
DPP v Baldwin [2000] RTR 314, QBD.. 10.11.3
DPP v Barker [2004] EWHC 2502 (Admin).. 10.13.1
DPP v Camp [2017] EWHC 3119 (Admin)... 10.11.3
DPP v Charlesworth [2022] EWHC 2835 (Admin)... 6.8.1
DPP v Christof [2015] EWHC 4096 (Admin).. 8.9.1
DPP v Collins [2006] UKHL 40... 7.12.2
DPP v Coyle [1996] RTR 287, CA... 10.11.3
DPP v Cuciurean [2022] EWHC 736 (Admin).. 7.17.4
DPP v Distill [2017] EWHC 2244 (Admin).. 7.6, 7.8
DPP v Furby [2000] RTR 181, QBD... 10.11.3
DPP v Garrett [1995] RTR 302, QBD... 10.11.3
DPP v H [1997] 1 WLR 1406, QBD... 10.11.1
DPP v Harris [1994] 158 JP 896, QBD... 10.6.1
DPP v Hastings (1993) 158 JP 118, QBD... 10.1.4
DPP v Hay [2005] EWHC 1395 (Admin) 10.9.2, 10.16.1
DPP v Houghton-Brown [2010] EWHC 3527 (Admin) 8.1.5
DPP v Janman [2004] EWHC 101 (Admin).. 10.11.1
DPP v Johnson (1994) 158 JP 891, QBD... 10.11.1
DPP v Kellet (1994) 158 JP 1138, QBD.. 11.6.5
DPP v King [2008] EWHC 447 (Admin).. 10.1.3
DPP v Little (1994) 95 Cr App R 28.. 2.1.1
DPP v Marshall [1988] 3 All ER 683, QBD... 9.3.1
DPP v McCarthy [1999] RTR 323.. 10.9.2
DPP v McFarlane [2002] EWHC 485 (Admin).. 7.10.4
DPP v Meadon [2003] EWHC 3005 (Admin).. 5.4.1
DPP v Mills [1996] 3 WLR 1093.. 4.8.1
DPP v Milton [2006] EWHC 242 (Admin)... 10.7.1
DPP v Mullally [2006] EWHC 3448 (Admin) 10.11.1
DPP v Nesbitt and Duffy [1995] 1 Cr App R 38.. 10.11.3
DPP v Pal [2000] EWHC 1575 (QB) 7.10.2
DPP v Parker [2005] RTR 16... 10.18
DPP v Parmenter [1991] 3 WLR 914, HL.. 2.3.1
DPP v Ramos [2000] Crim LR 768, QBD... 7.6, 7.10.4
DPP v Santa-Bermudez [2003] EWHC 2908 (Admin)...................................... 2.1.2
DPP v Smith, The Times, 1 June 1994, QBD 10.11.3
DPP v Smith [2006] 1 WLR 1571, QBD.. 2.1.2
DPP v Smith (Kingsley Anthony) [2017] EWHC 3193 (Admin) 7.12.2
DPP v Tilly and others [2001] EWHC Admin 821... 7.17.4
DPP v Wilson [1991] Crim LR 441, QBD.. 10.11.1

DPP v Wilson [2009] EWHC 1988 (Admin) 10.10.2
DPP v Woods [2002] EWHC 85 (Admin)................ 7.10.2
DPP v Wythe [1996] RTR 137, QBD 10.11.3
DPP v Ziegler and others [2021] UKSC 23................ 10.21

Edkins v Knowles [1973] 2 All ER 503, QBD 10.1.4

Fagan v Metropolitan Police Commissioner [1968] 3 All ER 442, QBD.......... 2.1.1
Felix v DPP [1998] Crim LR 657 .... 7.16.2
Francis v DPP [1997] RTR 113, QBD................ 10.11.3

Garry v CPS [2019] EWHC 636 (Admin)................ 8.9.1
Gearing v DPP [2008] EWHC 1695 (Admin)................ 10.10.2
Government of the United States of America v Dempsey [2018]
EWHC 1724 (Admin) 4.8.2

H v CPS [2010] EWHC 1374 (Admin)................ 2.1.2
H v DPP [2007] EWHC 960 (Admin) 2.1.2
Hague v DPP [1997] RTR 146, QBD................ 10.11.3
Hall v Cotton [1976] 3 WLR 681, QBD 8.1.5
Hallett v DPP [2011] EWHC 488 (Admin)................ 10.1.1
Harris v DPP [1993] 1 WLR 82, QBD 8.10.1
Harvey v DPP [2011] EWHC 3992 (Admin) 7.8
Hayes v CC of Merseyside Police [2011] EWCA Civ 911................ 1.3.2
Haystead v CC Derbyshire Police [2000] 3 All ER 890, QBD................ 2.1.1
Hewson v Commissioner of Police of the Metropolis [2018]
EWHC 471 (Admin) 7.11.1
Hobson v Gledhill [1978] 1 All ER 945, QBD................ 11.6.6
Hollingsworth v Howard [1974] RTR 58................ 10.10.2
Holmes v Chief Constable of Merseyside Police [2018]
EWHC 1026 (Admin) 2.6.1
Howard v DPP [2001] EWHC 17 (Admin)................ 7.11.2
Howarth v Commissioner of the Metropolitan Police [2011]
EWHC 2818 (Admin) 1.3.5
HSK v CPS [2022] EWHC 2213 (Admin) 7.10.2
Hudson v CPS [2017] EWHC 841 (Admin)................ 3.3.1
Hughes v DPP [2012] EWHC 606 (Admin)................ 7.6

I v DPP; M v DPP; H v DPP [2001] UKHL 10................ 7.5
Idrees v DPP [2011] EWHC 624 (Admin) 3.8.1
Ivey v Genting Casinos (UK) Ltd (trading as Crockfords) [2017] UKSC 67 .... 3.1.1

Jenkins v DPP [2020] EWHC 1307 (Admin)................ 8.1.1
John v Humphreys [1955] 1 All ER 793, QBD................ 10.14.1
Johnson v DPP [1994] Crim LR 673, QBD................ 4.4
Jones v Birmingham City Council and another [2023] UKSC 27 .... 7.4.2
Jones v Chief Constable of Bedfordshire [1987] RTR 332................ 10.16.1
Jones v CPS [2019] EWHC 2826 (Admin)................ 10.6.1
Jones v DPP [2010] EWHC 523 (Admin) 7.10.1

Kellett v DPP [2001] EWHC (Admin) 107 .... 7.11.1
Kendall v DPP [2008] EWHC 1848 (Admin)................ 7.8
Kennedy v DPP [2002] EWHC 2297 (Admin) 10.11.1
Kensington International Ltd v Congo and others [2007] EWCA Civ 1128 ..... 3.8.5
Kerr v Chief Constable of Surrey Police [2017] EWHC 2936 (Admin)............... 2.8
Kosar v Bank of Scotland [2011] EWHC 1050 (Admin) 7.11.1

L v CPS [2010] EWHC 341 (Admin) 11.6.3
Lafferty v DPP [1995] Crim LR 430, QBD 10.11.1
Langham v Crisp [1975] Crim LR 652 .... 10.21.4
Langley and others v Liverpool City Council [2006] 1 WLR 375, CA 2.4.2
Le Vine v DPP [2010] EWHC 1128 (Admin) 7.7
Lewis v Cox [1984] Crim LR 756, QBD 5.4.1
Loake v CPS [2017] EWHC 2855 (Admin) 7.11.1

M'Naghten's Case (1843) 10 Cl & F 200 .... 2.7.1, 7.11.1
Mantle v Jordan [1897] 1 QB 248 .... 8.8.8
Marland v DPP [2023] EWHC 1046 (Admin) 2.1.1
McDonnell v Commissioner of Police of the Metropolis and another [2015] EWCA Civ 573 .... 1.1
McKnight v Davies [1974] Crim LR 62, CA 4.3.1
McQuaid v Anderton [1980] 3 All ER 540, QBD 10.1.4
Mepstead v DPP [1996] Crim LR 111, QBD 2.1.1
Miller v DPP [2018] EWHC 262 (Admin) 10.11.3
Moore v Gooderham [1960] 3 All ER 575, QBD 8.1.1

Nagy v Weston [1965] 1 All ER 78, QBD 10.21.1
Neale v RMJE (a minor) (1985) 80 Cr App R 20 .... 7.2.1
Nelmes v Rhys Howells Transport Ltd [1977] RTR 266 .... 10.21.4
Nicolaou v Redbridge Magistrates' Court [2012] EWHC 1647 (Admin) 2.6.3
Norwood v DPP [2003] EWHC 1564 (Admin) 7.8

O'Hara v CC of the RUC [1997] 1 All ER 129, HL 1.3.5
O'Loughlin v CC of Essex [1998] 1 WLR 374, CA 1.4.2
Ohlson v Hylton [1975] 2 All ER 490, QBD 8.9.1
Osman v DPP (1999) 163 JP 725, QBD 1.3.5
Overd v CC of Avon and Somerset [2021] EWHC 3100 (QB) 7.13.2

Palmer v R [1971] AC 814, HL 1.1
Pappin v Maynard (1863) 27 JP 745 .... 10.21.3
Pattison v DPP [2005] EWHC 2938 (Admin) 10.13.1
Pegram v DPP [2019] EWHC 2673 (Admin) 2.2.2
Pendlebury v DPP [2018] EWHC 3567 (Admin) 7.11.4
Plavelil v DPP [2014] EWHC 736 (Admin) 7.11.1
Police Service for Northern Ireland v MacRitchie [2008] NICA 26 .... 6.8.1
Price v Cromack [1975] 1 WLR 988 .... 10.14.1
Pryor v CC of Greater Manchester Police [2011] EWCA Civ 749 .... 10.16.6
Pumbien v Vines [1996] Crim LR 124, QBD 10.16.1, 10.16.3

R v A [2020] EWCA Crim 407 .... 10.8.1
R v AAC [2023] EWCA Crim 15 .... 4.9.5
R v AAD and others [2022] EWCA Crim 106 .... 4.9.5
R v AAJ [2021] EWCA Crim 1278 .... 4.9.5
R v Abdullahi [2006] EWCA Crim 2060 .... 6.5.3
R v Abi-Khalil, R v Porja [2017] EWCA Crim 17 .... 5.1.1
R v AFU [2023] EWCA Crim 23 .... 4.9.3
R v AGM [2022] EWCA Crim 920 .... 5.1.1
R v Ali and another [2015] EWCA Crim 1279 .... 4.9.3
R v Altham [2006] EWCA Crim 7 .... 5.2.1
R v Ames [2023] EWCA Crim 1463 .... 3.8.4
R v Andrewes [2020] EWCA Crim 1055 .... 3.8.1
R v Ankerson [2015] EWCA Crim 432 .... 4.6
R v Archbold [2007] EWCA Crim 2137 .... 8.9.1

R v Auguste [2003] EWCA Crim 3929 .... 5.4.2
R v Baker and Wilkins [1997] Crim LR 497 .... 4.4
R v Bannister [2009] EWCA Crim 1571 .... 10.8.1
R v Barnes [2004] EWCA Crim 3246 .... 2.1.2, 2.3.2
R v Barreto [2019] EWHC 2044 (Admin) 10.4.2
R v Barton and another [2020] EWCA Crim 575 .... 3.1
R v Bassett [2008] EWCA Crim 1174 .... 6.8.1
R v Bater-James and another [2020] EWCA Crim 790 .... 6.1.1
R v Bett [1999] 1 All ER 600 .... 5.4.2
R v Bezzina; R v Codling; R v Elvin [1994] 3 All ER 964, CA 11.6.3
R v Blackfriars CC and the Commissioner of Police of the Metropolis [2014] EWHC 1541 (Admin) 1.5.2
R v Bloxham (1982) 74 Cr App R 279, HL 3.5
R v BM [2018] EWCA Crim 560 .... 2.3.2
R v Bogacki [1973] 2 All ER 864 .... 4.3.1
R v Bow Street Metropolitan Stipendiary Magistrate exp Government of the United States [1999] QB 847 .... 4.12.2
R v Bowden [2001] QB 88 .... 6.6.1
R v Bree [2007] EWCA Crim 804 .... 6.1.1
R v Bristol [2007] EWCA Crim 3214 .... 1.3.5, 5.4.1
R v Bristol CC, *ex parte* Bristol Press and Picture Agency (1986) 85 Cr App R 190 .... 1.5.4
R v Bristol Justices, *ex parte* Edgar [1998] 3 All ER 798 .... 4.1.1
R v Brock and Wyner (2001) 2 Cr App R 3 .... 5.4.2
R v Brooks and Brooks (1983) 76 Cr App R 66 .... 3.7
R v Brown and others [1994] 1 AC 212, HL 2.1.2, 2.3.1
R v Buchanan v CPS [2018] EWHC 1773 (Admin) 10.21.1
R v Buono [2005] EWCA Crim 1313 .... 10.8.1
R v Burke [2012] EWCA Crim 770 .... 6.8.1
R v Burstow [1997] 4 All ER 225, HL 2.3.1–2.3.2, 7.12.2
R v Buxton [2010] EWCA Crim 2923 .... 7.11.6
R v Cakmak and others [2002] EWCA Crim 500 .... 4.6
R v Caldwell [1981] 1 All ER 961 .... 4.4
R v Casserly [2024] EWCA Crim 25 .... 7.12.1
R v CC of Lancashire, *ex parte* Parker [1993] Crim LR 204, QBD 1.5.1
R v Chan-Fook [1994] 2 All ER 552, CA 2.1.2
R v Chapman [2017] EWCA Crim 1743 .... 5.3.5
R v Cheeseman [2019] EWCA Crim 149 .... 1.1, 2.3.2
R v Chilvers [2021] EWCA Crim 1311 .... 2.8
R v Chipunza [2021] EWCA Crim 587 .... 3.3.1
R v Ciccarelli [2011] EWCA Crim 2665 .... 6.3.1
R v Clancy [2012] EWCA Crim 8 .... 8.10.1
R v Clear [1968] 52 Cr App R 58 .... 3.2.2
R v Clouden [1987] Crim LR 56, CA 3.2.1
R v Coid [1998] Crim LR 199, CA 5.4.2
R v Coltman [2018] Crim 2059, CA 4.12.1
R v Cort [2003] 3 WLR 1300, CA 2.6.2
R v CS and another [2021] EWCA Crim 134 .... 4.9.5
R v Cunningham [1957] 2 All ER 412, CA 2.1.3, 2.3.1
R v Curtis [2010] EWCA Crim 123 .... 7.11.2
R v D [2019] EWCA Crim 45 .... 8.10.1
R v Dang and others [2014] EWCA Crim 348 .... 5.1.1, 5.3.1
R v Daubney (2000) 164 JP 519, CA 3.3.2
R v Davidoff [2022] EWCA Crim 1253 .... 6.8.1
R v Davis [2008] UKHL 26 .... 4.8.1
R v Day [2015] EWCA Crim 1646 .... 1.1

R v Deakin [1972] Crim LR 781, CA 3.5
R v Deyemi and Edwards [2007] All ER 369, CA 8.1.1
R v Dica [2005] EWCA Crim 2304 .... 2.3.1
R v Dooley [2005] EWCA Crim 3093 .... 6.6.1
R v Doyle [2000] 11 WLUK 291 .... 3.3.1
R v DPP, B v DPP [2007] EWHC 739 (Admin) 3.2.1
R v Dragjoshi v Croydon Magistrates' Court [2017] EWHC 2840 (Admin) 7.5
R v Drayton [2005] EWCA Crim 2013 .... 4.5.2
R v Duhaney, R v Stoddart (1998) 2 Cr App R 25 .... 8.3.6
R v Durkin [1973] 2 All ER 872, CA 3.1.2
R v Edwards [1998] Crim LR 207, CA 5.2.2
R v El-hakkaoui [1975] 2 All ER 146, CA 8.3.2
R v Elizabeth Forsyth [1997] 2 Cr App R 299 .... 3.5
R v Emmannuel [2022] EWCA Crim 1322 .... 6.3.1
R v Epping Justices, Ex p Quy [1998] RTR 158 .... 10.11.3
R v Evans [2009] EWCA Crim 650 .... 2.7.2
R v F [2010] EWCA Crim 2243 .... 6.7.2
R v Fellows [1997] 1 Cr App R 244 .... 6.6.1
R v Figures [1976] Crim LR 744 .... 3.5
R v Francis [2006] EWCA Crim 3323 .... 7.7
R v G [2008] UKHL 37 .... 6.1.2
R v G and R [2003] UKHL 50 .... 4.4
R v Gedminintaite and Collier [2008] EWCA Crim 814 .... 11.6.3
R v Ghosh [1982] 2 All ER 689, QBD 3.1.1
R v Gibson [1990] 2 QB 619 .... 6.7.2
R v Giles [2003] EWCA Crim 1287 .... 8.10.1
R v Gillard (1988) 87 Cr App Rep 189 .... 2.1.3, 6.10
R v Gilmartin [2013] EWCA Crim 2631 .... 7.5
R v Goodard [1992] Crim LR 588 .... 5.1.1
R v Golding [2014] EWCA Crim 889 .... 2.3.1
R v Golds [2016] UKSC 61 .... 2.7.1
R v Goodwin [2018] EWCA Crim 2287 .... 2.7.1
R v Gore [2007] EWCA Crim 2789 .... 2.7.6
R v Gore [2009] EWCA Crim 1424 .... 7.1.2
R v Griffiths [1998] Crim LR 567 CA 5.2.2
R v Grout [2011] EWCA Crim 299 .... 6.5.2
R v H [2005] 2 All ER 859 .... 6.3.1
R v Hale (1978) 68 Cr App R 415 .... 3.2.1
R v Hall (1985) 81 Cr App R 260 .... 3.5
R v Hamer [2023] EWCA Crim 516 .... 8.10.1
R v Hamilton [2007] EWCA Crim 2062 .... 6.7.2
R v Hanna [2023] EWCA Crim 33 .... 6.8.1
R v Haringey Magistrates' Court, *ex parte* Cragg (1996) 161 JP 61, QBD 11.6.5
R v Harris and Cox [1996] Crim LR 36 .... 5.1.1, 5.3.1
R v Harrison [1996] 1 Cr App R 138 .... 8.5
R v Hayes [2015] EWCA Crim 1944 .... 3.1.1
R v Heddell [2016] EWCA Crim 443 .... 8.1.1
R v Henderson [2016] EWCA Crim 965 .... 8.10.1
R v Hendy-Freegard [2007] EWCA Crim 1236 .... 2.6.2
R v Hepburn [2020] EWCA Crim 820 .... 6.1.1
R v Hichens [2011] EWCA Crim 1626 .... 1.1
R v Hinks [2000] 4 All ER 833, HL 3.1.1
R v Hodgson [2001] EWCA Crim 2697 .... 5.1.1
R v Holder [2023] EWCA Crim 5 .... 10.8.1
R v Howell [1982] QB 416 .... 7.3
R v Hughes [2013] UKSC 56 .... 10.8.3, 10.8.5, 10.13.2

R v Hunt [1987] 1 All ER 1, HL ... 5.1.1
R v Hunter and another [2021] EWCA Crim 1785 ... 3.8.6
R v Ireland [1998] AC 147, HL ... 2.3.1–2.3.2, 7.12.2
R v Jogee; R v Ruddock [2016] UKSC 8 ... 4.1.4
R v Jones [1995] QB 235 ... 8.5
R v Jones and others, Ayliffe and others v DPP, Swain v DPP [2006] UKHL 16 ... 1.1, 4.4
R v Kayani; R v Sollim [2011] EWCA Crim 2871 ... 2.6.3
R v Keal [2022] EWCA Crim 341 ... 2.7.1
R v Keane and McGrath [2010] EWCA Crim 2514 ... 1.1, 2.1.2
R v Kelly (1993) 97 Cr App R 245 ... 3.3.2
R v Kennedy [2007] UKHL 38 ... 2.1.3
R v Khan and others [2009] EWCA Crim 2 ... 2.7.4
R v Kish [2022] EWCA Crim 1161 ... 6.8.1
R v Klass [1998] 1 Cr App R 453 ... 3.3.2
R v Konzani [2005] EWCA Crim 706 ... 2.3.1
R v Kuddus [2019] EWCA Crim 837 ... 2.7.2
R v Lambert [2001] UKHL 37 ... 5.2.2
R v Latimer (1886) 17 QBD 359 ... 2.3.1
R v Lawrance [2020] EWCA Crim 971 ... 6.1.1
R v Leather [1993] 1 WLUK 699 ... 2.6.3
R v Lee (2000) 150 NLJ 1491, CA ... 2.2.1
R v Leeson [2000] 1 Cr App R 233 ... 5.1.1
R v Littleford [1978] CLR 48 ... 5.4.1
R v Loosely; Attorney-General's Reference (No 3 of 2000) [2001] UKHL 53 ... 9.3.1
R v Lunn [2008] EWCA Crim 2082 ... 5.4.2
R v Maginnis [1987] 1 All ER 907, HL ... 5.1.1
R v Mahroof [1988] 9 WLUK 97 ... 7.4.2
R v Major [2010] EWCA 3016 ... 7.11.6
R v Marron [2011] EWCA Crim 792 ... 5.1.1–5.1.2
R v Marsh [1996] 8 CL 54 ... 4.3.2
R v MacDonagh [1974] 2 All ER 257 ... 10.1.4
R v McCreadie and Tume [1992] Cr App Rep 143 ... 3.4
R v McCready [1978] 1 WLR 1376, CA ... 2.3.1
R v McFarlane [1994] QB 419 ... 6.11.1
R v McGee [2012] EWCA Crim 613 ... 5.4.2
R v McKay [2015] EWCA Crim 2098 ... 2.3.2
R v McKay (2015) unreported CA ... 10.3, 10.6.1
R v Melin [2019] EWCA Crim 557 ... 2.3.1
R v Miller [1976] Crim LR 147 ... 4.3.1
R v Miller [2010] EWCA Crim 2883 ... 6.6.2
R v Minett [2009] All ER (D) 215 ... 3.8.5
R v MK; R v Gega [2018] EWCA Crim 667 ... 4.9.5
R v Mohammed [2006] EWCA Crim 1107 ... 2.6.3, 6.5.4
R v Morris and King (1984) 149 JP 60, 79 Cr App Rep 104 ... 8.5
R v Musharraf [2022] EWCA Crim 1482 ... 7.11.4
R v Myers [2007] EWCA Crim 599 ... 10.5
R v Nelson [2000] All ER (D) 206 ... 8.3.5
R v Ngan [1998] 1 Cr App R 331 ... 3.1.1
R v NW [2010] EWCA Crim 404 ... 7.4.2
R v Okoro [2018] EWCA Crim 1929 ... 6.6.2
R v Owino [1996] 2 Cr App R 128 ... 2.1.2
R v Panton [2001] EWCA Crim 611 ... 5.1.1
R v Parker [1839] 173 ER 733 ... 4.5.2
R v Pawlicki and Swindell [1992] 3 All ER 903 ... 8.3.6

R v Pendlebury [2003] EWCA Crim 3426 .... 4.8.2
R v Pitchley [1972] Crim LR 705, CA 3.5
R v Pledge [2019] EWCA Crim 912 .... 10.5
R v Pleydell [2005] EWCA Crim 1447 .... 10.7.1
R v Porter [2006] EWCA Crim 560 .... 6.6.1–6.6.2
R v Qosja [2016] EWCA Crim 1543 .... 7.11.4
R v Rahman and Others [2023] EWCA Crim 1177 .... 8.3.3
R v Ray [2017] EWCA Crim 1391 .... 1.1
R v Richards [2020] EWCA Crim 95 .... 6.8.1
R v Roberts (1972) 56 Cr App R 95 .... 2.3.2
R v Robinson [1977] Crim LR 173 .... 3.2.1
R v Rochester [2018] EWCA Crim 1936 .... 5.3.5
R v Rogers [2007] UKHL 8 .... 7.10.1
R v Rose [2017] EWCA Crim 1168 .... 2.7.2
R v Rudling [2016] EWCA Crim 741 .... 2.7.2
R v Russell [1992] Crim LR 362 .... 5.1.1
R v Sadique [2013] EWCA Crim 1150 .... 4.1.4
R v Salih [2007] EWCA Crim 2750 .... 8.3.2
R v Sanchez [1996] Crim LR 572, CA 7.4.1
R v Saunders [1985] Crim LR 230, CA 2.3.1
R v Savage [1992] 1 AC 699, HL 2.3.1
R v Scott [1996] Crim LR 652, CA 5.2.2
R v Sheppard [2010] EWCA Crim 65 .... 7.9.2
R v Shivpuri [1986] UKHL 2, [1986] 2 All ER 334, HL 4.1.1, 5.1.1
R v Shorrock [1993] 3 All ER 917, CA 7.13.3
R v Singh (B), Singh (C) and Singh (J) [2000] Cr App R 31 .... 4.8.1
R v Smith [1959] 2 All ER 193, Court Martial CA 2.7.1
R v Smith; R v Jayson [2002] EWCA Crim 683 .... 6.6.1
R v Smith (Andrew) [2020] EWCA Crim 38 .... 3.8.6
R v Smith and others [2011] EWCA Crim 66 .... 3.1.1
R v Sookoo [2002] EWCA Crim 800 .... 4.8.2
R v Spence [1999] Crim LR 975, CA 10.1.2
R v Spurge [1961] 2 All ER 688, CA 10.7.1
R v Stamford [1972] 2 All ER 427 .... 6.6.1
R v Steele [1993] Crim LR 298 .... 8.1.1
R v Strong [1995] Crim LR 428, CA 10.7.1
R v Szewczyk [2019] EWCA Crim 1811 .... 8.10.1
R v T [2011] EWCA Crim 729 .... 4.8.2
R v Tagg [2001] EWCA Crim 1230 .... 7.2.1
R v Tait [1990] 1 QB 290 .... 2.5
R v Taj [2018] EWCA Crim 1743 .... 2.7.1
R v Tao [1976] 3 All ER 65 .... 5.4.2
R v Tas [2018] EWCA Crim 2603 .... 2.7.2
R v Taylor [2016] UKSC 5 .... 4.3.2
R v Toothill [1998] Crim LR 876 .... 4.1.1
R v Tosti and White [1997] EWCA Crim 222 .... 4.1.1
R v Townsend [2020] EWCA Crim 1343 .... 6.1.1
R v Trafford Magistrates' Court, *ex parte* Riley (1996) 160 JP 418, QBD 11.6.4
R v Tucker [2016] EWCA Crim 13 .... 8.9.1
R v Twigg [2019] EWCA Crim 1553 .... 10.8.2
R v Uddin [2017] EWCA Crim 1072 .... 2.7.4
R v Uxbridge Magistrates' Court, *ex parte* Sorani, Adimi and Kaziu [1999] 4 All ER 529, QBD 11.3.1
R v Vaid [2015] EWCA Crim 298 .... 4.3.1
R v Veasey [1999] Crim LR 158, CA 8.9.1
R v Veysey and others [2019] EWCA Crim 1332 .... 2.1.3

R v Vincent [2001] Crim LR 488 .... 3.7
R v Wabelua and others [2020] EWCA Crim 783 .... 4.9.4
R v Wakeman [2011] EWCA 1649 .... 2.6.3
R v Walker [1996] 1 Cr App R 111 .... 6.7.2
R v Webb [1995] 27 LS Gaz R 31, CA 11.4.2
R v Webster and others [1995] 2 All ER 168, CA 4.5.1
R v Weir [2005] EWCA Crim 2866 .... 6.3.2
R v Wenton [2010] EWCA Crim 2361 .... 4.5.1
R v Wheatley and another [2007] EWCA Crim 835 .... 4.3.2
R v Widdows [2011] EWCA Crim 1500 .... 7.11.2
R v Wilkinson [2018] EWCA Crim 2154 .... 2.6.1
R v Williams (1991) 92 Cr App R 158 .... 4.8.2
R v Wilson [1996] 2 Cr App R 241 .... 2.1.2
R v Wilson and Jenkins [1983] 3 All ER 448, HL 2.3.1–2.3.2
R v Winter [2010] EWCA Crim 1474 .... 2.7.3
R v Woodward [1995] 3 All ER 79, CA 10.7.1
R v Worthing Justices, *ex parte* Waste Management Ltd (1988) 152 JP 362, DC 10.21.2
R v ZN [2013] EWCA Crim 989 .... 4.8.1
R (on the application of A) v Central Criminal Court; C v Central Criminal Court [2017] EWHC 70 (Admin) 1.5.4
R (on the application of Andrews) v CC of Thames Valley [2022] EWHC 887 (Admin) 11.6.3
R (on the application of Bhatti) v Croydon MC [2010] EWHC 522 (Admin) 1.5.2
R (on the application of Chabloz) v CPS [2019] 10 WLUK 494 .... 7.12.2
R (on the application of Collins) v Secretary of State for Justice [2016] EWHC 33 (Admin) 1.1, 2.3.2
R (on the application of Dyer) v Watford MC [2013] EWHC 547 (Admin) 7.6
R (on the application of Eastenders Cash and Carry plc) v South Western Magistrates' Court [2011] EWHC 937 (Admin) 1.5.1
R (on the application of Faisaltex Ltd) v Preston CC [2008] EWHC 2832 (Admin) 1.4.4
R (on the application of H) v CPS [2005] EWHC 2459 (Admin) 7.2.1
R (on the application of Laporte) v CC of Gloucestershire [2006] UKHL 55 .... 7.3, 8.11.3
R (on the application of Lees) v Solihull MC [2013] EWHC 3779 (Admin) ... 1.5.2
R (on the application of Pinheiro) v North Tyneside Magistrates' Court and another [2022] EWHC 1176 (Admin) 6.8.2
R (on the application of R) v DPP [2006] EWHC 1375 (Admin) 7.7
R (on the application of Ricketts) v Basildon MC [2010] EWHC 2358 (Admin) 3.1.1
R (on the application of Roberts) v Commissioner of Police for the Metropolis [2015] UKSC 79 .... 8.11.3
R (on the application of Rutherford) v IPCC [2010] EWHC 2881 (Admin) 10.2.3
R (on the application of SF) v Secretary of State for the Home Department [2015] EWHC 2705 (Admin) 4.9.3
R (A and another) v Central Criminal Court and another; R (C and others) v Central Criminal Court and another [2017] EWHC 70 (Admin) 1.4.4
R (Cabot Global Ltd) v Barkingside Magistrates' Court [2015] EWHC 1458 (Admin) 1.4.4
Rawlins v CPS [2018] EWHC 2533 (Admin) 7.3
Reynolds and Warren v Metropolitan Police [1982] Crim LR 831, CC 4.2.1
Richardson v DPP [2019] EWHC 428 (Admin) 10.1.2

Riley and others v CPS [2016] EWHC 2513 (Admin) 11.6.1
Royal Mail Group Ltd v Watson [2021] EWHC 2098 (Admin) 11.6.3
RSPCA v Colchester Magistrates' Court and others [2015] EWHC 1418 (Admin) 11.6.1
RSPCA v McCormick and others [2016] EWHC 928 (Admin) 11.6.2

S v CPS [2008] EWHC 438 (Admin) 7.7
Sadiku v DPP [2000] RTR 155, QBD 10.1.1
Scottow v CPS [2020] EWHC 3421 (Admin) 7.12.2
Sharma v DPP [2018] EWHC 3330 (Admin) 8.10.1
Sharpe v DPP (1994) JP 158, QBD 10.11.1
Sheldrake v DPP (Attorney-General's Reference No 4 of 2002) [2005] 1 Cr App R 28 .... 10.10.1
Smith v ADVFN [2008] EWHC 1797 QBD 7.12.2
Sobczak v DPP [2012] EWHC 1319 (Admin) 2.2.2
Sowande v CPS [2017] EWHC 1234 (Admin) 1.3.4
Staffordshire Moorlands DC v Sanderson [2020] EWHC 962 (Admin) 7.16.1
Sutherland v HM Advocate [2020] UKSC 32 .... 6.5.4, 6.5.5
Swanston v DPP (1996) 161 JP 203, QBD 7.6
Syed v DPP [2010] EWHC 81 (Admin) 1.4.2

T v DPP [2003] EWHC 266 (Admin) 2.1.2
Taylor v DPP [2006] EWHC 1202 (Admin) 7.8
TBG v A Chief Constable [2022] EWHC 2665 (Admin) 6.8.1
Thomas v Hooper [1986] RTR 1, QBD 10.1.3
Thomas v News Group Newspapers Ltd [2001] EWCA Civ 1233 .... 7.11.7
Turner v Shearer [1973] 1 All ER 397 .... 2.2.4
Tyler v Whatmore [1976] RTR 83, QBD 10.1.4

Van Colle and another v Chief Constable of Hertfordshire [2008] UKHL 50 .... 4.8.1

Wade v DPP [1996] RTR 177, QBD 10.11.3
Wakolo v DPP [2012] EWHC 611 (Admin) 7.17.2
Walker v Commissioner of Police of the Metropolis [2014] EWCA Civ 897 .... 2.2.2, 7.3
West Sussex County Council and another v F and others [2018] EWHC 1702 (Fam) 4.11.2
Whittaker v Campbell [1983] 3 All ER 582, QBD 4.3.1
Williams v DPP [1992] 95 Cr App R 415 .... 7.2.1
Wood v DPP [2008] EWHC 1056 (Admin) 2.1.1
Wright v Reading Crown Court [2017] EWHC 2643 (Admin) 11.6.2
Wycombe District Council v Snowball [2020] EWHC 1656 (Admin) 7.15.2

York City Council v Poller [1976] RTR 37 .... 10.21.2

ZH v Metropolitan Police Commissioner [2012] EWHC 604 (Admin) 2.1.1

International

European Court of Human Rights

Austin v UK [2012] Crim LR 544 .... 2.6.1

Table of Legislation

Statutes

Abortion Act 1967
s 5(1) 2.7.6
Accessories and Abettors Act 1861
s 8 .... 4.1.1, 4.1.3
Administration of Justice (Miscellaneous Provisions) Act 1933
s 2(2)(b) 4.8.1
Air Traffic Management and Unmanned Aircraft Act 2021 .... 11.7.1
Ancient Monuments and Archaeological Areas Act 1979
s 28 .... 4.4
Animal Health Act 1981
s 61 .... 1.4.2
Animal Welfare Act 2006 .... 11.6, 11.6.1
s 4 .... 1.4.2, 11.6.1
s 4(1) 11.6.1
s 4(2) 11.6.1
s 4(3)(c)(ii) 11.6.1
s 4(3A) 11.6.1
s 5 .... 1.4.2
s 6(1) 1.4.2
s 6(2) 1.4.2
s 7 .... 1.4.2
s 8 .... 11.6.2
s 8(1) 1.4.2, 11.6.2
s 8(2) 1.4.2, 11.6.2
s 18 .... 11.6.2
s 19 .... 11.6.2
s 22 .... 11.6.2
s 22(1) 11.6.2
s 23 .... 11.6.2
s 54 .... 11.6.2
Anti-social Behaviour Act 2003
s 1 .... 7.13.4
s 2 .... 7.13.4
s 11A 7.13.4
s 11B 7.13.4
s 30 .... 7.15.1
s 40 .... 7.13.4
s 43(1) 11.1.2
s 54 .... 4.7.2
s 54(1) 4.7.2
Anti-social Behaviour, Crime and Policing Act 2014 .... 4.11, 7.13, 7.15.1, 7.16, 10.12.1
s 1 .... 7.13.1
s 4 .... 7.13.1
s 9(1) 7.13.1
s 34 .... 7.15.1
s 35 .... 7.15.1–7.15.2
s 35(1)(b) 7.15.1
s 36 .... 7.15.1
s 37 .... 7.15.1
s 39 .... 7.15.1, 11.1.3
s 39(1) 7.15.1
s 39(2) 7.15.1
s 39(3) 7.15.1
s 39(4) 7.15.1
s 43 .... 7.16.1
s 43(3) 7.16.1
ss 46–51 .... 7.16.1
s 46 .... 7.16.1
s 47 .... 7.16.1
s 48 .... 7.16.1
s 48(1) 7.16.1
s 48(3) 7.16.1
s 49 .... 7.16.1
s 50 .... 7.16.1
s 51 .... 7.16.1
s 52 .... 7.16.1
s 52(1) 7.16.1
s 59 .... 7.15.2
s 59(4) 7.15.2
s 62 .... 7.15.2
s 63 .... 7.15.2
s 63(1) 9.4.1
s 63(2) 9.4.2, 11.1.4
s 63(2)(b) 9.4.1
s 63(6) 9.4.2
s 67 .... 7.15.2
s 68 .... 7.15.2
s 76 .... 5.4.2, 7.13.4
s 77 .... 7.13.4
s 78 .... 7.13.4
s 79 .... 7.13.4
s 80 .... 7.13.4
s 81 .... 7.13.4
s 85(1) 7.13.4
s 86 .... 7.13.4
s 86(1) 7.13.4
s 86(2) 7.13.4

s 86(3) ... 7.13.4
s 86(4) ... 7.13.4
s 86(5) ... 7.13.4
s 106 ... 11.6.3
s 108 ... 8.1.1
s 116 ... 6.5.1
s 118(1) ... 6.5.1
s 121 ... 4.11.1
s 121(1) ... 4.11.1
s 121(1)(a) ... 4.11.1
s 121(3) ... 4.11.1
s 121(3A) ... 4.11.1
s 122A ... 4.11.2
s 176(6) ... 1.3.4
Sch 6A, para 1 ... 4.11.1
Sch 8 ... 11.3.1
Sch 8, para 2 ... 11.3.1
Sch 8, para 2(2)(a) ... 11.3.1
Sch 8, para 2(2)(c) ... 11.3.1
Sch 8, para 3 ... 11.3.1
Sch 8, para 3(3)(a) ... 11.3.1
Sch 8, para 3(3)(c) ... 11.3.1
Sch 8, para 3A ... 11.3.1
Sch 8, para 3A(2)(c) ... 11.3.1
Sch 8, para 4 ... 11.3.1
Sch 8, para 5 ... 11.3.1
Anti-terrorism, Crime and Security Act 2001 ... 7.12.2
s 114 ... 11.4.2
s 114(1) ... 11.4.2
s 114(2) ... 11.4.2
Assaults on Emergency Workers (Offences) Act 2018 ... 2.2.6
s 1 ... 2.2.6
s 1(1) ... 2.2.6
s 1(1)(b) ... 2.2.6
Aviation and Maritime Security Act 1990 ... 11.7.1
s 1 ... 11.7.1
Bail Act 1976
s 5B(7) ... 1.4.2
s 7(3) ... 1.4.2
s 30D(1) ... 1.4.2
s 30D(2A) ... 1.4.2
s 46A(1) ... 1.4.2
s 46A(1A) ... 1.4.2
British Nationality Act 1981 ... 4.11.1
British Transport Commission Act 1949
s 55(1) ... 7.1.1
s 56 ... 7.1.1
Broadcasting Act 1990 ... 7.12.2
Care Standards Act 2000
s 2 ... 11.2
s 3 ... 11.2
Child Abduction Act 1984 ... 2.6, 2.6.3
Pt 1 ... 8.3.5
s 1 ... 2.6.3
s 1(1) ... 2.6.3
s 1(2) ... 2.6.2–2.6.3
s 1(2)(c)–(e) ... 2.6.3
s 1(3) ... 2.6.3
s 2 ... 2.6.3
s 2(1) ... 2.6.3
s 2(2) ... 2.6.3
s 2(3) ... 2.6.3
s 2(3)(b) ... 2.6.3
s 5 ... 2.6.2–2.6.3
Children Act 1989 ... 2.4.1–2.4.2, 2.8
Pt 2 ... 2.6.3
s 1(1) ... 6.6.1
s 34 ... 2.4.2
s 43 ... 2.4.2
s 44 ... 2.4.2
s 46 ... 2.4.2
s 46(3)(e) ... 2.4.2
s 47 ... 2.4.2
s 48 ... 2.4.2
s 50 ... 2.4.2
s 51 ... 2.4.2
Children Act 2004 ... 6.1.2, 6.2.2, 6.3.2, 6.5.4
s 11 ... 6.6.1
s 58 ... 2.1.2
Children and Families Act 2014
s 91 ... 11.5.1
Children and Young Persons Act 1933 ... 2.4.1, 2.7.5, 11.5.1
Pt 1 ... 2.8
s 1 ... 2.1.2, 2.7.5, 2.8
s 1(1) ... 2.4.1
s 1(2)(b) ... 2.7.5
s 7 ... 11.5.1
s 7(3) ... 11.1.4
s 17 ... 2.4.1, 2.8
s 50 ... 2.7.1
Children and Young Persons Act 1969
s 32(1A) ... 1.4.2
Chronically Sick and Disabled Persons Act 1970
s 20 ... 10.1.3, 10.11.1
City of Westminster Act 1999 s 27(1) ... 11.1.2
Civil Partnership Act 2004
s 73 ... 2.8
Communications Act 2003 ... 7.12
s 125 ... 7.12.2
s 126 ... 7.12.2

s 127........... 2.5, 4.8.1, 6.5.5, 7.11.2, 7.11.4, 7.12.1–7.12.2
s 127(1)................................. 7.12.2
s 127(1)(a)............................. 7.12.2
s 127(2)...............7.1.1–7.1.2, 7.12.2
ss 128–130............................. 7.12.2
Computer Misuse Act 1990
s 1.............................. 4.12.1, 4.12.2
s 2.............................. 4.12.1, 4.12.2
s 3.. 4.12.1
Confiscation of Alcohol (Young Persons) Act 1997........... 9.5
s 1.. 11.1.4
s 1(1)........................... 9.5.1, 11.1.4
s 1(1AA)................................. 9.5.1
s 1(3)...................................... 9.5.1
Consumer Protection Act 1987...... 8.8
s 12(5).................................. 11.5.1
s 39(1).................................. 11.5.1
Copyright, Designs and Patents Act 1988
s 107(1)...................................... 5.5
s 107(2)...................................... 5.5
s 198(1)...................................... 5.5
s 297A.. 5.5
Coroners and Justice Act 2009.... 2.7.1
s 54(1).................................... 2.7.1
s 62.. 6.6.2
ss 74–85................................. 4.8.1
ss 86–97................................. 4.8.1
s 89.. 4.8.1
Corporate Manslaughter and Corporate Homicide Act 2007.................................. 2.7.3
s 1.. 2.7.3
s 2.. 2.7.3
s 2(1)(d).................................. 2.7.3
s 2(2).. 2.7.3
Sch 1.. 2.7.3
Counter-Terrorism Act 2008..... 11.1.1
Counter-Terrorism and Security Act 2015.................. 11.1.1
Countryside and Rights of Way Act 2000
Pt 2... 10.22
Courts Act 2003
ss 52–55A............................. 8.10.1
Crime and Disorder Act 1998
s 1.. 7.13.1
s 1B.. 7.13.1
s 28.. 7.10.1
ss 28–32.................................. 7.10
s 28(1).................................. 7.10.1
s 28(1)(a).........7.10.1, 7.10.3–7.10.4
s 28(1)(b).................... 7.10.1, 7.10.3
s 29......................2.1.1–2.1.2, 7.10.2
s 29(1).................................. 7.10.2
s 29(1)(a).............................. 7.10.2
s 29(1)(b).............................. 7.10.2
s 29(1)(c).............................. 7.10.2
s 30.. 7.10.3
s 30(1).................................. 7.10.3
s 31.......................... 7.7, 7.8, 7.10.4
s 31(1).................................. 7.10.4
s 31(1)(a)........................ 7.6, 7.10.4
s 31(1)(b).............................. 7.10.4
s 31(1)(c).............................. 7.10.4
s 32.. 7.10.5
s 32(1).................................. 7.10.5
s 32(1)(a).............................. 7.10.5
s 32(1)(b).............................. 7.10.5
Crime and Security Act 2010
ss 24–30...................................... 2.8
s 25(1)(b).................................... 2.8
Criminal Appeal Act 1995
s 9.. 4.8.1
s 11.. 4.8.1
Criminal Attempts Act 1981........................... 4.1.1, 4.2
s 1................ 3.1.1, 4.1.1, 4.1.3, 4.4, 5.2.1, 5.3.1
s 1(2)...................................... 4.1.1
s 8.. 4.1.1
s 9................................. 4.1.1, 4.2.1
s 22.. 4.1.1
Criminal Damage Act 1971
s 1............................. 4.4, 4.6, 8.3.5
s 1(1).................... 4.4, 7.1.1, 7.10.3
s 1(2)...................................... 4.5.1
s 1(3)............................... 4.4, 4.5.2
s 2.. 4.6
s 2(b).. 4.6
s 3.. 4.7.1
s 3(a)...................................... 4.7.1
s 3(b)...................................... 4.7.1
s 5............................. 4.4, 4.5.1, 4.6
s 5(2)(b)...................................... 4.4
s 6.. 4.4
s 10(1).. 4.4
Criminal Finances Act 2017........... 5.5
Criminal Justice Act 1967
s 8....................... 2.3.2, 2.7.1, 4.1.2
s 91................................. 7.1.1, 7.2
s 91(1)......................... 7.2.1, 7.18.2
Criminal Justice Act 1972
s 34.. 7.2.2
Criminal Justice Act 1988... 8.10, 8.11
s 39..............2.1, 2.1.1–2.1.2, 7.10.2
s 139................. 1.3.2, 8.9.5, 8.10.1, 8.10.4, 8.11.2
s 139(1)........................ 8.9.3, 8.10.1
s 139(5)................................ 8.10.1

s 139A 8.10.4–8.10.6, 8.11.2
s 139AA 1.3.2, 8.10.1, 8.10.4–8.10.6, 8.11.2
s 139AA(1) 8.10.4
s 139B 8.10.4–8.10.6, 8.11.2
s 139B(1) 8.11.2
s 139B(2) 8.11.2
s 141 .... 8.3.7, 8.9.2–8.9.3, 8.11.1
s 141(1) 8.9.2
s 141(2) 8.10.2, 8.10.3
s 141(11B) 8.9.2
s 141A 8.3.7, 8.10.2
s 141A(1) 8.10.2
s 141A(3) 8.10.2
s 141A(4) 8.10.2
s 142 .... 8.11.1
s 142(1) 8.11.1
s 160 .... 6.6.1–6.6.2
s 160(1) 6.6.2
s 160(2) 6.6.2
s 160A 6.6.2
s 160A(1)–(4) 6.6.2
Criminal Justice Act 1991 .... 8.3.5
Pt 4 .... 11.6.1
Criminal Justice Act 2003 .... 2.5
s 103(2)(b) 6.3.2
s 189 .... 8.3.1
Criminal Justice and Courts Act 2015 .... 8.3.5
s 17(3) 4.9.3
s 20 .... 4.10
s 20(1) 4.10
s 20(2) 4.10
s 21 .... 4.10
s 22 .... 4.10
s 36 .... 6.5.4
Sch 4 .... 4.10
Criminal Justice and Immigration Act 2008 .... 7.13
s 63 .... 6.6.2
s 65(2) 6.6.2
s 76 .... 1.1, 2.1.2
s 76(8B) 11.6.3
s 119 .... 7.13.5
s 120 .... 7.13.5
Criminal Justice and Police Act 2001 .... 1.4.4, 7.1.2
s 2 .... 7.1
s 39 .... 4.8.1
s 40 .... 4.8.1
s 42 .... 7.11, 7.11.8
s 42(4)(b) 7.11.8
s 42(7) 7.11.8
s 42(7A) 7.11.8
s 42A 7.11, 7.11.8
s 42A(1) 7.11.8
s 42A(1)(c) 7.11.8
s 42A(1)(d) 7.11.8
s 42A(1)(d)(i) 7.11.8
s 42A(2) 7.11.8
s 46 .... 6.11.1
s 50 .... 1.4.4
s 51 .... 1.4.4, 1.5.4
s 52 .... 1.4.4
Sch 1 Pt 1 .... 1.4.4
Sch 1 Pt 2 .... 1.4.4
Criminal Justice and Public Order Act 1994 .... 7.17.1, 8.3.5
s 51 .... 2.5, 4.8, 4.8.1, 7.11.2, 7.11.4, 7.12.2
s 51(1)(b) 4.8.1
s 51(1)(c) 4.8.1
s 51(7) 4.8.1
s 51(8) 4.8.1
s 51(9) 4.8.1
s 51(10) 4.8.1
s 60 .... 8.11.2–8.11.3, 8.13
s 60(1) 8.11.3
s 60(1)(a) 8.11.3
s 60(1)(aa) 8.11.3
s 60(1)(aa)(i) 8.11.3
s 60(1)(b) 8.11.3
s 60(5) 8.11.3
s 60(6) 8.11.3
s 60(8) 8.11.3
s 60AA 8.11.3
s 60AA(7) 8.11.3
s 61 .... 7.17.1
ss 61–62C 7.17
s 61(4) 7.17.1
s 62 .... 7.17.1
ss 62A–62C 7.17.1
s 76 .... 1.4.2
s 166 .... 7.18.2
Criminal Justice (International Co-operation) Act 1990
s 12 .... 5.5
s 19 .... 5.5
Criminal Law Act 1967
s 3 .... 1.1
s 3(1) 1.1
s 4 .... 4.1.3–4.1.4
s 4(1) 4.1.1
s 5(1) 4.1.1
s 5(2) 7.1.1–7.1.2, 11.4.1
s 6(3) 2.3.2
Criminal Law Act 1977 .... 7.12.2
s 1 .... 4.1.1, 4.1.4
s 1(1) 7.13.3
s 6 .... 1.4.2, 7.17, 7.17.1–7.17.2
s 6(1) 7.17.2
s 6(1A) 7.17.2

s 6(5) 7.17.2
s 7 .... 1.4.2, 7.17, 7.17.1, 7.17.3
s 7(1) 7.17.3
s 8 .... 1.4.2, 8.9.4
s 8(1) 8.9.4
s 10 .... 1.4.2
s 12A 7.17.2–7.17.3
s 51 .... 11.4.2
s 51(1) 11.4.2
s 51(2) 11.4.2
Crossbows Act 1987
s 1 .... 8.9.5
s 2 .... 8.9.5
s 3 .... 8.9.5
s 4 .... 8.9.5
Customs and Excise Management Act 1979
s 50(2) 5.5, 8.9.2
s 50(3) 5.5, 8.9.2
s 68(2) 5.5
s 170 .... 5.5
Dangerous Dogs Act 1989
s 1 .... 11.6.3
Dangerous Dogs Act 1991 .... 11.6.3, 11.6.5
s 1 .... 11.6.4, 11.6.5
s 1(1) 11.6.5
s 1(2) 11.6.5
s 1(2)(d) 11.6.5
s 1(3) 11.6.5
s 1(7) 11.6.5
s 3 .... 11.6.3
s 3(1) 11.6.3
s 3(1A) 11.6.3
s 3(1B) 11.6.3
s 4 .... 11.6.3
s 4(1)(b) 11.6.4
s 4A 11.6.5
s 5 .... 11.6.3
s 6 .... 11.6.5
Data Protection Act 2018 .... 4.12.2
s 170 .... 4.12.1
Deregulation Act 2015 .... 10.3
s 70 .... 9.1.7
Sch 23 .... 10.21.1
Dogs Act 1871
s 2 .... 11.6.3, 11.6.4
Dogs (Protection of Livestock) Act 1953
s 1 .... 11.6.3
s 2 .... 11.6.3
Domestic Abuse Act 2021 .... 2.1, 2.3, 2.4
Domestic Violence, Crime and Victims Act 2004
s 5 .... 2.7.4
s 5(1) 2.7.4
s 5(1)(d)(ii) 2.7.4
Domestic Violence, Crime and Victims (Amendment) Act 2012 .... 2.7.4
Education Act 1996
s 4 .... 8.10.5
s 444A 11.1.3
s 547 .... 8.10.6
s 547(1) 8.10.6
s 547(3) 8.10.6
s 548 .... 2.4.1
s 550ZA 8.10.6
s 550ZB 8.10.6
s 550ZC 8.10.6
s 550AA 8.10.6
Education and Inspections Act 2006
s 93 .... 8.10.6
Emergency Workers (Obstruction) Act 2006 .... 2.2.7
s 1 .... 2.2.7
s 1(1) 2.2.7
s 1(2) 2.2.7
s 1(3) 2.2.7
s 1(4) 2.2.7
s 2 .... 2.2.7
Employment and Training Act 1973
s 2 .... 4.10
Energy Act 2004
s 68 .... 2.2.2
Environmental Protection Act 1990 .... 7.16
s 79(1) 7.16.1
s 87 .... 7.16.2, 11.1.2
s 87(1) 7.1.1, 7.16.2
s 87(4A) 7.16.2
s 87(4A)(b) 7.16.2
s 88 .... 7.16.2, 11.1.2
s 88A 7.16.2
Equality Act 2010 .... 1.3.2
Explosives Act 1875
s 80 .... 7.1.1, 8.8.6
Family Law Act 1996 .... 4.11
s 63(1) 2.8
s 63A 4.11.2
ss 63A–63R 4.11.2
ss 63A–63S 4.11.2
s 63B 4.11.2
s 63C 4.11.2
s 63CA 4.11.1–4.11.2
s 63CA(1) 4.11.2
s 63CA(2) 4.11.2
s 63CA(3) 4.11.2
s 63CA(4) 4.11.2
s 63CA(5) 4.11.2

s 63D 4.11.2
s 63D(1) 4.11.2
s 63E 4.11.2
s 63F 4.11.2
s 63G 4.11.2
s 63J 4.11.2
s 63K 4.11.2
s 63L 4.11.2
s 63M 4.11.2
s 63O 4.11.2
s 63P 4.11.2
s 63Q 4.11.2
s 63R 4.11.2
s 63S 4.11.2
Finance Act 2014
Sch 19 .... 10.20.1
Fire and Rescue Services Act 2004 .... 7.12
s 49 .... 7.1.1–7.1.2, 7.12.3
s 49(1) 7.12.3
Firearms Act 1968 ..... 8.1, 8.1.1, 8.1.4, 8.2, 8.2.1, 8.4, 8.6, 8.6.3, 8.7, 8.7.2, 8.9.2
s 1 ..... 8.1.1–8.1.4, 8.2.1–8.2.2, 8.3.1, 8.3.3–8.3.4, 8.4.1–8.4.2, 8.5, 8.6.2, 8.7.1–8.7.3, Appendix 4
s 1(1) 8.1.1
s 1(2) 8.1.5
s 1(3) 8.7.4
s 1(3)(b) 8.7.2
s 2 .... 8.2.1–8.2.3
s 2(1) 8.2.1
s 2(2) 8.2.3
s 3(1) 5.5, 8.1.2
s 4 .... 8.1.2
s 4(2) 8.1.2
s 4(3) 8.1.4
s 4(4) 8.1.4
s 5 .... 8.1.1
s 5(1) 8.7.2
s 5(1)(af) 8.7.3
s 5(1)(ag) 8.7.3
s 5(1)(b) 8.1.1, 8.3.3
s 5(2A) 8.1.1
s 5(5) 8.1.1
s 5(6) 8.1.1
s 11 .... 8.1.3
s 11(6) 8.2.1
s 11A 8.1.3
s 16 .... 8.3.2
ss 16–20 .... 8.1.4
s 16A 8.3.3
s 17(1) 8.3.4
s 17(2) 3.3.1, 8.3.5
s 18 .... 8.3.6, 8.6.1
s 18(1) 8.3.6
s 19 .... 7.2.2, 8.5, 8.7.2
s 20 .... 8.4.1, 8.6.1
s 20(1) 8.4.1
s 20(2) 8.4.2
s 21 .... 8.3.1
s 21(1) 8.3.1
s 21(2) 8.3.1
s 21(2C) 8.3.1
s 21(3) 8.3.1
s 21(4) 8.3.1
s 21(5) 8.3.1
s 21(6) 8.3.1
s 21A(1) 8.7.2
s 21A(2) 8.7.2
s 22 .... 8.2.2, 8.7.1
s 22(1) 8.7.1
s 22(2) 8.1.3
s 22(3) 8.2.2, 8.6.3
s 22(4) 8.7.2
s 23 .... 8.7.2
s 23(1) 8.7.2
s 23(1A) 8.7.2
s 24 .... 8.2.2, 8.7.1–8.7.2
s 24(1) 8.7.1
s 24(2) 8.1.3
s 24(3) 8.2.2
s 24(4) 8.7.2
s 24(4)(b) 8.7.2
s 24(5) 8.1.3, 8.2.2, 8.7.1–8.7.2
s 24ZA 8.7.2
s 24ZA(1) 8.7.2
s 24A 8.7.1, 8.7.5
s 24A(1) 8.7.5
s 24A(2) 8.7.5
s 24A(3) 8.7.5
s 27(2) 8.1.5
s 28(1) 8.2.3
s 28(1A) 8.2.3
s 28A(7) 8.2.3
s 33 .... 8.1.2
s 40 .... 8.1.2
s 46 .... 1.5, 8.6.1, 8.6.3
s 46(1) 1.5.1, 8.6.3
s 46(2) 1.5.1, 8.6.3
s 46(5) 8.6.3
s 47 .... 8.1.4, 8.6.1
s 47(1) 8.6.1
s 47(2) 8.6.1
s 47(3) 8.6.1
s 47(4) 8.6.1
s 47(5) 8.6.1
s 48 .... 8.6.2
s 48(1) 8.6.2
s 48(2) 8.6.2
s 48(3) 8.6.2

s 48(4) ... 8.6.2
s 53 ... 8.7.2
s 54(3)(ba) ... 11.1.11
s 54(3)(g) ... 11.1.11
s 57(1) ... 11.1.11
s 57A ... 8.1.1
s 58 ... 8.1.1, 8.2.1
Sch 1 ... 8.3.5
Firearms Act 1982
s 1 ... 8.1.4
s 1(1) ... 8.1.4
s 1(5) ... 8.1.4
s 1(6) ... 8.1.4
Firearms (Amendment) Act 1988
s 14 ... 8.1.5
s 15 ... 8.1.3
Fireworks Act 2003 ... 8.8
s 11 ... 7.1.1
s 11(1) ... 8.8.2–8.8.4
Football (Offences) Act 1991 ... 7.18, 7.18.2
s 2 ... 7.18.2
s 2(a) ... 7.18.2
s 2(b) ... 7.18.2
s 3 ... 7.18.2
s 4 ... 7.18.2
Football Spectators Act 1989 ... 7.18, 7.18.2
s 14A ... 7.18.2
Sch 1 ... 7.18.2
Forgery and Counterfeiting Act 1981
s 14 ... 5.5
s 15 ... 5.5
s 16 ... 5.5
s 17 ... 5.5
Fraud Act 2006 ... 3.9
s 1 ... 3.8.1–3.8.4
ss 1–4 ... 3.8
s 2 ... 3.8.2
ss 2–4 ... 3.8.1
s 2(5) ... 3.8.2
s 3 ... 3.8.3
s 4 ... 3.8.4
s 5 ... 3.8.1
s 6 ... 3.8, 3.8.6
s 6(1) ... 3.8.6
s 7 ... 3.8, 3.8.7
s 7(1) ... 3.8.7
s 11 ... 3.9
s 12 ... 3.8
s 13 ... 3.8, 3.8.1, 3.8.5, 3.8.7
Further and Higher Education Act 1992
s 85A ... 8.10.6
s 85B ... 8.10.6
Gangmasters (Licensing) Act 2004
s 12(1) ... 5.5
s 12(2) ... 5.5
Goods Vehicles (Licensing of Operators) Act 1995
s 2(5) ... 10.4.1
Greater London Council (General Powers) Act 1974
s 15 ... 10.4.1
Guard Dogs Act 1975 ... 11.6.6
s 1 ... 11.6.6
s 1(1) ... 11.6.6
s 1(2) ... 11.6.6
s 1(3) ... 11.6.6
s 5 ... 11.6.6
Highways Act 1835
s 72 ... 10.4.1, 10.12, 10.12.4
Highways Act 1980 ... 8.8, 10.21
s 115E ... 9.4.1
s 137 ... 10.4.1, 10.21.1, 10.21.4
s 137(1) ... 10.21.1, 10.21.4
s 137ZA ... 10.21.1
s 139 ... 10.21.2
s 139(3) ... 10.21.2
s 139(4) ... 10.21.2
s 140 ... 10.21.2
s 161 ... 8.5, 10.21.3
s 161(1) ... 10.21.3
s 161(2) ... 8.8.7, 10.21.3
s 161(3) ... 10.21.3
s 161(4) ... 10.21.3
s 161A ... 10.21.3
s 162 ... 10.21.3
s 185 ... 7.16.2
Homicide Act 1957
s 2 ... 2.7.1
s 4(3) ... 2.7.1
Hovercraft Act 1968 ... 5.4.1
Human Rights Act 1998 ... 7.15.1, Appendix 1
s 3 ... 7.7
Identity Documents Act 2010
s 4 ... 11.3.1
s 6 ... 11.3.1
Immigration Act 1971
s 5 ... 11.3.2
s 24 ... 11.3.1
s 24(A1) ... 11.3.1
s 24(B1) ... 11.3.1
s 24(C1) ... 11.3.1
s 24(D1) ... 11.3.1
s 24(1) ... 11.3.1
s 24A(1) ... 11.3.2
s 24B ... 11.3.1
s 25 ... 5.5, 11.3.1
s 25A ... 5.5, 11.3.1

s 25D ... 11.3.1
Infant Life (Preservation) Act 1929 ... 2.7.6
s 1(1) ... 2.7.6
Infanticide Act 1938
s 1(1) ... 2.7.6
Investigatory Powers Act 2016
Pt 2, Ch 1 ... 11.1.1
s 19 ... 11.1.1
s 21 ... 11.1.1
Laser Misuse (Vehicles) Act 2018
s 1(1) ... 11.8
s 1(1)(a) ... 11.8
s 1(2) ... 11.8
s 2 ... 11.8
Legal Aid, Sentencing and Punishment of Offenders Act 2012 ... 10.7.2
s 91 ... 1.4.2
s 97(1) ... 1.4.2
s 144 ... 1.4.2, 7.17, 7.17.1
s 144(1) ... 7.17.1
s 144(1)(a) ... 7.17.1
s 144(2) ... 7.17.1
Licensing Act 1872 ... 10.12.3
s 12 ... 7.1.1, 7.2, 7.2.2, 7.18.2, 10.12.3
Licensing Act 1902
s 2 ... 7.2.2
Licensing Act 2003 ... 9.1–9.3, 9.3.2, 11.1.7
Pt 3 ... 7.13.5, 9.5.1, 9.5.2
Pt 4 ... 9.5.2
Pt 5 ... 9.1.1, 9.1.3, 9.5.1–9.5.2
s 3 ... 7.13.4
s 11 ... 8.8.9
s 97(1) ... 9.3.2
s 98(2)–(4) ... 9.3.2
s 140(1) ... 9.2.3
s 140(2) ... 9.2.3
s 141 ... 7.1.1, 11.1.3
s 141(1) ... 9.2.1
s 141(2) ... 9.2.1
s 141(2)(c) ... 11.1.3
s 141(3) ... 9.2.1, 11.1.3
s 142 ... 9.2.1, 11.1.3
s 143(1) ... 9.2.2
s 143(2) ... 9.2.2
s 145 ... 9.2.1
s 145(1) ... 9.1.1
s 145(3) ... 9.1.1, 9.2.3
s 145(4) ... 9.1.1
s 145(6)–(8) ... 9.1.1
s 146 ... 9.1.3, 9.3.3
s 146(1) ... 7.1.1, 9.1.2, 11.1.3
s 146(2) ... 9.1.2
s 146(3) ... 7.1.1, 9.1.2
s 146(4)–(6) ... 9.1.2
s 147 ... 9.3.3
s 147(1) ... 9.1.3
s 147(2) ... 9.1.3
s 147(3) ... 9.1.3
s 147A ... 9.1.3, 9.3.3
s 147B ... 9.1.3
s 148 ... 9.1.7
s 149 ... 9.1.4, 9.3.1
s 149(1) ... 9.1.4
s 149(1)(a) ... 9.1.4, 11.1.3
s 149(1)(b) ... 9.1.4
s 149(2) ... 9.1.4, 9.3.1
s 149(3) ... 9.1.4
s 149(3)(a) ... 7.1.1, 9.1.4, 11.1.3
s 149(3)(b) ... 9.1.4
s 149(4) ... 7.1.1, 9.1.4
s 149(4)(a) ... 9.1.4, 11.1.3
s 149(4)(b) ... 9.1.4
s 149(5) ... 9.1.4
s 149(6) ... 9.1.4
s 150 ... 9.1.5
s 150(1) ... 9.1.5, 11.1.3
s 150(2) ... 7.1.1, 9.1.5, 11.1.3
s 150(3) ... 9.1.5
s 150(3)(b) ... 11.1.3
s 150(4) ... 9.1.5
s 151 ... 7.1.1, 9.1.6
s 151(1) ... 9.1.6
s 151(1)(a) ... 9.1.6
s 151(2) ... 9.1.6
s 151(3) ... 9.1.6
s 151(4) ... 9.1.6
s 151(6) ... 9.1.6
s 152 ... 9.3.1
s 152(1) ... 9.1.7, 11.1.3
s 152(1)(b) ... 11.1.3
s 152(3) ... 9.1.7
s 152(4) ... 9.1.7, 9.3.1
s 153 ... 9.1.7
s 161 ... 7.13.4
s 165(2)(b) ... 7.13.4
s 165(2)(c) ... 7.13.4
s 165(2)(d) ... 7.13.4
s 169A(1) ... 9.3.3
s 169B ... 9.3.3
s 179(1) ... 9.3.2
s 180(1) ... 9.3.2
s 191 ... 9.1.1
Sch 1, para 2 ... 8.8.9
Litter Act 1983 ... 7.16
s 5(9) ... 7.16.2
Local Government Act 1972
s 72 ... 7.16.2
s 237A ... 11.1.2

Local Government and Housing Act 1989
s 4 .... 7.13.4
Local Government Byelaws (Wales) Act 2012
s 12 .... 11.1.2
London Local Authorities Act 1990
s 38(1) 11.1.2
London Local Authorities Act 2004
s 15 .... 11.1.2
Magistrates' Courts Act 1980
s 1 .... 4.8.1
s 22A 1.3.4, 3.1.1, 4.1.1
s 44 .... 4.1.3
s 76 .... 1.4.2
s 115 .... 7.3
s 115(1) 7.3
Malicious Communications Act 1988 .... 7.12
s 1 .... 2.5, 3.2.2, 4.8.1, 7.11.4, 7.12.1–7.12.2
s 1(1) 7.12.1
s 1(1)(a) 7.12.1
s 1(1)(b) 7.12.1
Mental Capacity Act 2005 .... 4.11.1
Mental Health Act 1983 .... 1.4.2, 2.4.2, 11.2
s 114(1) 11.2
s 118 .... 11.2
s 135 .... 11.2
s 136 .... 11.2
s 136(1) 11.2
s 136(2) 11.2
s 136(2A) 11.2
s 136(3) 11.2
s 136(4) 11.2
s 136A(1) 11.2
s 136A(2) 11.2
s 136B 11.2
s 136C 11.2
s 136C(1) 11.2
Merchant Shipping Act 1995 .... 10.16.1, 10.16.2
Misuse of Drugs Act 1971 .... 5.1, 5.1.1–5.1.2, 5.2, 5.2.2, 5.3.5, 11.1.5
s 2 .... 5.1.1
s 2A 5.1.1
s 4 .... 5.1, 5.1.1
s 4(1) 5.4.2
s 4(2) 5.1.1, 5.3.1, 5.5
s 4(2)(a) 5.1.1
s 4(2)(b) 5.1.1
s 4(3) 5.1.1, 5.5
s 4(3)(a) 5.1.1, 9.3.2
s 4(3)(b) 5.1.1, 9.3.2
s 4(3)(c) 5.1.1, 9.3.2
s 4A 5.1.1
s 5 .... 5.2.1
s 5(2) 2.7.5, 5.1.1, 5.2.1, 5.3.1, 7.1.1
s 5(3) 5.1.1, 5.2.2, 5.5
s 5(4) 5.2.1
s 6 .... 5.1.1, 5.3.1
s 6(2) 5.1.1
s 7 .... 5.1.1, 5.2.1, 5.3.1
s 7A 5.1.1
s 8 .... 5.4.2, 5.5
s 8(a)–(d) 5.4.2
s 8(b) 5.4.2
s 9 .... 5.1.1–5.1.2
s 9A 5.1, 5.1.2
s 18 .... 5.3.1
s 20 .... 5.5
s 23 .... 1.3.2, 1.5, 5.4.1
s 23(1) 5.4.1
s 23(2) 1.5.1, 5.1.1, 5.2.1–5.2.2, 5.4.1
s 23(2)(b) 5.4.1
s 23(3) 5.4.1, 5.4.2
s 23(4) 5.4.1
s 23(4)(b)–(c) 5.4.1
s 23A 5.4.1
s 23A(6) 5.4.1
s 28 .... 5.1.1, 5.2.1–5.2.2, 5.3.1, 7.8
s 37 .... 5.1.1
s 37(1) 5.1.1, 5.3.1
Sch 2 .... 5.1.1–5.1.2
Modern Slavery Act 2015 .... 4.9.1, 4.9.3
s 1 .... 4.9.2–4.9.3, 5.5
s 1(1) 4.9.2
s 1(1)(a) 4.9.2
s 1(1)(b) 4.9.2
ss 1–6 .... 4.9.1
s 2 .... 4.9.3, 5.5
s 2(1) 4.9.3
s 2(6) 4.9.3
s 3 .... 4.9.3
s 3(3)–(6) 4.9.2
s 3(5) 4.9.2
s 3(6) 4.9.2
s 4 .... 4.9.3
s 7 .... 4.9.3
s 11 .... 4.9.3
s 12 .... 4.9.3
s 14 .... 4.9.4
s 14(1) 4.9.4
s 14(2) 4.9.4
s 17 .... 4.9.4

s 23 .... 4.9.4
s 24 .... 4.9.4
s 45 .... 4.9.5
s 45(3) 4.9.5
s 52 .... 4.9.6
Sch 1 .... 4.9.4
National Health Service
Act 2006 .... 2.4.2, 7.13.5
s 12 .... 10.16.1
s 80 .... 10.16.1
National Health Service (Wales)
Act 2006
s 10 .... 10.16.1
s 38 .... 10.16.1
Offences Against the Person Act 1861
.... 2.1, 2.7.4
s 4 .... 2.7.1
s 16 .... 2.5, 4.8.1, 7.11.2, 7.11.4, 7.12.2
s 18 .... 2.1.1–2.1.2, 2.2.1, 2.3.1–2.3.2
s 20 .... 2.1.1–2.1.2, 2.3.1–2.3.2, 7.10.2, 7.12.3, 8.3.5
s 21 .... 8.3.5
s 22 .... 8.3.5
s 23 .... 5.1.1, 6.10
s 24 .... 2.1.3, 5.1.1, 6.10
s 29 .... 2.3.3
s 30 .... 8.3.5
s 32 .... 8.3.5
s 35 .... 10.7.3
s 38 .... 2.2.1, 8.3.5
s 44 .... 2.1.1
s 47 .... 2.1.1–2.1.2, 2.2.2, 2.3.1, 7.10.2, 8.3.5
s 58 .... 2.7.6
s 60 .... 2.7.6
Offensive Weapons Act 2019
s 54 .... 8.1.1
Official Secrets Act 1911 .... 11.1.1
Official Secrets Act 1920 .... 11.1.1
Official Secrets Act 1939 .... 11.1.1
Official Secrets Act 1989 .... 11.1.1
Online Safety Act 2023 .... 7.12
s 179(1) 7.12.3
s 179(7) 7.12.3
s 179(8) 7.12.3
s 179(1)(d) 7.12.3
s 180 .... 7.12.3, 7.12.4, 7.12.5, 7.12.6
s 181(1) 7.12.4
s 181(3) 7.12.4
s 182(7) 7.12.3
s 182(3) 7.12.3
s 182(4) 7.12.3
s 182(6) 7.12.3
s 182(7) 7.12.3
s 182(9) 7.12.3
s 183(1) 7.12.5
s 183(2) 7.12.5
s 183(3) 7.12.5
s 183(4) 7.12.5
s 183(6) 7.12.5
s 183(8) 7.12.5
s 183(11) 7.12.5
s 184(1) 7.12.6
s 184(2) 7.12.6
s 184(4) 7.12.6
s 184(5) 7.12.6
s 184(6) 7.12.6
s 184(7) 7.12.6
s 184(8) 7.12.6
s 184(9) 7.12.6
s 184(10) 7.12.6
s 184(11) 7.12.6
s 184(12) 7.12.6
s 185 .... 7.12.3, 7.12.4
Parks Regulation Act 1872 .... 11.1.3
Parks Regulation (Amendment)
Act 1926
s 2 .... 11.1.3
Police Act 1996 .... 2.2.7, 8.3.5
s 30 .... 2.2.2
s 53F 11.1.11
s 89(1) 2.2.2
s 89(2) 2.2.2–2.2.3
s 90 .... 2.2.4
s 90(1) 2.2.4
s 90(2) 2.2.4
s 90(3) 2.2.4
Police and Criminal Evidence Act
1984 .... 1.2, 1.3.2–1.3.4, 1.4.4, 1.5, 2.6.1, 3.1.1, 5.4.1, 8.6.1, 8.6.3, 11.2, 11.6.3
s 1 .... 1.3.2, 3.1.1, 3.3.1, 3.8.5, 4.3.1, 4.4, 8.9.1, 8.9.4–8.9.5, 8.13
s 1(3) 1.3.2
s 1(4) 1.3.2
s 1(5) 1.3.2
s 1(6) 1.3.2
s 1(7) 1.3.2, 2.3.3
s 1(8) 1.3.2
s 1(8A) 1.3.2, 8.10.1, 8.10.4
s 1(8B) 1.3.2, 8.8.2
s 2 .... 1.3.2, 2.2.2, 5.1.1, 5.2.1–5.2.2, 5.4.1
s 2(2) 1.3.2
s 2(10) 1.3.2
s 3 .... 1.2
s 8 .... 1.4.4, 1.5.1–1.5.2
s 8(1) 1.5.4

s 8(2) 1.5.1
s 8(4) 1.5.1
s 8(5) 1.5.1
s 9 .... 1.5.1, 1.5.4
s 10 .... 1.4.1
s 15 .... 1.5.1–1.5.2
s 15(1) 1.5.2
s 15(6)(b) 1.5.2
s 16 .... 1.5.1–1.5.3
s 16(3) 1.5.1
s 16(5) 1.5.2
s 17 .... 1.3.3, 1.4.2, 2.4.2, 7.7, 8.11.2
ss 17–22 .... 1.4
s 17(1) 1.4.2
s 17(1)(b) 2.8
s 17(1)(c)(ii) 1.4.2
s 17(1)(c)(iii) 7.6
s 17(1)(c)(iv) 1.4.2
s 17(1)(c)(v) 11.6.2
s 17(1)(c)(vi) 1.4.2, 7.17.1
s 17(1)(d) 1.4.2
s 17(1)(e) 1.4.2, 2.8
s 17(3) 1.4.2
s 17(6) 7.3
s 18 .... 1.4.3–1.4.4, 1.5.1, 1.5.4
s 18(1) 1.4.3
s 19 .... 1.4.4, 1.5.1, 5.3.1, 11.6.1
s 20 .... 1.4.4, 6.6.1–6.6.2
s 21 .... 1.4.4
s 22 .... 1.4.4, 5.3.1
s 24 .... 1.3, 1.3.1–1.3.2, 1.3.4, 7.1.2
s 24(4) 1.3.2
s 24(5) 1.3.2–1.3.3
s 24(5)(e) 1.3.1
s 24A 1.3, 1.3.1, 1.3.4
s 24A(1)(b) 1.3.4
s 28 .... 1.3.2, 2.2.2
ss 28–31 .... 1.3
s 29 .... 1.3.3
s 30 .... 1.3.3
s 30(1) 1.3.3
s 30(1A) 1.3.3
s 30A 1.3.3
s 30A(1) 1.3.3
s 30A(1A) 1.3.3
s 30A(3A) 1.3.3
s 30A(3B) 1.3.3
s 30B 1.3.3
s 30D(1) 1.3.3
s 31 .... 1.3.3
s 32 .... 1.4, 1.4.1, 1.4.3, 1.5.1, 1.5.4
s 32(2) 1.4.1
s 36(4) 11.1.1
s 55 .... 5.4.1
s 55(5) 11.1.1
s 55(6) 11.1.1
s 58 .... 10.10.2
s 61 .... 7.1.2
s 63B 5.2.1
s 64A(1B)(ca) 7.15.2
s 67(9A) 11.1.11
s 76 .... 1.3.2
s 78 .... 1.3.2, 9.3.1
s 117 .... 1.1
s 118 .... 1.3.2
Sch 1 .... 1.5.4
Sch 1, para 13 .... 1.4.4
Sch 2 .... 1.3.1
Code A 1.3.2
paras 2.2–2.11 .... 1.3.2
paras 2.12–2.14B 8.11.3
para 2.14C 8.12.3
para 3.8 .... 1.3.2
para 4.12 .... 1.3.2
Annex G 8.13
Code B 1.4.1–1.4.3, 1.5.1–1.5.4
Code C 1.3.1–1.3.3, 7.1.2
para 1.7 .... 1.3.2
Note 1F 1.3.2
para 3.16 .... 11.2
para 3.21 .... 1.3.2–1.3.3
para 10.1 .... 1.3.2
para 10.2 .... 1.3.2
para 10.4 .... 1.3.2
para 10.5 .... 1.3.2
para 10.7 .... 1.3.2
para 10.8 .... 1.3.2
para 10.10 .... 1.3.1
para 10.11 .... 1.3.1
Code D Pt 4 .... 7.1.2
Code E
Annex A, para 2.4(c)(iii) 3.1.1, 4.4, 5.2.1, 5.3.1
Code G 1.3.1
para 2.9 .... 1.3.1
para 2.9(e)(i) 1.3.3
para 4 .... 1.3.1
Code H 1.3.1
para 10.4 .... 1.3.2
Police, Crime, Sentencing and Courts Act
s 78 .... 7.13.3
Police Reform Act 2002 .... 7.13
Pt 2 .... 11.1.11
s 12(7)(d) 11.1.11
s 38 .... 2.2.5, 11.1, 11.1.1–11.1.2, 11.1.5–11.1.6, 11.1.11
s 38(6B) 11.1
s 38(6B)(a) 11.1.3–11.1.4
s 38(6B)(b) 11.1.8–11.1.10

s 38(7A) 11.1.11
s 38(8) 11.1.11
s 38(9) 11.1.11
s 38(9A) 11.1.11
s 38(9B) 11.1.11
s 38B 2.2.5
s 39 .... 2.2.5
s 40 .... 2.2.5
s 41 .... 2.2.5
s 41A 2.2.5
s 46 .... 2.2.5, 11.1.11
s 46(3) 2.2.5
s 47(1) 2.2.5
s 50 .... 7.13.2
s 50(1) 7.13.2
s 50(2) 7.13.2
s 59 .... 7.14, 7.14.1–7.14.2, 10.1.3, 10.22
s 59(3)(b) 7.14.2
s 59(4) 7.14.1
s 59(6) 7.14.1
Sch 3B 11.1.1
Sch 3B, Pt 1 .... 11.1.1
Sch 3B, Pt 2 .... 11.1.1
Sch 3B, Pt 2, para 8(1) 11.1.1
Sch 3C 11.1
Sch 3C, para 2 .... 11.1.3
Sch 3C, para 2(5) 11.1.2
Sch 3C, para 3 .... 11.1.3
Sch 3C, paras 3–9 .... 11.1.11
Sch 3C, para 3(1) 11.1.3
Sch 3C, para 3(1)(a) 11.1.3
Sch 3C, para 3(3)(e) 11.1.3
Sch 3C, para 3(4)(a) 11.1.7
Sch 3C, para 3(4)(c) 11.1.7
Sch 3C, para 3(4)(f) 11.1.7
Sch 3C, para 3(5) 11.1.3
Sch 3C, para 4 .... 11.1.4
Sch 3C, para 4(1) 11.1.4
Sch 3C, para 4(2) 11.1.4
Sch 3C, para 4(3) 11.1.4
Sch 3C, para 4(5) 11.1.4
Sch 3C, para 4(6) 11.1.4
Sch 3C, para 4(7) 11.1.4
Sch 3C, para 5 .... 5.4.1, 11.1.5
Sch 3C, para 5(1) 11.1.5
Sch 3C, para 5(2) 11.1.5
Sch 3C, para 5(2)(a) 11.1.5
Sch 3C, para 5(3) 11.1.5
Sch 3C, para 5(4) 11.1.5
Sch 3C, para 6 .... 11.1.6
Sch 3C, para 6(1) 11.1.6
Sch 3C, para 6(2) 11.1.6
Sch 3C, para 6(2)(a) 11.1.6
Sch 3C, para 6(3) 11.1.6
Sch 3C, para 6(4) 11.1.6
Sch 3C, para 6(5) 11.1.6
Sch 3C, para 6(7) 11.1.6
Sch 3C, para 7 .... 11.1.7, 11.1.11
Sch 3C, para 7(1) 11.1.7–11.1.9, 11.1.11
Sch 3C, para 7(2) 11.1.7
Sch 3C, para 7(3) 11.1.7–11.1.8, 11.1.11
Sch 3C, para 7(4) 11.1.7–11.1.9, 11.1.11
Sch 3C, para 7(5) 11.1.7, 11.1.11
Sch 3C, para 7(6) 11.1.7, 11.1.11
Sch 3C, para 8 .... 11.1.11
Sch 3C, para 8(1) 11.1.8
Sch 3C, para 8(2) 11.1.8
Sch 3C, para 8(3) 11.1.8
Sch 3C, para 8(4) 11.1.8
Sch 3C, para 8(5) 11.1.8
Sch 3C, para 8(6) 11.1.8
Sch 3C, para 8(7) 11.1.8
Sch 3C, para 9(1) 11.1.9
Sch 3C, para 9(2) 11.1.9
Sch 3C, para 9(3) 11.1.9
Sch 3C, para 10 .... 11.1.10
Sch 3C, para 11 .... 11.1.11
Sch 4, para 14 .... 11.1.11
Sch 5 .... 2.2.5
Police Reform and Social Responsibility Act 2011
Pt 1 .... 10.16.1
Policing and Crime Act 2009 .... 6.11.3
s 30 .... 9.5
s 30(1) 9.5.2
s 34 .... 7.4.2
ss 34–49 .... 7.4.2
Policing and Crime Act 2017 .... 5.5, 8.1.3, 11.1–11.2
s 134(1) 8.8.9
s 173 .... 4.11.2
Powers of Criminal Courts (Sentencing) Act 2000
s 92 .... 1.4.2
Prevention of Crime Act 1953 .... 8.9.1
s 1 .... 8.9.1, 8.10.3, 8.11.2
s 1(1) 8.9.1, 8.9.3
s 1A 8.9.1
s 1A(1) 8.9.1
Prison Act 1952
s 8 .... 2.2.7
s 40CB(1) 5.3.5
Proceeds of Crime Act 2002 .... 11.3.1
s 6 .... 5.5
s 70 .... 5.5
s 75 .... 5.5
s 327 .... 5.5
s 328 .... 5.5

s 362A(2) 5.5
s 362B 5.5
Sch 2 .... 3.2.2, 4.1.1, 4.1.4, 4.9.3, 5.1.1–5.2.2, 5.3.1, 5.4.2, 5.5, 6.5.3, 8.1.2, 11.3.1
Protection from Harassment Act 1997 .... 2.8, 7.1.2, 7.10.5, 7.11, 7.12.2
s 1 .... 7.7, 7.11.1, 7.11.6
s 1(1) 7.11.1, 7.11.3
s 1(1A) 7.11.1, 7.11.7
s 1(1A)(c) 7.11.7
s 1(3) 7.11.1
s 2 .... 7.10.5, 7.11.1–7.11.2, 7.11.4, 7.12.1
s 2(1) 7.11.1
s 2A 7.10.5, 7.11.1–7.11.5, 7.12.1
s 2A(3) 7.11.3
s 2B 7.11.3
s 3 .... 2.8, 7.11.7
s 3(3)(a) 7.11.7
s 3(6) 7.11.7
s 3A 7.11.7
s 4 .... 2.5, 4.8.1, 7.10.5, 7.11.2, 7.12.2
s 4(1) 7.11.2
s 4(3) 7.11.2
s 4A 2.5, 4.8.1, 7.10.5, 7.11.3–7.11.4, 7.12.2
s 4A(1) 7.11.4
s 4A(4) 7.11.4
s 4B 7.11.2, 7.11.4
s 5 .... 2.8, 7.10.5, 7.11.1, 7.11.6
s 5(3)–(7) 7.11.6
s 5(5) 7.11.6
s 5A 7.11.6
s 5A(2) 7.11.6
Protection of Children Act 1978 .... 6.6.1
s 1 .... 6.5.1, 6.6.1–6.6.2
s 1(1) 6.6.1
s 1(1)(a) 6.6.1
s 1(1)(b) 6.6.1
s 1(1)(c) 6.6.1
s 1(1)(d) 6.6.1
s 1(4) 6.6.1
s 1(4)(b) 6.6.1
s 1A 6.6.1
s 1B 6.6.1
Sch 6.6.1–6.6.2
Protection of Freedoms Act 2012
s 54 .... 10.22
Psychoactive Substances Act 2016 .... 5.3.2, 11.1.6
s 2 .... 5.3.5
s 2(2) 5.3.3
s 4 .... 5.3.3, 5.3.5, 5.5
ss 4–9 .... 5.3.5
s 5 .... 5.3.4, 5.3.5, 5.5
s 5(1) 5.3.4, 9.3.2
s 5(2) 5.3.4, 9.3.2
s 5(2)(b) 5.3.4
s 7 .... 5.3.5, 5.5
s 8 .... 5.3.5, 5.5
s 9 .... 5.3.4
s 11 .... 5.3.5
s 11(3) 5.3.5
s 23(3) 5.3.5
s 36 .... 11.1.6
ss 36–39 .... 5.3.5
s 43 .... 5.3.5
ss 49–53 .... 11.1.6
ss 49–51 .... 5.3.5, 11.1.6
s 50 .... 11.1.6
s 50(1)(b) 11.1.6
s 53 .... 5.3.5, 11.1.6
Sch 1 .... 5.3.3, 5.3.5
Sch 2 .... 5.3.5
Public Order Act 1936
s 1 .... 1.4.2
Public Order Act 1986 .... 2.1.1, 6.7.2, 7.4, 7.6
Pt 3A 7.9.2–7.9.3
s 1 .... 7.4.1
s 1(1) 7.4.1
s 1(3) 7.4.1
s 2 .... 7.4.1–7.4.2
s 2(1) 7.4.2
s 3 .... 7.4.1
s 3(1) 7.5
s 4 .... 1.4.2, 7.4.1, 7.6–7.7, 7.10.4
s 4(1) 7.6–7.7, 7.10.4
s 4(1)(a) 7.6
s 4(1)(b) 7.6
s 4(2) 7.6
s 4A 1.4.2, 7.7–7.8, 7.10.4, 7.11.1–7.11.4, 7.18.2
s 4A(1) 7.7
s 4A(1)(a) 7.7
s 4A(1)(b) 7.7
s 4A(3) 7.7
s 4A(3)(b) 7.7
s 5 .... 6.7.1, 7.1.1–7.1.2, 7.4.1, 7.7–7.8, 7.10.4, 7.18.2
s 5(1) 7.8
s 5(3) 7.8
s 6 .... 7.4.1
s 6(2) 7.4.2, 7.5
s 6(3) 7.6
s 6(4) 7.8
s 6(7) 7.4.2
s 11 .... 7.15.1

ss 17–23 .... 7.7
ss 17–29 .... 7.9, 7.18.2
ss 17–29N 1.3.4
s 18 .... 7.9.1
ss 18–23 .... 7.9.1
s 18(1) 7.9.1
s 18(4) 7.9.1
s 19 .... 7.9.1–7.9.2
s 19(1) 7.9.2
s 19(2) 7.9.2
s 20 .... 7.9.2
s 21 .... 7.9.1–7.9.2
s 22 .... 7.9.2
s 23 .... 7.9.1–7.9.2
s 28 .... 7.9.1
ss 29A–29N 7.9
s 29B 7.9.3
ss 29B–29G 7.9.3
s 29B(1) 7.9.3
s 29B(4) 7.9.3
s 29C 7.9.3
s 29D 7.9.3
s 29E 7.9.3
s 29F 7.9.3
s 29G 7.9.3
s 29I 7.9.3
s 29J 7.9.3
s 29JA 7.9.3
s 29M 7.9.3
s 38 .... 11.4.2
s 38(1) 11.4.2
s 38(2) 11.4.2
s 38(3) 11.4.2
Public Order Act 2023
s 1(1) 7.17.5
s 2(1) 7.17.5
s 3(1) 7.17.6
s 3(2) 7.17.6
s 3(5) 7.17.6
s 4(1) 7.17.6
s 4(2) 7.17.6
s 5(1) 7.17.6
s 6(1) 7.17.7
s 6(2) 7.17.7
s 7(1) 7.17.8
s 7(2) 7.17.8
s 11 .... 7.17.9
s 12 .... 7.17.9
s 13 .... 7.17.9
s 14 .... 7.17.9
s 34(2) 7.17.5
Public Passenger Vehicles Act 1981
Pt 2 .... 10.10.2
ss 6–29 .... 10.10.2
s 12(5) 10.4.1
Railways and Transport Safety Act 2003
s 68 .... 2.2.2, 2.2.4
Refuse Disposal (Amenity) Act 1978 .... 7.16
s 2 .... 7.16.3
s 2(1) 7.16.3
s 2A 7.16.3
Regulation of Investigatory Powers Act 2000
Pt 2 .... 5.1.1
Restriction of Offensive Weapons Act 1959 .... 8.11.1
s 1 .... 8.10.2, 8.10.3
Road Safety Act 2006 .... 10.4.3
Road Traffic Act 1988 .... 4.2, 10.2, 10.10.2
Pt 3 .... 10.14.1
Pt 5 .... 10.10.2
Pt 6 .... 10.16.2
s 1 .... 10.1.4, 10.6.1, 10.7.1, 10.8, 10.8.1, 10.8.4, 10.10.1, 10.12
s 1A 10.6.1, 10.7.1–10.7.2
s 2 .... 10.5, 10.6.1–10.6.2, 10.7.1–10.7.2, 10.12
s 2A 10.7.1
s 2B 10.6.1, 10.8, 10.8.4
s 3 .... 7.14.1, 10.4.1, 10.5–10.6, 10.6.1–10.6.2, 10.7.1–10.7.2, 10.8.5, 10.12
s 3ZA 10.6.1
s 3ZB 10.8, 10.8.5
s 3ZC 10.8, 10.8.3
s 3ZD 10.13.2
s 3A 10.6.1, 10.8, 10.8.2, 10.8.4, 10.11.3
s 3A(1) 10.8.2
s 3A(1)(b) 10.8.2
s 3A(1)(ba) 10.8.2
s 3A(1)(c) 10.8.2
s 3A(1)(d) 10.8.2
s 3A(3) 10.8.2
s 4 .... 1.4.2, 7.2.2, 7.18.2, 10.10.1, 10.11.2–10.11.3
s 4(1) 10.10.1
s 4(2) 10.10.1
s 4(3) 10.10.1
s 5 .... 7.18.2, 10.10.1–10.11.1, 10.11.3
s 5(1) 10.11.1
s 5(1)(a) 10.11.1
s 5(1)(b) 10.11.1
s 5(2) 10.11.1
s 5A 7.18.2, 10.10.1–10.11.3
s 5A(1)(a) 10.11.2
s 5A(1)(b) 10.11.2

s 5A(2) 10.11.2
s 5A(3) 10.11.2
s 5A(3)–(7) 10.11.2
s 6 .... 10.10.2
s 6(1)–(5) 10.10.2
s 6(5) 10.10.2
s 6(6) 10.10.2
s 6A 10.10.2
ss 6A–6C 10.10.2
s 6B 10.10.2
s 6C 10.10.2, 10.11.2
s 6D 10.10.2, 10.11.1–10.11.2
s 6D(1A) 10.10.2
s 6D(3) 10.10.2
s 6E 10.10.2, 10.11.1–10.11.2
s 6E(1) 10.10.2
s 7 .... 10.10.2, 10.11.3
s 7(6) 10.11.3
s 7A 10.11.3
s 7A(1) 10.11.3
s 7A(5) 10.11.3
s 7A(6) 10.11.3
s 13A(1) 10.6.1
s 14 .... 10.4.1, 10.17, 10.17.1
s 14(3) 10.17.1
s 15 .... 10.17, 10.17.2
s 15(1) 10.17.1–10.17.2
s 15(2) 10.4.1, 10.17.2
s 15(3) 10.17.2
s 15(3A) 10.17.2
s 15(4) 10.4.1, 10.17.2
s 16 .... 10.4.1, 10.18
s 16(4) 10.18
s 18(3) 10.4.1, 10.18
s 19 .... 10.4.1
s 22 .... 10.4.1, 10.5
s 23 .... 10.4.1
s 24 .... 10.4.1
s 25(1) 4.2.2
s 28 .... 10.5, 10.6.2, 10.7.1, 10.12, 10.12.1
s 28(1) 10.12.1
s 29 .... 10.5, 10.6.1–10.6.2, 10.12, 10.12.2
s 30 .... 10.12, 10.12.3
s 30(1) 10.12.3
s 34 .... 7.14.1, 10.4.1, 10.22
s 34(1) 10.22
s 34(3) 10.22
s 35 .... 10.2.1, 10.4.1, 10.5
s 35(1) 10.2.1
s 35(2) 10.2.1
s 36 .... 10.3, 10.4.1, 10.5
s 36(1) 10.3
s 37 .... 10.2.2
s 38(7) 10.6.1
s 40A 10.4.1
s 41 .... 10.4.2
s 41A 10.4.1
s 41B 10.4.1
s 41D 10.4.1–10.4.2
s 41D(a) 10.4.2
s 41D(b) 10.4.2
s 42 .... 10.4.1
s 44 .... 10.16.3
s 45 .... 10.20.2
s 47 .... 10.4.1, 10.16.3, 10.16.5
s 47(1) 10.16.3, 10.20.2
s 53 .... 10.16.3, 10.16.5
s 53(2) 10.16.3
s 71(1) 10.4.1
s 87 .... 10.14, 10.14.1
s 87(1) 10.4.1, 10.8.5, 10.13.1, 10.14.1
s 87(2) 10.14.1
s 88 .... 10.14.1
s 92(1) 10.15
s 96 .... 10.15
s 96(1) 10.15
s 96(2) 10.15
s 96(3) 10.15
s 101 .... 10.13.1
s 102 .... 10.13.1
s 103 .... 10.13.1
s 103(1) 10.13.1
s 103(1)(a) 10.13.1
s 103(1)(b) 10.8.3, 10.13.1–10.13.2
s 143 .... 10.4.1, 10.8.5, 10.16.1
s 143(1)(a) 10.16.1
s 143(3) 10.16.1
s 144 .... 10.16.1–10.16.2
s 144(2)(b) 10.16.1
s 144A 10.4.1, 10.16.2
ss 144A–144D 10.16.2
s 144A(1) 10.16.2
s 144B 10.16.2
s 163 .... 1.4.2, 10.2.3, 10.4.1, 10.12.1, 10.12.3, 10.16.6
s 164 .... 10.16.4, 10.16.6
s 164(1) 10.16.4
s 164(1)(d) 10.16.4
s 164(2) 10.16.4
s 164(3) 10.16.4
s 164(4) 10.16.4
s 164(4A) 10.16.4
s 164(5) 10.16.4
s 164(6) 10.16.4
s 165 .... 10.16.5–10.16.6
s 165(1) 10.16.5
s 165(2) 10.16.5
s 165(2)(a) 10.9.3
s 165(3) 10.16.5

s 165(4) ... 10.16.5
s 165(5) ... 10.16.5
s 165(6) ... 10.16.5
s 165A ... 10.8.5, 10.16.6
s 165B ... 10.16.6
s 168 ... 10.6, 10.6.1–10.6.2, 10.7.1, 10.12.1
s 170 ... 10.9, 10.9.2–10.9.3
s 170(1) ... 10.9.1
s 170(1)(a) ... 10.9.2
s 170(2) ... 10.9.3
s 170(3) ... 10.9.3
s 170(5) ... 10.9.2
s 170(6) ... 10.9.3
s 172 ... 10.4.1
s 185 ... 10.1.3, 10.13.1, 10.17.1
s 186(1) ... 10.1.3
s 187(1) ... 10.1.3
s 187(2) ... 10.1.3
s 188 ... 10.1.3
s 189 ... 10.1.3
s 192 ... 10.6.1, 10.7.1–10.7.2, 10.8.1–10.8.5, 10.9.1, 10.10.1, 10.11.1–10.11.2, 10.12.1–10.12.3, 10.13.1–10.13.2, 10.14.1, 10.15, 10.16.1, 10.19
s 192(1) ... 10.1.1, 10.1.4
Road Traffic (Foreign Vehicles) Act 1972
s 3(1) ... 10.4.1
Road Traffic Offenders Act 1988 ... 10.10.2
Pt 3 ... 10.4.1, 10.10.2
s 1 ... 10.5
s 1(1) ... 10.5
s 2 ... 10.5
s 15 ... 10.8.2
s 35 ... 10.4.1, 10.13.1
ss 51–90 ... 10.4
s 54 ... 10.4.1
s 62 ... 10.4.1
s 62(2) ... 10.4.1
s 67 ... 10.4.1
s 90A ... 10.4.3
ss 90A–90D ... 10.4.3
s 90B ... 10.4.3
s 90C ... 10.4.3
s 90D ... 10.4.3
s 90D(5) ... 10.4.3
s 90D(6) ... 10.4.1, 10.4.3
Sch 1 ... 10.5
Sch 3 ... 10.4.1
Road Traffic Regulation Act 1984 ... 10.10.2
s 5(1) ... 10.4.1
s 8(1) ... 10.4.1
s 11 ... 10.4.1
s 13 ... 10.4.1
s 16 ... 10.5
s 16(1) ... 10.4.1
s 17(4) ... 10.4.1, 10.5
s 18(3) ... 10.4.1
s 20(5) ... 10.4.1
s 25(5) ... 10.4.1
s 29(3) ... 10.4.1
s 35A(1) ... 10.4.1
s 47(1) ... 10.4.1
s 53(5) ... 10.4.1
s 53(6) ... 10.4.1
s 87 ... 10.3
s 88(7) ... 10.4.1, 10.5
s 89(1) ... 10.4.1, 10.5
s 99 ... 11.1.10
Royal Parks (Trading) Act 2000 ... 11.1.9
Scrap Metal Dealers Act 2013 ... 3.1.1
s 1 ... 3.1.1
s 12(1) ... 3.1.1
s 12(4) ... 3.1.1
s 13 ... 3.1.1
s 14 ... 3.1.1
s 15(6) ... 3.1.1
s 16 ... 3.1.1
s 16(13) ... 3.1.1
Sentencing Act 2020 ... 2.2.6
s 67 ... 2.2.6
s 70 ... 8.3.7
s 71 ... 5.1.1
s 72 ... 5.3.4
s 342E ... 8.13
s 342G(1) ... 8.13
Serious Crime Act 2007 ... 5.1.2
Pt 2 ... 2.2.6, 4.1.4
s 44 ... 4.1.4, 5.5
ss 44–49 ... 4.1.4
ss 44–67 ... 4.1.4
s 44(1) ... 4.1.4
s 45 ... 4.1.4
s 46 ... 4.1.4
s 47 ... 4.1.4
s 48 ... 4.1.4
s 49 ... 4.1.4
s 50 ... 4.1.4
s 51 ... 4.1.4
s 56 ... 4.1.4
s 58 ... 4.1.4
s 65 ... 4.1.4
Serious Crime Act 2015 ... 7.4.2
s 66 ... 2.4.1, 2.7.5
s 68(7) ... 6.11.1

s 69 ... 6.5.1
s 69(8) ... 4.9.3
s 76 ... 2.8
s 76(1) ... 2.8
s 76(1)(d) ... 2.8
s 76(2) ... 2.8
s 76(2)(b)(i) ... 2.8
s 76(3) ... 2.8
s 76(8) ... 2.8
s 76A(1) ... 2.8
s 79 ... 5.3.4
Serious Organised Crime and Police Act 2005
s 162 ... 11.1.9
Sexual Offences Act 1956
s 5 ... 6.1.2
s 33 ... 5.5
s 34 ... 5.5
Sexual Offences Act 2003 ... 3.2.2, 6.1, 6.7.2, 6.8.1, 7.13.3, 8.3.5
Pt 1 ... 6.5.1, 6.5.4
Pt 2A ... 6.11.3
s 1 ... 6.1.1–6.1.2, 6.10, 7.12.3
ss 1–79 ... 6.5.1, 6.5.4
s 1(1) ... 6.1.1
s 2 ... 6.1.1, 6.2, 6.2.2, 7.12.3
s 2(1) ... 6.2.1
s 3 ... 6.1.1, 6.3.1–6.3.2, 6.4
s 4 ... 6.1.1, 6.5.2
s 5 ... 6.1.1–6.1.2
s 5(1) ... 6.1.2
s 6 ... 6.2, 6.2.2
s 7 ... 6.3.2, 6.4
s 8 ... 6.5.1–6.5.2, 6.5.5
s 8(1) ... 6.5.2
s 8(2) ... 6.5.2
s 9 ... 6.4, 6.5.3
ss 9–13 ... 6.5.3
s 9(1) ... 6.4
s 9(2) ... 6.4
s 10 ... 6.5.1–6.5.3, 6.5.5
s 10(1) ... 6.5.1
s 10(2) ... 6.5.1
s 11 ... 6.5.3
s 12 ... 6.5.3
s 13 ... 6.5.3
s 14 ... 5.5, 6.5.3
s 14(1) ... 6.5.3
s 15 ... 6.5.4
s 15(1) ... 6.5.4
s 15(1)(a)(i)–(iii) ... 6.5.4
s 15A ... 6.5.5, 7.12.2
s 15A(1) ... 6.5.5
s 15A(2) ... 6.5.5
s 30 ... 6.1.1
s 47 ... 6.5.1, 6.11.1
s 48 ... 5.5, 6.5.1
ss 48–50 ... 6.5.1
s 49 ... 5.5, 6.5.1
s 50 ... 5.5, 6.5.1
s 51 ... 6.5.1
s 51(2) ... 6.5.1
s 51(2)(a) ... 6.5.1
s 51A ... 6.11.2
s 52 ... 5.5
s 53 ... 5.5, 6.11.3
s 53A ... 6.11.3
s 53A(1) ... 6.11.3
s 61 ... 6.10
s 61(1) ... 6.10
s 62 ... 6.10
s 63 ... 6.10
s 66 ... 6.7.1
s 66(1) ... 6.7.1
s 66A(1) ... 6.7.2
s 66A(2) ... 6.7.2
s 66A(5) ... 6.7.2
s 66B(1) ... 6.7.3
s 66B(2) ... 6.7.3
s 66B(3) ... 6.7.3
s 66B(4) ... 6.7.3
s 66B(6) ... 6.7.3
s 66B(7) ... 6.7.3
s 66B(8) ... 6.7.3
s 66C ... 6.7.3
s 67 ... 6.8, 6.8.1
s 67(1) ... 6.8.1
s 67(2) ... 6.8.1
s 67(3) ... 6.8.1
s 67(4) ... 6.8.1
s 67A ... 6.8.2
s 67A(1) ... 6.7.2, 6.8.2
s 67A(2) ... 6.8.2
s 71 ... 6.9
s 71(1) ... 6.9
s 72 ... 6.5.4
s 74 ... 6.1.1
ss 74–76 ... 6.1.1
s 75 ... 6.1.1, 6.2.1, 6.3.1
s 75(2) ... 6.1.1
s 75(2)(f) ... 6.1.1
s 75(3) ... 6.1.1
s 76 ... 6.1.1, 6.2.1, 6.3.1
s 76(1)(a) ... 6.10
s 77 ... 6.1.1
s 78 ... 6.1.1, 6.3.1
s 78(a) ... 6.2.1, 6.3.1
s 78(b) ... 6.2.1, 6.3.1
s 79(3) ... 6.2.1
s 103I(A1) ... 6.8.1
s 122H(A1) ... 6.8.2

ss 136A–136R 6.11.3
s 136B 6.11.3
s 136BA 6.11.3
Part 2 .... 6.9
Sch 2 .... 6.5.4
Sch 3 .... 6.8.1
Sch 5 .... 6.8.1
Sporting Events (Control of Alcohol) Act 1985 .... 7.18, 7.18.1
s 1 .... 7.18.1–7.18.2
s 1A 7.18.1
s 2 .... 7.18.1–7.18.2
s 2(1) 7.18.1
s 2(1)(a) 7.18.1
s 2(1)(b) 7.18.1
s 2(2) 7.18.1
s 2A 7.18.1–7.18.2
s 7 .... 7.18.1
Stalking Protection Act 2019 .... 7.11.1, 7.11.4, 7.11.5
s 1(1) 7.11.5
s 5(2) 7.11.5
s 8(1) 7.11.5
s 11 .... 7.11.5
Street Offences Act 1959
s 1 .... 6.11.1
s 1(1) 6.11.1
s 1A 6.11.1
Suicide Act 1961
s 2(1) 2.7.1–2.7.2, 4.1.1
Terrorism Act 2000 .... 1.1.1, 11.1.1
s 36 .... 11.1.11
s 40 .... 1.3.4
s 41 .... 1.3.1
s 43 .... 1.3.4, 1.4.1
s 43A 1.3.4
s 47 .... 1.3.4
s 56 .... 5.5
Sch 8 .... 1.3.1
Terrorism Act 2006 .... 11.1.1
Terrorism Prevention and Investigation Measures Act 2011 .... 11.1.1
Theft Act 1968 .... 3.1–3.4, 3.6, 8.3.5
s 1 .... 1.3.4, 3.1, 3.1.1
s 1(1) 3.1.1
ss 1–7 .... 7.1.1
s 2 .... 3.1.1
ss 2–6 .... 3.1.1
s 3 .... 3.1.1
s 4 .... 3.1.1
s 5 .... 3.1.1
s 6 .... 3.1.1
s 8 .... 3.2
s 8(1) 3.2.1
s 9 .... 3.3, 3.3.1
s 9(1)(a) 3.3.1–3.3.2
s 9(1)(b) 3.3.1–3.3.2
s 10 .... 3.3, 3.3.2
s 11 .... 3.1, 3.1.2
s 11(1) 3.1.2
s 11(2) 3.1.2
s 11(3) 3.1.2
s 12 .... 4.3.1
s 12(1) 4.2.1, 4.3.1–4.3.2
s 12(5) 4.3.1, 4.3.3
s 12(6) 4.3.1
s 12A 4.3.2
s 12A(2)(b) 4.3.2
s 12A(2)(c) 4.3.2
s 12A(3) 4.3.2
s 12A(5) 4.3.2
s 13 .... 3.4
s 21 .... 3.2, 3.2.2, 5.5
s 21(1) 3.2.2
s 21(1)(a) 3.2.2
s 21(1)(b) 3.2.2
s 22 .... 3.5
s 22(1) 3.5
s 23 .... 3.1
s 24(2) 3.5
s 24(3) 3.5
s 24A 3.4
s 25 .... 3.6
s 25(1) 3.6
s 27(3)(a) 3.5
s 27(3)(b) 3.5
s 31(1) 3.8.5
Theft Act 1978 .... 3.7
s 1 .... 3.9
s 3 .... 3.7
s 3(1) 3.7
s 3(3) 3.7
Town Police Clauses Act 1847 .... 8.8
s 28 .... 8.5, 8.8.8, 10.21.1
Trade Marks Act 1994
s 92(1) 5.5
s 92(2) 5.5
s 92(3) 5.5
Trade Union and Labour Relations (Consolidation) Act 1992
s 220 .... 7.11.8, 7.15.1
Traffic Management Act 2004
s 2 .... 10.2.1
Transport Act 1968
s 96(11) 10.4.1
s 96(11A) 10.4.1
s 97(1) 10.4.1
s 98(4) 10.4.1
s 99(4) 10.4.1

s 99ZD(1) 10.4.1
s 99C..................................... 10.4.1
Transport and Works Act 1992
s 27... 1.4.2
Tribunals, Courts and Enforcement Act 2007
Sch 12 para 68(1).................... 2.2.5
UK Borders Act 2007
ss 44–47 .... 11.3.1
Vagrancy Act 1824
s 3.............................. 11.1.3, 11.1.7
s 4.............................. 11.1.3, 11.1.7
Vehicle Excise and Registration Act 1994................. 10.1.1, 10.16.3, 10.19, 10.20
s 1(1B)......................... 10.1.3, 10.19
s 10...................................... 10.20.1
s 11.. 10.19
s 12(1)(a)................................ 10.19
s 12(1)(c)................................ 10.19
s 12(2)(b)................................ 10.19
s 21...................................... 10.16.2
s 21(1) 10.20.2
s 23...................................... 10.20.3
s 23(1) 10.20.2
s 28A 10.20.2
s 29........................... 10.19, 10.20.1
s 29(1) 10.20.1
s 33...................................... 10.20.1
s 34............... 10.4.1, 10.19, 10.20.1
s 34(1) 10.19
s 34(1)(a)................................ 10.19
s 34(1)(b)................................ 10.19
s 34(1)(c)................................ 10.19
s 42.......................... 10.4.1, 10.20.2
s 42(1) 10.20.2
s 42(6) 10.20.2
s 43.......................... 10.4.1, 10.20.3
s 43(1) 10.20.3
s 43(4) 10.20.3
s 43A 10.20.1
s 43C....................... 10.4.1, 10.20.3
s 44.. 10.19
s 53........................... 10.19, 10.20.1
s 59.. 10.4.1
s 62.. 10.19
Sch 2 .... 10.20.1
Vehicles (Crime) Act 2001 ...... 10.20.3
s 28...................................... 10.20.3
Violent Crime Reduction Act 2006
s 3.. 7.13.1
s 4.. 7.13.1
s 27.. 7.15.1
s 28.. 8.3.7
s 28(2) 8.3.7
s 28(3) 8.3.7
s 29.. 8.3.7
s 31.. 8.1.2
s 32.. 8.1.2
s 35.. 8.1.1
s 36.. 8.7.5
ss 36–41 .... 8.7.5
s 37.. 8.7.5
s 38.. 8.7.5
Voyeurism Act 2019.................... 6.8.1

Statutory Instruments

Air Navigation Order 2016 (SI 2016/765) 11.7
Arts 3, 4, 8, and 9 .... 11.7.1
Art 94A.................................. 11.7.1
Art 94A(1) 11.7.1
Art 94A(4) 11.7.1
Art 94A(7) 11.7.1
Art 240.................................. 11.7.1
Art 241 .... 11.7.1
Art 265B................................. 11.7.1
Anti-social Behaviour, Crime and Policing Act 2014 (Publication of Public Spaces Protection Orders) Regulations 2014 (SI 2014/2591) 7.15.2
Antique Firearms Regulations 2021 .... 8.1.1, 8.2.1
Cigarette Lighter Refill (Safety) Regulations 1999 (SI 1999/1844) 11.5.1
reg 2....................................... 11.5.1
Criminal Justice Act 1988 (Offensive Weapons) Order 1988 (SI 1988/2019) 8.9.2, 8.10.2
Criminal Justice Act 1988 (Offensive Weapons) (Exemption) Order 1996 (SI 1996/3064) 8.10.2
Dangerous Dogs (Designated Types) Order 1991 (SI 1991/1743) 11.6.5
Dangerous Dogs Exemption Schemes (England and Wales) Order 2015 (SI 2015/138)...... 11.6.5
Drug Driving (Specified Limits) Regulations 2014 (SI 2014/2868)
reg 2.................................... 10.11.2
European Commission implementing Regulation—Rules and Procedures for the operation of unmanned aircraft (EU) 2019/947. .... 11.7.1
Firearms (Amendment) Regulations 2010 (SI 2010/1759)...................8.7.1

Firearms Rules 1998
(SI 1998/1941) 8.1.5
Fireworks Regulations 2004
(SI 2004/1836) 1.3.5, 8.8, 8.8.2–8.8.3
reg 4 .... 8.8.2
reg 4(1)..................................... 8.8.2
reg 5 ....8.8.2–8.8.3
reg 6 ....8.8.2–8.8.3
reg 7(1)..................................... 8.8.4
reg 7(2)..................................... 8.8.4
Fixed Penalty Order 2000
(SI 2000/2792)
Sch 2 .... 10.4.3
Football (Offences) (Designation of Football Matches) Order 2004 (SI 2004/2410)
art 3... 7.18.2
Goods Vehicles (Community Authorisations) Regulations 1992 (SI 1992/3077)
reg 3 .... 10.4.1
reg 7 .... 10.4.1
Magistrates' Courts (Knife Crime Prevention Orders) Rules 2020 (SI 2020/210) 8.12
Misuse of Drugs Regulations 2001 (SI 2001/3998) 5.1.1, 5.2.1, 5.4.2
reg 4(2)..................................... 5.2.1
reg 5 .... 5.1.1
reg 6 .... 5.1.1, 5.2.1
reg 6A....................................... 5.1.2
reg 12 .... 5.3.1
reg 16A..................................... 5.2.1
Sch 2 .... 6.1.1
Sch 4 Pt 2................................. 5.2.1
Motor Cycles (Eye Protectors) Regulations 1999 (SI 1999/535)
reg 4 .... 10.18
Motor Cycles (Protective Helmets) Regulations 1998 (SI 1998/1807)
reg 4 .... 10.18
Motor Vehicles (Driving Licences) Regulations 1999 (SI 1999/2864)
reg 72 .... 10.15
reg 83(1).............................. 10.16.4
Motor Vehicles (Insurance Requirements) (Immobilisation, Removal and Disposal) Regulations 2011 (SI 2011/1120) 10.16.2
Motor Vehicles (Off Road Events) Regulations 1995 (SI 1995/1371) 10.6.1
Motor Vehicles (Tests) Regulations 1981 (SI 1981/1694)
reg 6(1)................................ 10.16.3
Motor Vehicles (Wearing of Seat Belts by Children in Front Seats) Regulations 1993 (SI 1993/31)
reg 5 .... 10.17.2
Police (Retention and Disposal of Motor Vehicles) Regulations 2002 (SI 2002/2095) 7.14, 7.14.2
reg 3(1).................................. 7.14.2
reg 5 .... 7.14.2
reg 7 .... 7.14.2
Policing and Crime Act 2017 (Possession of Pyrotechnic Articles at Musical Events) Regulations 2017 (SI 2017/306) 8.8.9
Public Service Vehicles (Community Licences) Regulations 1999 (SI 1999/1322)
reg 3 .... 10.4.1
reg 7 .... 10.4.1
Pyrotechnic Articles (Safety) Regulations 2015 (SI 2005/1553) 8.8, 8.8.5
reg 31 .... 8.8.5
reg 62 .... 8.8.5
reg 64 .... 8.8.5
Removal and Disposal of Vehicles Regulations 1986 (SI 1986/183) 10.21.4
Road Safety (Immobilisation, Removal and Disposal of Vehicles) Regulations 2009 (SI 2009/493) 10.4.3
Road Traffic Act 1988 (Retention and Disposal of Seized Motor Vehicles) Regulations 2005 (SI 2005/1606) 10.16.6
reg 4 .... 10.16.6
Road Transport (International Passenger Services) Regulations 1984 (SI 1984/748)
reg 19(1)................................ 10.4.1
reg 19(2)................................ 10.4.1
Road Transport (Passenger Vehicles Cabotage) Regulations 1999 (SI 1999/3413)
reg 3 .... 10.4.1
reg 4 .... 10.4.1
reg 7(1).................................. 10.4.1
reg 7(3).................................. 10.4.1

Road Vehicles (Construction and Use) Regulations 1986 (SI 1986/2695) 10.4.2, 10.21
reg 46 .... 10.17.1
reg 47(1) 10.17.1
reg 103 .... 10.21.4
reg 104 .... 10.4.2
reg 110 .... 10.4.2
reg 110(5) 10.4.2
reg 110 (5A) 10.4.2
Road Vehicles (Display of Registration Marks) Regulations 2001 (SI 2001/561) 10.20.2–10.20.3
Road Vehicles (Registration and Licensing) Regulations 2002 (SI 2002/2742) 10.19
Schools (Specification and Disposal of Articles) Regulations 2012 (SI 2012/951) 8.10.6
Special Constables Regulations 1965 (SI 1965/536) 11.1.11
Sports Grounds and Sporting Events (Designation) Order 2005 (SI 2005/3204)
Art 2 .... 7.18.1
Sch 1 .... 7.18.1
Sch 2 .... 7.18.1
Tobacco and Related Products Regulations 2016 (SI 2016/507) 11.5.1
Traffic Signs Regulations and General Directions 2016 (SI 2016/362) 10.3
Vehicle Drivers (Certificates of Professional Competence) Regulations 2007 (SI 2007/605)
reg 11(7) 10.4.1
Violent Crime Reduction Act 2006 (Realistic Imitation Firearms) Regulations 2007 (SI 2007/2606) 8.7.5
Weapons Amendment Order 2008 (SI 2008/973) 8.9.3
Zebra, Pelican and Puffin Pedestrian Crossings Regulations and General Directions 1997 (SI 1997/2400)
reg 23 .... 10.4.1
reg 24 .... 10.4.1
reg 25 .... 10.4.1
reg 26 .... 10.4.1

Home Office Circulars

82/1980 .... 5.1.1, 5.3.1
29/1997 .... 11.6.5
41/1998 .... 8.1.5
1/2004 .... 8.7.3
9/2005 .... 2.7.4
3/2007 .... 2.2.7
31/2007 .... 8.1.2, 8.7.2, 8.7.5
17/2008 .... 2.4.2
1/2009 .... 5.2.1
17/2009 .... 7.11.6
4/2010 .... 11.3.1
6/2010 .... 6.11.3
4/2011 .... 8.7.2
12/2011 .... 5.2.1, 5.4.1
9/2012 .... 5.2.1
15/2012 .... 5.2.1
18/2012 ....7.11.3–7.11.4
3/2013 .... 2.8
16/2013 .... 8.1.5
4/2014 .... 11.3.1
8/2014 .... 5.2.1
9/2014 .... 8.1.1
10/2014 .... 4.11.1
11/2014 .... 5.3.1
Annex B 5.3.1
13/2014 .... 5.2.1
14/2014 .... 5.1.2
8/2015 .... 2.4.1, 2.7.5, 5.1.2, 6.11.1, 7.4.2
24/2015 ....4.9.2–4.9.3
25/2015 .... 4.9.6

MOJ Circulars

8/2009 .... 4.8.1
3/2010 .... 2.7.1
6/2010 ....4.8.1, 6.6.1–6.6.2
13/2010 .... 2.7.1
7/2011 .... 2.7.3
3/2012 .... 2.7.4
4/2012 .... 7.17.1
8/2012 .... 8.9.1, 8.10.4, 10.7.2
2/2013 .... 1.1
1/2015 .... 4.10, 6.5.4
Annex A 10.8.3, 10.13.2

Codes of Practice

Code for Crown Prosecutors 6.1.2, 6.4, 7.1.2
Mental Health Act 1983: Codes of Practice (England) 2017 .... 11.2
Ch 16 .... 11.2
PACE Codes *see* Police and Criminal Evidence Act 1984

Table of Conventions

Council of Europe Convention on Action against Trafficking in Human Beings
- Art 4 .... 4.9
- Art 10 .... 4.9
- Art 26 .... 4.9

European Convention on Human Rights and Fundamental Freedoms 1950 .... 1.1, 1.3.2, 10.10.1, Appendix 1
- Art 2 .... 1.1
- Arts 2–12 .... Appendix 1
- Art 3 .... 1.1
- Art 4 .... 4.9.2
- Art 5 .... 2.6.1, 8.11.3
- Art 6 .... 7.8, 9.3.1
- Art 8 .... 6.1.2, 8.11.3
- Art 9 .... 7.12.1
- Art 10 .... 7.3, 7.7–7.8, 7.12.1, 7.15.1, 10.21.1
- Art 11 .... 7.3, 7.15.1, 10.21.1
- Art 14 .... Appendix 1

List of Abbreviations

A-G	Attorney General
ACPO	Association of Chief Police Officers (see NPCC)
ANPR	Automatic Number Plate Recognition (system/camera)
AOABH	assault occasioning actual bodily harm
ASBO	Anti-Social Behaviour Order
BB gun	ball bearing gun
BS	British Standard
BTP	British Transport Police
CBO	criminal behaviour order
CC	Chief Constable or County Court
CCTV	closed-circuit television
CED	conducted energy device
CEO	Chief Executive Officer
CEOP	Child Exploitation and On-line Protection Centre
CIE	Continuous Insurance Enforcement
CJA	Criminal Justice Act
COP	Code of Practice
CPN	community protection notice
CPS	Crown Prosecution Service
CS spray	named after the initials of the inventors—Corson and Staughton
CSE	child sexual exploitation
CSO	Community support officer
CSV	Community support volunteer
DBS	Disclosure and Barring Service (formerly ISA)
DC	Divisional Court
DEFRA	Department for Environment, Food, and Rural Affairs
DNA	deoxyribonucleic acid
DPP	Director of Public Prosecutions
DVLA	Driver and Vehicle Licensing Agency
DVPN	Domestic Violence Protection Notice
DVPO	Domestic Violence Protection Order
DVSA	Driver and Vehicle Standards Agency
ECHR	European Convention on Human Rights
ECtHR	European Court of Human Rights

EEA	European Economic Area
EU	European Union
FA	Football Association
FGM	female genital mutilation
FMU	Forced Marriage Unit at the Foreign and Commonwealth Office
FPN	fixed penalty notice
FTO	Foreign Travel Order
GB	Great Britain
GBH	grievous bodily harm
GHB	gamma-hydroxybutrate
GV	goods vehicle
HGV	heavy goods vehicle
HIV	human immunodeficiency virus
HL	House of Lords
HMCTS	His Majesty's Courts and Tribunals Service
HMRC	His Majesty's Revenue & Customs
HOC	Home Office Circular
HSE	Health and Safety Executive
IOPC	Independent Office for Police Conduct
ISA	Independent Safeguarding Authority (now DBS—above)
ISRO	interim Sexual Risk Order
KBD	King's Bench Division
LA	local authority
MC	magistrates' court
MIB	Motor Insurers' Bureau
MOD	Ministry of Defence
MoDP	Ministry of Defence Police
MOJ	Ministry of Justice
NCA	National Crime Agency
NHS	National Health Service
NIP	notice of intended prosecution
NPCC	National Police Chiefs' Council (formerly ACPO)
NRM	National Referral Mechanism (modern slavery and human trafficking)

OAPA	Offences Against the Person Act 1861
OFCOM	Office of Communications
OPL	over the prescribed limit
PACE	Police and Criminal Evidence Act 1984
PCSO	Police Community Support Officer
PNC	Police National Computer
PND	Penalty Notice for Disorder/Police National Database
PND-E	Penalty Notice for Disorder—Education option
PNLD	Police National Legal Database
POCA	Proceeds of Crime Act 2002
PSPO	public spaces protection order
PSV	public service vehicle
QBD	Queen's Bench Division
RTC	road traffic collision
SCGC	self-contained gas cartridge system
SHPO	Sexual Harm Prevention Order
SI	Statutory Instrument
SORN	Statutory Off-Road Notification
SPO	Stalking Protection Order
SRO	Sexual Risk Order
STPO	Slavery and Trafficking Prevention Order
STRO	Slavery and Trafficking Risk Order
TDA	taking and driving away
TFPN	traffic fixed penalty notice
TWOC	taking a conveyance without owner's consent
UAS	unmanned aircraft system
UK	United Kingdom
UKBA	UK Border Agency
UTMV	unlawful taking of a motor vehicle
VDRS	Vehicle Defect Rectification Scheme
VEL	Vehicle Excise Licence
VOSA	Vehicle and Operator Services Agency (now DVSA)
YOI	young offenders' institution

Icons List

PNLD	**Police National Legal Database document number.**
SSS	**Stop, search, and seize powers** under the Police and Criminal Evidence Act 1984, s 1 **or** stop, search, and seize powers under a statutory authority given within that Act.
E&S	**Entry and search powers** under the Police and Criminal Evidence Act 1984, ss 17, 18, and 32.
PND	**Penalty Notices for Disorder offences** under the Criminal Justice and Police Act 2001, s 1.
TFPN	**Traffic Fixed Penalty Notices** under the Road Traffic Offenders Act 1988.
RRA	**Racially or religiously aggravated offences** under the Crime and Disorder Act 1998, ss 28 to 32.
CHAR	**Offences where evidence of bad character can be introduced** under the Criminal Justice Act 2003, s 103.
TRIG	**Trigger offences**—when police can test (request to take samples) for presence of Class A drugs, under the Criminal Justice and Court Services Act 2000, Sch 6.

	Mode of trial Indictable, either way, or summary.
	Prosecution time limit The time limit allowed for submission of the file (laying of the information).
	Penalty Maximum sentence allowed by law.
NIP	**Notice of Intended Prosecution** to be issued under the Road Traffic Offenders Act 1988, s 1.

Chapter 1
Introduction

1.1 Powers of Arrest

Sections 24, 24A, and 28 to 31 of PACE deal with arrests made by a constable or other persons and other related matters.

1.1.1 Arrest without warrant: constables

Arrest without warrant

Section 24 of PACE provides the power of arrest for a constable without a warrant and the conditions that must apply before the arrest power can be used.

Powers of arrest

Arrest

(1) A constable may arrest without a warrant—
  - (a) anyone who is about to commit an offence;
  - (b) anyone who is in the act of committing an offence;
  - (c) anyone whom he has reasonable grounds for suspecting to be about to commit an offence;
  - (d) anyone whom he has reasonable grounds for suspecting to be committing an offence.

(2) If a constable has reasonable grounds for suspecting that an offence has been committed, he may arrest without a warrant anyone whom he has reasonable grounds to suspect of being guilty of it.

(3) If an offence has been committed, a constable may arrest without a warrant—
  - (a) anyone who is guilty of the offence;
  - (b) anyone whom he has reasonable grounds for suspecting to be guilty of it.

Necessity criteria

(4) But the power of summary arrest conferred by subsection (1), (2) or (3) is exercisable only if the constable has reasonable grounds for

believing that for any of the reasons mentioned in subsection (5) it is necessary to arrest the person in question.

Reasons

(5) The reasons are—

(a) to enable the name of the person in question to be ascertained (in the case where the constable does not know, and cannot readily ascertain, the person's name, or has reasonable grounds for doubting whether a name given by the person as his name is his real name);

(b) correspondingly as regards the person's address;

(c) to prevent the person in question—

(i) causing physical injury to himself or any other person;

(ii) suffering physical injury;

(iii) causing loss of or damage to property;

(iv) committing an offence against public decency (subject to subsection (6)); or

(v) causing an unlawful obstruction of the highway;

(d) to protect a child or other vulnerable person from the person in question;

(e) to allow the prompt and effective investigation of the offence or of the conduct of the person in question;

(f) to prevent any prosecution for the offence from being hindered by the disappearance of the person in question.

(6) Subsection (5)(c)(iv) applies only where members of the public going about their normal business cannot reasonably be expected to avoid the person in question.

Police and Criminal Evidence Act 1984, s 24

Explanatory notes

- The use of this arrest power is governed by PACE Code G.
- If a person is arrested on suspicion of being a terrorist, then Code H would apply in connection with the detention, treatment, and questioning for persons arrested under s 41 of, and Sch 8 to, the Terrorism Act 2000.
- If a person is arrested on suspicion of having committed a terrorist offence, but is arrested under s 24 of PACE, then PACE and Codes G and C will apply.
- The Director General of the NCA may confer some or all of the s 24 powers on NCA staff and nominate them as 'designated persons' (with powers of constable).
- The s 24 power means that a constable/designated person may only arrest persons without a warrant under this general power where:
  - ✦ they are about to commit/in the act of committing an offence;
  - ✦ there are reasonable grounds to suspect they are about to commit/ to be committing an offence;
  - ✦ there are reasonable grounds to suspect that an offence has been committed, there are reasonable grounds to suspect they are guilty of it;

- ✦ an offence has been committed: they are guilty of the offence; reasonable grounds to suspect they are guilty of it;

and the constable has reasonable grounds to believe (more than 'suspect') that it is **necessary** to arrest that person for any of the reasons listed.

- A lawful arrest requires both elements of:
  - ✦ a person's involvement or suspected involvement, or attempted involvement, in the commission of a criminal offence; **and**
  - ✦ reasonable grounds to believe that the arrest is necessary.
- The requirement for reasonable grounds makes this an **objective test**—that is, it requires some verifiable material fact other than the belief of the arresting officer.
- The exercise of these arrest powers will be subject to a test of necessity, based on the nature and circumstances of the offence, and the interests of the criminal justice system.
- An arrest will only be justified if the constable believes it is necessary for any of the reasons set out, **and** they had reasonable grounds on which that belief was based.
- Criteria for what may constitute necessity remain an operational decision at the discretion of the arresting officer.
- Paragraph 4 of Code G deals with 'Records of Arrest' in that:
  - ✦ the arresting officer is required to record in their pocketbook or other methods used for recording information:
    - ▪ the nature and circumstances of the offence leading to arrest;
    - ▪ the reason or reasons why arrest was necessary;
    - ▪ the giving of the caution;
    - ▪ anything said by the person at the time of arrest;
  - ✦ such record should be made at the time of arrest unless impracticable to do so, in which case to be completed as soon as possible thereafter.
- Some of the reasons to consider under s 24(5)(e), as to a prompt and effective investigation, are given in para 2.9 of Code G; these may be where there are reasonable grounds to believe that the person:
  - ✦ has made false statements;
  - ✦ has presented false evidence;
  - ✦ may steal or destroy evidence;
  - ✦ may collude or make contact with co-suspects or conspirators;
  - ✦ may intimidate or threaten, or make contact with, witnesses; or
  - ✦ where it is necessary to obtain evidence by questioning:
    - ▪ it is thought unlikely that the person would attend the police station voluntarily to be interviewed;
    - ▪ arrest would enable 'special warnings' to be given per Code C paras 10.10 and 10.11.
- If an arrest is for an indictable offence, there could be other reasons under s 24(5)(e) to consider, such as a need to:
  - ✦ enter and search any premises occupied or controlled by a person;
  - ✦ search the person (in respect of **any** offence, not just indictable);
  - ✦ prevent contact with others;

    + detaining the arrested person for more than twenty-four hours before charge.
- If arrest is for a recordable offence and it is necessary to secure and preserve evidence of that offence:
    + take fingerprints;
    + footwear impressions or samples;
    + if arrest is for any offence and it is necessary to search, examine, or photograph the person to obtain evidence;
    + compliance with statutory Class A drug-testing requirements.
- Apart from arrest, other options such as:
    + report for summons;
    + grant street bail;
    + issue a fixed penalty notice, PND; or
    + other methods of disposal;

  will have to be considered and excluded before arrest is decided upon.

Related cases

Alger v Commissioner of Police of the Metropolis [2023] EWHC 1582 (KB) In this case, AL, a window cleaner, attended voluntarily at a police station having heard the police wanted to speak to him about a dispute he was having with one of his customers. On arrival, he was arrested for the offence of malicious communications. It was held that the 'necessity' to arrest was not present where an individual was willingly assisting and cooperating with a police investigation and the arresting officer had failed adequately to consider whether attendance at a voluntary interview would have been a practical and sensible alternative option to arrest.

DE v Chief Constable of West Midlands [2023] EWHC 146 (KB) Dismissing a claim for false imprisonment, the court held that, objectively reviewed, the officer's belief in the necessity of the arrest under s 24 of PACE was based on reasonable grounds. Moreover, the officer's assessment of risk and the necessity for bail conditions were tangible and made with proper foundation. It followed that the arrest necessity criteria, specifically that contained within s 24(5)(e), were satisfied.

1.1.2 Information to be given on arrest

Cautions

Code C provides for when a caution must be given.

PACE Code C

Police officers and other persons subject to observing PACE should be aware of the following paragraphs in this Code:

- A person whom there are grounds to suspect of an offence must be cautioned before any questions about an offence or further questions if the answers provide the grounds for suspicion, are put to them if either the suspect's answers or silence (ie failure or refusal to answer or answer satisfactorily) may be given in evidence to a court in a prosecution.

A person need not be cautioned if questioned:
- solely to establish identity or ownership of any vehicle;
- to obtain information to comply with a statutory requirement;
- in furtherance of the proper and effective conduct of a search (eg to determine the need to search in the exercise of powers of stop and search or to seek cooperation while carrying out a search); or
- to seek verification of a written record (in accordance with para 11.13); or
- where it is impracticable to do so by reason of their condition or behaviour at the time; or
- they have already been cautioned immediately prior to arrest (para 10.1).

The **caution** that must be given on arrest; before a person is charged or informed, they may be prosecuted; and **should** (unless the restriction on drawing adverse inferences from silence applies) **be in the following terms:**

> You do not have to say anything. But it may harm your defence if you do not mention when questioned something which you later rely on in Court. Anything you do say may be given in evidence.
>
> *Code C para 10.5; for terrorism Code H para 10.5*

- Anyone who appears to be **under 18**, shall, in the absence of clear evidence that they are older, be treated as a juvenile and, where a caution is given, it must be done in the presence of an appropriate adult.
- An appropriate adult should be present when giving a caution to a vulnerable adult, being a person who, because of a mental health condition or mental disorder, may have difficulty in understanding or communicating effectively about the full implications for them of any procedures and processes, or does not appear to understand the significance of what they are told (see **PACE Code C para 1.13(d)**).

Meaning

Appropriate adult

PACE Code C (para 1.7) In the case of a juvenile (under 18):

(a) the parent, guardian or, if the juvenile is in the care of a local authority or voluntary organisation, a person representing that authority or organisation; or

(b) a social worker of a local authority; or

(c) failing these, some other responsible adult aged 18 or over who is not:
   - ✦ a police officer;
   - ✦ employed by the police;

- ✦ under the direction or control of the chief officer of a police force; or
- ✦ a person who provides services under contractual arrangements (but without being employed by the chief officer of a police force), to assist that force in relation to the discharge of its chief officer's functions, whether or not they are on duty at the time.

Note that a solicitor or independent custody visitor who is present at the police station and acting in that capacity may not be the appropriate adult (**Code C, Note 1F**).

Explanatory notes

- Whenever a person **not under arrest** is initially cautioned, or reminded that they are under caution, that person must at the same time be told that they are not under arrest and must be informed that they need to agree to be interviewed, how they may obtain legal advice according to whether they are at a police station or elsewhere, and the other rights and entitlements that apply to a voluntary interview (**Code C paras 3.21 and 10.2**).
- Minor deviations from the words of any caution given in accordance with Code C do not constitute a breach of this Code, provided the sense of the relevant caution is preserved (**Code C para 10.7**). If it appears that a person does not understand the caution, the person giving it should explain it in their own words.
- After any break in questioning under caution, the person being questioned must be made aware that they remain under caution. If there is any doubt, the relevant caution shall be given again in full when the interview resumes (**Code C para 10.8**). After a break in an interview or at the beginning of a subsequent interview, the interviewer should summarise the reason for the break and confirm this with the suspect.
- Failure to comply with cautioning procedures will allow the accused to claim a breach of this Code at any subsequent court proceedings. By virtue of s 76 or s 78 of PACE, the court may then exclude the evidence of any confession, or unfair evidence, so obtained.

Statutory requirements

Section 28 of PACE determines the information that must be given to a person when arrested.

Information to be given on arrest

(1) Subject to subsection (5) below, where a person is arrested, otherwise than by being informed that he is under arrest, the arrest is not lawful unless the person arrested is informed that he is under arrest as soon as is practicable after his arrest.

(2) Where a person is arrested by a constable, subsection (1) above applies regardless of whether the fact of the arrest is obvious.

(3) Subject to subsection (5) below, no arrest is lawful unless the person arrested is informed of the ground for the arrest at the time of, or as soon as practicable after, the arrest.

(4) Where a person is arrested by a constable, subsection (3) above applies regardless of whether the ground for the arrest is obvious.

(5) Nothing in this section is to be taken to require a person to be informed—
 (a) that he is under arrest; or
 (b) of the ground for the arrest,
 if it was not reasonably practicable for him to be so informed by reason of his having escaped from arrest before the information could be given.

Police and Criminal Evidence Act 1984, s 28

Explanatory notes

- A person who is arrested, or further arrested, must be informed at the time, or as soon as practicable thereafter, in a language they understand (see COP and the ECHR), that they are under arrest and the grounds for their arrest.
- When arresting using the power under s 24, the officer must tell the person not only the offence/suspected offence involved but also the reason why the officer believes that arrest is necessary. The necessity criteria (see **1.1.1**) must also be recorded by the officer.
- If it becomes apparent that a more serious offence may have been committed, the suspect must be made aware of these facts immediately (eg originally arrested and interviewed for sexual assault, which now transpires is rape).
- It would be manifestly unfair if the defendant did not know the true extent of the situation they were in, and any interviews could be excluded at trial.

Related cases

Blench v DPP [2004] EWHC 2717 (Admin) It was held in this case that it was possible to delay telling a detained person the reason for their arrest when it was not practicable to tell them at the time. The delay in giving reasons cannot retrospectively render unlawful an arrest that was correctly and lawfully made.

Hayes v CC of Merseyside Police [2011] EWCA Civ 911 The arresting officer must believe that the arrest is necessary under s 24(4) for a s 24(5) reason and this belief must be objectively reasonable.

Dhesi v CC of West Midlands Police [2000] All ER (D) 1172, CA The officer informing the offender that they were under arrest and giving the grounds does not have to be the same officer as the one who is physically detaining that person.

1.1.3 Arrest procedures

Arrest at police station—voluntary attendance

Where, for the purpose of assisting with an investigation, a person attends voluntarily at a police station or at any other place where a constable is present, or accompanies a constable to a police station or any such other place without having been arrested:

(a) he shall be entitled to leave at will unless he is placed under arrest;

(b) he shall be informed at once that he is under arrest if a decision is taken by a constable to prevent him from leaving at will.

Police and Criminal Evidence Act, s 29

Explanatory notes

- Confusion sometimes arises about the status of a suspect who has attended at a police station voluntarily. If the investigating officer concludes that the suspect should not be allowed to leave, and an arrest is **necessary**, then the officer should caution the suspect (unless recently cautioned) and inform the suspect that they are under arrest and take them before the custody officer.
- Ensure that the **necessity test** is satisfied (see **1.1.1**). Simply giving the grounds for the arrest as 'for the prompt and effective investigation' is not a good enough reason, without further explanation.
- Under s 29, a person is free to leave the station interview at any time. If they do, then it may be lawful to arrest, and the necessity criteria may be met. This is because, under para 2.9(e)(i) of Code G (see **1.1.1**), it may be 'necessary to obtain evidence by questioning', and here the person has refused or failed to comply with arrangements for voluntary attendance/interview.
- There is no provision to bail voluntary attenders at a police station, PACE only contains provisions for bail after arrest (including 'street bail') (see below). If you need to speak to the voluntary attender again and do not want to arrest them, then you can request that they re-attend at a set time and date, but there is no power to enforce this.
- When a person attends a police station as a volunteer and is not charged with an offence, there is no power to obtain biometric data; however, the taking of fingerprints etc may be done with a person's consent and an appropriate consent form should be provided and signed by the person.
- Where a person attends at a police station or elsewhere voluntarily, the suspect has a right to legal advice and all other rights and entitlements that apply to all voluntary interviews in accordance with Code C, irrespective of where the interview takes place. (For further guidance, see **Code C para 3.21**.)

- A voluntary interview is just as serious and important as being interviewed after arrest. The approach mirrors that which applies to detained suspects on arrival at the police station but with the interviewer rather than the custody officer setting out the rights, entitlements, and safeguards.

Arrest—not at a police station

Section 30 of PACE provides the procedure to be applied when a constable either makes an arrest or takes a person into custody after arrest by a person other than a constable (at any place other than a police station). The relevant points are:

- the arrested person must be taken to a police station as soon as practicable after arrest;
- this must be a police station designated for dealing with 'PACE' prisoners, unless:
  - ✦ it is anticipated that the arrested person will be dealt with in less than six hours at any police station;
  - ✦ the arrest/taken into custody is without the assistance of any other constable(s) and none were available to assist;
  - ✦ it is considered that the arrested person cannot be conveyed to a designated police station without the arrested person injuring themselves, the constable, or some other person;
- if the first police station to which an arrested person is taken after their arrest is not a designated police station, they shall be taken to a designated police station not more than six hours after their arrival at the first police station unless they have been released previously;
- prior to arrival at the police station, the arrested person must be released without bail if the constable is satisfied that there are no longer grounds for keeping them under arrest or releasing them on bail; if this occurs, the constable shall record the fact that they have done so and shall make the record as soon as practicable after release. This requirement should be read in conjunction with the necessity criteria as, once the relevant criterion making the arrest necessary has ceased, arguably the person should be released;
- a constable can delay taking a person to a police station or releasing them on bail if the presence of the arrested person at a place (other than a police station) is necessary in order to carry out such investigations as it is reasonable to carry out immediately; if such delay occurs, the reason(s) for the delay must be recorded when the person first arrives at a police station or (as the case may be) is released on bail.

Explanatory notes

- There is no requirement that a person must be taken to the nearest police station: s 30(1A) states that 'the person must be taken by a constable to a police station as soon as practicable after the arrest'—there is no mention of the word 'nearest'.

- The type of record that has to be made, if the arrested person is 'de-arrested' prior to arrival at the police station, is not specified but could, for example, include completing a formal custody record: this depends on individual force policies.

1.1.4 Release a person prior to arrival at a police station

Section 30A provides that a constable has power to release a person at any time prior to arrival at a police station without bail or on bail and, if on bail, with or without conditions.

Power

(1) A constable may release a person who is arrested or taken into custody in the circumstances mentioned in section 30(1)—
  (a) without bail unless subsection (1A) applies, or
  (b) on bail if subsection (1A) applies.

(1A) This subsection applies if—
  (a) the constable is satisfied that releasing the person on bail is necessary and proportionate in all the circumstances (having regard, in particular, to any conditions of bail which would be imposed), and
  (b) a police officer of the rank of inspector or above authorises the release on bail (having considered any representations made by the person).

Police and Criminal Evidence Act 1984, s 30A(1) and (1A)

Practical considerations

- A person may be released at any time before they arrive at a police station.
- If released on bail, the person must be required to attend at a police station.
- Under this section, bail cannot be granted with conditions, such as securities, sureties, or conditions of residence in a bail hostel as per s 30A(3A).
- However, under s 30A(3B) where a constable releases a person on bail under subsection (1), the constable may impose, as conditions of the bail, such requirements as appear to the constable to be necessary:
  (a) to secure that the person surrenders to custody;
  (b) to secure that the person does not commit an offence while on bail;

(c) to secure that the person does not interfere with witnesses or otherwise obstruct the course of justice, whether in relation to themselves or any other person; or
(d) for the person's own protection or, if the person is under the age of 18, for the person's own welfare or in the person's own interests.

Explanatory notes

- This power includes the power to grant 'street bail' and can only be used in the circumstances mentioned in s 30(1) ('only where a person is at any place other than a police station'); that means only prior to a person's arrival at the police station. Once a person has arrived at a police station, for example after an arrest or when answering bail, s 30A powers cannot be used and the requirement to attend a police station and any conditions would be invalid. The person could therefore not be arrested if in breach of bail.
- There is a presumption that where a police officer decides that it is appropriate to release an arrested person rather than take them to a police station, that release will be without bail, unless the requirements in s 30A(1A) are met.
- Officers can grant 'street bail' and consider attaching conditions relevant and proportionate to the suspect and the offence. The conditions that can be imposed must be necessary to secure that the person surrenders to custody, that the person does not commit an offence while on bail, or that the person does not interfere with witnesses or otherwise obstruct the course of justice. Where the person is under the age of 18, conditions may also be applied for their welfare, or in their own interest. No recognisance, security, or surety may be taken and no requirement to reside in a bail hostel may be imposed.
- Where a person has been bailed subject to conditions, they will have the right to apply for variation of conditions to a custody officer and to a magistrates' court. A record must be made of the exercise of the power and a copy provided to the person explaining their rights.
- The measures reflect bail provisions already available in relation to people at the charging stage of the process.
- Prior to release under s 30A, a constable must give a notice in writing setting out the offence for which they were arrested and the ground on which the arrest was made (see s 30B).
- Note that, under s 30D(1), where a person fails to surrender to bail granted under s 30A, either to attend at the police station or to attend at the specified time, a constable may arrest without warrant and the person must then be taken to a police station as soon as practicable after the arrest. A power of entry under s 17 of PACE may be used to effect the arrest (see **1.4.2**).

Arrest—for further offences

Where—
(a) a person—
  (i) has been arrested for an offence; and
  (ii) is at a police station in consequence of that arrest; and
(b) it appears to a constable that, if he were released from that arrest, he would be liable to arrest for some other offence,
he shall be arrested for that other offence.

Police and Criminal Evidence Act 1984, s 31

Explanatory notes

- Consider the necessity test under s 24(5) (see **1.1.1**).
- Consideration should be given to the custody clock and 'relevant times'.

1.1.5 Arrest without warrant: other persons

Section 24A of PACE provides a power of arrest without warrant to persons other than police officers.

Arrest power (other persons)

(1) A person other than a constable may arrest without a warrant—
  (a) anyone who is in the act of committing an indictable offence;
  (b) anyone whom he has reasonable grounds for suspecting to be committing an indictable offence.
(2) Where an indictable offence has been committed, a person other than a constable may arrest without a warrant—
  (a) anyone who is guilty of the offence;
  (b) anyone whom he has reasonable grounds for suspecting to be guilty of it.
(3) But the power of summary arrest conferred by subsection (1) or (2) is exercisable only if—
  (a) the person making the arrest has reasonable grounds for believing that for any of the reasons mentioned in subsection (4) it is necessary to arrest the person in question; and
  (b) it appears to the person making the arrest that it is not reasonably practicable for a constable to make it instead.
(4) The reasons are to prevent the person in question—
  (a) causing physical injury to himself or any other person;
  (b) suffering physical injury;
  (c) causing loss of or damage to property; or

> (d) making off before a constable can assume responsibility for him.
>
> (5) This section does not apply in relation to an offence under Part 3 or 3A of the Public Order Act 1986.
>
> Police and Criminal Evidence Act 1984, s 24A

Meaning of indictable offence

- An indictable offence includes triable 'either way offences'.
- The Anti-social Behaviour, Crime and Policing Act 2014, s 176(6) states:
  - any reference in PACE to an **indictable offence** has effect as if it included a reference to **low-value shoplifting**.
- The Magistrates' Courts Act 1980, s 22A states:
  - low-value shoplifting is triable only summarily—unless a person aged 18 or over elects trial at Crown Court before the summary trial begins;
  - **low-value shoplifting** means an offence under s 1 of the Theft Act 1968 where:
    - the value of the stolen goods does not exceed £200;
    - the goods were being offered for sale in a shop or any other premises, stall, vehicle, or place from which there is carried on a trade or business; and
    - at the time of the offence, the person accused was, or was purporting to be, a customer or potential customer of the person offering the goods for sale.

Explanatory note

- This power of arrest does not apply to offences under ss 17 to 29N of the Public Order Act 1986 (offences of racial/religious hatred, sexual orientation) (see **7.9**).

Related case

Sowande v CPS [2017] EWHC 1234 (Admin) Two security guards working at a shopping centre detained and arrested S, in accordance with s 24A(1)(b). S became violent and assaulted both guards. The convictions for two assaults against two security guards were safe when it was found that the security guards were acting lawfully under PACE when they arrested and detained a person they suspected of having committed an indictable offence (theft). The court confirmed that, for the purposes of s 24A(1)(b) in contrast to s 24A(2), it was not necessary for the arrested person to have committed an indictable offence: merely, that the arresting person had reasonable grounds for suspecting that the arrested person had committed such an offence. In addition, the court noted that there was an alternative basis, under s 3 of the Criminal Law Act 1967, to use reasonable force in the prevention of crime.

Practical considerations

- Consideration should be given to lawful authorities for using reasonable force.
- Arrest powers under ss 24 and 24A of PACE have effect in relation to any offence/indictable offence whenever committed.

1.2 Lawful Authorities—Use of Force

If a police officer uses force, this must be justified and reasonable and based on a lawful authority—otherwise it will be an assault and would, therefore, become an unlawful act. Statute, common law, and human rights set out the circumstances in which the use of force will be lawful, but each case will be decided upon its own peculiar facts.

Statute

Criminal Law Act 1967

(1) A person may use such force as is reasonable in the circumstances in the prevention of crime, or in effecting or assisting in the lawful arrest of offenders or suspected offenders or of persons unlawfully at large.

(2) Subsection (1) above shall replace the rules of the common law on the question when force used for a purpose mentioned in the subsection is justified by that purpose.

Criminal Law Act 1967, s 3

Police and Criminal Evidence Act 1984

Where any provision of this Act—

(a) confers a power on a constable; and

(b) does not provide that the power may only be exercised with the consent of some person, other than a police officer,

the officer may use reasonable force, if necessary, in the exercise of the power.

Police and Criminal Evidence Act 1984, s 117

Criminal Justice and Immigration Act 2008

The Act makes a number of provisions about criminal justice (including provision about the police), dealing with offenders and defaulters, and the management of offenders including the use of reasonable force for the purposes of 'self-defence'.

(1) This section applies where in proceedings for an offence—

  (a) an issue arises as to whether a person charged with the offence ('D') is entitled to rely on a defence within subsection (2), and

(b) the question arises whether the degree of force used by D against a person ('V') was reasonable in the circumstances.

(2) The defences are—
(a) the common law defence of self-defence;
(aa) the common law defence of defence of property; and
(b) the defence provided by section 3(1) of the Criminal Law Act 1967 (use of force in prevention of crime or making arrest).

(3) The question whether the degree of force used by D was reasonable in the circumstances is to be decided by reference to the circumstances as D believed them to be, and subsections (4) to (8) also apply in connection with deciding that question.

(4) If D claims to have held a particular belief as regards the existence of any circumstances—
(a) the reasonableness or otherwise of that belief is relevant to the question whether D genuinely held it; but
(b) if it is determined that D did genuinely hold it, D is entitled to rely on it for the purposes of subsection (3), whether or not—
(i) it was mistaken, or
(ii) (if it was mistaken) the mistake was a reasonable one to have made.

(5) But subsection (4)(b) does not enable D to rely on any mistaken belief attributable to intoxication that was voluntarily induced.

(5A) In a householder case, the degree of force used by D is not to be regarded as having been reasonable in the circumstances as D believed them to be if it was grossly disproportionate in those circumstances.

(6) In a case other than a householder case, the degree of force used by D is not to be regarded as having been reasonable in the circumstances as D believed them to be if it was disproportionate in those circumstances.

(6A) In deciding the question mentioned in subsection (3), a possibility that D could have retreated is to be considered (so far as relevant) as a factor to be taken into account, rather than as giving rise to a duty to retreat.

(7) In deciding the question mentioned in subsection (3) the following considerations are to be taken into account (so far as relevant in the circumstances of the case)—
(a) that a person acting for a legitimate purpose may not be able to weigh to a nicety the exact measure of any necessary action; and
(b) that evidence of a person's having only done what the person honestly and instinctively thought was necessary for a legitimate purpose constitutes strong evidence that only reasonable action was taken by that person for that purpose.

(8) Subsections (6A) and (7) are not to be read as preventing other matters from being taken into account where they are relevant to deciding the question mentioned in subsection (3).

(8A) For the purposes of this section a householder case is a case where—
(a) the defence concerned is the common law defence of self-defence;

(b) the force concerned is force used by D while in or partly in a building, or part of a building, that is a dwelling or is forces accommodation (or is both);
(c) D is not a trespasser at the time the force is used; and
(d) at that time D believed V to be in, or entering, the building or part as a trespasser.

(8B) Where—
(a) a part of a building is a dwelling where D dwells;
(b) another part of the building is a place of work for D or another person who dwells in the first part; and
(c) that other part is internally accessible from the first part,
that other part, and any internal means of access between the two parts, are each treated for the purposes of subsection (8A) as a part of a building that is a dwelling.

(8C) [*Relates to 'forces accommodation' under Armed Forces Act 2006, s 96.*]

(8D) Subsections (4) and (5) apply for the purposes of subsection (8A)(d) as they apply for the purposes of subsection (3).

(8E) The fact that a person derives title from a trespasser, or has the permission of a trespasser, does not prevent the person from being a trespasser for the purposes of subsection (8A).

(8F) In subsections (8A) to (8C) building includes a vehicle or vessel.

(9) This section, except so far as making different provision for householder cases, is intended to clarify the operation of the existing defences mentioned in subsection (2).

(10) In this section—
(a) 'legitimate purpose' means—
(i) the purpose of self-defence under the common law,
(ia) the purpose of defence of property under the common law, or
(ii) the prevention of crime or effecting or assisting in the lawful arrest of persons mentioned in the provisions referred to in subsection (2)(b);
(b) references to self-defence include acting in defence of another person; and
(c) references to the degree of force used are to the type and amount of force used.

Criminal Justice and Immigration Act 2008, s 76

Explanatory notes

- Section 76 provides a gloss on the common law of self-defence and the defence provided by s 3(1) of the Criminal Law Act 1967. It is intended to improve understanding of the practical application of these areas of the law. Much of it states what is already to be found in the case law to illustrate how the defence operates. As subsection (9) indicates, s 76 does not change the current test that allows the use of reasonable force, except in the case of householders. (Householders enjoy enhanced protection when acting in self-defence in that, in their case, the use of force is only regarded as unreasonable, and hence outside the scope of self-defence, where it is 'grossly disproportionate', whereas in all other cases force that is merely 'disproportionate' is regarded as unreasonable, and hence outside the scope of self-defence: see s 76(5A) and (6).)

- In both a non-householder case and a householder case, s 76 reaffirms that a person who uses force is to be judged on the basis of all the circumstances as they perceived them, that in the heat of the moment they will not be expected to have judged what action was called for, and that a degree of latitude may be given to a person who only did what they honestly and instinctively thought was necessary. A person is entitled to have their actions judged on their view of the facts as they honestly believed them to be, even if that belief was mistaken.
- In line with the case law, the defence will be available to a person if it is honestly believed that it was necessary to use force and if the degree of force used was not disproportionate in the circumstances as they viewed them (with the exception of householder cases). This reaffirms that a person who uses force is to be judged on the basis of the circumstances as they perceived them, that in the heat of the moment they will not be expected to have judged exactly what action was called for, and that a degree of latitude may be given to a person who only did what they honestly and instinctively thought was necessary. A defendant is entitled to have their actions judged based on a view of the facts as they honestly believed them to be, even if that belief was mistaken.
- The Criminal Law Act 1967, s 3 allows the use of reasonable force in the prevention of crime or in making, or assisting in, a lawful arrest and applies to any person. '**Crime**' does not cover crimes recognised as against international law; it only refers to crimes committed against domestic law either by statute or judicial decision (*R v Jones and others; Ayliffe and others v DPP, Swain v DPP* [2006] UKHL 16) (see **4.4**).
- Section 117 of PACE relates to the use of **reasonable force** by a police officer whilst exercising their (PACE) powers.
- The Criminal Justice Act and Immigration 2008, s 76 provides a statutory test as to using reasonable force for self-defence and defence of property at common law, preventing crime, or making an arrest. This does not alter common law and is not a complete statement of the law, but it does set out the basic principles (see *R v Keane and McGrath* [2010] EWCA Crim 2514).

Related cases

R v Cheeseman [2019] EWCA Crim 149 In this case, C and L were colleagues living in accommodation provided by the army. L became a trespasser when entering C's room and causing damage. Subsection (8A) provides for a belief at the time that the trespasser was 'in, or entering, the building or part as a trespasser' and this differs from the belief that a person entered as a trespasser. The householder defence would be available to a person who had caused injury to another who had entered the premises lawfully but thereafter became a trespasser.

R v Ray [2017] EWCA Crim 1391 It was held in this case that the jury must first determine the circumstances as the defendant believed them to be and then whether, in those circumstances, the amount of force used was reasonable. In determining the reasonableness of the degree of force, the jury must decide whether it was grossly disproportionate or not.

R (on the application of Collins) v Secretary of State for Justice [2016] EWHC 33 (Admin) It was held that a householder can use disproportionate force to defend themselves and would be acquitted of any offence of violence unless the prosecution could prove that the force used had been grossly disproportionate. Here it was found that the method of restraint used by the householder against C was proportionate. Also, it was held that the test of reasonableness in the circumstances did not breach Art 2 (see **Appendix 1**) of the Convention and there were sufficient safeguards regarding the defence to ensure this right was maintained. It was established that this defence was a mere refinement of the common law defence of self-defence.

R v Day [2015] EWCA Crim 1646 A guest in a dwelling could use reasonable force to protect themselves; self-defence was open not just to a property owner, but to a person in lawful occupation.

McDonnell v Commissioner of Police of the Metropolis and another [2015] EWCA Civ 573 An officer tackled M and brought him to the ground during his arrest resulting in the suspect breaking his shoulder. It was held not to be unreasonable or excessive use of force in accordance with s 117 of PACE and s 3 of the Criminal Law Act 1967. The injury had resulted from the tackle, but it was accidental and had not been deliberately inflicted.

R v Hichens [2011] EWCA Crim 1626 It was held in this case that self-defence and the defence of using reasonable force in the prevention of crime under the Criminal Law Act 1967, s 3 could extend to the use of force against an innocent third party to prevent a crime being committed by someone else.

Common law

- Whether force used is reasonable or excessive in the defence of self or property, the prevention of crime, or in making an arrest, will be determined by the court considering all the circumstances. The seminal words of Lord Morris in *Palmer v R* [1971] AC 814, HL emphasise the difficulties faced by a person confronted by an intruder or in taking any defensive action against attack.

If there has been an attack so that defence is reasonably necessary, it will be recognised that a person defending themselves cannot weigh to a nicety the exact measure of their defensive action. If the jury thought that in a moment of unexpected anguish a person attacked had only done what they honestly and instinctively thought necessary, that would be the most potent evidence that only reasonable defensive action had been taken.

- Although this area of law is addressed by statute, the wider issues of self-defence under common law may still be relevant (see **2.1.2**).

Human rights

- In addition, under the provisions of the ECHR (see **Appendix 1**), a further dimension in respect of the necessity and proportionality must be considered alongside the common law or statutory powers.
- Apart from using no more force than is necessary, considering proportionality will bring other factors into the equation, such as whether the force used is:
  - (a) proportionate to the wrong that it seeks to avoid or the harm it seeks to prevent;
  - (b) the least intrusive or damaging option available at the time.
- Striking a fair balance between the rights of the individual and the interests/rights of the community at large must be carefully considered.
- Any limited breaching of an individual's human rights must be both necessary and proportionate to the legitimate aim to be pursued (eg the lawful arrest or detention of that person is to pursue the legitimate aim of the prevention and detection of crime). Note, however, that certain Articles such as Art 3 cannot be lawfully breached.
- Therefore, any use of powers to cause inhuman or degrading treatment may amount to a breach. For example, words may be used to demean an individual such as in a prison situation. Under extreme circumstances, the use of words alone may suffice to constitute degrading treatment.
- If force is not used proportionately, then this may amount to a breach of various Articles of the ECHR (see **Appendix 1**).

Practical considerations

- Force used by an officer at an incident must be justified. When preparing evidence, state what the situation was like upon your arrival, the attitude of the individual(s) or group when they were approached, and what means were used (or attempted) to control the situation.
- Consider the College of Policing 'Public Order, Public Safety' tactical programme which provides guidance on public order policing.

Links to alternative subjects and offences

2.2.1 **Assault with intent to resist or prevent lawful arrest** 63
11.1 **Police Powers for Civilian Staff and Volunteers** 781
Appendix 1 **Human Rights** 839

1.3 Stop and Search Powers

1.3.1 Stop and search

PACE creates generic stop and search powers for a constable in places to which the public has access.

1.3.2 Search and detain

Section 1 of PACE creates the power for a constable to stop and search people and vehicles for stolen property, offensive weapons, bladed/pointed articles, or prohibited fireworks.

Power—search and detain

(1) A constable may exercise any power conferred by this section—
- (a) in any place to which at the time when he proposes to exercise the power the public or any section of the public has access, on payment or otherwise, as of right or by virtue of express or implied permission; or
- (b) in any other place to which people have ready access at the time when he proposes to exercise the power, but which is not a dwelling.

(2) Subject to subsection (3) to (5) below, a constable—
- (a) may search—
  - (i) any person or vehicle;
  - (ii) anything which is in or on a vehicle;

  for stolen or prohibited articles, any article to which subsection (8A), any substance to which subsection (8AA) below applies or any firework to which subsection (8B) below applies; and
- (b) may detain a person or vehicle for the purpose of such a search.

Police and Criminal Evidence Act 1984, s 1

Meanings

Vehicle

This is not defined. In the *Oxford English Dictionary*, it means 'a conveyance, usually with wheels, for transporting people, animals, goods or other objects and includes (amongst others) a car, cart, truck, bus, train carriage or sledge'. However, this power also applies to vessels including any ship, boat, raft, or other apparatus constructed or adapted for floating on water (under s 118 of the Act), aircraft, and hovercraft (under s 2(10) of the Act).

Stolen article (see **3.1**)

Prohibited articles

Prohibited articles given under s 1(7) and (8) means:

- an offensive weapon (see **8.9.1**);
- an article made or adapted for use in the course of or in connection with the following offences **or** intended by the person having it with them for such use by them or by some other person:
  - ✦ burglary (see **3.3.1**);
  - ✦ theft (see **3.1**);
  - ✦ taking a conveyance without consent (see **4.3**);
  - ✦ fraud (see **3.8**);
  - ✦ criminal damage (see **4.5**);
  - ✦ wilful obstruction of the highway (see **10.21.1**);
  - ✦ intentionally or recklessly causing public nuisance (see **7.13.3**);
  - ✦ public order offence of locking on (see **7.17.5**);
  - ✦ causing serious disruption by tunnelling (see **7.17.6**);
  - ✦ causing serious disruption by being present in a tunnel (see **7.17.6**);
  - ✦ obstruction etc of major transport works (see **7.17.7**); and
  - ✦ interference with use or operation of key national infrastructure (see **7.17.8**).

Article to which s 1(8A) applies

Any pointed or bladed article with which a person has committed, is committing, or is going to commit an offence under s 139 (see **8.10.1**) or s 139AA (see **8.10.6**) of the Criminal Justice Act 1988 (offences of having such articles in public place/on school premises).

Substance and article to which s 1(8AA) and s 1(8AB) apply

Any substance, or article which contains such a substance, in relation to which a person has committed, or is committing, or is going to commit an offence under s 6 (see **8.11.3**) of the Offensive Weapons Act 2019 (offence of having a corrosive substance in a public place).

Firework to which s 1(8B) applies

Any firework possessed in breach of prohibition imposed by fireworks regulations (see **8.8**).

Reasonable grounds for suspicion (subsection (3))

This section **does not** give a constable power to search a person or vehicle or anything in or on a vehicle **unless** they have **reasonable grounds** for suspecting that they will find stolen or prohibited articles, any article to which subsection (8A) applies, any substance to which subsection (8AA) applies, or any firework to which subsection (8B) applies.

Meaning of reasonable grounds

PACE Code A governs the exercise by police officers of statutory powers of stop and search. Paragraphs 2.2–2.11 provide an explanation of what are considered to be reasonable grounds for suspicion when conducting a search.

PACE Code of Practice A

Powers to stop and search must be used fairly, responsibly, with respect for people being searched, and without unlawful discrimination and ensure that in the discharge of their functions they have regard to the need to safeguard and promote the welfare of all persons under the age of 18.

Stop and search powers requiring reasonable grounds for suspicion—explanation

- Paragraph 2.2: reasonable grounds for suspicion is the legal test which a police officer must satisfy before they can stop and detain individuals or vehicles to search them under powers such as s 1 of PACE (to find stolen or prohibited articles) and s 23 of the Misuse of Drugs Act 1971 (to find controlled drugs). This test must be applied to the particular circumstances in each case and is in two parts:
  - (a) first, the officer must have formed a genuine suspicion in their own mind that they will find the object for which the search power being exercised allows them to search (see Annex A, second column, for examples); and
  - (b) secondly, the suspicion that the object will be found must be reasonable. This means that there must be an objective basis for that suspicion based on facts, information, and/or intelligence which are relevant to the likelihood that the object in question will be found, so that a reasonable person would be entitled to reach the same conclusion based on the same facts and information and/or intelligence.
- Officers must therefore be able to explain the basis for their suspicion by reference to intelligence or information about, or some specific behaviour by, the person concerned (see para 3.8(d) regarding the requirement to provide A clear explanation, para 4.6 regarding the record of the explanation of the grounds for the search, and para 5.5 for the requirement of police supervisors to monitor the use of stop and search powers by individual officers).
- Code A para 2.11 emphasises that there is no power to stop or detain a person in order to find grounds for a search. Police officers have many encounters with members of the public which do not involve detaining people against their will, and they do not require any statutory power in order to speak to a person (see para 4.12 and Note 1). However, if reasonable grounds for suspicion emerge during such an encounter, the officer may detain the person to search them, even though no grounds existed when the encounter began. As soon as detention begins, and before searching, the officer must inform the person that they are being detained for the purpose of a search and take action in accordance with paras 3.8 to 3.11 under 'Steps to be taken prior to a search'.

Summary of further provisions contained within this code (see Code A for full guidance and examples)

- Paragraph 2.2A: the exercise of these stop and search powers depends on the likelihood that the person searched is in possession of an item for which they may be searched; it does not depend on the person concerned being suspected of committing an offence in relation to the object of the search.

Personal factors can never support reasonable grounds for suspicion

- Paragraph 2.2B: reasonable suspicion can never be supported on the basis of personal factors. This means that unless the police have information or intelligence which provides a description of a person suspected of carrying an article for which there is a power to stop and search, the following cannot be used, alone or in combination with each other, or in combination with any other factor, as the reason for stopping and searching any individual, including any vehicle which they are driving or in which they are being carried:
  - ✦ a person's physical appearance with regard, for example, to any of the 'relevant protected characteristics' set out in the Equality Act 2010, s 149, which are age, disability, gender reassignment, pregnancy and maternity, race, religion or belief, sex, and sexual orientation (see para 1.1 and Note 1A), or the fact that the person is known to have a previous conviction; and
  - ✦ generalisations or stereotypical images that certain groups or categories of people are more likely to be involved in criminal activity.

Reasonable grounds for suspicion based on information and/or intelligence

- Paragraph 2.4: reasonable grounds for suspicion should normally be linked to accurate and current intelligence or information, relating to articles for which there is a power to stop and search, being carried by individuals or being in vehicles in any locality. This would include reports from members of the public or other officers describing:
  - ✦ a person who has been seen carrying such an article or a vehicle in which such an article has been seen;
  - ✦ crimes committed in relation to which such an article would constitute relevant evidence, for example property stolen in a theft or burglary, an offensive weapon or bladed or sharply pointed article used to assault or threaten someone, or an article used to cause criminal damage to property.
- Paragraph 2.4A: searches based on accurate and current intelligence or information are more likely to be effective. This does not, however, prevent stop and search powers being exercised in other locations where such powers may be exercised, and reasonable suspicion exists.

Reasonable grounds for suspicion and searching groups

- Paragraph 2.6: where there is reliable information or intelligence that members of a group or gang habitually carry knives unlawfully or weapons or controlled drugs, and wear a distinctive item of clothing or other means of identification in order to identify themselves as members of that group or gang, that distinctive item of clothing or other means of identification may provide reasonable grounds to stop and search any person believed to be a member of that group or gang.

- Paragraph 2.6A: a similar approach would apply to particular organised protest groups where there is reliable information or intelligence:
  - ✦ that the group in question arranges meetings and marches to which one or more members bring articles intended to be used to cause criminal damage and/or injury to others in support of the group's aims;
  - ✦ that at one or more previous meetings or marches arranged by that group, such articles have been used and resulted in damage and/or injury; and
  - ✦ that on the subsequent occasion in question, one or more members of the group have brought with them such articles with similar intentions.

These circumstances may provide reasonable grounds to stop and search any members of the group to find such articles. See also paras 2.12 to 2.18, 'Searches authorised under section 60 of the Criminal Justice and Public Order Act 1994', when serious violence is anticipated at meetings and marches.

Reasonable grounds for suspicion based on behaviour, time, and location

- Paragraph 2.6B: reasonable suspicion may also exist without specific information or intelligence and on the basis of the behaviour of a person. An officer who forms the opinion that a person is acting suspiciously, or that they appear to be nervous, must be able to explain, with reference to specific aspects of the person's behaviour or conduct which they have observed, why they formed that opinion. A hunch or instinct which cannot be explained or justified to an objective observer can never amount to reasonable grounds.

Securing public confidence and promoting community relations

- Paragraph 2.8A: all police officers must recognise that searches are more likely to be effective, legitimate, and secure public confidence when their reasonable grounds for suspicion are based on a range of objective factors.

Questioning to decide whether to carry out a search

- Paragraph 2.9: an officer who has reasonable grounds for suspicion may detain the person concerned in order to carry out a search. Before carrying out the search, the officer may ask questions about the person's behaviour or their presence in circumstances which gave rise to the suspicion. As a result of questioning the detained person, the reasonable grounds for suspicion necessary to detain that person may be confirmed or, because of a satisfactory explanation, be dispelled.

- Paragraph 2.10: if, as a result of questioning before a search, or other circumstances which come to the attention of the officer, there cease to be reasonable grounds for suspecting that an article of a kind for which there is a power to stop and search is being carried, no search may take place. In the absence of any other lawful power to detain, the person is free to leave at will and must be so informed.
- There is no power to stop or detain a person in order to find grounds for a search.

Restrictions in a garden/yard (subsections (4) and (5))

If a person or vehicle is in a garden or yard occupied with and used for the purposes of a dwelling or on other land so occupied and used, a constable may not search that person or vehicle, in exercising the power under s 1, unless the constable has reasonable grounds for believing that the suspect (or the person in charge of the vehicle):

- does not reside in the dwelling; **and**
- the vehicle or person is not in the place in question with the express or implied permission of a person who resides in the dwelling.

Power to seize

If in the course of such a search a constable discovers an article which he has reasonable grounds for suspecting to be a stolen or prohibited article, an article to which subsection (8A) applies, a substance to which subsection (8AA) applies or a firework to which subsection (8B) applies, he may seize it.

Police and Criminal Evidence Act 1984, s 1(6)

1.3.3 Conduct of a search

Section 2 of PACE provides safeguards for when a constable detains a person or vehicle under s 1 or in the exercise of any search powers prior to arrest. They are:

- a search can be abandoned if it is no longer required or it is impracticable;
- the time for which a person or vehicle may be detained for a search is as reasonably required to permit the search to be carried out, either at the place detained or nearby;
- a search and detain power does not authorise a constable to:
  - ✦ require a person to remove any of their clothing in public other than an outer coat, jacket, or gloves; or
  - ✦ stop a vehicle, if not in uniform;
- before commencing a search (excepting an unattended vehicle), a constable shall take reasonable steps to bring to the attention of the detainee or person in charge of the vehicle the following matters and provide the following details:

  - ✦ the constable's name and the name of the police station to which they are attached (plus identification if the constable is not in uniform);
  - ✦ the object of the proposed search;
  - ✦ the constable's grounds for proposing to make it; and
  - ✦ under s 3(7) and (8), entitlement to a copy of the written stop and search record, unless it appears to the constable that it will not be practicable to make/provide the record at the time of the search;
- where an unattended vehicle is searched, a constable shall leave a notice inside the vehicle (unless it would damage the vehicle) stating that they have searched it; giving the name of the police station to which they are attached; that an application for compensation for any damage caused by the search may be made to that police station; and, under s 3(8), the procedure as to the entitlement of a copy of the written stop and search record.

Meaning of vehicle (see 1.3.2)

1.3.4 Terrorism stop and search powers

- Under s 43 of the Terrorism Act 2000, a constable may stop and search a person whom they reasonably suspect to be a terrorist to discover whether they have in their possession anything which may constitute evidence that they are a terrorist. If a constable, in exercising the power to stop a person whom the constable reasonably suspects to be a terrorist, stops a vehicle, they may search the vehicle and anything in or on it to discover evidence that the person is a terrorist and may seize and retain anything which the constable discovers in the course of such a search, and reasonably suspects may constitute evidence that the person is a terrorist.
- This power to stop and search is much wider than under s 1 of PACE as no reason is needed other than a reasonable suspicion that the person is a terrorist as defined by s 40 of the Act.
- This power must not be used by PCSOs; it cannot be conferred on a person designated under s 38 of the Police Reform Act 2002.
- Section 43A of the Terrorism Act 2000 provides that a constable on reasonable suspicion that a vehicle is being used for the purposes of terrorism may stop and search the vehicle and driver, passenger, or anything in or on the vehicle or carried by the driver or a passenger to discover evidence that the vehicle is being used for the purposes of terrorism. A constable may seize and retain anything discovered in the course of such a search and reasonably suspects may be evidence that the vehicle is being used for the purposes of terrorism.
- In s 43A(5), driver, in relation to an aircraft, hovercraft, or vessel, means the captain, pilot, or other person with control of the aircraft, hovercraft, or vessel, or any member of its crew and, in relation to a train, includes any member of its crew.

- Section 43A may also be used to search unattended vehicles.
- Ensure compliance with the Code of Practice relating to the above stop and search powers under ss 43 and 43A.
- Section 43C provides similar powers to search terrorist offenders released on licence.
- Paragraph 4.13 of this Code deals with photography/film matters, as concerns had been raised among photographers and journalists about the use of stop and search powers in relation to photography. It is important to note that members of the public and media do not generally need any form of permit or express authority to take photographs nor is it an offence to take photographs/film in a public place or of a public building (unless there are any specific, advertised restrictions such as those applying to various Ministry of Defence buildings). Similarly, the police do not have any general power to stop people taking photographs.
- Digital images can be viewed as part of a search under s 43, 43A, or 47 to discover whether the person has in their possession anything which may constitute evidence that they are a terrorist, or to determine whether the images are of a kind which could be used in connection with terrorism.
- Film and memory cards may be seized as part of such a search if the police officer reasonably suspects they are evidence that the person is a terrorist, or a vehicle is being used for the purposes of terrorism, but officers do not have a power to delete images, destroy film, or to require the person to do so.
- For further information and guidance on Terrorism Act powers, see the *PNLD Counter-terrorism handbook* for further details.

1.3.5 Written records of stop and search

Section 3 of PACE details the following procedures to be adhered to when making written records of stop searches carried out by a constable, while exercising **any of their stop and search powers**, relating to a person or **vehicle**:

- If an arrest has been made as a result of a 'stop and search', a written record of the search must be included as part of the custody record. In any other case, if it is not practicable to make a record 'on the spot' then it shall be made as soon as practicable after the completion of the search.
- A record of the search of a person or vehicle shall include:
  - ✦ object of the search;
  - ✦ grounds for making it;
  - ✦ date and time made;
  - ✦ place where it was made;
  - ✦ except in the search of an unattended vehicle, the ethnic origins of the person searched or the person in charge of the vehicle searched (*ethnic origin is as described by that person, and if different as perceived by the constable*); and
  - ✦ shall identify the constable who carried out the search.

- Apart from the above mandatory fields, some forces continue to record all fields including name, outcome, and damage/injury caused.
- A person searched, or the owner/person in charge of a searched vehicle, is entitled to a copy of the record. This can be requested up to three months from the date when the search was made.

Explanatory notes

- Fireworks possessed in breach of prohibitions imposed by the Fireworks Regulations 2004 would give grounds for invoking the 'stop and search' powers (see **8.8** for details).
- Articles that are made, adapted, or intended for use for one of the listed offences could include:
  - ✦ crowbar/screwdriver (burglary);
  - ✦ car keys (for taking a vehicle without owner's consent);
  - ✦ stolen credit card (fraud); or
  - ✦ spray paint can/pens intending to cause graffiti (damage).
- This section does not give a constable power to search a person or vehicle, or anything in or on a vehicle unless they have reasonable grounds for suspecting that they will find stolen property or prohibited articles including fireworks.

Related cases (see also **5.4.1** cases)

Howarth v Commissioner of the Metropolitan Police [2011] EWHC 2818 (Admin) Based on intelligence, a police officer searched a protestor travelling to a demonstration for prohibited items which had been used to cause criminal damage at previous demonstrations. It was held that it was well recognised that the threshold for the existence of reasonable grounds for suspicion was low. It was accepted that it was not necessarily essential in all cases for the searching officer reasonably to suspect every individual member of a suspected group to be carrying the offending items before the search of members of the group was lawful.

B v DPP [2008] EWHC 1655 (Admin) Failure by a constable in plain clothes to produce their warrant card was a breach of s 2(2) of PACE and para 3.8 of Code A and, consequently, the drugs search was deemed unlawful.

R v Bristol [2007] EWCA Crim 3214 If a person is searched for drugs under s 23 of the Misuse of Drugs Act 1971 (see **5.4**), then s 2 of PACE applies. As the officer had failed to state their name and police station, then s 2 was breached, the search was unlawful, and the conviction was set aside (following *Osman v DPP* (1999) 163 JP 725, QBD).

O'Hara v CC of the RUC [1997] 1 All ER 129, HL Reasonable grounds for suspicion can arise from information/intelligence passed to an officer by a colleague, an informant, or anonymously. But the mere fact that an officer had been instructed is not sufficient; it is necessary that the arresting officer had in their own mind the relevant suspicion.

Practical considerations

- Paragraph 4.12 of Code A states that there is no national requirement for an officer who requests a person in a public place to account for themselves, ie their actions, behaviour, presence in an area, or possession of anything, to make any record of the encounter or to give the person a receipt. However, as detailed in guidance notes at para 22A of the Code, where there are concerns which make it necessary to monitor any local disproportionality, forces have discretion to direct officers to record the self-defined ethnicity of persons they request to account for themselves in a public place or whom they detain with a view to searching but do not search. Guidance should be provided locally, and efforts made to minimise the bureaucracy involved. Records should be closely monitored and supervised in line with paras 5.1 to 5.6, and forces can suspend or reinstate recording of these encounters as appropriate.
- A person who is asked to account for themselves should, if they request, be given information about how they can report their dissatisfaction about how they have been treated.
- Failing to comply with Codes of Practice could result in the CPS declining to institute or continue proceedings, or risk evidence being excluded at court. A court case may be lost through evidence being disallowed and the police officer could be subject to severe penalties.
- Officers must be fully aware and ready to take account of the special needs of juveniles and other vulnerable groups.

Links to alternative subjects and offences

5.4 **Search Powers for Controlled Drugs/Permit Use of Controlled Drugs on Premises** 263
8.12 **Stop and Search Powers—Knives and Weapons** 609
11.1.4 **Powers to search for and seize alcohol and tobacco** 787

1.4 Entry, Search, and Seizure Powers

Sections 32 and 17 to 22 of PACE deal with matters relating to searching people/premises, seizure and retention of property, plus entry and access for copying of seized items. These powers, without warrant, apply either upon or after arrest.

1.4.1 Search upon arrest

Section 32 of PACE creates powers of search relating to arrested persons before they are conveyed to a police station. The relevant points follow.

Person

A constable may search any person arrested at a place other than at a police station on reasonable grounds to believe that:

- the person may present a danger to themselves or others;
- concealed on the arrested person is anything which might be:
  - ✦ used to assist escape from lawful custody;
  - ✦ evidence relating to an offence.

Premises

- If a person is arrested for an **indictable offence**, at a place other than at a police station, a constable can enter and search any **premises** in which that person was:
  - ✦ when arrested;
  - ✦ immediately before they were arrested;

  for evidence relating to the indictable offence for which arrested, providing reasonable grounds exist to believe that the evidence is on the premises.
- If the premises consist of two or more separate dwellings, the power to search is limited to:
  - ✦ any dwelling in which the arrest took place or in which the person arrested was immediately before their arrest; **and**
  - ✦ any parts of the premises which the occupier of any such dwelling uses in common with the occupiers of any other dwellings comprised in the premises.

Seizure from person

A constable searching a person in the exercise of this power may seize and retain anything found on that person on reasonable grounds to believe that:

- the person might use it to cause physical injury to themselves or to any other person;
- the person might use it to assist them to escape from lawful custody;
- it is evidence of an offence or has been obtained in consequence of the commission of an offence (other than an item subject to **legal privilege**).

Meanings

Indictable offence (see **1.1.4**)

Premises

Premises includes any place, and in particular, includes:

- any vehicle, vessel, aircraft, or hovercraft;
- any offshore installation;
- any renewable energy installation; and
- a tent or movable structure.

Legal privilege

- Items subject to legal privilege relate to communications between:
  - the client and a professional legal adviser;
  - clients and any person representing them;
  - between such adviser/representative and any other person.
- This communication was made in connection with the:
  - giving of legal advice; or
  - contemplation of legal proceedings and for such purposes.
- It also includes items enclosed with or referred to in such communications when they are in the possession of a person who is entitled to them.
- Items held with the intention of furthering a criminal purpose are not items subject to legal privilege (s 10 of PACE).

Explanatory notes

- This power to search a person does not authorise a constable to require a person to remove any items of clothing in public other than an outer coat, jacket, or gloves.
- It does authorise a search of a person's mouth.
- The power to search premises is only to the extent that is reasonably required for the purpose of discovering any thing or any such evidence as mentioned in s 32(2).
- Any search of premises must comply with Code B.
- This power does not apply to an arrest which takes place at a police station.
- Items held subject to legal privilege cannot be seized when discovered during a premises search or executing a search warrant for an indictable offence.

- Legal privilege does not extend to a conveyancing document, solicitor's time sheets, fee records, appointment books, and other similar documents.
- Generally, an expert working for the defence is covered by the same legal privilege as the rest of a defence team.
- When seizing items found during the searching of premises under subsection 32(2)(b), the general power to seize property provided by s 19 of PACE will apply (see **1.4.4**).
- If it is suspected that the person is a terrorist then stop and search powers given under the Terrorism Act 2000, s 43 will apply.

1.4.2 **Power of entry to arrest, save life, or prevent damage**

Section 17 of PACE creates a power to enter and search premises to effect an arrest or to save life/prevent damage.

Power to enter premises

(1) Subject to the following provisions of this section, and without prejudice to any other enactment, a constable may enter and search any premises for the purpose—
 (a) of executing—
  (i) a warrant of arrest issued in connection with or arising out of criminal proceedings; or
  (ii) a warrant of commitment issued under section 76 of the Magistrates' Courts Act 1980;
 (b) of arresting a person for an indictable offence;
 (c) of arresting a person for an offence under—
  (i) section 1 (prohibition of uniforms in connection with political objects) of the Public Order Act 1936;
  (ii) any enactment contained in sections 6, 7, 8 or 10 of the Criminal Law Act 1977 (offences relating to entering and remaining on property);
  (iii) section 4 of the Public Order Act 1986 (fear or provocation of violence);
  (iiia) section 4 (driving etc when under influence of drink or drugs) or section 163 (failure to stop when required to do so by constable in uniform) of the Road Traffic Act 1988;
  (iiib) section 27 of the Transport and Works Act 1992 (which relates to offences involving drink or drugs);
  (iv) section 76 of the Criminal Justice and Public Order Act 1994 (failure to comply with interim possession order);
  (v) any of sections 4, 5, 6(1) and (2), 7 and 8(1) and (2) of the Animal Welfare Act 2006 (offences relating to the prevention of harm to animals);
  (vi) section 144 of the Legal Aid, Sentencing and Punishment of Offenders Act 2012 (squatting in a residential building);

(ca) of arresting, in pursuance of section 32(1A) of the Children and Young Persons Act 1969, any child or young person who has been remanded to local authority or youth detention accommodation under section 91 of the Legal Aid, Sentencing and Punishment of Offenders Act 2012;

(caa) of arresting a person for an offence to which section 61 of the Animal Health Act 1981 applies;

(cab) of arresting a person under any of the following provisions—

(i) section 30D(1) or (2A);

(ii) section 46A(1) or (1A);

(iii) section 5B(7) of the Bail Act 1976 (arrest where a person fails to surrender to custody in accordance with a court order);

(iv) section 7(3) of the Bail Act 1976 (arrest where a person is not likely to surrender to custody etc);

(v) section 97(1) of the Legal Aid, Sentencing and Punishment of Offenders Act 2012 (arrest where a child is suspected of breaking conditions of remand);

(cb) of recapturing any person who is, or is deemed for any purpose to be, unlawfully at large while liable to be detained—

(i) in a prison, young offender institution, secure training centre or secure college, or

(ii) in pursuance of section 92 of the Powers of Criminal Courts (Sentencing) Act 2000 (dealing with children and young persons guilty of grave crimes) or section 260 of the Sentencing Code (dealing with children and young persons guilty of grave crimes), in any other place;

(d) of recapturing any person whatever who is unlawfully at large and whom he is pursuing; or

(e) of saving life or limb or preventing serious damage to property. [See '**Explanatory notes**' below.]

(2) Except for the purpose specified in paragraph (e) of subsection (1) above, the powers of entry and search conferred by this section—

(a) are only exercisable if the constable has reasonable grounds for believing that the person whom he is seeking is on the premises; and

(b) are limited, in relation to premises consisting of two or more separate dwellings, to powers to enter and search—

(i) any parts of the premises which the occupiers of any dwelling comprised in the premises use in common with the occupiers of any other such dwelling; and

(ii) any such dwelling in which the constable has reasonable grounds for believing that the person whom he is seeking may be.

(3) The powers of entry and search conferred by this section are only exercisable for the purposes specified in subsection (1)(c)(ii), (iv) or (vi) above by a constable in uniform.

(4) The power of search conferred by this section is only a power to search to the extent that is reasonably required for the purpose for which the power of entry is exercised.
(5) Subject to subsection (6) below, all the rules of common law under which a constable has power to enter premises without a warrant are hereby abolished.
(6) Nothing in subsection (5) above affects any power of entry to deal with or prevent a breach of the peace.

Police and Criminal Evidence Act 1984, s 17

Conditions

- A concern for welfare may be too low a threshold for entry under s 17(1)(e) (see the ***Syed*** case, below), as this power is for saving life or limb or preventing serious damage to property.
- Apart from entry under s 17(1)(e), to save life or limb or prevent serious damage to property, the s 17(1) powers are only exercisable if the constable has reasonable grounds for believing that the person whom they are seeking is on the premises.
- In relation to premises consisting of two or more separate dwellings, these powers are limited to:
  - ✦ any parts of the premises which the occupiers of any dwelling comprised in the premises use in common with the occupiers of any other such dwelling; **and**
  - ✦ any such dwelling in which the constable has reasonable grounds for believing that the person whom they are seeking may be.
- The power to search is only given to the extent that is reasonably required for the purpose for which the power of entry is exercised.

Explanatory notes

- Code B must be complied with when this power is exercised.
- This section does not apply to s 4A of the Public Order Act 1986 (intentional harassment, alarm, or distress) (see **7.7**).
- Section 17(1)(e): life and limb refers to humans only but animals can be property.
- A **warrant of commitment** is a commitment warrant to prison issued under the Magistrates' Courts Act 1980, s 76 for failing to pay fines. It does not include 'default warrants' where an offender has defaulted on their payment of a fine.
- An **indictable offence** includes triable 'either way offences' and low-value shoplifting (see **1.1.4**).
- A designated CSO or CSV has the same powers as a police constable to enter and search premises for the purpose of saving life or limb or preventing serious damage to property (see **11.1.2**).
- Nothing in this section affects any power of entry to deal with or prevent a breach of the peace at common law (see **7.3**).

- The powers of entry and search conferred by this section are only exercisable for the purposes of subsection (1)(c)(ii), (iv), or (vi) by a constable in uniform (s 17(3)).

Related cases

Syed v DPP [2010] EWHC 81 (Admin) Officers said they had a power of entry as there were concerns for a person's welfare, but entry was refused. It was held that the police were not acting in the execution of their duty; there were no signs of the victim's injury, damage, or disturbance and the occupants had no complaints. Concern for welfare was too low a threshold for entry under s 17(1)(e).

Baker v CPS [2009] EWHC 299 (Admin) On a report that B had 'gone berserk with a knife' inside her home, officers entered the property 'to save life or limb' under s 17(1)(e). It was held that police could enter and search a premises without the consent of the occupier to save life or limb, including for the prevention of self-harm; and there was no need to give an explanation where it was impossible, impracticable, or undesirable to do so.

O'Loughlin v CC of Essex [1998] 1 WLR 374, CA When entry to premises is made to arrest a person for an offence, any occupier present should be informed of the reason for the entry, unless circumstances make it impossible, impracticable, or undesirable; otherwise, the constable would be acting unlawfully.

D'Souza v DPP [1992] 4 All ER 545, HL Entry was forced to a dwelling by police officers to recapture a person unlawfully at large from a secure hospital (under the Mental Health Act). Section 17(1)(d) of PACE gives a power of entry when in pursuit of persons unlawfully at large. The court ruled that the pursuit had to be within a few seconds or minutes of the entry (now known as 'immediate pursuit'). Officers were not entitled to form an intention to arrest and then go to premises where the person might be found. **Note**: this 'immediate pursuit' requirement does not apply to people unlawfully at large from prison/custody/remand/serving a sentence.

1.4.3 Searching of premises after arrest

Section 18 of PACE creates a power to enter and search premises after someone has been arrested for an indictable offence and provides a power to seize relevant items.

Power to enter/search after arrest

(1) Subject to the following provisions of this section, a constable may enter and search any premises occupied or controlled by a person who is under arrest for an indictable offence, if he has reasonable

grounds for suspecting that there is on the premises evidence other than items subject to legal privilege, that relates—
(a) to that offence; or
(b) to some other indictable offence which is connected with or similar to that offence.
(2) A constable may seize and retain anything for which he may search under subsection (1) above.
(3) The power to search conferred by subsection (1) above is only a power to search to the extent that is reasonably required for the purpose of discovering such evidence.
(4) Subject to subsection (5) below, the powers conferred by this section may not be exercised unless an officer of the rank of inspector or above has authorised them in writing.
(5) A constable may conduct a search under subsection (1)—
(a) before the person is taken to police station or released under section 30A; and
(b) without obtaining an authorisation under subsection (4), if the condition in subsection (5A) is satisfied.
(5A) The condition is that the presence of the person at a place (other than a police station) is necessary for the effective investigation of the offence.
(6) If a constable conducts a search by virtue of subsection (5) above, he shall inform an officer of the rank of inspector or above that he has made the search as soon as practicable after he has made it.
(7) An officer who—
(a) authorises a search; or
(b) is informed of a search under subsection (6) above, shall make a record in writing—
(i) of the grounds for the search; and
(ii) of the nature of the evidence that was sought.
(8) If the person who was in occupation or control of the premises at the time of the search is in police detention at the time the record is to be made, the officer shall make the record as part of his custody record.

Police and Criminal Evidence Act 1984, s 18

Meanings

Occupied

This refers to premises where the arrested person resides or works, and may include occupancy as an owner, tenant, or 'squatter'.

Controlled

This includes premises in which the arrested person holds some interest, such as owning, renting, leasing, or having use of the premises.

Indictable (see **1.1.4**)

Legal privilege (see **1.5.4**)

Explanatory notes

- A search should only be conducted if the officer has reasonable grounds for suspecting that evidence of that or another connected or similar indictable offence is on the premises.
- The search must be conducted in accordance with Code B.
- A person does not have to be in police detention before a s 18 authority can be issued, as s 18(1) just requires them to be arrested for an indictable offence.
- Another power to search premises immediately after arrest is created by s 32 (see **1.4**).

Related case

Cowan v Commissioner of the Metropolitan Police [2000] 1 WLR 254, CA Where a constable may seize 'anything' which is on premises, there is no reason why 'anything' could not mean 'everything' that is movable and it is practicable to remove. It does not matter that property itself could be considered to be premises, so the removal of a vehicle (being premises) is lawful and can be seized if necessary.

1.4.4 Powers of seizure from premises

Section 19 of PACE provides a constable who is lawfully on premises with a general power to seize property.

Power to seize

(1) The powers conferred by subsections (2), (3) and (4) below are exercisable by a constable who is lawfully on any premises.

(2) The constable may seize anything which is on the premises if he has reasonable grounds for believing—
  (a) that it has been obtained in consequence of the commission of an offence; and
  (b) that it is necessary to seize it in order to prevent it being concealed, lost, damaged, altered or destroyed.

(3) The constable may seize anything which is on the premises if he has reasonable grounds for believing—
  (a) that it is evidence in relation to an offence which he is investigating or any other offence; and
  (b) that it is necessary to seize it in order to prevent the evidence being concealed, lost, altered or destroyed.

(4) The constable may require any information which is stored in electronic form and is accessible from the premises to be produced

in a form in which it can be taken away and in which it is visible and legible or from which it can readily be produced in a visible and legible form, if he has reasonable grounds for believing—
(a) that—
(i) it is evidence in relation to an offence which he is investigating or any other offence; or
(ii) it has been obtained in consequence of the commission of an offence; and
(b) that it is necessary to do so in order to prevent it being concealed, lost, tampered with or destroyed.
(5) The powers conferred by this section are in addition to any power otherwise conferred.
(6) No power of seizure conferred on a constable under any enactment (including an enactment contained in an Act passed after this Act) is to be taken to authorise the seizure of an item which the constable exercising the power has reasonable grounds for believing to be subject to legal privilege.

Police and Criminal Evidence Act 1984, s 19

Explanatory notes

- Officers using this power can (while they are on the **premises lawfully**) seize any evidence whether it is owned by the defendant or by someone else, provided the seizure of it is necessary for the purpose(s) described. However, this Act does not provide a specific power for seizure of an innocent person's property when it is in a public place.
- As vehicles are deemed to be '**premises**' for the purposes of this Act, they can be seized under the same power (*Cowan v MPC* [2000] 1 WLR 254, CA).
- Motor vehicles, if owned by an innocent party and in a public place, may also be searched under authority of a s 8 warrant (see **1.5.1**) to search premises for evidence.
- A designated civilian investigating officer has the same seizure powers as a police constable.

Seizure of computerised information

Section 20 of PACE relates to the seizure of computerised information from premises.
(1) Every power of seizure which is conferred by an enactment to which this section applies on a constable who has entered premises in the exercise of a power conferred by an enactment shall be construed as including a power to require any information stored in any electronic form and accessible from the premises to be produced in a form in which it can be taken away and in which it is visible and legible or from which it can readily be produced in a visible and legible form.
(2) This section applies—
(a) to any enactment contained in an Act passed before this Act;

(b) to sections 8 and 18 above;
(c) to paragraph 13 of Schedule 1 to this Act; and
(d) to any enactment contained in an Act passed after this Act.

Police and Criminal Evidence Act 1984, s 20

Seizure of bulk material

The Criminal Justice and Police Act 2001 allows seizure of bulk material in order to examine it elsewhere ('seize and sift').

Premises

Section 50 of the 2001 Act allows a person who is lawfully on premises to seize bulk material when using existing seizure powers (listed in Part 1 of Sch 1 to the Act), providing:

- there are reasonable grounds to believe that it is or contains material which can be searched for and seized;
- in all the circumstances, it is not reasonably practicable for this to be ascertained whilst on the premises;
- where those conditions are met, the person is empowered by s 50 to seize so much of what they have found as is necessary to remove to determine whether that belief is correct (ie that it is or contains material which can be searched for and seized).

Person

Section 51 of the 2001 Act gives the police additional powers of seizure of bulk material from the person where there is an existing power to search as shown in Part 2 of Sch 1 to the Act:

Explanatory notes

- Powers given under s 50 also include any other authorised people such as HMRC or designated policing support officer.
- What is reasonably practicable will differ in each case. Factors to consider include the time to examine and separate the material, and the type and number of people involved. In addition, the need to reduce the risk of accidentally altering or damaging any of the material may be relevant.
- Where legally privileged material forms part of the 'whole thing' then this can be seized in order to separate it from the bulk of the material.
- The general principle is that anything that, on sifting, is found not to be seizable should be returned. However, there is an exception where that material is 'inextricably linked' to material that is seizable, in which case it may be retained subject to special rules about how it should be handled.
- Section 51 (seizure from person) could apply, for example, where a person has a briefcase containing bulk correspondence which cannot be examined in the street.

- Section 52 requires the occupier and/or some other person or persons from whom material has been seized to be given a notice specifying what has been seized and why, and that they can apply to a judge for the return of the material or for access to and copying of the seized material.
- Section 21 of PACE provides a person, from whom material has been lawfully seized by the police, with certain rights to access to and/or copies of it.
- Section 22 of PACE provides powers to retain items that have been seized by the police.

Related cases

R (A and another) v Central Criminal Court and another; R (C and others) v Central Criminal Court and another [2017] EWHC 70 (Admin) The approach in *Faisaltex* and *Cabot* applies to a s 9 PACE application.

R (Cabot Global Ltd) v Barkingside Magistrates' Court [2015] EWHC 1458 (Admin) The approach in *Faisaltex* applies to other electronica, including tablets, smart phones, or similar devices.

R (on application of Faisaltex Ltd) v Preston CC [2008] EWHC 2832 (Admin) A computer and hard drive counted as a single item within 'material' under s 8(1) of PACE. This power was sufficient without using s 51 of the Criminal Justice and Police Act 2001 as well.

1.5 **Enter and Search Warrants**

Procedures for premises search warrants, the application and execution process for warrants, and applying for access to excluded or special procedure material are all controlled by PACE.

There are several warrants provided under other legislation such as s 23 of the Misuse of Drugs Act 1971 and s 46 of the Firearms Act 1968. When executed, they should be conducted in accordance with PACE and the Codes of Practice, although they do retain individual powers peculiar to themselves.

1.5.1 **Premises search warrant**

Section 8 of PACE provides the grounds and procedure to be followed when applying for a search warrant relating to an indictable offence. It also provides a power to seize certain incriminating items.

Search warrant—application and procedure

(1) If on an application made by a constable a justice of the peace is satisfied that there are reasonable grounds for believing—
  (a) that an indictable offence has been committed; and
  (b) that there is material on premises mentioned in subsection (1A) below which is likely to be of substantial value (whether by itself or together with other material) to the investigation of the offence; and
  (c) that the material is likely to be relevant evidence; and
  (d) that it does not consist of or include items subject to legal privilege, excluded material or special procedure material; and
  (e) that any of the following conditions specified in subsection (3) below applies in relation to each set of premises specified in the application,

  he may issue a warrant authorising a constable to enter and search the premises.

(1A) The premises referred to in subsection (1)(b) above are—
  (a) one or more sets of premises specified in the application (in which case the application is for a 'specific premises warrant'); or
  (b) any premises occupied or controlled by a person specified in the application, including such sets of premises as are so specified (in which case the application is for an 'all premises warrant').

(1B) If the application is for an all premises warrant, the justice of the peace must also be satisfied—
  (a) that because of the particulars of the offence referred to in paragraph (a) of subsection (1) above, there are reasonable

grounds for believing that it is necessary to search premises occupied or controlled by the person in question which are not specified in the application in order to find the material referred to in paragraph (b) of that subsection; and

(b) that it is not reasonably practicable to specify in the application all the premises, which he occupies or controls and which might need to be searched.

(1C) The warrant may authorise entry to and search of premises on more than one occasion if, on the application, the justice of the peace is satisfied that it is necessary to authorise multiple entries in order to achieve the purpose for which he issues the warrant.

(1D) If it authorises multiple entries, the number of entries authorised may be unlimited, or limited to a maximum.

(2) A constable may seize and retain anything for which a search has been authorised under subsection (1) above.

(3) The conditions mentioned in subsection (1)(e) above are—

(a) that it is not practicable to communicate with any person entitled to grant entry to the premises;

(b) that it is practicable to communicate with a person entitled to grant entry to the premises, but it is not practicable to communicate with any person entitled to grant access to the evidence;

(c) that entry to the premises will not be granted unless a warrant is produced;

(d) that the purpose of a search may be frustrated or seriously prejudiced unless a constable arriving at the premises can secure immediate entry to them.

Police and Criminal Evidence Act 1984, s 8

Meanings

Indictable offence (see **1.1.4**)

Premises (see **1.4.1**)

Relevant evidence

In relation to an offence, means anything that would be admissible in evidence at a trial for the offence—s 8(4).

Legal privilege (see **1.5.4**)

Excluded material (see **1.5.4**)

Special procedure material (see **1.5.4**)

Specific premises warrant

This consists of one or more sets of premises named/specified in the application.

All premises warrant

Being all premises occupied or controlled by an individual.

Explanatory notes

- Section 8(5) states that the power to issue a warrant under this section is in addition to any other powers to issue warrants.
- Warrants under s 8 only apply to indictable offences, and can be for entry to:
  - named/specific premises—'**specific premises warrant**'; or
  - premises 'occupied or controlled by' an individual—'**all premises warrant**'.
- An all premises warrant will apply when it is necessary to search all premises occupied or controlled by an individual, but it is not reasonably practicable to specify all such premises at the time of application. The warrant will allow access to all premises occupied or controlled by that person, both those which are specified on the application and those which are not.
- Section 16(3) states that a warrant for entry and search must be executed within three months from the date of its issue.
- Where items falling outside those which may be seized under s 8(2) are found on the premises, consider the seizure provided by s 19 of PACE (see **1.4.4**).
- When applying for and executing warrants, s 15 (see **1.5.2**) and s 16 (see **1.5.3**), together with Code B, must be complied with in relation to application, safeguards, and execution.
- In any application, also consider the procedures for access to excluded material/special procedure material, if relevant, provided by s 9 of PACE (see **1.5.4**).
- Failure to comply with statutory requirements will make the entry, and subsequent seizure of property, unlawful (*R v CC of Lancashire, ex parte Parker* [1993] Crim LR 204, QBD).
- Officers should be aware of the extensive powers to search without a warrant on arrest under s 32 (see **1.4**) or after arrest under s 18 (see **1.4.3**).
- Warrants issued under the provision of s 8 authorise searching of the premises only, not people who are in them.
- Such people may be searched if another power applies—for example, post-arrest powers, but there can be a specific power to search people in warrants issued under s 23(2) of the Misuse of Drugs Act 1971 (see **5.5**) and s 46(2) of the Firearms Act 1968 (see **8.6.3**) (providing the application includes to search people in the premises).
- When applying for search warrants, 'reasonable grounds to believe' under s 8 of PACE imposes a higher threshold test than 'reasonable grounds to suspect' under s 46(1) of the Firearms Act 1968 (*R (on the application of Eastenders Cash and Carry plc) v South Western Magistrates' Court* [2011] EWHC 937 (Admin)).
- In relation to seizure and examination of bulk material, see **1.4.4**.

1.5.2 Application procedures for a search warrant

Section 15 of PACE sets out the procedure to be followed when applying for a search warrant. For quick reference, s 15 is given in bulleted form as follows:

Application procedure

- This section (and s 16) relates to the issue of warrants (**under any enactment**) for constables to enter and search premises.
- Entering or searching of premises under a warrant is unlawful unless it complies with this section and s 16 (see **1.5.3**).
- Where a constable applies for such warrant, the following details must be given:
  - ✦ grounds on which application made;
  - ✦ enactment under which the warrant would be issued;
  - ✦ identify (as far as practicable) the articles or persons sought.
- Furthermore, if the application is for:
  - ✦ a warrant authorising entry and search on more than one occasion:
    - ▪ the ground on which application made;
    - ▪ whether unlimited number of entries is sought; or
    - ▪ otherwise the maximum number of entries desired;
  - ✦ a 'specific premises warrant' (see **1.5.1**):
    - ▪ each set of premises to be entered and searched;
  - ✦ an 'all premises warrant' (see **1.5.1**):
    - ▪ specify (as far as reasonably practicable) the sets of premises to be entered and searched;
    - ▪ the person who is in occupation or control of those premises and any others which require entering and searching;
    - ▪ why it is necessary to search more premises than those specified; and
    - ▪ why it is not reasonably practicable to specify all the premises to be entered and searched.
- Such a warrant shall specify:
  - ✦ the name of the person who applied for it;
  - ✦ the date on which it is issued;
  - ✦ the enactment under which it is issued;
  - ✦ the articles or persons to be sought (identified as far as is practicable);
  - ✦ each set of premises to be searched;
  - ✦ in the case of an 'all premises warrant':
    - ▪ the person who is in occupation or control of premises to be searched, together with any premises under their occupation or control which can be specified and which are to be searched.

- The following points also have to be complied with:
  - ✦ applications shall be supported by an information in writing and made *ex parte* (subject does not have to be present);
  - ✦ the constable shall answer on oath any question that the justice of the peace or judge hearing the application puts to them;
  - ✦ a warrant shall authorise an entry on one occasion only—unless multiple entries are authorised, in which case it must specify whether the number of entries is unlimited or limited to a specified maximum;
  - ✦ two copies shall be made of a specific premises warrant that specifies only one set of premises and does not authorise multiple entries. Otherwise, as many copies as are reasonably required may be made of any other kind of warrant;
  - ✦ copies shall be clearly certified as copies.

Explanatory notes

- Advice and guidance are given in Code B, under search warrants.
- Where premises are multiple occupancy (eg a single house converted into flats), the warrant must specify all the rooms required to be searched (including the common living areas), and not just give the main address.
- Section 15(1) states that entering or searching premises under authority of a warrant is unlawful, unless procedures given in ss 15 and 16 (see **1.5.3**) are complied with.

Related cases

R (on the application of F, J and K) v Blackfriars CC and the Commissioner of Police of the Metropolis [2014] EWHC 1541 (Admin) A warrant was the authority to go on to premises; if s 15(6)(b) was not complied with (eg by failing to specify in detail the article(s) sought), then the warrant—and therefore the entry—could be invalidated.

R (on the application of Lees and others) v Solihull MC and another [2013] EWHC 3779 (Admin) Search warrants granted under s 8 to HMRC did not specify what material was sought. As a result, the entry, search, and seizure were unlawful because the warrants breached s 15(6)(b) by failing to identify the articles or persons sought.

R (on the application of Bhatti and others) v Croydon MC and another [2010] EWHC 522 (Admin) In an 'all premises warrant' issued under s 8, all premises that can be identified at the time of application must be so identified. Premises identified later must be added to the schedule attached to the warrant and signed by an inspector before attending the property. Failure to supply the occupier with a copy of the warrant/schedule at entry naming the premises or adding the address by hand as a warrant is executed breaches s 16(5), so entry, search, and seizure become unlawful under s 15(1).

1.5.3 Execution of search warrants

Section 16 of PACE sets out the procedure to be followed when executing a search warrant. For quick reference, s 16 is given in bulleted form as follows:

Execution procedure

A warrant to enter and search premises:

- may be executed by any constable;
- may authorise persons to accompany any constable who is executing it:
  such a person has the same powers as the constable, in relation to the execution of the warrant and seizure of anything to which the warrant relates, but only whilst in the company and under the supervision of a constable;
- must be executed within three months from the date of its issue;
- must be executed at a reasonable hour unless it appears that the purpose of a search may be frustrated on an entry at a reasonable hour;
- will only authorise a search to the extent required for the purpose for which the warrant was issued.

Specifically, no premises may be entered or searched unless an inspector (or above) authorises, in writing, entry for:

- an 'all premises warrant':
  - ✦ premises which are not specified;
- a 'multiple entries warrant':
  - ✦ for the second or subsequent entry and search.

Notification requirements exist when a constable is seeking to execute a warrant to enter and search premises, the constable shall:

- where the occupier is present:
  - ✦ identify themselves to the occupier. If not in uniform, documentary evidence produced to show that they are a constable;
  - ✦ produce the warrant and supply a copy of the warrant/schedule to the occupier;
- if the occupier is not present, but some other person is present who appears to the constable to be in charge of the premises:
  - ✦ the constable shall deal with that person as if they were the occupier and comply with the above requirements;
- if there is no person present (occupier or in charge):
  - ✦ the constable shall leave a copy of the warrant in a prominent place on the premises.

Where a constable has executed a warrant, they shall:

- endorse the warrant stating whether:
  - ✦ the articles or persons sought were found;
  - ✦ any articles were seized, other than articles which were sought;

- unless the warrant is for one set of premises only:
  - ✦ separately endorse each set of premises entered and searched providing the above details.

A warrant shall be returned to the **appropriate person**:
- when it has been executed;
- in the case of:
  - ✦ a 'specific premises warrant' **(not been executed)**;
  - ✦ an 'all premises warrant';
  - ✦ any warrant authorising multiple entries;

upon the expiry of the three-month period or sooner.

Meanings

Premises (see **1.4.1**)

All premises warrant (see **1.5.3**)

Multiple entries warrant (see **1.5.3**)

Appropriate person

If the warrant was issued by:
- a justice of the peace, it will be the designated officer for the local justice area in which the justice was acting when the warrant was issued;
- a judge, it will be the appropriate officer of the court from which the judge issued it.

Specific premises warrant (see **1.5.1**)

Explanatory notes

- A warrant returned to the appropriate person shall be retained by that person for twelve months from its return.
- An occupier of premises to which the warrant relates can inspect the warrant (and should be allowed to do so) during the twelve-month retaining period.
- When executing a search warrant, advice and guidance should be obtained from Code B, under search warrants.
- A person authorised in the warrant to accompany the constable may be an expert in computing or financial matters. Such an expert will then be able to take a more active role in the search and in seizing material, rather than merely being present in an advisory or clerical capacity.
- In practical terms, the supervising constable must identify any accompanying persons to the occupier of premises prior to the start of any search and explain that person's role in the process. The constable in charge will have overall supervisory responsibility and will be accountable for any action taken.

1.5.4 Access to excluded and special procedure material

Section 9 of PACE provides the procedures to be adopted to gain access to excluded material and special procedure material.

Access procedure

(1) A constable may obtain access to excluded material or special procedure material for the purposes of a criminal investigation by making an application under Schedule 1 and in accordance with that Schedule.

(2) Any Act (including a local Act) passed before this Act under which a search of premises for the purposes of a criminal investigation could be authorised by the issue of a warrant to a constable shall cease to have effect so far as it relates to the authorisation of searches—
   (a) for items subject to legal privilege; or
   (b) for excluded material; or
   (c) for special procedure material consisting of documents or records other than documents.

Police and Criminal Evidence Act 1984, s 9

Meanings

Excluded material

Defined by s 11 of PACE as:

- **personal records** which a person has acquired or created in the course of any trade, business, profession, or other occupation or for the purposes of any paid or unpaid office they hold in confidence;
- human tissue or tissue fluid which has been taken for the purposes of diagnosis or medical treatment and which a person holds in confidence;

For the purposes of these two categories, 'holds in confidence' means holds subject to:

  ✦ an express or implied undertaking to do so;
  ✦ a disclosure restriction or an obligation of secrecy contained in any enactment;

or

- **journalistic material** which consists of documents or records other than documents, being held or continuously held in confidence (by one or more persons);
- for the purposes of this category, 'holds in confidence' means: holds subject to an undertaking, restriction, or obligation of confidence

since it was first acquired or created for the purposes of journalism and for so long as it is continuously held by persons as such.

Personal records

Means documentary and other records concerning an individual (whether living or dead) who can be identified from them and relates to:
- their physical or mental health;
- spiritual counselling or assistance given/to be given to them; or
- counselling or assistance given/to be given for their personal welfare, by any voluntary organisation or individual who by reason of:
  - ✦ their office or occupation has responsibilities for this; or
  - ✦ an order by a court has responsibilities for their supervision.

Journalistic material

- Is material acquired or created for the purposes of journalism.
- Providing it is in the possession of a person who acquired or created it for that purpose.
- It will be acquired if a person receives the material from someone who intends that the recipient uses it for that purpose.

Special procedure material

- Includes journalistic material, other than excluded material.
- Includes material, other than items subject to legal privilege and excluded material, in the possession of a person who acquired or created it in the course of any trade, business, profession, or other occupation or for the purpose of any paid or unpaid office; and holds it in confidence subject to:
  - ✦ an express or implied undertaking to do so;
  - ✦ a disclosure restriction or an obligation of secrecy contained in any legislation.
- Where material is acquired by:
  - ✦ an employee from their employer in their course of employment;
  - ✦ a company from an associated company;

  it is only special procedure material if it was special procedure material immediately before the acquisition.
- Where material is created by:
  - ✦ an employee in the course of their employment;
  - ✦ a company on behalf of an associated company;

  it is only special procedure material if it would have been special procedure material had the employer/associated company created it.

Schedule 1

This gives full details of the procedure to be followed when making an application to a judge in order to gain access to excluded material or special procedure material.

Premises (see **1.4.1**)

Legal privilege (see **1.5.4**)

1.5.4 Access to excluded and special procedure material

Explanatory notes

- Code B provides guidance regarding the conduct of searches and advice on Sch 1 searches.
- The CPS makes Sch 1 applications and advice should be sought from them in any application.
- Case law has established that:
  - ✦ police cannot routinely examine hospital records;
  - ✦ a search warrant is not lawful without the proper paperwork;
  - ✦ a Sch 1 notice should specify the documents being sought.
- In relation to seizure and examination of bulk material, see **1.4.4**.
- Officers should be mindful of the powers to search (without a warrant) on arrest or after arrest (see **1.1**).
- Special procedure and excluded material can be searched for and seized under PACE, ss 18 and 32, provided:
  - ✦ lawful arrest is made, in good faith; **and**
  - ✦ the search is carried out strictly within the terms of those sections.

Related cases

R (on the application of A) v Central Criminal Court; C v Central Criminal Court [2017] EWHC 70 (Admin) A mobile phone could be the subject of a search warrant under s 9 of and Sch 1 to PACE, even where material that would be subject to legal privilege may be found on the phone.

R v Bristol CC, ex parte Bristol Press and Picture Agency (1986) 85 Cr App R 190 A 'Picture Agency' took photographs during two nights of rioting in Bristol. The police applied under s 9 of and Sch 1 to PACE for an order allowing them access to the pictures, on the grounds that the photographs might help the police to identify offences and offenders. It was held on appeal that the judge was entitled to grant the order as there were sufficient grounds in this case to believe that the photographs might help, and it was in the public interest to grant the order.

Chapter 2

Assaults and Violence

2.1 Assault (Common/Actual Bodily Harm)

A common assault under s 39 of the Criminal Justice Act 1988 is in fact two separate matters: an assault and/or a battery. This area of law is dealt with first, before covering the more serious assault occasioning actual bodily harm (AOABH) under the Offences Against the Person Act 1861. Defences which may be available to assaults are then discussed.

2.1.1 Common assault—battery

Offence

Common assault and battery shall be summary offences

Criminal Justice Act 1988, s 39

PNLD H4302, H4325

Points to prove

Assault

✓ assaulted
✓ another person

Battery

✓ all points above
✓ application of unlawful force (eg by beating)

Meanings

Assault

Any act, which **intentionally** or **recklessly**, causes another person to apprehend immediate and **unlawful** personal violence (*Fagan v Metropolitan Police Commissioner* [1968] 3 All ER 442, QBD).

Battery

Any intentional or reckless infliction of unlawful force or personal violence. Consequently, a battery may include an assault.

Intent (see **4.1.2**)

Reckless (see **2.3.1**)

Unlawful (see **2.3.1**)

Explanatory notes

- There are two distinct offences covered by this legislation: 'assault' and 'assault by beating' (battery).
- There is also a civil wrong of assault/battery.
- An 'assault' does not have to involve an actual application of force: it may just be threatening words used, although if violence is threatened, there must be the ability to carry out the threat at the time.
- The threat of physical contact, or the actual physical contact, requires a mental element which is an intention, or recklessness.
- Consent, actual or implied, is a defence to battery, and trivial touching of a kind which is generally acceptable in the ordinary conduct of daily life is regarded by the law as the use of lawful force, either because it is an exception in its own right, amounting to deemed consent, or because it is an example of implied consent. The line is drawn between acceptable and unacceptable force by having regard to the degree and duration of the force used.

Defences (see **2.1.2**)

Related cases

Marland v DPP [2023] EWHC 1046 (Admin) Implied or deemed consent could not be said to arise on the facts, where M applied force to C, his partner, when he knew that C had not consented, and the force could not be regarded as trivial. M applied force to C when she was walking down a road in the dark and she was drunk. Knowing that she did not consent, he grabbed her by both shoulders to guide her to his car and then let go of her, which caused her to fall to the ground. Since M knew that she did not consent, and his conduct was not the kind of trivial or inadvertent touching to which a person might be deemed to consent, no issue of implied or deemed consent arose. (Illustrations given of acceptable force that might, in contrast, give rise to an issue of implied or deemed consent were a touch to attract a person's attention or an inadvertent nudge occurring on busy public transport.)

ZH v Metropolitan Police Commissioner [2012] EWHC 604 (Admin) It was held in this case that when using force to detain a man, a police officer's failure to consider disabilities appropriately can result in liability for assault, false imprisonment, disability discrimination, and breaches of human rights.

Wood v DPP [2008] EWHC 1056 (Admin) A police officer, without any intention to arrest, grabbed a person's arm to stop them walking away to question them about an incident at a public house. It was held that this action amounted to an unlawful assault. Where a police officer restrains someone but does not at the time intend to arrest them, that police officer risks committing an assault, even if an arrest at a later time would have been justified.

Haystead v CC Derbyshire Police [2000] 3 All ER 890, QBD A mother was punched by her boyfriend and, as a result, dropped and injured the baby she was carrying. The defendant was convicted of assault by battery directly on the mother, and indirectly on the baby.

Mepstead v DPP [1996] Crim LR 111, QBD Police officers were issuing a fixed penalty notice to a car when the owner returned and became abusive to the officers. One officer took hold of his arm and told him to calm down. It was held that touching someone to draw their attention to what was being said was acceptable by the ordinary standards of everyday life.

Fagan v Metropolitan Police Commissioner [1968] 3 All ER 442, QBD It is irrelevant whether the battery is inflicted directly by the body of the offender or with a weapon or instrument such as a car.

Practical considerations

- If a common assault under this section is racially or religiously aggravated, you should consider the more serious version of this offence under s 29 of the Crime and Disorder Act 1998 (see **7.10.2**).
- Aggravated versions of the offences in this section apply if the common assault or battery is committed against an emergency worker (see **2.2.6**).
- An individual should be charged with either 'assault' or 'battery'—the inclusion of both in the same charge is bad for duplicity and could result in the charge being dismissed (*DPP v Little* (1994) 95 Cr App R 28).
- Ensure that visible injuries are photographed.
- Include in your CJA witness statement evidence as to intent or recklessness.
- Ascertain whether any of the defences could apply.
- The time limit for a prosecution of common assault or battery in domestic violence cases where the complainant has given a statement to the police or participated in a video witness interview with the police may be commenced at any time which is both within two years from the date of the offence and within six months from the first date of the statement being given or the video witness interview being conducted.
- Where the offence is committed against a person providing a public service, performing a public duty, or providing services to the public, the court must treat that fact as an aggravating factor, and must

state in open court that the offence is so aggravated (unless s 1 of the Assaults on Emergency Workers (Offences) Act 2018 applies—see 2.2.6).

Assault

- Unless extenuating circumstances apply, the police/CPS will invariably invite the aggrieved party to take their own action either by criminal prosecution or by civil action.
- Where a court decides that the assault or battery has not been proved or that it was justified, or so trifling as not to merit any punishment, it must dismiss the complaint and forthwith make out a certificate of dismissal. This certificate releases the defendant from any further proceedings (civil or criminal) (Offences Against the Person Act 1861, s 44).
- If the conduct involves threatening acts, words, gestures, or a combination of these, then consider alternative offences under the Public Order Act 1986, breach of the peace, or harassment (see 7.7).

Battery

- Ascertain the degree/severity of injury before charging.
- CPS guidelines specify the following injuries should normally be charged as battery: grazes, scratches, abrasions, minor bruising, swellings, reddening of the skin, superficial cuts, and a 'black eye'.

Consider s 47, s 20, or s 18 of the Offences Against the Person Act 1861 for more serious injuries.

SSS RRA

Summary

6 months

6 months' imprisonment and/or a fine

2.1.2 Assault occasioning actual bodily harm (AOABH)/Defences to assaults

Offences

Whosoever shall be convicted upon an indictment of any assault occasioning actual bodily harm shall be guilty of an offence.

Offences Against the Person Act 1861, s 47

PNLD H479

Points to prove

✓ assaulted
✓ another person
✓ occasioning them
✓ actual bodily harm

Meaning of actual bodily harm

Actual means that the harm should not be so trivial as to be effectively without significance; *bodily* means concerned with the body, and *harm* is not limited to injury but extends to hurt and damage. Actual bodily harm is not limited to harm to the skin, flesh, and bones of the victim, it applies to all parts of the body including the person's organs, nervous system, and brain.

Explanatory notes

- Bodily harm has its ordinary meaning and is that which is calculated to interfere with the health or comfort of the victim but must be more than transient or trifling.
- Examples of 'actual bodily harm' and physical/mental injuries are given in **Practical considerations**.
- A conviction can be obtained if actual bodily harm is caused to the victim by some action which is the natural and reasonably foreseeable result of what the defendant said or did.

Defences to assault

Consent

- Consent can be expressly given to an application of force (such as tattooing or an operation), providing the activity is not illegal itself (injection of illegal drugs) or it can be implied (by getting into a crowded train where contact is unavoidable).
- An honestly held belief that consent had been given (or would have been given—emergency surgery to save life).
- Submitting to an assault is not consent. Similarly, consent is negated if given due to duress or fraud (a trick), but the burden of proof is on the prosecution to prove that this was how consent was obtained.
- Consent cannot be given by a child or young person if they fail to understand the true nature of the act (what is involved).
- At a school for children with behavioural problems, where there is a higher risk of pupils becoming violent, it cannot be reasonably argued that a teacher's consent to being assaulted by the pupils can be implied (*H v CPS* [2010] EWHC 1374 (Admin)).
- Consent cannot be given to an assault that inflicts substantial bodily harm, such as in sadomasochism (*R v Brown and others* [1994] 1 AC 212, HL), although some body mutilation in limited and non-aggressive circumstances may be acceptable (*R v Wilson* [1996] 2 Cr App R 241).

Lawful sports

- Properly conducted lawful sports are considered to be for the public good and injuries received during the course of an event kept within the rules are generally accepted.
- Players are taken to have consented to any injuries which they might reasonably expect to suffer during the course of the match or contest.
- Criminal charges and proceedings should only be instigated in situations where the player acted outside the rules of the sport and the conduct was sufficiently serious as to be properly regarded as criminal.

Lawful correction

A parent or someone acting '*in loco parentis*' may administer reasonable physical punishment to a child under the doctrine of 'reasonable chastisement'. However, s 58 of the Children Act 2004 precludes the defence of reasonable chastisement from the following offences:

- s 18 or s 20 of the Offences Against the Person Act 1861 (wounding and causing grievous bodily harm);
- s 47 of that Act (assault occasioning actual bodily harm);
- s 1 of the Children and Young Persons Act 1933 (cruelty to persons under 16).

It follows that physical punishment of a child constitutes a criminal offence if it causes any injury or unnecessary suffering.

Self-defence (case law)

'A jury must decide whether a defendant honestly believed that the circumstances were such as required him to use force to defend himself from an attack or threatened attack; the jury has then to decide whether the force used was reasonable in the circumstances' (*R v Owino* [1996] 2 Cr App R 128 and *DPP v Armstrong-Braun* (1999) 163 JP 271, CA).

Self-defence (statutory test—reasonable force)

Criminal Justice and Immigration Act 2008, s 76 (see **1.2**).

Statutory authorities—using reasonable force (see **1.2**)

Related cases

R v Keane and McGrath [2010] EWCA Crim 2514 Self-defence could be available to an aggressor where the violence offered by the victim was so out of proportion that the roles were effectively reversed.

H v DPP [2007] EWHC 960 (Admin) It is not necessary to identify which injury was caused by which defendant, provided that some injury resulting in actual bodily harm was caused by the defendant.

DPP v Smith [2006] 1 WLR 1571, QBD Cutting hair, or applying some unpleasant substance that marked or damaged the hair, was capable of being AOABH. Harm is not limited to injury and includes hurt or damage.

R v Barnes [2004] EWCA Crim 3246 Provides guidance on consent in contact sports (see '**Defences to assaults—Lawful sport**').

DPP v Santa-Bermudez [2003] EWHC 2908 (Admin) Where someone, by act or word or a combination of the two, created a danger and thereby exposed another to a reasonably foreseeable risk of injury which materialised, there was an evidential basis for the actus reus of an assault occasioning actual bodily harm. However, it remained necessary for the prosecution to prove an intention to assault or the appropriate recklessness.

T v DPP [2003] EWHC 266 (Admin) Actual bodily harm can include loss of consciousness (even if there is no other physical injury) as it involves an impairment of the victim's sensory functions.

R v Chan-Fook [1994] 2 All ER 552, CA Actual bodily harm can include psychiatric injury, but does not include mere emotions such as fear, distress, or panic.

R v Brown and others [1994] 1 AC 212, HL Sadomasochists engaged in torture with each other cannot give consent, even though the 'victims' were all willing participants.

Practical considerations

- It is not a defence that V consented to the infliction of the serious harm (including actual bodily harm within the meaning of s 47 of the Offences Against the Person Act 1861) for the purposes of obtaining sexual gratification. However, this does not apply where the serious harm consists of, or is a result of, the infection of V with a sexually transmitted infection in the course of sexual activity and where V consented to the sexual activity in the knowledge or belief that D had the sexually transmitted infection (see s 71 of the Domestic Abuse Act 2021).
- If an assault under this section is racially or religiously aggravated, you should consider the more serious version of this offence under s 29 of the Crime and Disorder Act 1998 (see **7.10.2**).
- Aggravated versions of the offences in this section apply if the common assault or battery is committed against an emergency worker (see **2.2.6**).
- Where the offence is committed against a person providing a public service, performing a public duty, or providing services to the public, the court must treat that fact as an aggravating factor, and must state in open court that the offence is so aggravated.
- Ensure that visible injuries are photographed.
- Include in your CJA witness statement details of injuries, circumstances of the incident, and any evidence as to intent or recklessness.
- Obtain medical evidence (hospital or doctor).
- Could any of the defences apply or be used by the defendant?
- Examples of injuries which could amount to 'actual bodily harm':
  - ✦ loss or breaking of a tooth or teeth;

- ✦ temporary loss of sensory functions (includes loss of consciousness);
- ✦ extensive or multiple bruising;
- ✦ displaced broken nose;
- ✦ minor fractures;
- ✦ minor cuts (not superficial), may require stitches (medical treatment);
- ✦ psychiatric injury (proved by appropriate expert evidence) which is more than fear, distress, or panic.

- Consider s 20 or s 18 of the Offences Against the Person Act 1861 for more serious injuries (see **2.3**).

SSS E&S RRA

Either way

None

Summary: 6/12 months' imprisonment and/or a fine

Indictment: 5 years' imprisonment

2.1.3 Maliciously administering poison, etc, with intent

Section 24 of the Offences Against the Person Act 1861 makes it an offence to administer poison or other noxious substance with intent to injure, aggrieve, or annoy a person.

Offence

Whosoever shall unlawfully and maliciously administer to or cause to be administered to or taken by any other person any poison or other destructive or noxious thing, with intent to injure, aggrieve, or annoy such person, shall be guilty of an offence.

Offences Against the Person Act 1861, s 24

PNLD H2002

Points to prove

- ✓ date and location
- ✓ unlawfully and maliciously
- ✓ administered/caused to be administered/caused to be taken
- ✓ poison/destructive/noxious thing
- ✓ with intent to injure/aggrieve/annoy

Meanings

Unlawful

Means without excuse or justification at law. (See also *R v Kennedy* [2007] UKHL 38.)

Maliciously

'Maliciously requires either an actual intention to do the particular kind of harm that was done or recklessness as to whether any such harm should occur or not; it is neither limited to, nor does it require, any ill-will towards the person injured' (see *R v Cunningham* [1957] 2 All ER 412, CA).

Explanatory notes

- This section creates three offences:
  - ✦ administering a noxious thing to a person (substance is administered directly, ie injected);
  - ✦ causing a noxious thing to be administered to any other person (for example, substance is administered by an innocent third party); and
  - ✦ causing a noxious thing to be taken by any other person (for example, noxious substance is put in food then the food is eaten).
- In the dictionary, 'noxious' means harmful to living things; injurious to health. However, in legal terms a substance that may be harmless if taken in small quantities becomes noxious if administered in sufficient quantity to injure, aggrieve, or annoy. The purpose which the defendant has in view may also have a bearing on the nature of the substance in question. This can include the administration of a noxious thing that may not normally cause harm but is calculated to do so in the particular circumstances: for example, if sleeping tablets were put into a drink in a quantity that may not cause harm where the victim remains in the home, whereas if the victim was to drive or operate machinery this could be an entirely different matter with potentially disastrous consequences.

Related cases

R v Veysey and others [2019] EWCA Crim 1332 In this case, the defendant and two others were serving prisoners. Each was involved in throwing at a prison officer, or smearing a prison officer with, urine, faeces, or a mixture of the two, and each was prosecuted for the s 24 offence. It was held that where a substance was administered in a manner and a quantity which was harmful, and the requisite intent was proved, then the offence would be made out even though the same substance in a lesser quantity, or administered in a different manner, might not have been harmful. In addition, the court held that the offence extended to substances that were noxious in the sense that they were 'unwholesome'.

R v Gillard (1988) 87 Cr App Rep 189 'Administer' was held to include conduct that brings a noxious thing into contact with the victim's body, directly or indirectly, for example by spraying CS gas into the victim's face.

Practical considerations

- Note the more serious offence provided by s 23 for maliciously administering poison, etc, so as to endanger life or inflict grievous bodily harm.
- The s 24 offence has been successfully used in respect of 'spiked' drinks cases.
- Note also s 61 of the Sexual Offences Act 2003—administer substance with intent (see **6.10**).

SSS E&S

Indictable

None

5 years' imprisonment

Links to alternative subjects and offences

6.10 **Administer Substance Intending to Commit a Sexual Offence** 344
7.3 **Breach of the Peace** 362
7.8 **Threatening/Abusive Words/Behaviour** 380
7.10 **Racially/Religiously Aggravated Offences** 390
Appendix 1 **Human Rights** 839

2.2 Assault/Resist/Impersonate and Obstruct—Police or Designated/Accredited Person or Emergency Workers

This area of law concerns offences involving assault with intent to resist or prevent arrest; assault, resist, or wilfully obstruct a police constable, designated or accredited person in the execution of their duty; and obstruct or hinder emergency workers.

2.2.1 Assault with intent to resist or prevent lawful arrest

Section 38 of the Offences Against the Person Act 1861 creates the offence of 'assault with intent to resist or prevent lawful arrest'.

> **Offences**
>
> Whosoever shall assault any person with intent to resist or prevent the lawful apprehension or detainer of himself or of any other person for any offence shall be guilty of an offence.
>
> Offences Against the Person Act 1861, s 38

PNLD H2016

Points to prove

- ✓ assaulted
- ✓ with intent to resist/prevent
- ✓ the lawful apprehension/detention of
- ✓ self/other person
- ✓ for the offence of (specify)

Meanings

Assault (see **2.1.1**)

Intent (see **4.1.2**)

Resist or prevent

The *Oxford English Dictionary* offers the following meanings:

- resist—'to strive against, oppose, try to impede or refuse to comply with'.

- prevent—'stop from happening or doing something; hinder; make impossible'.

Explanatory notes

- The assault itself need not be any more serious than a common assault (which could be considered as an alternative charge).
- The intention to resist the lawful arrest (either of themselves or another person) must be proved.
- If any wound or grievous bodily harm has been caused by the person committing the offence, then a more serious offence under s 18 should be considered (see **2.3.2**).

Defences to assault (see **2.1.2**)

Related case

R v Lee (2000) 150 NLJ 1491, CA It is not a defence for the suspect/other person to hold an honest belief that a mistake is being made by the officers as to whether or not an offence has been committed by the suspect. The arrest itself must still be lawful.

Practical considerations

- It must be proved that:
  - the arrest/detention was lawful; and
  - the person concerned knew that an arrest was being made on them or another.
- Intention (at the time of commission of the offence) can be proved by:
  - interviewing the defendant—admissions made and explanations as to their state of mind, actions, and intentions; and/or
  - inferences drawn from the circumstances of the offence, evidence from witnesses, property found on defendant or in their control, and any other incriminating evidence.
- If this offence is committed by the person initially being arrested, the power of arrest comes from the original offence. Otherwise consider assaulting a police officer in the execution of their duty or breach of the peace.
- Could any of the general assault defences apply?
- Consider CPS guidelines and charging standards for assault with intent to resist arrest.

SSS E&S

Either way

None

Summary: 6/12 months' imprisonment and/or a fine

Indictment: 2 years' imprisonment

2.2.2 Assault constable in execution of duty

The Police Act 1996, s 89(1) provides the offences of assaulting a constable or person assisting a constable acting in the execution of their duty.

Offences

Any person who assaults a constable in the execution of his duty, or a person assisting a constable in the execution of his duty, shall be guilty of an offence.

Police Act 1996, s 89(1)

PNLD H901, H902

Points to prove

✓ assaulted a constable **or** person assisting a constable
✓ in execution of their duty

Meanings

Assault (see **2.1.1**)

Execution of duty

The officer must be acting lawfully and in the execution of their duty (see '**Related cases**').

Explanatory notes

- The duties of a constable have not been defined by any statute (see '**Related cases**').
- This offence also applies to police officers from Scotland or Northern Ireland (while in England or Wales) who are acting within statutory powers or executing a warrant.
- The offences also apply to a constable of the BTP (and includes Scotland for that purpose).
- Section 30 of the Police Act 1996 defines the jurisdiction of a constable as being throughout England and Wales and the adjacent UK waters. Special constables have the same jurisdiction, powers, and privileges of a constable.

Defences to assault (see **2.1.2**)

Related cases (see **2.1.1** and s 17 entry at **1.4.2** for more cases)

Pegram v DPP [2019] EWHC 2673 (Admin) It was held in this case that a police officer was deemed to be acting in the execution of their duty when, during a demonstration, the officer gripped the arm of a protester to warn them that they may be about to commit an offence. The officer was assaulted when the defendant's reaction was accidentally but recklessly to swing their arm and their hand made contact with the officer's face.

Dixon (Corey) v CPS [2018] EWHC 3154 (Admin) Where a constable was acting unlawfully, another constable nonetheless would act lawfully in assisting the first where there was an independent justification for their intervention in that they reasonably believed that the defendant might be about to use force which was excessive and which, regardless of the lawfulness of the detention by the first constable, would constitute an unlawful assault on the first constable.

Walker v Commissioner of Police of the Metropolis [2014] EWCA Civ 897 In this case, a police officer attended a domestic incident and restricted the suspect's movements in a doorway while appraising the situation. This action had not deprived the defendant of their liberty, albeit freedom of movement was restricted for a few seconds. The subsequent public order arrest had been lawful, but the common law power to detain, short of arrest, to prevent a breach of the peace (see **7.3**) can only apply if the officer had this power in mind at the relevant time.

Cumberbatch v Crown Prosecution Service; Ali v Director of Public Prosecutions [2009] EWHC 3353 (Admin) Where the arrest of an individual by a constable was unlawful, other constables who saw the incident and assisted the first were not acting in the execution of their duty and the individual, in using reasonable force to resist the assisting officers, was not guilty of the offence under s 89(2).

Practical considerations

- Officers should ensure they are acting within their powers and following relevant requirements or procedures (eg information to be given prior to search or at time of arrest under ss 2 and 28 of PACE (see **1.1.2**), otherwise they may no longer be acting within the execution of their duty (*Sobczak v DPP* [2012] EWHC 1319 (Admin)).
- The offence does not require proof that the defendant knew or ought to have known that the victim was a constable or that they were acting in the execution of their duty.
- A plain-clothes officer should produce identification, as a failure to do so could mean that the officer was acting outside the execution of their duty.
- Section 68 of the Railways and Transport Safety Act 2003 and s 68 of the Energy Act 2004 stipulate that the s 89(1) and s 89(2) (see **2.2.3**) offences also apply to BTP and members of the Civil Nuclear Constabulary.
- Do any of the general assault defences apply?
- Consider CPS guidelines and 2019 revised charging standards for this offence relating to injuries received amounting to a battery (see **2.1.1**).

- If the injuries justify a s 47 charge (see **2.1.2**) for a member of the public, then this will also be the appropriate charge for a constable.

SSS

Summary

6 months

6 months' imprisonment and/or a fine

2.2.3 Resist/obstruct constable in execution of duty

Section 89(2) of the Police Act 1996 deals with the offences of resisting or wilfully obstructing a constable in the execution of their duty.

Offences

Any person who resists or wilfully obstructs a constable in the execution of his duty, or a person assisting a constable in the execution of his duty, shall be guilty of an offence.

Police Act 1996, s 89(2)

PNLD **H903, H904**

Points to prove

✓ resisted/wilfully obstructed a constable or person assisting
✓ in the execution of constable's duty

Meanings

Resists (see **2.2.1**)

Wilful obstruction

In this context, it must be a deliberate obstruction.

Execution of duty (see **2.2.2**)

Explanatory notes

- Resists does not imply that any assault has taken place and where a person in the process of being lawfully arrested tears themselves away from the constable or person assisting, this will constitute resistance.
- The obstruction must be some form of positive act which prevents or impedes the officer in carrying out their duty.
- For the constable's duty and jurisdiction, see **2.2.2**.

- It must be proved that the officer was acting in the execution of their duty.

Related case

Aznanag v CPS [2015] EWHC 3017 (Admin) In this case, police officers were attempting to arrest a person inside premises. From outside, the defendant tried to push past a police officer to enter and the officer put their hand out to stop them. They ignored the request and grabbed the officer's wrist which caused pain. It was held that the police were acting in the exercise of their duty in trying to prevent people from moving forward and the officer had been entitled to try to stop the defendant.

Practical considerations (see 2.2.2)

SSS

Summary

6 months

1 month's imprisonment and/or a level 3 fine

2.2.4 Impersonate constable or wear/possess article of police uniform

Section 90 of the Police Act 1996 deals with the offences of impersonating a member of a police force or special constable or unlawfully wearing/being in possession of any article of police uniform.

Offences

(1) Any person who with intent to deceive impersonates a member of a police force or special constable or makes any statement or does any act calculated falsely to suggest that he is such a member or constable, shall be guilty of an offence.

(2) Any person who, not being a constable, wears any article of police uniform in circumstances where it gives him an appearance so nearly resembling that of a member of a police force as to be calculated to deceive shall be guilty of an offence.

(3) Any person who, not being a member of a police force or special constable, has in his possession any article of police uniform shall, unless he proves that he obtained possession of that article lawfully and has possession of it for a lawful purpose, be guilty of an offence.

Police Act 1996, s 90

PNLD **H905 to H909**

Points to prove

s 90(1) offence

✓ impersonated
✓ special constable/member of police force
✓ with intent to deceive

OR

✓ with intent to deceive
✓ made a statement/did an act
✓ which calculated falsely to suggest
✓ that you were a special constable/member of a police force

s 90(2) offence

✓ not being a constable
✓ wore article(s) of police uniform
✓ in circumstances which made you appear to resemble
✓ being a member of police force
✓ so as to be calculated to deceive

s 90(3) offence

✓ not being a special constable/member of police force
✓ possessed article(s) of police uniform

Meanings

With intent (see **4.1.2**)

Deceive

Means to induce a person to believe a thing to be true which is in fact false: in this case, that the person is a police officer.

Special constable

A special constable has the same jurisdiction, powers, and privileges as a constable.

Article of police uniform

Means any article of uniform or any distinctive badge, or mark, or document of identification usually issued to members of police forces or special constables, or anything having the appearance of such an article, badge, mark, or document.

Explanatory notes

- Section 68 of the Railways and Transport Safety Act 2003 states that s 90 (impersonation of constable) applies to a constable/special constable of the BTP.
- In s 90(2), 'calculated to deceive' has been held to mean 'likely to deceive' (*Turner v Shearer* [1973] 1 All ER 397), although this does not require the defendant to have a specific intent to deceive as with the more serious offence under s 90(1).

Defence—applicable to s 90(3) only

Proof that they obtained possession of the article of police uniform lawfully and possession of it was for a lawful purpose.

Related case

Cooke v DPP [2015] EWHC 3312 (Admin) The defendant was charged with an offence under s 90(3). Where the possession was for the purpose of sale to a person who, unknown to the seller, had an unlawful purpose, this would not be an offence under this section and the statutory defence would apply.

Practical considerations

- The burden of proof in relation to the defence of lawful possession under s 90(3) is on the defendant, to prove on the balance of probabilities.
- For the s 90(1) and s 90(2) offences, it is not necessary to prove intent to deceive a specific individual, or to prove that the person obtained any form of benefit or advantage as a result of the deception.

Summary

6 months

s 90(1)—6 months' imprisonment and/or a fine

s 90(2)—Level 3 fine

s 90(3)—Level 1 fine

2.2.5 Assault/resist/obstruct designated or accredited person in execution of duty

Section 46 of the Police Reform Act 2002 refers to offences in respect of suitably designated and accredited people as follows:

Offences

(1) Any person who assaults—
- (a) a designated person in the execution of his duty,
- (b) an accredited person in the execution of his duty,
- (ba) an accredited inspector in the execution of his duty, or
- (c) a person assisting a designated or accredited person or an accredited inspector in the execution of his duty, is guilty of an offence.

(2) Any person who resists or wilfully obstructs—
   (a) a designated person in the execution of his duty,
   (b) an accredited person in the execution of his duty,
   (ba) an accredited inspector in the execution of his duty, or
   (c) a person assisting a designated or accredited person or an accredited inspector in the execution of his duty, is guilty of an offence.

Police Reform Act 2002, s 46

PNLD H18929 to H18935

Points to prove

✓ assaulted or resisted/wilfully obstructed
✓ a designated/accredited person/accredited inspector/person assisting
✓ while in the execution of their duty

Meanings

Assaults (see **2.1.1**)

Designated person

(a) Designated persons are to be within the meaning given by s 47(1); and
(b) a person in relation to whom a designation under s 38B is for the time being in force.

Accredited person

Means a person accredited under s 41.

Accredited inspector

Means a weights and measures inspector accredited under s 41A.

Resists or wilfully obstructs (see **2.2.3**)

Explanatory notes

- Designated person under s 47(1) means person designated under s 38 or 39, and includes community support officer, policing support officer, community support volunteers, policing support volunteers, and contracted-out staff (see **11.1**).
- The term accredited person relates to community safety accreditation schemes set up by the chief officer under ss 40 and 41. The accredited person is given the powers defined in Sch 5.
- References to the execution of their duties relate to exercising any power or performing any duty by virtue of their designation or accreditation.

Defences to assault (see 2.1.2)

Related cases (see 2.2.2 and 2.2.3)

Practical considerations (see also 2.2.2 and 2.2.3)

- Given the extensive and detailed restrictions on the powers of these individuals, the precise activities that were involved at the time will be closely scrutinised by a court. It will be critical to establish that the person was acting within the lawful limits of their powers at the time.
- It is also an offence under s 46(3) for any person who, with intent to deceive, impersonates the above persons.
- It is a summary offence to intentionally obstruct a person acting lawfully as an enforcement agent (formerly certified bailiffs) under the Tribunals, Courts and Enforcement Act 2007, Sch 12, para 68(1).

SSS

Summary

6 months

Assaulted a designated or accredited person/accredited inspector or person assisting

6 months' imprisonment and/or a fine

Resisted/wilfully obstructed or resisted/obstructed a designated or accredited person/accredited inspector or person assisting

1 month's imprisonment and/or a level 3 fine

2.2.6 Assaults on emergency workers

The Assaults on Emergency Workers (Offences) Act 2018 makes provisions about offences when perpetrated against emergency workers, and persons assisting such workers; to make certain offences aggravated when perpetrated against such workers in the exercise of their duty; and for connected purposes.

Section 1 of the Act provides that when the offence of common assault or battery is committed against an emergency worker, acting in the exercise of their functions as such a worker, the offence shall be triable either way and, as such, carry a higher penalty (on summary conviction, a maximum of 6/12 months' imprisonment and/or a fine or, on indictment, a maximum of 2 years' imprisonment and/or a fine).

Section 67 of the Sentencing Act 2020 places a duty on the court when sentencing for certain offences to treat it as an aggravating factor where this offence is committed against emergency workers.

By s 67(3), the offences referred to are:

- (a) an offence under any of the following provisions of the Offences Against the Person Act 1861:
  - (i) s 16 (threats to kill) (see **2.5**);
  - (ii) s 18 (wounding with intent to cause grievous bodily harm) (see **2.3.2**);
  - (iii) s 20 (malicious wounding) (see **2.3.1**);
  - (iv) s 23 (administering poison etc) (see **5.1.1**);
  - (v) s 28 (causing bodily injury by gunpowder etc);
  - (vi) s 29 (using explosive substances etc with intent to cause grievous bodily harm);
  - (vii) s 47 (assault occasioning actual bodily harm) (see **2.1.2**):
- (aa) an offence under s 75A of the Serious Crime Act 2015 (strangulation or suffocation);
- (b) an offence under s 3 of the Sexual Offences Act 2003 (sexual assault) (see **6.1.1**);
- (c) manslaughter (see **2.7.2**);
- (d) kidnapping (see **2.6**);
- (e) any inchoate offence in relation to any of the preceding offences.

Meanings

Inchoate offence

In relation to an offence, means any of the following:

- (a) aiding, abetting, counselling, or procuring the commission of the offence (see **4.1**);
- (b) an offence under Part 2 of the Serious Crime Act 2007 (encouraging or assisting crime) in relation to the offence (see **4.1.4**);
- (c) attempting or conspiring to commit the offence (see **4.1.1**).

Emergency worker

- (a) a constable;
- (b) a person (other than a constable) who has the powers of a constable or is otherwise employed for police purposes or is engaged to provide services for police purposes;
- (c) a National Crime Agency officer;
- (d) a prison officer;
- (e) a person (other than a prison officer) employed or engaged to carry out functions in a custodial institution of a corresponding kind to those carried out by a prison officer;
- (f) a prisoner custody officer, so far as relating to the exercise of escort functions;
- (g) a custody officer, so far as relating to the exercise of escort functions;

(h) a person employed for the purposes of providing, or engaged to provide, fire services or fire and rescue services;
(i) a person employed for the purposes of providing, or engaged to provide, search services or rescue services (or both);
(j) a person employed for the purposes of providing, or engaged to provide:
  (i) NHS health services, or
  (ii) services in the support of the provision of NHS health services
and whose general activities in doing so involve face-to-face interaction with individuals receiving the services or with other members of the public.

Custodial institution

Means any of the following—
(a) a prison;
(b) a young offender institution, secure training centre, or secure college;
(c) a removal centre, a short-term holding facility, or pre-departure accommodation, as defined by s 147 of the Immigration and Asylum Act 1999;
(d) services custody premises, as defined by s 300(7) of the Armed Forces Act 2006.

Custody officer

Has the meaning given by s 12(3) of the Criminal Justice and Public Order Act 1994, being a person in respect of whom a certificate is for the time being in force certifying:
(a) that he has been approved by the Secretary of State for the purpose of performing any of the following—
  (i) escort functions;
  (ii) custodial duties at secure training centres; and
(b) that he is accordingly authorised to perform them.

NHS health services

Means any kind of health services provided as part of the health service continued under s 1(1) of the National Health Service Act 2006.

Explanatory notes

- The Sentencing Act does not create distinct offences but places a duty on the court to consider the fact that the offence was committed against an emergency worker as an aggravating factor.
- Section 1 of the Assaults on Emergency Workers (Offences) Act 2018 applies to an offence of common assault, or battery, that is committed against an emergency worker acting in the exercise of functions as such a worker.
- For the purposes of subsection (3), the circumstances in which an offence is to be taken as committed against a person acting in the exercise of functions as an emergency worker include circumstances

where the offence takes place at a time when the person is not at work but is carrying out functions which, if done in work time, would have been in the exercise of functions as an emergency worker.

- It is immaterial for the purposes of s 1(1) whether the employment or engagement is paid or unpaid.
- Where manslaughter is committed against emergency workers, a life sentence is required unless there are exceptional circumstances.

Related cases

R v Veysey and others [2019] EWCA Crim 1332 (see **2.1.3**).

DPP v Ahmed [2021] EWHC 2122 (Admin) In this case, the court discussed the scope of the term 'functions' and held that proportionate and good-faith actions undertaken by the police to assist those in distress or at risk of harm (to themselves or others) are likely to fall within the concept of 'functions'.

Campbell v CPS [2020] EWHC 3868 (Admin) It was held that the offence could be committed even if the worker was a police officer who might not have been acting in the execution of their duty at the material time. The phrase 'in the execution of his functions as an emergency worker' in s 1 of the Assaults on Emergency Workers (Offences) Act 2018 was not to be construed in the same way as the expression 'in the execution of his duty' in s 89(1) of the Police Act 1996 (see **2.2.2**) and imported no requirement that the emergency worker be acting lawfully.

Either way None

Summary: maximum 6/12 months' imprisonment and/or a fine

Indictment: maximum 2 years' imprisonment and/or a fine

2.2.7 Obstruct/hinder emergency workers and persons assisting

The Emergency Workers (Obstruction) Act 2006 creates offences of obstructing/hindering certain emergency workers responding to an emergency, and obstructing/hindering persons assisting such emergency workers.

Offence against emergency workers

A person who without reasonable excuse obstructs or hinders another while that other person is, in a capacity mentioned in subsection (2) below, responding to emergency circumstances, commits an offence.

Emergency Workers (Obstruction) Act 2006, s 1(1)

2.2.7 Obstruct/hinder emergency workers and persons assisting

PNLD H8810

Points to prove

- ✓ without reasonable excuse
- ✓ obstructed or hindered
- ✓ emergency worker as described in s 1(2) who is
- ✓ responding to emergency circumstances as given in s 1(3) and s 1(4)

Meanings

Capacity (of emergency worker)

(2) The capacity referred to in subsection (1) above is—

(a) that of a person employed by a fire and rescue authority in England and Wales;

(aa) that of a Ministry of Defence fire-fighter (as defined in section 16 of the Armed Forces Act 2016);

(b) in relation to England and Wales, that of a person (other than a person falling within paragraph (a) or (aa)) whose duties as an employee or as a servant of the Crown involve—

(i) extinguishing fires; or

(ii) protecting life and property in the event of a fire;

(c) that of a person employed by a **relevant NHS body** in the provision of ambulance services (including air ambulance services), or of a person providing such services pursuant to arrangements made by, or at the request of, a relevant NHS body;

(d) that of a person providing services for the transport of organs, blood, equipment or personnel pursuant to arrangements made by, or at the request of, a relevant NHS body;

(e) that of a member of [His] Majesty's Coastguard;

(f) that of a member of the crew of a vessel operated by—

(i) the Royal National Lifeboat Institution, or

(ii) any other person or organisation operating a vessel for the purpose of providing a rescue service,

or a person who musters the crew of such a vessel or attends to its launch or recovery.

Responding to emergency circumstances

(3) For the purposes of this section and section 2 of this Act, a person is **responding** to emergency circumstances if the person—

(a) is going anywhere for the purpose of dealing with emergency circumstances occurring there; or

(b) is dealing with emergency circumstances or preparing to do so.

(4) For the purposes of this Act, circumstances are '**emergency circumstances**' if they are present or imminent and—

(a) are causing or are likely to cause—

(i) serious injury to or the serious illness (including mental illness) of a person;

(ii) serious harm to the environment (including the life and health of plants and animals);
(iii) serious harm to any building or other property; or
(iv) a worsening of any such injury, illness or harm; or

(b) are likely to cause the death of a person.

Emergency Workers (Obstruction) Act 2006, s 1

Offence against person assisting emergency worker

(1) A person who without reasonable excuse obstructs or hinders another in the circumstances described in subsection (2) below commits an offence.

(2) Those circumstances are where the person being obstructed or hindered is assisting another while that other person is, in a capacity mentioned in section 1(2) of this Act, responding to emergency circumstances.

Emergency Workers (Obstruction) Act 2006, s 2

PNLD H8811

Points to prove

✓ without reasonable excuse
✓ obstructed or hindered
✓ a person who was assisting
✓ an emergency worker as described in s 1(2) who was
✓ attending/dealing/preparing to deal
✓ with emergency circumstances as given in s 1(3) and s 1(4)

Explanatory notes

- In s 1(2), a **'relevant NHS body'** includes the Secretary of State in the exercise of public health functions, a local authority in the exercise of public health functions, the National Health Service Commissioning Board, a clinical commissioning group, an NHS foundation trust, NHS trust, Special Health Authority, a clinical commissioning group, or Local Health Board.
- A person may be convicted of the offence under s 1 or s 2 of this Act notwithstanding that it is affected by: means other than physical means; or action directed only at any vehicle, vessel, apparatus, equipment, or other thing, or any animal used, or to be used by a person referred to in that section.
- For the purposes of ss 1 and 2, circumstances to which a person is responding are to be taken to be emergency circumstances if the person believes and has reasonable grounds for believing they are or may be emergency circumstances.
- Further details on this 2006 Act are dealt with in HOC 3/2007.

- The 2006 Act does not include police or prison officers because obstruction of a police constable is an offence under the Police Act 1996 (see **2.2.3**). The 1996 Act also covers prison officers by virtue of s 8 of the Prisons Act 1952 which stipulates that prison officers, whilst acting as such, shall have all the powers, authority, protection, and privileges of a constable.
- See **2.2.5** for assault or resist/wilfully obstruct a suitably designated or accredited person.

Summary

6 months

A fine

Links to alternative subjects and offences

7.3 **Breach of the Peace** 362
7.8 **Threatening/Abusive Words/Behaviour** 380
7.10 **Racially/Religiously Aggravated Offences** 390
11.1 **Police Powers for Civilian Staff and Volunteers** 781
Appendix 1 **Human Rights** 839

2.3 Wounding/Grievous Bodily Harm

2.3.1 Wounding or inflicting grievous bodily harm

Section 20 of the Offences Against the Person Act 1861 provides the offence of 'wounding or inflicting grievous bodily harm'.

Offences

Whosoever shall unlawfully and maliciously wound or inflict any grievous bodily harm upon any other person, either with or without any weapon or instrument shall be guilty of an offence.

Offences Against the Person Act 1861, s 20

PNLD H478

Points to prove

- ✓ unlawfully
- ✓ maliciously
- ✓ wounded **or** inflicted grievous bodily harm
- ✓ upon another person

Meanings

Unlawfully

Means without excuse or justification at law.

Maliciously

- Means malice must be present.
- For the meaning of 'malice', see **2.1.3** and the effect of *R v Cunningham* [1957] 2 All ER 412, CA.

Recklessness

It is not sufficient to show that if C had stopped to think, it would have been obvious to them that there was a risk. The prosecution has to prove that they were aware of the existence of the risk but nonetheless had gone on and taken it (*R v Cunningham* [1957] 2 All ER 412, CA).

Wound

Means any break in the continuity of the whole skin.

Inflict

- Inflict does not have as wide a meaning as 'cause'—grievous bodily harm can be inflicted without there being an assault.
- 'Grievous bodily harm may be inflicted either by: directly and violently assaulting the victim; or something intentionally done which although in itself is not a direct application of force to the body of the victim, does directly result in force being applied to the body of the victim so that he suffers grievous bodily harm' (*R v Wilson and Jenkins* [1983] 3 All ER 448, HL).

Grievous bodily harm

- Means 'serious or really serious harm' (*R v Saunders* [1985] Crim LR 230, CA).
- Bodily harm can include inflicting/causing a psychiatric harm/illness (silent/heavy breathing/menacing telephone calls—*R v Ireland* [1998] AC 147, HL) or include psychiatric injury, in serious cases, as well as physical injury (*R v Burstow* [1997] 4 All ER 225, HL).

Explanatory notes

- If it appears that the target of the attack was not the actual victim, then the 'doctrine of transferred malice' provides that if a person mistakenly causes injury to a person other than the person whom they intended to attack, they will commit the same offence as if they had injured the intended victim. The doctrine only applies if the crime remains the same and the harm done must be of the same kind as the harm intended (*R v Latimer* (1886) 17 QBD 359).
- As wounding and grievous bodily harm are both different, the distinction as to which offence is appropriate should be made.

Defences

May be available to a s 20 offence (see **2.1.2**).

Related cases

R v Melin [2019] EWCA Crim 557 Where an individual who consented to receive Botox was deceived by the person administering the treatment into believing that they were medically qualified, such deception amounts to a deception as to the treating person's identity, which is enough to vitiate consent.

R v Golding [2014] EWCA Crim 889 Where a defendant infected their partner with an incurable genital herpes, the court held that the 'serious harm' in an offence of grievous bodily harm did not have to be either permanent or dangerous and therefore the offence was made out.

R v Dica [2005] EWCA Crim 2304 Inflicting grievous bodily harm was held to include infecting the victim with HIV through unprotected consensual sexual intercourse.

R v Konzani [2005] EWCA Crim 706 For a valid defence, there must be a willing and informed consent by the other party to the specific risk of their contracting HIV—this cannot be inferred from consent to unprotected sexual intercourse alone.

R v Savage [1992] 1 AC 699, HL and **DPP v Parmenter [1991] 3 WLR 914, HL** In s 20 wounding/GBH cases, '*Cunningham* malice' will suffice. It is enough that the defendant should have foreseen that some physical harm might result—of whatever character.

R v Wilson and Jenkins [1983] 3 All ER 448, HL In this case, the victim, frightened by the defendant, jumped through a window and broke a leg. It was held that grievous bodily harm had been 'inflicted' by the offender by inducing substantial fear, even though there was no direct application of force.

R v Cunningham [1957] 2 All ER 412, CA Meaning of 'maliciously' and recklessness test (above).

Practical considerations

- It is not a defence that V consented to the infliction of the serious harm for the purposes of obtaining sexual gratification. However, this does not apply where the serious harm consists of, or is a result of, the infection of V with a sexually transmitted infection in the course of sexual activity, and where V consented to the sexual activity in the knowledge or belief that D had the sexually transmitted infection (see s 71 of the Domestic Abuse Act 2021).
- Consider the more serious racially/religiously aggravated offence (see **7.10**).
- Aggravated versions of the offences in this section apply if the offence is committed against an emergency worker (see **2.2.6**).
- Where the offence is committed against a person providing a public service, performing a public duty, or providing services to the public, the court must treat that fact as an aggravating factor, and must state in open court that the offence is so aggravated.
- In cases of 'transferred malice', the charge must specify at whom the intent was aimed (eg 'A wounded C with intent to cause GBH to B').
- The distinction between 'wound' and 'GBH' must be identified and considered, as they do not have the same meaning.
- Where both a wound and grievous bodily harm have been inflicted, choose which part of s 20 reflects the true nature of the offence (*R v McCready* [1978] 1 WLR 1376, CA).
- The s 18 offence requires intent while s 20 is 'unlawfully and maliciously'.
- Consider CPS advice and guidance for unlawful wounding or inflicting GBH:
    - ✦ The distinction between charges under s 18 and s 20 is one of **intent**. The gravity of the injury may provide some evidence of intent.

- ✦ Wounding means the breaking of the continuity of the whole of the outer skin, or the inner skin within the cheek or lip. It does not include the rupturing of internal blood vessels.
- ✦ Minor wounds, such as a small cut or laceration, should be charged under s 47. Section 20 should be reserved for those wounds considered to be serious (thus equating the offences with the infliction of grievous or serious bodily harm).
- ✦ Grievous bodily harm means serious bodily harm, such as:
  - injury resulting in permanent disability or permanent loss of sensory function; injury which results in more than minor permanent, visible disfigurement;
  - broken or displaced limbs or bones, including fractured skull, compound fractures, broken cheekbone/jaw/ribs;
  - injuries which cause substantial loss of blood, usually necessitating a transfusion, or resulting in lengthy treatment or incapacity;
  - psychiatric injury (expert evidence is essential to prove the injury).
- Obtain medical evidence to prove extent of injury.
- Obtain photographs of victim's injuries.

SSS E&S RRA

Either way

None

Summary: 6/12 months' imprisonment and/or a fine

Indictment: 5 years' imprisonment

2.3.2 Wounding or grievous bodily harm—with intent

Section 18 of the Offences Against the Person Act 1861 creates the offences of 'wounding or causing grievous bodily harm with intent'.

Offences

Whosoever shall unlawfully and maliciously by any means whatsoever wound or cause any grievous bodily harm to any person with intent to do some grievous bodily harm to any person, or with intent to resist or prevent the lawful apprehension or detainer of any person, shall be guilty of felony.

Offences Against the Person Act 1861, s 18

PNLD H476, H477, H2282, H2294, H5084

Points to prove

✓ unlawfully and maliciously
✓ caused grievous bodily harm or wounded a person
✓ with intent to
✓ do grievous bodily harm or resist/prevent lawful apprehension/ detention of self/another

Meanings

Unlawfully (see **2.3.1**)

Maliciously (see **2.3.1**)

Any means whatsoever

This is given its literal meaning. A connection between the means used and the harm caused must be proved.

Wound (see **2.3.1**)

Cause

Defined as 'anything that produces a result or effect'.

Grievous bodily harm (see **2.3.1**)

Intent (see **4.1.2**)

Resist or prevent (see **2.2.1**)

Explanatory notes

- 'Cause' has a wider meaning than 'inflict'. All that needs to be proved is some connection between the action (the means used) and the injury (sometimes called the chain of causation). There does not need to be a direct application of force.
- The issue of causation is separate from the test for intent.
- If appropriate, consider the 'causation test' (see *R v Roberts* (1972) 56 Cr App R 95—see '**Related cases**').
- Intent must be proved either from verbal admissions on interview and/or other incriminating evidence (eg subsequent actions).
- The statutory test under s 8 of the Criminal Justice Act 1967 must be considered (see **4.1.2**).
- In relation to the offence of wounding or causing GBH with intent to resist or prevent lawful arrest/detention, it must be proved:
  - ✦ arrest/detention was lawful;
  - ✦ defendant must have known that arrest was being made on them/ another person.

Defences (see **2.1.2**)

Related cases

R v Cheeseman [2019] EWCA Crim 149 In this case, the availability of the householder defence with respect to force used in self-defence against a person who entered premises lawfully, and became a trespasser thereafter, was confirmed.

R v BM [2018] EWCA Crim 560 Body modification, in this case removal of the ear and nipple, and splitting of the tongue, performed on a consenting adult still amounted to wounding with intent to do grievous bodily harm.

R (on the application of Collins) v Secretary of State for Justice [2016] EWHC 33 (Admin) (see **1.2**).

R v McKay [2015] EWCA Crim 2098 The defence of automatism induced through taking drink or drugs was not available to an offender.

R v Barnes [2004] EWCA Crim 3246 Provides guidance for contact sports as to when it is appropriate for criminal proceedings to be instituted after an injury (see **2.1.2**).

R v Roberts (1972) 56 Cr App R 95 In this case, a victim of an ongoing sexual assault jumped out of a car to escape and was seriously injured in doing so. The court considered the 'chain of causation' and applied the 'causation test':

- If the victim's actions are reasonable ones which could be foreseen and were acceptable under the circumstances, then the defendant will be liable for injuries resulting from them.
- If the harm/injury was caused by a voluntary act on the part of the victim, which could not reasonably be foreseen, then the chain of causation between the defendant's actions and the harm/injury received will be broken and the defendant will not be liable for them.

Practical considerations (see also **2.3.1**)

- It is not a defence that V consented to the infliction of the serious harm for the purposes of obtaining sexual gratification. However, this does not apply where the serious harm consists of, or is a result of, the infection of V with a sexually transmitted infection in the course of sexual activity, and where V consented to the sexual activity in the knowledge or belief that D had the sexually transmitted infection (see s 71 of the Domestic Abuse Act 2021).
- Section 18 does not come under racially or religiously aggravated assaults (see **7.10.2**), although this will be considered when determining sentence.
- Aggravated versions of the offences in this section apply if the offence is committed against an emergency worker (see **2.2.6**).
- Where the offence is committed against a person providing a public service, performing a public duty, or providing services to the public,

the court must treat that fact as an aggravating factor, and must state in open court that the offence is so aggravated.

- Knowledge that GBH was a virtually certain consequence of their action will not amount to an intention, but it **will** be good evidence from which a court can infer such intention.
- Other factors which may indicate the specific intent include:
    - ✦ a repeated or planned attack;
    - ✦ deliberate selection of a weapon or adaptation of an article to cause injury, such as breaking a glass before an attack;
    - ✦ making prior threats;
    - ✦ using an offensive weapon against, or kicking, the victim's head.
- Proof is required that the wound/GBH was inflicted maliciously. This means that the defendant must have foreseen some harm—although not necessarily the specific type or gravity of injury suffered or inflicted.
- Generally, an assault under this section may be:
    - ✦ wounding with intent to do GBH;
    - ✦ causing GBH, with intent to do GBH;
    - ✦ wounding with intent to resist or prevent the lawful arrest/ detention of self/any person;
    - ✦ maliciously causing GBH with intent to resist or prevent the lawful arrest of self/any person.
- Where evidence of intent is absent, but a wound or grievous bodily harm is still caused, then both s 18 and s 20 should be included on the indictment.
- Consider CPS advice and guidance for wounding/causing GBH with intent.
- In cases involving GBH, remember that s 20 requires the infliction of harm, whereas s 18 requires the causing of harm, although this distinction has been greatly reduced by the decisions in *R v Ireland* [1998] AC 147, HL and *R v Burstow* [1997] 4 All ER 225, HL (see **2.3.1**).
- Section 18 is of assistance in more serious assaults upon police officers where the evidence of an intention to prevent arrest is clear but the evidence of intent to cause GBH is in doubt.
- Section 6(3) of the Criminal Law Act 1967 permits a conviction for s 20 (inflicting GBH) in respect of a count for s 18 (causing GBH with intent), as 'cause' includes 'inflict' (*R v Wilson and Jenkins* [1983] 3 All ER 448, HL).
- Obtain medical evidence to prove extent of injury.
- Obtain photographs of victim's injuries.

SSS **RRA**

Indictable only

None

Life imprisonment

2.3.3 Use gunpowder and corrosive substances with intent to cause grievous bodily harm

Section 29 of the Offences Against the Person Act 1861 creates offences dealing with gunpowder and other corrosive substances.

Offences

Whosoever shall unlawfully and maliciously cause any gunpowder or other explosive substance to explode, or send or deliver to or cause to be taken or received by any person any explosive substance or any other dangerous or noxious thing, or put or lay at any place, or cast or throw at or upon or otherwise apply to any person, any corrosive fluid or any destructive or explosive substance, with intent in any of the cases aforesaid to burn, maim, disfigure, or disable any person, or to do some grievous bodily harm to any person, shall, whether any bodily injury be effected or not, be guilty of an offence.

Offences Against the Person Act 1861, s 29

PNLD **H1853, H1854 to H1858, H2062, H2255, H2256, H2259, H2281**

Points to prove

✓ unlawfully and maliciously applied/put/cast/lay/throw a corrosive fluid/explosive substance/destructive substance OR
✓ unlawfully and maliciously caused gunpowder/explosive substance to explode OR
✓ unlawfully and maliciously sent/delivered/caused to be taken/caused to be received by an explosive substance/dangerous or noxious thing
✓ with intent to burn/maim/disfigure/disable/do grievous bodily harm

Practical considerations

- There must be an intention in all cases to burn/maim/disfigure/do some grievous bodily harm or disable a person but there need not be any bodily injury caused.
- Section 1(7) of PACE creates the power for a constable to stop and search persons carrying prohibited articles that include offensive weapons. In relation to corrosive substances, it is noted that current powers only cover situations where an officer has reasonable grounds to suspect that an individual is carrying a prohibited article with the intent to cause injury, such as where the corrosive substance has been poured or decanted into another container to make it easier to use as a weapon; it does not cover situations, for

example, when the corrosive substance is being carried in its original packaging (see **1.3**).

SSS

Indictable only

None

Life imprisonment

Links to alternative subjects and offences

7.10 **Racially/Religiously Aggravated Offences** 390
Appendix 1 **Human Rights** 839

2.3.4 Non-fatal strangulation and non-fatal suffocation

Section 75A of the Serious Crime Act 2015 provides the offence of non-fatal intentional strangulation or intentional suffocation of another person.

Offence

(1) A person ('A') commits an offence if—
  (a) A intentionally strangles another person ('B'), or
  (b) A does any other act to B that—
    (i) affects B's ability to breathe, and
    (ii) constitutes battery of B.
(2) It is a defence to an offence under this section for A to show that B consented to the strangulation or other act.
(3) But subsection (2) does not apply if—
  (a) B suffers serious harm as a result of the strangulation or other act, and
  (b) A either—
    (i) intended to cause B serious harm, or
    (ii) was reckless as to whether B would suffer serious harm.
(4) A is to be taken to have shown the fact mentioned in subsection (2) if—
  (a) sufficient evidence of the fact is adduced to raise an issue with respect to it, and
  (b) the contrary is not proved beyond reasonable doubt.

Serious Crime Act 2015, s 75A

PNLD H100159, H100160

2.3.4 Non-fatal strangulation and non-fatal suffocation

Points to prove

Intentional strangulation

✓ intentionally
✓ strangled
✓ another person

Intentional suffocation

✓ did an act to a person that
✓ affected that person's ability to breathe AND
✓ constituted battery

Meanings

Serious harm

Serious harm means grievous bodily harm or wounding (see **2.3.1**), or actual bodily harm (see **2.1.2**).

Country

Country includes territory.

United Kingdom national

Means an individual who is a British citizen, a British Overseas Territories citizen, a British National (Overseas) or a British Overseas citizen, a person who under the British Nationality Act 1981 is a British subject, or a British protected person within the meaning of that Act.

Explanatory notes

- Strangulation occurs where pressure is applied to the neck to cause an obstruction or compression of blood vessels and/or the airways.
- Suffocation is a wider definition than strangulation and would include any act that is done to cause a deprivation of air to the other person which affects their normal breathing.
- Strangulation, or the other act that affects the person's ability to breathe, has to be intentional.
- Battery means the common law offence of battery.
- This offence will overlap with other assault offences, but the relevant offence and level of charge will usually be dictated by the injuries sustained and consideration of any aggravating features.
- If a person does an act in a country outside the UK and the act, if done in England and Wales, would constitute an offence under s 75A, and the person is a UK national or is habitually resident in England and Wales, the person is guilty in England and Wales of that offence (s 75B).

Defences (see **2.1.2**)

Unless serious harm was intended, or there was recklessness as to whether serious harm would be suffered, it is a defence to show that the victim consented to the strangulation or other act.

Related case

R v Brown and others [1994] 1 AC 212, HL (see **2.1.2**).

Practical considerations

- Consider the availability of the defence. Sufficient evidence that there was consent has to be provided by the defendant and the contrary not proved by the prosecution.
- Ensure that any visible injuries are photographed.
- Obtain medical evidence.
- Consider s 20 or s 18 of the Offences Against the Person Act 1861 for more serious injuries or aggravating features (see **2.3**).
- If a strangulation or suffocation under this section is racially or religiously aggravated, you should consider the more serious version of these offences under s 29 of the Crime and Disorder Act 1998 (see **7.10.2**).
- If a strangulation or suffocation is committed by a UK national, or a person who is habitually resident in England or Wales, outside the UK, then the person may be tried in England or Wales.

RRA CHAR

Either way

None

Summary: 6/12 months' imprisonment and/or a fine

Indictment: 5 years' imprisonment and/or a fine

Links to alternative subjects and offences

4.4 **Criminal Damage** 193
4.6 **Threats to Destroy or Damage Property** 203
4.7 **Custody/Control of Articles with Intent to Damage** 206
4.8.1 **Intimidation of a witness/juror** 210
4.11 **Forced Marriages** 230
6 **Sexual Offences and Assaults** 275
7.3 **Breach of the Peace** 362

2.3.4 Non-fatal strangulation and non-fatal suffocation

7.6 **Fear or Provocation of Violence** 373
7.7 **Intentional Harassment, Alarm, or Distress** 376
7.8 **Threatening/Abusive Words/Behaviour** 380
7.11 **Harassment/Stalking** 398
7.13 **Anti-Social Behaviour** 435
7.17.2 **Violent entry to premises** 479
Appendix 1 **Human Rights** 839

2.4 Child Cruelty and Taking a Child into Police Protection

2.4.1 Child cruelty

The Children and Young Persons Act 1933 was introduced to prevent children and young persons from being exposed to moral and physical danger. The Act addresses such problem areas as cruelty, neglect, safety, employment, and performing in entertainments. It also provides rules and guidance in relation to children and young persons who are involved in the criminal justice process.

Offences

If any person who has attained the age of 16 years and has responsibility for any child or young person under that age, wilfully assaults, ill-treats (whether physically or otherwise), neglects, abandons, or exposes him, or causes or procures him to be assaulted, ill-treated (whether physically or otherwise), neglected, abandoned, or exposed, in a manner likely to cause him unnecessary suffering or injury to health (whether the suffering or injury is of a physical or a psychological nature), that person shall be guilty of an offence.

Children and Young Persons Act 1933, s 1(1)

PNLD H100807, H100753

Points to prove

✓ being a person 16 years or over
✓ having responsibility
✓ for a child/young person (under 16 years)
✓ did wilfully or caused/procured the child/young person to be
✓ assaulted/ill-treated (whether physical or otherwise)/neglected/abandoned/exposed
✓ in manner likely to cause unnecessary suffering/injury (physical or psychological) to health

Meanings

Responsibility (s 17)

- The following shall be presumed to have responsibility for a child or young person:
  - (a) any person who:
    - (i) has **parental responsibility** for the child/young person; or

    (ii) is otherwise legally liable to maintain the child/young person; and
  (b) any person who has care of the child/young person.
- A person who is presumed to be responsible for a child or young person by virtue of (a) shall not be taken to have ceased to be responsible by reason only that they do not have care of the child/young person.

Parental responsibility

Means all the rights, duties, powers, responsibilities, and authority which by law a parent of a child has in relation to that child and their property.

Child

Means a person under 14 years of age.

Young person

Person who has attained the age of 14 but is under the age of 18 years.

Neglect in a manner likely to cause injury to health

- A parent or other person legally liable to maintain a child or young person, or the **legal guardian** of such a person, is deemed to have neglected in a manner likely to cause injury (physical or psychological) to health if they have failed to provide adequate food, clothing, medical aid, or lodging, or if, having been unable to do so, they have failed to take steps to procure it to be provided under relevant enactments.
- A person may be convicted of this offence:
  - ✦ even though actual suffering or injury (physical or psychological) to health, or the likelihood of it, was prevented by the action of another person;
  - ✦ notwithstanding the death of the child or young person in question.

Legal guardian

Means a **guardian** of a child as defined in the Children Act 1989.

Guardian

Includes any person who in the opinion of the court having cognisance of any case in relation to the child or young person or has for the time being the care of the child or young person.

Explanatory notes

- See HOC 8/2015 and also a 'Fact sheet: Serious Crime Act 2015—clarifying the criminal law on child cruelty'.
- The term 'ill-treated' is not specifically defined, but will include bullying, frightening, or any conduct causing unnecessary suffering or injury to physical or mental health.

- Battery of a child cannot be justified on the grounds of reasonable chastisement (see **2.1.2 'Defences to assault'**).

Practical considerations

- Section 548 of the Education Act 1996 prevents teachers in any school from giving corporal punishment.
- The prosecution must prove a deliberate or reckless act, or failure to act. The test is **subjective**, not based on the notion of a reasonable parent or person in charge.
- The courts have held that 'wilful' misconduct means 'deliberately doing something which is wrong, knowing it to be wrong or with reckless indifference as to whether it is wrong or not'. Although there is no definable threshold for when a minor neglectful act becomes a criminal offence, each single incident must be examined in the context of other acts or omissions and the possibility of a criminal offence should be considered.
- Consider taking the child/young person into police protection (see **2.4.2**).

E&S

Either way

None

Summary: 6/12 months' imprisonment and/or a fine

Indictment: 14 years' imprisonment and/or a fine

2.4.2 Taking a child at risk into police protection

The Children Act 1989, s 46 provides police powers to take children under 18 years old who are at risk of significant harm into police protection.

Powers

(1) Where a constable has reasonable cause to believe that a child would otherwise be likely to suffer significant harm, he may—
  (a) remove the child to suitable accommodation and keep him there; or
  (b) take such steps as are reasonable to ensure that the child's removal from any hospital, or other place, in which he is being accommodated is prevented.

(2) For the purposes of this Act, a child with respect to whom a constable has exercised his powers under this section is referred to as having been taken into police protection.

(3) As soon as is reasonably practicable after taking a child into police protection, the constable concerned shall—
   (a) inform the local authority within whose area the child was found of the steps that have been, and are proposed to be, taken with respect to the child under this section and the reasons for taking them;
   (b) give details to the authority within whose area the child is ordinarily resident ('the appropriate authority') of the place at which the child is being accommodated;
   (c) inform the child (if he appears capable of understanding)—
      (i) of the steps that have been taken with respect to him under this section and of the reasons for taking them; and
      (ii) of the further steps that may be taken with respect to him under this section;
   (d) take such steps as are reasonably practicable to discover the wishes and feelings of the child;
   (e) secure that the case is inquired into by an officer designated for the purposes of this section by the chief officer of the police area concerned; and
   (f) where the child was taken into police protection by being removed to accommodation which is not provided—
      (i) by or on behalf of a local authority; or
      (ii) as a refuge, in compliance with the requirements of section 51, secure that he is moved to accommodation which is so provided.

(4) As soon as is reasonably practicable after taking a child into police protection the constable concerned shall take such steps as are reasonably practicable to inform—
   (a) the child's parents;
   (b) every person who is not a parent of his but who has parental responsibility for the child; and
   (c) any other person with whom the child was living immediately before being taken into police protection,

   of the steps that he has taken under this section with respect to the child, the reasons for taking them and the further steps that may be taken with respect to him under this section.

(5) On completing any inquiry under subsection (3)(e), the officer designated conducting it shall release the child from police protection unless he considers that there is still reasonable cause for believing that the child would be likely to suffer significant harm if released.

(6) No child may be kept in police protection for more than 72 hours.

(7) While a child is being kept in police protection, the designated officer may apply on behalf of the appropriate authority for an emergency protection order to be made under section 44 with respect to the child.

(8) An application may be made under subsection (7) whether or not the authority knows of it or agree to its being made.

(9) While a child is being kept in police protection—
   (a) neither the constable concerned, nor the designated officer shall have parental responsibility for him; but

(b) the designated officer shall do what is reasonable in all the circumstances of the case for the purpose of safeguarding or promoting the child's welfare (having regard in particular to the length of the period during which the child will be so protected).

(10) Where a child has been taken into police protection, the designated officer shall allow—

(a) the child's parents;

(b) any person who is not a parent of the child but who has parental responsibility for him;

(c) any person with whom the child was living immediately before he was taken into police protection;

(d) any person named in a child arrangements order as a person with whom the child is to spend time or otherwise have contact;

(e) any person who is allowed to have contact with the child by virtue of an order under section 34; and

(f) any person acting on behalf of any of those persons,

to have such contact (if any) with the child as, in the opinion of the designated officer, is both reasonable and in the child's interests.

Children Act 1989, s 46

Meanings

Child

Means a person under the age of 18.

Hospital

Has the same meaning as in the Mental Health Act 1983, except that it does not include a hospital at which high-security psychiatric services are provided. The 1983 Act states that a hospital is: 'any health service hospital within the meaning of the National Health Service Act 2006 . .. and any accommodation provided by a local authority and used as a hospital by or on behalf of the Secretary of State under that Act'.

Explanatory notes

- The police have a duty to protect the child until more formal arrangements can be made. It is possible for a child to be in police protection without physically moving them. For example, if a child is in hospital having been battered, they may be taken into police protection while leaving the child in the hospital.
- All the parties involved, including the parents, child, and local authority, are to be kept informed and given reasons for any actions. The child's wishes must be listened to but do not have to be acted upon.

- This power is appropriate for detaining and returning children missing from home as long as they are at risk from significant harm.

Related case

Langley and others v Liverpool City Council [2006] 1 WLR 375, CA If practicable, removal of a child should be authorised by an emergency protection court order under s 44 and carried out by the local authority. If such an order is in force, the police should not exercise their s 46 powers, unless there are compelling reasons for doing so.

Practical considerations

- HOC 17/2008 provides guidance as follows:
  - ✦ The designated officer under s 46(3)(e) will usually be an officer of the rank of inspector.
  - ✦ These powers should only be used when the child would be likely to suffer significant harm.
  - ✦ Except in exceptional circumstances (eg imminent threat to a child's welfare), no child is to be taken into police protection until the initiating officer has seen the child and assessed their circumstances.
  - ✦ Consider entry powers under s 17 of PACE (see **1.4.2**) as no power of entry is provided under these police protection powers.
  - ✦ A police station is not suitable accommodation for these purposes but may be used as a temporary or emergency measure until suitable accommodation is identified.
- The Children Act 1989 includes other powers to protect children:
  - ✦ s 43—Child assessment orders;
  - ✦ s 44—Emergency protection orders;
  - ✦ s 47—Duty of local authority to investigate welfare;
  - ✦ s 48—Warrant/powers to ascertain if child requires protection;
  - ✦ s 50—Recovery of abducted children.
- A Local Safeguarding Children Board for each area should protect children from abuse and neglect. This involves a range of parties providing children's services and the police liaising with each other, including an information database whereby information can be shared between all partners.

Link to alternative offences

6.5 **Child Sexual Exploitation Offences** 297

2.5 **Threats to Kill**

Section 16 of the Offences Against the Person Act 1861 provides the offence of threats to kill.

Offences

A person who, without lawful excuse makes to another a threat intending that the other would fear it would be carried out, to kill that other or a third person shall be guilty of an offence.

Offences Against the Person Act 1861, s 16

PNLD H2144

Points to prove

✓ without lawful excuse
✓ made threat to kill
✓ intending to cause fear threat would be carried out

Meaning of intending (see 4.1.2)

Explanatory note

- There is no need to show that the defendant intended to kill anyone. The relevant intent must be that the person receiving the threat would fear the threat (to kill them or a third person) would be carried out.

Defences

- Having a lawful excuse, such as the prevention of crime or self-defence.
- It must be reasonable in all the circumstances to make the threat.

Related case

R v Tait [1990] 1 QB 290 An unborn child (foetus in utero) is not a third person distinct from its mother for the purposes of this section. Therefore, a threat to a pregnant woman to kill her unborn baby is not an offence under this section. However, it would appear that a threat to kill a child after its birth made at a time when it was still a foetus may come within the scope of this offence.

Practical considerations

- In order to establish that they had a lawful excuse, it is necessary for a person to show:
  - (a) that they honestly, but mistakenly, believed on reasonable grounds that the facts were of a certain order; and
  - (b) that if those facts had been of that order their conduct would have been lawful.
- The onus is on the prosecution to prove that there was no lawful excuse for making a threat and it is for the jury to decide what is reasonable and what amounts to a threat.
- Consider hearsay and bad character admissibility under the Criminal Justice Act 2003.
- Proof of the 'mens rea' ('guilty mind'), as to the intention that the other person would fear the threat would be carried out to kill that person or a third person, is required.
- Evidence of previous history between the parties is admissible as tending to prove that the defendant intended their words to be taken seriously.
- Detail in your file and CJA witness statements the following points:
  - ✦ nature of the threats made—exact words used and in what context, include any previous threats made;
  - ✦ the fact that the threat was **understood** by the person to whom it was made, and that the person feared the threat would be carried out;
  - ✦ describe the full circumstances of the incident and antecedent history details of the relationship between the defendant and complainant.
- Communications that constitute threats to another person may also amount to other offences. Consider intimidation of witnesses and jurors under s 51 of the Criminal Justice and Public Order Act 1994 (see **4.8.1**); threats of violence under ss 4 and 4A of the Protection from Harassment Act 1997 (see **7.11.2**); s 1 of the Malicious Communications Act 1988; and s 127 of the Communications Act 2003 (see **7.12.1**).
- Where the offence is committed against a person providing a public service, performing a public duty, or providing services to the public, the court must treat that fact as an aggravating factor, and must state in open court that the offence is so aggravated.

SSS E&S

Either way   None

Summary: 6/12 months' imprisonment and/or a fine

Indictment: 10 years' imprisonment

Links to alternative subjects and offences

4.11 Forced Marriages 230
7.3 Breach of the Peace 362
7.6 Fear or Provocation of Violence 373
7.8 Threatening/Abusive Words/Behaviour 380
7.11 Harassment/Stalking 398
7.12 Communications Causing Distress, Anxiety, or Serious Harm 418

2.6 False Imprisonment, Kidnapping, and Child Abduction

Contained within this topic area are the common law offences of kidnapping, false imprisonment, and child abduction under the Child Abduction Act 1984. Officers should be familiar with this area of law when dealing with any violent domestic incidents, sexual offences, or where people are taken against their will.

2.6.1 False imprisonment

False imprisonment is an offence at common law.

> **Offences**
>
> The unlawful and total restraint of the personal liberty of another, whether by constraining them or compelling them to go to a particular place or by confining them in a prison or police station or private place or by detaining them against their will in a public place.
>
> Common law

PNLD H2132

> **Points to prove**
>
> ✓ imprisoned, detained, or arrested
> ✓ another person
> ✓ against their will
> ✓ unlawfully

Explanatory notes

- The wrongful act ('actus reus') of false imprisonment is the act of placing an unlawful restriction on the victim's freedom in the absence of any legal right to do so.
- There must also have been an element of intent ('mens rea') to restrain, either deliberately or recklessly.
- There is no offence if the victim is not physically restrained unless the offender detains/intends to detain them by use of fear/threats. Unlawfully locking someone in a vehicle may be sufficient for this offence.

Defences

That the taking or detaining was in the course of a lawful arrest or detention under PACE (see **1.1**) or acting under another statutory or common law power.

Related cases

Holmes v Chief Constable of Merseyside Police [2018] EWHC 1026 (Admin) 'H' was a political campaigner who was protesting at a Labour Party conference and was arrested. It was held that there was no reasonable prospect of H establishing that the police officer, when arresting H, had not genuinely and reasonably believed that the officer had justification to do so because H was obstructing them in the execution of their duty. By their actions, the police officer had clearly considered that they had a duty to remove H from the place of protest where H wanted to be and prevent H from returning there from the designated area. The claim for false imprisonment therefore failed.

R v Wilkinson [2018] EWCA Crim 2154 A taxi driver was not able to rely on the defence of lawful excuse in relation to a charge of false imprisonment where, following a dispute over payment, R returned the passenger to her starting point.

Austin v UK [2012] Crim LR 544, ECtHR The police imposed a cordon to isolate and contain protestors in volatile and dangerous conditions to prevent serious injury or damage. It was held that, in the circumstances, an absolute cordon had been the least intrusive and most effective means to be applied. Those within the cordon had not been deprived of their liberty in breach of Art 5 (see **Appendix 1**).

Practical considerations

- A parent has no right to imprison their own child, although a parent is allowed to detain a child for purposes of reasonable parental discipline. Whether it is reasonable in all the circumstances is for a jury to decide.
- A victim could bring a civil action for damages (invariably after unlawful arrest by the police). Consider kidnapping (**2.6.2**) or child abduction (**2.6.3**) as alternatives.

E&S

Indictable | None

Life imprisonment and/or a fine

2.6.2 Kidnapping

Kidnapping is an offence at common law.

Offences

The taking or carrying away of one person by another, by force or fraud, without the consent of the person so taken or carried away, and without lawful excuse.

Common law

PNLD **H1877, H2156**

Points to prove

✓ without lawful excuse
✓ by force/fraud
✓ took/carried away
✓ another person
✓ without their consent

Meaning of fraud

Means deceit, guile, or trick. It should not be confused with the narrower meaning given to it for the purposes of consent in sexual offences.

Explanatory notes

- The important points to prove are the deprivation of liberty and carrying away even where a short distance is involved—and the absence of consent.
- In the case of a child, it is the child's consent that should be considered (rather than the parent/guardian) and, in the case of a very young child, absence of consent may be inferred.

Defences

Consent or lawful excuse.

Related cases

R v Hendy-Freegard [2007] EWCA Crim 1236 The offence of kidnapping must involve the deprivation of liberty and taking and carrying away.

R v Cort [2003] 3 WLR 1300, CA The defendant went to bus stops telling lone women that the bus they were waiting for had broken down and offering/providing lifts in his vehicle. It was held that the fact that the defendant had lied about the absence of the bus meant that, although they had got into the car voluntarily, the women had not given true consent to the journey and the offences of kidnap (and attempts) were complete.

Practical considerations

- A man or woman may be guilty of this offence in relation to their spouse or partner.
- Under s 5 of the Child Abduction Act 1984, consent of the DPP is required to prosecute for an offence of kidnapping if it was committed:
  - ✦ against a child under 16;
  - ✦ by a person connected with the child under s 1(2) (see **2.6.3**).
- In all other cases, the consent of the DPP is not required.

E&S

Indictable

None

Life imprisonment and/or a fine

2.6.3 **Child abduction**

The Child Abduction Act 1984 provides two distinct child abduction offences: s 1—person connected to child (parent/guardian) and s 2—committed by other persons.

Person connected with child

Offences

Subject to subsections (5) and (8) below, a person connected with a child under the age of 16 commits an offence if he takes or sends the child out of the United Kingdom without the appropriate consent.

Child Abduction Act 1984, s 1(1)

PNLD H2066, H2073

Points to prove

- ✓ being a parent/person connected with
- ✓ a child under 16 years of age
- ✓ took/sent that child
- ✓ out of the United Kingdom
- ✓ without the appropriate consent

2.6.3 Child abduction

Meanings

Person connected (s 1(2))

A **person connected** with a child for the purposes of this section is:
(a) a parent of the child; or
(b) in the case of a child whose parents were not married to each other at the time of birth, there are reasonable grounds for believing that he is the father of the child; or
(c) the guardian of the child; or
(ca) a special guardian of the child; or
(d) a person named in a child arrangements order as a person with whom the child is to live; or
(e) has custody of the child.

Takes

A person is regarded as **taking** a child if they cause or induce the child to accompany them, or any other person, or causes the child to be taken.

Sends

A person is regarded as **sending** a child if they cause the child to be sent.

Appropriate consent (s 1(3))

(a) This means the consent of each of the following:
  (i) the child's mother;
  (ii) the child's father, if he has parental responsibility for him;
  (iii) any guardian of the child;
  (iiia) any special guardian of the child;
  (iv) any person named in a child arrangements order as a person with whom the child is to live;
  (v) any person who has custody of the child; or
(b) the leave of the court granted under or by virtue of any provision of Part 2 of the Children Act 1989; or
(c) if any person has custody of the child, the leave of the court which awarded custody to him.

Explanatory notes

- A court could deal with a parent who had abducted their child in three ways. First, for contempt of court (flouting a court order); secondly, prosecution for an offence under the 1984 Act; and, thirdly, prosecution for kidnapping, either based on force, or fraud in achieving the removal of the child from the other parent (*R v Kayani; R v Sollim* [2011] EWCA Crim 2871).
- This offence can also be committed (subject to the statutory defences given below) when a child is in the care of a local authority or place of safety whilst subject to adoption proceedings.

Defences

(4) A person does not commit an offence under this section by taking or sending a child out of the United Kingdom without obtaining the appropriate consent if—
  (a) he is a person named in a child arrangements order as a person with whom the child is to live, and he takes or sends the child out of the United Kingdom for a period of less than one month; or
  (b) he is a special guardian of the child and he takes or sends the child out of the United Kingdom for a period of less than three months.

(4A) Subsection (4) above does not apply if the person taking or sending the child out of the United Kingdom does so in breach of an order under Part 2 of the Children Act 1989.

(5) A person does not commit an offence under this section by doing anything without the consent of another person whose consent is required under the forgoing provisions if—
  (a) he does it in the belief that the other person—
    (i) has consented; or
    (ii) would consent if he was aware of all the relevant circumstances; or
  (b) he has taken all reasonable steps to communicate with the other person but has been unable to communicate with him; or
  (c) the other person has unreasonably refused to consent.

(5A) Subsection (5)(c) above does not apply if—
  (a) the person who refused to consent is a person—
    (i) named in a child arrangements order as a person with whom the child is to live; or
    (ia) who is a special guardian of the child; or
    (iii) who has custody of the child; or
  (b) the person taking or sending the child out of the United Kingdom is, by so acting, in breach of an order made by a court in the United Kingdom.

(8) This section shall have effect subject to the provisions of the Schedule to this Act in relation to a child who is in the care of a local authority detained in a place of safety, remanded otherwise than on bail or the subject of proceedings or an order relating to adoption.

Child Abduction Act 1984, s 1

Abduction of child by another person

This is an offence in relation to the taking or detaining of a child where the offender is not connected with that child.

Offences

Subject to subsection (3) below, a person, other than one mentioned in subsection (2) below, commits an offence if, without lawful authority or reasonable excuse, he takes or detains a child under the age of 16—
(a) so as to remove him from the lawful control of any person having lawful control of the child; or
(b) so as to keep him out of the lawful control of any person entitled to lawful control of the child.

Child Abduction Act 1984, s 2(1)

PNLD H2065, H2067, H2075, H1650

Points to prove

- ✓ without lawful authority/reasonable excuse
- ✓ detained or took
- ✓ a child under 16 years of age
- ✓ so as to remove/keep them
- ✓ from/out of the lawful control
- ✓ of a person having/entitled to lawful control
- ✓ of that child

Meanings

Takes (see s **1(1)**)

Detains

A person is regarded as detaining a child if they cause the child to be detained or induce the child to remain with them or any other person.

Remove from lawful control

This can be satisfied if the child is induced to take some action that they would not normally have done (*R v Leather* [1993] 1 WLUK 699).

Explanatory notes

- The offence is subject to a statutory defence of consent (s 2(3)—below).
- This offence does not apply to persons listed in s 2(2) namely:
  - ✦ the child's father and mother—being married to each other, or civil partners, at the time of the birth;
  - ✦ the child's mother—where the father was not married to, or civil partners with, her at the time of the birth;
  - ✦ any other person mentioned in s 1(2)(c) to (e) above.

Defences

It shall be a defence for that person to prove—

(a) where the father and mother of the child in question were not married to, or civil partners of, each other at the time of his birth—
  (i) that he is the child's father
  (ii) that, at the time of the alleged offence, he believed, on reasonable grounds, that he was the child's father, or

(b) that, at the time of the alleged offence, he believed that the child had attained the age of 16 years.

Child Abduction Act 1984, s 2(3)

Related cases

Nicolaou v Redbridge Magistrates' Court [2012] EWHC 1647 (Admin) For the s 1 offence, it was held that a parent with the authority of a court order to take their child out of the UK for a specified period does not commit abduction of a child by not returning that child to the UK following expiry of that period.

R v Wakeman [2011] EWCA 1649 In this case, the defendant took the hands of two children and walked them 30 metres across a park to show them something interesting, without the consent of the parents. It was held that this can be an abduction. The prosecution need only prove an intentional or reckless taking, or detention, the consequence of which was removing a child from the control of any person having lawful control of that child.

R v Mohammed [2006] EWCA Crim 1107 (see **6.5.5**).

Practical considerations

- Child Abduction Warning Notices have provided useful evidence in many prosecutions, including large-scale 'grooming cases'. They have no statutory basis but, if properly used, can help to safeguard vulnerable youngsters and provide supportive evidence for criminal or other proceedings.
- Consider the more serious offence of kidnapping but be aware that consent from the DPP may be required under s 5 (see **2.6.2**).
- The s 1 offence (person connected with child) can only be committed by those people listed in s 1(2) **and** they must take or send that child out of the UK; the prosecution must rebut the defence of consent.
- Section 2 (other people not connected with the child) will cover the situation where an agent snatches a child for an estranged parent. The parent in such a case may commit the offence of aiding and abetting or the principal offence.

2.6.3 **Child abduction**

E&S

Either way

None

Summary: 6/12 months' imprisonment and/or a fine

Indictment: 7 years' imprisonment

Links to alternative subjects and offences

4.1 **Criminal Attempts** 173
4.11 **Forced Marriages** 230
7.6 **Fear or Provocation of Violence** 373
7.8 **Threatening/Abusive Words/Behaviour** 380
7.11 **Harassment/Stalking** 398
7.12 **Communications Causing Distress, Anxiety, or Serious Harm** 418
Appendix 1 **Human Rights** 839

2.7 Sudden and Unexplained Deaths

Police officers investigating sudden and unexplained deaths should have a basic knowledge of the relevant law and powers. Apart from informing supervision, following **force policies/procedures**, and requesting the assistance of scenes of crime officers, be mindful of scene preservation and the obtaining of forensic evidence.

2.7.1 Murder

The offence of murder comes under the common law and is defined as:

Offence

Where a person of sound mind and discretion unlawfully kills any reasonable creature in being and under the King's peace, with intent to kill or cause grievous bodily harm.

Common law

PNLD H2172, H2173

Points to prove

✓ unlawfully killed a human being
✓ with intent to kill or cause grievous bodily harm

Meanings

Sound mind and discretion

Every person of the age of discretion is presumed to be sane and accountable for their actions unless the contrary is proved. This means anyone who is not insane or anyone over 10 years old.

Unlawfully

Means without lawful authority, legal justification, or excuse.

Kills

This is 'the act' ('actus reus') which is the substantial cause of death (stabbed, shot, strangled, suffocated, poisoned, etc).

Reasonable creature in being

Any human being, including a baby born alive having an independent existence from its mother.

Under the King's peace

This is meant to exclude killing in the course of war. A British subject takes the King's peace with them everywhere in the world.

Intent

An intention to kill or to cause grievous bodily harm is the 'mens rea' of murder (see **4.1.2**).

Cause/causation

If there is an 'intervening factor' between the defendant's actions and the death of the victim, the jury will consider whether the defendant's act contributed significantly to the death.

Grievous bodily harm (see **2.3**)

Explanatory notes

- It shall be conclusively presumed that no child under the age of 10 years can be guilty of any offence (Children and Young Persons Act 1933, s 50).
- If a defendant wishes to plead **insanity**, they will be judged on the M'Naghten Rules from *M'Naghten's Case* (1843) 10 Cl & F 200. This examines the extent to which, at the time of the commission of the offence, the person was 'labouring under such defect of reason from disease of the mind that either: (a) the defendant did not know what they were doing, **or** (b) they did know what they were doing but did not know it was wrong'.
- If a person intentionally causes GBH and the victim subsequently dies as a result, that person is guilty of murder.
- The jury will consider whether the defendant's act **contributed significantly** to the death by applying the 'substantial test' as set out in *R v Smith* [1959] 2 All ER 193, Court Martial CA.
- Whether the defendant intended or foresaw the results of their actions will be determined by several factors including the statutory test under the Criminal Justice Act 1967, s 8 (see **4.1.2**).

Defences to murder

Insanity

See the meaning of 'sound mind and discretion' and '**Explanatory notes**' as to 'insanity'.

Lawful killing

Means with lawful authority; legal justification or excuse, including self-defence (see **1.2**).

At war

This is self-explanatory, not being under the 'King's peace' (see '**Meanings**').

Specific defences

Loss of control

Where a person ('D') kills or is a party to the killing of another ('V'), D is not to be convicted of murder if—

(a) D's acts and omissions in doing or being a party to the killing resulted from D's loss of self-control,
(b) the loss of self-control had a qualifying trigger, and
(c) a person of D's sex and age, with a normal degree of tolerance and self-restraint and in the circumstances of D, might have reacted in the same or in a similar way to D.

Coroners and Justice Act 2009, s 54(1)

Diminished responsibility

(1) A person ('D') who kills or is a party to the killing of another is not to be convicted of murder if D was suffering from an abnormality of mental functioning which—
  (a) arose from a recognised medical condition,
  (b) substantially impaired D's ability to do one or more of the things mentioned in subsection (1A), and
  (c) provides an explanation for D's acts and omissions in doing or being a party to the killing.

(1A) Those things are—
  (a) to understand the nature of D's conduct;
  (b) to form a rational judgment;
  (c) to exercise self-control.

Homicide Act 1957, s 2

Suicide pact

Means a common agreement between two or more persons having for its object the death of all of them, whether or not each is to take his own life, but nothing done by a person who enters into a suicide pact shall be treated as done by him in pursuance of the pact unless it is done while he has the settled intention of dying in pursuance of the pact.

Homicide Act 1957, s 4(3)

Related cases

R v Goodwin [2018] EWCA Crim 2287 Self-defence and the partial defence of loss of control are legally distinct. A loss of control defence must raise 'sufficient' evidence of the defence for it to be left to the jury. Evidence of a qualifying trigger is not of itself enough. Each element of the defence must be considered sequentially and separately. In this case, there was insufficient evidence that a person with a normal degree of tolerance and self-restraint would have reacted as the defendant did.

R v Taj [2018] EWCA Crim 1743 Self-defence was not available when a mistaken belief was attributable to voluntary intoxication even though there were no drugs or alcohol in the defendant's system, but they were still experiencing the effects from previous consumption.

R v Golds [2016] UKSC 61 The Supreme Court in this case clarified the meaning of 'substantially' in relation to a partial defence of diminished responsibility set out in s 2 of the Homicide Act 1957. Diminished responsibility involves an impairment of one or more of the abilities listed in the statute to an extent which the jury judges to be 'substantial' and which it is satisfied significantly contributed to the commission of the offence. Illustrative expressions, as an ordinary English word, of 'substantially' may be employed so the jury can clearly understand it, but the judge should not attempt to define the meaning.

R v Gnango [2011] UKSC 59 Two men had a gun fight with each other in a public place; both had the intent to kill the other. During the shooting, a shot from one of them accidentally killed a passer-by. It was held that, by virtue of transferred malice, both were guilty of the passer-by's murder.

R v Keal [2022] EWCA Crim 341 The defendant had a history of mental health problems and brutally attacked their father, mother, and grandmother and during the course of the attacks made comments indicating that K understood and regretted the actions but felt a compulsion to act. Charged with attempted murder, K pleaded insanity but was convicted. On appeal, it was held that under the M'Naghten Rules the defence of insanity was not available to a defendant who knew what they were doing was wrong but believed that they had no choice but to commit the act.

Practical considerations

- The killing must be causally related to the acts of the defendant and not through an intervening factor which breaks the chain of causation.
- If there is doubt whether death was caused by some supervening event (such as medical negligence when treated), the prosecution does not have to prove that the supervening event was not a significant cause of death.
- Intention 'mens rea' ('guilty mind')—has to be proved (see **4.1.2**).
- Consent of the A-G is required where:
  - ✦ the injury was sustained more than three years before death; **or**
  - ✦ the accused has been previously convicted of the offence alleged to be connected with the death.
- If a person is suffering from a terminal disease and receives a wound that hastens their death, this killing would (with the required intent) be murder or manslaughter.
- A murder or manslaughter committed by a British citizen outside the UK may be tried in this country as if it had been committed here.
- Motivation will form a key part of any prosecution and the availability of any defences should be considered.

- The meaning of '**qualifying trigger**' for the partial defence to murder is where the defendant lost self-control because:
  - ✦ of fear of serious violence against defendant or another person; **or**
  - ✦ it was attributable to things done or said (or both) which constituted circumstances of an extremely grave character and caused the defendant to have a justifiable sense of being seriously wronged.
- Guidance and details regarding the partial defences to murder for loss of control, diminished responsibility, and infanticide, made by the Coroners and Justice Act 2009, is given in MOJ Circular 13/2010.
- Offences Against the Person Act 1861, s 4 is the offence of soliciting to murder: 'Whosoever shall solicit, encourage, persuade, or endeavour to persuade, or shall propose to any person, to murder any other person, shall be guilty of an offence and liable to imprisonment for life.'
- Section 2(1) of the Suicide Act 1961 deals with encouraging or assisting suicide, whereby a person commits an offence if they do an act capable of encouraging or assisting suicide or attempted suicide of another person, and the act was intended to encourage or assist suicide or an attempt at suicide. See MOJ Circulars 2/2010 and 3/2010.
- Consider the CPS policy in respect of this offence, which requires DPP consent before prosecution.

SSS E&S

Indictable None

Life imprisonment

2.7.2 Manslaughter

Offence

Manslaughter is the unlawful killing of another human being which can either be a voluntary or involuntary manslaughter offence.

Common law

PNLD H2097, H2169

Points to prove

✓ unlawful act or gross negligence
✓ killed a human being

Meanings

Unlawful killing (see 2.7.1)

Voluntary manslaughter

When a murder charge is reduced to voluntary manslaughter by reason of one of the specific defences to murder (see **2.7.1**).

Involuntary manslaughter

An unlawful killing without an intention to kill or cause grievous bodily harm. Apart from the required intent, the elements of the offence are the same as for murder (see **2.7.1**).

Manslaughter can be caused by:

- **unlawful act** (not omission): the unlawful act must be unlawful in itself (eg another criminal offence such as an assault or a threat to kill) and must involve a risk that someone would be harmed by it;
- **gross negligence** (involving breach of duty): gross negligence manslaughter requires a breach of a duty of care owed by the defendant to the victim under circumstances where the defendant's conduct was serious enough to amount to a crime.

Related cases

R v Kuddus [2019] EWCA Crim 837 This was a gross negligence manslaughter case involving death related to the victim's nut allergy. It was argued that the defendant negligently breached a duty of care by failing to implement reasonable steps necessary to protect customers suffering with allergies. Due to this failure, customers were exposed to an obvious and serious risk of death. It was held that the offence does not require proof of serious and obvious risk of death to the individual who dies. The question that must be answered is whether the defendant's breach gave rise to a serious and obvious risk of death to the group or class of people to which the duty was owed.

R v Tas [2018] EWCA Crim 2603 It was held in this case that the fact that the jury could not be certain whether the defendant was aware of a knife being used by co-defendants as part of a joint enterprise did not undermine the conviction.

R v Rose [2017] EWCA Crim 1168 This case followed the test in *R v Rudling* (see below) that for gross negligence manslaughter there had to be a serious and obvious risk of death at the time of the statutory breach, not merely serious illness.

R v Rudling [2016] EWCA Crim 741 This case involved a charge of gross negligence manslaughter against a doctor. The offence requires a breach of an existing duty of care which is reasonably foreseeable as giving rise to the serious and obvious risk of death and the conduct of the defendant amounts to a criminal act or omission. It was held that in medical cases, that at the time of the breach of duty, a reasonably prudent person would conclude there was a risk of death and not merely serious illness.

R v Evans [2009] EWCA Crim 650 This case considered the duty required in gross negligence manslaughter. Where a person has contributed to a state of affairs which they knew or ought reasonably to have known had created a threat to life, a duty arose for them to act by taking all reasonable steps to save the life at risk.

Explanatory notes

- Where a person aged under 18 is convicted of a relevant offence of manslaughter of an emergency worker acting in the exercise of such functions, and where the offence occurred when the person was aged 16 or over, the court must impose a sentence of detention for life unless there are exceptional circumstances relating to the offence or offender and the courts can justify not doing so. The manslaughter conviction must not be by way of gross negligence, a defence of diminished responsibility, or loss of control to a murder charge or in pursuit of a suicide pact.
- Where a person aged 18 or over, but under 21, is convicted of a relevant offence of manslaughter of an emergency worker acting in the exercise of such functions, and where the offence occurred when the person was aged 16 or over, the court must impose a sentence of custody for life unless there are exceptional circumstances relating to the offence or offender and the courts can justify not doing so. The manslaughter conviction must not be by way of gross negligence, a defence of diminished responsibility, or loss of control to a murder charge or in pursuit of a suicide pact.
- Where a person aged 21 or over is convicted of a relevant offence of manslaughter of an emergency worker acting in the exercise of such functions, and where the offence occurred when the person was aged 16 or over, the court must impose a sentence of imprisonment for life unless there are exceptional circumstances relating to the offence or offender and the courts can justify not doing so. The manslaughter conviction must not be by way of gross negligence, a defence of diminished responsibility, or loss of control to a murder charge or in pursuit of a suicide pact.

Practical considerations (see also 2.7.1)

- Consider corporate manslaughter (see 2.7.3) in work-related deaths involving negligence by the company/organisation.
- Previous convictions or past behaviour of the defendant in homicide cases may well be relevant both to the issue of 'mens rea' (intent) and to sentence.
- The burden of proof in relation to claiming diminished responsibility or acting in pursuance of a suicide pact lies with the defendant.

- Section 2(1) of the Suicide Act 1961 gives an **offence** of encouraging or assisting suicide of another (see **2.7.1**).

SSS E&S

Indictable None

Life imprisonment

2.7.3 Corporate manslaughter

The Corporate Manslaughter and Corporate Homicide Act 2007 sets out the offence of corporate manslaughter for an organisation where a gross failure in the way its activities were managed or organised resulted in a person's death.

Offence

(1) An organisation to which this section applies is guilty of an offence if the way in which its activities are managed or organised—
  (a) causes a person's death, and
  (b) amounts to a gross breach of a relevant duty of care owed by the organisation to the deceased.

Corporate Manslaughter and Corporate Homicide Act 2007, s 1

PNLD H9076

Points to prove

✓ being an organisation to which s 1 applies
✓ managed or organised its activities
✓ in a way that caused the death of a person
✓ by an act or omission
✓ which amounted to a gross breach of a relevant duty of care owed to that person

Meanings

Organisations to which s 1 applies

- corporation;
- department or other body listed in **Sch 1**;
- police force;
- partnership, or a trade union or employers' association, that is an employer.

Schedule 1

This Schedule lists over forty government departments and other similar bodies, such as: CPS; DEFRA; Department for Transport; Department of Health; Foreign and Commonwealth Office; HMRC; Home Office; Ministry of Defence; and the Serious Fraud Office.

Explanatory notes

- An organisation will commit this offence if the way in which its activities are managed or organised causes a death and amounts to a gross breach of a duty of care owed to the deceased.
- The conduct must fall far below what would reasonably have been expected for it to be a gross breach. Any breaches of health and safety legislation will have to be considered—and how serious and dangerous those failures were.
- A duty of care exists, for example, in respect of the systems of work and equipment used by employees, the condition of work sites or premises occupied by the organisation, or to products or services supplied to customers.
- This Act does not create new duties; they are already owed in the civil law of negligence and the offence is based on these.

Practical considerations

- Officers dealing with fatal/potentially fatal work incidents that appear to involve negligence by the organisation should inform the HSE (see **Appendix 2**), as well as protecting the crime scene.
- Section 2 deals with the '**relevant duty of care**' owed by an organisation under the law of negligence to its employees or other persons working for it, as occupier of premises, or duty owed with the supply of goods or services, carrying out of any construction or maintenance operations or other commercial activity, or the use/keeping of any plant, vehicle, or other thing.
- This Act applies to a police force, so making it liable for the corporate manslaughter offence if a person dies whilst detained in police custody. MOJ Circular 7/2011 gives guidance in relation to deaths of persons in police custody under s 2(2) who are owed a duty of care under the Act.
- Section 2(1)(d) states that a duty owed to a person, being a person within s 2(2), is someone for whose safety the organisation is responsible.
- Directors, senior managers, or other individuals cannot be held liable for this offence. It will be the organisation that will be prosecuted. However, individuals can still be prosecuted for gross negligence manslaughter (*R v Winter* [2010] EWCA Crim 1474—see **2.7.2**) and for health and safety offences. Individuals will continue to be prosecuted where there is sufficient evidence and it is in the public interest to do so.

- Consent of the DPP is needed before a case of corporate manslaughter can be taken to court. Cases will be prosecuted by the CPS and Health and Safety charges will probably be dealt with at the same time.

Indictable

None

An unlimited fine

2.7.4 Death or serious physical harm to a child/vulnerable adult

Section 5 of the Domestic Violence, Crime and Victims Act 2004 creates the offences of causing or allowing the death of or serious physical harm to a child or a vulnerable adult by means of an unlawful act.

Offences

A person ('D') is guilty of an offence if—

(a) a child or vulnerable adult ('V') dies or suffers serious physical harm as a result of the unlawful act of a person who—
   (i) was a member of the same household as V, and
   (ii) had frequent contact with him,

(b) D was such a person at the time of that act,

(c) at that time there was a significant risk of serious physical harm being caused to V by the unlawful act of such a person, and

(d) either D was the person whose act caused the death or serious physical harm or—
   (i) D was, or ought to have been, aware of the risk mentioned in paragraph (c),
   (ii) D failed to take such steps as he could reasonably have been expected to take to protect V from the risk, and
   (iii) the act occurred in circumstances of the kind that D foresaw or ought to have foreseen.

Domestic Violence, Crime and Victims Act 2004, s 5(1)

PNLD H100755, H100754

Points to prove

- ✓ being a member of the same household and having had frequent contact with a person who was at that time a child/vulnerable adult
- ✓ caused that person's death OR
- ✓ caused that person to suffer serious physical harm OR
- ✓ was, or ought to have been, aware that there was a significant risk of serious physical harm being caused to that person

- ✓ by the unlawful act of a member of their household
- ✓ which occurred in circumstances of the kind that the defendant foresaw or ought to have foreseen and
- ✓ the defendant failed to take such steps as they could reasonably have been expected to take to protect them from that risk

Meanings

Child

Means a person under the age of 16 years.

Vulnerable adult

Means a person aged 16 or over whose ability to protect themselves from violence, abuse, or neglect is significantly impaired through physical or mental disability or illness, through old age, or otherwise. This includes a temporary vulnerability as well as one which is permanent.

Unlawful act (see **2.7.2**)

Act

This includes a course of conduct and includes omission.

Member of the same household

This includes people who do not live in that household, providing they visit often and for such periods of time that they are regarded as a member of it.

Serious physical harm

Means grievous bodily harm for the purposes of the Offences Against the Persons Act 1961 (see **2.3**).

Explanatory notes

- The meaning of a **vulnerable adult** also includes a temporary vulnerability as well as one which is permanent.
- If D was not the mother or father of V, D may not be charged with an offence under this section if they were under the age of 16 at the time of the act that caused the death or serious harm; and for the purposes of subsection (5)(d)(ii), D could not have been expected to take any such step as is referred to there before attaining that age.

Related cases

R v Uddin [2017] EWCA Crim 1072 The appeal in this case focused upon the interpretation of the phrase 'or otherwise' in the definition of 'vulnerable adult' in s 5 (see '**Meanings**' above). The meaning of 'otherwise' could be an external cause through which the victim's ability to protect themselves from violence, abuse, or neglect was significantly impaired. There are no limits to the facts or circumstances that might lead to the victim finding themselves in a state of impaired ability to obtain protection and would include those who are not suffering from illness, disability, or old age.

R v Khan and others [2009] EWCA Crim 2 There was a history of the defendant using violence against the victim and on this occasion the injuries he inflicted proved fatal. There was other medical evidence that suggested that she had sustained injuries from three previous attacks. It was held that this offence imposes a duty on members of the same household to protect children/vulnerable adults where their ability to protect themselves is impaired and vulnerability may be short- or long-term. Furthermore, the defendant was aware of the risk of serious harm and foresaw or ought reasonably to have foreseen that an unlawful act or course of conduct would result in death and failed to take reasonable steps to prevent the risk.

Practical considerations

- If V dies, the death should still be thoroughly investigated to establish whether the person is responsible for murder or manslaughter. As the offence is limited to an unlawful act, it will not apply to accidental or cot deaths.
- Further details on allowing/causing the death are dealt with in HOC 9/2005. MOJ Circular 3/2012 concerns the Domestic Violence, Crime and Victims (Amendment) Act 2012, which extended the original offence to include serious physical harm.

SSS E&S

Indictable

None

Causing/allowing death: Life imprisonment and/or a fine

Causing/allowing serious physical harm: 14 years' imprisonment and/or a fine

2.7.5 Overlaying/suffocation of infant under 3

The Children and Young Persons Act 1933 provides for circumstances where a child has been suffocated while lying next to an adult.

Offences

Where it is proved that the death of an infant under three years of age was caused by suffocation (not being suffocation caused by disease or the presence of any foreign body in the throat or air

> passages of the infant) while the infant was in bed with some other person who has attained the age of sixteen years, that other person shall, if he was, when he went to bed or at any later time before the suffocation, under the influence of drink or a prohibited drug, be deemed to have neglected the infant in a manner likely to cause injury to its health.
>
> Children and Young Persons Act 1933, s 1(2)(b)

PNLD H100807, H100753

Points to prove

- ✓ being a person 16 years or over
- ✓ caused the death of an infant under 3 years of age
- ✓ by suffocation
- ✓ while the infant was lying next to that person
- ✓ person under the influence of drink/prohibited drug
- ✓ when they went in to/on a bed/any furniture/surface for the purpose of sleeping

Meanings

In bed/went to bed

This includes a reference to the infant lying next to the adult in or on any kind of furniture or surface being used by the adult for the purpose of sleeping.

Prohibited drug

If possession of the drug immediately before taking it would be an offence under s 5(2) of the Misuse of Drugs Act 1971 (see **5.2.1**).

Explanatory notes

- See HOC 8/2015 for guidance on the addition of 'prohibited drug' to this offence.
- Consider a more serious charge, such as manslaughter (see **2.7.2**) or causing/allowing the death of a child (see **2.7.4**).
- Further details relating to s 1 are given at **2.4.1**.

E&S

Either way

None

Summary: 6/12 months' imprisonment and/or a fine

Indictment: 10 years' imprisonment and/or a fine

2.7.6 Infanticide/child destruction/ concealment of birth

This offence is committed by the mother of a child (under 12 months old), who by any wilful act or omission, causes the death of her child whilst mentally unbalanced (such as post-natal depression) due to childbirth or lactation.

Offence

Where a woman by any wilful act or omission causes the death of her child being a child under the age of twelve months, but at the time of the act or omission the balance of her mind was disturbed by reason of her not having fully recovered from the effect of giving birth to the child or by reason of the effect of lactation consequent upon the birth of the child, then, if the circumstances were such that but for this Act the offence would have amounted to murder or manslaughter, she shall be guilty of infanticide, and may for such offence be dealt with and punished as if she had been guilty of the offence of manslaughter of the child.

Infanticide Act 1938, s 1(1)

PNLD H2151

Points to prove

✓ a woman
✓ caused the death of her own child (being under 12 months of age) OR
✓ of which a person had been delivered
✓ by secret disposition of the dead body of child
✓ by wilful act/omission
✓ whilst balance of her mind disturbed

Practical considerations

- This offence reduces the act to manslaughter as the responsibility for her actions may have been reduced by the disturbance of her mind caused by childbirth.
- There is no reference to any intention to kill or cause serious bodily harm as required for the offence of murder, only a wilful act or omission (*R v Gore* [2007] EWCA Crim 2789).

Child destruction

- The Infant Life (Preservation) Act 1929, s 1(1) makes it an indictable offence for any person, by any wilful act, to intentionally destroy a child capable of being born alive, before it has an existence independent of its mother.

- Evidence that a woman had at any material time been pregnant for a period of twenty-eight weeks or more shall be prima facie proof that she was at that time pregnant with a child capable of being born alive.
- It has been held that a foetus of between eighteen and twenty-one weeks is not 'capable of being born alive' since it would be incapable of breathing even with the aid of a ventilator, and a termination of a pregnancy of that length is not an offence under this Act.
- No person shall be found guilty of this offence if it is proved that the act was done in good faith for saving the life of the mother.
- A registered medical practitioner does not commit this offence if the pregnancy is terminated in accordance with the provisions of the Abortion Act 1967, s 5(1).
- Section 58 of the Offences Against the Person Act 1861 relates to administering drugs or using instruments to procure a miscarriage (abortion) at any time between conception and the birth of the child alive; whereas the 1929 Act prohibits the killing of any child capable of being born alive.

Concealment of birth

- Under s 60 of the 1861 Act, if any woman delivers a child, every person who shall, by any *secret disposition* of the dead body of the said child, whether such child died before, at, or after its birth, endeavour to conceal the birth thereof, shall be guilty of an either way offence.
- This offence relates to secret disposal or hiding of the dead body of a baby where the baby has died before, at, or shortly after birth.
- If the living body of a child is concealed, which then dies where it is concealed, clearly a more serious offence of murder may be committed.
- The offence is specific in that it must be a '**secret disposition**' *after the child has died*, the test being whether there is likelihood that the body would be found.

SSS E&S

Indictable None

s 1(1) ***Infanticide/child destruction***

Indictment: Life imprisonment

Concealment of birth

Either way

Summary: 6/12 months' imprisonment and/or a fine

Indictment: 2 years' imprisonment

Links to alternative subjects and offences

4.1 Criminal Attempts 173
4.11 Forced Marriages 230
7.10 Racially/Religiously Aggravated Offences 390
10.8.1 Causing death by dangerous driving 691

2.8 Domestic Abuse

Coercive and controlling behaviour

The Serious Crime Act 2015, s 76 creates an offence in relation to a person who repeatedly or continuously engages in behaviour towards another (this person being personally connected to them) that is controlling or coercive.

Offence

A person (A) commits an offence if—

(a) A repeatedly or continuously engages in behaviour towards another person (B) that is controlling or coercive,

(b) at the time of the behaviour, A and B are personally connected (see subsection (6)),

(c) the behaviour has a serious effect on B, and

(d) A knows or ought to know that the behaviour will have a serious effect on B.

Serious Crime Act 2015, s 76(1)

PNLD H12042

Points to prove

✓ repeatedly/continuously engaged in controlling/coercive behaviour
✓ towards person to whom they were personally connected
✓ the behaviour had a serious effect on victim
✓ knew/ought to know the behaviour would have a serious effect

Meanings

Controlling behaviour

A range of acts designed to make a person subordinate and/or dependent by isolating them from sources of support, exploiting their resources and capacities for personal gain, depriving them of the means needed for independence, resistance and escape, and regulating their everyday behaviour.

Coercive behaviour

An act or a pattern of acts of assault, threats, humiliation and intimidation, or other abuse that is used to harm, punish, or frighten the victim.

This definition includes violence that is sometimes described as 'honour'-based violence, female genital mutilation (FGM), and forced marriage (see **4.11**), and it is clear that victims are not confined to one gender or ethnic group.

Personally connected

A and B are 'personally connected' if any of the following applies—

(a) they are, or have been, married to each other;
(b) they are, or have been, civil partners of each other;
(c) they have agreed to marry one another (whether or not the agreement has been terminated);
(d) they have entered into a civil partnership agreement (whether or not the agreement has been terminated);
(e) they are, or have been, in an intimate personal relationship with each other;
(f) they each have, or there has been a time when they each have had, a parental relationship in relation to the same child (see subsection (6A));
(g) they are relatives.

Serious Crime Act 2015, s 76(6)

For the purposes of subsection 6(f), a person has parental responsibility in relation to a child if the person is a parent of the child or the person has parental responsibility for the child.

But A does not commit an offence under this section if at the time of the behaviour in question:

(a) A has responsibility for B, for the purposes of Part 1 of the Children and Young Persons Act 1933 (see s 17 of that Act); (see **2.4.1**) and
(b) B is under 16.

Serious effect

A's behaviour has a 'serious effect' on B if:

(a) it causes B to fear, on at least two occasions, that violence will be used against B; or
(b) it causes B serious alarm or distress which has a substantial adverse effect on B's usual day-to-day activities.

For the purposes of subsection (1)(d), A 'ought to know' that which a reasonable person in possession of the same information would know.

Relative

A relative has the meaning given by s 63(1) of the Family Law Act 1996 which in relation to a person means:

(a) the father, mother, stepfather, stepmother, son, daughter, stepson, stepdaughter, grandmother, grandfather, grandson, or granddaughter of that person or of that person's spouse, former spouse, civil partner, or former civil partner; or

(b) the brother, sister, uncle, aunt, niece, nephew, or first cousin (whether of the full blood or of the half blood or by marriage or civil partnership) of that person or of that person's spouse, former spouse, civil partner, or former civil partner,

and includes, in relation to a person who is cohabiting or has cohabited with another person, any person who would fall within para (a) or (b) if the parties were married to each other or were civil partners of each other.

Civil partnership agreement

This has the meaning given by s 73 of the Civil Partnership Act 2004. It is a relationship between two people of the same sex (civil partners) registered as civil partners under the Act and ends only on death, dissolution, or annulment.

Child

This means a person under the age of 18 years.

Parental responsibility

This has the same meaning as in the Children Act 1989 (see **2.4.1**).

Defence

In proceedings for an offence under this section it is a defence for A to show that—

(a) in engaging in the behaviour in question, A believed that he or she was acting in B's best interests, and
(b) the behaviour was in all the circumstances reasonable.

Serious Crime Act 2015, s 76(8)

Explanatory notes

- The defence in subsection (8) is not available to A in relation to behaviour that causes B to fear that violence will be used against B.
- Any persons or agency investigating offences in relation to controlling or coercive behaviour under s 76 must have regard to the Home Office Guidance, 'Controlling or coercive behaviour: statutory guidance framework'.
- The s 76 offence would not apply where the behaviour in question is perpetrated by a parent, or a person who has parental responsibility, against a child under 16 (subsection (3)). This is because the criminal law, in particular the child cruelty offence in s 1 of the Children and Young Persons Act 1933, already covers such behaviour (see **2.4.1**).

- Abuse may take place through person-to-person contact, or through other methods, including, but not limited to, telephone calls, text, email, social networking sites, or use of GPS tracking devices.
- Section 76A(1) makes it an offence in England and Wales for a person who is a UK national or is habitually resident in England and Wales to engage in behaviour, wholly or partly in a country outside the UK, that would amount to an offence under this section.

Police powers of entry

- PACE, s 17(1)(b)—enter premises for the purpose of arresting a person for an indictable offence (see **1.4.2**).
- PACE, s 17(1)(e)—enter premises for the purpose of saving life or limb or preventing serious damage to property (see **1.4.2**).
- Breach of the peace—enter premises to prevent or deal with a breach of the peace (see **7.3**).

Restraining orders/injunctions

- Consider offences and powers available under the Protection from Harassment Act 1997 in relation to harassment or stalking (see **7.11**). This Act also deals with restraining orders (under s 5) and injunctions (under s 3).
- The victim should be made aware that they have certain rights enforceable in a civil court but should be advised that civil action can be costly and also the consequence of civil action instead of involving the police.
- Victims should be told that if a civil injunction is obtained under s 3 (see **7.11.6**) **with a power of arrest**, then details would be recorded on police computer systems.
- Sections 24 to 30 of the Crime and Security Act 2010 allow a Domestic Violence Protection Notice (DVPN) to be issued by a superintendent (or above) to an alleged domestic abuse perpetrator (P) if they have reasonable grounds to believe the person has threatened or used violence against the victim. If stated in the DVPN under s 25(1)(b), a constable can arrest P if the constable has reasonable grounds for believing that P is in breach of the DVPN. Within forty-eight hours of the DVPN being served, the police must make an application for a Domestic Violence Protection Order (DVPO) to a magistrates' court for the area, at which point the court can remand P for breach of such.
- Section 31(7) of the Domestic Abuse Act 2021 allows the county court to issue a DVPO against an individual involved in any relevant proceedings.
- A DVPN and DVPO could be issued where the victim did not consent and was not willing to attend court; all available material should be considered when making the decision (see *Kerr v Chief Constable of Surrey Police* [2017] EWHC 2936 (Admin)).
- The Domestic Abuse Act 2021 also makes provision in relation to domestic abuse, such as a definition of 'domestic abuse' for the purposes of the Act, the appointment of a Domestic Abuse Commissioner, etc.

Related case

R v Chilvers [2021] EWCA Crim 1311 The conviction for coercive and controlling behaviour was held to be safe where the jury did not have to be unanimous as to which particular kind of controlling or coercive behaviour they were satisfied had been established.

CHAR E&S

Either way

None

Summary: 6/12 months' imprisonment and/or a fine

Indictment: 5 years' imprisonment and/or a fine

Links to alternative subjects and offences

4.4 **Criminal Damage** 193
4.6 **Threats to Destroy or Damage Property** 203
4.8.1 **Intimidation of a witness/juror** 210
4.11 **Forced Marriages** 230
6 **Sexual Offences and Assaults** 275
7.3 **Breach of the Peace** 362
7.6 **Fear or Provocation of Violence** 373
7.7 **Intentional Harassment, Alarm, or Distress** 376
7.8 **Threatening/Abusive Words/Behaviour** 380
7.11 **Harassment/Stalking** 398
7.13 **Anti-Social Behaviour** 435
7.17.2 **Violent entry to premises** 479
Appendix 1 **Human Rights** 839

Chapter 3

Crime: Dishonesty

3.1 Theft

The Theft Act 1968 provides for the offence of theft and other connected offences. Section 1 of the Act provides for the offence of theft, while s 11 covers the offence of removing articles from places open to the public and s 23 concerns advertising rewards for the return of stolen or lost goods.

3.1.1 Theft (general)/theft of scrap metal

Theft is defined by s 1 of the Act, while ss 2 to 6 explain the elements contained within that definition.

Offences

A person is guilty of theft if he dishonestly appropriates property belonging to another with the intention of permanently depriving the other of it; and 'thief' and 'steal' shall be construed accordingly.

Theft Act 1968, s 1(1)

PNLD H2272

Points to prove

- ✓ dishonestly
- ✓ appropriates
- ✓ property
- ✓ belonging to another
- ✓ intention to permanently deprive the other of it

Meanings

Dishonestly

Section 2 defines what will not be considered as 'dishonest'.

A person's appropriation of property, belonging to another is not to be regarded as dishonest:

- if they appropriate the property in the belief that they have in law the right to deprive the other of it, on behalf of themselves or of a third person; or
- if they appropriate the property in the belief that they would have the other's consent if the other knew of the appropriation and the circumstances of it; or
- (except where the property came to them as trustee or personal representative) if they appropriate the property in the belief that the person to whom the property belongs cannot be discovered by taking reasonable steps.

  A person's appropriation of property belonging to another may be dishonest notwithstanding that they are willing to pay for the property.

Appropriates

'Appropriates' is defined in s 3.

- Any assumption by a person of the rights of an owner amounts to an appropriation and this includes, where they have come by the property (innocently or not) without stealing it, any later assumption of a right to it by keeping or dealing with it as owner.
- Where property or a right or interest in property is or purports to be transferred for value to a person acting in good faith, no later assumption by them of rights which they believed themselves to be acquiring shall, by reason of any defect in the transferor's title, amount to theft of the property.

Property

'Property' is defined by s 4.

- Property includes money and all other property (real or personal) including 'things in action' and other intangible property. Unless expressly excluded by s 4, 'property' covers all property even if possession or control of it is prohibited or unlawful (eg drugs).
- Land, or things forming part of it, and taken from it by a person or on their instructions, can only be stolen if:
  - ✦ the person is a trustee or personal representative, or is authorised by power of attorney, as a company liquidator, or in some other way, to sell or dispose of land belonging to somebody else, and they appropriate it or anything forming part of it by dealing with it in breach of the confidence entrusted in them; or
  - ✦ when the person is not in possession of the land, they appropriate anything forming part of it by severing it, causing it to be severed, or after it has been severed; or

  - ✦ when, being in possession of the land under a tenancy, they appropriate all or part of a fixture or structure let for use with that land.
- Mushrooms (and other fungi), flowers, plants (including shrubs and trees), and fruit or foliage from a plant are all capable of being 'property' for the purposes of theft. Picking mushrooms or flowers, fruit, or foliage from plants **growing wild** on land is not theft unless it is done for reward, sale, or other commercial purpose.
- Wild creatures, tamed or untamed, are regarded as property. However, a wild creature which is not tamed or normally kept in captivity (or the carcass of such animal) cannot be stolen unless it has been taken into possession by or on behalf of another, and such possession has not been lost or given up, or it is in the process of being taken into possession.

Belonging to another

'Belonging to another' is defined by s 5.

- Property shall be regarded as belonging to any person having possession or control of it or having in it any proprietary right or interest (not being an equitable interest arising only from an agreement to transfer or grant an interest).
- Where property is subject to a trust, ownership includes any individuals with the right to enforce that trust, and any intention to break it is regarded as intending to deprive a person having such right of the property.
- Where a person receives property from or on account of another and is under an obligation to the other to retain and deal with that property or its proceeds in a particular way, the property or proceeds shall be regarded (as against them) as belonging to the other.
- When a person obtains property because of another's mistake, and they are obliged to repay all or part of it, or its proceeds, or value then, to the extent of that obligation, the property or proceeds are regarded as belonging to the person entitled to restoration. Any intent not to repay shall be regarded accordingly as an intention to deprive that person of the property or proceeds.

Intention to permanently deprive

'Intention to permanently deprive' is defined by s 6.

- Section 6(1): a person appropriating property belonging to another without meaning the other permanently to lose the thing itself is nevertheless to be regarded as having the intention of permanently depriving the other of it if their intention is to treat the thing as their own to dispose of regardless of the other's rights; and a borrowing or lending of it may amount to so treating it if, but only if, the borrowing or lending is for a period and in circumstances making it equivalent to an outright taking or disposal.
- Section 6(2): without prejudice to the generality of subsection (1) above, where a person having possession or control (lawfully or not) of property belonging to another, parts with the property under a

condition as to its return which they may not be able to perform, this (if done for purposes of their own and without the other's authority) amounts to treating the property as their own to dispose of regardless of the other's rights.

Explanatory notes

- It is immaterial whether the appropriation is made with a view to gain or is made for the thief's own benefit.
- 'Things in action' include a cheque drawn to a payee, giving them an action (demand for payment) which they may enforce against the payer. It is, therefore, the property of the payee.
- 'Intangible property' includes patents, applications for patents, copyrights.
- 'Tenancy' means a tenancy for any period and includes a tenancy agreement, but a person who, when a tenancy ends, remains in possession as statutory tenant or otherwise will be treated as having possession under the tenancy.
- Possession, in general terms, means having the right to use property as your own without having any legal title to it (eg hiring a car—you have possession while legal ownership remains with the hire company).
- Possession may be 'actual' (an item in your hand or pocket) or 'constructive' (an item at your home while you are elsewhere).
- Control means having the power to use or manage items without having legal title to them (eg a delivery service having control of letters and packages for delivery—it does not actually own any of them and may not even have 'possession' at all times).
- Proprietary right or interest means ownership or having legal title to property or similar rights.
- An obligation to make restoration of property belonging to another must be a legal obligation, not a moral or social one.
- Simple and genuine borrowing of property is insufficient to constitute theft because the necessary 'mens rea' is missing, unless the person intends to return the property in such a state that it loses its value or goodness (eg exam papers borrowed for copying would not be 'stolen' as they have not lessened in their intrinsic value).
- The theft or attempted theft of mail bags or postal packages, or their contents, whilst in transit between British postal areas is, even if it happens outside England and Wales, triable in England and Wales.

Related cases

R v Barton and another [2020] EWCA Crim 575 In this case, the Court of Appeal confirmed that the test for dishonesty set out by the Supreme Court in *Ivey v Genting Casinos* was binding in criminal proceedings; and that, accordingly, a question of dishonesty should be decided by asking (i) what was the defendant's actual state of knowledge or belief as to the facts and (ii) whether, in the light of the defendant's state of knowledge or belief as to the facts, their conduct was dishonest by the standards of ordinary decent people.

Ivey v Genting Casinos (UK) Ltd (trading as Crockfords) [2017] UKSC 67 Where dishonesty is in question but s 2 of the Theft Act is of no assistance (s 2 will not cater for every circumstance), the magistrates/jury will first have to ascertain the actual state of the individual's knowledge or belief as to the facts (this does not have to be a reasonable belief—the question is whether the belief is genuinely held). Once their actual state of mind as to knowledge or belief is established, the question of whether their conduct was honest or dishonest was to be determined by the magistrates/jury by applying the (objective) standards of ordinary decent people. There is no requirement that the defendant had to appreciate that what they had done was, by those standards, dishonest. Taking this approach means that, to prove dishonesty, a prosecutor need only place before a court the facts of what the defendant did and thought and then invite the court to hold that they were dishonest according to the standards of ordinary decent people. This means that the subjective element of the test outlined in *R v Ghosh* [1982] 2 All ER 689 (specifically the second element of the test outlined by the case) can no longer be considered an accurate representation of the law on dishonesty.

R v Hayes [2015] EWCA Crim 1944 The defendant was charged with conspiracy to defraud by manipulating financial trade markets but the defence was that H had not acted dishonestly and what they had done was common practice and had been encouraged by managers. The conviction was upheld, and the court reaffirmed that that conduct should be tested by the standards of the first **objective** limb of *R v Ghosh* [1982] 2 All ER 689); ie by the ordinary standards of the honest and reasonable person and **not** by the standards of a particular market.

R v Smith and others [2011] EWCA Crim 66 It was held in this case that unless expressly excluded by s 4, 'property' covers all property even if possession or control of it is prohibited or unlawful (eg drugs).

R (on the application of Ricketts) v Basildon MC [2010] EWHC 2358 (Admin) Taking bags of donated items left outside a charity shop or from its waste bins was still theft.

R v Hinks [2000] 4 All ER 833, HL In this case, the defendant influenced, coerced, or encouraged the complainant who was naive, gullible, and of limited intelligence to hand over large sums of money. It was held that receiving a valid gift is appropriation. If the circumstances surrounding the acceptance of the property would be considered dishonest (by a reasonable person), then that conduct becomes theft.

R v Ngan [1998] 1 Cr App R 331 Appropriation must take place in England and Wales.

Practical considerations

- Consider stop, search, and seizure powers under s 1 of PACE (see **1.3**).

- All five of the elements contained within the theft definition must be proved to obtain a conviction.
- In the absence of a reliable admission of dishonesty, this evidence will have to be proved by other evidence such as: Where was the property found? Had it been hidden? What were the subsequent actions of the defendant?
- Other matters that should be addressed include:
  - Evidence of who owns the property and/or that the defendant does not.
  - Does the offender have any claim on the property?
  - Does the offender own any similar property/have the means to have paid for it?
  - Any attempts to alter the property or change its appearance.
  - Proof that only some of the property was stolen is sufficient for a conviction.
  - The current location of the property.
  - The value of the property stolen/recovered.
- The fact that a man and woman are married or are civil partners does not preclude one from stealing property belonging to the other.
  - A person is not exempt from answering questions in recovery proceedings on the grounds that to do so would incriminate them or their spouse or civil partner.
  - However, a statement or confession made in recovery proceedings is not admissible in proceedings for an offence under this Act as evidence against them or their spouse or civil partner.
- PACE Code E Annex A, para 2.4(c)(iii) provides exemption from the requirement to audio record interviews that are undertaken elsewhere than at a police station for certain indictable offences that include where a person has been cautioned for retail theft (shoplifting) contrary to s 1. This exemption is subject to a number of conditions, but the suspect must appear to be aged 18 years or over, and does not require an appropriate adult; the value of the property must not exceed £100 inclusive of VAT; the stolen property has been recovered and is fit for sale, and the suspect is not employed (whether paid or not) by the person, company, or organisation to which the property belongs. (See Code E for full details.)
- An interviewer who is not sure or has any doubt about the suitability of a place or location for carrying out an interview elsewhere than at a police station, should consult an officer of the rank of sergeant or above for advice.
- The above exemption to audio record interviews applies to an attempt to commit the offence under s 1 of the Criminal Attempts Act 1981 (see **4.1.1**).
- Consider issuing a PND for retail/commercial thefts under £100 (see **7.1.1**).
- Consider additional evidence (eg security video, CCTV footage).
- 'Low value' shoplifting (value that does not exceed £200) may be triable only as a summary offence under the Magistrates' Courts Act 1980, s 22A; but, as an either way offence, it is still considered an 'indictable offence' for PACE purposes (see **1.1.5**).

- Multiple charges of theft against a defendant may not be classified as low value where the aggregate value of charges exceeds £200 (*Candlish v DPP* [2022] EWHC 842 (Admin)).

Theft of scrap metal

- The Scrap Metal Dealers Act 2013 was passed in order to curb metal theft from a range of sectors—including the rail network, electric/telecommunication distribution, memorials, and street furniture.
- It is a summary offence under s 1 of the Act for a person to carry on business as a scrap metal dealer unless authorised by a licence under this Act. See PNLD **H10944**
- Section 21 states that a person carries on business as a scrap metal dealer if the person:
  - carries on a business which consists wholly or partly in buying or selling scrap metal, whether or not the metal is sold in the form in which it was bought; or
  - carries on business as a motor salvage operator.
- Scrap metal includes:
  - any old, waste, or discarded metal or metallic material; and
  - any product, article, or assembly which is made from or contains metal and is broken, worn out or regarded by its last holder as having reached the end of its useful life.
- But gold, silver, or alloy which contains by weight 2 per cent or more gold or silver is not scrap metal.
- Section 12(1) of the Act stipulates that a scrap metal dealer must not pay for scrap metal except by 'non-transferable' cheques or by an electronic transfer of funds (authorised by credit or debit card or otherwise). Payment cannot be made by cash or 'paying in kind' (with goods or services).
- Under s 12(4), if scrap metal is paid for in breach of s 12(1), the following commit a summary offence:
  - the scrap metal dealer;
  - the site manager (if payment on site);
  - any person who makes the payment acting for the dealer.

  See PNLD **H11034, H11035, H10959**
- It is a defence for the scrap metal dealer or site manager to prove that they:
  - made arrangements to ensure payment was not in breach of s 12(1); and
  - took all reasonable steps to ensure compliance with those arrangements.
- Section 15(6) makes it a summary offence if comprehensive records of receipt or disposal of scrap metal are not recorded as required by s 13 or s 14 or kept for three years from receipt or disposal. This ensures that the seller/purchaser of the scrap metal can be readily identified. See PNLD **H10966, H10968**
- Under s 16 of the Act, a constable or local authority officer may:
  - enter and inspect a licensed site at any reasonable time on notice to the site manager, but is not entitled to use force to enter the site unless in accordance with a warrant issued by a justice of the peace;

- ✦ require production of and inspect any scrap metal kept on site or records kept under s 13 or s 14 for receipt/disposal of scrap metal; and
- ✦ take copies/extracts from such records.
- It is a summary offence (s 16(13)) if a person: obstructs a right of entry or inspection, or fails to produce a record when so required, under the s 16 powers. See PNLD H10969, H10970

SSS E&S PND CHAR TRIG

Either way None

For offences contrary to ss 1(1) and 7 of the Theft Act 1968

Summary: 6/12 months' imprisonment and/or a fine

Indictment: 7 years' imprisonment and/or a fine

For s 16 of the Scrap Metal Dealers Act 2013

Summary: fine not exceeding level 3

For ss 1, 12, and 15 of the Scrap Metal Dealers Act 2013

Summary: a fine

3.1.2 Removal of articles from places open to the public

Section 11 of the Theft Act 1968 covers the offence of removing articles from places open to the public.

Offences

Subject to subsections (2) and (3) below, where the public have access to a building in order to view the building or part of it, or a collection or part of a collection housed in it, any person who without lawful authority removes from the building or its grounds the whole or part of any article displayed or kept for display to the public in the building or that part of it or in its grounds shall be guilty of an offence.

Theft Act 1968, s 11(1)

PNLD H2253

Points to prove

- ✓ without lawful authority
- ✓ removed from building/grounds of building
- ✓ to which public have access
- ✓ to view building/collection/part thereof
- ✓ the whole/part of article displayed/kept for display to public

Meaning of collection

This includes a collection displayed to the public for a temporary purpose (*R v Durkin* [1973] 2 All ER 872, CA), but references in this section to a collection do not apply to a collection made or exhibited for the sole purpose of effecting sales or other commercial dealings.

Explanatory notes

- Subsection 11(2) states that it is immaterial for the purposes of subsection (1) above, that the public's access to a building is limited to a particular period or particular occasion; but where anything removed from a building or its grounds is there otherwise than as forming part of, or being on loan for exhibition with, a collection intended for permanent exhibition to the public, the person removing it does not thereby commit an offence under this section unless they remove it on a day when the public have access to the building as mentioned in subsection (1) above.
- Access to grounds alone is insufficient. The public must have access to a building to view it, part of it, or a collection or part of it housed therein.
- Payment for the privilege of viewing the collection is irrelevant, as is whether such payment merely covers expenses or makes a profit.
- Articles displayed are not confined to works of art, the test being that the article, which may be priceless or valueless, is displayed or kept for public display.
- Note that this offence does not require any intent to permanently deprive the owner of the article taken.

Defences

A person does not commit an offence under this section if he believes that he has lawful authority for the removal of the thing in question or that he would have it if the person entitled to give it knew of the removal and the circumstances of it.

Theft Act 1968, s 11(3)

Defence notes

The burden is on the prosecution to prove the absence of genuine belief on the part of the defendant.

Practical considerations

- Ascertain the dates on which the building/articles is/are on display.
- Public access to a building for other purposes (eg a shopping mall) when a collection is displayed as an incidental to the main purpose of access (shopping) is unlikely to fall into this section. However, if the collection was displayed in a separate part of the building with access given purely to view it, it would fall into this section.

- Removal need not be during the times the public have access. It can occur even when the buildings/grounds are closed. However, per s 11(2), if the display is temporary, removal must take place on a day when the public have access to the buildings/grounds in order to view.
- Does the defendant have any claim on the property?
- Current location of the article(s).
- Value of property taken/recovered.
- Obtain CJA witness statements.
- Consider additional evidence (eg security video, CCTV footage).

E&S

Either way None

Summary: 6/12 months' imprisonment and/or a fine

Indictment: 5 years' imprisonment and/or a fine

Links to alternative subjects and offences

4.1 **Criminal Attempts** 173
4.2 **Vehicle Interference** 182
4.3 **Taking a Conveyance without Owner's Consent** 185
7.1 **Penalty Notices for Disorder** 351

3.2 Robbery

The Theft Act 1968 provides for the offence of theft and other connected offences. Section 8 provides for the offences of robbery and assault with intent to rob.

3.2.1 Robbery

Offences

A person is guilty of robbery if he steals, and immediately before or at the time of doing so, and in order to do so, he uses force on any person or puts or seeks to put any person in fear of being then and there subjected to force.

Theft Act 1968, s 8(1)

PNLD H432

Points to prove

- ✓ stole property
- ✓ immediately before/at the time of doing so
- ✓ and in order to do so
- ✓ used force on a person or put/sought to put person in fear of immediate force

Meanings

Steals (see **3.1.1**)

Force

Means the ordinary meaning and whether force has been used is a matter for the court to decide.

Explanatory notes

- The offence of theft must be proved before robbery can be substantiated.
- Force or the threat of force must be used immediately before or at the time of the theft. If, at the end of an assault, the offender, as an afterthought, decides to take their victim's wallet, that is not a robbery, it is separate offences of assault and theft.
- The use of force, or threat of force, must be to enable a theft.
- If the offence is carried out by a number of assailants, but only one uses violence towards the victim, the others cannot be held

responsible for the violence unless a prior agreement between them to use that degree of violence in order to achieve their objective is shown.
- It is not necessary to prove that the victim was actually put in fear, it is sufficient to prove that the offender sought to put them in fear (*R v DPP, B v DPP* [2007] EWHC 739 (Admin)).
- If a person, while stealing or attempting to steal mailbags or postal packages, or their contents, whilst in transit between British postal areas, commits robbery or attempted robbery, the offence is triable in England and Wales, even if it is committed outside England and Wales.

Defences

If an honest belief that a legal claim of right to the property exists (*R v Robinson* [1977] Crim LR 173).

Related case

R v Clouden [1987] Crim LR 56, CA 'Force' should be given its ordinary meaning. Very little force is required and a push or nudge to put the victim off balance to enable a theft to take place can be sufficient.

Practical considerations

- Ownership and value of any property stolen/recovered.
- The fear of being subjected to force must be genuine and can be proved in the victim's statement (although it is the defendant's intention to cause fear that is the key element). It is not necessary to prove somebody was put in fear, simply that the accused sought to put someone in fear of immediate force.
- Specific words used by the defendant will be critical.
- The use of force after the theft is complete is not robbery. However, 'appropriation' is a continuing process at all material times and robbery was committed where force was used to make an escape after a theft had occurred (*R v Hale* (1978) 68 Cr App R 415).
- A threat of force can also be implied if the victim believes that force will be used against them and therefore allows the theft to take place.
- An assault committed as an afterthought following a theft is not robbery, but it is assault and theft.
- Consider blackmail under s 21 of the Act (see **3.2.2**) when the threats are for force to be used on a future occasion.
- Any additional evidence (eg security video, CCTV footage).

SSS E&S CHAR TRIG

Indictable

None

Life imprisonment

3.2.2 Blackmail

Section 21 of the Theft Act 1968 deals with the offence of blackmail.

Offences

A person is guilty of blackmail if, with a view to gain for himself or another or with intent to cause loss to another, he makes any unwarranted demand with menaces; and for this purpose, a demand with menaces is unwarranted unless the person making it does so in the belief—
(a) that he has reasonable grounds for making the demands; and
(b) that the use of the menaces is a proper means of reinforcing the demands.

Theft Act 1968, s 21(1)

PNLD H444

Points to prove

✓ with view to gain for self/another or intent to cause loss to another
✓ made unwarranted demand with menaces

Meanings

Intent (see **4.1.2**)

Menaces

The ordinary meaning of menaces applies (eg threats).

Explanatory notes

- The nature of the act or omission demanded is immaterial.
- It is also immaterial whether the menaces relate to action to be taken by the person making the demand or a third party.
- The words 'with a view to gain' and 'with intent to cause loss' are alternative, separate, and distinct phrases.
- The gain can be either to the person making the threats or to a third party and likewise the loss can be by the third party. The offence is not confined to successfully obtaining physical possession of property by menaces, a demand is sufficient.
- Where a demand is made outside England and Wales to somebody inside the territory, the courts will have jurisdiction to try the offence pursuant to the Criminal Justice Act 1993 (*R v Pogmore* [2017] EWCA Crim 925).

Defences

In the belief that:

- they had reasonable grounds for making the demands; and
- the use of the menaces is a proper means of reinforcing the demands.

Defence notes

- Belief in both s 21(a) and (b) must be present for this defence. If only one is present, the offence of blackmail will still be made out.
- The onus is on the defendant to prove the belief, but the prosecution must cover this defence in interview or by other means to negate it.

Related case

R v Clear [1968] 52 Cr App R 58 The test to be applied to the meaning of 'menaces' is: it is immaterial whether the person threatened is actually frightened; and menaces must be words or conduct such as are likely to operate on the mind of the person of ordinary courage and firmness so as to make them accede unwillingly to the demand.

Practical considerations

- The menaces do not need to relate to action to be taken by the person making the demand.
- The offence does not include demanding sexual favours (which would almost certainly be attempted rape or a similar offence under the Sexual Offences Act 2003 (see **6.1**) as there could be no true consent). In some circumstances, the offence may include demanding sexual favours, such as a demand for a sexually explicit photograph, as a photograph would amount to property for the purpose of this offence.
- Cover the defence in interview or other means in order to negate it.
- If the evidence for 'gain' or 'loss' is vague, consider s 1 of the Malicious Communications Act 1988 (see **7.12**).
- Identify any evidence of contact/threats made to the complainant by the defendant (eg notes, letters, telephone, or social media).
- Consider confiscation of cash and property as this blackmail offence is listed as a 'criminal lifestyle' offence under Sch 2 to the Proceeds of Crime Act 2002 (see **5.5** for details).

E&S

Indictable | None

14 years' imprisonment

Links to alternative subjects and offences

2.1 Assault (Common/Actual Bodily Harm) 53
2.3 Wounding/Grievous Bodily Harm 79
2.5 Threats to Kill 97
4.1 Criminal Attempts 173
5.5 Proceeds of Crime 270

3.3 Burglary/Aggravated Burglary

Section 9 of the Theft Act 1968 creates the offence of burglary and s 10 aggravated burglary.

3.3.1 Burglary

Offences

(1) A person is guilty of burglary if—

(a) he enters any building or part of a building as a trespasser and with intent to commit any such offence as is mentioned in subsection (2) below; or

(b) having entered any building or part of a building as a trespasser he steals or attempts to steal anything in the building or that part of it or inflicts or attempts to inflict on any person therein any grievous bodily harm.

(2) The offences referred to in subsection (1)(a) above are offences of stealing anything in the building or part of a building in question, of inflicting on any person therein any grievous bodily harm or of doing unlawful damage to the building or anything therein.

Theft Act 1968, s 9

PNLD H2044, H2046

Points to prove

✓ entered a building/part of a building
✓ as a trespasser
✓ with intent
✓ to steal property therein/inflict grievous bodily harm on person therein/do unlawful damage to the building or anything therein

OR

✓ having entered a building/part of a building
✓ as a trespasser
✓ stole or attempted to steal anything therein/inflicted or attempted to inflict grievous bodily harm on any person therein

Meanings

Building

'Building' includes an outhouse, a shed, an inhabited vehicle, or a vessel irrespective of whether the resident is there or not.

Trespasser

Trespass means to pass over a limit or boundary or to enter another's building or land without permission. An offender must either know or be reckless as to whether they are a trespasser. Entry gained by fraud is still trespass.

Intent (see **4.1.2**)

Steal (see **3.1**)

Grievous bodily harm (see **2.3.1**)

Unlawful damage (see **4.4**)

Explanatory notes

- There does not have to be a forced entry into the building, merely proof that the person has entered as a trespasser.
- Entry into a building may be an actual physical entry, by use of an instrument (eg a hook on a stick through an open window) or by an innocent agent (eg a child under 10 years old). The term 'enter' does not require the whole of the person's body to be within the building (*R v Brown* [1985] Crim LR 212, CA).
- The offence does not differentiate between different types of building—but the punishment does.
- A person who has entered one part of a building legally and then enters into another part of the same building as a trespasser falls within this section.
- In s 9(1)(a), the original intention need not be completed—it is sufficient that the intention existed at the time of entry.
- In s 9(1)(b), no specific intention is required at the time of entry as the intruder commits one of the acts having entered as a trespasser.

Related cases

Hudson v CPS [2017] EWHC 841 (Admin) The defendants were charged with burglary contrary to s 9 having entered a fully furnished rental property with utilities connected but at the time there were no tenants. The court held that although vacated and not occupied, the property was still a dwelling ready for use as a home and the offence was complete. Deciding whether premises are a dwelling for the purpose of burglary is essentially a matter of fact and degree in each case.

R v Chipunza [2021] EWCA Crim 597 The defendant was charged with burglary of a hotel room. The issue in the case was whether the hotel room was a dwelling, an issue that makes a difference to the sentence that can be imposed (s 9(3) and (4)). The court held that this was a question of fact to be decided by the jury (and not the judge) but with a suitable direction from the judge as to the characteristics of a dwelling, such as that it is a place where people live, usually not transiently.

Practical considerations

- Consider stop, search, and seizure powers under s 1 of PACE (see **1.3**).
- Ensure a degree of entry into the building can be proved; otherwise consider other offences relevant to the circumstances.
- If satisfied the offender entered the building, gather evidence as to right to be there—CJA witness statements.
- A building may include structures made of wood, steel, or plastic, but it would not include a tent (inhabited or not), articulated trailer (on wheels), open-sided bus shelter, or carport.
- A static caravan permanently connected to mains water, sewers, and gas/electricity would probably be a building even when it was not occupied.
- A touring caravan parked in the driveway of a house is a vehicle. However, if it was no longer used for touring, and instead used for storage as a garden shed, it may well then be a building.
- A person who enters a shop legally and then goes into a private store room may be a trespasser.
- A person who legally enters premises and later becomes a trespasser due to hostilities by them does not become a trespasser for burglary. They must have been a trespasser at the time of entry into that part of the building.
- A person acting as a lookout should be treated as a joint principal.
- Is there any other evidence available (eg security video, CCTV)?
- If any person in the dwelling was subjected to violence (or threat) then the case is triable on indictment only.
- If the defendant had a firearm/imitation firearm with them, then consider also s 17(2) of the Firearms Act 1968 (see **8.3.5**).

SSS E&S CHAR TRIG

Either way

None

Summary: 6/12 months' imprisonment and/or a fine

Indictment: 10 years' imprisonment (dwelling—14 years' imprisonment)

3.3.2 Aggravated burglary

Section 10 of the Theft Act 1968 creates the offence of aggravated burglary, where the trespasser has with them, at the time of committing the burglary, one or more of the articles specified in s 10(1).

3.3.2 **Aggravated burglary**

Offences

A person is guilty of aggravated burglary if he commits any burglary and at the time has with him any firearm or imitation firearm, any weapon of offence, or any explosive.

Theft Act 1968, s 10

PNLD H2045, H2178, H2179

Points to prove

- ✓ committed burglary
- ✓ had with them at the time
- ✓ a firearm/imitation firearm/weapon of offence/explosive

Meanings

Burglary (see **3.3.1**)

Has with him

This phrase has a narrower meaning than 'possession' (see **8.3.6**).

Firearm (see **8.1.1**)
Includes an air gun or air pistol (see **8.7.2**).

Imitation firearm

Anything which has the appearance of being a firearm, whether capable of being discharged or not.

Weapon of offence

Any article made or adapted for use for causing injury to or incapacitating a person or intended by the person having it with them for such use.

Explosive

Means any article manufactured for the purpose of producing a practical effect by explosion or intended by the person having it with them for that purpose.

Related cases

R v Daubney (2000) 164 JP 519, CA Defendant must know that they had the article with them.

R v Klass [1998] 1 Cr App R 453 Entry into a building with a weapon is an essential element of this offence. Therefore, if there is only one weapon and it is with an accomplice who remains outside the building, neither of the offenders would commit aggravated burglary.

R v Kelly (1993) 97 Cr App R 245 A burglar who used a screwdriver to break into premises then, when challenged by the occupants, used that same screwdriver to threaten them, was held to have a weapon of offence with them at the time.

Practical considerations

- Was the burglary committed under s 9(1)(a) or (b)? This affects the point in time at which the offence occurred.
- If there is more than one offender, is there evidence that somebody entered the building with the weapon? If not, charge with burglary or the relevant offence.
- What reason did the offender have for possessing the article?
- Where it is unclear whether the offender had the article with them at the relevant time, charge them with burglary and charge possession of the article separately.
- The offence may be committed where the offender takes possession of an article in one part of a building and then enters another part of the building with it.
- Obtain evidence of ownership and right of entry into building.
- Is there any other evidence (eg security video, CCTV footage)?

SSS E&S CHAR TRIG

Indictable

None

Life imprisonment

Links to alternative subjects and offences

2.1.2 **Assault occasioning actual bodily harm** 56
2.3 **Wounding/Grievous Bodily Harm** 79
2.5 **Threats to Kill** 97
4.1 **Criminal Attempts** 173
4.5 **Damage with Intent to Endanger Life and Arson** 198
8.1 **'Section 1 Firearms' Offences** 507
8.2 **Shotgun Offences** 520
8.3 **Criminal Use of Firearms** 525
8.4 **Trespassing with Firearms** 537
8.5 **Possess Firearm or Imitation Firearm in a Public Place** 541

3.4 Dishonestly Abstracting Electricity

Section 13 of the Theft Act 1968 contains the offence of dishonestly abstracting electricity.

Offences

A person who dishonestly uses without due authority, or dishonestly causes to be wasted or diverted, any electricity commits an offence.

Theft Act 1968, s 13

PNLD H438

Points to prove

✓ dishonestly
✓ used without due authority or caused to be wasted/diverted
✓ electricity

Meanings

Dishonestly

This means a state of mind as opposed to conduct. See **3.1.1**.

Uses

Consumption of electricity that would not have occurred without an action by the accused.

Without due authority

Means without the proper authorisation.

Explanatory notes

- This section is made necessary by the fact that electricity does not fit into the definition of property under s 4 for theft (see **3.1.1**) and, therefore, it cannot be stolen. This also means that entering a building and abstracting electricity (or intending to) will not be burglary.
- Employees using their employer's electrically powered machinery for their own use would commit an offence under this section.
- It is not necessary for anybody to benefit from the wasted or diverted electricity. A person who, out of spite, switches on an electrical appliance before leaving a building would commit this offence.

Related case

R v McCreadie and Tume [1992] Cr App Rep 143 In this case, squatters were charged with abstracting electricity, but they argued that they had not tampered with the meter. It was held that it is sufficient for the prosecution to show that electricity was used without the authority of the electricity authority and that there was no intention to pay for it.

Practical considerations

- Obtain evidence of dishonest use, waste, or diversion of electricity (eg note the state of the meter, cash box missing).
- The person using the electricity does not have to be the person who reconnects the supply (eg a person using electricity with no intention to pay for it after a disconnected supply has been unlawfully reconnected by a third person would commit this offence).
- Check for sign of break-in to the premises, which may negate or support the story of the householder.
- Utilities bill may assist to prove diversion to bypass the meter.
- There is no requirement for the electricity to be supplied through the mains (eg it may be supplied from a car battery). Thus a person who takes a pedestrian-controlled electric vehicle which is not classed as a conveyance (see **4.3.1**) may commit this offence.
- Obtain CJA witness statement from electricity supplier.

E&S

Either way | None

Summary: 6/12 months' imprisonment and/or a fine

Indictment: 5 years' imprisonment

3.5 Handling Stolen Goods

Section 22 of the Theft Act 1968 creates various combinations of offences of handling stolen goods knowing or believing them to be stolen.

Offences

A person handles stolen goods if (otherwise than in the course of the stealing) knowing or believing them to be stolen goods he dishonestly receives the goods, or dishonestly undertakes or assists in their retention, removal, disposal or realisation by or for the benefit of another person, or he arranges to do so.

Theft Act 1968, s 22(1)

PNLD **H2137, H445**

Points to prove

✓ otherwise than in the course of stealing
✓ knowing/believing goods to be stolen
✓ dishonestly received them or
✓ dishonestly undertook/assisted
✓ in the retention/removal/disposal/realisation of them

OR

✓ arranged to do so
✓ by/for the benefit of another

Meanings

Stolen goods (s 24(2))

References to stolen goods shall include—**in addition** to the **goods** originally stolen and parts of them (whether in their original state or not)—**any other goods** which directly or indirectly represent or have at any time represented the stolen goods in the hands of the thief or handler of the goods (or any part of them) as being the proceeds of any disposal or realisation of the whole or part of the goods stolen or stolen goods handled by them of goods so representing the stolen goods.

Goods

Includes money and every other description of property except land, and includes things severed from the land by stealing (see **3.1.1**).

Knowing

Means actually having been told by somebody having first-hand knowledge (eg the thief or burglar) that the goods had been stolen (*R v Hall* (1985) 81 Cr App R 260).

Believing

Means the state of mind of a person who cannot be certain that goods are stolen, but where the circumstances indicate no other reasonable conclusion (*R v Elizabeth Forsyth* [1997] 2 Cr App R 299).

Dishonestly (see **3.1.1**)

Receives

Means gaining **possession** or control of the goods.

Possession

Means either actual physical possession or constructive possession (storing the goods in premises belonging to them).

Undertakes

Includes where the person agrees to perform the act(s) that constitute the offence.

Retention

Means keeping possession of, not losing, continuing to have (*R v Pitchley* [1972] Crim LR 705, CA).

Realisation

Means the conversion of the goods, invariably into money (*R v Deakin* [1972] Crim LR 781, CA).

Arranges to do so

Means arranging to receive, retain, remove, dispose, or convert the stolen goods. This can be done without seeing or having had anything to do with the goods.

Explanatory notes

- Where a person is being proceeded against for handling stolen goods only, s 27(3)(a) provides for '**special evidence**' (eg their previous dealings with stolen goods within the twelve months prior to the current incident) to be introduced into the proceedings. No charge or conviction regarding the previous incident is necessary.
- Similarly, s 27(3)(b) allows the introduction of evidence of a previous conviction for theft or handling within five years of the present incident. In this case, a notice must be served on the defence seven days prior to use of the evidence in court.
- Where the only evidence on a charge of handling stolen goods is circumstantial in that an accused person is in possession of property recently stolen (doctrine of recent possession), a court may infer guilty knowledge if: (a) the accused offers no explanation to account for their possession, or (b) the court is satisfied that the explanation they offer is untrue.

- Any benefit to the receiver is irrelevant.
- Someone who handles stolen goods, whilst having no knowledge or reason to believe them to be stolen, will not commit this offence.
- Actions taken for the benefit of another are only relevant in the offence of handling stolen goods—they have no significance in relation to the receiving of such goods.

Related cases

R v Bloxham (1982) 74 Cr App R 279, HL A person who innocently buys goods for value and later discovers they were, in fact, stolen goods cannot commit the offence of assisting in their disposal by selling them, as they benefited from their purchase not their sale.

R v Figures [1976] Crim LR 744 The defendant was found at Southampton to have in his possession goods that had been stolen in France. F admitted receiving them and paying for them in France knowing them to be stolen. F was charged with handling by assisting in their retention in England. The court dismissed the case and held that handling of goods stolen abroad is only an offence in England when the handling takes place in England. In this case, the offence was complete in France when the goods were received and paid for.

Practical considerations

- Under s 24(3), **goods** are **not regarded** as **still being stolen** goods after return to the person from whom stolen or to other lawful possession or custody, or after that person and any other person having a claim to them ceases, as regards those goods, to have any right to restitution regarding the theft.
- Ownership of the goods and evidence of theft must be established.
- Check for any evidence of previous dealings with stolen goods within the previous twelve months.
- Check previous convictions for theft or handling within the previous five years.
- Check for communications between the handler, the thief, or any potential buyers or distributors.
- Check for evidence of removal or alteration of identifying features.
- Obtain evidence of the true value of the goods.
- If the facts fit both theft and handling stolen goods, use the relevant alternative charges and let the court decide which offence, if any, is committed.
- Several people may be charged on one indictment, concerning the same theft, with handling all or some of the goods at the same or various times, and all such persons may be tried together. This does not apply to a summary trial.

SSS E&S CHAR TRIG

Either way None

Summary: 6/12 months' imprisonment and/or a fine

Indictment: 14 years' imprisonment

3.6 **Going Equipped**

The Theft Act 1968 provides for several other key offences of which theft is a constituent part. Section 25 creates the offences of going equipped for any burglary or theft.

> **Offences**
>
> A person shall be guilty of an offence if, when not at his place of abode, he has with him any article for use in the course of or in connection with any burglary or theft.
>
> Theft Act 1968, s 25(1)

PNLD **H421, H428, H429, H420**

> **Points to prove**
>
> ✓ not at place of abode
> ✓ had with them
> ✓ article(s) for use in course of/in connection with
> ✓ a burglary/theft

Meanings

Place of abode

This normally means the place or site where someone lives. Using its natural meaning, it normally includes the garage and garden of a house, but it is ultimately a matter for the court or jury to decide.

Has with him

This phrase has a narrower meaning than 'possession' (see **8.3.6**).

Article

This has a wide meaning. It may include a whole range of items and substances, from treacle and paper to assist in breaking a window quietly, a car jack for spreading bars, or pieces of spark plug ceramic for breaking car windows.

Burglary (see **3.3.1**)

Theft (see **3.1.1**)

Includes taking a conveyance without owner's consent (see **4.3.1**).

Explanatory notes

- Where a person is charged with an offence under this section, proof that they had with them any article made or adapted for use in

committing a burglary or theft shall be evidence that they had it with them for such use.
- It is not necessary to prove that the person found with the article intended to use it themselves—intended use by another will suffice.

Practical considerations

- What articles were with or available to the defendant?
- Where were the articles?
- What were their possible/intended uses?
- Did the defendant have a lawful purpose for having the article(s) in their possession at that particular time/place?
- Has the defendant used such articles in committing the offence previously?
- This offence caters for some preparatory acts prior to the commission of one or more of the specified acts.
- This offence can only be committed before the intended burglary or theft, not afterwards.
- Possession of the article(s) after arrest is not sufficient for this offence.
- When two or more people are acting in concert, the possession of housebreaking implements by one of them would be deemed to be possession by all of them.
- A person who has a relevant article with them but has not yet decided whether to use the article, does not have the necessary intent to commit the offence.
- Taking a conveyance without the owner's consent is, for the purposes of this section, to be treated as theft.

SSS E&S CHAR TRIG

Either way | None

Summary: 6/12 months' imprisonment and/or a fine

Indictment: 3 years' imprisonment

Links to alternative subjects and offences

4.1 **Criminal Attempts** 173
4.3 **Taking Conveyance without Owner's Consent** 185

3.7 Making off without Payment

Section 3 of the Theft Act 1978 creates the offence of making off without payment (also known as 'bilking').

Offences

Subject to subsection (3) below, a person who, knowing that payment on the spot for any goods supplied or service done is required or expected from him, dishonestly, makes off without having paid as required or expected and with intent to avoid payment of the amount due shall be guilty of an offence.

Theft Act 1978, s 3(1)

PNLD H460

Points to prove

- ✓ knowing a payment on the spot required/expected
- ✓ for goods supplied/service done
- ✓ dishonestly
- ✓ made off
- ✓ without having paid as required/expected
- ✓ with intent to avoid payment of amount due

Meanings

Payment on the spot

This includes payment at the time of collecting goods on which work has been done or in respect of which service has been provided. It can be commonly accepted practice, such as paying for a meal at a restaurant after it has been eaten.

Goods (see **3.5**)

Dishonestly (see **3.1.1**)

Intent (see **4.1.2**)

Explanatory notes

- The term **'goods supplied or service done'** will include making off without payment for fuel at a self-service petrol station, meals at restaurants, or hotel accommodation/services where the charge is levied after supplying the goods/service.
- If a motorist forgets to pay for petrol and drives off, but later remembers that they have not paid, and then returns to the filling

station to pay, they may not commit the offence due to lacking the necessary intent.
- Where there is an agreement to defer payment, any such agreement would normally eliminate the expectation of payment on the spot.

Defences

Subsection (1) above shall not apply where the supply of the goods or the doing of the service is contrary to law, or where the service done is such that payment is not legally enforceable.

Theft Act 1978, s 3(3)

Defence notes

A payment not being legally enforceable may be where the service provider breaks a contract (eg a taxi driver who fails to complete a journey) or where the contract cannot be enforced through the courts.

Related cases

R v Vincent [2001] Crim LR 488 Employing deceit which causes a victim to defer payment and then making off is not a 'dishonest making off' which is the key to this offence.

R v Brooks and Brooks (1983) 76 Cr App R 66 The words 'dishonestly makes off' were to be given their natural meaning (a departure from the spot where payment is required) and it was a matter of fact on which the jury could decide.

Practical considerations

- What goods or services have been provided?
- The goods or services provided must be specified in the charge.
- It is important to prove that the person knew that 'payment on the spot' was required.
- Did the accused have money or means with which to pay the bill?
- Is the payment legally enforceable?
- There must be an intention to avoid payment completely and not merely intent to defer or delay it.
- Is there any further evidence (eg CCTV footage)?

SSS CHAR

Either way None

Summary: 6/12 months' imprisonment and/or a fine

Indictment: 2 years' imprisonment

3.8 Fraud Offences

The Fraud Act 2006, ss 1 to 4 detail the three different ways of committing fraud: s 12 the liability of company officers, s 13 evidential matters relating to fraud, and ss 6 and 7 possess/make articles for use in fraud.

3.8.1 Fraud offence

Section 1 creates the general offence of fraud and ss 2 to 4 detail three different ways of committing fraud, namely by false representation, failing to disclose information, or by abuse of position.

Offences

(1) A person is guilty of fraud if he is in breach of any of the sections listed in subsection (2) (which provide for different ways of committing the offence).

(2) The sections are—
   (a) section 2 (fraud by false representation),
   (b) section 3 (fraud by failing to disclose information), and
   (c) section 4 (fraud by abuse of position).

Fraud Act 2006, s 1

PNLD **H8685, H8686, H8687**

Points to prove

False representation

✓ dishonestly made a false representation
✓ intending to make a gain for yourself/another or
✓ intending to cause loss to another/expose another to a risk of loss

Failing to disclose information

✓ dishonestly failed to disclose to another
✓ information which you were under a legal duty to disclose
✓ intending, by that failure
✓ to make a gain for yourself/another OR
✓ to cause loss to another/expose another to a risk of loss

Fraud by abuse of position

✓ occupying a position in which you were expected
✓ to safeguard, or not to act against, the financial interests of another
✓ dishonestly abused that position
✓ intending to make a gain for yourself/another OR
✓ intending to cause loss to another/expose another to a risk of loss

Meanings

Fraud by false representation (see **3.8.2**)

Fraud by failing to disclose information (see **3.8.3**)

Fraud by abuse of position (see **3.8.4**)

Gain and loss

(1) The references to gain and loss in sections 2 to 4 are to be read in accordance with this section.
(2) 'Gain' and 'loss'—
  (a) extend only to gain or loss in money or other property;
  (b) include any such gain or loss whether temporary or permanent; and 'property' means any property whether real or personal (including things in action and other intangible property).
(3) 'Gain' includes a gain by keeping what one has, as well as a gain by getting what one does not have.
(4) 'Loss' includes a loss by not getting what one might get, as well as a loss by parting with what one has.

Fraud Act 2006, s 5

Dishonestly (see **3.1.1**)

Intention (see **4.1.2**)

Explanatory notes

- All three fraud offences require an intention to make a gain for oneself or another or cause loss to another/expose another to a risk of loss.
- Similarly, intention must be proved (see **4.1.2**).
- Property covers all forms of property, including intellectual property, although in practice this is rarely 'gained' or 'lost'.
- Section 13 deals with evidential matters under this Act, conspiracy to defraud, or any other offences involving any form of fraudulent conduct or purpose (see **3.8.5**).

Related cases

R v Andrewes [2020] EWCA Crim 1055 In this case, the defendant obtained employment on the basis of false representations under s 2 of the Fraud Act 1968 (see **3.8.2**) relating to their qualifications. A confiscation order was made under s 6(5) of the Proceeds of Crime Act 2002 to recover the defendant's financial benefit from the employment over a ten-year period. On appeal, it was held that the order was disproportionate where the defendant had performed the employment competently giving full value for the renumeration received.

Darroux v The Crown [2018] EWCA Crim 1009 Where a person dishonestly completes claim forms and sends them to a service provider who then arranges to make payment to that person's bank account, the offence committed is one under the Fraud Act 2006.

Idrees v DPP [2011] EWHC 624 (Admin) Conviction for fraud was safe where there had been a case to answer when the defendant had allowed someone to impersonate them at a driving theory test, intending thereby to make a personal gain by obtaining a pass certificate for the test.

Either way

None

Summary: 6/12 months' imprisonment and/or a fine

Indictment: 10 years' imprisonment

3.8.2 Meaning of fraud by false representation

Meanings

Fraud by false representation

(1) A person is in breach of this section if he—
  (a) dishonestly makes a false representation, and
  (b) intends, by making the representation—
    (i) to make a **gain** for himself or another, or
    (ii) to cause **loss** to another or to expose another to a risk of loss.
(2) A representation is false if—
  (a) it is untrue or misleading, and
  (b) the person making it knows that it is, or might be, untrue or misleading.
(3) '**Representation**' means any representation as to fact or law, including a representation as to the state of mind of—
  (a) the person making the representation, or
  (b) any other person.
(4) A representation may be express or implied.
(5) For the purposes of this section a representation may be regarded as made if it (or anything implying it) is submitted in any form to any system or device designed to receive, convey or respond to communications (with or without human intervention).

Fraud Act 2006, s 2

Gain and loss (see **3.8.1**)

Dishonestly (see **3.1.1**)

Intention (see **4.1.2**)

Explanatory notes

- The person must make the representation with the intention of making a gain or causing loss or risk of loss to another. The gain or loss does not actually have to take place.
- There is no restriction on the way in which the representation may be expressed. It can be spoken, written (hardcopy or electronically), or communicated on a website or by conduct.
- An example of a representation by conduct is where a person dishonestly uses a credit card to pay for goods. By tendering the card, they are falsely representing that they have the authority to use it for that transaction. It is immaterial whether the retailer accepting the card is deceived by this representation.
- The practice of 'phishing' (eg sending an email purporting to come from a legitimate financial institution in order to obtain credit card and bank account details, so that the 'phisher' can access and fraudulently use those accounts) is another example of false representation.
- Subsection (5) is given in broad terms because it may be difficult to distinguish situations involving modern technology and/or human involvement. It could well be that the only recipient of the false statement is a machine or a piece of software, where a false statement is submitted to a system for dealing with electronic communications and not to a human being (eg postal or messenger systems). Another example of fraud by electronic means can be entering a number into a 'chip and pin' machine.

3.8.3 Meaning of fraud by failing to disclose information

Meanings

Fraud by failing to disclose information

A person is in breach of this section if he—

(a) dishonestly fails to disclose to another person information which he is under a legal duty to disclose, and

(b) intends, by failing to disclose the information—

 (i) to make a **gain** for himself or another, or

 (ii) to cause **loss** to another or to expose another to a risk of loss.

Fraud Act 2006, s 3(1)

Gain and loss (see **3.8.1**)

Dishonestly (see **3.1.1**)

Intention (see **4.1.2**)

Explanatory notes

- A legal duty to disclose information may include duties under both oral and/or written contracts.
- The concept of '**legal duty**' may derive from statute; a transaction that requires good faith (eg contract of insurance); express, or implied terms of a contract; custom of a particular trade/market; or a fiduciary relationship between the parties (eg between agent and principal).
- The failure of a solicitor to share vital information with a client within the context of their work relationship, in order to perpetrate a fraud upon that client, would be covered by this section.
- An example of an offence under this section could be where a person intentionally failed to disclose information relating to their physical condition when making an application for life insurance.

3.8.4 Meaning of fraud by abuse of position

Meanings

Fraud by abuse of position

(1) A person is in breach of this section if he—
  (a) occupies a **position** in which he is expected to safeguard, or not to act against, the financial interests of another person,
  (b) **dishonestly** abuses that position, and
  (c) **intends**, by means of the abuse of that position—
    (i) to make a **gain** for himself or another, or
    (ii) to cause **loss** to another or to expose another to a risk of loss.

(2) A person may be regarded as having **abused** his position even though his conduct consisted of an omission rather than an act.

Fraud Act 2006, s 4

Gain and loss (see **3.8.1**)

Dishonestly (see **3.1.1**)

Intention (see **4.1.2**)

Explanatory notes

- The offence of committing fraud by a person dishonestly abusing their **position** applies in situations where they are in a privileged position, and by virtue of this position are expected to safeguard another's financial interests or not act against those interests.
- The necessary relationship could be between trustee and beneficiary, director and company, professional person and client, agent and principal, employee and employer, or even between partners.

- It may arise otherwise, for example within a family or in the context of voluntary work or in any context where the parties are not at arm's length.
- Generally, this relationship will be recognised by the civil law as importing fiduciary duties. This relationship and the existence of their duty can be ruled upon by the judge or be the subject of directions to the jury.
- The defendant would be guilty of an offence if they abused their privileged position by dishonestly acting against the other's financial interests for their personal gain.
- The term '**abuse**' is not defined because it is intended to cover a wide range of conduct. Furthermore, the offence can be committed by omission as well as by positive action.
- Examples of offences under this section are:
  - ✦ an employee purposely failing to take up the chance of a crucial contract in order that an associate or rival company can take it up instead to the loss of their employer;
  - ✦ a software company employee uses their position to clone software products with the intention of selling the products to others;
  - ✦ where a carer for an elderly or disabled person has access to that person's bank account and abuses their position by transferring funds for their own gain.

3.8.5 Admissible evidence

Evidence

(1) A person is not to be excused from—
  (a) answering any question put to him in proceedings relating to property, or
  (b) complying with any order made in proceedings relating to property,
  on the ground that doing so may incriminate him or his spouse or civil partner of an offence under this Act or a related offence.

(2) But, in proceedings for an offence under this Act or a related offence, a statement or admission made by the person in—
  (a) answering such a question, or
  (b) complying with such an order,
  is not admissible in evidence against him or (unless they married or became civil partners after the making of the statement or admission) his spouse or civil partner.

(3) 'Proceedings relating to property' means any proceedings for—
  (a) the recovery or administration of any property,
  (b) the execution of a trust, or
  (c) an account of any property or dealings with property,

and 'property' means money or other property whether real or personal (including things in action and other intangible property).

(4) 'Related offence' means—
   (a) conspiracy to defraud;
   (b) any other offence involving any form of fraudulent conduct or purpose.

Fraud Act 2006, s 13

Explanatory notes

- This means that during any proceedings relating to property described above a person cannot be excused from answering any question or refusing to comply with any order made in those proceedings on the grounds of incrimination under this Act, conspiracy to defraud, or an offence involving any form of fraudulent conduct or purpose.
- However, any statement or admission made in answering such a question, or complying with such an order, is not admissible in evidence against them or their spouse or civil partner (unless they married or became civil partners after the making of such a statement or admission).
- Although this section is similar to s 31(1) of the Theft Act 1968 where a person/spouse/civil partner is protected from incrimination, while nonetheless being obliged to cooperate with certain civil proceedings relating to property, it goes beyond that section by removing privilege in relation to this Act, conspiracy to defraud, and any other offence involving any form of fraudulent conduct or purpose.
- A civil partnership is a relationship between two people of the same sex ('civil partners') registered as civil partners under the Civil Partnerships Act 2004 and ends only on death, dissolution, or annulment.

Related cases

R v Ames [2023] EWCA Crim 1463 The prosecution's case had been that AM had induced investors to enter into contracts for the purchase of off-plan properties, principally located in the Caribbean, when the true state of affairs concerning them had been such as to expose those investors to loss or a risk of loss. AM was convicted of two counts of fraud under s 4. It was held inter alia that it could not have been sensibly argued that AM had not intended to cause loss, and both the intention to make a gain and cause loss or expose investors to loss had been inherent in the very structure of AM's scheme. Further, as a matter of law, the two intentions specified in s 4(1)(c)(i) and (ii)—to make a gain etc or to cause a loss etc—were not separate ingredients that ordinarily required separate consideration by a jury but, rather, a single ingredient, namely, intention (by means of dishonest abuse of position) to cause financial gain or loss (or exposure to risk of loss), in other words, to have a financial impact; and whether the financial impact intended is gain, loss, or both, does not matter. (Separate consideration of those ingredients may, however, be required in rare cases—of which this was not one—in which distinct events or incidents were alleged for the purposes of either of the two intentions specified in s 4(1)(c)(i) and (ii).)

R v Minett [2009] All ER (D) 215 The defendant was in financial difficulties with their plumbing business and made fraudulent transactions using their customers' credit card details. It was held that this was a clear breach of trust. The defendant had been allowed into the victims' homes and been entrusted with their credit cards and details. The defendant had been under an obligation to deal honestly with them.

Kensington International Ltd v Congo and others [2007] EWCA Civ 1128 This case provides guidance relating to disclosure, evidence, and other aspects of s 13.

Practical considerations

- Consider stop, search, and seizure powers under s 1 of PACE (see **1.3**).
- The words used may be spoken or written. Alternatively, there may be nothing done or said in circumstances where a reasonable and honest person would have expected something to be said/done (eg to correct a mistake).
- The fraud may be proved by admissions, the defendant's actions, or a combination of both.
- Acts may be dishonest even if the perpetrator genuinely believed them to be morally justified.

3.8.6 Possess or control article for use in fraud

Section 6 deals with the offence of a person having in their possession or under their control an article for use in fraud.

> **Offences**
>
> A person is guilty of an offence if he has in his possession or under his control any article for use in the course of or in connection with any fraud.
>
> Fraud Act 2006, s 6(1)

PNLD H8688

3.8.6 Possess or control article for use in fraud

Points to prove

✓ had in your possession/under your control
✓ an article
✓ for use in the course of/in connection with a fraud

Meanings

Possession (see **8.1.1**)

Article

Means an article:

- made or adapted for use in the course of or in connection with an offence of fraud; or
- **intended** by the person having it with them for such use by them or by some other person.

It also includes any program or data held in electronic form.

Fraud (see **3.8.1**)

Intention (see **4.1.2**)

Explanatory notes

- Having the article after the commission of the fraud is not sufficient for this offence.
- The prosecution must prove that the defendant was in possession of the article and intended the article to be used in the course of or in connection with some future fraud. It is not necessary to prove that they intended it to be used in the course of or in connection with any specific fraud; it is enough to prove a general intention to use it for fraud.
- Similarly, it will be sufficient to prove that they had it with them with the intention that it should be used by someone else.
- Examples of electronic programs or data which could be used in fraud are: a computer program that can generate credit card numbers; computer templates that can be used for producing blank utility bills; computer files containing lists of other people's credit card details; or draft letters in connection with 'advance fee' frauds.

Related cases

R v Hunter and another [2021] EWCA Crim 1785 Ticket touting in breach of restrictions imposed by organisers was not subject to the limitations in the common law offence of conspiracy to defraud, there was no requirement for the prosecution to prove an intention to deceive.

R v Smith (Andrew) [2020] EWCA Crim 38 To be used in 'the course of or in connection with the fraud' could apply to articles used to mislead but also to articles created earlier with a view to them being used in the fraud or created later in order to disguise or mask the fraud.

SSS E&S TRIG

Either way — None

Summary: 6/12 months' imprisonment and/or a fine

Indictment: 5 years' imprisonment and/or a fine

3.8.7 Making or supplying article for use in fraud

Section 7 deals with the offences of making or supplying an article for use in fraud.

Offences

A person is guilty of an offence if he makes, adapts, supplies or offers to supply any article—

(a) knowing that it is designed or adapted for use in the course of or in connection with fraud, or

(b) intending it to be used to commit, or assist in the commission of, fraud.

Fraud Act 2006, s 7(1)

PNLD H8689

Points to prove

✓ made/adapted/supplied/offered to supply

✓ an article

✓ knowing that it was designed/adapted for use in the course of/in connection with fraud OR

✓ intending it to be used to commit/assist in the commission of fraud

Meanings

Article (see **3.8.6**)

Fraud (see **3.8.1**)

Intention (see **4.1.2**)

Explanatory note

- An example of this offence would be where a person makes devices which when attached to electricity meters cause the meter to malfunction. The actual amount of electricity used is concealed from the provider, who thus suffers a loss.

Practical considerations

- A general intention to commit fraud will suffice rather than a specific offence in specific circumstances (eg credit card skimming equipment may provide evidence of such an intention).
- Proof is required that the defendant had the article for the purpose of or with the intention that it be used in the course of or in connection with fraud, and a general intention to commit fraud will suffice.
- Section 13 deals with evidential matters for offences under this Act.

SSS **E&S** **TRIG**

Either way

None

Summary: 12 months' imprisonment and/or a fine

Indictment: 10 years' imprisonment and/or a fine

3.9 Obtaining Services Dishonestly

Section 11 of the Fraud Act 2006 makes it an offence for any person, by any dishonest act, to obtain services for which payment is required, with intent to avoid payment.

Offences

(1) A person is guilty of an offence under this section if he obtains services for himself or another—
   (a) by a dishonest act, and
   (b) in breach of subsection (2).
(2) A person obtains services in breach of this subsection if—
   (a) they are made available on the basis that payment has been, is being or will be made for or in respect of them,
   (b) he obtains them without any payment having been made for or in respect of them or without payment having been made in full, and
   (c) when he obtains them, he knows—
      (i) that they are being made available on the basis described in paragraph (a), or
      (ii) that they might be,
   but intends that payment will not be made, or will not be made in full.

Fraud Act 2006, s 11

PNLD H8691

Points to prove

✓ obtained services for yourself/another by a dishonest act
✓ services were available on the basis that payment made for/in respect of them
✓ you obtained them without any payment/in full
✓ when you obtained them, you knew that they were being/might be made available on the basis described above
✓ but you intended that payment would not be made/made in full

Meanings

Dishonest act (see **3.1.1**)

Intention (see **4.1.2**)

Explanatory notes

- This section makes it an offence for any person, by any dishonest act, to obtain services for which payment is required, with intent to avoid payment.
- This offence replaced the offence of obtaining services by deception in s 1 of the Theft Act 1978, although this offence contains no deception element.
- It is not possible to commit the offence by omission alone and it can be committed only where the dishonest act was done with the intent not to pay for the services as expected.

Practical considerations

- The person must know that the services are made available on the basis that they are chargeable, or that they might be.
- There is nothing to suggest that the services obtained need to be lawful for this offence to be committed (eg services of a prostitute).
- There must be some action or communication by the defendant rather than an error wholly initiated by the supplier of the service which is unaffected by behaviour on the part of the defendant.
- The offence is not inchoate. It requires the actual obtaining of the service, for example data or software that is only available on the internet once you have paid for access rights to that service.
- Examples of this offence would be where a person:
  - ✦ dishonestly uses false credit card details or other false personal information to obtain the service;
  - ✦ climbs over a wall and watches a sports event without paying the entrance fee—such a person is not deceiving the provider of the service directly, but is obtaining a service which is provided on the basis that people will pay for it;
  - ✦ attaches a decoder to a television set in order to view/have access to cable/satellite channels for which they have no intention of paying.

E&S

Either way

None

Summary: 6/12 months' imprisonment and/or a fine

Indictment: 5 years' imprisonment and/or a fine

Chapter 4

Crime: General

4.1 Criminal Attempts/Meaning of Intent/Meaning of Aid, Abet, Counsel, and Procure/ Encourage or Assist Crime

4.1.1 Criminal attempts

The Criminal Attempts Act 1981 creates an offence of 'attempting' to commit certain crimes. It is imperative to prove intent (mens rea) for attempt offences, as well as other offences requiring intent. Intent is therefore discussed in detail.

Offence

(1) If, with intent to commit an offence to which this section applies, a person does an act which is more than merely preparatory to the commission of the offence, he is guilty of attempting to commit the offence.

(2) A person may be guilty of attempting to commit an offence to which this section applies even though the facts are such that the commission of the offence is impossible.

(3) In any case where—

(a) apart from this subsection a person's intention would not be regarded as having amounted to an intent to commit an offence; but

(b) if the facts of the case had been as he believed them to be, his intention would be so regarded,

then, for the purposes of subsection (1) above, he shall be regarded as having had an intent to commit that offence.

Criminal Attempts Act 1981, s 1

4.1.1 Criminal attempts

Points to prove

✓ with intent
✓ attempted
✓ (wording of the offence attempted)

Meanings

Intent (see **4.1.2**)

Offence to which this section applies

- This section applies to any offence which if it were completed, would be triable as an indictable or an either way offence, **other than**:
  - ✦ conspiracy (at common law or under s 1 of the Criminal Law Act 1977 or any other enactment);
  - ✦ aiding, abetting, counselling, procuring, or suborning the commission of an offence (see **4.1.3**);
  - ✦ an offence under s 2(1) of the Suicide Act 1961 (encouraging or assisting suicide) (see **2.7.1**);
  - ✦ offences under s 4(1) (assisting offenders) or s 5(1) (accepting or agreeing to accept consideration for not disclosing information about a relevant offence) of the Criminal Law Act 1967;
  - ✦ an offence under s 184(1) of the Online Safety Act 2023 (encouraging or assisting serious self-harm).
- This section also applies to low-value shoplifting and is triable only summarily by virtue of s 22A of the Magistrates' Courts Act 1980 (see **1.1.5**).

(See Criminal Attempts Act 1981, s 1(4) and (5).)

More than merely preparatory (see '**Explanatory notes**' below)

Explanatory notes

- A person may attempt an offence that is either indictable or triable either way. Offences that are 'summary only' cannot be attempted.
- Whether an act is more than merely preparatory to the commission of an offence is ultimately for the jury/court to decide. The decision in *Davey v Lee* [1967] 2 All ER 423 states that the offence of attempt is complete if the defendant does an act which is a step towards the commission of the specific crime, which is immediately (and not just remotely) connected with the commission of it, the doing of which cannot reasonably be regarded as having any other purpose than the commission of the specific crime.
- Remember—a criminal **attempt** is not the same as having the **intent** to commit the offence. If an act is only preparatory (eg obtaining an insurance claim form to make a false claim), then it is not an attempt. There would have to be some other act such as actually filling the form out and posting it. Mere intent is not enough.

Related cases

R v Bristol Justices, ex parte Edgar [1998] 3 All ER 798 Even though damage under £5,000 in value can be dealt with at the magistrates' court 'as if it were triable summarily' (by virtue of s 22(2) of the Magistrates' Courts Act 1980), a suspect can still be charged with attempting to damage property under £5,000 because the attempted offence still satisfies the condition (under the Criminal Attempts Act 1981, s 1(4)) of being an 'either way' offence. It is not a purely summary offence in the normal sense.

R v Toothill [1998] Crim LR 876 Knocking on a door may be enough for an offence of attempted burglary.

R v Tosti and White [1997] EWCA Crim 222 The defendants were trying to break into premises, and it was held that the first action of examining the padlock amounted to an act that was more than merely preparatory to the commission of the substantive offence of burglary.

R v Shivpuri [1986] UKHL 2 The defendant was arrested by customs officers in possession of 'drugs' that turned out to be harmless powder, but by receiving and hiding the powder in the suitcase, S had completed an act that was more than merely preparatory to the commission of the offence. The court held that the defendant was guilty of attempting to import heroin—even by attempting what was impossible—under s 1(2).

Practical considerations

- Criminal attempt offences can only occur where the principal offence is either an indictable offence or one that is triable either way.
- Where a person commits the full offence of aid, abet, counsel, or procure, the offender should be charged as principal to the main offence where the offence is indictable or either way (Accessories and Abettors Act 1861, s 8).
- When investigating attempted murder, consideration must be given to the CPS advice offered in the assault charging standards (see **2.1 'Assault'** and **2.7.1 'Murder'**).
- Powers of arrest, search, mode of trial, penalty, and time limits are the same as those relating to the principal offence.
- Consider confiscation of cash and property for an offence of attempting, conspiring, or inciting the commission of a 'criminal lifestyle' offence under Sch 2 to the Proceeds of Crime Act 2002 (see **5.5** for details).

4.1.2 Meaning of intent

The mens rea, which is Latin for 'guilty mind', must be proved—more so in 'attempts' than in any other offence.

4.1.2 Meaning of intent

Intent

This can be proved by drawing on various sources of information:

- admissions made by the defendant in interview which reveal their state of mind at the time of the commission of the offence;
- answers given by the defendant to questions regarding their actions and intentions at the time of the offence;
- by inference from the circumstances of the offence;
- evidence from witnesses;
- actions of the defendant before, during, and after the event, and property found on them or in their control (such as a vehicle for transporting property).

To prove intent, you need to take all the above into account. However, the important thing is that you must **prove** the defendant's **state of mind** at the time. A jury/magistrates' court must consider the circumstances and decide by way of a subjective test whether the defendant would have intended or foreseen the results which occurred.

> **Statutory test**
>
> A court or jury in determining whether a person has committed an offence—
>
> (a) shall not be bound by law to infer that he intended or foresaw a result of his actions by reason only of its being a natural and probable consequence of those actions; but
>
> (b) shall decide whether he did intend or foresee that result by reference to all the evidence, drawing such inferences from the evidence as appear proper in the circumstances.
>
> Criminal Justice Act 1967, s 8

Subjective/objective tests

The difference between 'objective' and 'subjective' tests are important here. *Black's Law Dictionary* defines the terms as:

- ***Objective***: 'of, relating to, or based on externally verifiable phenomena, as opposed to an individual's perceptions, feelings, or intentions'. This is sometimes used in the context of the 'reasonable person' test—what would a reasonable person perceive to be the rights or wrongs of the matter in question or the likely outcome?
- ***Subjective***: 'based on an individual's perceptions, feelings, or intentions, as opposed to externally verifiable phenomena'. In a legal context, this is the opposite of objective. Instead of the hypothetical reasonable person, subjectivity requires a court to establish whether the offender was in fact conscious of a risk or other factor.

Strict liability

For some rare criminal offences, 'strict liability' will be enough to secure a conviction. The liability for committing this type of offence does not depend on an intention (eg causing harm) or state of mind (eg recklessness) but is based on the breach of a duty. Beyond road traffic offences, such as exceeding the speed limit, the occasions where strict liability offences will be encountered by police officers are few.

4.1.3 Meaning of aid, abet, counsel, and procure

To be convicted as an 'aider or abettor', a person must have knowledge of all the circumstances that constitute the offence. Whether the 'aider' realises that the circumstances constitute an offence is immaterial.

Offences

Whosoever shall aid, abet, counsel or procure the commission of any indictable offence whether the same be an offence at common law or by virtue of any Act passed or to be passed, shall be liable to be tried, indicted and punished as a principal offender.

Accessories and Abettors Act 1861, s 8

Meanings

Aid

This means to provide help or assistance to a principal offender, whether before or at the time of committing the offence.

Abet

This is somewhat difficult to describe, but abetting could include where an individual incites, instigates, or encourages the principal to commit the offence.

Counsel

This means to advise or solicit the commission of an offence.

Procure

Lord Widgery described this as 'to produce by endeavour'. It has also been defined as 'obtaining by care and effort'. A course of action is procured by setting out to see that it happens and taking the appropriate steps to produce that happening. A causal link must be established between what the procurer did and what the principal did.

Explanatory notes

- Section 44 of the Magistrates' Courts Act 1980 provides that it is an offence to aid, abet, counsel, or procure any offence that is triable summarily, including either way offences (unless specifically excluded by statute).

4.1.4 Encourage, assist, or accessory to commit crime

- Section 4 of the Criminal Law Act 1967 creates an offence of assisting a person who has committed a 'relevant' offence (see **4.1.1**), ie one to which s 1 of the Criminal Attempts Act 1981 applies.

4.1.4 Encourage, assist, or accessory to commit crime

Part 2 (ss 44 to 67) of the Serious Crime Act 2007 abolishes the common law offence of incitement and creates three encouraging or assisting crime offences. This area of law is far too wordy and involved to give full details here, but the relevant law is discussed to develop an understanding of the key issues as to what is involved.

Offences

A person commits an offence if—

(a) he does an act capable of encouraging or assisting the commission of an offence; and

(b) he intends to encourage or assist its commission.

Serious Crime Act 2007, s 44(1)

PNLD H9212, H9213, H9214

Points to prove

✓ did an act which was capable of encouraging or assisting
✓ in the commission of an offence, namely (detail offence)
✓ intending to
✓ encourage or assist in its commission

Meanings

Does an act

This includes a reference to a course of conduct.

Capable of encouraging or assisting

(1) A reference in this Part to a person's doing an act that is capable of encouraging the commission of an offence includes a reference to his doing so by threatening another person or otherwise putting pressure on another person to commit the offence.

(2) A reference in this Part to a person's doing an act that is capable of encouraging or assisting the commission of an offence includes a reference to his doing so by—

  (a) taking steps to reduce the possibility of criminal proceedings being brought in respect of that offence;

  (b) failing to take reasonable steps to discharge a duty.

(3) But a person is not to be regarded as doing an act that is capable of encouraging or assisting the commission of an offence merely because he fails to respond to a constable's request for assistance in preventing a breach of the peace.

Serious Crime Act 2007, s 65

Encouraging or assisting commission of an offence

Reference in Part 2 to encouraging or assisting the commission of an offence is to be read in accordance with s 47.

Intends (see **4.1.2**)

Explanatory notes

- A person is not taken to have intended to encourage or assist the commission of an offence merely because such encouragement or assistance was a foreseeable consequence of that person's act.
- If a person (D1) arranges for a person (D2) to do an act that is capable of encouraging or assisting the commission of an offence, and D2 does the act, D1 is also to be treated for the purposes of this Part as having done it.
- **Section 47** provides further meanings and assumptions and sets out what is required to prove intent or belief and whether an act would amount to the commission of an offence.

Accessory to an offence

Being an accessory to an offence can occur in three ways:

1. An accessory before the fact is a person who counsels or procures the commission of a crime (see **4.1.3**). Also, the offences of encouraging and assisting an offender (ss 44 to 49 of the Serious Crime Act 2007) and the offence of conspiracy under s 1 of the Criminal Law Act 1977.
2. Someone involved with the principal in a joint enterprise. Though not committing the crime itself, the person is involved with the principal offender to a greater or lesser degree at the time of the crime. If involved in that way, they are said to have secondary liability.
3. An accessory after the fact (replaced by the offence of 'assisting an offender' under s 4 of the Criminal Law Act 1967), states that where a person has committed a relevant offence, any other person who, knowing or believing them to be guilty of the offence or some other relevant offence, does without lawful authority or reasonable excuse, any act with intent to impede their apprehension or prosecution, shall be guilty of an offence.

For an accessory involved at the time of the offence as part of a joint enterprise (known as the doctrine of 'parasitic accessory liability'), the Supreme Court in the case of *R v Jogee; R v Ruddock* in 2016 is the leading precedent on this subject (see '**Related cases**' below).

Defence of acting reasonably

(1) A person is not guilty of an offence under this Part [*Part 2 of the Serious Crime Act 2007*] if he proves—
  (a) that he knew certain circumstances existed; and
  (b) that it was reasonable for him to act as he did in those circumstances.

(2) A person is not guilty of an offence under this Part if he proves—
  (a) that he believed certain circumstances to exist;
  (b) that his belief was reasonable; and
  (c) that it was reasonable for him to act as he did in the circumstances as he believed them to be.

(3) Factors to be considered in determining whether it was reasonable for a person to act as he did include—
  (a) the seriousness of the anticipated offence (or, in the case of an offence under section 46, the offences specified in the indictment);
  (b) any purpose for which he claims to have been acting;
  (c) any authority by which he claims to have been acting.

Serious Crime Act 2007, s 50

Related case

R v Jogee; R v Ruddock [2016] UKSC 8 The Supreme Court was asked to review the doctrine of parasitic accessory liability where defendants had acted in a joint enterprise. The Supreme Court held that it must be proved that the defendant *intended* that the offence should be committed and that mere foresight of what another might do was not enough.

Practical considerations

- Other sections worthy of note in Part 2 of the Act are as follows:
  - s 45—Encouraging or assisting an offence believing it will be committed;
  - s 46—Encouraging or assisting offences believing one or more will be committed;
  - s 47—Proving an offence under Part 2;
  - s 48—Proving an offence under s 46;
  - s 49—Supplemental provisions;
  - s 51—Protective offences: victims not liable;
  - s 56—Persons who may be perpetrators or encouragers etc.
- Consider confiscation of cash and property for an offence under s 44, which is listed as a 'criminal lifestyle' offence under Sch 2 to the Proceeds of Crime Act 2002 (see **5.5** for details). Similarly aiding, abetting, counselling, or procuring the commission of the s 46 offence is also listed under Sch 2.
- For a s 46 offence, a defendant might believe that their conduct would assist in the commission of one or more different offences by another individual without necessarily knowing, or being able to

identify, the precise offence or offences which the person to whom they offered encouragement or assistance intended to commit or would commit (*R v Sadique* [2013] EWCA Crim 1150).

s 46—Indictment

None

s 44 or s 45—Per anticipated offence

Variable as to trial venue

ss 44 to 46—Penalty per anticipated offence, subject to s 58

4.2 Vehicle Interference and Tampering with a Motor Vehicle

The Criminal Attempts Act 1981 and the Road Traffic Act 1988 create offences which protect motor vehicles such as vehicle interference and tampering with motor vehicles. Although a defendant may be trying to take a vehicle without the owner's consent, the 1981 Act does not allow 'criminal attempts' for purely summary offences.

4.2.1 Vehicle interference

Offences

(1) A person is guilty of the offence of vehicle interference if he interferes with a motor vehicle or trailer or with anything carried in or on a motor vehicle or trailer with the intention that an offence specified in subsection (2) below shall be committed by himself or some other person.

(2) The offences mentioned in subsection (1) above are—
- (a) theft of the motor vehicle or part of it;
- (b) theft of anything carried in or on the motor vehicle or trailer; and
- (c) an offence under section 12(1) of the Theft Act 1968 (taking a conveyance)

and if it is shown that a person accused of an offence under this section intended that one of those offences should be committed, it is immaterial that it cannot be shown which it was.

Criminal Attempts Act 1981, s 9

PNLD H446, H588

Points to prove

- ✓ interfere with a
- ✓ motor vehicle/trailer/part of/anything carried in/on it
- ✓ with intent that an offence of
- ✓ theft/taking and drive away without consent
- ✓ should be committed

Meanings

Interferes (see '**Related cases**' below)

Motor vehicle

Means a mechanically propelled vehicle intended or adapted for use on a road (see **10.1.3**).

Trailer

Means a vehicle drawn by a motor vehicle (see **10.1.3**).

Intention (see **4.1.2**)

Explanatory note

- This offence 'fits' between the offence of going equipped (an offence which may be committed prior to any contact with a 'conveyance') and the offence of taking a conveyance without the owner's consent or theft.

Related case

Reynolds and Warren v Metropolitan Police [1982] Crim LR 831, CC The suspects were seen to look into four vehicles. In each case, one of them touched one door handle (not always the driver's door). It was held that there was no case to answer on charges of interfering with vehicles contrary to s 9 of the 1981 Act and that more than looking into vehicles and touching them was necessary.

Practical considerations

- Has the suspect possession of any implements for use in the offence that would not necessarily complete the offence of going equipped?
- Is there any CCTV evidence available?
- Check on the availability of witness evidence for CJA statements.

SSS

Summary | 6 months

3 months' imprisonment and/or a level 4 fine

4.2.2 Tampering with motor vehicles

Offences

If, while a motor vehicle is on a road or on a parking place provided by a local authority, a person—

(a) gets on to the vehicle, or
(b) tampers with the brake or other part of its mechanism,
without lawful authority or reasonable cause he is guilty of an offence.

Road Traffic Act 1988, s 25(1)

4.2.2 Tampering with motor vehicles

PNLD H108

Points to prove

✓ without lawful authority or reasonable cause
✓ got on to/tampered with
✓ the brakes/other mechanism of a motor vehicle
✓ on a road/parking place provided by local authority

Meanings

Motor vehicle/vehicle (see **10.1.3**)

Road (see **10.1.1**)

Tampers

The word 'tamper' is not explained in the Act and therefore should be given its normal meaning: 'improperly interfering with something'.

Other part of its mechanism

Means any mechanical part and not just those of a similar type to the brake.

Explanatory notes

- The motor vehicle must be on a road (see **10.1.1**) and/or on a parking place provided by the local authority.
- It is for the prosecution to prove the above and that the accused got onto or tampered with the motor vehicle without lawful authority or reasonable cause.

Defences

People with lawful authority and reasonable cause will have a defence. Lawful authority might take the form of a police officer or firefighter releasing the brake of a vehicle to move it in an emergency.

Summary | 6 months

Level 3 fine

4.3 Taking a Conveyance without Owner's Consent

The following topic covers three aspects: taking a conveyance without the owner's consent (TWOC), aggravated vehicle-taking, and the taking of pedal cycles. TWOC can also be known as unlawful taking of a motor vehicle (UTMV) or taking and driving away (TDA).

4.3.1 Taking a conveyance without owner's consent

Offences

Subject to subsections (5) and (6) below, a person shall be guilty of an offence if, without having the consent of the owner or other lawful authority, he takes any conveyance for his own or another's use or, knowing that any conveyance has been taken without such authority, drives it or allows himself to be carried in or on it.

Theft Act 1968, s 12(1)

PNLD H430, H434, H435, H2108

Points to prove

There are several sets of circumstances depending on the role taken in the offence.

The following relates to the initial taker only:

✓ without the consent
✓ of the owner/other lawful authority
✓ took a conveyance
✓ for own/another's use

Meanings

Owner

If the conveyance is subject to a hiring or hire-purchase agreement, this means the person in possession of the conveyance under that agreement.

Takes

Some movement of the conveyance is essential (*R v Bogacki* [1973] 2 All ER 864).

4.3.1 Taking a conveyance without owner's consent

Conveyance

Means any conveyance constructed or adapted for the carriage of a person or persons whether by land, water, or air, **except** that it **does not include** a conveyance constructed or adapted for use only under the control of a person not carried in or on it.

Explanatory notes

- An important point is that the conveyance must be capable of carrying a person. A machine such as a small domestic lawnmower is not a conveyance, but one upon which the operator sits would be.
- A horse is an animal and therefore not 'constructed or adapted', so it is not a 'conveyance'.
- Pedal cycles are catered for in s 12(5) (see **4.3.3**).
- You must prove the use or intended use as a means of transport. If the conveyance is not used in this way (eg pushing a car away from a drive entrance to remove an obstruction), then there is no 'taking'.
- The term '**consent of the owner**' does not arise simply on occasions where specific permission has been given. Problems tend to arise where the owner has given some form of conditional consent; case law suggests that if the borrower of a car, for instance, makes a reasonable detour to their journey, then that detour will still be made 'with the consent of the owner'. However, using the conveyance for a wholly or substantially different purpose may well be an offence. This element is also relevant to one of the statutory defences.
- To prove the term '**allows himself**', it is necessary to show that the defendant knew that the conveyance had been taken without the consent of the owner or other lawful authority. The person may not know that when they get into the conveyance, but if they find out subsequently, they are expected to make some attempt to leave.
- The essential difference between this offence and the offence of theft is that in this offence there is an absence of any intention to permanently deprive the owner of their property.

Defence

A person does not commit an offence under this section by anything done in the belief that he has lawful authority to do it or that he would have the owner's consent if the owner knew of his doing it and the circumstances of it.

Theft Act 1968, s 12(6)

Defence notes

- The prosecution must prove that the defendant did not believe that they had lawful authority (such as a police or local authority power of removal or repossession by a finance company).
- Apart from the belief that the owner would have consented if they had known of the using of the conveyance, it must also be shown

that they believed that the owner would have consented had they known of the circumstances of the taking and the using of it.

Related cases

R v Vaid [2015] EWCA Crim 298 It was held that DNA evidence taken from an airbag after a vehicle had been involved in a collision to establish who had been driving at the time was admitted in offences of TWOC and dangerous driving.

R v Marchant and McAllister [1985] 80 Cr App R 361, CA The defendants were seen by police officers to push a car a few feet from where its owner had parked it. The owner did not realise it had been moved until told by police. It was held that even though the car had not been used, it had been taken and it had been intended for 'his own or another's use'.

Whittaker v Campbell [1983] 3 All ER 582, QBD In this case, the defendant used a driving licence belonging to another to hire a vehicle in the name shown on the licence. They were stopped by the police and charged and first convicted with taking a conveyance. On appeal, the conviction was quashed. It was held that, on the true construction of s 12(1), the consent of the owner of a motor vehicle to its use by another was not vitiated where that consent was obtained fraudulently.

R v Miller [1976] Crim LR 147 The term **'carried in or on'** requires some movement of the conveyance. A person found sitting in a boat that had been moored was found not guilty of the offence. The normal movement of the waves was deemed insufficient for the ingredients of the offence. However, the vertical movement of a hovercraft would be sufficient, because that is not a 'natural' movement taking place independently of the use of the conveyance.

McKnight v Davies [1974] Crim LR 62, CA The defendant was employed as a delivery driver and damaged the lorry after completing deliveries. Then they drove to a pub, took three friends home, drove to another pub, and then parked at home. The next morning, the defendant took the lorry back to the yard. It was held that the use of the vehicle exceeded the terms of consent to its use given by the defendant's employer and, as such, the offence under s 12 was committed. The defendant had 'taken' the vehicle when leaving the first pub, as they had then assumed possession in a legal sense.

Practical considerations

- Note that each deviation from the authorised route should not be regarded as 'taking' for s 12. So long as the driver is still performing the duties they are employed to perform, even if in an unauthorised manner, they are acting in the character of an employee. When the purpose of the journey is something other than the employer's business, as in this case, then they have 'taken' the vehicle.
- Consider stop, search, and seizure powers under s 1 of PACE (see **1.3**).

- If on the trial of an indictment for theft of a conveyance, the jury is not satisfied that the accused committed theft, it may find the accused guilty of the s 12(1) offence.
- As the offence is only summary, there is no such thing as an 'attempted taking of a conveyance' (see **4.1.1**).
- Consider the more serious offence of aggravated vehicle-taking (see **4.3.2**).
- In the interview, the situation where the person becomes aware that the conveyance has been taken after they had entered it should be covered along with any subsequent efforts to leave the conveyance.
- The Act allows for the extension of **prosecution time limits**, where proceedings shall not be commenced after the end of the period of three years beginning with the day on which the offence was committed. Subject to the three-year maximum period, proceedings may be commenced at any time within the period of six months beginning with the **relevant day**.
- The **'relevant day'** means the day on which sufficient evidence is available to justify proceedings.

SSS E&S CHAR TRIG

Summary

Complex—see '**Prosecution time limits**' in '**Practical considerations**' above

6 months' imprisonment and/or a fine

Discretionary disqualification

4.3.2 **Aggravated vehicle-taking**

Section 12A of the Theft Act 1968 creates the various offences of 'aggravated vehicle-taking'.

Offences

(1) Subject to subsection (3) [*defence*] a person is guilty of aggravated taking of a vehicle if—
   (a) he commits an offence under section 12(1) (*taking a conveyance without consent*) (in this section referred to as the 'basic offence') in relation to a mechanically propelled vehicle, and
   (b) it is proved that, at any time after the vehicle was unlawfully taken (whether by him or another) and before it was recovered, the vehicle was driven, or injury or damage was caused, in one or more of the circumstances set out in paragraphs (a) to (d) of subsection (2).

(2) The circumstances referred to in subsection (1)(b) above are—
   (a) that the vehicle was driven dangerously on a road or other public place;

(b) that, owing to the driving of the vehicle, an accident occurred by which injury was caused to any person;
(c) that, owing to the driving of the vehicle, an accident occurred by which damage was caused to any property, other than the vehicle;
(d) that damage was caused to the vehicle.

Theft Act 1968, s 12A

PNLD H4383, H4391, H4482

Points to prove

- ✓ without the consent
- ✓ of the owner/other lawful authority
- ✓ took (being the initial taker)
- ✓ a mechanically propelled vehicle for
- ✓ own/another's use
- ✓ (The 'basic offence')
- ✓ AND after it was taken and before it was recovered
- ✓ the vehicle was driven dangerously on a road/public place OR
- ✓ accident which caused injury to person(s), damage to any property or the vehicle

Meanings

Dangerously (see **10.7.1**)

A vehicle is driven dangerously if:
- it is driven in a way which falls far below what would be expected of a competent and careful driver; **and**
- it would be obvious to a competent and careful driver that driving the vehicle in that way would be dangerous.

Accident

Means 'any unintended occurrence which has an adverse physical result' and the legislation does not specify that it must occur on a road or even in a public place.

Damage

Means any damage not just criminal damage.

Explanatory notes

- 'Owner' has the same meaning as s 12(1) (see **4.3.1**).
- Consider the offence of dangerous driving (see **10.7.1**).
- A vehicle has been recovered once the police, owner, or some other person with the authority of the owner takes responsibility for the vehicle. However, if the police have been informed of the location of a taken vehicle, it has yet to be decided whether 'recovered' is from

the time of the call or the time the police arrive at the scene and take physical control.

- This offence only applies to mechanically propelled vehicles and not to all conveyances.
- Passengers in a vehicle involved in such an offence can also be liable to prosecution. Their culpability would be increased depending upon the extent or degree of encouragement they may have given to the driver.

Defences

A person is not guilty of an offence under this section if he proves that, as regards any such proven driving, injury or damage as is referred to in subsection (1)(b) (*aggravating factors*) above, either—

(a) the driving, accident or damage referred to above occurred before he committed the basic offence; or

(b) he was neither in, nor on, nor in the immediate vicinity of, the vehicle when that driving, accident or damage occurred.

Theft Act 1968, s 12A(3)

Related cases

R v Taylor [2016] UKSC 5 For an offence under s 12A and the circumstances listed in subsections (2)(b) and (c), there must be at least some act or omission in the control of the car which involves some element of fault in the driving that is more than minimal to contribute to the accident. The driving alone could not be said to be the cause of the accident if it merely explains how the vehicle came to be in the place where the accident occurred.

Dawes v DPP [1995] 1 Cr App R 65, QBD The defendant was arrested after unlawfully taking a vehicle that had been set up by the police with a device which automatically secured the car preventing his escape. During the short time before being arrested, the defendant damaged the car trying to get out. It was held that the subsequent damage caused was sufficient to create an offence under s 12A.

Practical considerations

- The fact that the person who originally took the vehicle is not the person who caused the accident resulting in personal injury is irrelevant—the initial taker can still be prosecuted for the aggravated offence. Nor is there any requirement that the driver of the 'taken vehicle' must be at fault when a personal injury accident occurs (*R v Marsh* [1996] 8 CL 54).
- Always bear in mind the above defences when interviewing.
- The aggravated offence never becomes statute-barred as it is an either way offence. Even if the damage caused is under £5,000 and the offence is triable only summarily, it is still an either way offence.

- By virtue of s 12A(5), a person who is found not guilty of this offence can still be found guilty of taking a vehicle without consent as an alternative.

SSS E&S CHAR TRIG

Either way

None

Summary: 6/12 months' imprisonment and/or a fine
Indictment: 2 years' imprisonment, **but** where a person dies as a result of an accident involving the offence, 14 years' imprisonment
Obligatory disqualification—licence endorsed 3 to 11 penalty points

4.3.3 Take pedal cycle without owner's consent

Taking or riding a pedal cycle without the consent of the owner or other lawful authority is an offence.

Offences

Taking a conveyance shall not apply in relation to pedal cycles; but, subject to subsection (6) below [*defences*], a person who, without having the consent of the owner or other lawful authority, takes a pedal cycle for his own or another's use, or rides a pedal cycle knowing it to have been taken without such authority, commits an offence.

Theft Act 1968, s 12(5)

PNLD H436, H437

Points to prove

✓ without consent of the owner/lawful authority
✓ takes/rides
✓ pedal cycle
✓ for own or other's use

Explanatory notes

- A pedal cycle is neither propelled by mechanical power nor is it electrically assisted.
- There are many types of 'hybrid' vehicles, such as motorised scooters, that may qualify as mechanically propelled vehicles or conveyances. Ultimately, this is a question of fact for the court to decide.

Defences (see **4.3.1**)

Practical considerations

- The prosecution must prove that the accused did not have lawful authority, such as a police or local authority power of removal or repossession by a finance company.
- As this is a summary offence, there is no offence of 'attempting to take a pedal cycle' (see **4.1.1**).

SSS CHAR TRIG

Summary

6 months

Level 3 fine

4.4 Criminal Damage

The offence of criminal damage is designed to protect people's property from the unlawful actions of others. Section 1 of the Criminal Damage Act 1971 creates the offence of simple 'criminal damage'.

Offences

A person who without lawful excuse destroys or damages any property belonging to another intending to destroy or damage any such property or being reckless as to whether any such property would be destroyed or damaged shall be guilty of an offence.

Criminal Damage Act 1971, s 1(1)

PNLD H2081, H2082, H2090

Points to prove

- ✓ without lawful excuse
- ✓ destroyed/damaged
- ✓ property to value of (specify value where known)
- ✓ intending to
- ✓ destroy/damage such property OR
- ✓ being reckless whether it was destroyed/damaged

Meanings

Destroyed

Means property which is incapable of being repaired and can only be replaced.

Damaged

Means property that has suffered some physical harm, impairment, or deterioration.

Property (s 10(1))

Means property of a tangible nature, whether real or personal, including money and:

(a) wild creatures which have been tamed or are ordinarily kept in captivity, and any other wild creatures or their carcasses if, but only if, they have been reduced into possession which has not been lost or abandoned or are in the course of being reduced into possession; but

(b) not including mushrooms growing wild on any land or flowers, fruit, or foliage of a plant growing wild on any land.

For the purposes of this subsection, mushroom includes any fungus and plant includes any shrub or tree.

Belonging to another

This is property that belongs to another person who has custody or control of it or who has a right or an interest in it or has a charge over it.

Intending (see **4.1.2**)

Reckless

The test set out in *R v G and R* [2003] UKHL 50 applies, which states that a person acts 'recklessly' for the purposes of s 1 with respect to:

- circumstances where that person is aware of a risk that exists or will exist;
- a result when they are aware of a risk that it will occur;

and it is, in the circumstances known to them, unreasonable to take the risk.

The **first part** provides for those existing or future circumstances known to the defendant which, in the circumstances as known to them, made it unreasonable to take the risk they took. An example would be a tramp taking shelter in a barn full of dry hay: aware of the risk, they light a fire to boil water for a cup of tea and set the barn alight.

The **second part** of the test applies if the person is aware that the result of their actions is a risk and, in the circumstances as known to them, it would be unreasonable to take that risk. An example would be an adult who lets off a large rocket and ignores instructions which state that the firework should be launched from a tube embedded in the ground and instead launches it from a bottle standing upright on the pavement. As a result, the rocket goes through the window of a house opposite and causes a fire.

The case of *G and R* involved two children aged 11 and 12 who set fire to a shop when lighting newspapers in a yard at the back. It was argued in their defence that, although the act might have been an obvious risk to the average person, it might not be obvious to such young children. The House of Lords agreed and overturned the previous '**objective**' test in the case of *R v Caldwell* [1981] 1 All ER 961.

Explanatory note

- The important thing to prove or disprove (in addition to the damage itself) is the state of mind (intent) or that the person was reckless in their actions, in destroying/damaging the property.

Defences

Lawful excuse

(1) This section applies to any offence under section 1(1) and any offence under section 2 or 3 other than one involving a threat by the person

charged to destroy or damage property in a way which he knows is likely to endanger the life of another or involving an intent by the person charged to use or cause or permit the use of something in his custody or under his control so to destroy or damage property.

(2) A person charged with an offence to which this section applies shall, whether or not he would be treated for the purposes of this Act as having a lawful excuse apart from this subsection, be treated for those purposes as having a lawful excuse—

(a) if at the time of the act or acts alleged to constitute the offence he believed that the person or persons whom he believed to be entitled to consent to the destruction of or damage to the property in question had so consented, or would have so consented to it if he or they had known of the destruction or damage and its circumstances; or

(b) if he destroyed or damaged or threatened to destroy or damage the property in question or, in the case of a charge of an offence under section 3, intended to use or cause or permit the use of something to destroy or damage it, in order to protect property belonging to himself or another or a right or interest in property which was or which he believed to be vested in himself or another, and at the time of the act or acts alleged to constitute the offence he believed—

(i) that the property, right or interest was in immediate need of protection; and

(ii) that the means of protection adopted or proposed to be adopted were or would be reasonable having regard to all the circumstances.

(3) For the purposes of this section it is immaterial whether a belief is justified or not if it is honestly held.

Protect life or property

(4) For the purposes of subsection (2) above a right or interest in property includes any right or privilege in or over land, whether created by grant, licence or otherwise.

(5) This section shall not be construed as casting doubt on any defence recognised by law as a defence to criminal charges.

Criminal Damage Act 1971, s 5

Defence notes

Damage caused to protect life, prevent injury, or stop unlawful imprisonment of a person is also a valid defence (*R v Baker and Wilkins* [1997] Crim LR 497).

Related cases

Attorney-General's Reference (No 1 of 2022) [2022] EWCA Crim 1259 The court outlined the relevant considerations in cases involving criminal damage caused during protests. It was held, inter alia, that

Convention rights under Arts 9, 10, and 11 (see **Appendix 1**) did not provide protection to those who cause criminal damage during a protest, which was violent or not peaceful, although it was at least theoretically possible that, where the damage caused was minor or trivial, the Convention required a proportionality assessment to protect a person from prosecution and conviction. However, prosecution and conviction for causing significant damage to property, even if inflicted in a way which was 'peaceful', could not be disproportionate in Convention terms.

R v Jones and others, Ayliffe and others v DPP, Swain v DPP [2006] UKHL 16 The defendants took part in protests at military bases against the war in Iraq and damaged the perimeter fence and vehicles. It was claimed that the damage done was to prevent the international crime of aggression and so was a 'lawful excuse' under s 5. It was held that the right of citizens to use force or cause damage on their own initiative is limited when not defending their own person or property and furthermore it does not cover customary international law.

Chamberlain v Lindon [1998] 2 All ER 538, QBD The defendant destroyed a wall erected by their neighbour which obstructed a right of access to their property. It was held that the defendant had a lawful excuse for their action because the obstruction to the complainant's rights had already happened and they believed those rights would be further prejudiced if the wall remained in place.

Johnson v DPP [1994] Crim LR 673, QBD The defendant was a squatter and damaged a door in a house which they occupied. The defence was that J had a lawful excuse under s 5(2)(b). The appeal against conviction was rejected. It was held that when lawful excuse is the defence, two questions need to be asked. The first is an objective question (ie whether the act of damage was done to protect property); *and* the second, a subjective question (whether the defendant believed that the property was in immediate need of protection and the means of protection used were reasonable).

Practical considerations

- Consider stop, search, and seizure powers under s 1 of PACE (see **1.3**).
- If property has been destroyed, the value specified in the charge should reflect the full replacement cost.
- Charging that property was both 'destroyed' and 'damaged' is an unnecessary duplication, so wherever possible a choice should be made.
- Consider applying for a warrant (under s 6) to search for and seize anything in the custody or control of suspect on their premises.
- If the destruction or damage has been caused by fire, an offence of arson under s 1(3) should be charged (see **4.5.2**).
- Consider the more serious offence of racially or religiously aggravated criminal damage (see **7.10**).
- PACE Code E Annex A, para 2.4(c)(iii) provides exemption from the requirement to audio record interviews that are undertaken

elsewhere than at a police station for certain indictable offences that include where a person has been cautioned for criminal damage to property contrary to s 1(1). This exemption is subject to a number of conditions, but the suspect must be aged 18 years or over and does not require an appropriate adult, the value of the damage must not exceed £300, and the suspect is not employed (whether paid or not) by the person, company, or organisation to which the property belongs. (See **Code E** for full details.)

- The above exemption to audio record interviews applies to an attempt to commit the offence under s 1 of the Criminal Attempts Act 1981 (see **4.1.1**).
- Consider issuing a PND if damage value is below £300 (see **7.1.1**).
- If the full offence is not committed, consider attempt at criminal damage (see **4.1**).
- The same incident may involve separate activities, some causing ordinary damage and some damage by fire (eg protestors break into a laboratory building, smash laboratory equipment, and set fire to some files). In such circumstances, they are separate offences and best charged as such.
- There is a special offence of criminal damage to an ancient monument under the Ancient Monuments and Archaeological Areas Act 1979, s 28. The advantage of using this offence is that the owner can also be liable for damaging the protected monument which they own.
- Consider the offences of having an article with intent to commit damage (see **4.7**) or making threats to cause damage (see **4.6**).

SSS E&S RRA NIP

Either way

None

Summary: *Value below* £5,000—3 months' imprisonment and/or a level 4 fine

Either way: *Value* £5,000 *or above*—6/12 months' imprisonment and/or a fine
Indictment: 10 years' imprisonment

Links to alternative subjects and offences

7.1 **Penalty Notices for Disorder** 351
7.10 **Racially/Religiously Aggravated Offences** 390
7.13 **Anti-Social Behaviour** 435

4.5 Damage with Intent to Endanger Life and Arson

Damage with intent to endanger life is also known as aggravated damage. This and arson are serious offences because of their potential to have disastrous effects on other people's lives and the wider community.

This section is presented in two parts: damage with intent to endanger life and then arson.

4.5.1 Damage with intent to endanger life

Section 1(2) of the Criminal Damage Act 1971 creates the serious offence of destroying or damaging property intending that or being reckless as to whether life will be endangered.

Offences

A person who without lawful excuse, destroys or damages any property, whether belonging to himself or another—

(a) intending to destroy or damage any property or being reckless as to whether any property would be destroyed or damaged; and

(b) intending by the destruction or damage to endanger the life of another or being reckless as to whether the life of another would be thereby endangered;

shall be guilty of an offence.

Criminal Damage Act 1971, s 1(2)

PNLD H4369

Points to prove

- ✓ without lawful excuse
- ✓ destroy/damage
- ✓ property
- ✓ whether belonging to self or another
- ✓ with intent destroy/damage or reckless destroy/damage and
- ✓ intending by destruction/damage to endanger life of another OR
- ✓ being reckless as to whether such life would thereby be endangered

Meanings

Lawful excuse (see '**Defences**' below)

Intent (see **4.1.2**)

Destroy (see **4.4**)

Damage (see **4.4**)

Property (see **4.4**)

Belonging to another (see **4.4**)

Endanger life

Does not require an attempt to kill or injury to occur. It is sufficient that life was endangered.

Reckless (see **4.4**)

Explanatory notes

- Consider attempted murder or manslaughter (see **4.1** and **2.7**).
- No actual injury need occur; all that is required is evidence that life was endangered. For example, if a jealous person cuts the brake pipe of their rival's car, no harm may come to the intended victim, but the potential for harm exists. Either intention to endanger the life of another or recklessness in that regard must be proved and the potential for harm to someone other than the defendant must be proved.
- The actual damage caused must also be the cause of the danger. For example, shooting at a person in a room (through a window) both endangers life and damages the window, but it is not the damage that endangers the life.

Defences

- Lawful excuse could be attempting to effect, a rescue to save life, but in doing so it could endanger life.
- The statutory lawful excuse defence for damage given in s 5 (see **4.4**) specifically precludes damage with intent to endanger life and arson.

Related cases

R v Wenton [2010] EWCA Crim 2361 The defendant smashed a house window, after which an open can of petrol was thrown through the window along with a piece of paper that had been set alight. The petrol spilled, but did not ignite, so there was no fire. The house had a family with children living in it at the time of the attack. The defendant was charged and convicted of the s 1(2) offence. However, on appeal, it was held that any endangerment to life must directly arise from the act of damage/destruction. The damage to the window was unrelated to the incident which gave rise to the risk of danger to life and consequently the appeal was allowed, and the conviction quashed.

R v Webster and others [1995] 2 All ER 168, CA In this case, a coping stone was pushed from a bridge onto a moving train. It landed on top of a carriage, piercing through the outer skin, and showering the passengers with debris. However, no one was injured. The defendants were charged and convicted of 'damage with intent to endanger life'. It was held that where the intention was for the stone to injure the passengers, the damage caused was not relevant and that the correct offence was 'recklessness causing damage which could endanger life'.

Practical considerations

- The same incident may involve separate activities, some causing ordinary damage and some damage by fire (eg protestors break into a laboratory building, smash laboratory equipment, and set fire to files). In such circumstances, they are separate offences and should be charged as such.
- Damage by fire is arson (see **4.5.2**).

SSS E&S RRA

Indictable

None

Life imprisonment

4.5.2 **Arson**

Section 1(3) of the Criminal Damage Act 1971 creates the offence of 'arson'.

> **Offences**
>
> An offence committed under this section by destroying or damaging property by fire shall be charged as arson.
>
> Criminal Damage Act 1971, s 1(3)

PNLD H470, H20247

Points to prove

Arson

- ✓ without lawful excuse
- ✓ destroy/damage
- ✓ by fire
- ✓ property with intent to destroy/damage it OR
- ✓ being reckless whether such property was destroyed/damaged

Arson—endanger life

- ✓ all points to prove for arson (above) and
- ✓ intending by destruction/damage to endanger life of another OR
- ✓ being reckless as to whether such life would be endangered

Meanings

Destroy (see **4.4**)

Damage (see **4.4**)

Property (see **4.4**)

Explanatory note

- For the offence to be complete, some of the damage must be by fire; this does not include smoke damage. It is enough, however, that wood is charred (*R v Parker* [1839] 173 ER 733).

Defences

There is no specific defence for arson.

Related case

R v Drayton [2005] EWCA Crim 2013 A charge of causing criminal damage by fire under s 1(3) still constitutes a charge of arson even if 'arson' is not specifically stated in the charge.

Practical considerations

- Intention or recklessness must be proved. A burglar who accidentally dropped a lighted match used for illumination could be reckless.
- The same incident may involve separate activities, some causing ordinary damage and some damage by fire. These are separate offences and should be so charged.
- Most arsons involve the use of '**accelerants**' such as petrol or lighter fuel to start the fire. If it is suspected that accelerants might have been used, special procedures need to be implemented to obtain forensic samples.
- An accelerant is used to increase the speed of a chemical reaction. For police purposes, this usually means something to speed up the spread of a fire during an arson attack. Accelerants are volatile and will evaporate if left in the open air. Do not confuse accelerants with oils and greases, which demand different treatment.
- Procedures for the careful preservation and packaging which must be carried out to enable the detection of accelerants can be divided into three basic areas:
  - ✦ clothing;
  - ✦ at the scene;
  - ✦ fragile items.
- Submit the control sample of the suspected accelerant in a clean metal container with a well-fitting cap, sealed inside a **nylon bag**. If no metal can is available, use a clean glass container but protect any rubber insert in the cap with a nylon film. For this purpose, cut up part of one of the nylon bags and use the rest as a control—see below. Isolate from all other samples.

- Control sample of nylon bag used to seal any sample: in a case where a nylon bag has been employed to seal a sample, a control nylon bag from the same batch as the one used to contain the samples should be submitted. This should be sealed but should only contain air.
- Important—never dry out items suspected of containing fire accelerants before packaging. Never store or transport items for examination for the presence of fire accelerant materials near a control sample of fire accelerant or anything taken from the defendant. Even a suspicion of contamination will destroy the evidential value of the samples.

SSS E&S RRA

Either way

None

Summary: 6/12 months' imprisonment and/or a fine

Indictment: Life imprisonment

4.6 Threats to Destroy or Damage Property

Section 2 of the Criminal Damage Act 1971 creates specific offences relating to threats to destroy or damage property.

Offences

A person who without lawful excuse makes to another a threat, intending that the other would fear it would be carried out,—
(a) to destroy or damage any property belonging to that other or a third person; or
(b) to destroy or damage his own property in a way which he knows is likely to endanger the life of that other or a third person;
shall be guilty of an offence.

Criminal Damage Act 1971, s 2

PNLD H2278, H2280

Points to prove

✓ without lawful excuse
✓ threatened to destroy/damage property of a person
✓ intending
✓ a person would fear that the threat would be carried out

Threaten damage to own property to endanger life

✓ without lawful excuse
✓ threatened to destroy/damage
✓ own property
✓ which they knew
✓ was likely to endanger life of another
✓ intending a person would fear threat would be carried out

Meanings

Lawful excuse (see 'Defences' **4.4**)

Intending (see **4.1.2**)

Destroy (see **4.4**)

Damage (see **4.4**)

Property (see **4.4**)

Endanger life (see **4.5.1**)

Explanatory notes

- It does not matter that the defendant may not actually intend to carry out the threats and/or the victim may not even believe them. The offender's **intention** to create such a fear is sufficient—and necessary—to complete the offence.
- The test for whether the action amounts to a threat is objective (ie 'would the reasonable person conclude that a threat had been made?') (*R v Cakmak and others* [2002] EWCA Crim 500). Only intention will do; unlike s 1, there is no mention of 'reckless' in this section.
- The threat must be to another person and can relate to a third party—such as 'I will smash up your son's car if you don't do what I say'—the threat is to one person about their or a third person's property.
- In s 2(b) above, the offender can threaten to damage their own property in a way that is likely to endanger the life of another, such as a landlord threatening to burn down a house they own if a tenant will not leave.
- There is no specific requirement for the threat to be carried out immediately, each case will depend on the circumstances surrounding it.
- In relation to the meaning of 'threats in criminal damage', two points must be considered:
  - ✦ *the type of conduct threatened*—this must amount to an offence under s 1 of the Criminal Damage Act 1971, either simple criminal damage or criminal damage where life is endangered; and
  - ✦ *the threat itself*—the person making the threats must intend their victim to fear that damage will be done. It does not matter that they may not actually intend to carry out the threats and/or the victim may not believe them. The offender's intention to create such a fear is sufficient to complete the offence.

Defence

Having a lawful excuse will be a defence under s 5 (see **4.4**).

Related case

R v Ankerson [2015] EWCA Crim 432 The defendant made threats to burn down his estranged wife's house regardless of whether their children were inside or not. It was held that the intention of the defendant must have been to create a genuine fear that the threat might be carried out, even where the listener was not certain that the threat would be carried out. The critical word was 'fear'. It was enough if the intention was to create in the mind of an objective listener the genuine fear that the threat might be carried out. The listener could have that fear, even where they were not certain that the threat would be carried out.

SSS E&S

Either way

None

Summary: 6/12 months' imprisonment and/or a fine

Indictment: 10 years' imprisonment

Links to alternative subjects and offences

2.5 **Threats to Kill** 97
2.8 **Domestic Violence** 125
7.7 **Intentional Harassment, Alarm, or Distress** 376
7.13 **Anti-Social Behaviour** 435

4.7 Custody/Control of Articles with Intent to Damage and Sale of Paint Aerosols to Persons under 16

Even when criminal damage has not been committed or threatened, there may be an offence of possessing articles with an intention to cause damage. An offence of selling paint aerosols to children is designed to curb criminal damage to property by way of graffiti.

4.7.1 Custody/control of articles with intent to damage

Section 3 of the Criminal Damage Act 1971 creates the offence of 'going equipped' intending to destroy or damage property.

Offences

A person who has anything in his custody or under his control intending without lawful excuse to use it or cause or permit another to use it—
(a) to destroy or damage any property belonging to some other person; or
(b) to destroy or damage his own or the user's property in a way which he knows is likely to endanger the life of some other person;
shall be guilty of an offence.

Criminal Damage Act 1971, s 3

PNLD H474, H475

Points to prove

- ✓ had in custody/control
- ✓ an article/object/substance/anything at all
- ✓ intending
- ✓ without lawful excuse
- ✓ to destroy/damage or to cause/permit another to use the article, etc
- ✓ property belonging to another/own or user's property
- ✓ knowing life of another is likely to be endangered

Meanings

Anything

Has its natural/everyday meaning and can range from explosives to a box of matches or a hammer.

Custody or control

This is a wider term than possession and could cover occasions where the defendant does not have the article with them. Custody means safekeeping. Control means the power to manipulate property without having legal title or possession, such as the dispatcher of a parcel-delivery company who has control of the distribution of the parcels without ownership, custody, or possession.

Intent (see **4.1.2**)

Lawful excuse (see **4.4**)

Cause

Means some degree of dominance or control, or some express or positive authorisation from the person who 'causes'.

Permit

Requires general or particular permission, as distinguished from authorisation, and the permission may be express (eg verbal/written) or implied (eg the person's actions). A person cannot permit unless they are in a position to forbid and no one can permit what they cannot control.

Destroy (see **4.4**)

Damage (see **4.4**)

Property (see **4.4**)

Belonging to another (see **4.4**)

Endanger life (see **4.5.1**)

Explanatory notes

- The offence is split into two parts, but certain elements are common to both. Intent to use/cause/permit must be proved in all cases, as must the element of having anything in the defendant's custody/control and the absence of lawful excuse.
- The act intended does not have to be immediate; it can be at some time in the future (eg someone storing bomb-making materials for future use).
- The only difference between s 3(a) and s 3(b) offences is that in (b) there is an element of knowledge of the likelihood of endangering the life of someone else and the offender's own property can be the object of the intended damage (eg a person carrying a can of petrol to set fire to their own house with their partner inside).

Defence

Having a lawful excuse (see **4.4**).

SSS E&S

Either way — None

Summary: 6/12 months' imprisonment and/or a fine
Indictment: 10 years' imprisonment

4.7.2 Sale of aerosol paints to children

Section 54 of the Anti-social Behaviour Act 2003 makes it an offence to sell aerosol spray paints to persons under 16, to reduce the incidence of graffiti criminal damage caused by young persons.

Offence

A person commits an offence if he sells an aerosol paint container to a person under the age of sixteen.

Anti-social Behaviour Act 2003, s 54(1)

PNLD H5636

Points to prove

✓ sold
✓ an aerosol paint container
✓ to a person under the age of 16

Meaning of aerosol paint container

Means a device which contains paint stored under pressure and is designed to permit the release of the paint as a spray.

Defences

(4) It is a defence for a person charged with an offence under this section in respect of a sale to prove that—
   (a) he took all reasonable steps to determine the purchaser's age, and
   (b) he reasonably believed that the purchaser was not under the age of sixteen.

(5) It is a defence for a person charged with an offence under this section in respect of a sale effected by another person to prove that he (the defendant) took all reasonable steps to avoid the commission of an offence under this section.

Anti-social Behaviour Act 2003, s 54

Practical considerations

- You will need to show that the sale was concluded, rather than simply the advertising or negotiating.
- There is no need to prove any intention by the purchaser or any specific knowledge/suspicion of intended knowledge on the part of the seller.
- Age to be proved by birth certificate or valid ID card.

Summary

6 months

Level 4 fine

4.8 Intimidation of a Witness/ Juror and Perverting the Course of Justice

Witnesses and/or jurors involved in the investigation or trial of criminal offences are protected from intimidation and/or threat by s 51 of the Criminal Justice and Public Order Act 1994. This area of law is presented in two parts: intimidation of a witness/juror and perverting the course of justice.

4.8.1 Intimidation of a witness/juror

Offences

Intimidation

(1) A person commits an offence if—

- (a) he does an act which intimidates, and is intended to intimidate, another person ('the victim'),
- (b) he does the act knowing or believing that the victim is assisting in the investigation of an offence or is a witness or potential witness or a juror or potential juror in proceedings for an offence, and
- (c) he does it intending thereby to cause the investigation or the course of justice to be obstructed, perverted or interfered with.

Threats

(2) A person commits an offence if—

- (a) he does an act which harms, and is intended to harm, another person or, intending to cause another person to fear harm, he threatens to do an act which would harm that other person,
- (b) he does or threatens to do the act knowing or believing that the person harmed or threatened to be harmed ('the victim'), or some other person, has assisted in an investigation into an offence or has given evidence or particular evidence in proceedings for an offence, or has acted as a juror or concurred in a particular verdict in proceedings for an offence; and
- (c) he does or threatens to do it because of that knowledge or belief.

Criminal Justice and Public Order Act 1994, s 51

PNLD H1809, H2234, H2235

Points to prove

Intimidate a witness/juror

- ✓ knew/believed person was
- ✓ assisting investigation of offence or a witness/potential witness or juror/potential juror

- ✓ in proceedings for offence
- ✓ did an act which
- ✓ intimidated that person and was intended to do so
- ✓ intending to cause investigation/course of justice to be obstructed or perverted or interfered with

Harm/threaten a witness/juror

- ✓ knew/believed person or another had assisted in investigation/ given evidence in proceedings/acted as juror/concurred in particular verdict
- ✓ because of that knowledge/belief
- ✓ threatened/did an act which
- ✓ harmed/was intended to harm/would have harmed person

Meanings

Investigation into an offence

Means such an investigation by the police or other person charged with the duty of investigating offences or charging offenders.

Offence

Includes an alleged or suspected offence.

Potential juror

Means a person who has been summonsed for jury service at the court at which proceedings for the offence are pending.

Act intending to intimidate

If, in proceedings against a person for an **offence under subsection (1)**, it is proved that he did an act falling within paragraph (a) with the knowledge or belief required by paragraph (b), he shall be presumed, unless the contrary is proved, to have done the act with the intention required by paragraph (c) of that subsection.

Criminal Justice and Public Order Act 1994, s 51(7)

Intended (see **4.1.2**)

Act intending to threaten/harm

In proceedings against a person for an offence under subsection (2) (**threats**), it is proved that within the **relevant period**:

(a) he did an act which harmed, and was intended to harm, another person, or
(b) intending to cause another person fear of harm, he threatened to do an act which would harm that other person,

he did (as the case may be) or threatened to do an act described by (a) above with the knowledge or belief of (b) above, then he shall be presumed, unless the contrary is proved, to have done the act or threatened to do the act with the motive required by (c) above.

Criminal Justice and Public Order Act 1994, s 51(8)

The relevant period

In this section 'the relevant period'—

(a) in relation to a witness or juror in any proceedings for an offence, means the period beginning with the **institution of the proceedings** and ending with the first anniversary of the conclusion of the trial or, if there is an appeal or a reference under section 9 or 11 of the Criminal Appeal Act 1995, of the conclusion of the appeal;
(b) in relation to a person who has, or is believed by the accused to have, assisted in an investigation into an offence, but was not also a witness in proceedings for an offence, means the period of one year beginning with any act of his, or any act believed by the accused to be an act of his, assisting in the investigation; and
(c) in relation to a person who both has, or is believed by the accused to have, assisted in the investigation into an offence and was a witness in proceedings for the offence, means the period beginning with any act of his, or any act believed by the accused to be an act of his, assisting in the investigation and ending with the anniversary mentioned in paragraph (a) above.

Criminal Justice and Public Order Act 1994, s 51(9)

Institution of proceedings

For the purposes of the definition of the relevant period in subsection (9) above—

(a) proceedings for an offence are instituted at the earliest of the following times:
   (i) when a justice of the peace issues a summons, or warrant under section 1 of the Magistrates' Courts Act 1980 in respect of the offence;
   (ii) when a person is charged with the offence after being taken into custody without a warrant;
   (iii) when a bill of indictment is preferred by virtue of section 2(2)(b) or (ba) of the Administration of Justice (Miscellaneous Provisions) Act 1933;
(b) proceedings at a trial of an offence are concluded with the occurrence of any of the following, the discontinuance of the prosecution, the discharge of the jury without a finding, the acquittal of the accused or the sentencing of or other dealing with the accused for the offence of which he was convicted; and
(c) proceedings on an appeal are concluded on the determination or abandonment of the appeal.

Criminal Justice and Public Order Act 1994, s 51(10)

Explanatory notes

- For equivalent offences in some civil proceedings, see ss 39 and 40 of the Criminal Justice and Police Act 2001.
- In respect of the relevant period, this subsection means that the statutory presumption can only be used during the relevant period. It is still possible to bring a prosecution for this offence many years after that period, but the prosecution will not have the advantage of being able to use this presumption.
- In relation to both offences, it will be immaterial whether the act is (or would be) done, or that the threat is made:
  - ✦ otherwise than in the presence of the victim; or
  - ✦ to a person other than the victim.
- Two cases regarding the above provision have determined the following:
  - ✦ Relating to both offences, the person making the threats still commits an offence if they use a third party to convey them to the witness/juror. The 'messenger' could be an innocent agent (eg a victim's relative) who simply passes on a message without understanding its meaning or effect (*A-G's Reference (No 1 of 1999)* [2000] QB 365).
  - ✦ The threats can be made by telephone, letter, or by other means. It is not necessary for the offender and victim to be in the same place at the same time (*DPP v Mills* [1996] 3 WLR 1093).
- The harm done or threatened may be financial as well as physical (whether to the person or a person's property) and the same applies regarding any intimidatory act that consists of threats.
- This offence is in addition to, and does not necessarily replace, any offence which currently exists at common law (eg perversion of the course of justice, which is usually charged as an attempt or conspiracy).
- Communications that constitute threats to another person may also amount to other offences. Consider threats to kill under s 16 of the Offences Against the Person Act 1861 (see **2.5**); threats of violence under ss 4 and 4A of the Protection from Harassment Act 1997 (see **7.11.2**); s 1 of the Malicious Communications Act 1988; and s 127 of the Communications Act 2003 (see **7.12.1** and **7.12.2**).

Related cases

R v ZN [2013] EWCA Crim 989 In order to secure a conviction, it must be proved that the victim was in fact 'intimidated'. If the victim was not intimidated, then consider an offence of attempting witness intimidation (see **4.8.1**).

Van Colle and another v Chief Constable of Hertfordshire [2008] UKHL 50 There is a general duty on the police to suppress crime, but this does not carry with it liability to individuals for injury caused to them by criminals whom the police failed to apprehend or deter when it was possible to do so.

R v Singh (B), Singh (C) and Singh (J) [2000] Cr App R 31 The defendants visited the victim and threatened them. The men were prosecuted for witness intimidation contrary to s 51(1)(b). It was held that to prove the case there must be evidence that the investigation had started. This is required as an objective fact under s 51(1)(c). It is not sufficient for the defendant to believe there is an investigation underway.

Practical considerations

- *R v Davis* [2008] UKHL 26 concerned the use of anonymous witness evidence at trial. The House of Lords judgment placed a restriction on the court's ability to allow evidence to be given anonymously during criminal trials; as a result, protection is now provided through s 89 of the Coroners and Justice Act 2009.
- Sections 74 to 85 of the Coroners and Justice Act 2009 deal with anonymity in criminal investigations for murder/manslaughter where a firearm or knife was used, and the issue of investigation anonymity orders to prohibit disclosure of information to prevent identification of potential witnesses. MOJ Circular 6/2010 provides guidance on these orders.
- Sections 86 to 97 of the Coroners and Justice Act 2009 concern the anonymity of witnesses and the issue, discharge, or variation of witness anonymity orders to protect a witness or prevent the identity of a witness in criminal proceedings being disclosed. MOJ Circular 8/2009 provides guidance on these witness anonymity provisions.

E&S

Either way None

Summary: 6/12 months' imprisonment and/or a fine
Indictment: 5 years' imprisonment and/or a fine

4.8.2 **Perverting the course of justice**

Offences

Committed where a person or persons:
- acts or embarks upon a course of conduct
- which has a tendency to, and
- is intended to pervert,
- the course of public justice.

Common law

PNLD H613

Points to prove

- ✓ with intent to pervert
- ✓ the course of public justice
- ✓ do an act/series of acts
- ✓ tending to pervert course of public justice

Explanatory notes

- Examples where conduct is capable of amounting to this offence are:
  - making false allegations;
  - perjury;
  - concealing offences;
  - obstructing the police;
  - assisting others to evade arrest;
  - failing to prosecute;
  - procuring and indemnifying sureties;
  - interference with witnesses, evidence, and jurors;
  - publication of matters calculated to prejudice a fair trial.
- A positive act is required (eg failing to respond to a summons was insufficient to warrant a charge of perverting the course of justice).
- Any act or course of conduct that tends or is intended to interfere with the course of public justice can amount to an offence. To get a conviction, it is not sufficient to prove that the conduct did, or tended to, pervert the course of justice. The evidence must prove that the offender intended that it would do so.
- It is not necessary for the offender's motives to be the procurement of a false verdict or the defeat of the ends of justice. Trying to introduce genuine evidence by unlawful means is perverting the course of justice (eg a witness takes incriminating photos but refuses to give evidence). Steps are then taken by the investigator to get another witness to introduce them as evidence (*A-G's Reference (No 1 of 2002)* [2002] EWCA Crim 2392).

Related cases

Government of the United States of America v Dempsey [2018] EWHC 1724 (Admin) The mere fact of lying to the police may not itself be enough to make out the offence of perverting the course of justice. It may or may not intend to pervert the course of justice, but the lie can be enough on particular facts.

R v T [2011] EWCA Crim 729 The defendant deleted child pornography files from a memory stick, intending to prevent a criminal investigation against her husband. It was held that an act which might mislead the police or make their investigation more difficult could pervert the course of justice.

Practical considerations

- Putting the term 'attempting to pervert the course of justice' in a common law indictment is misleading because it is a substantive rather than an inchoate (incomplete) offence. It should be charged as 'doing acts tending and intended to pervert the course of justice' (*R v Williams* (1991) 92 Cr App R 158).

- Perverting the course of justice is usually charged as an attempt, conspiracy, or incitement.
- There has been comment by the courts where this offence has been used for relatively minor attempts to pervert the course of justice and it is charged alongside an offence that is serious enough to permit the offender's conduct to be considered when sentencing for the main offence. In *R v Sookoo* [2002] EWCA Crim 800, a shoplifter had attempted to hide their identity and inevitably failed, and the prosecutors should not have included a specific count of perverting the course of justice. Such conduct may serve to aggravate the original offence and the judge may increase the sentence as a result. However, in *R v Pendlebury* [2003] EWCA Crim 3426, P gave a positive breath test but a false name to police and had four previous convictions for doing the same thing. P argued that they should not be charged with perverting the course of justice, and it should simply be an aggravating factor. Held that P's conduct was not too trifling to amount to the offence because it was the third occasion on which they had given false particulars against a background of persistent and serious offending.
- A more appropriate use for this offence will be where a great deal of police time and resources are involved in putting the matter right, or there may be cases where innocent members of the public have their names given and they have been the subject of questioning and even detention.

E&S

Indictable

None

Life imprisonment

4.9 Slavery and Human Trafficking

Article 4 of the Council of Europe Convention on Action against Trafficking in Human Beings defines **human trafficking** as:

- recruiting, transporting, harbouring, or receiving of people;
- by threatening or using:
  - force or other forms of coercion;
  - abduction;
  - fraud;
  - deception;
  - the abuse of power or a position of vulnerability; or
  - the giving or receiving of payments or benefits;
- to achieve the consent of a person having control over another person;
- for the purpose of exploitation.

Exploitation shall include, at a minimum, the exploitation of the prostitution of others or other forms of sexual exploitation, forced labour or services, slavery or practices similar to slavery, servitude, or the removal of organs.

Article 10 of the Convention requires the UK to adopt legislative or other measures to identify, support, and protect victims of trafficking.

Article 26 of the Convention requires that the UK allows for the possibility of not imposing penalties on human trafficking victims if they have been compelled to break the law.

4.9.1 The Modern Slavery Act 2015

The Modern Slavery Act ensures that the National Crime Agency, the police, and other law enforcement agencies have the powers they need to pursue, disrupt, and bring to justice those engaged in human trafficking and slavery, servitude, and forced or compulsory labour. The 2015 Act also introduces measures to enhance the protection of victims of slavery and trafficking.

Sections 1 to 6 consolidate and simplify existing slavery and trafficking offences into one Act. This aims to provide clarity and focus when investigating and prosecuting those involved in modern slavery offences. It also clarifies important aspects of the existing offences, for example to make it clearer that the offences can be used effectively where the victim is vulnerable, such as a child.

The Act includes two main modern slavery offences and creates a defence for victims.

4.9.2 Slavery, servitude, and forced or compulsory labour

Section 1(1) provides an offence of slavery, servitude, and forced or compulsory labour.

Offences

A person commits an offence if—
(a) the person holds another person in slavery or servitude and the circumstances are such that the person knows or ought to know that the other person is held in slavery or servitude, or
(b) the person requires another person to perform forced or compulsory labour and the circumstances are such that the person knows or ought to know that the other person is being required to perform forced or compulsory labour.

Modern Slavery Act 2015, s 1(1)

PNLD H12165, H12166

Points to prove

For s 1(1)(a)

✓ held person in slavery or servitude
✓ knew or ought to have known that the person was in slavery or solitude

For s 1(1)(b)

✓ required person to perform forced/compulsory labour
✓ knew or ought to have known that they were being required to perform
✓ forced/compulsory labour

Meaning of slavery, servitude, and forced or compulsory labour

Have the same meaning as they have for the purposes of Art 4 ECHR agreed by the Council of Europe at Rome on 4 November 1950 as it has effect for the time being in relation to the UK.

Explanatory notes

- The s 1 offence is committed where a person holds another person in slavery or servitude or requires another person to perform forced or compulsory labour, and the first person knows or ought to know that the second person is being held in slavery or servitude or is being required to perform forced or compulsory labour.
- In determining whether a person has been subjected to slavery, servitude, or forced or compulsory labour, regard may be had

to all the circumstances including any of the person's personal circumstances (such as the person's age, the person's family relationships, and any physical or mental disability or illness) that significantly impair the person's ability to protect themselves from being subjected to slavery, servitude, or forced or compulsory labour.

- An individual's consent to the conduct alleged to amount to slavery, servitude, or forced or compulsory labour does not prevent the offence being committed. This provision could be particularly relevant in cases where the victim is vulnerable to abuse, for example a child (a person under the age of 18).
- In relation to the forced or compulsory labour offence, the court can consider any work or services provided by the person including any work or services provided in circumstances that amount to exploitation under s 3(3)–(6). This makes it clear that the forced and compulsory labour offence can cover a broad range of types of work and services, such as begging or picking pockets, that could amount to exploitation under s 3(5) or s 3(6).
- See HO Circular 024/2015.

4.9.3 Human trafficking

The Modern Slavery Act 2015 provides for a single offence of human trafficking covering sexual and non-sexual exploitation.

Offence

A person commits an offence if the person arranges or facilitates the travel of another person ('V') with a view to V being exploited.

Modern Slavery Act 2015, s 2(1)

PNLD H12167

Points to prove

✓ being a UK national (see '**Explanatory notes**' below regarding non-UK nationals)
✓ arranged or facilitated the **travel** of another person with a view to
✓ them being exploited

Meanings

Travel

This means:

- arriving in, or entering, any country;
- departing from any country;
- travelling within any country.

Arrange or facilitate

Section 2 clarifies that it is irrelevant whether or not V consents to the travel and that, in particular, a person may arrange or facilitate V's travel by recruiting V, transporting or transferring V, harbouring or receiving V, or transferring or exchanging control over V.

Exploit

For the offences in s 2, s 3 defines 'exploit' as including slavery, servitude, and forced or compulsory labour; sexual exploitation; removal of organs; securing services, etc by force, threats, or deception; and securing services, etc from children and vulnerable persons.

Explanatory notes

- Section 2(6) provides that a UK national commits an offence regardless of: where in the world the arranging or facilitating takes place; or the countries of arrival, entry, travel, or departure. For example, a UK national who traffics a person from Spain to France could be prosecuted in England and Wales for this offence.
- Under s 4, committing one offence with a view to going on to commit a trafficking offence under s 2 is a separate offence. Thus, preparatory criminal conduct that constitutes a lesser offence can attract higher penalties. For example, if someone supplies false documents intending them to be used to facilitate human trafficking or steals a vehicle intending to use it to traffic individuals, that person can be tried *both* for the lesser offence (supplying false documents; vehicle theft) *and* for an offence preparatory to human trafficking.
- Section 2(7) provides that a person who is not a UK national commits an offence under this section if:
  (a) any part of the arranging or facilitating takes place in the UK; or
  (b) the travel consists of arrival in or entry into, departure from, or travel within, the UK.
- See HO Circular 024/2015.

Related cases

R v AFU [2023] EWCA Crim 23 A conviction for conspiracy to produce Class B drugs was unsafe. Prosecuting authorities had failed to follow CPS guidelines relating to the prosecution of suspects who might be victims of trafficking. Although the status as a victim of trafficking does not always preclude a prosecution, where a victim has been compelled to commit criminal acts and where those criminal acts are attributable to slavery, then a prosecution will be unlikely to succeed. Case law refers to there being a necessary degree of nexus between the trafficking and the offence in such cases, often evidenced by the extent of a defendant's compulsion to act.

R v Ali and another [2015] EWCA Crim 1279 This case considered (among other issues) the meaning of 'trafficking', in which the defendants were convicted of various sexual offences arising out of the grooming of young girls for sexual purposes. It was held that the key factor was travel and that a journey was contemplated. The fact that the journey might be short did not affect whether the offence had been committed. The legislation does not specify a minimum distance or duration and, therefore, victims could be 'trafficked' within or across a small geographical area. The case relates to the previous offence of trafficking contained in s 59A of the Sexual Offences Act 2003; however, it is thought that the details of this case in relation to the meaning of 'trafficking' are still applicable to the newer offence under s 2 of the Modern Slavery Act 2015.

R (on the application of SF) v Secretary of State for the Home Department [2015] EWHC 2705 (Admin) In determining whether a 17-year-old girl (SF) had been trafficked, it was held that the competent authority had wrongly attached significant weight to a police inspector's conclusion that there was insufficient evidence of trafficking. The decision that SF had not been trafficked had to be quashed, as the CA had failed to take into account the evidence of the experts, fortified by the guidance, relating to the reasons why an honest person who had been trafficked might give inconsistent or late evidence.

Practical considerations

What to look for—indications that a person might be a victim of trafficking

Trafficking victims are often arrested on the following charges:

- cannabis cultivation;
- drug importation;
- immigration offences;
- document offences;
- prostitution;
- dishonesty offences, including theft, picking pockets, and begging.

The following is a non-exhaustive list of common factors that may also help identify possible victims:

- from a place known to be a source of human trafficking;
- possession of false identity or travel documents;
- showing signs of fear or anxiety;
- exhibiting distrust of the authorities;
- evidence of violence or threats of violence;
- fear of revealing immigration status;
- lack of knowledge of home or work address;
- signs that the individual's movements are being controlled or that they are taking instructions from a third party;
- inconsistent about name and age.
- Both the s 1 offence (slavery, servitude, and forced or compulsory labour) and the s 2 offence (human trafficking) are 'criminal lifestyle' offences under Sch 2 to the Proceeds of Crime Act 2002 (POCA) (see **5.5**).

- Sections 1 and 2 of the Modern Slavery Act 2015 are on the list of either way offences, so a simple caution can only be used in exceptional circumstances and with the agreement of an **inspector**, in accordance with s 17(3) of the Criminal Justice and Courts Act 2015.
- In relation to the s 2 offence and child sexual exploitation, also consider the Serious Crime Act 2015, s 69(1), which makes it an offence to be in possession of any item that contains advice or guidance about abusing children sexually (see **6.5.1**).
- Sections 11 and 12 of the Modern Slavery Act 2015 allow a senior immigration officer or **constable** to detain a **land vehicle, ship, or aircraft** where a person has been arrested for a s 2 offence (human trafficking) and there are reasonable grounds to believe that a forfeiture order could be made if that person was convicted.

Either way None

For both s 1 and s 2 offences:

Summary: 6/12 months' imprisonment and/or a fine

Indictment: Life imprisonment

4.9.4 Slavery and trafficking prevention orders on sentencing

Section 14 of the Modern Slavery Act 2015 provides for slavery and trafficking prevention orders (STPO) on conviction.

A court may make a slavery and trafficking prevention order against a person ('the defendant') where it deals with the defendant in respect of—
(a) a conviction for a slavery or human trafficking offence,
(b) a finding that the defendant is not guilty of a slavery or human trafficking offence by reason of insanity, or
(c) a finding that the defendant is under a disability and has done the act charged against the defendant in respect of a slavery or human trafficking offence.

Modern Slavery Act 2015, s 14(1)

Explanatory notes

- The prohibitions that may be included in the order are those which the court is satisfied are necessary for the purpose of protecting persons generally, or particular persons, from the physical or psychological harm which would be likely to occur if the defendant committed a slavery or human trafficking offence.
- Section 14(2) provides that the court may make the order only if it is satisfied that:

(a) there is a risk that the defendant may commit a slavery or human trafficking offence; and
(b) it is necessary to make the order for the purpose of protecting persons generally, or particular persons, from the physical or psychological harm which would be likely to occur if the defendant committed such an offence.

- A slavery or human trafficking offence means an offence listed in Sch 1 to the Act.
- Section 17 of the Act provides that the STPO may prohibit the defendant from doing things in any part of the UK, and anywhere outside the UK and will have effect for a fixed period of at least five years (save for restrictions on foreign travel) or until a further order is made.
- The STPO is intended to restrict the activity of individuals who have been convicted of a slavery or human trafficking offence, including an equivalent offence in a country outside the UK.
- A court may make an STPO against an individual when sentencing that person for a slavery or human trafficking offence. Alternatively, a **chief officer of police**, an immigration officer, or the Director General of the National Crime Agency can apply to a magistrates' court for an STPO.
- An STPO can be used for individuals under 18. In these cases, the application will be dealt with by a youth court.
- Under s 23, a slavery and trafficking risk order (STRO) can be made by a magistrates' court. The court may make the order only if it is satisfied that the defendant has acted in a way which means that:
  (a) there is a risk that the defendant will commit a slavery or human trafficking offence; and
  (b) it is necessary to make the order for the purpose of protecting persons generally, or particular persons, from the physical or psychological harm which would be likely to occur if the defendant committed such an offence.
- Section 24 gives the effect to an STRO to prohibit the defendant from doing anything described in the order for a fixed period of at least two years or until a further order is made.

Related case

R v Wabelua and others [2020] EWCA Crim 783 The court summarised the eight principles applicable when making a slavery and tracking prevention order pursuant to s 14(1) of the Modern Slavery Act 2015.

4.9.5 Defence for victims of slavery or trafficking

Section 45 of the 2015 Act provides a defence for victims of slavery or trafficking who have committed a criminal offence. The defence is intended to provide further encouragement to victims to come forward and give evidence without fear of being prosecuted and convicted for offences connected to their slave or trafficked status.

The statutory defence set out in s 45 applies a different test in the defence for people aged 18 or over and those under the age of 18. This emphasises that children can be influenced into committing crimes without compulsion being used and reflects DPP guidance.

Defence

For a person under the age of 18 when an act that constitutes an offence is committed, s 45 defence applies where:

- the child commits the offence as a direct consequence of their being a victim of slavery or relevant exploitation; and
- a reasonable person in the same situation and having the child's relevant characteristics (including their age) would have committed the offence.

Where a person is aged 18 or over when an act that constitutes an offence is committed, s 45 defence applies where that person:

- commits the offence because they were compelled to do so;
- was compelled as a result of slavery or relevant exploitation (compulsion is further defined at s 45(3)); and
- a reasonable person in the same situation and having the relevant characteristics would have committed the offence.

Related cases

R v AAC [2023] EWCA Crim 15 Convictions relating to the applications for false identity documents, and the use of these to commit fraud, were not safe where the defendant was found to be a victim of human trafficking. Although AAC had pled guilty and the offending took place prior to the defence available in s 45 of the Modern Slavery Act 2015 coming into force, Art 26 of the Council of Europe Convention on Action against Trafficking in Human Beings requires state parties to provide for the possibility of not proposing penalties on victims of trafficking for their involvement in unlawful activities, to the extent that they have been compelled to do so. The court accepted AAC's evidence in its entirety and accepted that they were a victim of trafficking and so accepted that, for some of the offences, AAC did not commit the offences and so the conviction was unsafe, and the appeal could be allowed.

R v AAD and others [2022] EWCA Crim 106 The judgment in this case sets out guidance from the Court of Appeal on trafficking and modern slavery cases, including admissibility of conclusive grounds decisions, abuse of process considering the s 45 defence, and circumstances where a victim could argue that a guilty plea was unsafe.

R v AAJ [2021] EWCA Crim 1278 Where offending occurred before the Modern Slavery Act 2015 came into force, the defence under s 45 does not have retrospective effect. Where that is so, the old case law applies. It establishes that there is no blanket immunity; the central question is whether there is a reasonable nexus of connection between the offence and the trafficking so as to make the trafficked person a victim of the offence in question and diminish or extinguish their culpability; and, in such a case, the prosecutor must consider whether it is in the public interest to prosecute.

R v CS and L [2021] EWCA Crim 134 Section 45 of the Modern Slavery Act 2015 does not have retrospective effect. There was no factor which positively indicated that Parliament intended the defence under s 45 to be available in respect of offences committed by victims of trafficking before the Act came into force.

R v MK; R v Gega [2018] EWCA Crim 667 Section 45 does not require the defendant to bear the legal burden of proof. What is required is that the relevant issue is raised by evidence. The defence must then apply the criminal standard to disprove each element of the defence.

4.9.6 Duty to notify the Home Office of suspected victims of slavery or human trafficking

Section 52 introduced a duty to notify the Home Office about suspected victims of slavery or human trafficking. Potential victims should be referred to the National Referral Mechanism (NRM). The duty is placed on specified public authorities to which the section applies and is triggered where that authority has reasonable grounds to believe that a person may be a victim of slavery or human trafficking.

Explanatory notes

- The public authorities to which the duty applies currently include a chief officer of police for a police area, the Chief Constable of the BTP, the NCA, the Gangmasters and Labour Abuse Authority, and council authorities.
- The NRM team has a target date of five working days from receipt of referral in which to decide whether there are reasonable grounds to believe the individual is a potential victim of human trafficking. This may involve seeking additional information from the first responder or from specialist non-governmental organisations, social services, or the individual's legal representative. Following a positive 'reasonable grounds' decision, the NRM team have at least forty-five working days to determine whether 'on the balance of probabilities' there are sufficient grounds to decide that the individual is a victim of modern slavery.
- See HO Circular 025/2015.

4.9.6 **Notification of suspected victims of slavery or human trafficking**

Links to alternative subjects and offences

2.6.2 **Kidnapping** 102
2.6.3 **Child abduction** 103
5.5 **Proceeds of Crime** 270
6.11.3 **Paying for sexual services of a prostitute subject to exploitation** 349
7.6 **Fear or Provocation of Violence** 373
Appendix 1 **Human Rights** 839

4.10 Ill-treatment or Neglect by a Care Worker

Offence

It is an offence for an individual who has the care of another individual by virtue of being a care worker to ill-treat or wilfully to neglect that individual.

Criminal Justice and Courts Act 2015, s 20(1)

PNLD H12029

Points to prove

✓ has the care of another
✓ by virtue of being a care worker
✓ ill-treated/wilfully neglected that individual

Meanings

Care worker

An individual who, as **paid work**, provides:

(a) **health care** for an **adult** or **child**, other than excluded health care, or
(b) **social care** for an adult,

including an individual who, as paid work, supervises or manages individuals providing such care or is a director or similar officer of an organisation that provides such care.

Paid work

An individual does something as paid work if they receive or are entitled to payment for doing it other than:

(a) payment of reasonable expenses;
(b) payment to which the individual is entitled as a foster parent;
(c) a social security benefit; or
(d) a payment made under s 2 of the Employment and Training Act 1973 (arrangements to assist people to select, train for, obtain, and retain employment).

Health care

This includes:
(a) all forms of health care provided for individuals relating to physical or mental health, and care provided for or in connection with the protection or improvement of public health; and

(b) procedures similar to forms of medical or surgical care that are not provided in connection with a medical condition, and 'excluded health care' is defined in Sch 4.

Social care

This includes all forms of personal care and other practical assistance provided for individuals who need such care or assistance by reason of age, illness, disability, pregnancy, childbirth, dependence on alcohol or drugs, or any similar circumstances.

Adult

This means an individual aged 18 or over.

Child

This means an individual aged under 18.

Explanatory notes

- Section 20 makes it an offence for an individual who has the care of another individual by virtue of being a care worker to ill-treat or wilfully neglect that individual. The offence applies in England and Wales.
- A person providing health care or social care that is merely incidental to the person's other activities is not included. So, for example, a prison officer who assisted a prisoner in adjusting a hearing aid, could be perceived as providing practical assistance within the definition of 'social care'; but, in this example, the prison officer would have provided the assistance incidentally to their custodial duties not by virtue of being a care worker. The same principles would apply, for example, to police officers and office workers in similar circumstances.
- The *care provider* may also commit an offence under s 21 of the Act (subject to s 22).
- The definition of 'care worker' is intended to ensure that the individual offence can apply to any individual perpetrator not just those on the 'front line' of care provision. However, it will only apply where the individual supervisor, director, etc has themselves directly committed ill-treatment or wilful neglect. They will not commit the individual offence by virtue of the acts or omissions of others they supervise or manage.
- The offence is limited to those performing 'paid work', as defined, to ensure that informal carers, such as unpaid family and friends, are not captured by the offence. The intention is also to exclude from the definition situations where an individual works as an unpaid volunteer but, for example, travel costs to and from the place where they volunteer are reimbursed. Similarly, this exclusion would also cover a family carer who occasionally receives a contribution towards the personal costs they incur in providing that care from the person for whom they care. Such reimbursement is not to be treated

as amounting to paid work. The intention is also to exclude any social security benefit where, for example, claimants are required to undertake unpaid work as a condition of receiving that benefit. So, for example, an individual working in an adult care home as part of the Department for Work and Pensions' 'Work Programme' will not be treated as being in paid work.

- 'Health care' includes services provided as part of the protection or improvement of public health, for example smoking cessation support, and is also intended to capture services, such as cosmetic surgery, that are not necessarily directly related to a medical condition.
- For more information, see MOJ Circular 2015/01.

E&S CHAR

Either way

None

Summary: 6/12 months' imprisonment and/or a fine

Indictment: 5 years' imprisonment and/or a fine

Links to alternative subjects and offences

2.1 **Assault (Common/Actual Bodily Harm)** 53
2.4 **Child Cruelty** 91
2.8 **Domestic Abuse** 125
7.3 **Breach of the Peace** 362
7.8 **Threatening/Abusive Words/Behaviour** 380
7.10 **Racially/Religiously Aggravated Offences** 390

4.11 Forced Marriages

The Anti-social Behaviour, Crime and Policing Act 2014 deals with the criminal offence of forced marriage. In addition, the Family Law Act 1996 provides civil remedies regarding forced marriage and the offence of breaching a forced marriage protection order.

4.11.1 Forced marriage offences

Section 121 of the Anti-social Behaviour, Crime and Policing Act 2014 gives various offences relating to forced marriage.

Offences

(1) A person commits an offence under the law of England and Wales if he or she—
  (a) uses violence, threats or any other form of coercion for the purpose of causing another person to enter into a marriage, and
  (b) believes, or ought reasonably to believe, that the conduct may cause the other person to enter into the marriage without free and full consent.

(3) A person commits an offence under the law of England and Wales if he or she—
  (a) practises any form of deception with the intention of causing another person to leave the United Kingdom, and
  (b) intends the other person to be subjected to conduct outside the United Kingdom that is an offence under subsection (1) or would be an offence under that subsection if the victim were in England or Wales.

(3A) A person commits an offence under the law of England and Wales if he or she carries out any conduct for the purpose of causing a child to enter into a marriage before the child's eighteenth birthday (whether or not the conduct amounts to violence, threats, any other form of coercion or deception, and whether or not it is carried out in England and Wales).

Anti-social Behaviour, Crime and Policing Act 2014, s 121

PNLD H11462, H11463, H100800

Points to prove

s 121(1) offence

✓ used violence/threats/other form of coercion
✓ in order to cause a person to enter into marriage
✓ believed/ought reasonably to have believed

✓ this conduct may cause that person
✓ to marry without free and full consent

s 121(3) offence

✓ practised any form of deception
✓ with intent to cause a person to leave UK
✓ intending that person to be subject of s 121(1) offence outside UK OR
✓ would be subject to s 121(1) offence if victim were in England and Wales

s 121 (3A) offence

✓ carried out conduct
✓ for the purpose of causing a child
✓ to enter into a marriage
✓ before that child's eighteenth birthday

Meanings

Child

A person under the age of 18 years.

Marriage

This means any religious or civil ceremony of marriage (whether or not legally binding).

Explanatory notes

- The offence of forced marriage catches a person who intentionally forces a person to enter into marriage, believing the person does not consent, or a person who deceives someone into going abroad for the specific purpose of forcing them to marry. An offence is committed whether or not the forced marriage goes ahead.
- If the intended victim lacks capacity (under the Mental Capacity Act 2005) to consent to marriage, the offence under s 121(1) is capable of being committed by any conduct carried out for the purpose of causing the victim to enter into a marriage (whether or not the conduct amounts to violence, threats, or any other form of coercion).
- It is irrelevant whether the conduct mentioned in s 121(1)(a) or (3A) is directed at the victim of the offence or another person for the purposes of either of those subsections.

Practical considerations

- A person commits an offence under s 121(1) or (3) only if, at the time of the conduct or deception:
  - ✦ the person or the victim or both of them are in England or Wales;
  - ✦ neither the person nor the victim is in England or Wales but at least one of them is habitually resident in England and Wales; or
  - ✦ neither the person nor the victim is in the UK but at least one of them is a **UK national**.

- A person commits an offence under subsection (3A) only if:
  - the conduct is for the purpose of causing the child to enter into a marriage in England or Wales;
  - at the time of the conduct, the person or child is habitually resident in England and Wales; or
  - at the time of the conduct, the child is a UK national who:
    - has been habitually resident in England and Wales; and
    - is not habitually resident or domiciled in Scotland or Northern Ireland.
- The term **UK national** means an individual who is:
  - a British citizen, a British Overseas Territories citizen, a British National (Overseas), or a British Overseas citizen;
  - a person who under the British Nationality Act 1981 is a British subject; or
  - a British protected person within the meaning of that Act.
- HOC 10/2014 provides guidance and further information.
- If a forced marriage protection order is breached, then this is an offence under s 63CA of the Family Law Act 1996 (see **4.11.2**).
- Schedule 6A (para 1) to the Anti-social Behaviour, Crime and Policing Act 2014 provides for the anonymity of victims of forced marriage in England and Wales. It creates a prohibition (summary offence) on the identification of victims in publications; penalties where the prohibition is breached; but also a defence to a defendant who can prove that at the time of the alleged offence, they were not aware, and did not suspect or have reason to suspect, that the publication included the matter in question or that the allegation in question had been made.

Either way

None

Summary: 6/12 months' imprisonment and/or a fine

Indictment: 7 years' imprisonment

4.11.2 Forced marriage: protection orders

Section 63CA of the Family Law Act 1996 provides for forced marriage protection orders to protect a person from being forced into marriage or from any attempt to be forced into a marriage, or to protect a person who has been forced into a marriage.

Powers and Offences

The Act provides powers for the courts to issue protection orders, and deal with other associated matters, together with the offence of breaching a marriage protection order, as follows:

- s 63A—Forced marriage protection orders;

- s 63B—Contents of orders;
- s 63C—Applications and other occasions for making orders;
- s 63CA—Offence of breaching order:
  - ✦ s 63CA(1): a person who without reasonable excuse does anything that the person is prohibited from doing by a forced marriage protection order is guilty of an offence;
  - ✦ s 63CA(2): where an order is made under s 63D(1), a person is liable for the s 63CA offence only if that person was aware of the existence of the order;
  - ✦ s 63CA(3): if a person is convicted of the s 63CA offence, that conduct is not punishable as a contempt of court;
  - ✦ s 63CA(4): if any conduct has been punished as a contempt of court, a person cannot be convicted of the s 63CA offence.

Related case

West Sussex County Council and another v F and others [2018] EWHC 1702 (Fam) A loosely arranged 'engagement' without the victim's consent, but not with the intention subsequently of her being forced to marry, whether she wanted to or not, did not amount to a forced marriage or any imminent risk of that. There is a distinction between consensual arranged marriages and forced marriages involving serious human rights abuses. This case was far closer to the arranged marriage end of the spectrum. The nature of the arrangement was such that, had it endured to an age when the victim might legally have married, she would have had a say and, had she not wished it, it would not have proceeded.

Practical considerations

- It is important that the difference between an arranged marriage and a forced marriage is recognised and understood.
  - ✦ An arranged marriage is an agreement between both parties (usually prompted by the parents) entered into freely and is a practice that has worked successfully in several cultures for many centuries.
  - ✦ A forced marriage, for the purpose of the Act, is when a person ('A') is forced into a marriage by another person ('B'), whether the marriage is to B or another person, without A's free and full consent.
- There are criminal offences that can be committed by the family and (potential) husband/wife of the person when forcing someone into marriage such as forced marriage (see **4.11.1**), assaults (see **2.1**), false imprisonment or kidnapping (see **2.6**), and sexual offences (see **Chapter 6**).
- There are different types of situations where the issue of forced marriage can arise:
  - ✦ fear of being forced to marry in the UK or abroad;
  - ✦ already in a forced marriage;
  - ✦ a third-party report;
  - ✦ a spouse brought from abroad.

4.11.2 **Forced marriage: protection orders**

- Section 173 of the Policing and Crime Act 2017 has improved the protection to victims of forced marriages by providing them with lifelong anonymity by inserting s 122A of the Anti-social Behaviour, Crime and Policing Act 2014.
- With the victim's consent, refer them to local and national support groups (eg Honour Network or Forced Marriage Unit (FMU) at the Foreign and Commonwealth Office—see **Appendix 2**).
- Make a referral to social services and Child Protection Department if the victim is, or has children, under 18.
- Although it is mostly women who are affected by this, there are cases of men who are also forced to marry, and they should be treated in the same way as a woman making the report.

For the offence of breaching an order under s 63CA

Either way　　None

Summary: 6/12 months' imprisonment and/or a fine

Indictment: 5 years' imprisonment and/or a fine

Links to alternative subjects and offences

2.6 **False Imprisonment, Kidnapping, and Child Abduction** 100
2.8 **Domestic Abuse** 125
6 **Sexual Offences and Assaults** 275
7.6 **Fear or Provocation of Violence** 373
7.7 **Intentional Harassment, Alarm, or Distress** 376
7.11 **Harassment/Stalking** 398
Appendix 1 **Human Rights** 839
Appendix 2 **Useful Contacts and Links** 845

4.12 Computer Misuse

This legislation makes provisions for the securing of computer material against unauthorised access or modification. It is intended to be used against 'hackers' (ie people who break into computer systems without authority either externally or within an organisation).

4.12.1 Unauthorised access to computer material

Offence

A person is guilty of an offence if—

(a) he causes a computer to perform any function with intent to secure access to any program or data held in any computer, or to enable any such access to be secured;

(b) the access he intends to secure, or to enable to be secured, is unauthorised; and

(c) he knows at the time when he causes the computer to perform the function that that is the case.

Computer Misuse Act 1990, s 1(1)

PNLD H8770

Points to prove

- ✓ caused a computer to perform a function
- ✓ with intent to secure authorised access to
- ✓ a program/data held in the computer or to enable any such access to be so secured

Explanatory notes

- The intent a person has to have to commit an offence under this section need not be directed at any particular program or data; a program or data of any particular kind; or a program or data held in any particular computer.
- The offence would be committed where the person's intention is to enable someone else to secure unauthorised access to a computer or to enable the person themselves to secure unauthorised access to a computer at some later time.
- A person secures access to a program or data held in a computer if by causing a computer to perform a function they:
  - (a) alter or erase the program or data;
  - (b) copy or move it to a storage medium other than that in which it is held or to a different location in the storage medium in which it is held;

(c) use it; or
(d) have it output from the computer in which it is held (whether by having it displayed or in any other manner).

- References to a program or data held in a computer include references to a program or data held in a removable storage medium which is for the time being in the computer; and a computer is to be regarded as containing a program or data held in such a medium.
- No damage, loss, or gain need be proven. These are aspects of the offence under s 2 (see **4.12.2**) that prohibit unlawful access and might be said inherently to cause damage to the security and integrity of a computer system.
- Where access is the issue, it is the access which must be unauthorised to commit this offence. If an authorised person later misuses information, there is no offence under s 1 or 2 of the Act (see **4.12.2**) but there may be an offence under s 3 depending on the circumstances.

Related cases

R v Coltman [2018] Crim 2059 There is no public interest defence available to an allegation under s 1(1) of the Computer Misuse Act 1990.

Attorney-General's Reference (No 1 of 1991) [1993] QB 94 The computer which a person causes to perform a function with the required intent does not have to be a different computer from the one into which they intend to secure unauthorised access.

Practical considerations

- Where a computer is used to access personal data, consideration should be given to s 170 of the Data Protection Act 2018 which criminalises the deliberate or reckless obtaining, disclosing, or procuring disclosure to another and retention of personal data without the consent of the data controller.
- Personal data comprises data which relates to a living individual who can be identified from that data. As personal data is increasingly stored, processed, and exchanged on the internet and as such often exists in an international environment, this Act was introduced to interlock the UK's data protection laws with international data protection arrangements.

4.12.2 Unauthorised access with intent to commit further offence

Offence

A person is guilty of an offence under this section if he commits an offence under section 1 ('the unauthorised access offence') with intent—
(a) to commit an offence to which this section applies; or

(b) to facilitate the commission of such an offence (whether by himself or by any other person);

and the offence he intends to commit or facilitate is referred to below in this section as the further offence.

Computer Misuse Act 1990, s 2

PNLD H4201, H4202

Points to prove

✓ caused a computer to perform a function
✓ with intent to secure authorised access to
✓ a program/data held in the computer
✓ with intent to commit offence under s 2 OR
✓ with intent to facilitate the commission of an offence under s 2

Explanatory notes

- This section applies to offences for which the sentence is fixed by law; or for which a person of 21 years of age or over (and has no previous convictions) may be sentenced to imprisonment for a term of five years.
- It is immaterial for the purposes of this section whether the further offence is to be committed on the same occasion as the unauthorised access offence or on any future occasion.
- A person may be guilty of an offence under this section even though the commission of the further offence is impossible.

Related case

Attorney-General's Reference (No 1 of 1991) [1993] QB 94 (see **4.12.1**).

Practical considerations

- In *R v Bow Street Metropolitan Stipendiary Magistrate, ex p Government of the United States* [1999] QB 847, it was determined that ss 1 and 2 can include individuals who have lawful access to specific files on a system, but then look at other material on the same system (eg an operator is given a number of computer files to work upon but then accesses other files).
- Also note practical considerations at **4.12.1**.

4.12.2 Unauthorised access with intent to commit further offence

Either way

Offence under s 1

Time Limit: None

Summary: 6/12 months' imprisonment and/or a fine

Indictment: 2 years' imprisonment and/or a fine

Offence under s 2

Time Limit: Complex (see legislation)

Summary: 6/12 months' imprisonment and/or a fine

Indictment: 5 years' imprisonment and/or a fine

Chapter 5

Controlled Drugs

5.1 Produce/Supply a Controlled Drug and Supply of Articles

The Misuse of Drugs Act 1971 regulates certain drugs and designates which drugs are controlled by assigning them to certain categories (A, B, or C). If the drug is a controlled drug, it will be unlawful, with exceptions, to import, export, produce, supply, or possess that drug. Section 4 deals with producing or supplying a controlled drug and s 9A supplying or offering articles for the purpose of administering or preparing controlled drugs.

5.1.1 Produce/supply a controlled drug

Section 4 of the Misuse of Drugs Act 1971 provides a prohibition on the production, supply, and offering to supply of controlled drugs, with offences for contravening such prohibitions.

Offences

(1) Subject to any regulations under section 7 of this Act, or any provision made in a temporary class drug order by virtue of section 7A for the time being in force, it shall not be lawful for a person—
   (a) to produce a controlled drug; or
   (b) to supply or offer to supply a controlled drug to another.
(2) Subject to section 28 of this Act, it is an offence for a person—
   (a) to produce a controlled drug in contravention of subsection (1) above; or
   (b) to be concerned in the production of such a drug in contravention of that subsection by another.
(3) Subject to section 28 of this Act, it is an offence for a person—
   (a) to supply or offer to supply a controlled drug to another in contravention of subsection (1) above; or

(b) to be concerned in the supplying of such a drug to another in contravention of that subsection; or

(c) to be concerned in the making to another in contravention of that subsection of an offer to supply such a drug.

Misuse of Drugs Act 1971, s 4

PNLD H1924, H1939, H2351, H2356, H5077

Points to prove

s 4(2)(a) offence

✓ produced
✓ controlled drug of Class A/B/C

s 4(2)(b) offence

✓ concerned in the production
✓ by another of
✓ controlled drug of Class A/B/C

s 4(3)(a) offence

✓ supply or offered to supply (type of drug)
✓ a controlled drug of Class A/B/C

s 4(3)(b) offence

✓ was concerned in
✓ supplying (type of drug)
✓ a controlled drug of Class A/B/C

s 4(3)(c) offence

✓ was concerned in making an offer
✓ to supply (type of drug)
✓ a controlled drug of Class A/B/C

Meanings

Regulations under section 7

Misuse of Drugs Regulations 2001—see '**Defences**' below.

Temporary class drug order

This is an order under s 2A that temporarily makes a substance or product a Class A, B, or C controlled drug, until it may then be formally classified and added to Sch 2 to the Act. See HOC 012/11 for further information.

Provision made by virtue of s 7A

Section 7A provides the Secretary of State with the power to make further provision in relation to a drug subject to temporary control.

Produce

Means producing a controlled drug by manufacture, cultivation, or any other method, and 'production' has a corresponding meaning.

Stripping a cannabis plant of its leaves comes within the term 'any other method' for the purposes of production (*R v Harris and Cox* [1996] Crim LR 36).

Defendants who supply hydroponic equipment have been convicted of conspiracy to be concerned in the production of cannabis by another (*R v Dang and others* [2014] EWCA Crim 348).

Controlled drug

Means (per s 2) a substance or product that is classified under Class A, B, or C in Sch 2 to the Act; or a drug subject to a temporary class drug order.

Supply

Furnishing or providing a person with something that person wants or requires for their purpose. Including where an offender is looking after drugs whether voluntarily or involuntarily if they intend returning them to the person for whom they were being 'minded' or even anyone else (*R v Maginnis* [1987] 1 All ER 907 (voluntary minding) and *R v Panton* [2001] EWCA Crim 611 (involuntary minding, eg after threats have been made against them)). Section 37 (interpretation) states that supplying includes distributing.

Subject to section 28 (see '**Defences**' below)

Explanatory notes

- The offence of offering to supply a controlled drug is complete when the offer is made. It does not matter whether the defendant intended ever to follow the offer through (see *R v Goodard* [1992] Crim LR 588).
- Undercover or 'test purchase' officers are trained to a National Standard and comply with NPCC guidelines. Where appropriate, authority is obtained under Part 2 of the Regulation of Investigatory Powers Act 2000, before surveillance takes place.

Defences

Section 28 of the Misuse of Drugs Act 1971

This applies to offences under s 4(2) and (3), s 5(2) and (3), s 6(2), and s 9 of this Act and provides that it shall be a defence if the defendant proves that they:

- neither believed nor suspected nor had reason to suspect that the substance or product in question was a controlled drug; or
- believed the substance or product in question to be a controlled drug or a controlled drug of a description such that, if it had been that controlled drug or a controlled drug of that description, they would not at the material time have been committing any offence to which this section applies.

Regulation 5 of the Misuse of Drugs Regulations 2001—Licences to produce, supply, possess

Where any person is authorised by a licence of the Secretary of State issued under this regulation and for the time being in force to produce, supply, offer to supply or have in his possession any controlled drug, it shall not, by virtue of section 4(1) or 5(1) of the Act, be unlawful for that person to produce, supply, offer to supply or have in his possession that drug in accordance with the terms of the licence and in compliance with any conditions attached to the licence.

Misuse of Drugs Regulations 2001, reg 5

Regulation 6 of the Misuse of Drugs Regulations 2001—General authority to supply and possess

(1) Notwithstanding the provisions of section 4(1)(b) of the Act, any person who is lawfully in possession of a controlled drug may supply that drug to the person from whom he obtained it.
(2) Notwithstanding the provisions of section 4(1)(b) of the Act, any person who has in his possession a drug specified in Schedule 2, 3, 4 or 5 which has been supplied by or on the prescription of a practitioner, a registered nurse, a pharmacist independent prescriber, a supplementary prescriber or a person specified in Schedule 8 acting in accordance with a patient group direction for the treatment of that person, or of a person whom he represents, may supply that drug to any doctor, dentist or pharmacist for the purpose of destruction.
(3) Notwithstanding the provisions of section 4(1)(b) of the Act, any person who is lawfully in possession of a drug specified in Schedule 2, 3, 4 or 5 which has been supplied by or on the prescription of a veterinary practitioner or veterinary surgeon for the treatment of animals may supply that drug to any veterinary practitioner, veterinary surgeon or pharmacist for the purpose of destruction.
(4) It shall not by virtue of section 4(1)(b) or 5(1) of the Act be unlawful for any person in respect of whom a licence has been granted and is in force under section 16(1) of the Wildlife and Countryside Act 1981 to supply, offer to supply or have in his possession any drug specified in Schedule 2 or 3 for the purposes for which that licence was granted.
(5) Notwithstanding the provisions of section 4(1)(b) of the Act, any of the persons specified in paragraph (7) may supply any controlled drug to any person who may lawfully have that drug in his possession.
(6) Notwithstanding the provisions of section 5(1) of the Act, any of the persons so specified may have any controlled drug in his possession.
(7) The persons referred to in paragraphs (5) and (6) are—
    (a) a constable when acting in the course of his duty as such;
    (b) a person engaged in the business of a carrier when acting in the course of that business;
    (c) a person engaged in the business of a postal operator (within the meaning of the Postal Services Act 2000) when acting in the course of that business;

(d) an officer of customs and excise when acting in the course of his duty as such;
(e) a person engaged in the work of any laboratory to which the drug has been sent for forensic examination when acting in the course of his duty as a person so engaged;
(f) a person engaged in conveying the drug to a person who may lawfully have that drug in his possession.

Misuse of Drugs Regulations 2001, reg 6

Related cases

R v AGM [2022] EWCA Crim 920 After pleading guilty to being concerned in the production of cannabis, AGM was sentenced to eighteen months' imprisonment. On appeal, it was argued that AGM's conviction on their own plea was unsafe because, if it had been known that AGM was a victim of trafficking, either AGM would not have been prosecuted or the proceedings, which took place before the passing of the Modern Slavery Act 2015, would have been stayed as an abuse of process. The appeal was allowed and the court held, inter alia, that AGM was more likely than not to be a victim of trafficking. There was not a direct causal nexus between the fact that AGM had previously been a victim of slavery and exploitation and the commission of the offence. Therefore, the defence under s 45 of the Act was not available. However, the conviction was unsafe where the defendant was more likely than not to have been a victim of trafficking and so it would not have been in the public interest to prosecute them.

R v Abi-Khalil, R v Porja [2017] EWCA Crim 17 Two defendants cannot be concerned in the supply of drugs to another, where the supply is to one of the defendants themselves, unless the facts suggest an onward supply of the drugs.

R v Marron [2011] EWCA Crim 792 At the airport, M's luggage was found to contain 44 kg of a fine white powder. M was convicted of conspiracy to supply cocaine, by importing a non-controlled drug (Phenacetin) that is used as a 'cutting agent' for cocaine.

R v Hodgson [2001] EWCA Crim 2697 The number of visitors, for short periods, to a property may be evidence from which drug dealing may be inferred.

R v Leeson [2000] 1 Cr App R 233 It does not matter whether a person thinks they are dealing in a specific type of controlled drug if they are in fact dealing in another.

R v Russell [1992] Crim LR 362 Making crack from cocaine is 'producing'.

R v Shivpuri [1986] 2 All ER 334, HL Attempting to supply something that in fact was not a controlled drug can nevertheless be a criminal attempt.

R v Hunt [1987] 1 All ER 1, HL The onus is on the prosecution to prove all elements, including the fact that the drug could not be lawfully possessed by the defendant in the circumstances.

5.1.1 **Produce/supply a controlled drug**

R v Maginnis [1987] 1 All ER 907, HL This case involved possession of a packet of cannabis that was being kept for a friend (a drug trafficker). The return of the drugs to the trafficker was deemed to be supply.

Practical considerations

- Consider offences under s 23 or s 24 of the Offences Against the Person Act 1861 relating to maliciously administering poison or noxious things, etc to another (see **2.1.3**).
- Section 71 of the Sentencing Act 2020 sets out how a court must treat as an aggravating factor the fact that the offence of supplying a controlled drug was committed by an adult either in the vicinity of school premises or by using a courier under the age of 18.
- HOC 82/1980 recommends that cultivation of cannabis (see **5.3.1**) be charged under s 4 instead of s 6 of the Misuse of Drugs Act 1971 in view of s 37(1) of this Act which provides a definition of 'produce'.
- The specific power to search, detain a person or vehicle/vessel, and seize any drugs is given in s 23(2) (see **5.4.1**). Ensure that s 2 of PACE (see **1.3.3**) is complied with.
- Fungus (of any kind) that contains psilocin or an ester of psilocin, commonly known as 'magic mushrooms', is a Class A drug under the Misuse of Drugs Act 1971.
- Consider confiscation of cash and property for the s 4(2) and (3) offences of unlawful production/supply of controlled drugs; these are listed as 'criminal lifestyle' offences under Sch 2 to the Proceeds of Crime Act 2002 (see **5.5** for details).

E&S TRIG

Either way, unless the defendant could receive the minimum sentence of seven years for a third drug trafficking offence under s 313 of the Sentencing Code in which case the offence is triable only on indictment

None

Class A drug
Summary: 6/12 months' imprisonment and/or a fine
Indictment: Life imprisonment and/or a fine

Class B drug
Summary: 6/12 months' imprisonment and/or a fine
Indictment: 14 years' imprisonment and/or a fine

Class C drug
Summary: 3 months' imprisonment and/or a fine
Indictment: 14 years' imprisonment and/or a fine

5.1.2 Supply articles to administer or prepare drugs/drug-cutting agents

Section 9A of the Misuse of Drugs Act 1971 creates a prohibition on the supply or offering to supply articles for administering or preparing a controlled drug.

Offences

(1) A person who supplies or offers to supply any article which may be used or adapted to be used (whether by itself or in combination with another article or other articles) in the administration by any person of a controlled drug to himself or another, believing that the article (or the article as adapted) is to be so used in circumstances where the administration is unlawful, is guilty of an offence.

(3) A person who supplies or offers to supply any article which may be used to prepare a controlled drug for administration by any person to himself or another believing that the article is to be used in circumstances where the administration is unlawful is guilty of an offence.

Misuse of Drugs Act 1971, s 9A

PNLD **H1833, H1835, H2267, H2268**

Points to prove

- ✓ supplied/offered to supply article(s)
- ✓ which might be used/adapted
- ✓ for administration of a controlled drug
- ✓ to self/another
- ✓ believing article(s)
- ✓ was/were to be used
- ✓ in circumstances where administration unlawful

Meanings

Supplies (see **5.1.1**)

Offers (see **'Related cases' 5.1.1**)

Controlled drug (see **5.1.1**)

Administration

Includes a person administering it to themselves with the assistance of another.

Defences

(2) It is not an offence under subsection (1) above to supply or offer to supply a hypodermic syringe, or any part of one.

(4) For the purposes of this section, any administration of a controlled drug is unlawful except—
   (a) the administration by any person of a controlled drug to another in circumstances where the administration of the drug is not unlawful under section 4(1) of this Act,
   (b) the administration by any person of a controlled drug, other than a temporary class drug, to himself in circumstances where having the controlled drug in his possession is not unlawful under section 5(1),
   (c) the administration by any person of a temporary class drug to himself in circumstances where having the drug in his possession is to be treated as excepted possession for the purposes of this Act (see section 7A(2)(c)).

Misuse of Drugs Act 1971, s 9A

Practical considerations

- The scope of the 'article(s)' is wide and includes, for example, plastic bottles which are intended to be used or adapted for smoking controlled drugs.
- Specified health care professionals are exempted from s 9A regarding certain articles per reg 6A of the Misuse of Drugs Regulations 2001; this includes their supplying aluminium foil as part of a drug treatment plan; see HOC 14/2014 for further details.
- Section 9 of the Misuse of Drugs Act 1971 provides for offences related to opium.

Drug-cutting and drug-cutting agents

- A drug-cutting agent is defined as a substance which is added to a controlled drug in connection with the unlawful supply or exportation of the drug. They are added to drugs by dealers in order to increase the volume of a drug to maximise their profits—drug-cutting. Drug-cutting agents can be any substance intended for use in this way. For example, benzocaine and lidocaine and phenacetin are regularly added to cocaine without the user noticing.
- Substances used as drug-cutting agents are often themselves not illegal; for example, lidocaine and benzocaine when used in health and veterinary care. However, Part 4 of the Serious Crime Act 2015 (ss 52 to 56) confers powers on a constable, officer of the NCA, or HMRC customs officer to seize, retain, and destroy substances intended to be used as cutting agents for controlled drugs (in Sch 2 or subject to a temporary class drug order) under the Misuse of Drugs Act 1971 (see **5.1.1**).
- A police or customs officer may enter and search premises for suspected drug-cutting agents, pursuant to a search and seizure warrant under s 52, and to seize and retain these substances. The process for application and execution of the warrant mirrors that given in the 1971 Act. When lawfully on premises (eg at a port),

police and customs officers can seize substances under s 56 on reasonable grounds to suspect they are intended for use as drug-cutting agents.

- It is a summary offence for a person, without reasonable excuse, to obstruct a police or customs officer executing or seeking to execute a search and seizure warrant (PNLD **H11864**).
- Consider the offence of conspiracy to supply Class A drugs (*R v Marron* [2011] EWCA Crim 792—see **5.1.1**) or assisting in the commission of an offence under the Serious Crime Act 2007 (see **4.1.3**).
- See 'Guidance on Part 4 of the Serious Crime Act 2015: The seizure and forfeiture of drug-cutting agents' (Home Office, April 2015) and HOC 8/2015.

SSS

Summary

6 months

6 months' imprisonment and/or a fine

Links to alternative subjects and offences

1.1 **Powers of Arrest** 1
4.1 **Criminal Attempts** 173
6.10 **Administer Substance Intending to Commit a Sexual Offence** 344

5.2 Possession of/with Intent to Supply a Controlled Drug

The Misuse of Drugs Act 1971 makes a distinction between people who are lawfully allowed to possess controlled drugs and people who are unlawfully in possession of such drugs. Possession (unless exempt) of a controlled drug is unlawful, as is possession of controlled drugs with intent to supply.

5.2.1 Possessing a controlled drug

Offences

(1) Subject to any regulations under section 7 of this Act for the time being in force, it shall not be lawful for a person to have a controlled drug in his possession.

(2) Subject to section 28 of this Act and to subsection 5(4), it is an offence for a person to have a controlled drug in his possession in contravention of subsection 5(1) above.

(2A) Subsections (1) and (2) do not apply in relation to a temporary class drug.

Misuse of Drugs Act 1971, s 5

PNLD H2360 to H2390

Points to prove

✓ possess [name of drug]
✓ a controlled drug of Class A/B/C

Meanings

Regulations under s 7 (see 5.1.1)

Controlled drug (see 5.1.1)

Possession

Proof of unlawful possession requires the following three elements:

- the drug must be in the custody or control (actual or **constructive**) of the defendant;
- the defendant must know or suspect the existence of the drug in question;
- the drug must be a controlled drug within the meaning of the Act.

Temporary class drug (see 5.1.1)

Constructive control/possession

The defendant does not have immediate physical possession of the drugs but has almost as much control over them (see '**Explanatory notes**').

Explanatory notes

- Simple possession of a temporary class drug will not be an offence. However, all other offences will apply to temporary class drugs; see HOC 12/2011 for further details.
- An example of 'constructive possession' is where a person leaves drugs in a 'left luggage' locker and retains the keys. Although they no longer have 'actual' custody of the drugs, they have a high degree of control over them which amounts to possession. If the defendant handed the keys to an innocent agent who holds them as a favour, the defendant still has constructive possession. Similarly, if that other person knows that drugs are in the locker then, by keeping the keys, they are also in constructive possession of the drugs.

Defences

Section 28 and Regulations under s 7 (see **'Defences' 5.1.1**)

In any proceedings for an offence under subsection (2) above in which it is proved that the accused had a controlled drug in his possession, it shall be a defence for him to prove—

(a) that, knowing or suspecting it to be a controlled drug, he took possession of it for the purpose of preventing another from committing or continuing to commit an offence in connection with that drug and that as soon as possible after taking possession of it he took all such steps as were reasonably open to him to destroy the drug or to deliver it into the custody of a person lawfully entitled to take custody of it; or

(b) that, knowing or suspecting it to be a controlled drug, he took possession of it for the purpose of delivering it into the custody of a person lawfully entitled to take custody of it and that as soon as possible after taking possession of it he took all such steps as were reasonably open to him to deliver it into the custody of such a person.

Misuse of Drugs Act 1971, s 5(4)

Defence notes

The defence under s 5(4) is to cater for situations such as:

- a parent discovers their child has a controlled drug, takes possession of it, and flushes it down the lavatory;
- a passer-by discovers heroin lying on the pavement, takes possession of it, and then gives it to the police.

Related cases

R v Altham [2006] EWCA Crim 7 Using cannabis to alleviate chronic pain is still unlawful possession.

5.2.1 **Possessing a controlled drug**

Adams v DPP [2002] EWHC 438 (Admin) The defendant's flat was searched on a drug warrant while they were present with some visitors. Heroin was found on the sofa between two guests, and the defendant said it was the defendant's. They withdrew the admission when they were interviewed. It was held that 'possession' means (in brief): actual or potential physical control; and an intention to possess. The defendant's knowledge that one of the visitors to their home had brought heroin, and that one had intended to take the heroin, was insufficient to conclude that the defendant had control over the drugs to establish the offence under s 5.

Practical considerations

- For produce/supply a controlled drug, see **5.1.1**.
- Cannabis and its derivatives are Class B controlled drugs. HOC 1/2009 provides guidance on cannabis offences.
- The Misuse of Drugs Act 1971 (Amendment) Order 2023 now classifies nitrous oxide as a Class C drug under para 1(a) of Part 3 of Sch 2 to the Misuse of Drugs Act 1971.
- Regulation 4(2) of the Misuse of Drugs Regulations 2001 deals with drugs in Part 2 of Sch 4 (anabolic steroids and human growth hormones) and states that the importation or exportation of these drugs is to be carried out in person and only for that person's use. This prevents access to these drugs through postal, freight, or courier services. HOC 9/2012 provides further details.
- Regulation 6 of the Misuse of Drugs Regulations 2001 allows a person to possess certain specified drugs for certain legitimate reasons (see **'Defences' 5.1.1**). For example, a 'cannabis-based product' for medicinal use in humans by prescription only—Sch 2. 'A cannabis-based product' is defined as being a product: (i) that is or contains cannabis, cannabis resin, cannabinol, or a cannabinol derivative; **and** (ii) is produced for medicinal use in humans; **and** (iii) is a product that is regulated as a medicinal product, or an ingredient of a medicinal product. Additional access and administration restrictions are imposed in relation to this product. HOC 018/2018 provides further detail on this. Possession and supply of such specified drugs in specified circumstances is not an offence.
- Regulation 16A of the Misuse of Drugs Regulations 2001 in part states that a person shall not self-administer a 'cannabis-based product' for medicinal use in humans by the smoking of the product, other than for research purposes.
- HOC 15/2012 states that substances suspected to be controlled drugs must be sent to a forensic science laboratory for analysis unless they are seizures of:
  - cannabis, including cannabis resin but excluding cannabis (hash) oil; or
  - a small quantity (for personal use only) of certain controlled drugs, which gave a positive result when tested with a Home Office-approved kit (see below).

This is providing the case is dealt with at the magistrates' court (in some cases, the Crown Court), a trained law enforcement member confirms that it is that drug, and the identification of the drug is not in dispute.

- Section 63B of PACE provides for the testing of adult persons for specified Class A drugs. The test can be carried out when a person has been arrested for or charged with **either** a 'trigger' offence (Sch 6 to the Criminal Justice and Court Services Act 2000 lists offences that are 'trigger' offences) **or** any offence when authorised by a police officer of inspector rank or above who has reasonable grounds to suspect that misuse of a specified Class A drug caused or contributed to the offence.
- Home Office-approved kits (operated by trained officers) (HOC 13/2014) can be used to identify the following drugs for evidential purposes: heroin, morphine, amphetamine, cocaine, MDMA (ecstasy), ketamine (a Class B drug—see HOC 8/2014 for details), and methylmethcathinone (including mephedrone).
- The specific power to search, detain a person or vehicle/vessel, and seize any drugs is given in s 23(2) (see **5.4.1**). Ensure that s 2 of PACE (see **1.3**) is complied with.
- PACE Code E Annex A, para 2.4(c)(iii) provides exemption from the requirement to audio record interviews that are undertaken elsewhere than at a police station for specified indictable offence types. The exemption is subject to a number of conditions. An example where this exemption applies is where a person has been cautioned for possession of a controlled drug under s 5(2) if the drug is cannabis or khat (but not cannabis oil) and possession is for personal use. A condition is that the suspect appears to be aged 18 years or over and there is no reason to suspect that they are a vulnerable person and therefore an appropriate adult is not required (see Code E for full details of this exemption).
- The above exemption to audio record interviews applies to an attempt to commit the offence under s 1 of the Criminal Attempts Act 1981 (see **4.1.1**).
- Possession of cannabis under s 5(2) can be dealt with by PND for offenders aged 18 and over. ACPO guidance gives a three-stage escalation procedure (see **7.1.2**).

PND (Cannabis) **SSS** **E&S** **TRIG**

Either way None

Class A
Summary: 6/12 months' imprisonment and/or a fine
Indictment: 7 years' imprisonment and/or a fine

Class B
Summary: 3 months' imprisonment and/or a level 4 fine
Indictment: 5 years' imprisonment and/or a fine

Class C
Summary: 3 months' imprisonment and/or a level 3 fine
Indictment: 2 years' imprisonment and/or a fine

5.2.2 Possession with intent to supply

Section 5(3) of the Misuse of Drugs Act 1971 creates a specific offence of possessing a controlled drug with intent to supply it.

Offences

Subject to section 28 of this Act, it is an offence for a person to have a controlled drug in his possession, whether lawfully or not, with intent to supply it to another in contravention of section 4(1) of this Act.

Misuse of Drugs Act 1971, s 5(3)

PNLD **H2322 to H2327, H2492, H2493**

Points to prove

- ✓ possesses
- ✓ [name of drug]/an unspecified controlled drug of class A/B/C
- ✓ with intent to supply

Meanings

Section 28 (see **5.1.1**)

Controlled drug (see **5.1.1**)

Possession (see **5.2.1**)

Intent (see **4.1.2**)

Supply (see **5.1.1**)

Section 4 (see **5.1.1**)

Explanatory notes (see 5.1.1 and 5.2.1)

Defences

Section 28 (lack of knowledge defence) (see **5.1.1**)

Related cases (see also 5.1.1 and 5.2.1 cases)

R v Lambert [2001] UKHL 37 A judge must treat the s 28 defence as an evidential burden on the defendant rather than a legal requirement to be proved on the balance of probabilities.

R v Griffiths [1998] Crim LR 567 CA Evidence of large sums of cash in the defendant's house along with the drugs may be used as part of the prosecution case to show that the defendant was in possession of those drugs with intent to supply.

R v Scott [1996] Crim LR 652, CA Lifestyle may prove possession, but not intent to supply.

Practical considerations (see also **5.1.1** and **5.2.1**)

- Lifestyle/paraphernalia can sometimes be used to help prove the 'possession' element but not 'intent to supply' where dealers are being prosecuted (*R v Edwards* [1998] Crim LR 207, CA).
- Provided a controlled drug is involved, it does not matter that a dealer thought they were supplying another controlled drug.
- The specific power to search, detain a person or vehicle/vessel, and seize any drugs is given in s 23(2) (see **5.4.1**). Ensure that s 2 of PACE (see **1.3**) is complied with.
- Consider confiscation of cash and property for the s 5(3) offence of possession of controlled drug with intent to supply; this is listed as a 'criminal lifestyle' offence under Sch 2 to the Proceeds of Crime Act 2002 (see **5.5** for details).

E&S TRIG

Either way

None

Class A
Summary: 6/12 months' imprisonment and/or a fine
Indictment: Life imprisonment and/or a fine

Class B
Summary: 6/12 months' imprisonment and/or a fine
Indictment: 14 years' imprisonment and/or a fine

Class C
Summary: 3 months' imprisonment and/or a level 4 fine
Indictment: 14 years' imprisonment and/or a fine

Links to alternative subjects and offences

2.7 **Sudden and Unexplained Deaths** 109
4.1 **Criminal Attempts** 173

5.3 Cultivate Cannabis, Possess Khat, and Psychoactive Substances

This chapter deals with the offences of cultivating cannabis, possessing khat, and possessing or dealing in psychoactive substances.

5.3.1 Cultivate cannabis

Section 6 of the Misuse of Drugs Act 1971 makes it an offence to cultivate cannabis plants.

Offences

(1) Subject to any regulations under section 7 of this Act for the time being in force, it shall not be lawful for a person to cultivate any plant of the genus cannabis.

(2) Subject to section 28 of this Act, it is an offence to cultivate any such plant in contravention of subsection (1) above.

Misuse of Drugs Act 1971, s 6

PNLD H9733, H9741

Points to prove

✓ cultivation of cannabis plant(s) being a Class B drug

Meanings

Regulations under s 7 (see **5.1.1**)

Allow cultivation of the cannabis plant under licence (see '**Defences**' below).

Cannabis

Means any plant of the genus *Cannabis* or and any part of any such plant (by whatever name designated).

Section 28 (see '**Defences**' below)

Explanatory notes

- The mere growing of the cannabis plant is regarded as an act of 'production'.

- It is necessary to prove that the defendant gave some attention to the plant in order to show 'cultivation'—watering, heating, and lighting would be common examples.

Defences

Section 28 (lack of knowledge)* (see 5.1.1) *Regulations under s 7

Where any person is authorised by a licence of the Secretary of State issued under this regulation and for the time being in force to cultivate plants of the genus Cannabis, it shall not by virtue of section 6 of the Act be unlawful for that person to cultivate any such plant in accordance with the terms of the licence and in compliance with any conditions attached to the licence.

Misuse of Drugs Regulations 2001, reg 12

Defence notes

- Acting without a valid licence or failing to comply with the conditions of the licence is an offence under s 18 of the Misuse of Drugs Act 1971 (although other more serious offences may also have been committed).
- Certain people can lawfully possess/supply a controlled drug and/or can be licensed to do so (see **5.1.1**).
- There is no general defence of medical necessity to the offence of production/possession/supply of cannabis (*Attorney-General's Reference (No 2 of 2004)* [2005] EWCA Crim 1415).

Practical considerations

- Cultivation of cannabis also falls within the scope of the offences of 'producing cannabis' or 'concerned in the production of cannabis' as under s 37(1) the definition of 'produce' has a much wider meaning than just chemically making a drug, and means by manufacture, cultivation, or any other method. The cultivation of cannabis offence in s 6 is not a lifestyle offence, whereas production is. Production falls under the lifestyle offences within Sch 2 to the Proceeds Act 2002, allowing the courts to make wider confiscation orders where it is shown that the defendant has benefited from their criminal conduct. Therefore, advice from the CPS should be sought on the most appropriate offence to charge.
- Stripping a cannabis plant of its leaves comes within the term 'any other method' for the purposes of production (*R v Harris and Cox* [1996] Crim LR 36).
- Any equipment used at 'cannabis farms', which usually consists of hydroponic equipment to provide the lighting and heating, electrical fans, air ventilation systems, transformers. And other equipment can be seized under s 19 of PACE (see **1.4.4**).
- Instead of storing this bulky equipment, which has been seized as evidence, consider s 22 of PACE which states that photographs of the equipment will be sufficient evidence.

- Supplying hydroponic equipment could be an offence of conspiring to be concerned in the production of cannabis by another (*R v Dang and others* [2014] EWCA Crim 348—see **5.1.1** for details).
- In order to ascertain whether a building is being used as a 'cannabis farm', consider the use of a thermal camera or heat-seeking equipment to detect high infrared values; for example, in the roof area. This is due to the intensive use of heating and lighting equipment in the growing environment.
- Cannabis and its derivatives are classified as Class B controlled drugs. As regards possession under s 5(2) (see **5.2.1**), ACPO guidance gives a three-stage escalation procedure which involves issuing a PND for offenders 18 and over (see **7.1.2**).

E&S

Either way

None

Summary: 6/12 months' imprisonment and/or a fine

Indictment: 14 years' imprisonment and/or a fine

5.3.2 **Possess khat**

Practical considerations

- Possession of khat (a product that is from the leaves and shoots of the shrub *Catha edulis* and is classified as a Class C controlled drug) is an offence under s 5(2) of the 1971 Act (see **5.2.1**) and can be dealt with by a (lower tier) PND (see **7.1.1**), although with the bulky nature of khat and its reliance on international freight, law enforcement will also focus on UK borders.
- HOC 11/2014 provides further details and gives a three-stage escalation procedure for dealing with possession for personal use only—not for possession with intent to supply or other offences. This is similar to that used for possession of cannabis (see **7.1.2**): with a 'khat warning' for a first offence, PND for a second offence, and prosecution for a third offence.
- Annex B of HOC 11/2014 provides guidelines for identifying khat, being visual for khat warnings and PND issue, but in other cases done forensically.
- PACE Code E Annex A, para 2.4(c)(iii) provides exemption from the requirement to audio record interviews undertaken elsewhere than at a police station for four specified offences, one being where a person has been cautioned for possession of khat (see **5.2.1**).
- The above exemption to audio record interviews applies to an attempt to commit the offence under s 1 of the Criminal Attempts Act 1981 (see **4.1.1**).

5.3.3 Psychoactive substances

The Psychoactive Substances Act 2016 contains several offences (subject to statutory exemptions) that include the production, supply, or offer to supply any psychoactive substance, and possession of a substance with intent to supply, if the substance is likely to be used for its psychoactive effects, regardless of its potential for harm. Note that there is no offence of possession of a psychoactive substance for personal use in the same way that there is for controlled drugs, except for possession while in a custodial institution, where separate provisions are made.

5.3.4 Producing a psychoactive substance

Section 4 of the Psychoactive Substances Act 2016 provides for an offence of producing a psychoactive substance.

Offences

(1) A person commits an offence if—
- (a) the person intentionally produces a psychoactive substance,
- (b) the person knows or suspects that the substance is a psychoactive substance, and
- (c) the person—
  - (i) intends to consume the psychoactive substance for its psychoactive effects, or
  - (ii) knows, or is reckless as to whether, the psychoactive substance is likely to be consumed by some other person for its psychoactive effects.

Psychoactive Substances Act 2016, s 4

PNLD H12520

Points to prove

✓ date and location
✓ intentionally produce psychoactive substance
✓ knows/suspects it is a psychoactive substance
✓ intends to consume it for psychoactive effects
OR
✓ knows/is reckless as to whether
✓ it is likely to be consumed by other person for psychoactive effects

Meanings

Psychoactive substance

Means any substance that:

(a) is capable of producing a psychoactive effect in a person who consumes it, and

(b) is not an exempted substance (see **'Other useful information'** 5.3.5).

Psychoactive effect

A substance produces a psychoactive effect in a person if, by stimulating or depressing the person's central nervous system, it affects the person's mental functioning or emotional state; and references to a substance's psychoactive effects are to be read accordingly (s 2(2)).

Consumes

A person consumes a substance if they cause or allow the substance, or fumes given off by the substance, to enter their body in any way. For example, this includes injecting, eating or drinking, snorting, inhaling, and smoking.

Exempted substance

Means a substance listed in Sch 1 to the Psychoactive Substances Act 2016. These are substances that are either controlled through existing legislation (alcohol, tobacco, medicines, and controlled drugs) or are substances that produce a negligible psychoactive effect in a person (caffeine and foodstuffs such as nutmeg and chocolate).

Explanatory note

- The main effect of psychoactive substances is on a person's brain, the major part of the central nervous system. By speeding up or slowing down activity in the central nervous system, psychoactive substances cause an alteration in the individual's state of consciousness by producing a range of effects including, but not limited to, hallucinations; changes in alertness, perception of time and space, mood or empathy with others; and drowsiness.

Either way

None

Summary: 6/12 months' imprisonment and/or a fine

Indictment: maximum 7 years' imprisonment and/or a fine

Region: UK

5.3.5 Supply of a psychoactive substance and offering to supply a psychoactive substance

Section 5 of the Psychoactive Substances Act 2016 provides for two separate offences, namely supply of a psychoactive substance and offering to supply a psychoactive substance.

Offences

(1) A person commits an offence if—
- (a) the person intentionally supplies a substance to another person,
- (b) the substance is a psychoactive substance,
- (c) the person knows or suspects, or ought to know or suspect, that the substance is a psychoactive substance, and
- (d) the person knows, or is reckless as to whether, the psychoactive substance is likely to be consumed by the person to whom it is supplied, or by some other person, for its psychoactive effects.

(2) A person ('P') commits an offence if—
- (a) P offers to supply a psychoactive substance to another person ('R'), and
- (b) P knows or is reckless as to whether R, or some other person, would, if P supplied a substance to R in accordance with the offer, be likely to consume the substance for its psychoactive effects.

Psychoactive Substances Act 2016, s 5

PNLD H12521, H12522

Points to prove

s 5(1) offence

✓ date and location
✓ offer to supply psychoactive substance
✓ to another
✓ knowing/being reckless as to whether that/another person would
✓ if supplied in accordance with offer
✓ be likely to consume it for psychoactive effects

s 5(2) offence

✓ date and location
✓ intentionally supply a substance to another
✓ the substance was psychoactive substance
✓ knows/suspects/ought to know/suspect the substance was psychoactive substance
✓ knows/was reckless as to whether substance likely to be consumed for psychoactive effects

Meanings

Psychoactive substance (see **5.3.4**)

Psychoactive effect (see **5.3.4**)

Consumes (see **5.3.4**)

Explanatory notes

- For the purposes of s 5(2)(b), the reference to a substance's psychoactive effects includes a reference to the psychoactive effects that the substance would have if it were the substance that P had offered to supply to R.
- Section 72 of the Sentencing Act 2020 sets out how the court must treat as an aggravating factor the fact that the offence of supplying psychoactive substances was committed by an **adult** either in the vicinity of school premises or by using a courier under the age of 18 or within a custodial institution.
- For custodial institutions, the same offence of possession with intent to supply exists, which is aggravated if the supply occurs on the premises of the institution. There is an additional offence for a detained person to possess a psychoactive substance in a custodial institution under s 9 of the Act.
- Section 40CB of the Prison Act 1952 provides an offence to throw or project any article or substance into a prison and this will include drugs, mobile phones, and psychoactive substances.

Either way

None

Summary: 6/12 months' imprisonment and/or a fine

Indictment: maximum 7 years' imprisonment and/or a fine

Region: UK

5.3.6 Possession with intent to supply psychoactive substances

Section 7 of the Psychoactive Substances Act 2016 provides for an offence of possession with intent to supply psychoactive substances.

Offences

A person commits an offence if—

(a) the person is in possession of a psychoactive substance,

(b) the person knows or suspects that the substance is a psychoactive substance, and

(c) the person intends to supply the psychoactive substance to another person for its consumption, whether by any person to whom it is supplied or by some other person, for its psychoactive effects.

Psychoactive Substances Act 2016, s 7

PNLD H12523

Points to prove

- ✓ date and location
- ✓ possession of psychoactive substance
- ✓ knows/suspects it is a psychoactive substance
- ✓ intends to supply substance to another
- ✓ for its consumption
- ✓ for psychoactive effects

Meanings

Psychoactive substance (see **5.3.4**)

Psychoactive effect (see **5.3.4**)

Consumes (see **5.3.4**)

Explanatory note

- Section 7 is a possession offence but is aimed at those in the supply chain. Simple possession of a psychoactive substance for personal use would not be caught by this offence and is only criminalised by the Act when it occurs in a custodial institution. The offence in this section would, however, cover social supply—that is, circumstances where a person acquires a psychoactive substance on behalf of a group of friends and then supplies the substance to those friends.

Other useful information

- Offences under ss 4, 5, 7, and 8 are lifestyle offences for the purposes of confiscation proceedings (see **5.5**).
- Section 11 provides the exceptions to offences under the Act: including the offences under ss 4, 5, and 7: it is not an offence for a person to carry on any activity listed in s 11(3) if, in the circumstances in which it is carried on by that person, the activity is an exempted activity. In this section, 'exempted activity' means an activity listed in Sch 2.
- Any substance that is a controlled drug will be covered by the provisions of the Misuse of Drugs Act 1971 and the Misuse of Drugs Regulations 2001 (see **5.2**).
- Exemptions include medicinal products, alcohol, nicotine, tobacco, caffeine, and foods.
- Sections 36 to 39 inclusive provide powers to stop and search persons, vehicles, vessels, aircraft, and premises where an officer has reasonable grounds to suspect that a person has committed, or is likely to commit, an offence under any of ss 4 to 9.
- Community Support Officers (CSOs) and Community Support Volunteers (CSVs) may seize and retain a psychoactive substance where they find a psychoactive substance in a person's possession (whether or not the CSO or CSV finds it in the course of searching the person in the exercise of a power or duty conferred or imposed by their designation (see **11.1.6**)).

5.3.6 **Possession with intent to supply psychoactive substances**

- There is no power to stop and search where an officer suspects that a person has in their possession a psychoactive substance intended for personal use; the officer will need to have reasonable grounds to suspect that the person has committed or is likely to commit an offence under the Act: for example, the person is likely to commit the offence of possession with intent to supply a psychoactive substance.
- Section 43 provides a power to seize and retain anything found during the course of a search which the officer believes is a psychoactive substance.
- Retention and disposal of psychoactive substances are covered by ss 49 to 51 and 53 but should also be undertaken in accordance with force policy.
- There are no Home Office kits to identify psychoactive substances, with forensic testing being the only option. In terms of other offences, consider selling/supplying controlled drugs (see **5.1.1**), drugs articles (see **5.1.2**), supplying intoxicating substances (see **11.5.1**), or breaching consumer protection legislation.
- Test purchases could establish if an item sold as a psychoactive substance contains controlled drugs (including temporary controlled drugs) by forensic testing, in which case a s 23(3) drugs warrant (see **5.4.1**) can be applied for.
- Consider approaching the local authority for it to issue a PSPO (see **7.15.2**) which could ban people using psychoactive substances in a public place, with a power to seize such substances and, if appropriate, to issue a fixed penalty notice.

Related cases

R v Rochester [2018] EWCA Crim 1936 A substance will fall within the definition of a psychoactive substance whether it produces its effect by directly or indirectly stimulating or depressing the central nervous system.

R v Chapman [2017] EWCA Crim 1743 In this case, it was held that possession of nitrous oxide with intent to supply for recreational purposes is an offence under the Psychoactive Substances Act 2016; it was only an exempted substance for medicinal purposes.

Either way   None

Summary: 6/12 months' imprisonment and/or a fine

Indictment: maximum 7 years' imprisonment and/or a fine

Region: UK

Links to alternative subjects and offences

4.1 **Criminal Attempts** 173
11.1 **Police Powers for Civilian Staff and Volunteers** 781

5.4 Search Powers for Controlled Drugs/Permit Use of Controlled Drugs on Premises

5.4.1 Power to search, detain, and seize drugs

Search powers under s 23 or s 23A of the Misuse of Drugs Act 1971 confer powers on a constable to stop, detain, and search a person, vehicle, or vessel for controlled drugs and an obstruction offence for failing to comply.

Power to search, detain, and seize drugs

If a constable has reasonable grounds to suspect that any person is in possession of a controlled drug in contravention of this Act or of any regulations or orders made thereunder, the constable may—

(a) search that person, and detain him for the purpose of searching him;
(b) search any vehicle or vessel in which the constable suspects that the drug may be found, and for that purpose require the person in control of the vehicle or vessel to stop it;
(c) seize and detain, for the purposes of proceedings under this Act, anything found in the course of the search, which appears to the constable to be evidence of an offence under this Act.

Misuse of Drugs Act 1971, s 23(2)

Offences

A person commits an offence if he—

(a) intentionally obstructs a person in the exercise of his powers under this section.

Misuse of Drugs Act 1971, s 23(4)

PNLD H2112

Points to prove

✓ intentionally obstructed
✓ constable/authorised person in exercise of s 23 powers

Meanings

Reasonable grounds (see 1.1)

Controlled drug (see 5.1.1)

5.4.1 **Power to search, detain, and seize drugs**

Vehicle (see **10.1.3**)

Vessel

Includes a hovercraft within the meaning of the Hovercraft Act 1968.

Intentionally obstructs

Where a person deliberately does an act which, though not necessarily aimed at or hostile to the police, makes it more difficult for the police to carry out their duty and they intentionally do the act knowing that their conduct will have an obstructive effect (*Lewis v Cox* [1984] Crim LR 756, QBD).

Explanatory notes

- Section 23(1) gives a constable/authorised person power to enter premises relating to producing or supplying (eg chemists) any controlled drugs, to inspect the drug stocks or demand production and inspection of books or documents regarding dealings in such drugs.
- Where a person is acting under s 23(1), it is an offence (s 23(4)(b)–(c)) to conceal books, documents, stocks, or drugs; or when demanded, to fail (without reasonable excuse) to produce the books or documents.
- Section 23A provides further powers to search and detain for the purpose of searching a person (or vehicle or vessel) where a constable has reasonable grounds to suspect that the person is in possession of a temporary class drug (see **5.1.1**). Also, to seize, detain, and dispose of such a drug. It is an offence under s 23A(6) to intentionally obstruct a constable exercising this power; guidance is provided in HOC 12/2011 regarding temporary class drug offences and powers.
- These powers are exercisable *anywhere* and must be conducted in accordance with the related COP and PACE (see **1.3**).
- Paragraph 5 of Sch 3C to the Police Reform Act 2002 confers powers for CSOs and CSVs to seize and detain controlled drugs found in the possession of a person (see **11.1.5**).

Related case

R v Bristol [2007] EWCA Crim 3214 The officer failed to give their name and police station prior to a s 23 drug search, in breach of s 2 of PACE (see **1.1.2**), making the search unlawful. As a result, the officer was not acting in the execution of their duty and the s 23(4) offence was not committed.

Practical considerations

Personal safety

- Contact with the blood or saliva of drug abusers (particularly those users who inject) carries a risk of infection with serious diseases such as AIDS, HIV, and hepatitis.
- Every effort should be made to avoid such fluids entering your own body through cuts, eyes, or the mouth. Should such contact occur,

the possibility of infection is minimised by the contact area being thoroughly washed immediately and medical advice sought as soon as practicable.

Searching of suspects

- Care should always be taken to avoid unguarded needles piercing the skin; if such an event does occur, seek medical advice as soon as practicable.
- When conducting a search initially request the suspect/prisoner to turn out their own pockets, before patting the outside of pockets to detect the presence of a syringe.
- Drug abusers will go to extreme lengths to conceal drugs on or in their bodies. Drugs are commonly found in body orifices (s 55 of PACE provides the circumstances in which intimate searches can be carried out).
- Search a person meticulously: small amounts of drugs can be concealed, for example, in the lining of clothing, under plasters supposedly covering an abrasion, or stuck to the skull under the hairline.
- Searching inside a person's mouth does not constitute an intimate search.

Handling of drugs

- Certain drugs may be absorbed through the skin; it is therefore always advisable to wear gloves when handling drugs.
- Never under any circumstances taste the drugs.
- There will be occasions when the name of the drug seized is unknown and there is doubt as to whether it is controlled. Always seek advice and assistance from a supervisory officer or the drug squad.

Drug abusers' equipment

- Abusers use a wide range of paraphernalia to prepare and administer their drugs. The following list (which is not exhaustive) may provide evidence of that activity where premises are searched:
  - ✦ syringes and needles; scorched tinfoil and spoons; small mirrors, razors, and straws; tubes of tinfoil; ligatures; lemon juice or citric acid; cigarette papers and home-made cigarettes; bloodstained swabs; square folds of paper which may contain powder; cling film; small self-sealing bags; weighing scales; hookah pipes.

General

- Section 23(3) of the Misuse of Drugs Act 1971 allows a warrant to be issued for any constable to enter (if need be by force) premises named in the warrant and to search the premises and any persons found therein for evidence of offences relating to controlled drugs (see **1.4** for application procedures).
- Ensure all s 23(3) search powers are in the warrant; a warrant authorising a premises search only does not give grounds to search people found therein (*CC of Thames Valley v Hepburn* [2002] EWCA

Civ 1841). If the warrant authorises the search of premises and people, it is reasonable to restrict their movement to conduct a proper search (*DPP v Meadon* [2003] EWHC 3005 (Admin)).
- Comply with PACE and the COP for the grounds for: searching people, conduct of the search, and completion of a search record (see **1.3.5**); using reasonable force to detain and carry out the search (see **1.2**).
- When using s 23 search powers, ensure that the s 2 PACE requirements are met (see **1.3**) (eg police officer fails to state name and police station), otherwise the search will be deemed unlawful and may affect the admissibility of any evidence obtained.
- Although s 23(2) authorises detention of a suspect for the purpose of searching, it does not give the officer a general right to question the suspect. However, they may ask questions incidental to exercising that power.
- Section 23(2)(b) does not give an officer the right to stop a vehicle or to search it simply because they suspect the vehicle (not the occupants) has been used in connection with a drug offence on a previous occasion (*R v Littleford* [1978] CLR 48).
- Nothing in s 23(2) prejudices any other powers available to a constable to search or seize/detain property.
- Consider road traffic law to stop the vehicle (see **10.2**).

E&S

Either way

None

Summary: 6/12 months' imprisonment and/or a fine
Indictment: 2 years' imprisonment and/or a fine

5.4.2 Occupier/manager permits drug use on premises

Section 8 of the Misuse of Drugs Act 1971 makes it an offence for occupiers and managers of premises to permit certain activities relating to controlled drugs to take place on those premises.

Offences

A person commits an offence if, being the occupier or concerned in the management of any premises, he knowingly permits or suffers any of the following activities to take place on those premises, that is to say—
(a) producing or attempting to produce a controlled drug in contravention of section 4(1) of this Act;
(b) supplying or attempting to supply a controlled drug to another in contravention of section 4(1) of this Act, or offering to supply a controlled drug to another in contravention of section 4(1);

(c) preparing opium for smoking;
(d) smoking cannabis, cannabis resin or prepared opium.

Misuse of Drugs Act 1971, s 8

PNLD H9739, H15141, H15848

Points to prove

- ✓ being the occupier/concerned in managing of premises
- ✓ knowingly
- ✓ permitted/suffered to take place
- ✓ on premises
- ✓ the production/attempted production OR
- ✓ supplying/attempted to supply/offering to supply to another
- ✓ Class A/B/C drug namely [if known] OR
- ✓ preparing of opium for smoking OR
- ✓ smoking of cannabis, cannabis resin, or prepared opium

Meanings

Occupier

Whether a person is in lawful occupation of premises has created some difficulty. In *R v Tao* [1976] 3 All ER 65, a college student who paid rent for a room on the campus was deemed to be the occupier of that room; Lord Justice Roskill commented that it would be 'somewhat astonishing' if a squatter could not be an 'occupier' under the Act. Similarly, there may be different occupiers at different times or an occupier who only had that status for certain periods. The question was always one of fact (*R v Coid* [1998] Crim LR 199, CA).

Management

Implies a degree of control over the running of the affairs of the venture or business. If a person controls premises by running, planning, or organising them, they will be managing. Sharing or assisting in the running of premises is sufficient for the purposes of 'being concerned in the management'.

Knowingly (see **9.1.3**)

Permits (see **10.14.1**)

Suffers

Means an unwillingness or failure to prevent.

Producing (see **5.1.1**)

Controlled drug (see **5.1.1**)

Section 4(1) (see **5.1.1**)

Supplying (see **5.1.1**)

Explanatory notes

- This offence is limited to the activities specified at (a) to (d). It is not committed, for example, by a landlord who knows that one of their tenants is in their room injecting themselves with amphetamines. They may commit the offence if, for example:
  - ✦ a drug is being supplied to others on the premises;
  - ✦ a controlled drug is being produced on the premises;
  - ✦ the occupants are smoking cannabis.
- The Misuse of Drugs Regulations 2001 allow a person to possess some drugs for certain legitimate reasons (eg medicinal, research) (see **'Defences' 5.1.1**).

Related cases

R v McGee [2012] EWCA Crim 613 Where a person permits the supply of Class A drugs to take place on their premises, the prosecution must prove that the supply took place 'on the premises' rather than 'from the premises'.

R v Lunn [2008] EWCA Crim 2082 It is more serious where the manager of a public house allows premises to be used for drugs compared to the owner of a private house.

R v Auguste [2003] EWCA Crim 3929 During a police raid, a block of cannabis resin and two reefers were found. Although several people were in the house, there was no smell of cannabis having been smoked. It was held that activity of actually smoking cannabis must be carried out before this offence is committed.

R v Brock and Wyner (2001) 2 Cr App R 3 The offence under s 8(b) has two elements: (i) knowingly permits—knowledge of the dealing, which could be actual knowledge or the defendant closing their eyes to the obvious; or (ii) suffers—unwillingness to prevent the dealing, which could be inferred from the failure to take reasonable steps to prevent it. A person's belief that they have taken reasonable steps does not provide them with a defence.

R v Bett [1999] 1 All ER 600 If the defendant is aware that the premises are being used to supply controlled drugs, it does not matter, for the purposes of establishing guilt, which type of drug is involved.

Practical considerations

- Whenever the decision to search premises can be planned, a warrant should be obtained under the Misuse of Drugs Act 1971, s 23(3) (see **5.4.1** and **1.5**).
- The police have a power to close premises associated with nuisance or disorder by issuing a closure notice under the Anti-social Behaviour, Crime and Policing Act 2014, s 76 (see **7.13.4**).
- Consider confiscation of cash and property for premises relating to controlled drugs under s 8, as this is listed as a 'criminal lifestyle' offence under Sch 2 to the Proceeds of Crime Act 2002 (see **5.5** for details).

E&S TRIG

Either way None

Class A/B
Summary: 6/12 months' imprisonment and/or a fine
Indictment: 14 years' imprisonment and/or a fine

Class C
Summary: 3 months' imprisonment and/or a fine
Indictment: 14 years' imprisonment and/or a fine

Link to alternative subject

7.13.4 **Closure of premises (nuisance/disorder)** 441

5.5 **Proceeds of Crime**

The Proceeds of Crime Act 2002 provides for confiscation orders in relation to persons who benefit from criminal conduct, restraint orders to prohibit dealing with property relating to unlawful conduct, freezing orders, unexplained wealth orders, and creates the offence of money laundering. It gives law enforcement agencies and partners capabilities and powers to recover the proceeds of crime and to tackle money laundering, corruption, and terrorist financing. Section 75 of the Act sets out the criteria for a 'criminal lifestyle'. Schedule 2 lists the 'criminal lifestyle' offences and s 6 sets out the confiscation procedure.

Criminal lifestyle criteria

(1) A defendant has a criminal lifestyle if (and only if) the following condition is satisfied.

(2) The condition is that the offence (or any of the offences) concerned satisfies any of these tests:—
- (a) it is specified in Schedule 2;
- (b) it constitutes conduct forming part of a course of criminal activity;
- (c) it is an offence committed over a period of at least six months and the defendant has benefited from the conduct which constitutes the offence.

(3) Conduct forms part of a course of criminal activity if the defendant has benefited from the conduct and—
- (a) in the proceedings in which he was convicted he was convicted of three or more other offences, each of three or more of them constituting conduct from which he has benefited, or
- (b) in the period of six years ending with the day when those proceedings were started (or, if there is more than one such day, the earliest day) he was convicted on at least two separate occasions of an offence constituting conduct from which he has benefited.

(4) But an offence does not satisfy the test in subsection (2)(b) or (c) unless the defendant obtains relevant benefit of not less than £5,000.

(5) Relevant benefit for the purposes of subsection (2)(b) is—
- (a) benefit from conduct which constitutes the offence;
- (b) benefit from any other conduct which forms part of the course of criminal activity and which constitutes an offence of which the defendant has been convicted;
- (c) benefit from conduct which constitutes an offence which has been or will be taken into consideration by the court in sentencing the defendant for an offence mentioned in paragraph (a) or (b).

(6) Relevant benefit for the purposes of subsection (2)(c) is—
(a) benefit from conduct which constitutes the offence;
(b) benefit from conduct which constitutes an offence which has been or will be taken into consideration by the court in sentencing the defendant for the offence mentioned in paragraph (a).

Proceeds of Crime Act 2002, s 75

Criminal lifestyle offences

Schedule 2 to the Proceeds of Crime Act 2002 lists offences relating to 'criminal lifestyle' defined by s 75.

Drug trafficking

Misuse of Drugs Act 1971

- s 4(2) or (3) (unlawful production/supply of controlled drugs) (see **5.1.1**);
- s 5(3) (possession of controlled drug with intent to supply) (see **5.2.2**);
- s 8 (premises relating to controlled drugs) (see **5.4.2**);
- s 20 (assisting/inducing offence outside UK).

Psychoactive Substances Act 2016

- s 4 (producing a psychoactive substance) (see **5.3.4**);
- s 5 (supplying, or offering to supply, a psychoactive substance) (see **5.3.5**);
- s 7 (possession of psychoactive substance with intent to supply) (see **5.3.6**);
- s 8 (importing or exporting a psychoactive substance).

Customs and Excise Management Act 1979

Committed in breach of import or export drug restriction:

- s 50(2) or (3) (improper importation of goods);
- s 68(2) (exportation of prohibited or restricted goods);
- s 170 (fraudulent duty evasion).

Criminal Justice (International Co-operation) Act 1990

- s 12 (manufacture/supply of a substance specified in Sch 2 to that Act);
- s 19 (using a ship for illicit traffic in controlled drugs).

Money laundering

Proceeds of Crime Act 2002

- s 327 (concealing, etc criminal property);
- s 328 (assisting another to retain criminal property).

Slavery etc

Modern Slavery Act 2015

- s 1 (slavery, servitude, and forced or compulsory labour).

Directing terrorism

Terrorism Act 2000

- s 56 (directing the activities of a terrorist organisation).

People trafficking

- Offence under s 25 or 25A of the *Immigration Act 1971* (assisting unlawful immigration, etc) (see **11.3**);
- An offence under s 2 of the *Modern Slavery Act 2015* (human trafficking) (see **4.9**).

Arms trafficking

An offence under either of the following provisions of the *Customs and Excise Management Act 1979* if it is committed in connection with a firearm or ammunition:

- s 68(2) (exportation of prohibited goods);
- s 170 (fraudulent evasion of duty, etc).

Firearms Act 1968, s 3(1) (dealing in firearms or ammunition by way of trade or business) (see **8.1.2**).

Counterfeiting

Forgery and Counterfeiting Act 1981

- s 14 (making counterfeit notes or coins);
- s 15 (passing, etc counterfeit notes or coins);
- s 16 (having counterfeit notes or coins);
- s 17 (make/possess materials or equipment for counterfeiting).

Intellectual property

Copyright, Designs and Patents Act 1988

- s 107(1) (make/deal in article which infringes copyright);
- s 107(2) (make/possess article designed or adapted to make copy of a copyright work);
- s 198(1) (making or dealing in an illicit recording);
- s 297A (making or dealing in unauthorised decoders).

Trade Marks Act 1994

- s 92(1), (2), or (3) (unauthorised trade mark use).

Prostitution and child sex

Sexual Offences Act 1956

- s 33 or 34 (keeping or letting premises for use as a brothel).

Sexual Offences Act 2003

- s 14 (arranging or facilitating commission of a child sex offence) (see **6.5.3**);
- s 48 (causing or inciting sexual exploitation of a child);
- s 49 (controlling a child in relation to sexual exploitation);
- s 50 (arranging or facilitating sexual exploitation of a child);

- s 52 (causing or inciting prostitution for gain);
- s 53 (controlling prostitution for gain) (see **6.11.3**).

Blackmail

Theft Act 1968

- s 21 (blackmail) (see **3.2.2**).

Gangmasters

Gangmasters (Licensing) Act 2004

- s 12(1) or (2) (acting as a gangmaster without a licence, possession of false documents).

Inchoate offences

- offence of attempting, conspiring, or inciting the commission of an offence specified in this Sch (see **4.1.1**);
- offence under s 44 of the Serious Crime Act 2007 of doing an act capable of encouraging or assisting the commission of an offence specified in this Schedule (see **4.1.3**).
- offence of aiding, abetting, counselling, or procuring the commission of such an offence.

Explanatory notes

- The criminal lifestyle tests are designed to identify individuals who may be living off crime and make them account for their assets, which are liable to be confiscated if the person is unable to account for their lawful origin.
- The first test is that they are convicted of an offence specified in Sch 2.
- The second test is that the defendant is convicted of an offence of any description, provided it was committed over a period of at least six months, and obtained not less than £5,000 from that offence and/or any others taken into consideration by the court on the same occasion.
- The third test is that the defendant is convicted of a combination of offences amounting to 'a course of criminal activity'.
- This third test is more complicated than the other two. The defendant satisfies it if they have been convicted in the current proceedings:
    - of four or more offences of any description from which they have benefited; or
    - of any one such offence and has other convictions for any such offences on at least two separate occasions in the last six years. In addition, the total benefit from the offence(s) and/or any others taken into consideration by the court must be not less than £5,000.
- The purpose of confiscation proceedings under s 6 is to recover the financial benefit that the offender has obtained from their criminal conduct. Proceedings are conducted according to the civil standard of proof, being on the balance of probabilities.

- In certain circumstances, the court is empowered to assume that the defendant's assets, and their income and expenditure during the period of six years before proceedings were brought, have been derived from criminal conduct and to calculate the confiscation order accordingly.
- Confiscation orders may be made in the Crown Court following conviction. Where the conviction takes place in the magistrates' court, a confiscation order can only be made if the defendant is committed to the Crown Court either for sentence or for sentence and confiscation under s 70.
- Sections 362A and 362B of the Proceeds of Crime Act 2002 provide for 'unexplained wealth orders'. The High Court may make an unexplained wealth order in respect of property that requires the respondent to provide a statement setting out the nature and extent of their interest in the property and to explain how the property was obtained, etc. To make the order, the court must be satisfied that the respondent holds the property and the property must have a value greater than £50,000.

Links to alternative subjects and offences

3.2.2 **Blackmail** 142
4.1 **Criminal Attempts** 173
4.9 **Slavery and Human Trafficking** 217
6.5 **Child Sexual Exploitation Offences** 297
8.1 **'Section 1 Firearms' Offences.** 507
11.3 **Illegal Entry into the UK/Identity Documents** 802

Chapter 6

Sexual Offences and Assaults

6.1 Rape Offences

Rape and other sexual offences were consolidated by the Sexual Offences Act 2003.

6.1.1 Rape

The offence of rape is covered by ss 1 (rape) and 5 (rape of a child under 13—see **6.1.2**) of the Sexual Offences Act 2003.

Offences

A person (A) commits an offence if—
(a) he intentionally penetrates the vagina, anus or mouth of another person (B) with his penis,
(b) B does not consent to penetration, and
(c) A does not reasonably believe that B consents.

Sexual Offences Act 2003, s 1(1)

PNLD H5651, H5652, H5653, H5654

Points to prove

- ✓ intentionally
- ✓ without consent
- ✓ penetrated anus/vagina/mouth
- ✓ of another person
- ✓ with the defendant's penis
- ✓ not reasonably believing that they had consented

Meanings

Intentionally (see also **4.1.2**)

This means deliberate penetration. If the defendant intended to penetrate but was physically unable to do so or the defendant admitted that it was their intent, then the law states that they still had the necessary intent.

Penetration (s 79(2))

Means a continuing act from entry to withdrawal.

Vagina (s 79(9))

Includes vulva.

Consent

Both s 75 (evidential presumptions about consent) and s 76 (conclusive presumptions about consent) apply to this offence (see '**Defences**' below).

Reasonable belief

Whether a belief is reasonable is to be determined having regard to all the circumstances, including any steps A has taken to ascertain whether B consents.

Explanatory notes

- As the definition of vagina includes vulva, then full penetration is not essential to commit rape.
- The offence of rape includes penile penetration not only of the vagina and anus but also of the mouth as this act could be just as traumatising and damaging for the victim.
- Where a person consents to penetration at the time of entry, but then withdraws their consent and the penetration continues, the person penetrating may be guilty of rape or assault by penetration.
- The offence covers surgically reconstructed genitalia, eg as a result of gender reassignment surgery (s 79(3)). It therefore protects transsexuals, but also means that a person with a surgically constructed penis can commit the offence.
- As penetration can be proved by reference to scientific evidence (semen, bruising, etc), consent often becomes the major, if not only, issue.

Defences

A critical issue in rape cases is consent and ss 74 to 76 deal specifically with this.

Consent (s 74)

For the purposes of this Part, a person consents if he agrees by choice, and has the freedom and capacity to make that choice.

Sexual Offences Act 2003, s 74

Evidential presumptions about consent

(1) If in proceedings for an offence to which this section applies it is proved—
   (a) that the defendant did the relevant act,
   (b) that any of the circumstances specified in subsection (2) existed, and
   (c) that the defendant knew that those circumstances existed,

The complainant is to be taken not to have consented to the relevant act unless sufficient evidence is adduced to raise an issue as to whether he consented, and the defendant is to be taken not to have reasonably believed that the complainant consented unless sufficient evidence is adduced to raise an issue as to whether he reasonably believed it.

(2) The circumstances are that—
   (a) any person was, at the time of the relevant act or immediately before it began, using violence against the complainant or causing the complainant to fear that immediate violence would be used against him;
   (b) any person was, at the time of the relevant act or immediately before it began, causing the complainant to fear that violence was being used, or that immediate violence would be used, against another person;
   (c) the complainant was, and the defendant was not, unlawfully detained at the time of the relevant act;
   (d) the complainant was asleep or otherwise unconscious at the time of the relevant act;
   (e) because of the complainant's physical disability, the complainant would not have been able at the time of the relevant act to communicate to the defendant whether the complainant consented;
   (f) any person had administered to or caused to be taken by the complainant, without the complainant's consent, a substance which, having regard to when it was administered or taken, was capable of causing or enabling the complainant to be stupefied or overpowered at the time of the relevant act.

(3) In subsection (2)(a) and (b), the reference to the time immediately before the relevant act began is, in the case of an act that is one of a continuous series of sexual activities, a reference to the time immediately before the first sexual activity began.

Sexual Offences Act 2003, s 75

Conclusive presumptions about consent

(1) If in proceedings for an offence to which this section applies it is proved that the defendant did the relevant act and that any of the circumstances specified in subsection (2) existed, it is to be conclusively presumed—
   (a) that the complainant did not consent to the relevant act, and
   (b) that the defendant did not believe that the complainant consented to the relevant act.

(2) The circumstances are that—
  (a) the defendant intentionally deceived the complainant as to the nature or purpose of the relevant act;
  (b) the defendant intentionally induced the complainant to consent to the relevant act by impersonating a person known personally to the complainant.

Sexual Offences Act 2003, s 76

Defence notes

Meaning of 'relevant act' (s 77)

References to the term 'relevant act' in ss 75 and 76 vary according to the offence committed and are where the defendant intentionally:

- 'penetrates, with his penis, the vagina, anus or mouth of another person' (*Rape (s 1)*);
- 'penetrates, with a part of his body or anything else, the vagina or anus of another person, where the penetration is sexual' (*Assault by penetration (s 2)*);
- 'touches another person, where the touching is sexual' (*Sexual assault (s 3)*);
- 'causes another person to engage in a sexual activity' (*Causing a person to engage in activity without consent (s 4)*).

Consent in s 74

The **freedom** to **agree** is intended to stress that a lack of protest, resistance, or injury by the victim does not necessarily signify consent.

- Freedom is not defined in the Act so it must be a matter of fact as to whether the victim was free to agree or whether pressure or threats ruled out that agreement.
- A person might not have sufficient **capacity** if they suffer from a mental disorder, are incapacitated due to drink/drugs, or their age prevents them from making a free choice.
- Section 30 of the 2003 Act creates the offence of sexual activity with a person who has a mental disorder which impedes their choice.
- Capacity is not defined so it will be for the court to decide from all the available evidence.

Evidential presumptions about consent in s 75

- The term '**substance**' in s 75(2)(f) is not defined, so anything capable of stupefying or overpowering would be covered; this would include substances such as alcohol, GHB, or Rohypnol.
- Section 75(3) covers the situation where there have been a number of sexual acts, of which penetration is the culmination, and the defendant is being prosecuted for them and the threats occurred immediately before the first sexual act. In that case, the presumption still applies.
- Where the prosecution proves that the defendant did a **relevant act** (in this case rape), and the situations described in s 75(2)

existed and the defendant knew they existed, then the complainant will be presumed not to have consented and the defendant will be presumed not to have reasonably believed the complainant consented (s 75(1)).

Conclusive presumptions about consent in s 76

- To use the conclusive presumption provided in s 76, evidence as to the existence of the intentional deception will be critical.
- Deceiving the complainant as to the nature or purpose of the act could be where the complainant is told that digital penetration of her vagina is necessary for medical reasons when in fact it is only for sexual gratification of the defendant.
- Impersonation would cover circumstances where the defendant deceives the complainant into believing that he is her partner causing the complainant to consent to the sexual act.

General

- If none of the situations described in ss 75 and 76 apply, then the prosecution must show that the circumstances of the offence were such that the defendant could not reasonably believe that the complainant consented.
- If the defendant states that they did reasonably believe that the complainant consented, then it would be a matter for the jury to decide as to whether a reasonable person would come to the same belief having regard to all the circumstances. In interview, they should be asked what assured them that the victim consented or that it was consensual.
- The circumstances will include the personal characteristics of the defendant: the defendant's age, general sexual experience, sexual experience with this complainant, learning disability, and any other factors that could have affected the defendant's ability to understand the nature and consequences of their actions which may be relevant depending on the circumstances of the case.
- The Act makes it clear there is an onus on parties involved in a relevant sexual activity to ensure that they have the true consent of the other person(s) and that they took reasonable steps to make sure true consent was freely given prior to any sexual act taking place.

Related cases

R v Bater-James and another [2020] EWCA Crim 790 The court issued guidance in relation to digital and electronic communications held by a witness on devices such as mobile telephones, and the disclosure thereof. The court emphasised that merely speculative defence enquiries would not give rise to a reasonable line of enquiry requiring the examination of the device by an investigator; and that what did amount to a reasonable line of enquiry would depend on the facts and issues in the individual case, including any potential defence. The court also considered the ways in which the destruction of, or refusal to provide, data might be managed without derailing the case, including by summons of the witness, cross-examination, and judicial direction. (See also Home Office Extraction of Information from electronic devices: code of practice 2022.)

R v Lawrance [2020] EWCA Crim 971 This case considered the issue of consent. The defendant gave a false assurance to the complainant that they had had a vasectomy. Consequently, she consented to sexual intercourse without the use of contraception. However, she became pregnant and underwent a termination. It was held that the deception about fertility was one which related not to the physical performance of the sexual act but to risks or consequences associated with it. The question of consent could not be affected by whether pregnancy followed or not. This is different to a lie about whether a condom is being worn during sex, from engaging in intercourse not intending to withdraw having promised to do so, and from engaging in sexual activity having misrepresented one's gender.

R v Hepburn [2020] EWCA Crim 820 A conviction for oral rape but acquittal for vaginal rape during a continuous incident were not irreconcilable where the victim had been asleep at commencement of the oral rape and had mistaken the offender for her boyfriend.

R v Townsend [2020] EWCA Crim 1343 Video footage demonstrating a sexual act performed on an unknown person could amount to a sexual assault where the jury could conclude that the person had not consented.

R v Bree [2007] EWCA Crim 804 This case considered the issue of consent where the complainant had consumed a considerable amount of alcohol. It was held that if, as a result of consuming alcohol or for any other reason, capacity to choose whether to have sexual intercourse was temporarily lost, then no consent was present and dependent upon enquiries into the state of mind of the victim, if intercourse takes place, then it would be rape.

Practical considerations

- For the meaning of sexual, see **6.2.1**.
- Ejaculation does not have to occur for the rape to be committed.
- All reports of rape must be treated as genuine and the victims treated with sensitivity. Only a suitably trained or qualified person should be used to take a statement or obtain evidence from the victim.
- The crime scene should be identified and preserved, ensuring that cross-contamination does not occur (see **1.3.3**).
- Evidence of the offence should be seized, including clothing and any articles used, such as condoms.
- Consider medical and forensic examination of the victim and offender.
- CPS guidance on Rape and Sexual Offences 2021—
  Chapter 6: 'Consent'—contains guidance regarding consent that should be carefully considered when deciding not only what offence to charge but also whether it is in the public interest to prosecute.

- HOC 1/2015 gives guidance on the 'date rape' drug GHB, under Sch 2 to the Misuse of Drugs Regulations 2001, so ensuring stricter control to reduce the risks of diversion and misuse. More recent concerns regarding spiking of drinks or needles have led the Home Office to propose new measures to address the problem including, inter alia, spike testing kits and the training of door supervisors.
- The other main substances used in drug-facilitated sexual assaults are benzodiazepines, Rohypnol, and ketamine; sometimes taken within a 'chemsex' setting. Victims of rape and/or sexual assaults committed in such settings may be reluctant to engage with prosecution for fear of disclosing drug offences they themselves may have committed. See also **6.10**.
- Obtain evidence of first complaint if appropriate and available.
- Advise the victim not to shower, bathe, drink, or smoke and to retain the clothing they were wearing at the time of the attack.
- Consider CCTV and other potential evidence from independent witnesses.

E&S CHAR

Indictable

None

Life imprisonment

6.1.2 **Rape of a child under 13**

This is covered by s 5 of the Sexual Offences Act 2003.

Offences

A person commits an offence if—
(a) he intentionally penetrates the vagina, anus or mouth of another person with his penis, and
(b) the other person is under 13.

Sexual Offences Act 2003, s 5(1)

PNLD H5667, H5669

Points to prove

✓ intentionally
✓ penetrated the anus/vagina/mouth
✓ of a person under 13
✓ with the defendant's penis

6.1.2 **Rape of a child under 13**

Meanings

Intentionally (see **6.1.1**)

Penetrates (see **6.1.1**)

Vagina (see **6.1.1**)

Explanatory notes

- There is no issue of consent under this section. Whether the child consented or not is irrelevant, making this almost an offence of 'strict liability'.
- This section also includes not only penetration of the vagina and anus but also penile penetration of the mouth as in s 1.
- As with the s 1 offence of rape, the offence covers surgically reconstructed genitalia, for example as a result of gender reassignment surgery.

Related case

R v G [2008] UKHL 37 The defendant, aged 15, had intercourse with a girl aged 12 in his room with her consent. At the time the defendant believed her to be aged 15. It was held that reasonable belief as to consent or age was irrelevant as the offence was absolute and imposed strict liability.

Practical considerations

- Full penetration does not have to occur and it is not necessary to prove any additional consequences (eg that the hymen was broken).
- Once it can be proved that penetration occurred, it will be very hard to show that this was anything other than intentional but it is still a necessary ingredient of the offence.
- Prove age of child. Only a suitably trained or qualified person should be used to take a statement or obtain evidence from the child/victim.
- Whilst offences between adults and children will always be viewed as serious, account should be taken of Art 8 ECHR (respect for private life) in relation to the criminalisation of consenting children.
- For information for professionals working with children, including the police, when dealing with online safety issues such as cyberbullying, grooming, sexting, etc a Professionals Online Safety Helpline (POSH) is a charity which is part of the UK Safer Internet Centre funded by the EU (see **Appendix 2**).
- Consider CPS charging principles based on the Code for Crown Prosecutors.
- Consider all the evidential responsibilities highlighted as with the s 1 offence of rape.

E&S CHAR

Indictable None

Life imprisonment

Links to alternative subjects and offences

2.6 **False Imprisonment/Kidnap** 100
2.8 **Domestic Abuse** 125

6.2 Sexual Assault by Penetration

These offences are covered by ss 2 and 6 (child under 13) of the Sexual Offences Act 2003.

6.2.1 Assault by penetration of a person aged 13 or over

Section 2 of the Sexual Offences Act 2003 covers the situation where a person intentionally (and not just recklessly) penetrates the vagina or anus of another person.

Offences

A person (A) commits an offence if—
(a) he intentionally penetrates the vagina or anus of another person (B) with a part of his body or anything else,
(b) the penetration is sexual,
(c) B does not consent to the penetration, and
(d) A does not reasonably believe that B consents.

Sexual Offences Act 2003, s 2(1)

PNLD H5659, H5660

Points to prove

✓ intentionally
✓ sexually penetrated
✓ the anus/vagina of another person aged 13 or over
✓ with a part of the body and/or a thing
✓ without consent
✓ not reasonably believing that they had consented

Meanings

Intentionally (see **6.1.1**)

Penetration (see **6.1.1**)

Vagina (see **6.1.1**)

Part of the body (see s 79(3))

References to a part of the body include references to a part surgically constructed (in particular, through gender reassignment surgery).

Anything else

This term has not been defined but it is an extremely wide category and will cover anything that can be used to penetrate the body of another.

Sexual

Section 78 of the Sexual Offences Act 2003 defines 'sexual' for the purposes of Part 1 (ss 1 to 79) (with the exception of s 71 which has a separate definition). For the purposes of this Part (except ss 15A, 66B to 66D, and 71), penetration, touching, or any other activity is sexual if a reasonable person would consider that:

(a) whatever its circumstances or any person's purpose in relation to it, it is because of its nature sexual; or
(b) because of its nature, it may be sexual and because of its circumstances or the purpose of any person in relation to it (or both) it is sexual.

Consent (see **6.1.1**)

Reasonable belief (see **6.1.1**)

Explanatory notes

- Section 79(3) takes into account surgically reconstructed genitalia. Medical examination could reveal that a person has undergone reconstructive surgery.
- Once penetration has been proved, it will be difficult for the defendant to show that it was not their intention to do this. However, as partial penetration will suffice, there may be occasions (such as during sporting or gymnastic contact) where the defendant claims partial penetration by, say, a finger was inadvertent. It would then be for the prosecution to prove otherwise.
- If the defendant states that they reasonably believed that the complainant consented, then it will be a matter for the jury to decide whether a reasonable person would come to the same belief having regard to all the circumstances.
- The circumstances include the personal characteristics of the defendant: the defendant's age, general sexual experience, sexual experience with this complainant, learning disability, and any other factor that could have affected their ability to understand the nature and consequences of their actions may be relevant depending on the circumstances of the case.
- Parties to relevant sexual activity must ensure that they have the true consent of the other person(s) and that they took reasonable steps to make sure true consent had been freely given prior to any sexual act taking place.
- This offence carries the same penalty as rape (life imprisonment), thus reflecting its gravity.

6.2.1 **Assault by penetration of a person aged 13 or over**

- Determining what is '**sexual**' is a mixed test consisting of an objective test based on what a reasonable person would consider to be sexual and the purpose of the person involved:
  - subsection (a) where there is no doubt that the activity is sexual, such as oral sex or penetration by vibrator; and
  - subsection (b) where the activity could also have some purpose apart from a sexual one, and where the defendant's act was not sexually motivated. This would cover situations where the defendant penetrates their victim with an object with the sole intent of committing a violent act, not a sexual one (eg penetration with the handle part of a knife to humiliate and assert their power over the victim).
- The defendant may not have intended the act to be sexual but, from a reasonable person's point of view and because of its nature, a reasonable person would consider that it might be sexual.
- Medical examinations or intimate searches by the relevant authorities (such as police and customs), or such other treatment where penetration is involved but is not sexual (eg in colonic irrigation), will not normally be deemed sexual.
- Unlike rape, this offence can be committed by digital penetration and penetration by any other part of the body, such as a fist, tongue, and toes.
- Full penetration is not essential to commit the offence.
- Items included in the term 'anything else' can be such objects as bottles, vibrators, and other similar objects and substances.

Defences

Sections 75 and 76 apply to this offence; see **6.1.1 'Defences'** for further details.

Practical considerations

- Any reports of serious sexual assault must be treated as genuine and the victims treated with sensitivity.
- Evidence of the offence should be seized and includes clothing, condoms, and articles used.
- Ensure cross-contamination does not occur.
- Obtain evidence of the first complaint if appropriate and available.
- Advise the victim not to shower, bathe, drink, or smoke and to retain the clothing they were wearing at the time of the attack.
- Consider CCTV and other evidence from potential witnesses.

E&S CHAR

Indictable | None

Life imprisonment

6.2.2 Assault by penetration of a child under 13

Section 6 of the Sexual Offences Act 2003 is the same as s 2 above, except that the complainant is under 13 and there is no issue of consent.

Offences

A person commits an offence if—
(a) he intentionally penetrates the vagina or anus of another person with a part of his body or anything else,
(b) the penetration is sexual, and
(c) the other person is under 13.

Sexual Offences Act 2003, s 6(1)

PNLD H5671, H5672

Points to prove

✓ intentionally
✓ sexually penetrated
✓ anus/vagina of a girl aged under 13 OR
✓ anus of a boy aged under 13
✓ with a part of the body and/or a thing

Meanings

Intentionally (see **6.1.1**)

Penetrates (see **6.1.1**)

Vagina (see **6.1.1**)

Part of his body (see **6.2.1**)

Anything else (see **6.2.1**)

Sexual (see **6.2.1**)

Explanatory notes (see **6.2.1 'Explanatory notes'**)

Practical considerations (also see **6.2.1 'Practical considerations'**)

- This is an offence of strict liability (see **6.1.2**).
- It is not necessary for the victim to know or explain what they were penetrated with.

6.2.2 **Assault by penetration of a child under 13**

- The offence can be used in cases where the child does not possess the knowledge to identify the nature of what they had been penetrated with.
- Prove age of child. Only a suitably trained or qualified person should be used to take a statement or obtain evidence from the victim.

E&S CHAR

Indictable | None

Life imprisonment

6.3 Sexual Assault by Touching

6.3.1 Sexual assault by touching a person aged 13 or over

This offence is covered by s 3 of the Sexual Offences Act 2003.

Offences

A person (A) commits an offence if—
(a) he intentionally touches another person (B),
(b) the touching is sexual,
(c) B does not consent to the touching, and
(d) A does not reasonably believe that B consents.

Sexual Offences Act 2003, s 3(1)

PNLD H5661, H5662

Points to prove

✓ intentionally touched
✓ another person aged 13 or over
✓ that touching was sexual
✓ other person did not consent
✓ not reasonably believing that they were consenting

Meanings

Intentionally (see **6.1.1**)

Touching (s 79(8))

This includes touching:

- with any part of the body;
- with anything else;
- through anything;

and in particular includes touching amounting to penetration.

Sexual (see **6.2.1**)

Consent (see **6.1.1**)

Reasonable belief (see **6.1.1**)

Explanatory notes

- This section covers non-penetration sexual assaults on another person aged 13 or over. It will cover a wide spectrum of behaviour that would include the defendant rubbing up against the complainant's private parts through the person's clothes for their sexual gratification.

- Touching includes touching through clothes which does not have to involve using the hands and can involve any part of the body being used or touched or even an object such as a sex toy.
- The offence does not require that the defendant intended that the touching be sexual, only that the touching itself was intentional. The sexual aspect of the touching is a separate element.
- Whilst there could not be many examples of 'accidental' or inadvertent penetration, accidental touching occurs all the time. Jostling in a crowded street, travelling on a busy train or bus, and attending sports events can all lead to some form of contact with others.
- It will normally be apparent that the defendant intentionally touched the victim (because of the part of the body touched or used or because of accompanying circumstances) but there will still be far more room for a defence of lack of intent than in penetration offences.
- In most cases of sexual assault, the sexual element will be non-contentious. For example, where a man gropes a female's genitals, it would be hard to imagine a set of circumstances where this would not be sexual and in those cases s 78(a) (see **6.2.1**) will be relied on.
- If, with regard to all the circumstances, the purpose and nature of the touching, a reasonable person would consider it sexual then it will be covered by s 78(b).
- It is not certain if the more obscure sexual fantasies would be covered at all by s 78. Would a reasonable person consider the removal of a shoe as sexual, looking at the purpose and nature of it? If not, then this would not constitute 'sexual' touching even if the offender received sexual gratification from doing it. This reflects the former common law position with regard to such offences.

Defences

Sections 75 and 76 apply—see **6.1.1 'Defences'** for further details.

Related cases

R v Emmannuel [2022] EWCA Crim 1322 For a conviction for sexual assault, it was for the jury to determine if the touching had been sexual.

Attorney General's Reference (No 1 of 2020) [2020] EWCA Crim 1665 It is not necessary for the prosecution to prove, as an element of this offence, that the defendant intended the touching of the person to be sexual.

R v Ciccarelli [2011] EWCA Crim 2665 The defendant claimed that, at a party, the complainant had touched them between the legs and tried to kiss them. Later, while the complainant was asleep, the defendant went to the complainant's bedroom and climbed into bed, and touched them again with an erect penis from behind, tried to pull the complainant's knickers down, and climbed on top. The complainant woke up and made the defendant leave the room. The defendant was convicted of sexual assault but appealed on a question of consent. Because the defendant made no attempt to awaken the complainant prior to the sexual advances, it was held that there was insufficient evidence to raise the issue of reasonable belief under s 75.

R v H [2005] 2 All ER 859 The defendant made a sexual suggestion before touching the complainant over tracksuit bottoms. It was held that in this type of scenario two questions had to be answered in the affirmative to find guilt;

1. would they consider that the touching could be sexual because of its nature and surrounding circumstances; and
2. given the circumstances or the purpose of the touching, whether the jury was convinced that the touching had in fact been sexual.

In borderline cases, intent can be used to determine whether touching was sexual, and this includes anything said; however, in the majority of cases, the answer would be the same whether the two-question approach were used or where the matter is considered as a whole.

Practical considerations

- Reports of serious sexual assault must be treated as genuine and the victims treated with sensitivity.
- As with all serious sexual offences, identify any scene, preserve it, and seize any articles or associated items relevant to the offence for which the offender has been arrested.
- Prevent any potential for cross-contamination.
- Keep the offender and victim separate.
- Consider medical and forensic examination for victim and offender.

SSS E&S CHAR

Either way

None

Summary: 6/12 months' imprisonment and/or a fine

Indictment: 10 years' imprisonment

6.3.2 Sexual assault by touching a child under 13

This offence is covered by s 7 of the Sexual Offences Act 2003; the elements are the same as for s 3 but there is no need to prove lack of consent by the child; any such consent is irrelevant.

6.3.2 Sexual assault by touching a child under 13

Offences

A person commits an offence if—
(a) he intentionally touches another person,
(b) the touching is sexual, and
(c) the other person is under 13.

Sexual Offences Act 2003, s 7(1)

PNLD H5673, H5674

Points to prove

✓ intentionally touched
✓ a child aged under 13
✓ the touching was sexual

Meanings

Intentionally (see **6.1.1**)

Touching (see **6.3.1**)

Sexual (see **6.2.1**)

Explanatory notes

- Consent is not an issue as this is an offence of strict liability (see **6.1.2**).
- Points raised in **6.3.1** relating to the touching and its sexual nature are still relevant to this offence.

Related case

R v Weir [2005] EWCA Crim 2866 The defendant was on trial for sexual assault by touching a 10-year-old girl. Despite not being the same offence category, a previous caution for taking an indecent photograph of a child was disclosed at court under s 103(2)(b) of the Criminal Justice Act 2003. This was allowed as it showed a propensity to commit the s 7 offence.

Practical considerations

- Prove the age of the child. Only a suitably trained or qualified person should be used to take a statement or obtain evidence from the victim.
- If possible, identify and preserve a scene and seize any articles suspected of being used in the offence. Always consider the potential for cross-contamination (see **1.3.3**).

E&S CHAR

Either way

None

Summary: 6/12 months' imprisonment and/or a fine
Indictment: 14 years' imprisonment

6.4 Sexual Activity with a Child

This offence is covered by s 9 of the Sexual Offences Act 2003.

Offences

(1) A person aged 18 or over (A) commits an offence if—
  (a) he intentionally touches another person (B),
  (b) the touching is sexual, and
  (c) either—
    (i) B is under 16 and A does not reasonably believe that B is 16 or over, or
    (ii) B is under 13.

(2) A person guilty of an offence under this section, if the touching involved—
  (a) penetration of B's anus or vagina with a part of A's body or anything else,
  (b) penetration of B's mouth with A's penis.
  (c) penetration of A's anus or vagina with a part of B's body, or
  (d) penetration of A's mouth with B's penis.

is liable, on conviction on indictment, to imprisonment for a term not exceeding 14 years.

Sexual Offences Act 2003, s 9(1) and (2)

PNLD **H5679 to H5682, H5687 to H5690**

Points to prove

Non-penetrative

✓ defendant aged 18 or over
✓ intentionally touched
✓ child under 13 OR
✓ a child aged 13/14/15, not reasonably believing they were 16 or over
✓ the touching was sexual

Penetrative

✓ defendant aged 18 or over
✓ intentionally touched
✓ a child under 13 OR
✓ a child aged 13/14/15, not reasonably believing they were 16 or over
✓ that touching was sexual and involved penetration of:
  ✦ complainant's anus/vagina with part of D's body or thing OR
  ✦ complainant's mouth with D's penis OR
  ✦ D's anus/vagina with part of complainant's body OR
  ✦ D's mouth with complainant's penis

Meanings

Intentionally (see **6.1.1**)

Touching (see **6.3.1**)

Sexual (see **6.2.1**)

Reasonable belief (see '**Defences**' below)

Explanatory note

- This offence is very similar to ss 3 and 7 (see **6.3**), but the defendant is aged 18 or over and touching involved in s 9(2) is specified in terms of what was used on/in what part of the body.

Defences

Proving a reasonable belief that the child was 16 or over at the time. This only applies if the victim is aged between 13 and 15. If under 13 the offence is one of strict liability.

Defence notes

- In deciding whether it is in the public interest to prosecute this offence, where there is enough evidence to provide a realistic prospect of conviction prosecutors may take into consideration factors which include the age and emotional maturity of the parties, whether they entered into the sexual relationship willingly, any coercion or corruption by a person, the relationship between the parties, and whether there was any existence of a duty of care or breach of trust.
- If the victim is aged between 13 and 15, the prosecution must provide evidence that the defendant's belief was not reasonable. For example, that the defendant knew that the child attended school and had not yet taken their GCSE examinations.
- If the prosecution can provide such evidence, it is open to the defendant to rebut it, if they can show on the balance of probabilities that their belief was reasonably held.
- However, if the defendant and the complainant met for the first time over the internet, the complainant provided photographs of themselves in which they looked much older than they in fact were, and if they told the defendant that they were 18 and did look 18, then the belief might be reasonable.

Practical considerations

- This offence is gender-neutral.
- Identify and preserve any scene. Prevent cross-contamination.
- Seize any articles/clothing or associated equipment which is relevant.
- Consider charging principles in the Code for Crown Prosecutors.

6.4 Sexual Activity with a Child

- Consider factors which include the age and emotional maturity of the parties, whether they entered into the sexual relationship willingly, any coercion or corruption by a person, relationship between the parties, and whether there was any existence of a duty of care or breach of trust.
- The discretion of the CPS not to charge where it is not in the public interest would be partially relevant where the two parties were close in age, for instance an 18-year-old and a 15-year-old, and had engaged in mutually agreed sexual activity.

E&S CHAR

s 9(1) offence

Either way

None

Summary: 6/12 months' imprisonment and/or a fine

Indictment: 14 years' imprisonment

s 9(2) offence

Indictable

None

14 years' imprisonment

6.5 Child Sexual Exploitation Offences

6.5.1 Cause/incite child under 16 to engage in sexual activity

Section 10 of the Sexual Offences Act 2003 makes it an offence for a person aged 18 or over intentionally to cause or incite a child aged under 16 to engage in sexual activity. Where the child is aged 13, 14, or 15, the prosecution must prove that the defendant did not reasonably believe that they were 16 or over.

Offences

(1) A person aged 18 or over (A) commits an offence if—
- (a) he intentionally causes or incites another person (B) to engage in an activity,
- (b) the activity is sexual, and
- (c) either—
  - (i) B is under 16 and A does not reasonably believe that B is 16 or over, or
  - (ii) B is under 13.

(2) A person guilty of an offence under this section, if the activity caused or incited involved—
- (a) penetration of B's anus or vagina,
- (b) penetration of B's mouth with a person's penis,
- (c) penetration of a person's anus or vagina with a part of B's body or by B with anything else, or
- (d) penetration of a person's mouth with B's penis,

is liable, on conviction on indictment, to imprisonment for a term not exceeding 14 years.

Sexual Offences Act 2003, s 10(1) and (2)

PNLD H5691 to H5698

Points to prove

Non-penetration

✓ offender aged 18 or over
✓ intentionally
✓ caused/incited
✓ a child aged 13/14/15, not reasonably believing they were 16 or over OR
✓ a child under 13

6.5.1 Cause/incite child under 16 to engage in sexual activity

✓ to engage in sexual activity
✓ of a non-penetrative nature

Penetration

✓ per first six points of '**Non-penetration**'
✓ involving the penetration of
✓ child's anus/vagina OR
✓ child's mouth with another person's penis OR
✓ a person's anus/vagina with part of child's body or by child with anything else OR
✓ a person's mouth with the boy's penis

Meanings

Intentionally (see **6.1.1**)

Causes

Defined by the *Concise Oxford Dictionary* as 'be the cause of, make happen'. This implies that the defendant must take some positive action rather than omit acting. Examples could be the use of force, threats, deception, or intimidation but also promising a reward, persuading the child that the behaviour is perfectly acceptable behaviour that other children also engage in, alleging to check for bruises or lice or to try on clothes.

Incites

Defined by the *Concise Oxford Dictionary* as 'encourage, stir up, urge or persuade'. Examples could be bribery, threats, or pressure.

Sexual (see **6.2.1**)

Reasonably believe (see **6.4**)

Explanatory notes

- The sexual activity that is caused or incited involves the victim being engaged in that sexual activity. This can be, for example, where the defendant causes or incites the child to sexually touch themselves or the child to masturbate or strip for the defendant's sexual gratification.
- It may be with a third person (eg where the defendant causes or incites the child to have oral sex with the penis of another person).
- The incitement itself is an offence so the sexual activity does not have to take place for the offence to be committed, for example where someone intervenes.
- Section 10(2) replicates some of the other offences covered in the Act, such as rape, assault by penetration. This duplication is intended to cover every possible scenario that could be envisaged, ensuring that offenders do not escape prosecution because of a loophole in the law.

- Where the child is under 13, the offender should be charged with the s 8 offence (see **6.5.3**), especially if it involves penetration, as it then carries life imprisonment. However, s 10 might be used where the offender is under 18 or the child is under 13 and it only became known during trial that the child was under 13. The extension of s 10 to under-13s now means that the trial could continue with the original charge where necessary, thus closing a potential loophole in the law.

Practical considerations

- Section 10 is not intended to cover health professionals or anyone providing sex education, advice, or contraception to children.
- This offence could be considered where the offender and victim are very close in age (eg an offender of 18 and a victim of 15) and are in a relationship, and both have entered into a sexual relationship willingly.
- Where the child is aged 13 or over, but under 16, the prosecution must prove that the defendant did not reasonably believe that they were 16 or over. If the child is under 13, the offence is one of strict liability.
- The Serious Crime Act 2015, s 69(1), makes it an either way offence to be in possession of any item that contains advice or guidance about abusing children sexually (the so-called paedophile manual). This covers offences under Part 1 (ss 1 to 79) of the 2003 Act, the Protection of Children Act 1978, s 1 (see **6.6.1**), and the Modern Slavery Act 2015, s 2 (see **4.9.3**), committed with a view to exploitation that consists of or includes behaviour within s 3(3) of that Act (sexual exploitation).
- It is a defence for a person (D) charged with an offence under s 69 (above) to prove that D had a legitimate reason for being in possession of the item and D did not know, and had no reason to suspect, that it contained advice or guidance about abusing children sexually; or the item was sent to D without any request made by D or on D's behalf, and D did not keep it for an unreasonable time.

E&S CHAR

s 10(1) offence

Either way — None

Summary: 6/12 months' imprisonment and/or a fine

Indictment: 14 years' imprisonment

s 10(2) offence

Indictable — None

14 years' imprisonment

6.5.2 Paying for sexual services of a child

Section 47 of the Sexual Offences Act 2003 makes it an offence for any person intentionally to obtain for themselves the sexual services of a child aged under 18, where those services have been paid for or where payment has been promised.

Offences

A person (A) commits an offence if—

(a) he intentionally obtains for himself the sexual services of another person (B),

(b) before obtaining those services, he has made or promised payment for those services to B or a third person, or knows that another person has made or promised such a payment, and

(c) either—

(i) B is under 18, and A does not reasonably believe that B is 18 or over, or

(ii) B is under 13.

Sexual Offences Act 2003, s 47(1)

PNLD H5790 to H5799

Points to prove

Penetration/child under 13: s 47(1)(a), (b), (c)(ii), (3), and (6)

✓ intentionally
✓ obtained for yourself the sexual services of a child under 13
✓ involving the penetration of
✓ the child's vagina/anus with a part of your body/a thing OR
✓ the child's mouth with your penis OR
✓ your vagina/anus with a part of the child's body/by the child with a thing OR
✓ your mouth with the child's penis
✓ having previously made/promised to make payment to them OR
✓ having previously made/promised to make payment to another person
✓ knowing that another person had previously made/promised to make payment to them OR
✓ knowing that another person had previously made/promised to make payment to a third person for those services

Non-penetration/child under 13: s 47(1)(a), (b), (c)(ii), and (4)(b)

✓ intentionally
✓ obtained for yourself the sexual services of a child under 13
✓ having previously made/promised to make payment to them OR
✓ having previously made/promised to make payment to another person OR

✓ knowing that another person had previously made/promised to make payment to them OR
✓ knowing that another person had previously made/promised to make payment to a third person for those services

For an offence under s 47(1)(c)(i)—child under 18, in addition to the above

✓ obtained for yourself the sexual services of a child 13/14/15/16/17
✓ when you did not reasonably believe them to be aged 18 or over

Meanings

Payment (s 47(2))

Means any financial advantage, including the discharge of an obligation to pay or the provision of goods or services (including sexual services) gratuitously or at a discount.

Explanatory notes

- Where the victim is 13 or over, the offence will not be committed where the defendant reasonably believes that the victim is 18 or over. (It will be for the prosecution to prove that the defendant did not reasonably believe that the victim was 18 or over.) However, where the victim is under 13, the defendant will commit the offence regardless of any reasonable belief they may have had about the victim's age.
- This offence can be committed by a male or female against a male or female.
- Under s 51(2), for the purposes of ss 48 to 50 (causing, inciting, controlling, arranging, or facilitating sexual exploitation of a child), a person (B) is sexually exploited if:
  (a) on at least one occasion and whether or not compelled to do so, B offers or provides sexual services to another person in return for payment or a promise of payment to B or a third person; or
  (b) an indecent image of B is recorded or streamed or otherwise transmitted;

  and 'sexual exploitation' is to be interpreted accordingly.
- Section 51(2)(b) ensures that the definition of sexual exploitation also covers a situation where indecent images of children are not only recorded but also streamed, eg via the internet, or transmitted by some other technological means, such as CCTV.
- Section 116 of the Anti-social Behaviour, Crime and Policing Act 2014 provides that a police officer (inspector or above) may issue a notice to the owner, operator, or manager of a hotel, on reasonable belief that the hotel has been or will be used for the purposes of child sexual exploitation (CSE) or conduct preparatory to or connected with CSE.
- A constable may require a person issued with such a notice to provide the police with the name and details of address of guests staying at the hotel. Failure to comply is a summary offence under s 118(1) of that Act.

- For information for professionals working with children, including the police, when dealing with online safety issues such as cyberbullying, grooming, sexting, etc, contact Professionals Online Safety Helpline (POSH), a charity which is part of the UK Safer Internet Centre (see **Appendix 2**).

Indictable | None

Victim under 13 at time of offence and involving penetration

s 47(1), (3), and (6) offence

Indictment: life imprisonment

Victim under 16 at time of offence and involving penetration

s 47(1), (4)(a) and (6) offence

Indictment: maximum 14 years' imprisonment

Either way | None

Victim under 16 at time of offence—no penetration

s 47(1) and (4)(b) offence

Summary: maximum 6/12 months' imprisonment and/or a fine

Indictment: maximum 14 years' imprisonment

Victim under 18 at time of offence

s 47(1) and (5) offence

Summary: maximum 6/12 months' imprisonment and/or a fine

Indictment: maximum 7 years' imprisonment

6.5.3 Cause/incite child under 13 to engage in sexual activity

The offence of causing/inciting a child under 13 to engage in sexual activity is covered by s 8 of the Sexual Offences Act 2003.

Offences

(1) A person commits an offence if—
  (a) he intentionally causes or incites another person (B) to engage in an activity,
  (b) the activity is sexual, and
  (c) B is under 13.

(2) A person is guilty of an offence under this section, if the activity caused or incited involved—
  (a) penetration of B's anus or vagina,

(b) penetration of B's mouth with a person's penis,
(c) penetration of a person's anus or vagina with a part of B's body or by B with anything else, or
(d) penetration of a person's mouth with B's penis.

Sexual Offences Act 2003, s 8

PNLD H5675 to H5678

Points to prove

Non-penetration

✓ intentionally caused/incited
✓ a child under 13
✓ to engage in sexual activity
✓ of a non-penetrative nature

Penetration

✓ the first three points of '**Non-penetration**'
✓ involving the penetration of
✓ child's anus/vagina OR
✓ child's mouth with another person's penis OR
✓ a person's anus/vagina with a part of child's body or by child with anything else OR
✓ a person's mouth with the boy's penis

Meanings

Intentionally (see **6.1.1**)

Cause (see **6.5.1**)

Incite (see **6.5.1**)

Sexual (see **6.2.1**)

Explanatory notes

- This offence is the same as the s 10 offence save that the defendant can be of any age and that the victim is under 13.
- In relation to sexual activity caused or incited, the offence covers the same situations as the offence under s 4 except that, for this offence, consent is irrelevant.

Practical considerations

- Section 8 consists of four separate offences: causing or inciting penetrative or non-penetrative sexual activity; you must specify which offence it is. The sexual activity must be of the child (*R v Grout* [2011] EWCA Crim 299).
- If possible, identify and preserve the crime scene and seize any articles and documentation relevant to the offence.

- Prove the age of the child. Only a suitably trained or qualified person should be used to take a statement or obtain evidence from the victim.

SSS E&S CHAR

s 8(1) offence

Either way | None

Summary: 6/12 months' imprisonment and/or a fine
Indictment: 14 years' imprisonment

s 8(2) offence

Indictable | None

Life imprisonment

6.5.4 Arrange/facilitate commission of a child sex offence

Offences

A person commits an offence if—
(a) he intentionally arranges or facilitates something that he intends to do, intends another person to do, or believes that another person will do, in any part of the world, and
(b) doing it will involve the commission of an offence under any of sections 5 to 13.

Sexual Offences Act 2003, s 14(1)

PNLD **H100735, H100737, H100738 to H100742**

Points to prove

✓ intentionally
✓ arranged/facilitated
✓ an act which the defendant
✓ intended to do OR
✓ intended/believed another person would do
✓ in any part of the world
✓ doing it would involve the commission of an offence under any of ss 5 to 13

Meanings

Intentionally (see 6.1.1)

Arranges

Organise, plan, or reach agreement about an action or event in advance.

Facilitates

Make it happen, make it easier to achieve or promote.

Explanatory notes

- The defendant does not have to be the one who will commit the sexual offence; it will be enough if they intended/believed that they or another person would commit the relevant offence in any part of the world.
- The offence covers a situation where the defendant takes a person to a place where there is a child in the belief that the person is likely to engage in sexual activity with that child.
- It also caters for situations where the defendant arranges for themselves or another the procurement of a child with whom they propose to engage in sexual activity. For example, the defendant is going on holiday and plans to engage in sexual activity with children whilst there and so arranges through an agency to meet children.
- The sexual activity does not have to occur for the offence to be committed.
- The relevant offences are—
  - ✦ s 5—Rape of a child under 13 (see **6.1.2**);
  - ✦ s 6—Assault a child under 13 by penetration (see **6.2.2**);
  - ✦ s 7—Sexual assault of a child under 13 (see **6.3.2**);
  - ✦ s 8—Causing or inciting a child under 13 to engage in sexual activity (see **6.5.3**);
  - ✦ s 9—Sexual activity with a child (see **6.4**);
  - ✦ s 10—Causing or inciting a child to engage in sexual activity (see **6.5.1**);
  - ✦ s 11—Engaging in sexual activity in the presence of a child;
  - ✦ s 12—Causing a child to watch a sexual act;
  - ✦ s 13—Child sex offences committed by children or young persons.

Defences

(2) A person does not commit an offence under this section if—
- (a) he arranges or facilitates something that he believes another person will do, but that he does not intend to do or intend another person to do, and
- (b) any offence within subsection (1)(b) would be an offence against a child for whose protection he acts.

> (3) For the purposes of subsection (2), a person acts for the protection of a child if he acts for the purposes of—
> (a) protecting the child from sexually transmitted infection,
> (b) protecting the physical safety of the child,
> (c) preventing the child from becoming pregnant, or
> (d) promoting the child's emotional well-being by the giving of advice,
>
> and not for the purpose of obtaining sexual gratification or for the purpose of causing or encouraging the activity constituting the offence within subsection (1)(b) or the child's participation in it.
>
> Sexual Offences Act 2003, s 14(2) and (3)

Defence notes

This is intended to protect those people such as health care workers who are aware that a person is having sex with a child under 16 and gives them condoms as they believe that if they do not do so the child will have unprotected sex. It appears that the health care worker must warn the person that what they are doing is illegal but can give the condoms without committing an offence under this section.

Related case

R v Abdullahi [2006] EWCA Crim 2060 Nothing in s 12 (causing a child to watch a sexual act) stated that the offence could only be committed where the display of the material or act was contemporaneous with, or simultaneous to, the sexual gratification. The form which the sexual gratification could take was not defined, so it could take any one of countless forms. There was nothing to prevent the sexual gratification from extending into a scheme to obtain further gratification by committing a sexual act with the child.

Practical considerations

- The specified offence (under ss 5 to 13) does not have to take place. Once the intention to commit the offence is proved, it is immaterial that it is impossible to commit the substantive offence.
- Offenders who are caught in undercover operations will be prosecuted in every case for the same offence as those who meet real-life victims. The evidence obtained by the police or other activist groups will result in substantive charges of arranging or facilitating a child sex offence.
- Obtain any evidence which proves the links (eg advertisement, emails, and bookings for hotels).
- Seize mobile phone, computer hard drive, and any other physical evidence relevant to the offence.
- This offence is listed as a 'criminal lifestyle' offence under Sch 2 to the Proceeds of Crime Act 2002 (see **5.5** for details).

- For the Home Office 'Child sex offender disclosure scheme guidance', see web link at **Appendix 2**.

E&S CHAR

Either way

None

Same penalty as for offence within subsection (1)(b)

6.5.5 Meeting a child following sexual grooming

This offence is covered by s 15 of the Sexual Offences Act 2003.

Offences

A person aged 18 or over (A) commits an offence if—

(a) A has met or communicated with another person (B) on one or more occasions and subsequently—
  (i) A intentionally meets B,
  (ii) A travels with the intention of meeting B in any part of the world or arranges to meet B in any part of the world, or
  (iii) B travels with the intention of meeting A in any part of the world,

(b) A intends to do anything to or in respect of B, during or after the meeting mentioned in paragraph (a)(i) to (iii) and in any part of the world, which if done will involve the commission by A of a relevant offence,

(c) B is under 16, and

(d) A does not reasonably believe that B is 16 or over.

Sexual Offences Act 2003, s 15(1)

PNLD H12210, H12211

Points to prove

✓ being a person 18 or over (A)
✓ has on one or more occasions met/communicated
✓ with a person under 16
✓ not reasonably believing that person to be 16 or over
✓ intentionally met or travelled intending to meet, or arranged to meet, that person or that person has travelled with the intention of meeting (A)
✓ in any part of the world

✓ intending to do anything to/in respect of that person ✓ during/after the meeting and in any part of the world ✓ which if done would involve commission by A ✓ of a relevant offence

Meanings

Has met or communicated (s 15(2)(a))

The reference to A having met or communicated with B is a reference to A having met B in any part of the world or having communicated with B by any means from, to, or in any part of the world.

Intentionally (see **6.1.1**)

Relevant offence (s 15(2)(b))

Means an offence under Part 1 (ss 1 to 79 inclusive) and anything done outside England and Wales which is not an offence under that Part but would be if done in England and Wales.

Reasonably believe (see '**Defences**' below)

Explanatory notes

- A defendant must have communicated on one or more occasions or had one prior meeting with the person. The communication could be by telephone, texting, email, chat rooms, game chat, etc. These communications do not have to contain sexually explicit language or pornography but could, for example, be something as seemingly innocuous as the offender giving the victim swimming lessons or meeting them incidentally through a friend.
- Where person A has met, or communicated with, person B only once before the event mentioned in s 15(1)(a)(i)–(iii), an offence under s 15 is committed only if those events took place on or after 13 April 2015, when s 15 was amended by the Criminal Justice and Courts Act 2015, s 36. Prior to that date, it would have to be 'on at least two occasions'.
- They must intentionally meet or travel with the intention of meeting or arrange to meet each other. This meeting can take place anywhere in the world as long as some part of the journey took place in England, Wales, or Northern Ireland.
- The meeting itself does not have to take place, arranging will suffice, although the intent to commit the relevant offence (in any part of the world) will have to be proved.
- This offence is intended to deal with predators who groom young children by gaining their trust, lying about their age, then arranging to meet them to sexually abuse them. This offence is preventative, in that the relevant sexual offence does not have to occur for the offence to be committed.

Defences

Reasonable belief that the victim is 16 or over (see **6.4 'Defence notes'**).

Related cases

Sutherland v HM Advocate [2020] UKSC 32 The conviction was safe where the evidence provided by a 'paedophile hunter' group had been correctly admitted into evidence and did not breach rights under Art 8 ECHR: the right to respect for a private and family life (see **Appendix 1**).

R v G [2010] EWCA Crim 1693 The defendant communicated with the victim and arranged to meet at the victim's school. It was held that there is no requirement that communication is sexual in nature, but a sexual intent must exist at the time of arranging the meeting. The statutory offence does not require the meeting to take place; it is sufficient if, with the intention of meeting, A travels to B or B travels to A. In each case, however, A must intend to commit a relevant (sexual) offence. A's sexual intention must be proved to have been formed either when A travels to B, waits for B to arrive, or at the moment of meeting. It is not enough that during the course of a meeting, which started without any such intention, A then decides to take advantage of the situation and commit an offence: the crime then will be the commission of or the attempt to commit that offence. The offence contained within s 15 is not engaged.

R v Mohammed [2006] EWCA Crim 1107 The defendant, M, sent intimate text messages to a vulnerable 13-year-old with severe learning difficulties and behavioural problems. Both were found together 8 miles from the complainant's foster home. M confirmed that the complainant had visited their home; the abduction was short-lived, with the complainant being willing and initiating contact, but no sexual act taking place. It was held that the defendant's motivation was sexual, and they had blatantly taken the complainant from the control of carers and the conviction was upheld.

Practical considerations

- Prove that the victim is under 16. Only a suitably trained or qualified person should be used to take a statement or obtain evidence from the victim.
- Any articles in the defendant's possession such as condoms, pornography, rope, and lubricant could help to prove intent.
- Offence applies to all offences in Part 1 of the Act (ss 1 to 79).
- All evidence in relation to the grooming should be seized (eg any communications, bookings, or other documents which link the defendant and victim).
- Consider CCTV evidence.
- Seize any computer and mobile phone that could have been used.

E&S CHAR

Either way

None

Summary: 6/12 months' imprisonment and/or a fine

Indictment: 10 years' imprisonment

6.5.6 Sexual communication with a child

The offence of sexual communication with a child helps to ensure that young people are fully protected by the law and allows the authorities to intervene earlier to prevent more serious offending against children.

Offence

A person aged 18 or over (A) commits an offence if—

(a) for the purpose of obtaining sexual gratification, A intentionally communicates with another person (B),

(b) the communication is sexual or is intended to encourage B to make (whether to A or to another) a communication that is sexual, and

(c) B is under 16 and A does not reasonably believe that B is 16 or over.

Sexual Offences Act 2003, s 15A(1)

PNLD H12043

Points to prove

- ✓ being a person 18 or over
- ✓ for the purpose of obtaining sexual gratification
- ✓ intentionally communicated with a person under 16
- ✓ who they did not reasonably believe to be 16 or over
- ✓ the communication being sexual/intended to encourage recipient to make sexual communication

Meanings

Sexual communication/activity (s 15A(2))

A communication is sexual if—

(a) any part of it relates to sexual activity, or

(b) a reasonable person would, in all the circumstances but regardless of any person's purpose, consider any part of the communication to be sexual;

and in paragraph (a) sexual activity means an activity that a reasonable person would, in all the circumstances but regardless of any person's purpose, consider to be sexual.

Related case

Sutherland v HM Advocate [2020] UKSC 32 (see **6.5.5**).

Practical considerations

- This offence criminalises conduct where an adult intentionally communicates (eg by message, chat, written note, or orally) with a child under 16 (whom the adult does not reasonably believe to be aged 16 or over) for the purpose of obtaining sexual gratification if the communication is sexual or intended to encourage the child to make a communication that is sexual (s 15A(1) and (2)), often referred to as 'sexualised chat'.
- This offence means that action can be taken at a much earlier stage in the grooming process and/or in cases where the suspect does not intend or go on to arrange to meet a child.
- There are other offences under ss 8 and 10 of the Sexual Offences Act 2003 (see **6.5.1** and **6.5.3**) that make it an offence to cause or incite a child under 13 or 16 respectively to engage in sexual activity. However, these offences are unlikely to apply if a communication (eg in the form of an email or a text message) sent to a child contains sexual content but does not in any way ask the child to engage in sexual activity but the offence in s 15A covers such scenarios.
- Scenarios likely to be covered by the offence include talking sexually to a child via a chat room or sending sexually explicit text messages to a child as well as inviting a child to communicate sexually (irrespective of whether the invitation is itself sexual).
- This offence is designed to ensure that it does not criminalise, for example, ordinary social or educational interactions between children and adults or communications between young people themselves.
- Section 127 of the Communications Act 2003 (see **7.12.2**) makes it an offence to send a message by means of a public electronic communications network (including the internet) if its content is grossly offensive, indecent, obscene, or menacing. Depending on the content of the message, this offence could apply where sexual messages are sent to a child by some form of electronic communication, such as text, email, or phone (although it would not cover non-electronic written messages or verbal communication, or electronic messages sent by a private network such as a school intranet). However, this offence is not a sexual offence and does not attract sex offender registration. It would not be appropriate to change that position as the offence criminalises behaviour that may not be sexual in any way.

6.5.6 Sexual communication with a child

E&S CHAR

Either way | None

Summary: 6/12 months' imprisonment and/or a fine

Indictment: 2 years' imprisonment

6.6 Indecent Photographs/Images: Persons under 18/Disclose with Intent to Cause Distress

6.6.1 Take, make, distribute, publish indecent photographs of person under 18

This offence is covered by s 1 of the Protection of Children Act 1978.

Offences

Subject to sections 1A and 1B [defences], it is an offence for a person—

(a) to take, or permit to be taken or to make, any indecent photograph or pseudo-photograph of a child; or
(b) to distribute or show such indecent photographs or pseudo-photographs; or
(c) to have in his possession such indecent photographs or pseudo-photographs, with a view to their being distributed or shown by himself or others; or
(d) to publish or cause to be published any advertisement likely to be understood as conveying that the advertiser distributes or shows such indecent photographs or pseudo-photographs or intends to do so.

Protection of Children Act 1978, s 1(1)

PNLD H1629, H2009, H2101, H2105, H2222, H4373, H4433, H4434

Points to prove

s 1(1)(a), (b)

✓ took/permitted to be taken/made/distributed/showed
✓ indecent photograph(s)/pseudo-photograph(s)
✓ of a child/children

s 1(1)(c)

✓ possessed
✓ indecent photograph(s)/pseudo-photograph(s)
✓ of a child/children
✓ with a view to it/them being distributed/shown by yourself or another

s 1(1)(d)

✓ published/caused to be published
✓ an advertisement likely to be understood as conveying
✓ that the advertiser

6.6.1 Take, make, distribute, publish indecent photographs

✓ distributed/showed or intended to distribute/show ✓ indecent photograph(s)/pseudo-photograph(s) ✓ of a child/children

Meanings

Make

Includes downloading images from the internet and storing or printing them (*R v Bowden* [2001] QB 88). See also *R v Smith; R v Jayson* [2002] EWCA Crim 683 below.

Indecent photographs (s 7(2) and (3))

- Includes indecent **film**, a copy of an indecent photograph or film, and an indecent photograph comprised in a film.
- Photographs (including those comprised in a film) shall, if they show children and are indecent, be treated for all purposes of this Act as indecent photographs of children and so as respects pseudo-photographs.

Photograph (s 7(4) and (4A))

References to a photograph include:
- the negative as well as the positive version; and
- data stored on a computer disc or by other electronic means which is capable of conversion into a photograph;
- a tracing or other image, whether made by electronic or other means (of whatever nature):
  - ✦ which is not itself a photograph or pseudo-photograph; but
  - ✦ which is derived from the whole or part of a photograph or pseudo-photograph (or a combination of either or both); and
  - ✦ data stored on a computer disc or by other electronic means which is capable of conversion into the above tracing or image.

Notes: If the impression conveyed by a pseudo-photograph is that of a child, the pseudo-photograph shall be treated as showing a child and so shall a pseudo-photograph where the predominant impression conveyed is that the person shown is a child notwithstanding that some of the physical characteristics shown are those of an adult (s 7(8)).

Film (s 7(5))

This includes any form of video-recording.

Pseudo-photograph (s 7(7))

Means an image, whether made by computer graphics or otherwise howsoever, which appears to be a photograph.

Indecent pseudo-photograph (s 7(9))

This includes a copy of an indecent pseudo-photograph; and data stored on a computer disc or by other electronic means which is capable of conversion into an indecent pseudo-photograph.

Child (s 7(6))

A person under the age of 18.

Distribute (s 1(2))

Means to part with possession to another person or expose or offer for acquisition by another person.

Shown by himself

Means shown by the defendant to other people.

Explanatory note

- The image does not have to be stored in a way that allows it to be retrieved. However, the image must be made deliberately. Innocently opening a file from the internet may not be an offence: see s 1(4)(b) in '**Defences**' below.

Defences

1(4) Where a person is charged with an offence under subsection 1(b) or (c), it shall be a defence for him to prove—
  (a) that he had a legitimate reason for distributing or showing the photographs or pseudo-photographs or (as the case may be) having them in his possession; or
  (b) that he had not himself seen the photographs or pseudo-photographs and did not know, nor had any cause to suspect, them to be indecent.

Marriage and partnership

1A(1) This section applies where, in proceedings for an offence under section 1(1)(a) of taking or making an indecent photograph or pseudo-photograph of a child, or for an offence under section 1(1)(b) or (c) relating to an indecent photograph or pseudo-photograph of a child, the defendant proves that the photograph or pseudo-photograph was of the child aged 16 or over, and that at the time of the offence charged the child and he—
  (a) were married or civil partners of each other, or
  (b) lived together as partners in an enduring family relationship.

(2) Subsections (5) and (6) also apply where, in proceedings for an offence under section 1(1)(b) or (c) relating to an indecent photograph or pseudo-photograph of a child, the defendant proves that the photograph or pseudo-photograph was of the child aged 16 or over, and that at the time when he obtained it the child and he—
  (a) were married or civil partners of each other, or
  (b) lived together as partners in an enduring family relationship.

(3) This section applies whether the photograph or pseudo-photograph showed the child alone or with the defendant, but not if it showed any other person.

(4) In the case of an offence under section 1(1)(a), if sufficient evidence is adduced to raise an issue as to whether the child consented to the photograph or pseudo-photograph being taken or made, or as to whether the defendant reasonably believed that the child so consented, the defendant is not guilty of the offence unless it is proved that the child did not so consent and that the defendant did not reasonably believe that the child so consented.

(5) In the case of an offence under section 1(1)(b), the defendant is not guilty of the offence unless it is proved that the showing or distributing was to a person other than the child.

(6) In the case of an offence under section 1(1)(c), if sufficient evidence is adduced to raise an issue both—

- (a) as to whether the child consented to the photograph or pseudo-photograph being in the defendant's possession, or as to whether the defendant reasonably believed that the child so consented, and
- (b) as to whether the defendant had the photograph or pseudo-photograph in his possession with a view to its being distributed or shown to anyone other than the child,

the defendant is not guilty of the offence unless it is proved either that the child did not so consent, and that the defendant did not reasonably believe that the child so consented, or that the defendant had the photograph or pseudo-photograph in his possession with a view to its being distributed or shown to a person other than the child.

Instances when defendant is not guilty of the offence

1B(1) In proceedings for an offence under section 1(1)(a) of making an indecent photograph or pseudo-photograph of a child, the defendant is not guilty of the offence if the defendant proves that—

- (a) it was necessary for the defendant to make the photograph or pseudo-photograph for the purposes of the prevention, detection or investigation of crime, or for the purposes of criminal proceedings, in any part of the world,
- (b) at the time of the offence charged the defendant was a member of the Security Service or the Secret Intelligence Service, and it was necessary for the defendant to make the photograph or pseudo-photograph for the exercise of any of the functions of that Service, or
- (c) at the time of the offence charged the defendant was a member of GCHQ, and it was necessary for the defendant to make the photograph or pseudo-photograph for the exercise of any of the functions of GCHQ, or
- (d) the defendant—
  - (i) was at the time of the offence charged a member of OFCOM, employed or engaged by OFCOM, or assisting OFCOM in the exercise of any of their online safety functions (within the meaning of section 235 of the Online Safety Act 2023), and
  - (ii) made the photograph or pseudo-photograph for the purposes of OFCOM's exercise of any of those functions.

(2) In this section 'GCHQ' has the same meaning as in the Intelligence Services Act 1994.
(3) In this section 'OFCOM' means the Office of Communications.

Protection of Children Act 1978, ss 1(4), 1A, and 1B

Defence notes

- The defence given in s 1(4)(b) as to 'not seeing and did not know, nor had any cause to suspect, them to be indecent' would cover situations where an email attachment was opened innocently and not subsequently deleted owing to a genuine lack of IT skills (eg may still be in a 'deleted' directory, 'recycle bin', or other 'temporary' directory), or innocently downloading an image from the web, then immediately deleting the image without realising that it was also stored as a back-up copy in a temporary internet directory.
- There are some authoritative factors in deciding whether a defence may apply, depending on whether the person(s):
  - ✦ acted reasonably in all the circumstances;
  - ✦ reported the photographs or pseudo-photographs as soon as was practicable and to the appropriate authority;
  - ✦ stored the photographs or pseudo-photographs in a secure and safe manner;
  - ✦ copied or distributed the photographs or pseudo-photographs unnecessarily.

Related cases

R v Porter [2006] EWCA Crim 560 If a person cannot gain access to retrieve deleted images on a computer, then they were no longer in custody or control of those images.

R v Dooley [2005] EWCA Crim 3093 If downloaded material was accessible to all club members, then it is downloaded with a view to its distribution or showing to others.

R v Smith; R v Jayson [2002] EWCA Crim 683 Deliberately opening an indecent computer email attachment or downloading an indecent image from the internet, so it can be viewed on a screen, is 'making' a photograph.

R v Fellows [1997] 1 Cr App R 244 It was held that a digital image held on a computer for display over the 'internet' was a photograph for the purposes of this legislation.

R v Stamford [1972] 2 All ER 427 What is indecent is for the jury to decide and witnesses should not be called to persuade them.

Practical considerations

- Problems arise when young people take and share indecent self-generated photos of themselves (known as 'sexting'), and if prosecuted for the s 1 offence the young person would be placed on the sex offenders register.

- NPCC and CEOP consider that a safeguarding approach should apply to children and young people involved in 'sexting'. The Children Act 1989, s 1(1) states that with statutory intervention the welfare of the child is paramount; this is reinforced by the Children Act 2004, s 11, which places a duty on key persons and bodies, including the police, to safeguard and promote the welfare of children.
- It is not an offence under this Act to possess photographs to show to yourself although this is an offence under s 160 of the Criminal Justice Act 1988 (see **6.6.2**).
- Proceedings for this offence require the consent of the DPP.
- Ascertain how the photographs or pseudo-photographs were made, discovered, and whether stored.
- Seize all computer equipment as evidence under s 20 of PACE (see **1.4.4**).
- The Schedule to the 1978 Act permits forfeiture of indecent images of children and the devices that hold them without the involvement of a court, unless the owner or other person with an interest in the material gives notice of a legitimate claim to the property.

E&S CHAR

Either way | None

Summary: 6/12 months' imprisonment and/or a fine

Indictment: 10 years' imprisonment

6.6.2 Possession of indecent photograph(s) of person under 18

Section 160 of the Criminal Justice Act 1988 concerns the offence of simple possession of indecent photographs or pseudo-photographs of a person under 18.

Offences

Subject to section 160A, it is an offence for a person to have any indecent photograph or pseudo-photograph of a child in his possession.

Criminal Justice Act 1988, s 160(1)

PNLD H2205

Points to prove

✓ possessed
✓ indecent photograph(s)/pseudo-photograph(s)
✓ of a child/children

Meanings

Section 160A

(see '**Defences**' below)

Photograph (see **6.6.1**)

Indecent photograph (see **6.6.1**)

Pseudo-photograph (see **6.6.1**)

Child (see **6.6.1**)

Explanatory note

- Where there is evidence of intent to distribute or show then the offence under s 1 of the Protection of Children Act 1978 (see **6.6.1**) should be used.

Defences

160(2) Where a person is charged with an offence under subsection (1) above, it shall be a defence for him to prove—
   (a) that he had a legitimate reason for having the photograph or pseudo-photograph in his possession; or
   (b) that he had not himself seen the photograph or pseudo-photograph and did not know, nor had any cause to suspect, it to be indecent; or
   (c) that the photograph or pseudo-photograph was sent to him without any prior request made by him or on his behalf and that he did not keep it for an unreasonable time.

160A(1) This section applies where, in proceedings for an offence under section 160 relating to an indecent photograph or pseudo-photograph of a child, the defendant proves that the photograph or pseudo-photograph was of the child aged 16 or over, and that at the time of the offence charged the child and he—
   (a) were married or civil partners of each other, or
   (b) lived together as partners in an enduring family relationship.

(2) This section also applies where, in proceedings for an offence under section 160 relating to an indecent photograph or pseudo-photograph of a child, the defendant proves that the photograph or pseudo-photograph was of the child aged 16 or over, and that at the time when he obtained it the child and he—
   (a) were married or civil partners of each other, or
   (b) lived together as partners in an enduring family relationship.

(3) This section applies whether the photograph or pseudo-photograph showed the child alone or with the defendant, but not if it showed any other person.

(4) If sufficient evidence is adduced to raise an issue as to whether the child consented to the photograph or pseudo-photograph being in the defendant's possession, or as to whether the defendant reasonably believed that the child so consented, the defendant is not guilty of the offence unless it is proved that the child did not so consent and that the defendant did not reasonably believe that the child so consented.

Criminal Justice Act 1988, ss 160(2) and 160A

Defence notes

The conditions for the defence are listed under s 160A(1)–(4). If any of these conditions are not satisfied, the prosecution need only prove the offence as set out in s 160. But if the three conditions are satisfied, the defendant is not guilty of the offence unless the prosecution proves that the child did not consent and that the defendant did not reasonably believe that the child consented.

Related cases

R v Okoro [2018] EWCA Crim 1929 It was not necessary to establish that the defendant knew they had each individual image but simply that they had a group of images for the s 160 offence to be made out. The burden to establish a statutory defence under s 160(2) of the Criminal Justice Act 1988 and s 65(2) of the Criminal Justice and Immigration Act 2008 (defences relating to the offence of possession of extreme pornographic images, see '**Practical considerations**' below) passed to the defendant.

R v Miller [2010] EWCA Crim 2883 A conviction for possession of indecent computer images of children was safe despite the fact that the images had been deleted from the active part of the hard drive before the computer's seizure.

R v Porter [2006] EWCA Crim 560 (see **6.6.1**).

Atkins v DPP and Goodland v DPP [2000] 2 All ER 425 Images stored in a temporary directory unbeknown to the defendant did not amount to possession; knowledge was required.

Practical considerations

- Ensure that the photographs or pseudo-photographs are seized.
- It is for a jury to decide the age of an unknown child seen in a photograph.
- Seize the computer or storage mechanism as evidence under s 20 of PACE (see **1.4.4**).
- The Schedule to the Protection of Children Act 1978 permits forfeiture of indecent images of children and the devices that hold them without the involvement of a court, unless the owner or some other person with an interest in the material gives notice of a legitimate claim to the property.

- Check on the audit chain for the photograph and documents relating to them to ensure possession is the only suitable charge.
- Consent of the DPP is required.
- Section 62 of the Coroners and Justice Act 2009 creates the offence of possession of a prohibited **image** of a person under 18, being a non-photographic image, which is pornographic and is grossly offensive, disgusting, or otherwise of an obscene character, also includes an image solely of a child's genitals or anal region or any sexual acts. Any such image found in possession of a school pupil by a member of staff at the school can be given to a police constable (see **8.10.8**).
- Section 63 of the Criminal Justice and Immigration Act 2008 provides the offence of possession of **extreme pornographic images**, being an image that portrays, in an explicit and realistic way, any act which involves:
  - ✦ threatening a person's life;
  - ✦ serious injury, or is likely to result in serious injury to a person's anus, breasts, or genitals;
  - ✦ sexual interference with a human corpse;
  - ✦ a person performing intercourse or oral sex with an animal (whether dead or alive);
  - ✦ non-consensual penetration of a person's vagina, anus, or mouth by another with the other person's penis; or
  - ✦ non-consensual penetration of a person's vagina or anus by another with a part of the other person's body or anything else,

  and a reasonable person looking at the image would think that any such person or animal was real. Any such images found in possession of a school pupil by a member of staff at the school can be given to a police constable (see **8.10.8**).

E&S CHAR

Either way

None

Summary: 6/12 months' imprisonment and/or a fine

Indictment: 5 years' imprisonment and/or a fine

6.7 Indecent Exposure, Images, Public Decency, and Voyeurism

6.7.1 Indecent exposure

This offence is covered by s 66 of the Sexual Offences Act 2003.

Offences

A person commits an offence if—
(a) he intentionally exposes his genitals, and
(b) he intends that someone will see them and be caused alarm or distress.

Sexual Offences Act 2003, s 66(1)

PNLD H5816

Points to prove

✓ intentionally
✓ exposed genitals
✓ intending
✓ someone would see them
✓ be caused alarm/distress

Meanings

Intentionally (see **6.1.1**)

Genitals

Means external male or female sexual organs.

Explanatory notes

- Exposure of the genitals must be intentional and not accidental.
- The offence applies to either sex. However, genitals do not include a female's breasts or the buttocks of either sex, so a female flashing her breasts or someone mooning (exposing their buttocks) will not be caught within this offence.
- Offence can be committed anywhere and is not restricted to public places.

Practical considerations

- As per CPS guidance, although every case should be considered according to its own facts and merits, in the absence of any sexual context and in relation to nudity where the person has no intention

to cause alarm or distress, it will normally be appropriate to take no action unless members of the public were actually caused harassment, alarm, or distress (as opposed to considering the likelihood of this). In this case, such conduct should be regarded as at most amounting to an offence under s 5 of the Public Order Act 1986 (see **7.8**).
- 'Disorderly' may describe this behaviour as normal standards of society expect people to be clothed in public.
- Proof of the relevant intent (both as to the genitals being seen and alarm or distress being caused thereby) will be critical to a successful prosecution.
- The precise location and the time of day could be important in showing a likely intention by the defendant.
- The accompanying words/conduct of the defendant will be relevant here, along with any preparatory or subsequent actions.

E&S CHAR

Either way

None

Summary: 6/12 months' imprisonment and/or a fine

Indictment: 2 years' imprisonment

6.7.2 Sending etc photograph or film of genitals

Section 66A of the Sexual Offences Act 2003 creates the offence of sending a photograph or film of genitals, otherwise referred to as 'cyber flashing'.

Offences

A person (A) who intentionally sends or gives a photograph or film of any person's genitals to another person (B) commits an offence if—
(a) A intends that B will see the genitals and be caused alarm, distress or humiliation, or
(b) A sends or gives such a photograph or film for the purpose of obtaining sexual gratification and is reckless as to whether B will be caused alarm, distress or humiliation.

Sexual Offences Act 2003, s 66A(1)

PNLD H101569

Points to prove

✓ intentionally
✓ sent/gave to a person
✓ photograph(s)/film(s)/combination of photograph and film

6.7.2 Sending etc photograph or film of genitals

> ✓ of any person's genitals
> ✓ intending that the person would see the genitals and be caused alarm/distress/humiliation OR
> ✓ for the purpose of obtaining sexual gratification and being reckless as to whether that person would be caused alarm/distress/humiliation

Meanings

Photograph (s 66A(3))

Includes the negative as well as the positive version.

Film (s 66A(4))

A moving image.

Genitals

Male or female sexual organs.

Explanatory notes

- This offence is intended to cover conduct often referred to as cyber flashing, referring to the act of sending unsolicited sexual images to other persons online or otherwise—for example, via social media or dating apps—but can also cover data-sharing services such as Bluetooth and Airdrop.
- The offence is committed where a person (A) intentionally sends or gives a photograph or film of any person's genitals to another person (B) and either A intends that B will see the genitals and be caused alarm, distress, or humiliation or A sends or gives the photograph or film for the purpose of obtaining sexual gratification and is reckless as to whether B will be caused alarm, distress, or humiliation (s 66A(1)).
- 'Sending or giving' a photograph or film includes, in particular, sending it to another person by any means, electronically or otherwise, showing it to another person, and placing it for a particular person to find, see s 66A(2). The meaning of sending or giving is intended to be technologically neutral; it does not matter over or through what an image is sent.
- References to a photograph or film also include an image, whether made or altered by computer graphics or in any other way, which appears to be a photograph or film, a copy of a photograph, film, or image within s 66A(1)(a), and data stored by any means which is capable of conversion into a photograph, film, or image within s 66A(1)(a) (see s 66A(5)).
- The definitions and clarity offered within this section are intended to account for advances in 'deepfake' technology that make it easier to create images where it is almost impossible to tell whether they are real or fake, and ensuring the sending or giving of such is captured.

- See also s 66B of the Sexual Offences Act 2003 providing for offences relating to the sharing of, or threatening to share, intimate photographs or films (see **6.7.3**).

Either way | None

Summary: maximum 6/12 months' imprisonment and/or a fine
Indictment: maximum 2 years' imprisonment and/or a fine

6.7.3 Sharing or threatening to share intimate photograph or film

Section 66B of the Sexual Offences Act 2003 creates the offences of sharing or threatening to share intimate photographs or film.

Offences

(1) A person (A) commits an offence if—
  (a) A intentionally shares a photograph or film which shows, or appears to show, another person (B) in an intimate state,
  (b) B does not consent to the sharing of the photograph or film, and
  (c) A does not reasonably believe that B consents.

(2) A person (A) commits an offence if—
  (a) A intentionally shares a photograph or film which shows, or appears to show, another person (B) in an intimate state,
  (b) A does so with the intention of causing B alarm, distress or humiliation, and
  (c) B does not consent to the sharing of the photograph or film.

(3) A person (A) commits an offence if—
  (a) A intentionally shares a photograph or film which shows, or appears to show, another person (B) in an intimate state,
  (b) A does so for the purpose of A or another person obtaining sexual gratification,
  (c) B does not consent to the sharing of the photograph or film, and
  (d) A does not reasonably believe that B consents.

(4) A person (A) commits an offence if—
  (a) A threatens to share a photograph or film which shows, or appears to show, another person (B) in an intimate state, and
  (b) A does so—
    (i) with the intention that B or another person who knows B will fear that the threat will be carried out, or
    (ii) being reckless as to whether B or another person who knows B will fear that the threat will be carried out.

Sexual Offences Act 2003, s 66B(1)–(4)

6.7.3 Sharing or threatening to share intimate photograph or film

PNLD H101570, H101571, H101572, H101573

Points to prove

s 66B(1) offence

- ✓ intentionally
- ✓ shared
- ✓ photograph(s)/film(s)/combination of photograph and film
- ✓ which showed/appeared to show
- ✓ another person
- ✓ in an intimate state
- ✓ without that person's consent
- ✓ not reasonably believing that the person consented

s 66B(2) offence

- ✓ intentionally
- ✓ shared
- ✓ photograph(s)/film(s)/combination of photograph and film
- ✓ which showed/appeared to show
- ✓ another person
- ✓ in an intimate state
- ✓ where the sharing of that photograph/film was without that person's consent
- ✓ intending to cause that person alarm/distress/humiliation

s 66B(3) offence

- ✓ intentionally
- ✓ shared
- ✓ photograph(s)/film(s)/combination of photograph and film
- ✓ which showed/appeared to show
- ✓ another person
- ✓ in an intimate state
- ✓ where the sharing of that photograph/film was without that person's consent
- ✓ not reasonably believing that the person consented
- ✓ for the purpose of obtaining sexual gratification for himself/herself/another person

s 66B(4) offence

- ✓ threatened to share
- ✓ photograph(s)/film(s)/combination of photograph and film
- ✓ which showed/appeared to show
- ✓ another person
- ✓ in an intimate state
- ✓ intending/being reckless as to whether
- ✓ that person OR
- ✓ another person who knew that person
- ✓ would fear that the threat will be carried out

Meaning of consent (for the purposes of subsections (1)–(3))

Includes general consent covering the particular act of sharing as well as specific consent, and whether a belief is reasonable is to be determined having regard to all circumstances including any steps the person has taken to ascertain whether the other person consents (see s 66B(6)).

Explanatory notes

- Section 66B(1) creates an offence which is committed if a person (A) intentionally shares a photograph or film which shows, or appears to show, another person (B) in an intimate state, without the consent, or a reasonable belief in the consent, of that person. There is no requirement to prove that the sharing was done for a particular purpose.
- Section 66B(2) creates an offence which is committed if a person (A) intentionally shares a photograph or film which shows, or appears to show, another person (B) in an intimate state, without the consent of B, with the intent to cause alarm, distress, or humiliation to B.
- Section 66B(3) creates an offence of intentionally sharing a photograph or film which shows, or appears to show, another person (B) in an intimate state, without the consent and without a reasonable belief in the consent of B, for the purpose of obtaining sexual gratification for the person doing the sharing or another person.
- Section 66B(4) creates an offence of threatening to share a photograph or film which shows or appears to show another person (B) and where the perpetrator intended that B or someone who knows B will fear the threat will be carried out or was reckless as to that result.
- Where a person is charged with an offence under subsection (4), it is not necessary for the prosecution to prove that the photograph or film mentioned in the threat exists, or if it does exist, that it is in fact a photograph or film which shows or appears to show a person in an intimate state (see s 66B(7)).
- The focus on photographs and films which 'shows or appears to show' ensures that the offence is made out, not just in scenarios where the photograph or film shared is a genuine photograph or film of B, but also, for example, where the photograph or film shows someone who appears to be B but might not, in fact, be B (for example, if the photograph or film depicts either B or B's identical twin C) and photographs and film that have been altered or manufactured so that it appears to be a genuine photograph or film of B. This approach is taken in all the offences in this section.
- It is a defence to the offence to prove a reasonable excuse for sharing the photograph or film (see s 66B(8)). Examples of a reasonable excuse might include where it was necessary for the

prevention or detection of a crime to share an intimate photo or film with a police officer.

- Section 66C provides for exemptions to the offences under this section.

E&S CHAR

s 66B(1) offence

Summary — 6 months

Summary: maximum 6 months' imprisonment and/or a fine

s 66B(2), (3), and (4) offences

Either way — None

Summary: maximum 6/12 months' imprisonment and/or a fine
Indictment: maximum 2 years' imprisonment and/or a fine

6.7.4 Outraging public decency

This is an offence at common law.

Offences

It is an offence to commit an act of a lewd, obscene, or disgusting nature, which is capable of outraging public decency, in a public place where at least two members of the public who were actually present at the time could have witnessed it, even if they had not actually seen it.

Common law

PNLD H6007

Points to prove

✓ in a public place
✓ committed an act capable of being seen by two or more persons
✓ of a lewd/obscene/disgusting nature thereby outraging public decency
✓ by behaving in an indecent manner

Meanings

Lewd

Means lustful or indecent.

Obscene

Means morally repugnant or depraved.

Disgusting

Means repugnant or loathsome.

Public place

Means a place to which the public have access or a place which is visible to the public.

Explanatory notes

- Consider if statutory offences would be more suitable, such as the Sexual Offences Act 2003, the Public Order Act 1986, or Obscene Publications Act 1959.
- Such conduct can also be an offence of public nuisance under s 78 of the Police, Crime, Sentencing and Courts Act 2022 (see **7.13.3**).

Related cases

R v F [2010] EWCA Crim 2243 It was held in this case that the two-person rule applicable to outraging public decency had not been satisfied where, on the agreed evidence, the defendant had stopped the act of masturbating in his car whenever other people came into the area but continued once they had gone.

R v Hamilton [2007] EWCA Crim 2062 Filming up women's skirts in a supermarket outrages public decency. In this case, the victim was a teenage girl and one image taken was of her upper thighs. Although the image was not of genitals, it did amount to indecency for this offence (note also the voyeurism offence under s 67A(1) Sexual Offences Act 2003 (see **6.7.3**)).

R v Walker [1996] 1 Cr App R 111 The defendant exposed himself and masturbated in front of two young girls in his living room. It was held that as the public could not see into his living room it was not a public place for this offence.

R v Gibson [1990] 2 QB 619 The 'act' does not have to be a 'live' activity nor does it have to be of a sexual nature. It may be the act of putting a disgusting object on public display, such as displaying a sculpted head with a real human foetus dangling from it in a public art gallery.

Practical considerations

- More than one person must be able to witness the lewd act.
- Conduct must grossly cross the boundaries of decency and be likely to seriously offend the reasonable person (rather than simply upsetting or even shocking).
- There is no requirement to prove that those persons who witnessed the act were actually disgusted or outraged by it. The test is an objective one based on whether a reasonable person would be

disgusted. However, the reasonable person must be from that section of the public likely to be exposed to the offending material. The prospect of outrage is linked to the time and place of the exhibition, thus nudist camps, although not generally open to the public, are lawful because all those present consent to their own observation of nakedness.
- It has been held that, in order to outrage, exposure of the naked body (male or female) must grossly transgress accepted limits of decency and be likely to gravely offend a reasonable person. Therefore, in cases involving nudity, this offence will usually only be suitable if masturbation or sexual intercourse occurs alongside the nudity. Where a person intentionally exposes their genitals intending that someone will see them and be caused alarm or distress, the offence of exposure under s 66 of the Sexual Offences Act 2003 applies (see **6.7.1**).
- Where the circumstances are appropriate, positive evidence of disgust can be given by a police officer.
- In most cases, offences under the Public Order Act 1986, Sexual Offences Act 2003, or Obscene Publications Act 1959 would be more appropriate than this common law offence.

E&S CHAR

Either way

None

Summary: 6 months' imprisonment and/or a fine

Indictment: Imprisonment and/or a fine

Links to alternative subjects and offences

7.3 **Breach of the Peace** 362
7.8 **Threatening/Abusive Words/Behaviour** 380
7.11 **Harassment/Stalking** 398
7.12.6 **Offence of encouraging or assisting serious self-harm** 430

6.7.5 **Voyeurism**

Section 67 of the Sexual Offences Act 2003 makes it an offence for a person to observe, for the purpose of their own sexual gratification, another person doing a private act, for instance by looking through a window or peephole at someone having sexual intercourse, where they know the person observed does not consent to being looked at for this purpose.

Offences

(1) A person commits an offence if—
  (a) for the purpose of obtaining sexual gratification, he observes another person doing a private act, and
  (b) he knows that the other person does not consent to being observed for his sexual gratification.
(2) A person commits an offence if—
  (a) he operates equipment with the intention of enabling another person to observe, for the purpose of obtaining sexual gratification, a third person (B) doing a private act, and
  (b) he knows that B does not consent to his operating equipment with that intention.
(3) A person commits an offence if—
  (a) he records another person (B) doing a private act,
  (b) he does so with the intention that he or a third person will, for the purpose of obtaining sexual gratification, look at an image of B doing the act, and
  (c) he knows that B does not consent to his recording the act with that intention.
(4) A person commits an offence if he instals equipment, or constructs or adapts a structure or part of a structure, with the intention of enabling himself or another person to commit an offence under subsection (1).

Sexual Offences Act 2003, s 67(1)–(4)

PNLD H5817 to H5820

Points to prove

Observing (s 67(1))

✓ for purpose of obtaining sexual gratification
✓ observed another person
✓ doing a private act
✓ knowing that the person did not consent to being observed for defendant's sexual gratification

Operating equipment to observe (s 67(2))

✓ operated equipment
✓ with the intention of enabling another person
✓ for the purpose of obtaining sexual gratification
✓ to observe a third person doing a private act
✓ knowing that person did not consent to defendant operating equipment with that intention

Recording a private act (s 67(3))

✓ recorded another person doing a private act
✓ with intention that
✓ defendant/a third person
✓ would for the purpose of obtaining sexual gratification
✓ look at an image of that other person doing the act

✓ knowing that the other person did not consent to defendant recording the act with that intention

Install equipment/construct/adapt a structure (s 67(4))

✓ installed equipment OR
✓ constructed/adapted a structure/part of a structure
✓ with intention to enable defendant/third person to commit an offence under s 67(1)

Meanings

Private act (s 68(1))

A person is doing a private act if they are in a place where they could reasonably expect privacy and their genitals, breasts, or buttocks are exposed or covered only by underwear, they are using the toilet, or doing a sexual act that is not normally done in public.

Consent

Defendant must **know** that the person does not consent to being observed for **sexual gratification**. They may have consented to being observed for some other reason.

Sexual gratification

In s 67(1), the sexual gratification must be for the defendant; in s 67(2), it is for a third person's sexual gratification; in the other subsections, it could be for the defendant's or a third party's sexual gratification.

Structure (s 68(2))

Includes a tent, vehicle, or vessel or other temporary or movable structure.

Explanatory notes

- For s 67(2)–(4), it is irrelevant whether or not any third parties knew that the person did not consent.
- Section 67(2) is aimed at those who install webcams or other recording equipment for the gratification of others. An image is defined as 'a moving or still image and includes an image produced by any means and, where the context permits, a three-dimensional image' (s 79(4)).
- Section 67(4) would cover a person who installed a two-way mirror or a spy-hole in a hotel room. The offender would commit the offence even if the peephole or mirror was discovered before it was ever used.
- For the purposes of s 67, operating equipment includes enabling or securing its activation by another person without that person's knowledge (s 68(1A)).

Related cases

R v Richards [2020] EWCA Crim 95 The complainants worked as escorts or prostitutes and had had intercourse with the appellant in their bedrooms in return for payment. R had deliberately and covertly filmed the sexual activity. The issue whether the two complainants had consented to the filming was for the jury to resolve. An act can be a private act even where the defendant was one of the participants.

R v Burke [2012] EWCA Crim 770 In relation to voyeurism under s 67, the jury had to be satisfied not only that the observation was deliberate but also that it was for the purpose of sexual gratification.

Police Service for Northern Ireland v MacRitchie [2008] NICA 26 The defendant placed their mobile telephone underneath the gap between the wall of changing cubicles having activated the video recording function. The images caught the victim wearing a bikini and the defendant was charged with an offence under s 67(3). While swimwear if worn as underwear could be within the term 'underwear' in the definition of 'private act' in s 68, this was not the case in this instance. At the relevant time, the victim wore the bikini as swimwear rather than as underwear. However, an attempt to commit the full offence that could not be perpetrated was nevertheless an attempted s 67 offence.

R v Bassett [2008] EWCA Crim 1174 Whether a person had a reasonable expectation of privacy would depend on the facts and would be closely related to the nature of the observation taking place. The parts of the body that fall within the scope of the 2003 Act are those parts for which people conventionally expect privacy. 'Breasts' were to mean female breasts as opposed to the bare male chest.

Practical considerations

- Any equipment used requires seizing.
- CCTV footage may be of use.
- Search for films made and evidence of equipment hire.
- Medium/equipment used for recording/storing image can be seized for examination and evidence.

E&S CHAR

Either way | None

Summary: 6/12 months' imprisonment and/or a fine

Indictment: 2 years' imprisonment

6.7.6 Voyeurism offences: operating equipment and recording images

Section 67A of the Sexual Offences Act 2003 provides additional voyeurism offences where equipment is used to observe, or images recorded of, a person's genitals, buttocks, or underwear (including so-called 'upskirting'), or a person who is breast-feeding a child, for the purposes of obtaining sexual gratification or humiliating, alarming, or distressing that person.

Offences

(1) A person (A) commits an offence if—
  (a) A operates equipment beneath the clothing of another person (B),
  (b) A does so with the intention of enabling A or another person (C), for a purpose mentioned in subsection (3), to observe—
    (i) B's genitals or buttocks (whether exposed or covered with underwear), or
    (ii) the underwear covering B's genitals or buttocks,
  in circumstances where the genitals, buttocks or underwear would not otherwise be visible, and
  (c) A does so—
    (i) without B's consent, and
    (ii) without reasonably believing that B consents.

(2) A person (A) commits an offence if—
  (a) A records an image beneath the clothing of another person (B),
  (b) the image is of—
    (i) B's genitals or buttocks (whether exposed or covered with underwear), or
    (ii) the underwear covering B's genitals or buttocks,
  in circumstances where the genitals, buttocks or underwear would not otherwise be visible,
  (c) A does so with the intention that A or another person (C) will look at the image for a purpose mentioned in subsection (3), and
  (d) A does so—
    (i) without B's consent, and
    (ii) without reasonably believing that B consents.

(2A) A person (A) commits an offence if—
  (a) A operates equipment,
  (b) A does so with the intention of enabling A or another person (C), for a purpose mentioned in subsection (3), to observe another (B) while B is breast-feeding a child, and
  (c) A does so—
    (i) without B's consent, and
    (ii) without reasonably believing that B consents.

(2B) A person (A) commits an offence if—
  (a) A records an image of another (B) while B is breast-feeding a child,
  (b) A does so with the intention that A or another person (C) will look at the image for a purpose mentioned in subsection (3), and
  (c) A does so—
    (i) without B's consent, and
    (ii) without reasonably believing that B consents.

Sexual Offences Act 2003, s 67A(1)–(2B)

PNLD H19989, H19990, H100749, H100750

Points to prove

Upskirting

✓ operated equipment
✓ beneath the clothing of another person
✓ with the intention of enabling yourself/another to observe OR
✓ recorded image beneath the clothing of another person of
✓ the genitals/buttocks/underwear of that person
✓ in circumstances where they would not otherwise be visible
✓ for the purposes of obtaining sexual gratification for yourself/another OR
✓ for the purpose of humiliating/alarming/distressing the person filmed/recorded
✓ without that person's consent
✓ without reasonably believing that person consented

Observe breast-feeding

✓ operated equipment
✓ with the intention of enabling yourself/another
✓ to observe another person while that person was breast-feeding a child
✓ without consent
✓ without reasonably believing that person consented
✓ for the purpose of obtaining sexual gratification OR
✓ humiliating/alarming/distressing the other person

Meanings

Image (s 79(4))

Means a moving or still image and includes an image produced by any means and, where the context permits, a three-dimensional image.

Explanatory notes

- The purposes referred to in subsections (1) and (2B) are:
  - (a) obtaining sexual gratification (whether for the defendant or another person);
  - (b) humiliating, alarming, or distressing the victim.
- For the purposes of s 67A, operating equipment includes enabling or securing its activation by another person without that person's knowledge (*s 68(1A)*).
- Breast-feeding a child includes rearranging one's clothing in the course of preparing to do so or having just finished breast-feeding (*s 67A(3A)*).
- It is irrelevant in regard to a person breast-feeding whether the person is in a public place, whether or not the breasts are exposed, and what part of the person's body is, or is intended by the

perpetrator to be, visible in the recorded image or is intended by the perpetrator to be observed (*s 67A(3B)*).

- The offences can be committed against any gender and in any location (regardless of whether it is a public or private place) and cover a broad range of behaviour, ranging from watching someone doing a private act, or recording them doing so, to arranging for a third person to watch, and installing equipment that allows the person to be observed or recorded.

Practical considerations

(See s 67 offence, at **6.7.6**.)

E&S CHAR

Either way None

Summary: 6/12 months' imprisonment and/or a fine

Indictment: 2 years' imprisonment

Links to alternative subjects and offences

7.3 **Breach of the Peace** 362
7.11 **Harassment/Stalking** 398

6.8 Sexual Harm Prevention Orders and Sexual Risk Orders

Part 2 of the Sexual Offences Act 2003 provides for orders which can be applied to relevant sex offenders and those who pose a risk of harm: Sexual Harm Prevention Orders and Sexual Risk Orders.

The orders can place a range of restrictions and/or positive requirements on individuals depending on the nature of the case, such as limiting their internet use or preventing travel abroad.

6.8.1 Sexual Harm Prevention Orders

Sexual Harm Prevention Orders (SHPOs) and interim SHPOs set out in ss 103A to 103K of the 2003 Act are intended to protect the public from physical or psychological harm from an offender (a full list of offences is contained in Schs 3 and 5 to the Act) who poses a risk to the public by placing restrictions and/or positive requirements on their behaviour. The SHPO and interim SHPO also require the offender to notify their details to the police for the duration of the order.

Section 103I of the Sexual Offences Act 2003 makes it an offence to breach a SHPO, interim SHPO, or Foreign Travel Order (FTO).

Offences

(A1) A person who, without reasonable excuse—

- (a) does anything that the person is prohibited from doing by a sexual harm prevention order or an interim sexual harm prevention order, or
- (b) fails to do something that the person is required to do by a sexual harm prevention order or an interim sexual harm prevention order,

commits an offence.

Sexual Offences Act 2003, s 103I(A1)

PNLD H101094

Points to prove

- ✓ without reasonable excuse
- ✓ did anything prohibited by OR
- ✓ failed to do something required by
- ✓ SHPO/interim SHPO

Meanings

Sexual harm s 103B(1)

From a person means physical or psychological harm caused:

(a) by the person committing one or more offences listed in Sch 3 to the Sexual Offences Act 2003 (sexual offences for the purposes of Part 2 of that Act); or
(b) (in the context of harm outside the UK) by the person doing, outside the UK, anything which would constitute an offence listed in that Schedule if done in any part of the UK.

Explanatory notes

- An SHPO can be made by a court dealing with an individual who has been found to be not guilty by reason of insanity or found to be under a disability and to have done the act charged, in respect of an offence listed in Sch 3 or Sch 5 to the 2003 Act or on application in respect of a 'qualifying offender' (this includes anyone convicted or cautioned of such offences). The individual must pose a risk of sexual harm to the public in the UK or children or vulnerable adults abroad.
- An SHPO may impose any restriction and/or positive requirement the court deems necessary for the purpose of protecting the public from sexual harm and makes the offender subject to the notification requirements for the duration of the order. SHPOs are available to the court when dealing with an offender or on a free-standing application to the magistrates' court by the police, NCA, BTP, or MoD Police after the time of the conviction, caution, or finding.
- On conviction, by provision of s 345 of the Sentencing Act 2020, SHPOs are available at the point of sentencing by the court without application; however, the prosecutor may wish to invite the court to consider making an order in appropriate cases. A breach of such Orders is an offence under s 354 of that Act (see PNLD **H101093**).
- The minimum duration for a full order is five years. The lower age limit is 10, which is the age of criminal responsibility, but where the defendant is under the age of 18 an application for an order should only exceptionally be considered.
- For further information, see Chapter 2 of the Home Office 'Guidance on Part 2 of the Sexual Offences Act 2003'.

Related cases

R v Hanna [2023] EWCA Crim 33 Appeal against the imposition of an SHPO was successful where the test in s 346 of the Sentencing Act 2020 had not been met as there was no basis on which to infer a real risk of sexual offending against children.

TBG v A Chief Constable [2022] EWHC 2665 (Admin) The magistrates' court had been right to conclude that the licence conditions after release from a sentence of life imprisonment for murder did not sufficiently address the risks of sexual harm that were posed to members of the public and it was entitled to find that the SHPO and associated conditions were necessary.

R v Davidoff [2022] EWCA Crim 1253 Conviction only for an offence or offences listed in Sch 5 to the Sexual Offences Act 2003 is not a bar to the making of a SHPO, but there must be a focus on whether the terms of s 344 of the Sentencing Act 2020 are met.

DPP v Charlesworth [2022] EWHC 2835 (Admin) Although it is generally preferable for courts to make behavioural orders at the time of sentencing, the magistrates' court could consider making a SHPO after a sentence has been imposed.

R v Kish [2022] EWCA Crim 1161 An SHPO can only be made where it is necessary to protect the public from sexual harm from the offender, therefore, it was not the intention of Parliament to include animals as beneficiaries of SHPOs.

Either way | None

Summary: 6/12 months' imprisonment and/or a fine

Indictment: 5 years' imprisonment and/or a fine

6.8.2 **Sexual Risk Orders**

A Sexual Risk Order (SRO) is a civil order which can be sought by the police against an individual who has not been convicted, cautioned, etc of a Sch 3 or Sch 5 offence (or any other offence) but who has done an act of a sexual nature which has given rise to a reasonable belief that an SRO is necessary to protect from harm to the public in the UK or children or vulnerable adults abroad.

Section 122H of the Sexual Offences Act 2003 makes it an offence to breach an SRO or interim SRO, etc.

Offences

A person who, without reasonable excuse—

(a) does anything that the person is prohibited from doing by a sexual risk order or an interim sexual risk order, or

(b) fails to do something that the person is required to do by a sexual risk order or an interim sexual risk order,

commits an offence.

Sexual Offences Act 2003, s 122H(A1)

PNLD H101096

6.8.2 Sexual Risk Orders

Points to prove

s 122H(A1)

✓ without reasonable excuse
✓ did something prohibited by OR
✓ failed to do something required by
✓ sexual risk order/interim sexual risk order

Explanatory notes

- As with SHPOs, an SRO may impose any restriction and/or positive requirement the court deems necessary for the purpose of protecting the public from sexual harm and makes the offender subject to the notification requirements for the duration of the order. SHPOs are available to the court on application by the police, NCA, BTP, or MoD Police.
- Breach of an order also results in the defendant becoming subject to the notification requirements (as set out in s 122F) for the remaining duration of the order.
- An order, whether full or interim, prohibits the offender from, or requires the offender to do, anything described in it. The prohibitions and/or requirements must be necessary to protect the public in the UK or children or vulnerable adults abroad from harm from the offender. As a result of changes made by the Police, Crime, Sentencing and Courts Act 2022, an order can require the offender to comply with conditions requiring positive action. (See Chapter 2 of the Home Office 'Guidance on Part 2 of the Sexual Offences Act 2003', see online link in **Appendix 2**.)

Related case

R (on the application of Pinheiro) v North Tyneside Magistrates' Court and another [2022] EWHC 1176 (Admin) P had arranged parties and for young women to attend. There was a risk of them being sexually assaulted and raped, groomed, recruited, and trafficked for sexual exploitation. The interim SRO (ISRO) included a prohibition to have contact with any female under the age of 18 other than inadvertently and not reasonably avoidable in the course of normal daily life. P argued that this was unreasonable in that it extended to young women 'over 16' and specifically P's 'girlfriend', Y, and accordingly the ISROs had breached P's rights under Art 8 ECHR. The court held, among other things, that there was an evidential basis and a reasonable justification when making and upholding an ISRO, that there had been 'action of a sexual nature' by P, and a 'necessity' to protect young women from harm from him arising from further such action. If an ISRO did involve a serious intrusion in a relationship of a boyfriend and a girlfriend, then Art 8 rights would have been interfered with, but there had been no evidence of an interference with a relationship of P and Y as boyfriend and girlfriend. Note that this decision referred to an ISRO only and therefore had not been a decision on the substantive application for an SRO.

Either way

None

Summary: maximum 6/12 months' imprisonment and/or a fine
Indictment: maximum 5 years' imprisonment

6.9 Sexual Activity in a Public Lavatory

This offence is covered by s 71 of the Sexual Offences Act 2003.

Offences

A person commits an offence if—

(a) he is in a lavatory to which the public or a section of the public has or is permitted to have access, whether on payment or otherwise,

(b) he intentionally engages in an activity, and,

(c) the activity is sexual.

Sexual Offences Act 2003, s 71(1)

PNLD H5841

Points to prove

✓ being in a lavatory
✓ to which the public/a section of the public have/are permitted to have access
✓ whether on payment/otherwise
✓ intentionally
✓ engaged in a sexual activity

Meanings

Intentionally (see **6.1.1**)

Sexual activity (s 71(2))

For the purposes of this section, an activity is sexual if a reasonable person would, in all the circumstances but regardless of any person's purpose, consider it to be sexual activity. (*Note this differs to the use of this expression elsewhere in the Act* (see s 78 of the Sexual Offences Act 2003 at **6.2.1**).

Explanatory notes

- The offence would cover staff toilets in large/small premises where the public could have access.
- The sexual activity does not have to be specified; it would be enough to record details of what was seen or heard.
- There is no requirement to prove that anyone was alarmed or distressed by the activity.
- The common law offence of 'outraging public decency' has also been used to prosecute sexual activity in a public lavatory. This offence

carries an unlimited penalty, but it must not be disproportionate to remain within legitimate exceptions to restraints on 'private life within the Human Rights Act'. It differs from the s 71 offence in that the act must be of a lewd, obscene, and disgusting nature, which is capable of outraging public decency, in a public place where at least two members of the public could have witnessed it. It is not necessary for any members of the public to have witnessed the act (see **6.7.4**).

Practical considerations

- The sexual activity could be committed by a male or female against a male or female.
- If possible obtain independent evidence.

Summary

6 months

6 months' imprisonment and/or a fine

6.10 Administer Substance Intending to Commit a Sexual Offence

This offence is covered by s 61 of the Sexual Offences Act 2003.

Offences

A person commits an offence if he intentionally administers a substance to, or causes a substance to be taken by, another person (B)—

(a) knowing that B does not consent, and

(b) with the intention of stupefying or overpowering B, so as to enable any person to engage in a sexual activity that involves B.

Sexual Offences Act 2003, s 61(1)

PNLD H5811

Points to prove

✓ intentionally
✓ administered a substance to OR
✓ caused a substance to be taken by
✓ another person
✓ knowing that they did not consent
✓ with intention of stupefying/overpowering
✓ so as to enable any person to engage in a sexual activity involving them

Meanings

Intentionally (see **6.1.1**)

Administer

Includes conduct that brings a substance into contact with the victim's body, directly or indirectly, for example by spraying CS gas into the victim's face (*R v Gillard* (1988) 87 Cr App R 189 on s 24 of the Offences Against the Person Act 1861, see **2.1.3**).

Causes to be taken

This would cover such conduct as slipping a date rape drug directly into a drink or deceiving the victim as to the nature of the substance (eg telling the victim it is a painkiller when in fact it is a sedative).

Sexual (see **6.2.1**)

Explanatory notes

- This offence is intended to cover situations where so-called 'date rape' drugs (such as Rohypnol or GHB (gamma-hydroxybutyrate)—see **6.1.1**) are given to a person to allow the defendant or someone else to engage in sexual activity with them. It also covers the spiking of a person's drink with alcohol when they believed they were drinking a soft drink.
- It does not matter how the substance is administered (eg by drink, injection). The offence has a very wide ambit in that it allows for one person to administer the substance or cause the substance to be taken and another to engage in the sexual activity (although no sexual activity need take place).
- The required consent refers to the taking/administering of the substance as opposed to the intended sexual activity. In s 75(2)(f), there is an evidential presumption that the victim does not consent to the sexual activity under ss 1 to 4 (see **6.1.1**, **6.2.1**, and **6.3.1**) where a substance which would stupefy or overpower has been administered.

Practical considerations

- The offence is committed whether or not there is any sexual activity as long as the substance was administered and there was the relevant intention.
- If there was no sexual activity, it may be hard to prove this offence. However, consider offences under s 23 or s 24 of the Offences Against the Person Act 1861 as to administering a poison or other noxious thing (see **2.1.3** and **5.1.1**).
- Also consider offences under s 63 of the Sexual Offences Act 2003 for trespass with intent to commit a sexual offence and s 62 of that Act to commit an offence with intent to commit a sexual offence.
- If there was sexual activity, then consider further offences.
- Consider taking samples and medical examinations where appropriate.
- Gather evidence by seizing any appropriate documentation.
- Seize mobile phones where there is evidence of a link between the defendant and victim at the relevant time.
- Consider CCTV footage.

E&S CHAR

Either way | None

Summary: 6/12 months' imprisonment and/or a fine

Indictment: 10 years' imprisonment

Link to alternative offence

2.1.3 **Maliciously administering poison, etc, with intent** 60

6.11 Prostitution: Soliciting and Paying for Services of Prostitute (Subject Exploitation)

6.11.1 Persistently loitering/soliciting in street/public place for prostitution

This offence is contrary to s 1 of the Street Offences Act 1959.

Offences

It shall be an offence for a person aged 18 or over (whether male or female) persistently to loiter or solicit in a street or public place for the purpose of prostitution.

Street Offences Act 1959, s 1(1)

PNLD H10148, H10149

Points to prove

- ✓ person aged 18 or over
- ✓ persistently
- ✓ loitered/solicited
- ✓ in street/public place
- ✓ for purpose of prostitution

Meanings

Persistently (s 1(4)(a))

Conduct is persistent if it takes place on two or more occasions in any period of three months

Loiter

Means to dawdle or linger idly about a place, proceeding with frequent pauses.

Solicit

Means to accost and offer oneself.

Street (s 1(4)(c))

Includes any bridge, road, lane, footway, subway, square, court, alley, or passage, whether a thoroughfare or not, which is for the time being open to the public; and the doorways and entrances of premises abutting on a street, and any ground adjoining and open to a street.

Public place

Defined in the Crime and Disorder Act 1998, a public place is 'any highway and any place to which at the material time the public has access, on payment or otherwise, as of right or by virtue of express or implied permission'.

Explanatory notes

- Section 68(7) of the Serious Crime Act 2015 amended this offence to apply only to persons aged 18 and over, thus recognising that a person under 18 is a victim (child sexual exploitation). It is an offence to pay for the sexual services of a child under the Sexual Offences Act 2003, s 47 (see **6.5.1**). HOC 8/2015 provides guidance on this matter.
- Any reference to a person loitering or soliciting for the purposes of prostitution is a reference to a person loitering or soliciting for the purposes of offering services as a prostitute (s 1(4)(b)).

Related case

R v McFarlane [1994] QB 419 This case defines a prostitute as 'any person who offers sexual services for reward', whether the offer is intended to be performed or not.

Practical considerations

- A court can make an order under ss 1(2A)–(2D) and 1A of the Act requiring a person convicted of this offence to attend three meetings with a named supervisor or with such other person as the supervisor may direct. If such order is made, the court may not impose any other penalty for the offence.
- The purpose of this order is to assist the offender by addressing the cause and finding ways to cease engaging in such conduct in the future.
- Official guidelines for dealing with prostitution ensure that all the relevant agencies work in partnership to ensure that individuals do not become involved in prostitution in the first place or to create opportunities to leave prostitution.
- **Prostitution adverts**: s 46 of the Criminal Justice and Police Act 2001 makes it an offence to place on, or in the immediate vicinity of, a public telephone an advertisement relating to prostitution services, with the intention that the advertisement should come to the attention of any prospective customers.
- Consider seizing CCTV for evidential purposes.

Summary — 6 months

Level 2 fine (after a previous conviction: level 3)

6.11.2 Soliciting to obtain services of a prostitute

This offence is covered by s 51A of the Sexual Offences Act 2003.

Offences

It is an offence for a person in a street or public place to solicit another (B) for the purpose of obtaining B's sexual services as a prostitute.

Sexual Offences Act 2003, s 51A(1)

PNLD H10153

Points to prove

- ✓ solicited
- ✓ another person (B)
- ✓ for purpose of obtaining
- ✓ B's sexual services as a prostitute
- ✓ in a street or public place

Meanings

Solicit (see **6.11.1**)

Prostitute (s 54(2))

Means a person (A) who, on at least one occasion and whether or not compelled to do so, offers or provides sexual services to another person in return for payment or a promise of payment to A or a third person; and 'prostitution' is to be interpreted accordingly.

Payment (s 54(3))

Means any financial advantage, including the discharge of an obligation to pay or the provision of goods or services (including sexual services) gratuitously or at a discount.

Street (see **6.11.1**)

Public place (see **6.11.1**)

Explanatory note

- The reference to a person in a street or public place includes a person in a vehicle in a street or public place (s 51A(2)).

Summary

6 months

Level 3 fine

6.11.3 Paying for sexual services of a prostitute subject to exploitation

Section 53A of the Sexual Offences Act 2003 makes it an offence for a person to pay or promise payment for sexual services of a prostitute who has been subject to exploitative conduct.

Offences

A person (A) commits an offence if—

(a) A makes or promises payment for the sexual services of a prostitute (B),

(b) a third person (C) has engaged in exploitative conduct of a kind likely to induce or encourage B to provide the sexual services for which A has made or promised payment, and

(c) C engaged in that conduct for or in the expectation of gain for C or another person (apart from A or B).

Sexual Offences Act 2003, s 53A(1)

PNLD H9908

Points to prove

✓ made/promised payment for the sexual services of a prostitute
✓ a third person engaged in exploitative conduct
✓ likely to induce/encourage that prostitute to provide sexual services
✓ in the expectation of gain for yourself/another person

Meanings

Payment (see **6.11.2**)

Prostitute (see **6.11.2**)

Exploitative conduct (s 53A(3))

Conduct which involves the use of force, threats (whether or not relating to violence), any other form of coercion, or any form of deception.

Gain (s 54(1))

Means any financial advantage, including the discharge of an obligation to pay or the provision of goods or services (including sexual services) gratuitously or at a discount; or the goodwill of any person which is or appears likely, in time, to bring financial advantage.

6.11.3 **Paying for sexual services of a prostitute**

Explanatory notes

- It is irrelevant where in the world the sexual services are to be provided and whether those services are provided, and whether A is, or ought to be, aware that C has engaged in exploitative conduct (s 53A(2)).
- This is a strict liability offence which is committed if someone pays or promises payment for sexual services of a prostitute who has been subject to exploitative conduct.
- The person responsible for the exploitative conduct must have been acting for or in the expectation of gain for themselves or another person, other than the payer or the prostitute.
- The use of threats is not restricted to threats of physical violence: it could be 'psychological' threats, such as threatening to inform immigration/police, to withdraw accommodation or financial support, or to stop supplying drugs.

Practical considerations

- This offence is aimed at protecting vulnerable/exploited females by trying to reduce the demand for prostitution by placing the emphasis of the law on the user rather than the prostitute.
- HOC 6/2010 provides guidance on the Policing and Crime Act 2009 provisions relating to prostitution: paying for sexual services of a prostitute subject to exploitation; loitering for purposes of prostitution; soliciting; and closure notices/orders.
- Section 53 of the Sexual Offences Act 2003 makes it an offence for a person to intentionally control another person's activities relating to prostitution, in any part of the world, where the defendant does so for, or in the expectation of, gain for themselves or a third party.
- Part 2A (ss 136A to 136R) of the Sexual Offences Act 2003 deals with court orders and closure notices (issued by a superintendent or above) for premises used for specified prostitution or pornography offences under s 136B or specified child sex offences under s 136BA.

Summary

6 months

Level 3 fine

Links to alternative subjects and offences

4.9 **Slavery and Human Trafficking** 217
5.5 **Proceeds of Crime** 270

Chapter 7

Public Disorder/Nuisance

7.1 Penalty Notices for Disorder

Penalty Notices for Disorder (PNDs) were established by s 2 of the Criminal Justice and Police Act 2001. For a full list of all upper and lower tier offences, refer to the Ministry of Justice 'Penalty notices for disorder: guidance for police officers' (see **Appendix 2**).

7.1.1 Penalty notices for disorder offences

A PND can only be issued to an offender who is aged 18 or over. Offences for which a PND can be issued are as follows:

Upper tier

Penalty—£90 (18 and over)

Possession of a category 4 firework

Fireworks Act 2003, s 11(1) (see **8.8.3**).

Throwing fireworks in a thoroughfare

Explosives Act 1875, s 80 (see **8.8.6**).

Wasting police time or giving false report

Criminal Law Act 1967, s 5(2) (see **11.4.1**).

Disorderly behaviour while drunk in a public place

Criminal Justice Act 1967, s 91 (see **7.2.1**).

Theft (under £100 retail/commercial only) (see **7.1.2 'Shoplifting and criminal damage'** for guidance)

Theft Act 1968, ss 1 to 7 (see **3.1.1**).

7.1.1 **Penalty notices for disorder offences**

Destroying or damaging property (under £300) (see 7.1.2 'Shoplifting and criminal damage' for guidance)

Criminal Damage Act 1971, s 1(1) (see **4.4**).

Possess cannabis and its derivatives, being a Class B controlled drug ('Cannabis possession' for guidance)

Misuse of Drugs Act 1971, s 5(2) (see **5.2.1** and **5.3.1**).

Behaviour likely to cause harassment, alarm, or distress

Public Order Act 1986, s 5 (see **7.7**).

Sale of alcohol anywhere to a person under 18

Licensing Act 2003, s 146(1) (see **9.1.2**).

Supply of alcohol by or on behalf of a club to a person aged under 18

Licensing Act 2003, s 146(3) (see **9.1.2**).

Buy or attempt to buy alcohol on behalf of a person under 18

Licensing Act 2003, s 149(3)(a) (see **9.1.4**).

Buy/attempt to buy alcohol for consumption by under 18 on relevant premises

Licensing Act 2003, s 149(4) (see **9.1.4**).

Sell or attempt to sell alcohol to a person who is drunk

Licensing Act 2003, s 141 (see **9.2.1**).

Deliver/allow delivery of alcohol to person under 18

Licensing Act 2003, s 151 (see **9.1.6**).

Knowingly give a false alarm of fire

Fire and Rescue Services Act 2004, s 49 (see **7.12.7**).

Lower tier

Penalty—£60 (18 and over)

Being drunk in a highway, public place, or licensed premises

Licensing Act 1872, s 12 (see **7.2.2**).

Trespassing on a railway

British Transport Commission Act 1949, s 55(1).

Throw stone, matter, or thing at a train/apparatus on railway

British Transport Commission Act 1949, s 56.

Possess khat or preparation/product containing khat, being a Class C controlled drug ('Khat possession' for guidance)

Misuse of Drugs Act 1971, s 5(2) (see **5.3.1**).

Leave/deposit litter

Environmental Protection Act 1990, s 87(1) (see **7.16.2**)—issuing restrictions apply (see **7.16** and **11.1.2**).

Allow person under 18 to consume alcohol on relevant licensed premises

Licensing Act 2003, s 150(2) (see **9.1.5**).

7.1.2 Police operational guidance for issuing PNDs

Police operational guidance on PNDs is published by the MOJ (see **Appendix 2**).

PND scheme

- The main aim of the PND scheme is to provide a quick and effective alternative disposal option for dealing with low-level, anti-social, and nuisance offending. The PND is a type of fixed penalty notice for specified offences (see **7.1.1**). It does not prevent other means of disposal and arrest should be considered where appropriate.
- A person has twenty-one days from being issued the PND to either pay the penalty or request a court hearing or (in some cases—see '**Educational course schemes**' below) attend an educational course. Failure to do this, within this period, will result in a fine being registered for enforcement at the magistrates' court (where the person resides) of one and a half times the penalty.
- Payment of the penalty or completing the course is not an admission of guilt and will discharge any liability to be convicted of the offence. A PND is not a criminal conviction, but for recordable offences a PNC entry may be made which may be disclosed under an enhanced DBS check.
- PNDs can be issued by constables (including special constables), CSOs, CSVs (see **11.1.2**), trading standards officers, or accredited persons for certain offences. No one can demand a PND; similarly, no one should be forced to accept a PND. Where a person is uncooperative, consider an alternative disposal.
- PNDs are only available to a person aged 18 or over, providing they are suitable (see '**Persons**' below), and the evidential test in the Code for Crown Prosecutors is satisfied. The PND may be given either on the spot, at a police station, or any other place later.

7.1.2 Police operational guidance for issuing PNDs

Preconditions for issuing a PND

A PND may **only** be issued where:

- there is reason to believe a person has committed a PND offence and there is sufficient evidence to support a successful prosecution (interviews and questioning must be consistent with the practice and procedures established by PACE Code C);
- the offence is not too serious and is suitable for being dealt with by PND;
- the suspect is suitable, compliant, and able to understand what is going on;
- a second or subsequent offence, which is known, does not overlap with the PND offence (see '**Offences**' below);
- the offence(s) involve(s) no one below the age of 18;
- sufficient evidence as to the suspect's age, identity, and place of residence exists.

Offences

A PND will not be appropriate where:

- there has been any injury (or any realistic threat or risk of injury) to any person;
- there has been a substantial financial/material loss to the private property of an individual;
- a penalty offence is committed in association with another offence, including a penalty offence;
- the provisions of the Protection from Harassment Act 1997 might apply;
- the offence involves domestic violence;
- offences are football-related;
- an offence has been committed jointly with a person below the age of 18 years;
- any designated premises supervisor has committed an offence (but may be appropriate for bar staff when taking action against premises found or known to be serving alcohol to underage drinkers).

Shoplifting and criminal damage

- PND (Code DA12) disposal for 'shoplifting' will only be appropriate where the value of goods does not exceed £100 inclusive of VAT. The property must be recovered and remains fit for sale unless the items stolen comprise drink or food and have been consumed and that the person suspected of stealing the property is not employed (whether paid or not) by the person, company, or organisation to which the property belongs.
- Label swapping can be dealt with by PND if it is opted to deal with the offence as theft. A PND cannot be issued for the offence of making off without payment (see **3.7**).
- Only ONE PND should ever be issued to an individual for retail theft.

- PND (Code DA11) disposal may only be used for criminal damage up to the value of £300 so long as the suspect is not employed (as above).
- PND disposal for shop theft/criminal damage will not be appropriate for substance misusers. The reason is that they may be better dealt with by court or conditional caution which can direct the person to treatment.
- Where a PND is issued, it should be recorded on PNC within twenty-four hours.

Throwing fireworks

A PND may be appropriate where fireworks are thrown to cause annoyance and nuisance, but this will not be the case if it is part of a pattern of intimidation or there was intention to cause harm.

False reports

- When dealing with offences under the Communications Act 2003, s 127(2), the Criminal Law Act 1967, s 5(2), and the Fire and Rescue Service Act 2004, s 49, a PND may be appropriate if the 999 service is misused or the person has made nuisance calls, but this will not be the case for serious misuse such as making a hoax bomb threat.
- A PND may be issued without DPP consent for wasting police time. Where the offender requests a hearing, a summons will be raised in the normal way and the CPS will give delegated DPP consent.

Possession of cannabis or khat

- A PND (Code DA22) may be issued for possession of cannabis (which is not cannabis oil) or khat and any preparation or other product containing khat for personal use. A PND cannot be given for other drug offences or possession with intent to supply.
- ACPO guidance on cannabis possession and the national framework guidance on khat possession for personal use provides a three-stage escalation procedure where an offender will receive a cannabis or khat warning for a first offence, a PND for a second offence, and prosecution for a third or subsequent offence.

Associated with other offences

- If a PND offence is clearly associated with another offence, including a penalty offence, a PND should not be issued and the offences should be charged together (eg drunk and disorderly and damage, due to being drunk).
- A PND may be issued if a penalty offence does not 'overlap with' or is 'associated with' another offence—for example, a PND s 5 public order offence then found in possession of stolen credit cards—for which a charge is deemed appropriate.

7.1.2 Police operational guidance for issuing PNDs

- A PND may be issued in addition to dealing with a second or subsequent offence in another way, although ensure that a PND is not issued in addition to dealing with a very serious offence.
- Where a PND is issued for a penalty offence and it subsequently comes to light after the incident that a more serious or non-penalty offence was committed on the same occasion, officers may bring a charge for the subsequent offence. Payment of a penalty does not discharge liability to conviction for a more serious offence (*R v Gore* [2009] EWCA Crim 1424). Ultimately, it will be for the CPS to determine, based on the facts of the case, whether a prosecution may be brought in respect of a subsequent or more serious offence.

Persons

A PND will not be appropriate where the suspect is:

- below the age of 18;
- unable to provide a satisfactory address for enforcement purposes;
- unable to understand the language, PND procedure, or what is being given to them;
- under the influence of drugs or alcohol, in which case consider arrest or issuing the PND at another time;
- a known Class A drug or substance misuser, then it would be better dealt with by court or a conditional caution which can direct a person to suitable substance treatment;
- uncooperative, non-compliant, or presents a considerable risk of not paying the penalty or completing the educational course;
- subject to: a custodial sentence, including home detention curfew, or a suspended sentence order; or a community penalty other than a fine, community protection notice (CPN) or criminal behaviour order (CBO);
- known to have previous convictions for disorder offences, recently issued with a PND, or given a simple or conditional caution for such offences—but consideration could be given to issuing a PND, depending on the circumstances.

Jointly committed offences

Where a person under 18 and a person aged 18 or over jointly commit a penalty offence, then a PND will not be appropriate for the person aged 18 or over. In such cases, other forms of disposal should be considered.

Identification

- Age, identity, and address checks must be rigorous. The PNC and PentiP (the national system for recording the issuing and collection of penalty notices and the collection of related penalties) must be thoroughly checked, including the disposals page. If doubt as to identity exists, consider exercising s 24 PACE arrest powers.
- Fingerprints may be taken with consent under s 61 of PACE and Part 4 of Code D; this will support identification for any PND issued for a penalty offence.

Victims

- Consider the seriousness of the offence and its effect on the victim. Consult with the victim about the potential issue of a PND and take their views into account before reaching a decision.
- Be mindful that PND disposal removes the possibility of a compensation order, although the victim can still seek redress through civil litigation. The victim should be made aware of this.

Educational course schemes

- The Criminal Justice and Police Act 2001 permits a chief officer of police to establish a PND educational course scheme in relation to one or more penalty offences, but this is not mandatory. It means a constable can give a person a PND with an education option (**PND-E**) where appropriate.
- A PND-E gives a person the opportunity to discharge their liability to be convicted of the penalty offence by paying for and completing an educational course that relates to the penalty offence (although a record of the PND-E will remain on PentiP and the PNC (if given for a recordable offence) as with a 'standard' PND). Alternatively, a person can opt to pay the penalty in full or request to be tried (as with a PND).

Links to alternative subjects and offences

3.1 **Theft** 130
4.4 **Criminal Damage** 193
5.2.1 **Possessing a controlled drug** 248
5.3.1 **Cultivate cannabis** 254
8.8 **Fireworks** 561
9.1 **Alcohol Restrictions on Persons under 16/18** 619
9.2.1 **Sale of alcohol to person who is drunk** 633
9.4 **Public Spaces Protection Order—Alcohol Restrictions** 643
11.1 **Police Powers for Civilian Staff and Volunteers** 781
11.4 **Wasting Police Time** 810

7.2 Drunkenness in Public Places

Section 91 of the Criminal Justice Act 1967 and s 12 of the Licensing Act 1872 deal with offences relating to drunkenness in public places, namely those of being drunk and disorderly and of being drunk in a highway.

7.2.1 Drunk and disorderly

Offences

Any person who in any public place is guilty, while drunk, of disorderly behaviour shall be guilty of an offence.

Criminal Justice Act 1967, s 91(1)

PNLD H517

Points to prove

✓ while in a public place
✓ whilst drunk
✓ guilty of disorderly behaviour

Meanings

Disorderly behaviour

Is defined by the *Oxford English Dictionary* as 'unruly, unrestrained, turbulent, riotous or offensive behaviour'.

Public place

Includes any highway and other premises or place to which at the material time the public have or are permitted to have access, whether on payment or otherwise.

Drunk

Drunk is defined by the *Collins* and *Oxford English Dictionaries* as 'intoxicated with alcohol to the extent of losing control over normal physical and mental functions' and 'having drunk intoxicating liquor to an extent which affects steady self-control' (*R v Tagg* [2001] EWCA Crim 1230).

Explanatory notes

- It does not apply to a person who is disorderly because of **sniffing glue** or **using drugs**. The common meaning of 'drunk' does not cater for such conduct, as confirmed by *Neale v RMJE (a minor)* (1985) 80 Cr App R 20.

- If the offender has taken liquor and drugs, the court must be satisfied that the loss of self-control was due to the liquor and not the drugs.
- Whether or not someone is in a state of drunkenness is a matter of fact for the court/jury to decide.

Related cases

R (on the application of H) v Crown Prosecution Service [2005] EWHC 2459 (Admin) The conduct must be disorderly while the defendant is drunk to satisfy the offence. The offence is not committed if the defendant only becomes disorderly after the arrest.

Williams v DPP [1992] 95 Cr App R 415 It was held in this case that the landing in a block of flats with restricted access was not a public place because only people with implied consent, or those who had been given admission by one of the occupiers (such as building maintenance), could have access.

Practical considerations

- This offence can be dealt with by PND (see **7.1.1**).
- Home Office guidance relates to issuing a PND for this offence (see **7.1.2**).
- Comply with CPS public order charging standards and guidance for drunk and disorderly.

PND

Summary

6 months

Level 3 fine

7.2.2 **Drunk on a highway**

Section 12 of the Licensing Act 1872 creates the offences of being 'drunk and incapable' in a highway, public place, or licensed premises, whilst in possession of a loaded firearm or being in charge of various conveyances or animals.

7.2.2 Drunk on a highway

Offences

Every person found drunk in any highway or other public place, whether a building or not, or on any licensed premises, shall be liable to a penalty. Every person who is drunk while in charge on any highway or other public place of any carriage, horse, cattle, or steam engine, or who is drunk when in possession of any loaded firearms, shall be liable to a penalty.

Licensing Act 1872, s 12

PNLD H124, H516, H3041

Points to prove

Drunk and incapable

- ✓ drunk and incapable
- ✓ highway/public place/licensed premises

Other drunk offences

- ✓ drunk
- ✓ whilst in charge of
- ✓ pedal cycle/carriage/horse/cattle/steam engine **or** when in possession of a loaded firearm
- ✓ on/in a highway/public place

Meanings

Drunk (see **7.2.1**)

Highway/public place (see **7.2.1**)

Incapable

Means 'incapable of looking after oneself and getting home safely'.

Carriage

Includes vehicles such as trailers and bicycles (whether being ridden or pushed).

Cattle

Includes sheep and pigs.

Firearm (see **8.1.1**)

Explanatory notes

- A motor vehicle is a 'carriage'. However, it may be more appropriate to consider the offences of driving or being in charge while under the influence of drink or drugs, under s 4 of the Road Traffic Act 1988, or over the prescribed limit under s 5 (see **10.10**).

- Case law suggests that residents in licensed premises cannot be convicted of this offence outside the permitted hours when the premises are closed to the public. However, the duty of the licensee to prevent drunkenness on the premises is unaffected.
- See also the related offences of drunk and disorderly in a public place (see **7.2.1**).
- Section 2 of the Licensing Act 1902 makes it an offence to be drunk in charge of a child who appears to be under the age of 7 years.

Practical considerations

- This offence can be dealt with by means of a PND (see **7.1.1**).
- If this offence involves a firearm, consider s 19 of the Firearms Act 1968 (carrying a firearm in a public place) which has a far greater penalty (see **8.5**).
- Officers should frequently assess the condition of drunks which can sometimes be life threatening (eg inhalation of vomit).
- Be aware that other medical conditions could give the impression that somebody is drunk (eg diabetic coma). It is best to convey the person to hospital if there are any doubts.
- Section 34 of the Criminal Justice Act 1972 provides a police constable with a power to take a drunken offender to a 'detoxification' or alcohol treatment centre. While a person is being so taken, they shall be deemed to be in lawful custody.

PND

Summary

6 months

Drunk and incapable

Level 1 fine

Drunk in charge of firearm/carriage/horse/steam engine

1 month's imprisonment or a level 1 fine

Links to alternative subjects and offences

9.2 **Drunkenness on Licensed Premises** ... 633

9.3 **Powers to Enter/Close Licensed Premises and Test Purchases** ... 638

9.4 **Public Spaces Protection Order—Alcohol Restrictions** ... 643

9.5 **Alcohol in Public Place (under 18)—Offences/Confiscation** ... 646

10.10 **Drive/Attempt/in Charge of Vehicle While Unfit** ... 705

7.3 Breach of the Peace

'Breach of the peace' is a common law concept which involves various powers in order to prevent a breach of the peace in both public and private places: these are arrest, intervene, or detain by force.

It is not a criminal offence but a 'complaint' laid before the court with an application made for a person to be bound over to keep the peace.

Complaint

Breach of the peace

The power of a magistrates' court on the complaint of any person to adjudge any other person to enter into a recognizance, with or without sureties, to keep the peace or to be of good behaviour towards the complainant shall be exercised by order on complaint.

Magistrates' Courts Act 1980, s 115(1)

PNLD H4636, H4637

Points to prove

✓ behave in a manner
✓ whereby breach of the peace
✓ was occasioned/likely to be occasioned

Meaning of breach of the peace

A breach of the peace may occur where harm is done or is likely to be done to a person, or to their property in their presence, or they are in fear of being harmed through assault, affray, riot, or other disturbance (*R v Howell* [1982] QB 416).

Court powers

- Section 115 of the Magistrates' Courts Act 1980 provides magistrates' courts with the power to order a person to be 'bound over' to keep the peace and/or be of good behaviour towards a particular person.
- The power of a magistrates' court on the complaint of any person to adjudge any other person to enter into a recognizance, with or without sureties, to keep the peace or to be of good behaviour towards the complainant shall be exercised by order on complaint.
- If any person fails to comply with the order, the court may commit that person to custody for a period not exceeding six months or until they comply with the order.

Explanatory note

- Notwithstanding that for some purposes proceedings under s 115 are treated as criminal proceedings, since the procedure is by way of complaint it is primarily a civil process. The jurisdiction of the justices does not depend on a summons being issued nor does the absence of a complaint in the form prescribed invalidate the procedure.

Related cases

Rawlins v CPS [2018] EWHC 2533 (Admin) Police officers attended the defendant's home following a call from their father, claiming that the defendant was being aggressive. An officer told the defendant that if they did not leave, they would potentially be arrested for breach of the peace, as the officer believed that either party may come to harm if one of them remained. The appellant stood up with clenched fists and moved towards the officers aggressively. It was held that the officers had been acting in the execution of their duty when they arrested the appellant for aggression that could properly be regarded as making a breach of the peace imminent, namely their physical aggression towards the officers.

R (on the application of Laporte) v CC of Gloucestershire [2006] UKHL 55 In this case, three coaches were stopped by police and searched under a s 60 authority (see **8.12.3**) based on intelligence that occupants would cause disorder at an RAF base in Gloucestershire. They were turned back and escorted back to London. Although the police actions were based on a reasonable and honestly held belief in preventing an apprehended breach of the peace, they had acted unlawfully and disproportionately because a breach of the peace was not 'imminent' at the time the coaches were stopped; thus, interfering with the protesters' rights under Arts 10 and 11 (see **Appendix 1**).

CC of Cleveland Police v McGrogan [2002] EWCA Civ 86 If a person is detained for an actual or threatened breach of the peace, then continued detention is limited to circumstances where there is a real, rather than a fanciful, fear, based on all the circumstances, that if released the detained person would commit/renew a breach of the peace within a relatively short time. It cannot be justified solely on the ground that sooner or later the prisoner, if released, is likely to breach the peace. The officer must have an honest belief, based on objectively reasonable grounds, that further detention is necessary to prevent such a breach of the peace.

Practical considerations

- A breach of the peace is not an offence so bail cannot be given.
- Breach of the peace can occur on private premises. If the police have genuine grounds to apprehend such a breach, they have a power of entry to deal with or prevent a breach of the peace (see s 17(6) of

PACE, **1.4.2**). This right of entry is not absolute but must be weighed against the degree of disturbance that is threatened.

- A police officer must not remain on private premises once a breach has finished (assuming it is not likely to reoccur) but, as long as the officer is lawfully on the premises in the first instance, they are entitled to be given the opportunity to withdraw.
- Officers attending private premises with officials such as bailiffs may have to enter them to prevent a breach of the peace while a court order is being enforced.
- An individual arrested to prevent a breach of the peace does not have to be taken before a court. There is no power to continue the person's detention beyond the time where a recurrence or renewal of the breach of the peace is likely. If there is such danger, they should be detained for court (see *CC of Cleveland Police v McGrogan* [2002] EWCA Civ 86, CA above).
- There is a continuing role for the common law power to detain short of arrest in order to prevent a breach of the peace, although in order for it to apply an officer would need to have it in mind at the relevant time (*Walker v Commissioner of Police of the Metropolis* [2014] EWCA Civ 897—see **2.2.2**).
- Release may occur at any stage: at the scene, after the person has been taken from the scene, or at the police station.

Summary

6 months

Breach of the order may result in up to 6 months' imprisonment

Links to alternative subjects and offences

2.8 **Domestic Abuse** 125
9.2 **Drunkenness on Licensed Premises** 633
11.1 **Police Powers for Civilian Staff and Volunteers** 781
Appendix 1 **Human Rights** 839

7.4 Riot and Violent Disorder

The Public Order Act 1986 provides the statutory offences of riot and violent disorder.

7.4.1 Riot

Offences

Where twelve or more persons who are present together use or threaten unlawful violence for a common purpose and the conduct of them (taken together) is such as would cause a person of reasonable firmness present at the scene to fear for his personal safety, each of the persons using unlawful violence for the common purpose is guilty of riot.

Public Order Act 1986, s 1(1)

PNLD H2011

Points to prove

- ✓ used unlawful violence for a common purpose
- ✓ 12 or more persons present together used/threatened unlawful violence for common purpose
- ✓ conduct would cause fear for personal safety to a person of reasonable firmness

Meanings

Present together

Means that all the people concerned were actually present at the scene of the incident, aiming for a common purpose.

Common purpose (s 1(3))

The common purpose may be inferred from conduct.

Violence

Includes violent conduct towards property as well as violent conduct towards persons. It is not restricted to conduct causing, or intended to cause, injury or damage, but includes any other violent conduct (eg throwing at or towards a person a missile of a kind capable of causing injury, which does not hit or falls short).

Person of reasonable firmness

This test is an objective one by which the court can judge the seriousness of the disturbance using a fixed standard—namely, whether or not a person of reasonable firmness would be put in fear by the conduct.

Explanatory notes

- It is immaterial whether or not the 12 or more use or threaten unlawful violence simultaneously.
- No **person of reasonable firmness** need actually be, or be likely to be, present at the scene.
- A court will not consider this hypothetical person (of reasonable firmness) to be someone who is the target for the people who are involved in the disturbance but someone who is a bystander to the incident (*R v Sanchez* [1996] Crim LR 572, CA).
- Riot may be committed in private as well as in public places.
- The common purpose can be either lawful or unlawful and must be proved either by admission or as above by inference from conduct.

Defences

Intention

(1) A person is guilty of riot only if he intends to use violence or is aware that his conduct may be violent.

(2) Subsections (1) and (2) do not affect the determination for the purposes of riot or violent disorder of the number of persons who use or threaten violence.

Effect of intoxication

(3) For the purposes of this section a person whose awareness is impaired by intoxication shall be taken to be aware of that of which he would be aware if not intoxicated, unless he shows either that his intoxication was not self-induced or that it was caused solely by the taking or administration of a substance in the course of medical treatment.

(4) In subsection (5) 'intoxication' means any intoxication, whether caused by drink, drugs or other means, or by a combination of means.

Public Order Act 1986, s 6

Defence notes

- Intent or awareness must be proved. Even if intent can only be proved against two people but they were part of a group of, say, 13 who can be shown to have used unlawful violence, the two can still be convicted of riot.
- The intoxication defence applies to the following offences:
  - ✦ s 1—Riot—unlawful violence;
  - ✦ s 2—Violent disorder—unlawful violence;
  - ✦ s 3—Affray—unlawful violence;

✦ s 4—Threatening words or behaviour; and
✦ s 5—Harassment, alarm, or distress.

Practical considerations

- Refer to **8.12** for details of powers to stop and search when it is anticipated that serious violence may take place, and to remove masks.
- Consent of the DPP is required.
- Consider the CPS public order charging standards.
- The person who was feeling threatened does not actually have to be a 'person of reasonable firmness', but their evidence may support other evidence that will satisfy the court that such a person would have been in fear of their personal safety had they been present.

This evidence could be provided by:

- witnesses including police officers and bystanders (who may or may not be of reasonable firmness);
- the types of injuries sustained;
- damage to property;
- security cameras;
- news photographs or film footage.

SSS E&S

Indictable only

None

10 years' imprisonment

7.4.2 Violent disorder

Offences

Where three or more persons who are present together use or threaten unlawful violence and the conduct of them (taken together) is such as would cause a person of reasonable firmness present at the scene to fear for his personal safety, each of the persons using or threatening unlawful violence is guilty of violent disorder.

Public Order Act 1986, s 2(1)

PNLD H700

Points to prove

✓ used/threatened unlawful violence
✓ three persons present together

✓ use/threaten unlawful violence and their conduct (taken together)
✓ would cause a person of reasonable firmness present at the scene
✓ to fear for their personal safety

Meanings

Present together

Means being in the same place at the same time (see *R v NW* [2010] EWCA Crim 404 below).

Person of reasonable firmness (see **7.4.1**)

Violence (see **7.4.1**)

Explanatory notes

- It is immaterial whether or not the three or more use or threaten unlawful violence simultaneously.
- No **person of reasonable firmness** need actually be, or likely to be, present at the scene.
- Violent disorder may be committed in private as well as in public places.
- If three or more people had been present together and using violence, even if intent can only be proved against one person, then that person can be convicted—it is not necessary that 'three or more persons' be charged with the offence. Following *R v Mahroof* [1988] 9 WLUK 97, it is good practice to specify 'others' in the charge, even if their identity is not known and they were not arrested.

Defences

Intention (see s 6(2) and s 6(7), **7.4.1**)

Effect of intoxication (see **7.4.1**)

Defence notes

Intent

Intent to use or threaten violence must, therefore, be proved for each individual. This means that even if only one person has the intent, they can still be charged if it can be proved that at least two others were using or threatening violence and they were present together. Words alone may suffice for the threats. **Intention** (see s 6(2) and s 6(7), **7.4.1**).

Related case

R v NW [2010] EWCA Crim 404 The term 'present together' in s 2 is intended to mean no more than being in the same place at the same time. There is no requirement that there be a common purpose among those using or threatening the use of violence. Therefore, the offence which it created was not confined to situations in which the individual members of the crowd were acting together to achieve a common aim or even with a common motive. The phrase did not require any degree of cooperation between those using or threatening violence.

Practical considerations

- Refer to **8.12** for details of powers to stop and search when it is anticipated that serious violence may take place and for powers to remove masks.
- Consider CPS public order charging standards for violent disorder.
- Sections 34 to 49 of the Policing and Crime Act 2009 deal with injunctions to prevent gang-related violence. The Serious Crime Act 2015 substituted s 34 so it now includes drug-dealing activity as well. HOC 8/2015 provides guidance on this matter. The standard of proof applicable to the granting of injunctions concerning gangs was the civil standard (on the balance of probabilities) (see *Jones v Birmingham City Council and another* [2023] UKSC 27).

SSS E&S

Either way | None

Summary: 6/12 months' imprisonment and/or a fine

Indictment: 5 years' imprisonment and/or a fine

Links to alternative subjects and offences

2.2 **Assault/Resist Arrest** ... 63
2.3 **Wounding/Grievous Bodily Harm** ... 79
4.4 **Criminal Damage** ... 193
4.5.1 **Damage with intent to endanger life** ... 198
4.6 **Threats to Destroy or Damage Property** ... 203
4.7 **Custody/Control of Articles with Intent to Damage** ... 206
8.12 **Stop and Search Powers—Knives and Weapons** ... 609
11.1 **Police Powers for Civilian Staff and Volunteers** ... 781

7.5 **Affray**

The purpose of the offence of affray is to prevent incidents of public disorder and the fear of it. For the offence of affray to be committed, the threat of violence needs to be capable of affecting others.

Offences

A person is guilty of affray if he uses or threatens unlawful violence towards another and his conduct is such as would cause a person of reasonable firmness present at the scene to fear for his personal safety.

Public Order Act 1986, s 3(1)

PNLD H2010

Points to prove

✓ used/threatened unlawful violence towards another
✓ and their conduct was such as would cause
✓ a person of reasonable firmness to fear for personal safety

Meanings

Threatens

A threat cannot be made by the use of words alone.

Violence

See **7.4**, except affray **does not include** violent conduct towards property.

Conduct

Where two or more persons use or threaten the unlawful violence, it is the conduct of them taken together that must be considered for the purpose of the offence.

Person of reasonable firmness

No person of reasonable firmness need actually be, or be likely to be, present at the scene. **The concept meets the same criteria as riot** (see **7.4.1**).

Explanatory notes

- Affray may be committed in private as well as in public places.
- Notionally there are at least three parties involved in an affray:
  - ✦ the individual making threats;
  - ✦ the person subject to the threats;

✦ the bystander of reasonable firmness who does not need to be physically present as long as evidence is available to prove that such a person would be affected.

Defences

Intent (see **s 6(2), 7.4.1**)

Effects of intoxication (see **'Defences' 7.4.1**)

Defence notes (see **'Defence notes' 7.4.2**)

Related cases

R v Dragjoshi v Croydon Magistrates' Court [2017] EWHC 2840 (Admin) Where an affray was committed by a group of people, all of whom took part in unlawful violence, it was held that it was not necessary to attribute particular acts to any individual.

R v Gilmartin [2013] EWCA Crim 2631 It was not inconsistent to acquit two offenders of possession of an offensive weapon but convict them of an affray during which they had threatened the victims with weapons.

I v DPP; M v DPP; H v DPP [2001] UKHL 10 The mere possession of a weapon, without the threatening situation, would not be enough to constitute a threat of unlawful violence. Affray requires that the offender must be 'using/threatening unlawful violence towards another'. What amounted to such a threat was a question of fact in each case, but in this instance, there were no threats made and no violence was used.

Practical considerations

- Unlike riot and violent disorder, affray can be committed by one person acting alone. However, where two or more people are involved in the violence or threatened violence, it is the conduct of them taken together that will determine whether the offence is made out.
- Refer to **8.12.3** for details of powers to stop and search when it is anticipated that serious violence may take place and to remove masks.
- Consider CPS public order charging standards for affray.
- For powers to stop and search for knives and offensive weapons, see **1.3.1**.
- The person feeling threatened does not have to be a 'person of reasonable firmness', but evidence may support other evidence that will satisfy the court that a 'person of reasonable firmness' would have been in fear of their personal safety (see **7.4.1** for 'other evidence' examples).

7.5 **Affray**

SSS E&S

Either way

None

Summary: 6/12 months' imprisonment and/or a fine

Indictment: 3 years' imprisonment

7.6 Fear or Provocation of Violence

Section 4 creates the offence of causing fear or provocation of violence, often known as 'threatening behaviour'.

Offences

A person is guilty of an offence if he—

(a) uses towards another person threatening, abusive or insulting words or behaviour, or

(b) distributes or displays to another person any writing, sign or other visible representation which is threatening, abusive or insulting,

with intent to cause that person to believe that immediate unlawful violence will be used against him or another by any person, or to provoke the immediate use of unlawful violence by that person or another, or whereby that person is likely to believe that such violence will be used or it is likely that such violence will be provoked.

Public Order Act 1986, s 4(1)

PNLD H701, H702

Points to prove

s 4(1)(a) offence

- ✓ use towards another person
- ✓ threatening/abusive/insulting words or behaviour
- ✓ with intent to EITHER
- ✓ cause that person to believe
- ✓ that immediate unlawful violence
- ✓ would be used against them or another
- ✓ by any person OR
- ✓ provoke the immediate use of unlawful violence
- ✓ by that person/another OR
- ✓ that person was likely to believe
- ✓ that such violence would be used OR
- ✓ likely that such violence would be provoked

s 4(1)(b) offence

- ✓ distribute/display
- ✓ to another
- ✓ a writing/sign/visible representation
- ✓ which was threatening/abusive/insulting
- ✓ with intent to EITHER
- ✓ (continue from this point in above offence—to end)

Meanings

Threatening

Includes verbal and physical threats, and also violent conduct.

Abusive

Means using degrading or reviling language.

Insulting

Has been held to mean scorning, especially if insolent or contemptuous.

Intent (see '**Defences**' and '**Intent**' below)

Distribute

Means spread or disperse.

Display

Means a visual presentation.

Explanatory notes

- An offence under this section may be committed in a public or a private place, except that no offence is committed where the words or behaviour are used, or the writing, sign, or other visible representation is distributed or displayed, by a person inside a **dwelling** and the other person is also inside that or another dwelling (s 4(2)).
- **Dwelling** means any **structure** or part of a structure occupied as a person's home or as other living accommodation (whether the occupation is separate or shared with others) but does not include any part not so occupied and, for this purpose, 'structure' includes a tent, caravan, vehicle, vessel, or other temporary or movable structure.
- No offence will be committed if the display is inside a dwelling and if it is displayed only to people also inside, although if it is displayed from inside to people outside the dwelling, then an offence under s 4 may be committed.

Defences

Intent

A person is guilty of an offence under s 4 only if he intends [see **4.1.2**] his words or behaviour, or the writing, sign or other visible representation, to be threatening, abusive or insulting, or is aware that it may be threatening, abusive or insulting.

Public Order Act 1986, s 6(3)

Intoxication (see **'Defences' 'Effect of intoxication' 7.4.1**)

Related cases

R v Distill [2017] EWHC 2244 A domestic garden would generally not fall within the definition of a dwelling or part of a structure for the purposes of the Act.

Hughes v DPP [2012] EWHC 606 (Admin) A blow delivered in such a way as to avoid giving the victim any advanced warning or perception that immediate unlawful violence was going to be used against them could not constitute an offence under s 4(1).

DPP v Ramos [2000] Crim LR 768, QBD If the victim believes that the threatened violence will occur at any moment, this will be sufficient for the 'immediacy' requirement.

Swanston v DPP (1996) 161 JP 203, QBD A witness (such as a police officer) who was present when the offence took place can give evidence to prove the threatening behaviour and intent, even if the victim does not give evidence.

Atkin v DPP [1989] Crim LR 581, QBD The threatening words must be addressed directly to another person who is present and either within earshot or aimed at someone thought to be in earshot.

Brutus v Cozens [1972] 2 All ER 1297, HL Whether behaviour is insulting or not is a question of fact for the justices/court to decide.

Practical considerations

- Section 17(1)(c)(iii) of PACE gives a constable a specific power to enter and search premises for the purpose of arresting a person for an offence under s 4 (see **1.4.2**).
- If this offence is **racially or religiously aggravated**, the more serious offence under s 31(1)(a) of the Crime and Disorder Act 1998 should be considered (see **7.10.4**). It is not open to the court to convict on both the simple and aggravated offences if they arise out of the same facts (*R (on the application of Dyer) v Watford MC* [2013] EWHC 547 (Admin)).
- Consider religious or racial hatred offences (see **7.9**).
- It is not duplicitous if the three alternatives 'threatening, abusive or insulting' are charged, though all three need not be present.
- Consider CPS public order charging standards.

RRA SSS

Summary — 6 months

6 months' imprisonment and/or a fine

7.7 Intentional Harassment, Alarm, or Distress

Section 4A of the Public Order Act 1986 creates the offences of intentionally causing a person harassment, alarm, or distress by using threatening, abusive, insulting words or behaviour, or disorderly behaviour; or displaying any writing, sign, or other visible representation that is threatening, abusive, or insulting.

Offences

(1) A person is guilty of an offence if, with intent to cause a person harassment, alarm or distress, he—
  (a) uses threatening, abusive or insulting words or behaviour, or disorderly behaviour, or
  (b) displays any writing, sign or other visible representation which is threatening, abusive or insulting,

thereby causing that or another person harassment, alarm or distress.

(2) An offence under this section may be committed in a public or a private place, except that no offence is committed where the words or behaviour are used, or the writing, sign or other visible representation is displayed, by a person inside a dwelling and the person who is harassed, alarmed or distressed is also inside that or another dwelling.

Public Order Act 1986, s 4A

PNLD H350, H351

Points to prove

s 4A(1)(a) offence

✓ used threatening/abusive/insulting words or behaviour OR
✓ used disorderly behaviour towards another person
✓ with intent to cause harassment/alarm/distress
✓ and actually caused harassment/alarm/distress

s 4A(1)(b) offence

✓ displayed writing/sign/other visible representation
✓ causing harassment/alarm/distress
✓ with intent to cause harassment/alarm/distress

Meanings

Harassment

Means to subject someone to constant and repeated physical and/or verbal persecution.

Alarm

Means a frightened anticipation of danger.

Distress

Means to cause trouble, pain, anguish, or hardship.

Intent (see **4.1.2**)

Threatening (see **7.6**)

Abusive (see **7.6**)

Insulting (see **7.6**)

Disorderly behaviour

The *Oxford English Dictionary* states 'unruly, unrestrained, turbulent or riotous behaviour'.

Explanatory notes

- This offence is similar to the s 5 offence (except 'insulting'—see **7.8**), but this offence requires proof of **intent** to cause alarm, harassment, or distress.
- An offence under this section may be committed in a public or private place but no offence is committed if it takes place inside a dwelling and the affected person is also inside that or another dwelling.
- Although this offence can be committed on private premises, there is no specific power of entry.

Defences

It is a defence for the accused to prove—

(a) that he was inside a dwelling and had no reason to believe that the words or behaviour used, or the writing, sign or other visible representation displayed, would be heard or seen by a person outside that or any other dwelling, or

(b) that his conduct was reasonable.

Public Order Act 1986, s 4A(3)

Related cases

Le Vine v DPP [2010] EWHC 1128 (Admin) A communally used laundry room within self-contained flats is not a dwelling.

S v CPS [2008] EWHC 438 (Admin) When posting offensive material on the internet, the defendant had the required intent and had taken the risk that the intended harm would be caused to the complainant. The fact that the complainant had not seen the material until being shown it by the police later did not break the chain of causation for the purposes of this offence.

R v Francis [2006] EWCA Crim 3323 The defendant was being detained in a police cell and allegedly made a racially obscene remark to a police officer. They were charged with the s 4A offence. It was held that the exception in the Public Order Act 1986, s 4A, was not available, since a police cell was not a home or 'other accommodation where a person lives', notwithstanding the fact that a person detained in a police cell might from time to time do the same things which they might do in their own home or in the place where they live.

R (on the application of R) v DPP [2006] EWHC 1375 (Admin) It was held in this case that for a police officer to be distressed, evidence of real emotional disturbance or upset is required, showing more than is normally experienced during their course of duty.

Practical considerations

- There must be evidence of intent to cause harassment, alarm, or distress and one of those forms of abuse must be caused to someone (not necessarily the person who was its original target).
- Consider s 5 (see **7.8**) where there is no evidence of intent.
- Where the extent of the behaviour results in the fear or realisation of violence, consider s 4(1) (see **7.6**) or assault charges (see **2.1**, **2.2**, or **2.3**).
- If there is repeated harassment, consider s 1 of the Protection from Harassment Act 1997 (see **7.11.1**).
- If a power of entry is required, consider s 17 of PACE (see **1.4.2**). Note that there is no power of entry for s 4A but consider an ongoing breach of the peace (see **7.3**) or a power of entry related to s 4 of the Public Order Act 1986 (see **7.6** and **1.4.2**).
- Consider the behaviour in the context of the circumstances—behaviour that causes distress to an elderly woman may not be distressing to a young man.
- If other people, besides the police officer and the defendant, are present include that fact in your evidence.
- If this offence is racially and/or religiously aggravated, consider the more serious offence under s 31 of the Crime and Disorder Act 1998 (see **7.10.4**) or ss 17 to 23 of the Public Order Act 1986 which relate to racial hatred offences (see **7.9**).

CHAR

Summary — 6 months

6 months' imprisonment and/or a fine

Links to alternative subjects and offences

2.1.1 **Common assault—battery** ... 53
2.5 **Threats to Kill** ... 97
2.8 **Domestic Abuse** ... 125
4.8.1 **Intimidation of a witness/juror** ... 210
11.1 **Police Powers for Civilian Staff and Volunteers** ... 781

7.8 Threatening/Abusive Words/Behaviour

Section 5 of the Public Order Act 1986 creates an offence of being threatening or abusive in a way which is likely to cause harassment, alarm, or distress.

Offences

A person is guilty of an offence if he—
(a) uses threatening or abusive words or behaviour, or disorderly behaviour, or
(b) displays any writing sign or other visible representation which is threatening or abusive,
within the hearing or sight of a person likely to be caused harassment, alarm or distress thereby.

Public Order Act 1986, s 5(1)

PNLD H11412, H11413

Points to prove

✓ used threatening/abusive words/behaviour or disorderly behaviour OR
✓ displayed writing/sign/visible representation
✓ which was threatening or abusive
✓ within hearing/sight of a person
✓ likely to be caused harassment/alarm/distress
✓ intending that those words/that behaviour etc was threatening; OR
✓ being aware that such words/behaviour/writing/sign, etc
✓ was likely to have that effect

Meanings

Threatening or abusive (see 7.6)

Harassment, alarm, and distress (see 7.7)

Disorderly behaviour (see 7.7)

Explanatory notes

- What may distress a woman of 75 years might not distress a man of 20 years. The conduct must be **likely to cause** distress. However, you can fear for the safety of someone else (particularly if you are a police officer) and it does not necessarily have to be for yourself.

- An offence under this section may be committed in a public or a private place except that no offence is committed when the words or behaviour are used or the writing, sign, or other visible representation is displayed, by a person inside a dwelling and the other person is also inside that or another dwelling. Subject to particular facts, a dwelling does not include a garden to the front or rear of a property (see *DPP v Distill* [2017] EWHC 2244 (Admin)).

Defences

Specific

5(3) It is a defence for the accused to prove—

(a) that he had no reason to believe that there was any person within hearing or sight who was likely to be caused harassment, alarm or distress; or

(b) that he was inside a dwelling and had no reason to believe that the words or behaviour used, or the writing, sign or other visible representation displayed, would be heard or seen by a person outside that or any other dwelling; or

(c) that his conduct was reasonable.

Intent

6(4) A person is guilty of an offence under section 5 only if he intends his words or behaviour, or the writing, sign, or other visible representation, to be threatening, or abusive, or is aware that it may be threatening, or abusive, or (as the case may be) he intends his behaviour to be or is aware that it may be disorderly.

Public Order Act 1986, ss 5(3) and 6(4)

Intoxication (see **'Defences' 'Effect of intoxication' 7.4.1**)

Defence notes

Article 6 (right to a fair trial—see **Appendix 1**) does not prohibit rules which transfer the burden of proof to the accused, provided it is only an 'evidential burden' where the defendant only needs to give believable evidence which justifies the defence and does not need to reach any specific standard of proof. Proving the guilt of the defendant still remains with the prosecution (eg s 28 of the Misuse of Drugs Act 1971—see **5.1.1**).

Related cases

Harvey v DPP [2011] EWHC 3992 (Admin) The defendant objected to a cannabis drug search and said, 'Fuck this man, I ain't been smoking nothing.' A warning was given about swearing but they continued and were arrested for s 5. It was held that police officers regularly hear this language so are unlikely to be affected by it. The swearing had not caused the officers, young people in the group, or anyone in the area harassment, alarm, or distress.

Abdul and others v DPP [2011] EWHC 247 (Admin) This case involved a group of five people who hurled abuse and waved placards with offensive slogans such as 'Butchers of Basra', 'British soldiers go to hell', 'terrorists', and 'cowards' at soldiers marching through a town on return from Afghanistan. Freedom of expression under Art 10 (see **Appendix 1**) was not an unqualified right. It was held that not all speech is protected by freedom of expression rights and that not all protest is legitimate in the eyes of the state. The words in question went well beyond legitimate protest and there was a very clear threat to public order. Their words were 'potentially defamatory and undoubtedly inflammatory'.

Kendall v DPP [2008] EWHC 1848 (Admin) A conviction for a racially aggravated s 5 offence was safe where the posters had been put up in the street with the awareness that the display as a whole was both threatening and abusive and that the posters were likely to cause alarm or distress.

Taylor v DPP [2006] EWHC 1202 (Admin) The court considered the wording 'within the sight or hearing of a person'. It was held that this requires evidence that there was someone able to hear or see the conduct but the prosecution does not have to call evidence to prove that the words were heard or behaviour seen. It is not sufficient that a person may have happened upon the scene and observed what was occurring but, where there are several people at the scene near enough to hear, this equates to being able to hear and so falls within the requirement of 'within the hearing of'.

Norwood v DPP [2003] EWHC 1564 (Admin) The defendant displayed a poster in their flat window, visible from the street, which said 'Islam out of Britain' and 'Protect the British People'. It bore a reproduction of one of the 'Twin Towers' in flames along with a crescent and star surrounded by a prohibition sign. It was held that the poster was capable of causing harassment, alarm, or distress. The defence of reasonable conduct and the rights of freedom of expression under Art 10 carry a duty to avoid unreasonable or disproportionate interference with the rights of others; if they do interfere disproportionately, the state has a duty to intervene.

Practical considerations

- If an offence under this section is racially or religiously aggravated, consider the more serious version of this offence under s 31 of the Crime and Disorder Act 1998 (see **7.10**).
- Consider racial and religious hatred offences (see **7.9**).
- Ensure any possible defences raised are covered in interview or rebutted by other evidence.
- The s 5 offence should be distinguished from the similar s 4A offence, which requires specific intent (see **7.7**).
- Words or behaviour are alternatives and one or other should be specified in the charge and must be proved.
- Consider issuing a PND for this offence (see **7.1**).

- It is not duplicitous if both alternatives are charged, 'threatening or abusive', though both need not be used.
- When investigating this offence, consideration must be given to the CPS public order charging standards (available at www.cps.gov.uk).

PND **RRA**

Summary

6 months

Level 3 fine

Links to alternative subjects and offences

2.1.1 **Common assault—battery** 53
2.2.1 **Assault with intent to resist or prevent lawful arrest** 63
2.8 **Domestic Abuse** 125
4.6 **Threats to Destroy or Damage Property** 203
11.1 **Police Powers for Civilian Staff and Volunteers** 781

7.9 Racial, Religious, or Sexual Orientation Hatred Offences

Sections 17 to 29 of the Public Order Act 1986 relate to racial hatred offences and ss 29A to 29N refer to religious or sexual orientation hatred offences.

7.9.1 Use of words/behaviour or display of written material (racial)

Section 18 creates the offence of using words or behaviour, or displaying written material, intending or likely to stir up racial hatred.

Offences

A person who uses threatening, abusive or insulting words or behaviour, or displays any written material which is threatening, abusive or insulting, is guilty of an offence if—

(a) he intends thereby to stir up racial hatred, or
(b) having regard to all the circumstances racial hatred is likely to be stirred up thereby.

Public Order Act 1986, s 18(1)

PNLD H2430, H2444

Points to prove

✓ used/displayed threatening/abusive/insulting
✓ words/behaviour/written material
✓ intended/likely to stir up racial hatred

Meanings

Threatening, abusive, and insulting (see 7.6)

Display (see 7.6)

Written material

Includes any sign or other visible representation.

Intention (see 4.1.2)

Racial hatred

Means hatred against a group of persons defined by reference to colour, race, nationality (including citizenship), or ethnic or national origins.

Explanatory notes

- Racial hatred can be directed against a racial or religious group outside Great Britain.
- 'Insulting' does not mean behaviour which might give rise to irritation or resentment.
- The offence may be committed in a public or private place, but if committed inside a dwelling then the s 18(4) defence may apply—see below.
- An intention to stir up racial hatred must be proved, or if having regard to all the circumstances, racial hatred is likely to be stirred up.

Defences

(4) For the accused to prove that he was inside a dwelling and had no reason to believe that the words or behaviour used, or the written material displayed, would be heard or seen by a person outside that or another dwelling.

(5) A person who is not shown to have intended to stir up racial hatred is not guilty of an offence under this section if he did not intend his words or behaviour, or the written material, to be, and was not aware that it might be, threatening, abusive or insulting.

Public Order Act 1986, s 18

Defence notes

For the meaning of 'dwelling', see **7.6 'Explanatory notes'**.

Practical considerations

- If the s 18, s 19, s 21, or s 23 offences relate to the display of written racial hatred material, the court may order forfeiture of the material.
- The following applies to all racially aggravated offences:
  - ✦ every section from s 18 to s 23 creates a separate offence (see **7.9.2** list) and one or more such offences may be charged together;
  - ✦ if the offence is committed by a body corporate, with the consent or connivance of a director, manager, company secretary, or other similar officer or person acting as such, then under s 28 they as well as the company are guilty of the offence;
  - ✦ consider the CPS public order charging standards for racial hatred offence;
  - ✦ consent of Attorney General/Solicitor General required.

E&S RRA

Either way

None

Summary: 6/12 months' imprisonment and/or a fine

Indictment: 7 years' imprisonment and/or a fine

7.9.2 Publishing/distributing written material (racial)

Section 19 of the Public Order Act 1986 creates the offence of publishing or distributing written material intending or likely to stir up racial hatred.

Offences

A person who publishes or distributes written material which is threatening, abusive or insulting is guilty of an offence if—

(a) he intends thereby to stir up racial hatred, or
(b) having regard to all the circumstances racial hatred is likely to be stirred up thereby.

Public Order Act 1986, s 19(1)

PNLD H2240, H2241

Points to prove

✓ published/distributed
✓ threatening/abusive/insulting written material
✓ intended/likely to stir up racial hatred

Meanings

Publishes or distributes

Means its publication or distribution to the public or a section of the public.

Written material (see 7.9.1)

Threatening, abusive, or insulting (see 7.6)

Intends (see 4.1.2)

Racial hatred (see 7.9.1)

Defences

For accused who is not shown to have intended to stir up racial hatred to prove that he was not aware of the content of the material and did not suspect nor had reason to suspect, that it was threatening, abusive or insulting.

Public Order Act 1986, s 19(2)

Related case

R v Sheppard [2010] EWCA Crim 65 Publishing racially inflammatory material on a website, even if the server is in the USA, is an offence under s 19.

Practical considerations (see 7.9.1)

- References to publication and distribution of written material are to its publication or distribution to the public or a section of the public.
- Other racial hatred offences under Part 3A are:
  - ✦ public performance of play—s 20;
  - ✦ distributing, showing, or playing a recording—s 21;
  - ✦ broadcasting or including programme in programme service—s 22;
  - ✦ possession of racially inflammatory material—s 23.

E&S RRA

Either way

None

Summary: 6/12 months' imprisonment and/or a fine

Indictment: 7 years' imprisonment and/or a fine

7.9.3 Religious or sexual orientation hatred offences

Section 29B creates the offence of using words or behaviour, or displaying written material, intending or likely to stir up religious or sexual orientation hatred.

Offences

A person who uses threatening words or behaviour, or displays any written material which is threatening, is guilty of an offence if he intends thereby to stir up religious hatred or hatred on the grounds of sexual orientation.

Public Order Act 1986, s 29B(1)

PNLD **H6657, H6658**

7.9.3 Religious or sexual orientation hatred offences

Points to prove

✓ used threatening words or behaviour or displayed threatening written material
✓ intended to stir up religious or sexual orientation hatred

Meanings

Threatening (see **7.6**)

Displays (see **7.6**)

Written material (see **7.9.1**)

Intention (see **4.1.2**)

Religious hatred

Means hatred against a group of persons defined by reference to religious belief or lack of religious belief.

Hatred on the grounds of sexual orientation

Means hatred against a group of persons defined by reference to sexual orientation (whether towards persons of the same sex, the opposite sex, or both).

Explanatory note

- Racial or sexual orientation hatred may be committed in a public or a private place but, if committed inside a dwelling, the s 29B(4) defence may apply.

Defences

For the accused to prove that he was inside a dwelling and had no reason to believe that the words or behaviour used, or the written material displayed, would be heard or seen by a person outside that or another dwelling.

Public Order Act 1986, s 29B(4)

Defence notes (see 7.9.1)

Practical considerations

- If the offence under s 29B relates to the display of written material, the court may, under s 29I, order forfeiture of the material. Forfeiture applies to publishing or distributing written material (s 29C), distributing/showing/playing a recording (s 29E), and possession of inflammatory material (s 29G).

- The following apply to religious or sexual orientation hatred offences:
  - ✦ every section from s 29B to s 29G creates a separate offence and one or more such offences may be charged together;
  - ✦ if the offence is committed by a body corporate with the consent or connivance of a director, manager, company secretary, or other similar officer or person acting as such, then under s 29M, they as well as the company are guilty of the offence;
  - ✦ consider CPS public order charging standards;
  - ✦ consent of the Attorney General is required.
- Consider the CPS Racist and Religious Hate Crime—Prosecution Guidance (see **Appendix 2**).

Protection for freedom of expression

Religious hatred

Section 29J states that nothing in Part 3A shall be read or given effect in a way which prohibits or restricts discussion, criticism, or expressions of antipathy, dislike, ridicule, insult, or abuse of particular religions, or the beliefs or practices of their adherents, or of any other belief system, or the beliefs or practices of its adherents, or proselytising, or urging adherents of a different religion or belief system to cease practising their religion or belief system.

Sexual orientation

Section 29JA states that in Part 3A, for the avoidance of doubt, the discussion or criticism of sexual conduct or practices, or the urging of persons to refrain from or modify such conduct or practices, shall not be taken of itself to be threatening or intended to stir up hatred.

- Other religious or sexual orientation hatred offences under Part 3A are:
  - ✦ publishing or distributing written material—s 29C;
  - ✦ public performance of play—s 29D;
  - ✦ distributing, showing, or playing a recording—s 29E;
  - ✦ broadcasting or including programme in programme service—s 29F; and
  - ✦ possession of inflammatory material—s 29G.

They are all either way offences and carry the same penalty as s 29B offence.

E&S RRA

Either way

None

Summary: 6/12 months' imprisonment and/or a fine

Indictment: 7 years' imprisonment and/or a fine

7.10 Racially/Religiously Aggravated Offences

Sections 28 to 32 of the Crime and Disorder Act 1998 relate to racially or religiously aggravated offences.

7.10.1 Meaning of 'racially or religiously aggravated'

Section 28 states when a specific offence is deemed 'racially or religiously aggravated'.

Definition

An offence is racially or religiously aggravated for the purposes of sections 29 to 32 below if—

(a) at the time of committing the offence, or immediately before or after doing so, the offender demonstrates towards the victim of the offence hostility based on the victim's membership (or presumed membership) of a racial or religious group; or

(b) the offence is motivated (wholly or partly) by hostility towards members of a racial or religious group based on the membership of that group.

Crime and Disorder Act 1998, s 28(1)

Meanings

Membership

In relation to a racial or religious group, includes association with members of that group.

Presumed

Means presumed by the defendant (even if it is a mistaken presumption).

Racial group

Means a group of people defined by reference to race, colour, nationality (including citizenship), or ethnic or national origins.

Religious group

Means a group of people defined by religious belief or lack of religious belief.

Explanatory note

- It is immaterial whether or not the offender's hostility is also based, to any extent, on any other factor not mentioned in s 28(1).

Related cases

Jones v DPP [2010] EWHC 523 (Admin) The motive does not have to be proved for each limb of s 28(1). No subjective intent is required for s 28(1)(a) as the test is objective, with just the need to show racial hostility. However, under s 28(1)(b) the motivation behind the behaviour must be proved.

R v Rogers [2007] UKHL 8 The defendant called three Spanish women 'bloody foreigners' and told them to 'go back to their own country' before pursuing them in an aggressive manner. It was held that it is immaterial whether the hostility was based on factors other than simple racism or xenophobia. The denial of equal respect and dignity to people seen as different can be more deeply hurtful, damaging, and disrespectful than if it were based on a more specific racial characteristic.

7.10.2 Racially or religiously aggravated assaults

Section 29 relates to racially or religiously aggravated assault offences.

Offences

A person is guilty of an offence under this section if he commits—

(a) an offence under section 20 of the Offences Against the Person Act 1861 [see **2.3.1**]; or

(b) an offence under section 47 of that Act [see **2.1.2**];

(ba) an offence under section 75A of the Serious Crime Act 2015 (strangulation or suffocation); or

(c) a common assault [see **2.1.1**],

which is racially or religiously aggravated for the purposes of this section.

Crime and Disorder Act 1998, s 29(1)

PNLD H10007, H10009, H10010

Points to prove

- ✓ committed offence under s 20 or s 47 of OAPA 1861 or s 39 of CJA 1988
- ✓ such offence was racially/religiously aggravated

7.10.2 Racially or religiously aggravated assaults

Meaning of racially or religiously aggravated (see 7.10.1)

Explanatory note

- If, on the trial on indictment of a person charged with this offence, the jury finds the defendant not guilty of the offence charged, it may find them guilty of the relevant 'basic' offence (eg s 20 or s 47 of the OAPA 1861; or s 39 of CJA 1988).

Related cases

HSK v Crown Prosecution Service [2022] EWHC 2213 (Admin) The defendant was one of a group of white youths who assaulted K causing grievous bodily harm. During the assault, at least one member of the group said to K that they did not want 'your coronavirus in my country' (referring to Covid-19 having originated in China and the assumption of the speaker of the words that K was of Chinese heritage). The question for the court related to whether the assault by the defendant, who had no recollection of using those words, could be held to be racially aggravated. The High Court held that the justices could have convicted HSK of the aggravated offence if they had found that the attack was motivated by K's assumed racial origin either because all of the group had that motivation or because they found that the defendant had had that motivation. In this case, it could not be established that the attack by the defendant was motivated by racial hostility. HSK had pleaded guilty to s 20 assault and was sentenced for that offence accordingly.

DPP v Woods [2002] EWHC 85 (Admin) A doorman at licensed premises was called a 'black bastard' and assaulted by the defendant. It was held that although the words were used out of frustration and the victim was unconcerned and did not consider the words racially offensive, the offence of racially aggravated common assault was still committed.

DPP v PAL [2000] EWHC 1575 (QB) An Asian youth, P, was accused of assaulting and verbally abusing an Asian man, E, using the phrases 'white man's arse licker' and 'brown Englishman'. It is necessary to prove racial hostility towards the victim and the use of racially abusive insults would ordinarily be sufficient for that purpose but that would not be so in all cases. In this case, although the words used would have had no meaning but for the race of E, what P was demonstrating was not hostility towards Asians but hostility towards E's conduct.

Practical considerations

Always charge the defendant with the relevant 'basic' offence as there is no provision for an alternative verdict at a magistrates' court.

SSS E&S RRA

Either way

None

Offence under s 29(1)(a), (b), or (ba)

Summary: 6/12 months' imprisonment and/or a fine
Indictment: 7 years' imprisonment and/or a fine

Offence under s 29(1)(c)

Summary: 6/12 months' imprisonment and/or a fine
Indictment: 2 years' imprisonment and/or a fine

7.10.3 Racially or religiously aggravated criminal damage

Section 30 creates an offence of racially or religiously aggravated criminal damage.

Offences

A person is guilty of an offence under this section if he commits an offence under section 1(1) of the Criminal Damage Act 1971 (destroying or damaging property belonging to another) which is racially or religiously aggravated for the purposes of this section.

Crime and Disorder Act 1998, s 30(1)

PNLD H10011

Points to prove

✓ committed s 1(1) criminal damage offence (see **4.4**)
✓ offence was racially/religiously aggravated

Meaning of racially or religiously aggravated (see 7.10.1)

Explanatory notes

- For the purposes of this section, s 28(1)(a) (see **7.10.1**) has effect as if the person to whom the property belongs or is treated as belonging for the purposes of that Act was the victim of the offence.
- If, on the trial on indictment of a person charged with this offence, the jury finds the defendant not guilty of the offence charged, it may find them guilty of the relevant 'basic' offence.

Practical considerations

- Where this offence is shown to be motivated by racial hostility under s 28(1)(b) (see **7.10.1**), there is no need to identify a specific victim (eg painting racist graffiti on a wall would be likely to constitute this offence).
- This offence is triable either way irrespective of the value of the damage caused (unlike the relevant 'basic' offence).

SSS E&S RRA

Either way

None

Summary: 6/12 months' imprisonment and/or a fine

Indictment: 14 years' imprisonment and/or a fine

7.10.4 Racially or religiously aggravated public order offences

Section 31 relates to racially or religiously aggravated public order offences. Section 30 creates an offence of racially or religiously aggravated criminal damage.

Offences

A person is guilty of an offence under this section if he commits—

(a) an offence under section 4 of the Public Order Act 1986 (fear/provocation of violence) [see **7.6**]; or

(b) an offence under section 4A of that Act (intentional harassment, alarm, or distress) [see **7.7**]; or

(c) an offence under section 5 of that Act (harassment, alarm, distress) [see **7.8**],

which is racially or religiously aggravated for the purposes of this section.

Crime and Disorder Act 1998, s 31(1)

PNLD H1003, H10004, H18313

Points to prove

- ✓ committed an offence
- ✓ under s 4, s 4A, or s 5 of the Public Order Act 1986
- ✓ such offence was racially/religiously aggravated

Meaning of racially or religiously aggravated (see 7.10.1)

Explanatory notes

- If, on the trial on indictment of a person charged with an offence under s 31(1)(a) or (b), the jury finds them not guilty of the offence charged, it may find that person guilty of the 'basic' offence.
- For the purposes of s 31(1)(c), s 28(1)(a) (see **7.10.1**) shall have effect as if the person likely to be caused harassment, alarm, or distress were the victim of the offence.

Related cases

DPP v McFarlane [2002] EWHC 485 (Admin) During an argument over a disabled parking bay, the defendant (a white man) referred to the complainant (a black man) as a 'jungle bunny', a 'black bastard', and a 'wog' and was charged with racially aggravated threatening behaviour. It was held that the words used by the defendant had been racially inspired and anger about another's inconsiderate behaviour was not an excuse for racial comments.

DPP v Ramos [2000] Crim LR 768, QBD After a serious bomb attack, threatening letters were sent to an organisation which offered help and advice to the Asian community making threats that a bombing hate campaign would be started, although no time frame was specified. Because there was no threat of immediate unlawful violence, the defendant was acquitted. The appeal by the DPP was allowed and it was held that for the purposes of s 4(1) it was the state of mind of the victim which was central rather than the statistical likelihood of violence taking place within a short space of time. Where the wording of a letter was very threatening and suggested that immediate violence may occur, it was open to the magistrate to decide whether or not the victim believed or was likely to believe that something could happen at any time.

Practical considerations

If the defendant is found not guilty of the offence charged under s 31(1)(a) or (b) at the magistrates' court, there is no provision for an alternative verdict, therefore it is good practice to include the relevant 'basic' offence as an alternative charge.

E&S RRA

Offence under s 31(1)(a) or (b)

Either way — None

Summary: 6/12 months' imprisonment and/or a fine

Indictment: 2 years' imprisonment and/or a fine

Offence under s 31(1)(c)

Summary — 6 months

Level 4 fine

7.10.5 Racially or religiously aggravated harassment/stalking

Section 32 concerns the offences of harassment/stalking or putting a person in fear of violence or stalking involving fear of violence or serious alarm or distress which is racially or religiously aggravated.

Offences

A person is guilty of an offence under this section if he commits—

(a) an offence under section 2 or 2A of the Protection from Harassment Act 1997 (offences of harassment and stalking); or

(b) an offence under section 4 or 4A of that Act (putting people in fear of violence and stalking involving fear of violence or serious alarm or distress),

which is racially or religiously aggravated for the purposes of this section.

Crime and Disorder Act 1998, s 32(1)

PNLD H10006, H18819

Points to prove

- ✓ committed an offence
- ✓ under s 2, s 2A, s 4, or s 4A of the Protection from Harassment Act 1997
- ✓ such offence was racially/religiously aggravated

Meaning of racially or religiously aggravated (see 7.10.1)

Explanatory notes

- Offences relating to the Protection from Harassment Act 1997 (above) are harassment (s 2—see **7.11.1**), stalking (s 2A—see **7.11.3**), putting people in fear of violence (s 4—see **7.11.2**), and stalking involving fear of violence or serious alarm or distress (s 4A—see **7.11.4**).
- If, on the trial on indictment of a person charged with an offence under s 32(1)(a), the jury finds them not guilty of the offence charged, it may find them guilty of the basic offence. Similarly, if found not guilty of an offence under s 32(1)(b), it may find them guilty of an offence under s 32(1)(a).
- If the matter is dealt with at the magistrates' court (summary) for an offence under s 32(1)(a) and found not guilty, there is no provision for an alternative verdict, so it is good practice to include the relevant basic offence as an alternative. Similarly, for a s 32(1)(b) offence, include the s 32(1)(a) offence as an alternative.

Practical considerations

- This is a distinct offence with a higher maximum penalty than for general harassment offences. For other offences, or where the hostility is related to disability, sexual orientation, or transgender identity, such hostility constitutes an aggravating factor when sentencing for the offence, see s 66 of the Sentencing Act 2020.
- Section 360 of the Sentencing Act 2020 provides a court with the power to make a restraining order (see **7.11.6**).

E&S RRA

Either way

None

Offence under s 32(1)(a)

Summary: 6/12 months' imprisonment and/or a fine

Indictment: 2 years' imprisonment and/or a fine

Offence under s 32(1)(b)

Summary: 6/12 months' imprisonment and/or a fine

Indictment: 14 years' imprisonment and/or a fine

7.11 Harassment/Stalking

The Protection from Harassment Act 1997 provides criminal and civil remedies to restrain conduct amounting to harassment or stalking. Sections 42 and 42A of the Criminal Justice and Police Act 2001 concern prevention of harassment of a person in their own home.

7.11.1 Harassment—no violence

Section 1 prohibits harassment, while s 2 creates the offence of harassment.

Offences

1(1) A person must not pursue a course of conduct—
  (a) which amounts to harassment of another, and
  (b) which he knows or ought to know amounts to harassment of the other.

1(1A) A person must not pursue a course of conduct—
  (a) which involves harassment of two or more persons, and
  (b) which he knows or ought to know amounts to harassment of those persons, and
  (c) by which he intends to persuade any person (whether or not one of those mentioned above)—
    (i) not to do something that he is entitled or required to do, or
    (ii) to do something that he is not under any obligation to do.

2(1) A person who pursues a course of conduct in breach of section 1(1) or (1A) is guilty of an offence.

Protection from Harassment Act 1997, ss 1(1), 1(1A), and 2(1)

PNLD H5

Points to prove

- ✓ pursued a course of conduct
- ✓ which amounted to harassment
- ✓ and which they knew/ought to have known amounted to harassment

Meanings

Course of conduct

- Must involve in relation to a single person under s 1(1), conduct on at least two occasions in relation to that person, **or** to two or more

persons under s 1(1A), conduct on at least one occasion in relation to each of those persons.
- Conduct includes speech.

Harassment

Includes causing the person(s) alarm or distress.

Explanatory notes

- There is no requirement under the Protection from Harassment Act 1997 that a harassment warning be given prior to any arrest being made. Some forces may have adopted the warning scheme as policy but there is no legal requirement to do so.
- If a reasonable person in possession of the same information as the defendant would think the course of conduct amounted to harassment, then the offender should have realised this as well (*Kellett v DPP* [2001] EWHC Admin 107).
- A person may be subjected to harassment by writing (eg emails or letters), orally (eg in person or by telephone), or by conduct.
- An offender does not have to act in a malicious, threatening, abusive, or insulting way. It could be that they may be infatuated with the victim and intend them no harm.
- The court can issue a 'restraining order' against the defendant. If required, ask the CPS to apply for one (see **7.11.6**).
- Note that protection orders are available under the Stalking Protection Act 2019, including an offence of breaching a stalking order (see **7.11.5**).

Defences

Section 1(1) or (1A) does not apply to a course of conduct if the person who pursued it shows—

(a) that it was pursued for the prevention or detection of crime,

(b) that it was pursued under any enactment or rule of law or to comply with any condition or requirement imposed by any person under any enactment, or

(c) that in the particular circumstances the pursuit of the course of conduct was reasonable.

Protection from Harassment Act 1997, s 1(3)

Defence notes

- These defences would apply to the police, customs, and security services, including the private sector (eg private detective or store detective).
- A suspect suffering from some form of obsessive behaviour or schizophrenia cannot use their mental illness as a defence because of the 'reasonable person' test.

Related cases

Hewson v Commissioner of Police of the Metropolis [2018] EWHC 471 (Admin) The interference with human rights under Arts 8 and 10 ECHR (see **Appendix 1**), by issuing a prevention of harassment letter, had been proportionate at the time the letter was issued.

Loake v Crown Prosecution Service [2017] EWHC 2855 (Admin) The defence of insanity (see **2.7.1**) established by the *M'Naghten's Case* (1843) 10 Cl & F 200, is available for the s 2 offence of harassment.

Plavelil v DPP [2014] EWHC 736 (Admin) The fact that repeated untrue malicious allegations might be easily rebutted did not mean that they were not oppressive harassment within s 1 of the Protection from Harassment Act 1997.

Kosar v Bank of Scotland [2011] EWHC 1050 (Admin) A company was not precluded from being able to commit a criminal offence of harassment contrary to s 2(1) of the 1997 Act.

DPP v Baker [2004] EWHC 2782 (Admin) Harassment may occur either continuously or intermittently over a period of time, providing at least one of the incidents relied on by the prosecution occurred within the six-month limitation period.

Practical considerations

- Evidence of previous complaints of harassment to prove continuance of the harassment on at least two separate occasions.
- Two isolated incidents do not constitute a course of conduct.
- Consider serving a harassment warning notice on the suspect. Have any previous warning notices been served on the suspect?
- A campaign of collective harassment applies equally to two or more people as it does to one. Namely, conduct by one person shall also be taken, at the time it occurs, to be conduct by another if it is aided, abetted, counselled, or procured by that other person (s 7(3A) of the 1997 Act).
- Consider the intentional harassment, alarm, or distress offence under s 4A of the Public Order Act 1986 (see **7.7**).
- If it is racially or religiously aggravated harassment, see **7.10.5**.
- Obtain CJA witness statements.
- Obtain all available evidence (eg other witnesses, CCTV camera footage, detailed telephone bills, entries in domestic violence registers, harassment notice).
- The court can also impose a restraining order on anyone convicted of this offence. A breach of such order is in itself an offence under s 363 of the Sentencing Act 2020 (see **7.11.6**).
- Consider the offence of stalking under s 2A (see **7.11.3**).

RRA

Summary

6 months

6 months' imprisonment and/or a fine

7.11.2 Harassment (fear of violence)

Section 4 relates to a course of conduct which, on at least two occasions, causes another to fear that violence will be used against them.

Offences

A person whose course of conduct causes another to fear, on at least two occasions, that violence will be used against him is guilty of an offence if he knows or ought to know that his course of conduct will cause the other so to fear on each of those occasions.

Protection from Harassment Act 1997, s 4(1)

PNLD H18816

Points to prove

- ✓ caused fear of violence
- ✓ by a course of conduct
- ✓ knew/ought to have known
- ✓ would cause fear of violence on each occasion

Meaning of course of conduct (see **7.11.1**)

Explanatory notes

- The person whose course of conduct is in question ought to know that it will cause another to fear that violence will be used against them on any occasion if a reasonable person with the same information would think it would cause the other so to fear on that occasion.
- A defendant found not guilty of this offence (at trial on indictment) may be convicted of s 2 harassment (see **7.11.1**) or s 2A stalking (see **7.11.3**).

- The court can issue a 'restraining order' against the defendant (see **7.11.6**).
- Communications that constitute threats to another person may also amount to other offences. Consider threats to kill under s 16 of the Offences Against the Person Act 1861 (see **2.5**); intimidation of witnesses and jurors under s 51 of the Criminal Justice and Public Order Act 1994 (see **4.8.1**); s 127 of the Communications Act 2003 (see **7.12.2**); and s 181 of the Online Safety Act 2023 (see **7.12.4**).

Defences

It is a defence for a person charged with an offence under this section to show that—

(a) his course of conduct was pursued for the purpose of preventing or detecting crime,

(b) his course of conduct was pursued under any enactment or rule of law or to comply with any condition or requirement imposed by any person under any enactment, or

(c) the pursuit of his course of conduct was reasonable for the protection of himself or another or for the protection of his or another's property.

Protection from Harassment Act 1997, s 4(3)

Defence notes (see **7.11.1**)

Related cases

R v Widdows [2011] EWCA Crim 1500 A charge of harassment is not normally appropriate for use as a means of criminalising conduct during incidents in a long and predominantly affectionate relationship in which both parties persisted and wanted to continue.

R v Curtis [2010] EWCA Crim 123 The prosecution must establish that a course of conduct amounts to harassment. The conduct must be an oppressive, unreasonable, and unacceptable campaign, to a degree that would be a criminal matter.

Howard v DPP [2001] EWHC 17 (Admin) A family suffered continual abuse from their neighbours. One of the many threats made by the defendant was to kill their dog. It was held that this was sufficient grounds for the family to fear violence being used against them.

Practical considerations (see also **7.11.1**)

- Offence could cover long-standing disputes where fear of violence is a possibility against one of the parties.
- Consider stalking involving fear of violence or serious alarm or distress (see **7.11.4**) or intentional harassment, alarm, or distress offence under s 4A of the Public Order Act 1986 (see **7.7**).

- Section 4B of the Act also allows for prosecution of a UK national or a person habitually resident in England and Wales who pursues, wholly or partly in a country outside the UK, a course of conduct which constitutes an offence under this section.

E&S

Either way

None

Summary: 6/12 months' imprisonment and/or a fine

Indictment: 10 years' imprisonment and/or a fine

7.11.3 **Stalking**

Section 2A creates the offence of stalking.

Offences

(1) A person is guilty of an offence if—

    (a) the person pursues a course of conduct in breach of section 1(1), and

    (b) the course of conduct amounts to stalking.

(2) For the purposes of subsection (1)(b) (and section 4A(1)(a)) a person's course of conduct amounts to stalking of another person if—

    (a) it amounts to harassment of that person,

    (b) the acts or omissions involved are ones associated with stalking, and

    (c) the person whose course of conduct it is knows or ought to know that the course of conduct amounts to harassment of the other person.

Protection from Harassment Act 1997, s 2A

PNLD H10641

Points to prove

✓ pursued a course of conduct in breach of s 1(1)
✓ and that conduct amounted to stalking
✓ and which you knew/ought to have known
✓ amounted to harassment

Meanings

Breach of section 1(1) (see **7.11.1**)

7.11.3 **Stalking**

Harassment (see **7.11.1**)
Includes causing the person(s) alarm or distress.

Acts or omissions (s 2A(3))

The following are examples which, in particular circumstances, are associated with stalking:

- following a person;
- contacting, or attempting to contact, a person by any means;
- publishing any statement or other material—relating or purporting to relate to a person or purporting to originate from a person;
- monitoring the use by a person of the internet, email, or any other form of electronic communication;
- loitering in any place (whether public or private);
- interfering with any property in the possession of a person;
- watching or spying on a person.

Explanatory notes

- Stalking is most often found where a person is fixated and/or obsessed with another. This can manifest itself in a pattern of persistent and repeated contact, or attempts to contact, the victim. Examples of behaviours associated with stalking are given in s 2A(3) (above).
- An offender does not have to act in a malicious, threatening, abusive, or insulting way. It could be that they may be infatuated with the victim and intend them no harm.
- Although the Sentencing Act 2020 and the Protection from Harassment Act 1997 provide that the court can issue a 'restraining order' against the defendant (see **7.11.6**), the Stalking Protection Act 2019 allows for protection orders to be made specific to this offence (see **7.11.5**).

Practical considerations

- The CPS and NPCC have published a protocol on the appropriate handling of stalking offences. Refer the victim to relevant support agencies: National Stalking Helpline or Paladin, including victim support (see **Appendix 2**) and local domestic violence support groups.
- Section 2B allows a justice of the peace to issue a warrant which authorises a constable to enter and search premises on reasonable grounds for believing that:
  - ✦ a stalking offence under s 2A has been, or is being, committed; and
  - ✦ there is material on the premises which is likely to be of substantial value (whether by itself or together with other material) to the investigation of the offence.
- Section 4A concerns the offence of stalking involving fear of violence or serious alarm or distress (see **7.11.4**).
- HOC 18/2012 provides further details concerning the s 2A and s 4A stalking offences and power of entry under s 2B. See also Stalking or Harassment, Crown Prosecution Service (www.cps.gov.uk).

- If it is racially or religiously aggravated stalking, see **7.10.5**.
- Consider the offence of intentional harassment, alarm, or distress under s 4A of the Public Order Act 1986 (see **7.7**).

Summary

6 months

6 months' imprisonment and/or a fine

7.11.4 Stalking (fear of violence/serious alarm or distress)

Section 4A is a more serious stalking offence of causing another to fear, on at least two occasions, that violence will be used against them or causes them serious alarm or distress which has a substantial adverse effect on their usual day-to-day activities.

Offences

A person (A) whose course of conduct—
(a) amounts to stalking, and
(b) either—
  (i) causes another (B) to fear, on at least two occasions, that violence will be used against B, or
  (ii) causes B serious alarm or distress which has a substantial adverse effect on B's usual day-to-day activities,
is guilty of an offence if A knows or ought to know that A's course of conduct will cause B so to fear on each of those occasions or (as the case may be) will cause such alarm or distress.

Protection from Harassment Act 1997, s 4A(1)

PNLD H18817, H18818

Points to prove

- ✓ course of conduct that amounted to stalking
- ✓ caused another to fear on at least two occasions that violence would be used OR
- ✓ caused serious alarm/distress which had a substantial adverse effect on B's usual day-to-day activities
- ✓ which knew/ought to have known
- ✓ would cause either fear of violence on each occasion or serious alarm/distress

Meaning of stalking (see 7.11.3)

7.11.4 **Stalking (fear of violence/serious alarm or distress)**

Explanatory notes

- The phrase '**substantial adverse effect** on the usual day-to-day activities' is not defined in s 4A. HOC 18/2012 states that evidence of a substantial adverse effect may include the victim:
  - changing their routes to work, work patterns, or employment;
  - arranging for friends or family to pick up children from school;
  - installing additional security in/around their home;
  - suffering from physical or mental ill-health;
  - suffering from stress due to deterioration in performance at work;
  - moving home; or
  - stopping/changing the way they socialise.
- If the victim continues with their existing routines in defiance of a stalker, they may still be able to evidence the substantial impact on their usual day-to-day activities.
- The person whose course of conduct is in question ought to know that it will cause another to fear that violence will be used against them on any occasion if a reasonable person in possession of the same information would think the course of conduct would cause the other to fear on that occasion.
- For the purposes of this section, the person whose course of conduct is in question ought to know that their course of conduct will cause the victim serious alarm or distress which has a substantial adverse effect on the victim's usual day-today activities if a reasonable person in possession of the same information would think the course of conduct would cause the victim such alarm or distress.
- Other offences that may be considered in appropriate circumstances include threats to kill under s 16 of the Offences Against the Person Act 1861 (see **2.5**); intimidation of witnesses and jurors under s 51 of the Criminal Justice and Public Order Act 1994 (see **4.8.1**); s 1 of the Malicious Communications Act 1988 (see **7.12.1**); s 127 of the Communications Act 2003 (see **7.12.2**); and threatening communications under s 181 of the Online Safety Act 2023 (see **7.12.4**).

Defences

It is a defence for A to show that—

(a) A's course of conduct was pursued for the purpose of preventing or detecting crime,

(b) A's course of conduct was pursued under any enactment or rule of law or to comply with any condition or requirement imposed by any person under any enactment, or

(c) the pursuit of A's course of conduct was reasonable for the protection of A or another or for the protection of A's or another's property.

Protection from Harassment Act 1997, s 4A(4)

Defence notes (see 7.11.1)

Related cases

R v Musharraf [2022] EWCA Crim 1482 In this case, the Court of Appeal considered written complaints in the context of stalking, and that requiring a course of conduct is defined as conduct on at least two occasions. The legislation provides that stalking covers behaviour directed at a particular person and the Court of Appeal deemed there to be no issue in determining that the offence could cover false complaints to a person's employer or regulator. The natural meaning of the term stalking did not exclude such actions.

R v Qosja [2016] EWCA Crim 1543 It was held that the offence was wide enough to cover a person who is caused to fear on a particular occasion that violence will be used on an uncertain future date. This does not need to be a specific threat of violence but the requirement is that they fear that violence will (rather than may be) used.

Pendlebury v DPP [2018] EWHC 3567 (Admin) Section 4A requires no objective conduct on the part of a defendant beyond stalking. The remainder of the statutory test is concerned with the effect on the mind of the complainant and the knowledge, or constructive knowledge, of the defendant. The offence requires proof of a specific state of mind on the part of the complainant, not merely proof of circumstances that might reasonably engender that state of mind.

Practical considerations (see also **7.11.3**)

- If on the trial on indictment of a person charged with a s 4A offence the jury finds that person not guilty, it may find the person guilty of an offence under s 2 (see **7.11.1**) or s 2A (see **7.11.3**).
- Although the Sentencing Act 2020 and the Protection from Harassment Act 1997 provide that the court can issue a 'restraining order' against the defendant (see **7.11.6**), the Stalking Protection Act 2019 allows for protection orders to be made specific to this offence (see **7.11.5**).
- If it is racially or religiously aggravated stalking, see **7.10.5**.
- Consider intentional harassment, alarm, or distress offence under s 4A of the Public Order Act 1986 (see **7.7**).
- Section 4B of the Act also allows for prosecution of a UK national or a person habitually resident in England and Wales who pursues, wholly or partly in a country outside the UK, a course of conduct which constitutes an offence under s 4A of the Protection from Harassment Act 1997.

E&S

Either way

None

Summary: 6/12 months' imprisonment and/or a fine

Indictment: 10 years' imprisonment and/or a fine

7.11.5 Stalking Protection Orders

The Stalking Protection Act 2019 creates provisions for offences and orders to protect persons from the risks associated with stalking occurring outside the domestic abuse context (although there is nothing preventing them being used in this manner). Interim orders can be made by the court allowing the police safeguarding and pre-conviction intervention.

Offences

A person who, without reasonable excuse, breaches a stalking protection order or an interim stalking protection order commits an offence.

Stalking Protection Act 2019, s 8(1)

PNLD H20164

Points to prove

✓ date and location
✓ a person
✓ without reasonable excuse
✓ conducted an act they were prohibited from doing by
✓ a stalking protection order OR
✓ an interim stalking protection order
✓ breaching s 8(1) of the Stalking Protection Act 2019

Meanings

Stalking protection order

Has the same meaning given by s 1(1) in that it is an order which, for the purpose of preventing the defendant from carrying out acts associated with stalking, (a) prohibits the defendant from doing anything described in the order or (b) requires the defendant to do anything described in the order.

Interim protection order

Has the same meaning given by s 5(2) being an order that is made (a) at the same time and by the same chief officer of police as the main application or (b) if the main application has already been made, by the chief officer of police who made that application.

Explanatory notes

- A chief officer of police may apply to a magistrates' court in respect of a person (the defendant) if it appears that:
  (a) the defendant has carried out acts associated with stalking;
  (b) the defendant poses a risk associated with stalking to another person (which may be in respect of physical or psychological harm

and which may arise from acts the defendant knows or ought to know are unwelcome to the person even if, in other circumstances, the acts would appear harmless in themselves); and

(c) there is reasonable cause to believe the proposed order is necessary to protect another person from such a risk (whether or not the other person was the victim of the acts mentioned in (a) above).

- Where an application is made to magistrates for a Stalking Protection Order (SPO), it will usually remain in place for two years.
- An individual protected by an order does not have to be the victim of stalking themselves; for example, it may be that a perpetrator is stalking people connected to the individual.
- Interim orders provide powers to prevent stalkers from contacting or approaching their victims while police investigate suspected offences providing immediate protection for victims while a decision for an SPO is being made.
- The Act does not specifically define stalking; however, s 2A of the Protection from Harassment Act 1997 provides some examples of what has previously been deemed as stalking 'behaviour' (see **7.11.3**).

Practical considerations

- The Act outlines the notification requirements for a defendant subject to a full or interim order including a requirement to provide their name and address within three days of the date of service. Section 11 creates further offences for failing to make the relevant notifications.
- Where the police become aware of a breach, positive action should be taken to arrest as soon as possible to protect the victim. Any breach can then be used as bad character evidence in subsequent proceedings.
- In proceedings for an offence under this section, a copy of the original stalking protection order/interim stalking protection order (certified by the designated officer for the court which made it) is admissible as evidence of it having been made and of its contents. This is to the same extent that oral evidence would be admissible in such proceedings.

Either way

None

Summary: 6/12 months' imprisonment and/or a fine

Indictment: 5 years' imprisonment and/or a fine

7.11.6 **Restraining orders**

Restraining orders can be made on conviction, under s 360 of the Sentencing Act 2020, for the purpose of protecting a victim or victims of an offence, or any other person mentioned in the order, from conduct which amounts to harassment or will cause a fear of violence. Such orders were previously provided for under s 5 of the Protection from Harassment Act 1997 which is now repealed. Section 5A of the Protection from Harassment Act 1997 still provides for restraining orders to be made on acquittal.

Offences

It is an offence for a person who is subject to a restraining order without reasonable excuse to do anything prohibited by the restraining order.

Sentencing Act 2020, s 363(1)

It is an offence for the defendant, without reasonable excuse, to do anything that the defendant is prohibited from doing by an order under this section.

Protection from Harassment Act 1997, s 5A(2D)

PNLD **H22092, H22093, H22152**

Points to prove

- ✓ without reasonable excuse
- ✓ being subject to a restraining order
- ✓ imposed by a magistrates' court/Crown Court
- ✓ did something prohibited by a restraining order

Explanatory notes

- A court sentencing or otherwise dealing with a defendant convicted of **any offence** may, as well as sentencing or dealing with the defendant in any other way, make a restraining order under s 360 of the Sentencing Act 2020 or s 5A of the Protection from Harassment Act 1997.
- The views of the victim should be sought when considering making an order but their consent is not required.
- The order may prohibit the defendant from doing anything described in the order for the purpose of protecting the victim(s), or any other person mentioned in the order, from further conduct which amounts to harassment or will cause a fear of violence.
- Where the parties are to continue or resume a relationship, courts may consider a prohibition within the restraining order not to molest the victim as an alternative to a prohibition on contacting the victim.
- The order may last for a specified period or until a further order is made.
- The prosecutor, defendant, or any person named therein may apply for it to be varied or discharged by a further order.

Related cases

R v Buxton [2010] EWCA Crim 2923 A restraining order can be made to protect a company.

R v Major [2010] EWCA 3016 If a court issues a restraining order on acquittal, there must be clear evidence that the victim needs protection from harassment from the defendant.

Practical considerations

- One incident is sufficient to breach an order.
- These are criminal matters and should not be confused with civil injunctions.
- When an order is made, it must identify the protected parties so ensure the details are available.
- Include a copy of the original order in the file for CPS attention.
- If you require a further order, you must request the CPS to apply for one.

E&S

Either way None

Summary: 6/12 months' imprisonment and/or a fine

Indictment: 5 years' imprisonment and/or a fine

7.11.7 Civil remedies

Section 3 provides a civil remedy for harassment, allowing the victim to obtain damages and/or an injunction. Section 3A provides for injunctions to protect persons from harassment within s 1(1A).

Offences

Where—

(a) the High Court or a county court grants an injunction for the purpose mentioned in subsection (3)(a), and

(b) without reasonable excuse the defendant does anything which he is prohibited from doing by the injunction,

he is guilty of an offence.

Protection from Harassment Act 1997, s 3(6)

PNLD H6

Points to prove

✓ without reasonable excuse

✓ pursued course of conduct prohibited by injunction
✓ granted by High Court/county court

Meanings

Injunction

An order or decree issued by a court for a person to do or not do that which is specified for a specified amount of time.

Subsection (3)(a)

In such proceedings, the High Court or a county court grants an injunction for the purpose of restraining the defendant from pursuing any conduct which amounts to harassment.

Reasonable excuse (see '**Defence**' below)

Explanatory notes

- An actual or perceived breach of s 1 may result in a claim in civil proceedings by the victim of the course of conduct in question.
- On such a claim, damages may be awarded for, among other things, any anxiety caused by, and financial loss resulting from, the harassment.
- Where, in such proceedings, the court grants an injunction restraining the defendant from pursuing any conduct amounting to harassment, and the plaintiff considers that the defendant has done anything prohibited by the injunction, they may apply to have a warrant issued for the arrest of the defendant.
- The warrant application must be made to the court that issued the injunction.
- Section 3A stipulates that where there is an actual or apprehended breach of s 1(1A) (see **7.11.1**) by the relevant person, then any person who is or may be:
  - ✦ a victim of the course of conduct in question; or
  - ✦ a person falling within s 1(1A)(c)

  may apply to the High Court or a county court for an injunction restraining the relevant person from pursuing any conduct which amounts to harassment in relation to any person or persons mentioned or described in the injunction.

Defences

The defence of reasonable excuse was meant for a life-saving situation such as a rescue from a burning house or something similar.

Related case

Thomas v News Group Newspapers Ltd [2001] EWCA Civ 1233 A national newspaper and journalists were sued for harassment under s 3 after publishing an article about police discipline which gave the complainant's name, place of work, and described them as 'a black clerk'. It was held that it was not the conduct of the offender that created the offence or civil wrong of harassment but the effect of that conduct. There was a sound argument that the reference by the newspaper to the complainant's skin colour was not reasonable. Furthermore, it could be argued that the newspaper could have foreseen that some of its readers would send hate mail after the articles.

Practical considerations

If a person is convicted of a breach of an injunction under this section, their conduct is not punishable as a contempt of court, or vice versa.

Either way None

Summary: 6/12 months' imprisonment and/or a fine

Indictment: 5 years' imprisonment and/or a fine

7.11.8 Harassment of person in their home

Sections 42 and 42A of the Criminal Justice and Police Act 2001 give the police power to direct a person to leave a dwelling to prevent harassment and an offence of harassing a person in their home.

Offences

42(7) Any person who knowingly fails to comply with a requirement in a direction given to him under this section (other than a requirement under subsection (4)(b)) shall be guilty of an offence.

(7A) Any person to whom a constable has given a direction including a requirement under subsection (4)(b) commits an offence if he—

(a) returns to the vicinity of the premises in question within the period specified in the direction beginning with the date on which the direction is given; and

(b) does so for the purpose described in subsection (1)(b).

42A(1) A person commits an offence if—

(a) that person is present outside or in the vicinity of any premises that are used by any individual ('the resident') as his dwelling;

(b) that person is present there for the purpose (by his presence or otherwise) of representing to the resident or another individual (whether or not one who uses the

premises as his dwelling), or of persuading the resident or such another individual—
- (i) that he should not do something that he is entitled or required to do; or
- (ii) that he should do something that he is not under any obligation to do;

(c) that person—
- (i) intends his presence to amount to the harassment of, or to cause alarm or distress to, the resident, or
- (ii) knows or ought to know that his presence is likely to result in the harassment of, or to cause alarm or distress to, the resident; and

(d) the presence of that person—
- (i) amounts to the harassment of, or causes alarm or distress to, any person falling within subsection (2); or
- (ii) is likely to result in the harassment of, or to cause alarm or distress to, any such person.

Criminal Justice and Police Act 2001, ss 42, 42A

PNLD **H1300, H6639, H6640**

Points to prove

s 42(7) offence

- ✓ outside/in vicinity of premises
- ✓ knowingly
- ✓ contravened the direction of a constable

s 42(7A) offence

- ✓ having been given a direction by a constable
- ✓ to leave the vicinity of premises
- ✓ not to return within a specified period
- ✓ returned there within that period
- ✓ to persuade the resident/another individual
- ✓ not to do something they are entitled to do/do something not obliged to do

s 42A(1) offence

- ✓ present outside/in vicinity of a dwelling
- ✓ to persuade resident/other individual
- ✓ not to do something entitled/required to do/to do something not obliged to do
- ✓ intended to harass/cause alarm/distress to the resident
- ✓ knew/ought to have known such presence was likely to do so
- ✓ and their presence amounted to harassment/caused alarm/distress/likely to do so

Meanings

Directions

(1) Subject to the following provisions of this section, a constable who is at the scene may give a **direction** under this section to any person if—
  (a) that person is present outside or in the vicinity of any premises that are used by any individual ('the resident') as his **dwelling**;
  (b) that constable believes, on reasonable grounds, that that person is present there for the purpose (by his presence or otherwise) of representing to the resident or another individual (whether or not one who uses the premises as his dwelling), or of persuading the resident or such another individual—
    (i) that he should not do something that he is entitled or required to do; or
    (ii) that he should do something that he is not under any obligation to do; and
  (c) that constable also believes, on reasonable grounds, that the presence of that person (either alone or together with that of any other persons who are also present)—
    (i) amounts to, or is likely to result in, the **harassment** of the resident; or
    (ii) is likely to cause alarm or distress to the resident.

(2) A direction under this section is a direction requiring the person to whom it is given to do all such things as the constable giving it may specify as the things he considers necessary to prevent one or both of the following—
  (a) the harassment of the resident; or
  (b) the causing of any alarm or distress to the resident.

(3) A direction under this section may be given orally; and where a constable is entitled to give a direction under this section to each of several persons outside, or in the vicinity of, any premises, he may give that direction to those persons by notifying them of his requirements either individually or all together.

(4) The requirements that may be imposed by a direction under this section include—
  (a) a requirement to leave the vicinity of the premises in question, and
  (b) a requirement to leave that vicinity and not to return to it within such period as the constable may specify, not being longer than 3 months;

  and (in either case) the requirement to leave the vicinity may be to do so immediately or after a specified period of time.

(5) A direction under this section may make exceptions to any requirement imposed by the direction, and may make any such

exception subject to such conditions as the constable giving the direction thinks fit; and those conditions may include—
   (a) conditions as to the distance from the premises in question at which, or otherwise as to the location where, persons who do not leave their vicinity must remain; and
   (b) conditions as to the number or identity of the persons who are authorised by the exception to remain in the vicinity of those premises.

(6) The power of a constable to give a direction under this section shall not include—
   (a) any power to give a direction at any time when there is a more **senior ranking** police officer at the scene; or
   (b) any power to direct a person to refrain from conduct that is lawful under section 220 of the Trade Union and Labour Relations (Consolidation) Act 1992 (right peacefully to picket a work place);

but it shall include power to vary or withdraw a direction previously given under this section.

Criminal Justice and Police Act 2001, s 42

Dwelling

Means any structure or part of a structure occupied as a person's home or as other living accommodation (whether the occupation is separate or shared with others) but does not include any part not so occupied, and for this purpose 'structure' includes a tent, caravan, vehicle, vessel, or other temporary or movable structure.

Harassment (see **7.11.1**)

Explanatory notes

- A requirement in a direction under s 42(4)(b) means to leave that vicinity immediately or after a specified period of time and not to return within a specified period (no more than three months).
- Under the s 42A(1)(d)(i) offence, a person falls within s 42A(2) if they are the resident, a person in the resident's dwelling, or a person in another dwelling in the vicinity of the resident's dwelling.
- Under s 42, a constable in attendance may give a direction to any person if that person is outside or in the vicinity of premises used by a resident as their dwelling, having reasonable grounds to believe that the person's presence amounts to harassment of the resident or is likely to cause them alarm or distress.
- Such a direction requires the person to whom it is given to do everything specified by the constable as necessary to prevent the harassment of and/or the causing of alarm or distress to the resident.
- A direction under s 42 may include a requirement to leave:
  - ✦ the vicinity of the premises in question; and
  - ✦ not return to it within such period as the constable may specify, not being longer than three months.

- The references in s 42A(1)(c) and (d) to a person's presence refer to their presence either alone or together with any other person(s) also present.
- For the s 42A offence, a person ought to know that their presence is likely to result in the harassment of, or cause alarm or distress to, a resident if a reasonable person possessing the same information would think that their presence would likely have that effect.

Practical considerations

- Directions given under this section may be given orally but it is important that the direction must be both heard and understood by the person concerned.
- If a direction is given to more than one person, the constable may give it to them either individually or all together.
- The power of a constable to give a direction under s 42 does not include where there is a more **senior-ranking** officer present. If the senior officers are of the same rank, then the greater length of service in that rank determines who should give the direction.
- Similarly, a constable cannot give a direction if the person(s) are exercising their right to peacefully picket a workplace.
- A constable may vary or withdraw any direction previously given.

Either way

None

Offence under s 42(7)

3 months' imprisonment and/or a level 4 fine

Offence under s 42(7A) or s 42A

12 months' imprisonment and/or a level 4 fine

Links to alternative subjects and offences

2.1.1 **Common assault—battery** 53
2.5 **Threats to Kill** 97
2.8 **Domestic Abuse** 125
4.6 **Threats to Destroy or Damage Property** 203
4.8.1 **Intimidation of a witness/juror** 210

7.12 Communications Causing Distress, Anxiety, or Serious Harm

The Malicious Communications Act 1988 concerns the sending and delivery of letters or other articles to cause distress or anxiety; the Communications Act 2003 regulates all types of media, including the sending of grossly offensive material via the public electronic communications network; and the Online Safety Act 2023 creates further offences for false communications and for those who threaten death or serious harm. The offence of giving or causing to give a false alarm of fire is dealt with by the Fire and Rescue Services Act 2004.

7.12.1 Sending letters etc with intent to cause distress or anxiety

Section 1 of the Malicious Communications Act 1988 creates offences relating to the sending of indecent, offensive, or threatening letters, electronic communications, or articles with intent to cause distress or anxiety to the recipient.

Offences

Any person who sends to another person—

(a) a letter, electronic communication or article of any description which conveys—

  (i) a message which is indecent or grossly offensive;

(b) any article or electronic communication which is, in whole or part, of an indecent or grossly offensive nature,

is guilty of an offence if his purpose, or one of his purposes, in sending it is that it should, so far as falling within paragraph (a) or (b) above, cause distress or anxiety to the recipient or to any other person to whom he intends that it or its contents or nature should be communicated.

Malicious Communications Act 1988, s 1(1)

PNLD H12178, H12179

Points to prove

s 1(1)(a) offence

✓ sent a letter/an electronic communication/an article
✓ which conveyed an indecent/grossly offensive message
✓ for the purpose of causing distress/anxiety

✓ to the recipient/any other person
✓ to whom its contents/nature were intended to be communicated

s 1(1)(b) offence

✓ sent to another person an article
✓ in whole/in part of an indecent/grossly offensive nature
✓ for the purpose of causing distress/anxiety to the recipient/any other person
✓ to whom you intended it/its contents/nature were intended to be communicated

Meanings

Electronic communication

Includes:
- any oral or other communication by means of an **electronic communications network**; and
- any communication (however sent) that is in electronic form.

Electronic communications network

Means:
- a transmission system for the conveyance, by the use of electrical, magnetic, or electro-magnetic energy, of signals of any description; and
- such of the following as are used, by the person providing the system and in association with it, for the conveyance of the signals:
  - ✦ apparatus comprised in the system;
  - ✦ apparatus used for the switching or routing of the signals;
  - ✦ software and stored data; and
  - ✦ other resources, including network elements which are not active.

Grossly offensive

This has to be judged by the standards of an open and just multiracial society. Whether a message falls into this category depends not only on its content but on the circumstances in which the message has been sent.

Explanatory notes

- Sending includes delivering or transmitting and causing to be sent, delivered, or transmitted; 'sender' will be construed accordingly.
- The offence is completed once the communication is sent (eg letter is posted; email/text/tweet sent). The section does not include a requirement that the intended victim has to receive the communication. It is merely the sending and intended purpose of the offender which constitutes the offence.
- There is no need to identify the other person but the communication must be sent to another person.
- There is no need for text. A picture or a sound file is still a communication.

Related cases

R v Casserly [2024] EWCA Crim 25 In this case, the recipient of a communication was an elected town councillor who had received an email from a constituent (C) challenging the councillor's ability to conduct their role. The email referenced the fact that the councillor was deaf, partially sighted, and had limited reading ability. C was charged with the s 1(1)(b) offence. An appeal against conviction was allowed and the court held inter alia that the email had been sent in a political context and, where that is the case, the law expects those involved to have a 'thicker skin' than ordinary citizens and, as such, language used may not necessarily amount to the offence charged. It was clear that there was a higher threshold to be met in the present case and the jury had to be absolutely sure that C's objective was to cause distress and anxiety.

Connolly v DPP [2007] EWHC 237 (Admin) The defendant telephoned chemist shops to ascertain whether they stocked the morning-after pill, sending pictures of aborted foetuses to those that did. These pictures were indecent and grossly offensive with the purpose of causing distress or anxiety. It was held that rights of expression under Art 9 or Art 10 ECHR (see **Appendix 1**) did not excuse the distress and anxiety caused, and conviction was necessary in a democratic society. The words 'indecent' and 'grossly offensive' have their ordinary meaning.

Practical considerations

- As well as letters and telephone systems, this offence would include emails, fax, text messages, Facebook, X (formally known as Twitter), or other social media.
- If the intent is to cause the victim annoyance, inconvenience, or needless anxiety, then consider the offence under s 127 of the Communications Act 2003 (see **7.12.2**).
- If there has been more than one incident, an offence under s 2 or s 2A of the Protection from Harassment Act 1997 may be appropriate (see **7.11.1** or **7.11.3**).
- If any threat used includes an unwarranted demand, consider the more serious offence of blackmail (see **3.2.2**).

E&S

Either way

None

Summary: 12 months' imprisonment and/or a fine

Indictment: 2 years' imprisonment and/or a fine

7.12.2 Improper use of electronic public communications network

Section 127 of the Communications Act 2003 creates offences regarding improper use of a public electronic communications network.

Offences

(1) A person is guilty of an offence if he—
  (a) sends by means of a public electronic communications network a message or other matter that is grossly offensive or of an indecent, obscene or menacing character; or
  (b) causes any such message or matter to be so sent.
(2) A person is guilty of an offence if, for the purpose of causing annoyance, inconvenience or needless anxiety to another, he—
  (c) persistently makes use of a public electronic communications network.

Communications Act 2003, s 127

PNLD H5555, H5556, H5559

Points to prove

s 127(1) offence

- ✓ sent
- ✓ by means of a public electronic communications network
- ✓ a message/other matter
- ✓ that was grossly offensive/indecent/obscene/menacing character OR
- ✓ caused such a message/matter to be so sent

s 127(2)(c)offence

- ✓ persistently made use
- ✓ of a public electronic communications network
- ✓ for the purpose of causing annoyance/inconvenience/needless anxiety
- ✓ to another

Meanings

Public electronic communications network

Means an **electronic communications network** provided wholly or mainly for the purpose of making electronic communications services available for use by members of the public.

Electronic communications network (see **7.12.1**)

Grossly offensive (see **7.12.1**)

Menacing

Means a message which conveys a threat; which seeks to create a fear in or through the recipient that something unpleasant is going to happen. Here the intended or likely effect on the recipient must ordinarily be a central factor.

Persistently

Includes any case in which the misuse is repeated on a sufficient number of occasions for it to be clear that the misuse represents a pattern of behaviour, or practice, or recklessness as to whether people suffer annoyance, inconvenience, or anxiety.

Explanatory notes

- 'Public electronic communications network' covers current and future developments in communication technologies (eg telephone, computers (internet), satellites, mobile terrestrial networks, emails, text messages, fax, and radio).
- Subsections (1) and (2) do not apply to anything done in the course of providing a programme service within the meaning of the Broadcasting Act 1990. However, it is unclear how this provision will apply as an exemption or not to online broadcasting by internet bloggers or on YouTube etc.
- These offences do not apply to anything done in the course of providing a broadcasting service, such as a television programme, public teletext, digital television, radio programme, or sound provided by the BBC.
- Sections 128 to 130 empower OFCOM (Office of Communications) to enforce this Act to stop a person persistently misusing a public electronic communications network or services.

Related cases

Scottow v CPS [2020] EWHC 3421 (Admin) There was no offence of posting annoying tweets. To be regarded as a 'persistent' use of a public electronic communications network for the purposes of s 127(2)(c), a series of communications had to have an element of frequency and a connecting theme or factor. Examples would be repeated instances of prank calls, silent calls, heavy breathing, and other common forms of nuisance phone call containing no meaningful content.

DPP v Smith (Kingsley Anthony) [2017] EWHC 3193 (Admin) It was held in this case that for s 127(1)(a) when deciding whether a particular message is *grossly offensive*, a court needs to be careful not to criminalise speech that, however contemptible, is no more than offensive. It has to be asked whether taking account of the context and all relevant circumstances by applying the standards of a reasonable person in a multiracial and multifaith society that a message was grossly offensive to those whom it related and whether it would have created a sense of apprehension or fear in a person of reasonable fortitude who received or read it.

Chambers v DPP [2012] EWHC 2157 (Admin) It was confirmed that Twitter was a public electronic communications network and a message sent, intended to be a joke, even if it was a bad joke made in bad taste, lacked the mens rea required to create fear, and in this case it did not amount to an offence under s 127.

DPP v Collins [2006] UKHL 40 The test is whether a message is liable to cause gross offence to those to whom it relates. Further, for an offence to be made out under s 127(a) of the 2003 Act the accused must intend for the words to be grossly offensive to those to whom they relate or must be aware that they may be taken as such.

R v Ireland [1998] AC 147, HL and **R v Burstow [1997] 4 All ER 225, HL** Silent telephone calls which caused psychiatric injury to a victim were capable of being an AOABH (see **2.1**) or grievous bodily harm (see **2.3**) if they caused the victim to fear imminent violence on themselves. Expert evidence confirmed that the victims had suffered palpitations, breathing difficulties, cold sweats, anxiety, sleeplessness, dizziness, and stress.

R v Johnson [1996] 2 Cr App R 434 Making numerous obscene/offensive telephone calls can amount to a public nuisance (see **7.13.3**).

Practical considerations

- The CPS suggests that a relevant communication should be more than offensive, shocking, disturbing, satirical, or rude.
- These offences do not apply to a private/internal network. In these instances, consider s 1 of the Malicious Communications Act 1988 (see **7.12.1**).
- Under subsection (1), there is no requirement to show any specific purpose or intent by the defendant.
- Consider s 1 of the Malicious Communications Act 1988 (see **7.12.1**) if the offence involves intent to cause the victim distress or anxiety.
- Also consider an offence under the Protection from Harassment Act 1997 (see **7.11**).
- If threats or information relate to bombs, noxious substances, or the placing of dangerous articles, consider offences under the Antiterrorism, Crime and Security Act 2001 and the Criminal Law Act 1977 (see **11.4.2**).
- Section 125 creates the offence of dishonestly obtaining an electronic communications service with intent to avoid the applicable payment.
- Possession or control of apparatus which may be used dishonestly to obtain an electronic communications service, or in connection with obtaining such a service, is also an offence under s 126.
- If communication is with a child for the purposes of sexual gratification, consider the offence under s 15A of the Sexual Offences Act 2003 (see **6.5.5**).

- Communications that constitute threats to another person may also amount to other more serious offences. Consider threats to kill under s 16 of the Offences Against the Person Act 1861 (see **2.5**); intimidation of witnesses and jurors under s 51 of the Criminal Justice and Public Order Act 1994 (see **4.8.1**); and threats of violence under ss 4 and 4A of the Protection from Harassment Act 1997 (see **7.11.2**).
- A PND may be issued by a police officer, CSO, or other accredited person for an offence under s 127(2) (see **7.1.1**).
- Prosecutions, if in the public interest, should only proceed with cases under s 1 of the Malicious Communications Act 1988 (see **7.11.1**) or under this section where there is sufficient evidence that the communication is more than offensive, shocking, disturbing, satirical, iconoclastic, or rude; or the expression of unpopular or unfashionable opinion about serious or trivial matters, or banter or humour (see also *Smith v ADVFN* [2008] EWHC 1797 (QBD)).

PND

Summary

Normally 6 months but no more than 3 years after the offence

6 months' imprisonment and/or a fine

7.12.3 Send false communication with intent to cause harm

Section 179 of the Online Safety Act 2023 creates a false communications offence.

Offences

A person commits an offence if—
(a) the person sends a message (see section 182),
(b) the message conveys information that the person knows to be false,
(c) at the time of sending it, the person intended the message, or the information in it, to cause non-trivial psychological or physical harm to a likely audience, and
(d) the person has no reasonable excuse for sending the message.

Online Safety Act 2023, s 179(1)

PNLD H101561

Points to prove

- ✓ without reasonable excuse
- ✓ sent a message conveying information known to be false
- ✓ intending, at the time of sending it, the message, or the information in it, to cause non-trivial psychological or physical harm to a likely audience

Meanings

Person

Includes (in addition to an individual and a body of persons corporate or unincorporate) any organisation or association of persons.

Likely audience

For the purposes of this offence, an individual is a 'likely audience' of a message if, at the time the message is sent, it is reasonably foreseeable that the individual would encounter the message, or in the online context, would encounter a subsequent message forwarding or sharing the content of the message.

Sends a message

A person sends a message if the person sends, transmits, or publishes a communication (including an oral communication) by electronic means or sends, or gives to an individual, a letter or a thing of any other description, and references to a message are to be read accordingly (s 182(2)). A person also sends a message if the person causes a communication (including an oral communication) to be sent, transmitted, or published by electronic means or causes a letter or a thing of any other description to be sent or given to an individual (s 182(3)).

Sending

Includes 'giving'.

Explanatory notes

- Section 179(3) states that in a case where several or many individuals are a likely audience, it is not necessary for the purposes of subsection (1)(c) that the person intended to cause harm to any one of them in particular (or to all of them).
- The prosecution must prove that the sender lacked a reasonable excuse for sending the message (s 179(1)(d)).
- It does not matter whether the content of a message is created by the person who sends it (so, for example, in the online context, an offence may be committed by a person who forwards another person's direct message or shares another person's post) (see s 182(6)).
- In the application of ss 179 to 181 to the sending by electronic means of a message consisting of or including a hyperlink to other

content, references to the message are to be read as including references to content accessed directly via the hyperlink.
- Section 185 of the Online Safety Act 2023 provides extraterritorial application and jurisdiction for certain offences under Part 10 of the Act, including that under s 179(1).
- Section 182(9) provides that in the online context the date on which a person commits an offence in relation to a message is the date on which the message is first sent by the person.
- See s 180 for exemptions from the offence under this section, for example a recognised news publisher cannot commit an offence under s 179.
- A provider of an internet service by means of which a communication is sent, transmitted, or published is not to be regarded as a person who sends a message (see s 182(4)).

Summary — Complex (see s 179(7) and (8))

Maximum 6 months' imprisonment and/or a fine

7.12.4 Send communication threatening death or serious harm

Section 181 of the Online Safety Act 2023 creates an offence of threatening communications, committed where a person sends a message conveying a threat of death, serious injury, rape, assault by penetration, or serious financial loss, and intends that (or is reckless as to whether) someone encountering the message will fear the threat will be carried out.

Offences

A person commits an offence if—
(a) the person sends a message (see section 182),
(b) the message conveys a threat of death or serious harm, and
(c) at the time of sending it, the person—
  (i) intended an individual encountering the message to fear that the threat would be carried out (whether or not by the person sending the message), or
  (ii) was reckless as to whether an individual encountering the message would fear that the threat would be carried out (whether or not by the person sending the message).

Online Safety Act 2023, s 181(1)

PNLD H101562

Points to prove

- ✓ sent a message that conveyed
- ✓ a threat of death OR serious harm
- ✓ intending, or being reckless as to whether, an individual encountering the message would fear that the threat would be carried out

Meanings

Serious harm

Serious injury amounting to grievous bodily harm within the meaning of the Offences against the Person Act 1861 (see **2.3.1**), rape (see **6.1**), assault by penetration within the meaning of s 2 of the Sexual Offences Act 2003 (see **6.1.1**), or serious financial loss.

Encounter

In relation to a message, means read, view, hear, or otherwise experience the message.

Explanatory notes

- In proceedings for an offence under this section relating to a threat of serious financial loss, it is a defence for the person to show that the threat was used to reinforce a reasonable demand and the person reasonably believed that the use of the threat was a proper means of reinforcing the demand (see s 181(3)).
- For further notes, see **7.12.3**.
- Section 185 of the Act provides extraterritorial application and jurisdiction for certain offences under Part 10 of the Act, including that under s 181(1).

Either way None

Summary: maximum 6/12 months' imprisonment and/or a fine

Indictment: maximum 5 years' imprisonment and/or a fine

7.12.5 **Sending or showing flashing images electronically**

Section 183 of the Online Safety Act 2023 creates offences relating to the sending or showing of flashing images electronically to people with epilepsy, intending to cause them harm.

7.12.5 Sending or showing flashing images electronically

Offences

A person (A) commits an offence if—

(a) A sends a communication by electronic means which consists of or includes flashing images (see subsection (13)),
(b) either condition 1 or condition 2 is met, and
(c) A has no reasonable excuse for sending the communication.

Online Safety Act 2023, s 183(1)

A person (A) commits an offence if—

(a) A shows an individual (B) flashing images by means of an electronic communications device,
(b) when showing the images—
 (i) A knows that B is an individual with epilepsy, or
 (ii) A suspects that B is an individual with epilepsy,
(c) when showing the images, A intends that B will suffer harm as a result of viewing them, and
(d) A has no reasonable excuse for showing the images.

Online Safety Act 2023, s 183(8)

PNLD **H101563, H101564, H101565**

Points to prove

s 183(1) and (2) condition 1 offence

✓ without reasonable excuse
✓ sent a communication by electronic means
✓ consisting of or including flashing images
✓ at the time it was sent, it was reasonably foreseeable that an individual with epilepsy would be among individuals who would view it
✓ intending that such an individual would suffer harm as a result of viewing the flashing images

s 183(1) and (3) condition 2 offence

✓ without reasonable excuse
✓ sent a communication by electronic means
✓ consisting of or including flashing images
✓ believing that a named individual would or might view the communication
✓ knowing or suspecting them to be an individual with epilepsy
✓ intending that that individual would suffer harm as a result of viewing the flashing images

s 183(8) offence

✓ without reasonable excuse
✓ showed
✓ to a named individual
✓ flashing images

- ✓ by means of an electronic communications device
- ✓ knowing/suspecting that individual was an individual with epilepsy
- ✓ intending that that individual would suffer harm as a result of viewing the flashing images

Meanings

Person (see **7.12.2**)

Electronic communications device

Equipment or a device that is capable of transmitting images by electronic means.

Flashing images

Images which carry a risk that an individual with photosensitive epilepsy who viewed them would suffer a seizure as a result.

Harm

Means a seizure, or alarm or distress.

Individual with epilepsy

Includes, but is not limited to, an individual with photosensitive epilepsy.

Send

Includes transmit and publish (and related expressions are to be read accordingly).

Content

Anything communicated by means of an internet service, whether publicly or privately, including written material or messages, oral communications, photographs, videos, visual images, music, and data of any description.

Explanatory notes

- For s 183(1), condition 1 is that at the time the communication is sent, it was reasonably foreseeable that an individual with epilepsy would be among the individuals who would view it, and A sends the communication with the intention that such an individual will suffer harm.
- Condition 2 is that, when sending the communication, A believes that an individual whom the sender knows or suspects to be an individual with epilepsy will, or might, view it and intends that individual to suffer harm as a result of viewing the flashing images.
- 'Viewing a communication' in the context of the offence also includes where a communication is forwarded or shared further.

As such, the offence within s 183(1) may be committed where a person forwards or shares a communication (as well as by the person sending it) (s 183(4)).

- Section 183(8) creates an offence of showing another person flashing images by means of an electronic communications device. The offence is committed if a person shows an individual flashing images, for example on a mobile phone screen, and when showing the images knows or suspects that the individual concerned is an individual with epilepsy, intends that that individual will suffer harm as a result of viewing them, and if the person has no reasonable excuse for showing the images.
- It does not matter whether images may be viewed immediately or only after some action, such as pressing play, is performed (s 183(11)).
- Section 180 provides exemptions to the offences in the same way as they apply to s 179 (see **7.12.3**).
- In relation to offences under s 183(1), a provider of an internet service by means of which a communication is sent is not to be regarded as a person who sends a communication (s 183(6)).
- Further to s 183(1), a communication consisting of or including a hyperlink to other content, references to the communication are to be read as including references to content accessed directly via the hyperlink.
- An offence under subsection (1) or (8) cannot be committed by a health care professional acting in that capacity.
- It does not matter for the purposes of this section whether flashing images may be viewed at once (eg a GIF that plays automatically) or only after some action is performed (eg pressing play).
- Any references to sending a communication include references to causing a communication to be sent; and references to showing flashing images include references to causing flashing images to be shown.

Either way | None

Summary: maximum 6/12 months' imprisonment and/or a fine

Indictment: maximum 5 years' imprisonment and/or a fine

7.12.6 Offence of encouraging or assisting serious self-harm

Section 184 of the Online Safety Act 2023 provides for the offence of encouraging or assisting serious self-harm.

Offences

A person (D) commits an offence if—
(a) D does a relevant act capable of encouraging or assisting the serious self-harm of another person, and
(b) D's act was intended to encourage or assist the serious self-harm of another person.

Online Safety Act 2023, s 184(1)

PNLD H101568

Points to prove

✓ communicated in person with a person OR
✓ sent/transmitted/published a communication by electronic means OR
✓ showed to a person a communication that had been sent/transmitted/published by electronic means OR
✓ published material other than by electronic means OR
✓ sent/gave/showed/made available to a person material published other than by electronic means OR
✓ sent/gave/showed/made available to a person a form of correspondence OR
✓ sent/gave/made available to a person an item on which data was stored electronically
✓ in such a way that was capable of encouraging/assisting the serious self harm of another person
✓ with the intention that it would do so

Meaning of serious self-harm

Self-harm amounting to grievous bodily harm within the meaning of the Offences Against the Person Act 1861 includes successive acts of self-harm which cumulatively reach that threshold (see **2.3.1**).

Explanatory notes

- D does a relevant act if D:
  - (a) communicates in person;
  - (b) sends, transmits, or publishes a communication by electronic means;
  - (c) shows a person such a communication;
  - (d) publishes material by any means other than electronic means;
  - (e) sends, gives, shows, or makes available to a person:
    - (i) material published as mentioned in para (d); or
    - (ii) any form of correspondence; or

(f) sends, gives, or makes available to a person an item on which data is stored electronically (see s 184(2)).

- A person committing the offence need not know, or even be able to identify, the person or persons who receive the communication. So, a person who intends that a recipient or recipients of their communication will seriously harm themselves is guilty of an offence, even though they may never know the identity of those who receive the communication (see s 184(4)).
- D may commit an offence under this section whether or not serious self-harm occurs (see s 184(5)).
- If a person (D1) arranges for a person (D2) to do an act that is capable of encouraging or assisting the serious self-harm of another person and D2 does that act, D1 is to be treated as also having done it (see s 184(6)).
- In the application of subsection (1) to an act by D involving an electronic communication or a publication in physical form, it does not matter whether the content of the communication or publication is created by D (so, for example, in the online context, the offence under this section may be committed by forwarding another person's direct message or sharing another person's post) (see s 184(7)).
- In the application of subsection (1) to the sending, transmission, or publication by electronic means of a communication consisting of or including a hyperlink to other content, the reference in subsection (2)(b) to the communication is to be read as including a reference to content accessed directly via the hyperlink (see s 184(8)).
- Where a person sends, gives, or makes available an item on which data is stored electronically (such as a USB stick), they may commit the offence where the item contains material intended to encourage or assist self-harm (see ss 184(2)(f) and 184(9)).
- A means of which a communication is sent, transmitted, or published is not to be regarded as a person who sends, transmits, or publishes it (see s 184(10)).
- Any reference in this section to doing an act that is capable of encouraging the serious self-harm of another person includes a reference to doing so by threatening another person or otherwise putting pressure on another person to seriously self-harm. 'Seriously self-harm' is to be interpreted consistently with subsection (3) (see s 184(11)).
- Any reference to an act in this section, except in subsection (3), includes a reference to a course of conduct, and references to doing an act are to be read accordingly (see s 184(12)).
- In subsection (3), 'act' includes omission (see s 184(13)).

Either way | None

Summary: maximum 6/12 months' imprisonment and/or a fine.

Indictment: maximum 5 years' imprisonment and/or a fine.

7.12.7 Gives/causes to be given false alarm of fire

Section 49 of the Fire and Rescue Services Act 2004 creates the offences of giving a false alarm and causing to be given a false alarm of fire.

Offences

A person commits an offence if he knowingly gives or causes to be given a false alarm of fire to a person acting on behalf of a fire and rescue authority.

Fire and Rescue Services Act 2004, s 49(1)

PNLD H4695, H4696

Points to prove

- ✓ knowingly
- ✓ gave/caused to be given
- ✓ a false alarm of fire
- ✓ to a person acting on behalf of a fire and rescue authority

Meanings

Knowingly (see **9.1.3**)

Fire and rescue authority

A fire and rescue authority for the county/county borough/area or the London Fire Commissioner.

Practical considerations

- The prosecutor may apply to the court for an **injunction** (see **7.13.1**).
- PND can be issued by a police officer/CSO (see **7.1.1**).

PND

Summary | 6 months

51 weeks' imprisonment and/or a fine not exceeding level four on the standard scale.

7.12.7 Gives/causes to be given false alarm of fire

Links to alternative subjects and offences

2.5 Threats to Kill 97
4.6 Threats to Destroy or Damage Property 203
6.7.2 Sending etc photograph or film of genitals 323
6.7.3 Sharing or threatening to share intimate photograph or film 325
11.4.1 Wasting police time 810

7.13 Anti-Social Behaviour

Anti-social behaviour is dealt with in this chapter under the Anti-social Behaviour, Crime and Policing Act 2014, the Criminal Justice and Immigration Act 2008, and the Police Reform Act 2002.

7.13.1 Injunctions—application/breach

Section 1 of the Anti-social Behaviour, Crime and Policing Act 2014 allows a court to grant an injunction against a person involved in anti-social behaviour for the purpose of preventing further behaviour and, if there is a risk of violence, s 4 allows a court to attach a power of arrest to the injunction.

Power to grant injunctions

(1) A court may grant an injunction under this section against a person aged 10 or over ('the respondent') if two conditions are met.
(2) The first condition is that the court is satisfied, on the balance of probabilities, that the respondent has engaged or threatens to engage in antis-social behaviour.
(3) The second condition is that the court considers it just and convenient to grant the injunction for the purpose of preventing the respondent from engaging in anti-social behaviour.
(4) An injunction under this section may for the purpose of preventing the respondent from engaging in anti-social behaviour—
  (a) prohibit the respondent from doing anything described in the injunction;
  (b) require the respondent to do anything described in the injunction.

Anti-social Behaviour, Crime and Policing Act 2014, s 1

Meanings

Anti-social behaviour

Means conduct:

- that has caused, or is likely to cause, harassment, alarm, or distress to any person;
- capable of causing nuisance or annoyance to a person in relation to that person's occupation of residential premises; or
- capable of causing **housing-related** nuisance or annoyance to any person.

Housing-related

Means directly or indirectly relating to the housing management functions of a housing provider or a local authority.

Explanatory notes

- This civil injunction could be used to deal with anti-social nuisance or annoyance across a wide range of behaviours. This can include vandalism, public drunkenness, drug issues, aggressive begging, irresponsible dog owners, noisy or abusive behaviour, or bullying against neighbours or others.
- If the county court or High Court (youth court if under 18) issues an injunction, this will prohibit the person from doing and require them to do what is described in the injunction, with the intention of addressing their anti-social behaviour.
- The injunction can provide protection for victims and communities and set a clear standard of behaviour in order to prevent escalation.
- If an injunction includes a requirement, it must specify the person responsible for ensuring compliance with the requirement. The person may be an individual or an organisation.
- Before including a requirement, the court must receive evidence about its suitability and enforceability. If two or more requirements are included, the court must consider their compatibility with each other.
- A respondent subject to a requirement must keep in touch with the person responsible for ensuring compliance regarding any instructions given by that person, and notify that person of any change of address. These obligations are requirements of the injunction.
- These are civil proceedings but the standard of proof is to the criminal standard.
- An injunction may be granted only on the application of: a local authority; a housing provider; the chief officer of police for a police area; the chief constable of the BTP; Transport for London; the Environment Agency; the Natural Resources Body for Wales; the Secretary of State; a Special Health Authority; or the Welsh Ministers.
- The court may vary or discharge an injunction under the application of the person who applied for the injunction, or the respondent.
- Under s 4, a court granting an injunction may attach a power of arrest to a prohibition or **requirement** of the injunction if the court thinks that:
  - ✦ the respondent has engaged or threatened to engage in violence against other persons; or
  - ✦ there is a significant risk of **harm** to other persons from the respondent.

- **Harm** includes serious ill-treatment or abuse, whether physical or not.

Arrest without warrant—breach of injunction

> Where a power of arrest is attached to a provision of an injunction under section 1, a constable may arrest the respondent without warrant if he or she has reasonable cause to suspect that the respondent is in breach of the provision.
>
> Anti-social Behaviour, Crime and Policing Act 2014, s 9(1)

Practical considerations

- A person arrested under s 9(1) must, within twenty-four hours from the time of the arrest, be brought before the appropriate judge of the High Court or county court. Christmas Day, Good Friday, and any Sunday are to be disregarded when calculating the twenty-four hours.
- Examples of injunction requirements could be attending dog training or alcohol awareness classes or mediation sessions with neighbours or victims.
- Prohibitions or requirements in the injunction can be for a fixed or indefinite period but must have a specified time limit to a maximum of twelve months if the respondent is under 18.
- Although breach of an injunction is not a criminal offence, the breach procedure is to the criminal standard of proof. Breach is treated as contempt of court and sanctions could be up to two years' imprisonment and/or an unlimited fine or, if under 18, supervision, detention, curfew, or activity requirement.
- An injunction may have the effect of excluding the respondent from the place where they normally live ('the premises') only if:
  - ✦ the respondent is aged 18 or over;
  - ✦ the injunction is granted on the application of a local authority, the chief officer of police for the area where the premises are located, or, if the premises are owned or managed by a housing provider, that housing provider; and
  - ✦ the court thinks that the respondent has used or threatened to use violence against other persons or there is a significant risk of harm to other persons from the respondent.
- Although s 1 and s 1B of the Crime and Disorder Act 1998 are no longer in force, an Anti-Social Behaviour Order issued whilst these sections were in force will be effective for the length of time stipulated in the order itself.
- Although s 3 and s 4 of the Violent Crime Reduction Act 2006 are no longer in force, a Drink Banning Order issued whilst these sections were in force will be effective for the length of time stipulated in the order itself.

7.13.2 Act in anti-social manner—fail to give name/address

Section 50 of the Police Reform Act 2002 empowers a police officer (in uniform) to request the name and address of a person behaving in an anti-social manner and creates an offence of failing to comply with that request.

Offences

Any person who—
(a) fails to give his name and address when required to do so under subsection (1), or
(b) gives a false or inaccurate name or address in response to a requirement under that subsection,
is guilty of an offence.

Police Reform Act 2002, s 50(2)

PNLD H18885

Points to prove

- ✓ being a person whom a constable had reason to believe
- ✓ had been/was acting in anti-social manner
- ✓ failed or gave false/inaccurate details
- ✓ when required by the constable to provide their name and address

Meanings

Required to do so under subsection (1)

If a constable in uniform has reason to believe that a person has been acting, or is acting, in an **anti-social manner**, they may require that person to give their name and address to the constable.

Anti-social manner (behaviour) (see **7.13.1**)

Explanatory note

- A person who fails to give their name and address **or** provides a false or inaccurate name or address will commit an offence.

Related case

Overd v CC of Avon and Somerset [2021] EWHC 3100 (QB) It was held that an arrest on suspicion of an offence under s 50 was a finding of fact that was plainly open to the arresting officer on the evidence. There was no authority to the effect that unless a person was warned that a failure to give their name would provide reasonable grounds to suspect them of committing an offence under s 50, and might result in their arrest, their arrest would be unlawful. It would be good practice to give such a warning where practical but that was not the same thing.

Summary

6 months

Level 3 fine

7.13.3 Intentionally or recklessly causing a public nuisance

'Public nuisance' is no longer an offence at common law having been abolished and replaced with a new statutory offence under s 78 of the Police, Crime, Sentencing and Courts Act 2022.

Offences

78(1) A person is guilty of this offence if
- (a) the person—
  - (i) does an act, or
  - (ii) omits to do an act that they are required to do by any enactment or rule of law,
- (b) the person's act or omission—
  - (i) creates a risk of, or causes, serious harm to the public or a section of the public, or
  - (ii) obstructs the public or a section of the public in the exercise or enjoyment of a right that may be exercised or enjoyed by the public at large, and
- (c) the person intends that their act or omission will have a consequence mentioned in paragraph (b) or is reckless as to whether it will have such a consequence.

(2) In subsection (1)(b)(i) 'serious harm' means—
- (a) death, personal injury or disease,
- (b) loss of, or damage to, property, or
- (c) serious distress, serious annoyance, serious inconvenience or serious loss of amenity.

Police, Crime, Sentencing and Courts Act 2022, s 78

PNLD H100671

7.13.3 Intentionally or recklessly causing a public nuisance

Points to prove

✓ did an act OR omitted to do an act required by any enactment/rule of law
✓ creating a risk of/causing serious harm to the public or a section of the public OR
✓ obstructing the public/section of the public in the exercise/enjoyment of a right
✓ that may be exercised/enjoyed by the public at large
✓ intending/being reckless that the act or omission
✓ had the consequence of serious harm

Explanatory notes

- This offence requires an act, or omission of an act required by law, which creates a risk of serious harm to the public or a section of the public or obstructs them from the exercise or enjoyment of a right they may enjoy.
- The person must intend that the act or omission in question will have such a consequence or have been reckless as to whether it would.
- The common law offence will apply to any act or omission of an act which occurred before 28 June 2022.
- Section 78(8) clarifies that only the liability for a common law offence of nuisance is affected by s 78. The tort of public nuisance (civil remedy) and ability to take action under any enactment against a person for an act or omission within s 78(1) are not abolished.
- For Public Order Act 2023 stop and search powers relevant for this offence, see **7.17.9**.

Related case

R v Shorrock [1993] 3 All ER 917, CA The defendant leased a field at their farm for a weekend which was used for an acid house party/rave while they were away and the defendant denied any knowledge that a public nuisance would be committed on the land. Upholding the conviction, it was held that it was not necessary to prove that the defendant had actual knowledge of the nuisance, but merely that they were responsible for a nuisance which they knew or ought to have known (in the sense that the knowledge was available to them) would be the consequences of activities on the land.

Practical considerations

- For extreme acts of unpleasantness or lewdness, consider offences under the Sexual Offences Act 2003 (see **Chapter 6**) or the common law offence of outraging public decency (see **6.7.4**).
- Conspiracy to commit this offence is contrary to s 1(1) of the Criminal Law Act 1977.

E&S

Either way | None

Summary: 6/12 months' imprisonment and/or a fine

Indictment: 10 years' imprisonment and/or a fine

7.13.4 Closure of premises (nuisance/disorder)

Section 76 of the Anti-social Behaviour, Crime and Policing Act 2014 provides a power to issue closure notices in respect of premises associated with nuisance or disorder. Section 86 creates closure notice/order offences.

Offences

(1) A person who without reasonable excuse remains on or enters premises in contravention of a closure notice (including a notice continued in force under section 81) commits an offence.

(2) A person who without reasonable excuse remains on or enters premises in contravention of a closure order commits an offence.

(3) A person who without reasonable excuse obstructs a person acting under section 79 or 85(1) commits an offence.

Anti-social Behaviour, Crime and Policing Act 2014, s 86

PNLD H11457, H11458, H11459

Points to prove

Closure notice s 86(1)

✓ without reasonable excuse
✓ remained on/entered premises
✓ in contravention of a closure notice or s 81 continue notice

Closure order s 86(2)

✓ without reasonable excuse
✓ remained on/entered premises
✓ in contravention of a closure order

Obstruction s 86(3)

✓ without reasonable excuse
✓ obstructed person
✓ acting under
✓ s 79 (service notice)/s 85(1) (order enforcement)

7.13.4 Closure of premises (nuisance/disorder)

Meanings

Premises

Includes any:
- land or other place (whether closed or not);
- outbuildings that are, or are used as, part of premises.

Closure notice (power to issue)

(1) A police officer of at least the rank of inspector, or the **local authority**, may issue a closure notice if satisfied on reasonable grounds—
 (a) that the use of particular premises has resulted, or (if the notice is not issued) is likely soon to result, in nuisance to members of the public, or
 (b) that there has been, or (if the notice is not issued) is likely soon to be, disorder near those premises associated with the use of those premises,

 and that the notice is necessary to prevent the nuisance or disorder from continuing, recurring or occurring.

(2) A closure notice is a notice prohibiting access to the premises for a period specified in the notice. For the **maximum period**, see section 77.

(3) A closure notice may prohibit access—
 (a) by all persons except those specified, or by all persons except those of a specified description;
 (b) at all times, or at all times except those specified;
 (c) in all circumstances, or in all circumstances except those specified.

(4) A closure notice may not prohibit access by—
 (a) people who habitually live on the premises, or
 (b) the owner of the premises,

 and accordingly, they must be specified under subsection (3)(a).

(5) A closure notice must—
 (a) identify the premises;
 (b) explain the effect of the notice;
 (c) state that failure to comply with the notice is an offence;
 (d) state that an application will be made under section 80 for a closure order;
 (e) specify when and where the application will be heard;
 (f) explain the effect of a closure order;
 (g) give information about the names of, and means of contacting, persons and organisations in the area that provide advice about housing and legal matters.

(6) A closure notice may be issued only if reasonable efforts have been made to inform—
 (a) people who live on the premises (whether habitually or not), and

(b) any person who has control of or responsibility for the premises or who has an interest in them,

that the notice is going to be issued.

(7) Before issuing a closure notice the police officer or local authority must ensure that any body or individual the officer or authority thinks appropriate has been consulted.

Anti-social Behaviour, Crime and Policing Act 2014, s 76

Local authority

In England: district council, county council (for area with no district council), London borough council, Common Council of the City of London, or the Council of the Isles of Scilly.

In Wales: a county council or a county borough council.

Maximum period (s 77—Duration of closure notices)

- The maximum period that may be specified in a closure notice is twenty-four hours. An extension notice may extend this for up to a further twenty-four hours, by a superintendent (issued by police) or CEO of the authority (issued by local authority).
- The maximum period of a notice issued by a superintendent or CEO is forty-eight hours. In calculating when the period of forty-eight hours ends, Christmas Day is to be disregarded.

The local authority CEO means the head of the paid service of the authority designated under s 4 of the Local Government and Housing Act 1989.

Notice continued in force under s 81

Where application has been made to a magistrates' court under s 80 for a closure order, if the court does not make a closure order it may instead order that the closure notice shall continue for a specified further period (maximum forty-eight hours) if satisfied that conditions for making a s 76 notice are met and that the continuation of the notice is necessary to prevent the nuisance or disorder from continuing, recurring, or occurring.

Similarly, the court may adjourn the application hearing for up to fourteen days to enable the occupier of the premises, the person in control of or responsible for the premises, or any other person with an interest in the premises to show why a closure order should not be made. If adjourned, the closure notice will continue in force until the end of the adjournment period.

Closure order (power of court to make order)

(1) Whenever a closure notice is issued an application must be made to a magistrates' court for a closure order (unless the notice has been cancelled under section 78).

(2) An application for a closure order must be made—
   (a) by a constable, if the closure notice was issued by a police officer;
   (b) by the authority that issued the closure notice, if the notice was issued by a local authority.

(3) The application must be heard by the magistrates' court not later than 48 hours after service of the closure notice.

(4) In calculating when the period of 48 hours ends, Christmas Day is to be disregarded.

(5) The court may make a closure order if it is satisfied—
   (a) that a person has engaged, or (if the order is not made) is likely to engage, in disorderly, offensive or criminal behaviour on the premises, or
   (b) that the use of the premises has resulted, or (if the order is not made) is likely to result, in serious nuisance to members of the public, or
   (c) that there has been, or (if the order is not made) is likely to be, disorder near those premises associated with the use of those premises,
   (d) and that the order is necessary to prevent the behaviour, nuisance, or disorder from continuing, recurring, or occurring.

(6) A closure order is an order prohibiting access to the premises for a period specified in the order. The period may not exceed 3 months.

(7) A closure order may prohibit access—
   (a) by all persons, or by all persons except those specified, or by all persons except those of a specified description;
   (b) at all times, or at all times except those specified;
   (c) in all circumstances, or in all circumstances except those specified.

(8) A closure order—
   (a) may be made in respect of the whole or any part of the premises;
   (b) may include provision about access to a part of the building or structure of which the premises form part.

(9) The court must notify the relevant licensing authority if it makes a closure order in relation to premises in respect of which a premises licence is in force.

Anti-social Behaviour, Crime and Policing Act 2014, s 80

Premises licence

Means a licence granted under Part 3 of the Licensing Act 2003, in respect of any premises, which authorises the premises to be used for one or more licensable activities.

Person acting under s 79 (service of notice)

(1) A closure notice, an extension notice a cancellation notice, or a variation notice must be served by—
  (a) a constable, in the case of a notice issued by a police officer;
  (b) a representative of the authority that issued the notice, in the case of a notice issued by a local authority.
(2) The constable or local authority representative must if possible—
  (a) fix a copy of the notice to at least one prominent place on the premises,
  (b) fix a copy of the notice to each normal means of access to the premises,
  (c) fix a copy of the notice to any outbuildings that appear to the constable or representative to be used with or as part of the premises,
  (d) give a copy of the notice to at least one person who appears to the constable or representative to have control of or responsibility for the premises, and
  (e) give a copy of the notice to the people who live on the premises and to any person who does not live there but was informed (under section 76(6)) that the notice was going to be issued.
(3) If the constable or **local authority representative** reasonably believes, at the time of serving the notice, that there are persons occupying another part of the building or other structure in which the premises are situated whose access to that part will be impeded if a closure order is made under section 80, the constable or representative must also if possible serve the notice on those persons.
(4) The constable or local authority representative may enter any premises, using reasonable force if necessary, for the purposes of complying with subsection (2)(a).

Anti-social Behaviour, Crime and Policing Act 2014, s 79

Local authority representative

Means an employee of the authority, or a person, or employee of a person, acting on behalf of the authority.

Person acting under s 85(1) (enforcement of closure orders)

An authorised person may—
(a) enter premises in respect of which a closure order is in force;
(b) do anything necessary to secure the premises against entry.

Anti-social Behaviour, Crime and Policing Act 2014, s 85(1)

7.13.4 Closure of premises (nuisance/disorder)

Authorised person

In relation to a closure order made on the application of a constable or a local authority:

- a constable means a constable or a person authorised by the chief officer of police for the area in which the premises are situated;
- a local authority means a person authorised by that authority.

Explanatory notes

- The closure notice is a fast, flexible power that allows the police or council to protect victims and communities by quickly closing premises that are causing, or likely to cause, nuisance or disorder.
- A closure notice is issued by the police/council in the first instance, then if required a closure order can be applied for through the courts.
- The closure notice can close premises for up to forty-eight hours but cannot stop the owner or those who habitually live there accessing the premises; whereas an order can close the premises for up to six months and can restrict all access.
- Both the notice and order can cover any land or any other place, whether enclosed or not, including residential, business, non-business, and licensed premises.
- Under s 78, where a closure notice is in force and the police/authority decide to cancel the notice, they can issue a cancellation notice (all the premises) or variation notice (if part of the premises). The court should then be informed prior to the hearing for the closure order.

Defences

Having a reasonable excuse for remaining on or entering premises in contravention of a closure notice/order or obstructing a person under section 79 or section 85(1) (as the case may be).

Anti-social Behaviour, Crime and Policing Act 2014, s 86

Practical considerations

- Consultation is required as part of the closure notice process. This should include the victim, others who may be affected, community representatives, other organisations and bodies, the police or local council (if not the issuing body), or others using the premises. Consider those who use the premises to access other premises which are not subject to the closure notice.
- The method of consultation will depend on the situation and urgency. A record must be kept of those consulted if the case is challenged in court.
- Include in the closure notice the following information:
  - identify the premises;
  - explain the effect of the notice;
  - state that failure to comply with the notice is an offence;

- ✦ state that an application will be made for a closure order;
- ✦ specify when and where the application will be heard;
- ✦ explain the effect of the closure order; and
- ✦ contact details of providers giving advice about housing and legal matters.
- A criminal offence is committed when a person, without reasonable excuse:
  - ✦ remains on or enters premises in contravention of a closure notice/order;
  - ✦ obstructs a police officer or local council employee who is: serving a closure notice, cancellation notice, or variation notice; entering the premises; or securing the premises.
- A closure notice cannot be appealed. A closure order can be appealed to the Crown Court within twenty-one days from the date of the decision to which the appeal relates.
- Notices under ss 1 and 11A of the Anti-social Behaviour Act 2003; orders under ss 2, 11B, and 40 of the 2003 Act; and orders under ss 161 and 165(2)(b), (c), or (d) of the Licensing Act 2003 will continue to be effective for as long as the notice or order is in force.

Summary 6 months

s 86(2) or (5)—51 weeks' imprisonment and/or a fine

s 86(1), (3), or (4)—3 months' imprisonment and/or a fine

7.13.5 Causing nuisance/disturbance on NHS premises

Sections 119 and 120 of the Criminal Justice and Immigration Act 2008 create both the offence of causing a nuisance or disturbance to NHS staff on NHS premises and the power to remove a person suspected of committing or having committed the offence.

Offences

(1) A person commits an offence if—
  (a) the person causes, without reasonable excuse and while on NHS premises, a nuisance or disturbance to an NHS staff member who is working there or is otherwise there in connection with work,
  (b) the person refuses, without reasonable excuse, to leave the NHS premises when asked to do so by a constable or an NHS staff member, and
  (c) the person is not on the NHS premises for the purpose of obtaining medical advice, treatment or care for himself or herself.

Criminal Justice and Immigration Act 2008, s 119

7.13.5 Causing nuisance/disturbance on NHS premises

PNLD H9776

Power to remove

(1) If a constable reasonably suspects that a person is committing or has committed an offence under section 119, the constable may remove the person from the NHS premises concerned.

(2) If an authorised officer reasonably suspects that a person is committing or has committed an offence under section 119, the authorised officer may—
  (a) remove the person from the NHS premises concerned, or
  (b) authorise an appropriate NHS staff member to do so.

(3) Any person removing another person from NHS premises under this section may use reasonable force (if necessary).

(4) An authorised officer cannot remove a person under this section or authorise another person to do so if the authorised officer has reason to believe that—
  (a) the person to be removed requires medical advice, treatment or care for himself or herself, or
  (b) the removal of the person would endanger the person's physical or mental health.

Criminal Justice and Immigration Act 2008, s 120

Points to prove

- ✓ while on NHS premises
- ✓ other than for the purpose of obtaining medical advice or treatment/care for self
- ✓ caused without reasonable excuse while on those premises
- ✓ a nuisance OR
- ✓ a disturbance to an NHS staff member who is working there OR
- ✓ was otherwise there in connection with work
- ✓ refused without reasonable excuse to leave the premises
- ✓ when asked to do so by a constable/NHS staff member

Meanings

NHS premises

Means:

- any hospital vested in, or managed by, a **relevant NHS body**;
- any building or other structure, or **vehicle**, associated with the hospital and situated on **hospital grounds** (whether or not vested in, or managed by, a relevant NHS body); and
- the hospital grounds.

Relevant NHS body

Means:

- a National Health Service trust (see National Health Service Act 2006) all or most of whose hospitals, establishments, and facilities are situated in England;
- an NHS foundation trust (England).

Vehicle

Includes an air ambulance.

Hospital grounds

Means land in the vicinity of a hospital and associated with it.

NHS staff member

Means a person employed by a relevant English body or otherwise working for such a body (whether as or on behalf of a contractor, as a volunteer, or otherwise).

Authorised officer

Means any NHS staff member authorised by a relevant NHS body to exercise the powers which are conferred by this section on an authorised officer in respect of NHS premises.

Explanatory notes

- For the purposes of s 119, a person ceases to be on NHS premises for the purpose of obtaining medical advice, treatment, or care for themselves once the person has received the advice, treatment, or care, or if the person has been refused the advice, treatment, or care during the last eight hours.
- This offence addresses behaviour which disrupts NHS staff in the performance of their duties. There is no requirement that the delivery of health care is impeded.
- This offence is quite restricted as it does not apply to a person who is on the premises for the purpose of obtaining medical advice, treatment, or care, patients, and those attending for consultations, to collect medication or test results, or convalescing after treatment.

Practical considerations

- Although the offence/power relates to England and Wales, it is currently (May 2024) only in force for England.
- A nuisance or disturbance can include any form of non-physical behaviour which breaches the peace, such as verbal aggression or intimidating gestures towards NHS staff.
- A person will not commit the offence if they have a reasonable excuse. Behaviour consequent to the receipt of upsetting news or bereavement may, for example, constitute a reasonable excuse.

7.13.5 Causing nuisance/disturbance on NHS premises

- The nuisance or disturbance must be towards a NHS staff member rather than any other person. The NHS staff member must either be working at the premises or be there for some other purpose relating to their work, such as walking between buildings or taking a break.
- Where NHS bodies wish to have the option to exercise the power of removal without recourse to police, they will need to authorise a member of staff (known as the '**authorised officer**') to exercise the powers of removal. Any person exercising the power of removal may use reasonable force if necessary.

Summary

6 months

Level 3 fine

7.14 Vehicles Causing Annoyance

Section 59 of the Police Reform Act 2002 empowers police officers to seize motor vehicles used in a way as to cause alarm, distress, or annoyance to members of the public. The Police (Retention and Disposal of Motor Vehicles) Regulations 2002 govern how such seized vehicles should be retained and disposed of.

7.14.1 Vehicles used in a manner causing alarm, distress, or annoyance

Section 59 of the Police Reform Act 2002 concerns the use of vehicles in a manner that causes alarm, distress, or annoyance to members of the public.

Police powers

(1) Where a constable in uniform has reasonable grounds for believing that a motor vehicle is being used on any occasion in a manner which—
- (a) contravenes section 3 or 34 of the Road Traffic Act 1988 (careless and inconsiderate driving and prohibition of off-road driving), and
- (b) is causing, or is likely to cause, alarm, distress or annoyance to members of the public,

he shall have the powers set out in subsection (3).

(2) A constable in uniform shall also have the powers set out in subsection (3) where he has reasonable grounds for believing that a motor vehicle has been used on any occasion in a manner falling within subsection (1).

(3) Those powers are—
- (a) power, if the motor vehicle is moving, to order the person driving it to stop the vehicle;
- (b) power to seize and remove the motor vehicle;
- (c) power, for the purposes of exercising a power falling within paragraph (a) or (b), to enter any premises on which he has reasonable grounds for believing the motor vehicle to be;
- (d) power to use reasonable force, if necessary, in the exercise of any power conferred by any of paragraphs (a) to (c).

(4) A constable shall not seize a motor vehicle in the exercise of the powers conferred on him by this section unless—
- (a) he has warned the person appearing to him to be the person whose use falls within subsection (1) that he will seize it, if that use continues or is repeated; and

- (b) it appears to him that the use has continued or been repeated after the warning.

(5) Subsection (4) does not require a warning to be given by a constable on any occasion on which he would otherwise have the power to seize a motor vehicle under this section if—
- (a) the circumstances make it impracticable for him to give the warning;
- (b) the constable has already on that occasion given a warning under that subsection in respect of any use of that motor vehicle or of another motor vehicle by that person or any other person;
- (c) the constable has reasonable grounds for believing that such a warning has been given on that occasion otherwise than by him; or
- (d) the constable has reasonable grounds for believing that the person whose use of that motor vehicle on that occasion would justify the seizure is a person to whom a warning under that subsection has been given (whether or not by that constable or in respect of the same vehicle or the same or a similar use) on a previous occasion in the previous twelve months.

(6) Subsection (3)(c) does not authorise entry into a private dwelling house.

Police Reform Act 2002, s 59

Offence

A person who fails to comply with an order under subsection (3)(a) is guilty of an offence.

Police Reform Act 2002, s 59(6)

PNLD H4179

Points to prove

- ✓ failed to stop a moving vehicle on the order of a police constable in uniform
- ✓ they having reasonable grounds for believing
- ✓ that the vehicle was being used in a manner which contravened s 3/34 RTA 1988 AND
- ✓ was causing alarm, distress or annoyance to members of the public OR
- ✓ was likely to cause alarm, distress, or annoyance to members of the public

Meanings

Motor vehicle

Any mechanically propelled vehicle whether or not it is intended or adapted for use on roads (see **10.1.3**).

Driving (see **10.1.4**)

Private dwelling house

Does not include any garage or other structure occupied with the dwelling house or any land appurtenant to the dwelling house.

Explanatory notes

- An offence is committed if the driver of the moving motor vehicle fails to stop the vehicle when ordered to do so by a constable in uniform.
- A constable in uniform has the power to seize the vehicle but only after warning the person. If, after the warning has been given, the driving continues or is repeated then the vehicle can be seized.
- The requirement to give the warning does not apply where it is impracticable to do so or where it has been given on a previous occasion in the previous twelve months.
- The powers under this section cannot be exercised unless the driver is **both** using the vehicle anti-socially **and** is driving contrary to s 3 (careless and inconsiderate driving, see **10.6.1**) or s 34 (prohibition of off-road driving, see **7.14.1**) of the Road Traffic Act 1988.

Practical considerations

- The warning under s 59(4) **must** be given and ignored before the vehicle can be seized (see **7.14.2**). Therefore, it is important that the warning is both heard and understood.
- A warning given within the last twelve months does not have to have been given in respect of the same vehicle.
- Where a motor vehicle is seized, a seizure notice must be given to the person who appears to be the owner of the vehicle.
- A previous warning given on the same occasion need not have been given by the same constable nor does it have to have been given to the same person **or** in respect of the same vehicle. It could have been given to the same person using another vehicle or to a different person using the same vehicle. This covers situations where people use their vehicles anti-socially and swap them around.
- Consider the dispersal powers or powers under a PSPO (see **7.15**) or the public nuisance offence (see **7.13.3**).

Summary | 6 months

Level 3 fine

7.14.2 Retention/disposal of seized motor vehicle

The Police (Retention and Disposal of Motor Vehicles) Regulations 2002 relate to vehicles seized under s 59 of the Police Reform Act 2002 (see **7.14.1**).

> **Power**
>
> A relevant motor vehicle shall be passed into and remain in the custody of a constable or other person authorised under this regulation by the chief officer of the police force for the area in which the vehicle was seized ('the authority') until—
>
> (a) the authority permit it to be removed from their custody by a person appearing to them to be the owner of the vehicle; or
>
> (b) it has been disposed of under these Regulations.
>
> Police (Retention and Disposal of Motor Vehicles) Regulations 2002, reg 3(1)

Meanings

Relevant motor vehicle

As seized and removed under s 59(3)(b) of the Police Reform Act 2002 (see **7.14.1**).

The authority

Means a constable or other person authorised by the chief officer.

Explanatory notes

- A relevant motor vehicle will pass into and remain in the custody of a constable or other person authorised under this regulation by the chief officer of police in the area in which it was seized, until the authority permits a person appearing to them to be the owner of it to remove it or it has been disposed of under these regulations.
- While the vehicle is in the custody of the authority, it must take any necessary steps for its safe keeping.
- As soon as reasonably practicable after taking a vehicle into its custody, the authority must take reasonable steps to serve a seizure notice on the person who is, or appears to be, the owner, except where the vehicle has been released from its custody.
- If a person satisfies the authority that they are the owner of the vehicle and pays the charges accrued concerning its removal and retention, the authority shall permit them to remove it from custody.
- A person otherwise liable to pay charges concerning the removal and retention of the vehicle will not be liable if they were not the user when it was seized under s 59 and they did not know of its use

leading to the seizure, had not consented to such use, and could not, by reasonable steps, have prevented such use.

- Where it has not been possible to serve a seizure notice on the relevant person, or such a notice has been served and the vehicle has not been released from the authority's custody under these regulations, the authority may dispose of the vehicle in accordance with reg 7.
- The authority may not dispose of the vehicle under reg 7:
  - (a) during the period of fourteen days, starting with the date of seizure;
  - (b) if the fourteen-day period has expired, until after the deadline specified in the seizure notice;
  - (c) if (a) or (b) does not apply, during the period of seven working days starting with the date on which the vehicle is claimed.
- Where the authority disposes of the vehicle by way of selling, it must pay the net proceeds of the sale to any person who, within a year of the sale, satisfies it that they were the vehicle owner at the time of the sale.

Practical considerations

- A seizure notice may be served by personal delivery to the person addressed in it by leaving it at their usual or last known address or by registered delivery to their last known address.
- If the owner is a body corporate (eg a company), the notice must be served or sent to the company secretary or clerk at its registered office.
- The seizure notice must inform the owner that they have seven working days to collect the vehicle and that charges are payable from when the vehicle is claimed by the owner under reg 5.

Links to alternative subjects and offences

10.1 Meanings: Roads, Public Places, Vehicles, and Drives 651
10.2 Powers to Stop/Direct Vehicles and Pedestrians 658
10.4 Traffic Fixed Penalty Notices 666
10.6 Driving without Due Care and Attention 680
10.21 Obstruction of the Road/Footpath 769

7.15 Dispersal Powers/Public Spaces Protection Orders

7.15.1 Dispersal powers

Sections 34 and 35 of the Anti-social Behaviour, Crime and Policing Act 2014 provide, if the proper authority is in place, police powers to direct a person in a public place to leave the area for up to forty-eight hours and return persons under the age of 16 to their place of residence or a place of safety. Failure to comply is an offence under s 39.

Authorisation

(1) A police officer of at least the rank of inspector may authorise the use in a specified locality, during a specified period of not more than 48 hours, of the powers given by section 35.
(2) An officer may give such an authorisation only if satisfied on reasonable grounds that the use of those powers in the locality during that period may be necessary for the purpose of removing or reducing the likelihood of—
  (a) members of the public in the locality being harassed, alarmed or distressed, or
  (b) the occurrence in the locality of crime or disorder.
(3) In deciding whether to give such an authorisation an officer must have particular regard to the rights of freedom of expression and freedom of assembly set out in articles 10 and 11 of the Convention.
(4) An authorisation under this section—
  (a) must be in writing,
  (b) must be signed by the officer giving it, and
  (c) must specify the grounds on which it is given.

Anti-social Behaviour, Crime and Policing Act 2014, s 34

Directions to exclude person

(1) If the conditions in subsections (2) and (3) are met and an authorisation is in force under section 34, a constable in uniform may direct a person who is in a public place in the locality specified in the authorisation—
  (a) to leave the locality (or part of the locality), and
  (b) not to return to the locality (or part of the locality) for the period specified in the direction ('the exclusion period').
(2) The first condition is that the constable has reasonable grounds to suspect that the behaviour of the person in the locality has contributed or is likely to contribute to—
  (a) members of the public in the locality being harassed, alarmed or distressed, or
  (b) the occurrence in the locality of crime or disorder.

(3) The second condition is that the constable considers that giving a direction to the person is necessary for the purpose of removing or reducing the likelihood of the events mentioned in subsection (2)(a) or (b).
(4) The exclusion period may not exceed 48 hours. The period may expire after (as long as it begins during) the period specified in the authorisation under section 34.
(5) A direction under this section—
   (a) must be given in writing, unless that is not reasonably practicable;
   (b) must specify the area to which it relates;
   (c) may impose requirements as to the time by which the person must leave the area and the manner in which the person must do so (including the route).
(6) The constable must (unless it is not reasonably practicable) tell the person to whom the direction is given that failing without reasonable excuse to comply with the direction is an offence.
(7) If the constable reasonably believes that the person to whom the direction is given is under the age of 16, the constable may remove the person to a place where the person lives or a place of safety.
(8) Any constable may withdraw or vary a direction under this section; but a variation must not extend the duration of a direction beyond 48 hours from when it was first given.
(9) Notice of a withdrawal or variation of a direction—
   (a) must be given to the person to whom the direction was given, unless that is not reasonably practicable, and
   (b) if given, must be given in writing unless that is not reasonably practicable.

Anti-social Behaviour, Crime and Policing Act 2014, s 35

Directions to surrender property

(1) A constable who gives a person a direction under section 35 may also direct the person to surrender to the constable any item in the person's possession or control that the constable reasonably believes has been used or is likely to be used in behaviour that harasses, alarms or distresses members of the public.
(2) A direction under this section must be given in writing, unless that is not reasonably practicable.
(3) A constable who gives a person a direction under this section must (unless it is not reasonably practicable)—
   (a) tell the person that failing without reasonable excuse to comply with the direction is an offence, and
   (b) give the person information in writing about when and how the person may recover the surrendered item.
(4) The surrendered item must not be returned to the person before the end of the exclusion period.
(5) If after the end of that period the person asks for the item to be returned, it must be returned (unless there is power to retain it under another enactment).

(6) But if it appears to a constable that the person is under the age of 16 and is not accompanied by a parent or other responsible adult, the item may be retained until the person is so accompanied.
(7) If the person has not asked for the return of the item before the end of the period of 28 days beginning with the day on which the direction was given, the item may be destroyed or otherwise disposed of.

Anti-social Behaviour, Crime and Policing Act 2014, s 37

Offences

(1) A person given a direction under section 35 who fails without reasonable excuse to comply with it commits an offence.
(3) A person given a direction under section 37 who fails without reasonable excuse to comply with it commits an offence.

Anti-social Behaviour, Crime and Policing Act 2014, s 39

PNLD **H11452, H11453**

Points to prove

✓ failed
✓ without reasonable excuse
✓ to comply with a direction given under s 35 or s 37

Meanings

Specified

Means specified in the authorisation.

Convention (see **Appendix 1**)

Public place

Means a place to which at the material time the public or a section of the public has access, on payment or otherwise, as of right or by virtue of express or implied permission.

Exclusion period (see **s 35(1)(b) 'Directions to exclude person'** above)

Explanatory notes

- If there is likely to be anti-social behaviour, crime, or disorder in an area and it may be necessary to use the dispersal power, an inspector can authorise officers to use the power for a period of up to forty-eight hours.

- If a person's behaviour is causing or likely to cause harassment, alarm, or distress, or crime or disorder in the public place specified in the authorisation, then under s 35 a police officer can issue a direction for that person to leave the area.
- A CSO or CSV has a power to require the names and addresses of persons believed to have committed the s 39 offence. Failing to provide name and address is an offence and the CSO or CSV can detain a person for 30 minutes pending the arrival of a constable (see **11.1.3** and **11.1.7**).
- A direction can be issued to anyone over the age of 10, and if they are under 16 they can be taken home or to a place of safety.
- The direction must be given in writing, unless impracticable to do so. A written notice must specify the relevant area, when they must leave the area, and the route they must take. Any item possessed/ under the control of that person can be confiscated under s 37. The person must also be told that failure to comply with the direction (excluded from area and/or surrender of such item) without reasonable excuse is an offence.
- The information provided in the direction should be as clear as possible, ensuring that the person has understood it. If the direction is given verbally, a written record of it must be kept in order to enforce it in the event that it is breached and to be able to monitor use of the power. The written notice can be admitted in evidence in breach proceedings.
- Section 64A(1B)(ca) of PACE provides the power to photograph elsewhere than at a police station, person(s) who are given a direction by a constable under s 35.

Defences

Having a reasonable excuse for failing to comply with a direction given under s 35 (exclude from area) or s 37 (surrender property).

Anti-social Behaviour, Crime and Policing Act 2014, s 39

Practical considerations

- When authorising the dispersal power, the inspector (or above) must have regard to Arts 10 and 11 ECHR which provide for the rights to freedom of expression and freedom of assembly. Ensure that this power is used proportionately and reasonably so it is compatible with the Human Rights Act 1998 (see **Appendix 1**).
- When pre-authorising or authorising an area, the locality should be clearly defined as a specific geographic location, for example by listing the streets to which it applies or the streets which form the boundary of the area. The authorisation should not cover an area larger than necessary.
- This power can only be used in the specific location authorised, so if the behaviour occurs outside the authorised area, the inspector (or

above) will have to increase the area or the officer cannot issue the dispersal.

- The exclusion period may not exceed forty-eight hours and it may be that this period expires after (as long as it begins during) the period specified in the authorisation under s 34.
- The police officer can require the person given the direction to hand over items causing or likely to cause anti-social behaviour under s 37. These items could be alcohol, fireworks, offensive material, noisy equipment, eggs, or spray paint, for example.
- An officer can confiscate an item handed over to them but there is no power to seize the item, although the person will commit an offence under s 39 if they do not hand over the item when directed to do so.
- Surrendered items can be collected at the expiry of the direction period but if the item is not collected within twenty-eight days it can be destroyed or disposed of. A person under the age of 16 can be required to be accompanied by a parent/responsible adult to collect the item, thus ensuring that the adult is made aware of the incident to encourage parental responsibility.
- Section 36 places restrictions so that a direction cannot be given to someone engaged in lawful conduct: peaceful picketing (Trade Union and Labour Relations (Consolidation) Act 1992, s 220) or taking part in a public procession (Public Order Act 1986, s 11). In addition, the direction cannot restrict access to where a person lives or works or prevent them from attending court/tribunal or education/training or from receiving medical treatment during the direction timer period.
- A person who is given a direction and feels they have been incorrectly dealt with should speak to the duty inspector at the local police station. Details should be given to the person on the written notice.
- This dispersal power is a more flexible tool for officers to deal with anti-social behaviour, crime, and disorder. This is not only when they have occurred or are occurring but also when they are likely to occur and, in any locality, thus extending the capability of the police to prevent incidents before they happen.

Summary | 6 months

s 39(1) and (2)—3 months' imprisonment or a level 4 fine

s 39(3) and (4)—Level 2 fine

7.15.2 Public spaces protection orders (PSPOs)

Section 59 of the Anti-social Behaviour, Crime and Policing Act 2014 provides the local authority (LA) with power to make a public spaces protection order (PSPO) with regard to activities in a public place that have a detrimental effect on the quality of life of those in the locality. It is an offence to fail to comply with a PSPO; breach can also be dealt with by a fixed penalty notice (FPN) under s 68. Under s 59A of the Act, the LA may make an expedited order in relation to a public place in the vicinity of a school, NHS vaccine site, or test and trace site within the LA's area.

Power to make public spaces protection orders

(1) A local authority may make a public spaces protection order if satisfied on reasonable grounds that two conditions are met.
(2) The first condition is that—
  (a) activities carried on in a public place within the authority's area have had a detrimental effect on the quality of life of those in the locality, or
  (b) it is likely that activities will be carried on in a public place within that area and that they will have such an effect.
(3) The second condition is that the effect, or likely effect, of the activities—
  (a) is, or is likely to be, of a persistent or continuing nature,
  (b) is, or is likely to be, such as to make the activities unreasonable, and
  (c) justifies the restrictions imposed by the notice.
(4) A public spaces protection order is an order that identifies the public place referred to in subsection (2) ('the restricted area') and—
  (a) prohibits specified things being done in the restricted area,
  (b) requires specified things to be done by persons carrying on specified activities in that area, or
  (c) does both of those things.
(5) The only prohibitions or requirements that may be imposed are ones that are reasonable to impose in order—
  (a) to prevent the detrimental effect referred to in subsection (2) from continuing, occurring or recurring, or
  (b) to reduce that detrimental effect or to reduce the risk of its continuance, occurrence or recurrence.
(6) A prohibition or requirement may be framed—
  (a) so as to apply to all persons, or only to persons in specified categories, or to all persons except those in specified categories;
  (b) so as to apply at all times, or only at specified times, or at all times except those specified;
  (c) so as to apply in all circumstances, or only in specified circumstances, or in all circumstances except those specified.
(7) A public spaces protection order must—
  (a) identify the activities referred to in subsection (2);
  (b) explain the effect of section 63 (where it applies) and section 67;
  (c) specify the period for which the order has effect.
(8) A public spaces protection order must be published in accordance with regulations made by the Secretary of State.

Anti-social Behaviour, Crime and Policing Act 2014, s 59

7.15.2 **Public spaces protection orders (PSPOs)**

Offences

(1) It is an offence for a person without reasonable excuse—
  (a) to do anything that the person is prohibited from doing by a public spaces protection order or an expedited order or
  (b) to fail to comply with a requirement to which the person is subject under a public spaces protection order or an expedited order.

Anti-social Behaviour, Crime and Policing Act 2014, s 67

PNLD H100724

Points to prove

✓ without reasonable excuse
✓ failed to comply with a public spaces protection order

Meanings

Local authority (LA) (see **7.13.4**)

Public place (see **7.15.1**)

Section 63 (see **9.4**)

Section 67 (see '**Offences**' above)

Explanatory notes

- A PSPO can deal with a nuisance/problem in a public area which is detrimental to the local community and quality of life by imposing conditions on using the specified area which apply to everyone, intending that the law-abiding majority can use and enjoy public spaces safe from anti-social behaviour.
- LA are responsible for making the PSPO, although enforcement of the order will be broader, involving LA officials, police officers, designated groups, and officers accredited under the community safety accreditation scheme.
- Before a PSPO can be made, the LA must be satisfied, on reasonable grounds, that activities in a public space have had or will be likely to have a detrimental effect on the quality of life of those in the locality; it is likely to be persistent or continuing in nature, so making the activities unreasonable; and the order justifies the restrictions imposed.
- The meaning of a public space is wide and includes any place to which the public or any section of the public has access, on payment or otherwise, as of right or by virtue of express or implied permission, for example a shopping centre.
- Prior to making a PSPO, the LA must consult with the police, the landowner or occupier, together with appropriate community

representatives (eg residents association). It could include an individual or group of individuals, for instance regular users of a park, or specific activities such as busking or other type of street entertainment.

- An expedited PSPO can only be made if protest activity in the public place has had, or is likely to be having, the effect of causing harassment, intimidation, or impediment to those working or volunteering at, or using the services of, the site or the school in question.

Defences

(1) Having a reasonable excuse for failing to comply with a public spaces protection order.

(3) A person does not commit an offence under this section by failing to comply with a prohibition or requirement that the local authority did not have power to include in the public spaces protection order.

Anti-social Behaviour, Crime and Policing Act 2014, s 67

Related case

Wycombe District Council v Snowball [2020] EWHC 1656 (Admin) It was held in this case that the offence was complete when a police officer or other authorised individual reasonably formed the belief that an individual was drinking alcohol and had a container for alcohol, in breach of a PSPO. Once the belief had been established, it did not matter whether the individual later established that the relevant container did not contain alcohol as all the elements of the offence had been satisfied at the time the notice was issued.

Practical considerations

- The maximum duration of a PSPO is three years but this can be for a shorter period if required. If considered necessary, the LA can extend a PSPO before its expiry by up to three years, and if appropriate further consultation should again take place.
- The maximum duration of an expedited PSPO is six months but this may be extended before expiration if reasonable and necessary (s 60A).
- If required, a PSPO can be varied, such as changing the size of the restricted area or the specific requirements or restrictions. For example, a PSPO deals with controlling dogs in a park, but a year later, groups now congregate in the park drinking alcohol, so the LA could vary the PSPO to deal with both issues. The LA can also discharge a PSPO at any time.
- Section 63 can restrict the consumption of alcohol in a public space subject to a PSPO, and s 62 provides details of premises and places where a PSPO cannot apply. For details of restrictions and enforcing the order, see **9.4**.

7.15.2 Public spaces protection orders (PSPOs)

- In relation to dogs and their owners, a PSPO could, for example, exclude dogs from designated areas (eg a children's play area in a park); require dog faeces to be picked up by owners; require dogs to be kept on leads; and restrict the number of dogs that can be walked by one person at any one time.
- A PSPO must be published in accordance with regulations (SI 2591/2014), identifying the activities subject to the order, sanctions for breach, and the duration of the PSPO. The LA should publish details of making, extending, varying, or discharging a PSPO on its website and display notices with details of the PSPO at the public place to which the order relates.
- The PSPO or variation can be challenged in the High Court by an interested person (person who lives or regularly works in or visits the area) within six weeks of it being made/varied. Grounds could be that the LA did not have power to make the order, or include certain prohibitions or requirements, or that proper consultation had not taken place. The High Court can uphold the PSPO, quash it, or vary it.
- A person who fails to comply with a PSPO, without reasonable excuse, will commit an offence; except breach of a PSPO by consuming alcohol which is an offence under s 63 (see **9.4**). Both the s 63 and s 67 offences can be dealt with by a FPN (up to £100) under s 68.
- Current designated public place orders, gating orders, and dog control orders could remain in force for three years from the commencement day of PSPOs (20 October 2014).
- A PSPO takes precedence over a by-law in the restricted area if the by-law prohibits the same activity that is now covered by the PSPO.

Summary

6 months

Level 3 fine

7.16 Community/Environmental Protection

The Anti-social Behaviour, Crime and Policing Act 2014 deals with issuing a community protection notice (CPN) for environmental nuisances; other matters such as litter, abandoned vehicles, and refuse are dealt with by the Environmental Protection Act 1990, the Litter Act 1983, and the Refuse Disposal (Amenity) Act 1978.

7.16.1 Community protection notices (CPN)

Section 43 of the Anti-social Behaviour, Crime and Policing Act 2014 gives an authorised person power to issue a CPN to a person or body if their conduct is unreasonable and it has a detrimental effect on the quality of life of those in the locality. Failure to comply with a CPN is an offence under s 48, and breach can be dealt with by a fixed penalty notice (FPN) under s 52.

Power to issue notices

(1) An authorised person may issue a community protection notice to an individual aged 16 or over, or a body, if satisfied on reasonable grounds that—
- (a) the conduct of the individual or body is having a detrimental effect, of a persistent or continuing nature, on the quality of life of those in the locality, and
- (b) the conduct is unreasonable.

(3) A community protection notice is a notice that imposes any of the following requirements on the individual or body issued with it—
- (a) a requirement to stop doing specified things;
- (b) a requirement to do specified things;
- (c) a requirement to take reasonable steps to achieve specified results.

(4) The only requirements that may be imposed are ones that are reasonable to impose in order—
- (a) to prevent the detrimental effect referred to in subsection (1) from continuing or recurring, or
- (b) to reduce that detrimental effect or to reduce the risk of its continuance or recurrence.

(5) A person (A) may issue a community protection notice to an individual or body (B) only if—
- (a) B has been given a written warning that the notice will be issued unless B's conduct ceases to have the detrimental effect referred to in subsection (1), and

(b) A is satisfied that, despite B having had enough time to deal with the matter, B's conduct is still having that effect.

(6) A person issuing a community protection notice must before doing so inform any body or individual the person thinks appropriate.

(7) A community protection notice must—
- (a) identify the conduct referred to in subsection (1);
- (b) explain the effect of sections 46 to 51.

(8) A community protection notice may specify periods within which, or times by which, requirements within subsection (3)(b) or (c) are to be complied with.

Anti-social Behaviour, Crime and Policing Act 2014, s 43

Offences

A person issued with a community protection notice who fails to comply with it commits an offence.

Anti-social Behaviour, Crime and Policing Act 2014, s 48(1)

PNLD **H11454, H11509**

Points to prove

✓ an individual
✓ failed to comply with a community protection notice

Meanings

Authorised person

Means a constable or person designated by the relevant local authority (eg housing providers).

Local authority (LA) (see **7.13.4**)

Community protection notice (CPN) (see **s 43(3)** above)

Conduct

This includes a failure to act.

Sections 46 to 51

These sections relate to the following:
- s 46—Appeals against notices;
- s 47—Remedial action by local authority;
- s 48—Offence of failing to comply with notice;
- s 49—Remedial orders;
- s 50—Forfeiture of item used in offence; and
- s 51—Seizure of item used in offence.

Explanatory notes

- A CPN cannot be issued until a written warning has been given to the person/body; this must make it clear that if they do not stop the anti-social behaviour, a CPN could be issued. Identify in the written warning the behaviour that has to be changed and give a time period for it to be achieved, advising them of potential sanctions on breaching a CPN if a notice is then issued.
- When a written warning has been issued, enough time should be given to allow the person or body to deal with the matter before issuing a CPN. This will be on a case-by-case basis; for example, where an area is to be cleared several days or weeks may be required, but in a case of playing loud music this could require the behaviour to stop immediately.
- A CPN can be issued by a LA enforcement officer, social landlord (designated by LA), constable against a person aged 16 or over, business, or organisation, if satisfied on reasonable grounds that their conduct is having a detrimental effect on the quality of life of those in the locality, is persistent or continuing in nature, and is unreasonable.
- A CPN requirement should be appropriate to the situation; it could be to stop doing or to do specified things, or to take reasonable steps to achieve specified results. This means that not only can the officer stop someone being anti-social but they can also put steps in place to ensure the behaviour does not recur.
- If a body, the CPN should be given to the most appropriate person, such as the shop owner or a store manager. The issuing officer has to be satisfied that the person can be reasonably expected to control, affect, or deal with the behaviour. The notice can be given directly to the person in question, posted to them, or posted on the premises (if the owner or occupier is not known).

Defences

A person does not commit an offence under this section if—

(a) the person took all reasonable steps to comply with the notice, or

(b) there is some other reasonable excuse for the failure to comply with it.

Anti-social Behaviour, Crime and Policing Act 2014, s 48(3)

Related case

Staffordshire Moorlands DC v Sanderson [2020] EWHC 962 (Admin)
It was held in this case that s 43 does not create a power to issue a CPN in the name of an individual (a parent) concerning the conduct of a different individual (their child).

Practical considerations

- Consider if a requirement or timescale is reasonable and achievable before issuing the notice. Furthermore, a CPN is designed to deal with short- or medium-term issues, and while restrictions and requirements may be similar to those in civil injunctions (see **7.13.1**), more serious conditions, such as attending a drug rehabilitation course, should be dealt with by a court order.
- Failing to comply with a CPN is an offence under s 48(1). If appropriate, a police officer or LA officer could issue a FPN (up to £100) under s 52(1) for failing to comply with a CPN. Other options to consider could be remedial action or a court remedial, forfeiture, or seizure order.
- Remedial action could be the LA or its agent clearing a garden on the perpetrator's behalf and when completed charging the perpetrator with the cost for the clearance, which could include officer time, equipment, labour, and administration costs. Work undertaken on land 'open to the air' can be done without the consent of the owner or occupier but any indoor work will require the permission of the owner or occupier.
- Issuing a CPN does not discharge the LA from its duty to issue an Abatement Notice if it is a statutory nuisance as listed in s 79(1) of the Environmental Protection Act 1990.
- On conviction for failing to comply with a CPN, the prosecutor may ask the court to impose a remedial and/or a forfeiture order as:
  - ✦ it is a serious matter that requires a court order;
  - ✦ remedial work is in an area that requires consent from the owner/occupier and this is not forthcoming; or
  - ✦ forfeiture or seizure of items may be required as a result of the behaviour (eg sound-making equipment).
- The court can order the forfeiture of items used in committing the s 48 CPN offence; this might be spray paints, sound equipment, or a dog (owner unable to control the dog). Forfeited items can be destroyed or disposed of appropriately (including rehoming a dog). A warrant issued under s 51 can authorise seizure of such items and an officer may use reasonable force, if necessary, to do this.
- Failure to comply with any of the requirements in the court order constitutes contempt of court and could lead to a custodial sentence.
- Anyone issued with a CPN can appeal to a magistrates' court but this must be within twenty-one days of issue of the notice. Appeal could be on the grounds that the behaviour: did not take place; was not persistent or continuing; was not unreasonable; or did not have a detrimental effect on the quality of life of those in the locality. Other grounds for appeal might be: unreasonable CPN requirements; was issued to the wrong person; or the individual cannot reasonably be expected to control or affect the behaviour.

Summary

6 months

Level 4 fine (person) or fine (body)

7.16.2 Leaving litter/removing or interfering with litter bins

Section 87 of the Environmental Protection Act 1990 creates the offence of depositing litter in a public place which is open to the air.

Offences

A person is guilty of an offence if he throws down, drops or otherwise deposits any litter in any place to which this section applies, and leaves it.

Environmental Protection Act 1990, s 87(1)

PNLD H579

Points to prove

✓ threw down/dropped/deposit in and leave
✓ in a place
✓ to which s 87 Environmental Protection Act applied

Meanings

Deposits

Means to place or put down.

Litter

Includes the discarded ends of cigarettes, cigars, and like products, chewing gum, and the remains of other products designed for chewing.

Place

- Any place in the area of a **principal litter authority** that is open to the air. Land shall be treated as 'open to the air' notwithstanding that it is covered, providing it is open to the air on at least one side.
- This section does not apply to a place which is 'open to the air' if the public does not have access to it, with or without payment.

Principal litter authority

Means a county council, county borough council, district council, London borough council, Common Council of the City of London, and the Council of the Isles of Scilly.

7.16.2 Leaving litter/removing or interfering with litter bins

Explanatory notes

- It is immaterial whether the litter is deposited on land or in water, so the offence extends to dropping or depositing litter in bodies of water such as rivers and lakes.
- Under s 88, an authorised officer of a litter authority or a suitably designated constable may, if they have reason to believe that a person has committed an offence under s 87, issue a fixed penalty notice to that person.

Defences

No offence is committed under subsection (1) above where the depositing of the litter is—

(a) authorised by law, or

(b) done with the consent of the owner, occupier or other person having control of the place where it is deposited.

Environmental Protection Act 1990, s 87(4A)

Defence notes

A person may only give consent under s 87(4A)(b) in relation to the depositing of litter in a lake, pond, or watercourse if they are the owner, occupier, or other person having control of all the land adjoining that lake, pond, or watercourse and all the land through or into which water in that lake, pond, or watercourse directly or indirectly discharges, otherwise than by means of a public sewer.

Related case

Felix v DPP [1998] Crim LR 657 The defendant left three cards advertising the services of prostitutes in a telephone kiosk which was enclosed by three sides, a roof, and a door, and had a 6-inch gap at the bottom. It was held that a telephone kiosk did not fall within the definition of an 'open public space' for the purposes of s 87.

Practical considerations

- The area of a local authority which is on the coast extends down to the low-water mark (s 72 of the Local Government Act 1972). Therefore, it is an offence to deposit litter on the beach.
- Consider issuing a PND (see **7.1**) for this litter offence (applies to constable only).
- If a **fixed penalty notice** is issued under s 88, a copy of it must be sent to the relevant litter authority within twenty-four hours.
- **Littering from vehicles**—s 88A provides that the Secretary of State may make regulations under which a vehicle keeper may be required to pay a fixed penalty notice where a littering offence has been

committed in respect of the vehicle. A littering offence is committed in respect of a vehicle if an offence under s 87(1) occurs as a result of litter being thrown, dropped, or otherwise deposited from the vehicle (whether or not by the vehicle's keeper).

Meanings

Keeper

In relation to a vehicle, means the person by whom the vehicle is kept at the time when the littering offence in question occurs, which in the case of a registered vehicle is to be presumed, unless the contrary is proved, to be the registered keeper.

Removing or interfering with litter bins

It is a summary offence under s 5(9) of the Litter Act 1983 for any person to wilfully remove or otherwise interfere with any litter bin or notice board provided or erected under this section or s 185 of the Highways Act 1980.

PND

Summary — 6 months

Level 4 fine

7.16.3 Unauthorised dumping/abandoned vehicles/fly tipping

Section 2 of the Refuse Disposal (Amenity) Act 1978 creates an offence of abandoning motor vehicles or any other thing on land in the open (fly tipping).

Offences

Any person who, without lawful authority—

(a) abandons on any land in the open air, or on any other land forming part of a highway, a motor vehicle or any thing which formed part of a motor vehicle and was removed from it in the course of dismantling the vehicle on the land; or

(b) abandons on any such land any thing other than a motor vehicle, being a thing C it there,

shall be guilty of an offence.

Refuse Disposal (Amenity) Act 1978, s 2(1)

7.16.3 Unauthorised dumping/abandoned vehicles/fly tipping

PNLD H4043

Points to prove

- ✓ without lawful authority
- ✓ abandoned on land in open air/forming part of highway
- ✓ a motor vehicle OR
- ✓ part of a motor vehicle removed in the course of dismantling the vehicle on the land OR
- ✓ an item brought to the land
- ✓ for the purpose of abandoning it there

Meanings

Motor vehicle

Means a mechanically propelled vehicle intended or adapted for use on roads, whether or not it is in a fit state for such use, and includes any trailer intended or adapted for use as an attachment to such a vehicle, any chassis or body, with or without wheels, appearing to have formed part of such a vehicle or trailer and anything attached to such a vehicle or trailer.

Abandoned

A person who leaves any thing on any land in such circumstances or for such a period that they may reasonably be assumed to have abandoned it or to have brought it to the land for the purpose of abandoning it there shall be deemed to have abandoned it there or, as the case may be, to have brought it to the land for that purpose unless the contrary is shown.

Explanatory note

- In addition to any penalty, the court may order the defendant to pay any costs involved in the removal and disposal of the offending article.

Practical considerations

- Removal and disposal of items under this section are the responsibility of the local authority.
- Section 2A of the Refuse Disposal (Amenity) Act 1978 gives an authorised officer of a local authority the power to issue a fixed penalty in respect of the offence of abandoning a vehicle.
- Before contacting the local authority, consider checking the motor vehicle to ascertain whether it is stolen or used for involvement in crime.

Summary

6 months

3 months' imprisonment and/or a level 4 fine

Fixed penalty £200 or such amount as the appropriate person of a local authority may determine.

Links to alternative subjects and offences

4.3 **Taking a Conveyance without Owner's Consent** 185
4.4 **Criminal Damage** 193
10.1 **Meanings: Roads, Public Places, Vehicles, and Drives** 651
10.21 **Obstruction of the Road/Footpath** 769
10.22 **Off-Road Driving** 778
11.1 **Police Powers for Civilian Staff and Volunteers** 781

7.17 Trespassing on Premises/Land

Section 144 of the Legal Aid, Sentencing and Punishment of Offenders Act 2012 relates to squatting in a residential building. Sections 61 to 62C of the Criminal Justice and Public Order Act 1994 deal with trespassers residing on land who fail to leave, whereas ss 6 and 7 of the Criminal Law Act 1977 concern the use or threat of violence to secure entry into premises and unauthorised entry or remaining on premises.

7.17.1 Trespassers (squatting) in residential building/residing on land (failing to leave)

Section 144 of the Legal Aid, Sentencing and Punishment of Offenders Act 2012 creates the offence of squatting in a residential building.

Offences

A person commits an offence if—

(a) the person is in a residential building as a trespasser having entered it as a trespasser,

(b) the person knows or ought to know that he or she is a trespasser, and

(c) the person is living in the building or intends to live there for any period.

Legal Aid, Sentencing and Punishment of Offenders Act 2012, s 144(1)

PNLD H10402

Points to prove

✓ being in a residential building

✓ having entered it as a trespasser

✓ lived/intended to live in the building

Meanings

Residential building

A building is residential if it is designed or adapted, before the time of entry, for use as a place to live.

Building

Includes any structure or part of a structure (including a temporary or moveable structure).

Trespasser

Someone who wrongfully enters onto someone else's premises.

Explanatory notes

- The fact that a person derives title from a trespasser, or has permission from a trespasser, does not prevent the person from being a trespasser.
- For the purposes of s 144(1)(a) (above), it is irrelevant whether the person entered the building as a trespasser before or after this section came into force.

Defence

The offence is not committed by a person holding over after the end of a lease or licence (even if the person leaves and re-enters the building).

Legal Aid, Sentencing and Punishment of Offenders Act 2012, s 144(2)

Practical considerations

- MOJ Circular 2012/04 provides further details regarding this squatting offence, which requires that the trespasser 'is living' or 'intends to live' in the building for any period.
- Section 17(1)(c)(vi) of PACE provides a power of entry to arrest a person for the offence of squatting in a residential building (see **1.4.2**).
- Section 6 of the Criminal Law Act 1977 provides the offence of using or threatening violence to secure entry to premises (see **7.17.2**), but the police still have lawful authority to enter the property to arrest for the s 144 squatting offence.
- Section 7 of the 1977 Act concerns the offence of failing to leave residential premises once the lawful occupiers have gained legitimate entry (see **7.17.3**).

Residing on land without consent in or with a vehicle

Section 60C of the Criminal Justice and Public Order Act 1994 creates a summary offence of residing, or intending to reside, on land (including common land) without the consent of the occupier of the land in or with a vehicle where certain conditions are satisfied.

7.17.1 Trespassers (squatting) in residential building etc

Offences

(1) Subsection (2) applies where—
  (a) a person aged 18 or over ('P') is residing, or intending to reside, on land without the consent of the occupier of the land,
  (b) P has, or intends to have, at least one vehicle with them on the land [vehicle includes caravans],
  (c) one or more of the conditions mentioned in subsection (4) [see below] is satisfied, and
  (d) the occupier, a representative of the occupier or a constable requests P to do either or both of the following—
    (i) leave the land;
    (ii) remove from the land property that is in P's possession or under P's control.

(2) P commits an offence if—
  (a) P fails to comply with the request as soon as reasonably practicable, or
  (b) P—
    (i) enters (or having left, re-enters) the land within the prohibited period with the intention of residing there without the consent of the occupier of the land, and
    (ii) has, or intends to have, at least one vehicle with them on the land.

(3) The prohibited period is the period of 12 months beginning with the day on which the request was made.

Criminal Justice and Public Order Act 1994, s 60C

PNLD **H100680, H100684**

Points to prove

s 60C(2)(a)

✓ failed to leave the land or failed to remove property from the land
✓ as soon as reasonably practicable
✓ following a request made by the occupier/representative of the occupier/constable under s 60C of the Criminal Justice and Public Order Act 1994

s 60C(2)(b)

✓ having been requested within the previous 12 months
✓ to leave/remove property from land
✓ under s 60C(1) of the Criminal Justice and Public Order Act 1994
✓ by the occupier/representative of the occupier/a constable
✓ entered/re-entered that land
✓ with the intention of residing there without the owner's consent
✓ and had or, intended to have
✓ at least one vehicle on the land

Meanings

Land

Does not include buildings other than agricultural buildings within the meaning of paras 3 to 8 of Sch 5 to the Local Government Finance Act 1988.

Occupier

Means the person entitled to possession of the land by virtue of an estate or interest held by the person.

Vehicle

Includes any vehicle, whether or not it is in a fit state for use on roads, and includes any chassis or body, with or without wheels, appearing to have formed part of such a vehicle, and any load carried by, and anything attached to, such a vehicle, and a caravan as defined in s 29(1) of the Caravan Sites and Control of Development Act 1960.

Explanatory notes

- For the purposes of this section, a person is to be considered as residing or having the intention to reside in a place even if that residence or intended residence is temporary, and a person may be regarded as residing or having an intention to reside in a place notwithstanding that the person has a home elsewhere.
- Section 60D makes provision for the seizure and retention of relevant property where a constable reasonably suspects that an offence under this section has been committed.
- Section 60E provides that a court that convicts a person of an offence under this section may order certain property to be forfeited.

Summary

6 months

3 months' imprisonment and/or a fine

Trespassers residing on land—failing to leave

- The Criminal Justice and Public Order Act 1994 gives the police powers for dealing with people, vehicles, and caravans trespassing on land.
- Section 61 of this Act gives the police power to direct two or more people trespassing on land, intending to reside there for a period of time, to leave that land and to remove any vehicles or other property they have with them on the land. This is providing that reasonable steps have been taken by or on behalf of the occupier to ask them to leave, and they have:
  - ✦ in the case of persons trespassing on land in England and Wales, caused damage, disruption, or distress; or

- six or more vehicles on the land between them.
- It is a summary offence under s 61(4) if a person, knowing that a direction has been given which applies to them, either:
  - fails to leave the land as soon as is reasonably practicable; or
  - having left, again enters the land as a trespasser within the period of twelve months beginning with the day on which the direction was given.
- Section 62 provides that a constable may seize and remove a vehicle if a direction has been given under s 61 and they reasonably suspect that a person to whom it applies has, without reasonable excuse, failed to remove a vehicle which appears to belong to them or to be in their possession or under their control; or they have entered the land as a trespasser with a vehicle within twelve months of the direction being given.
- Sections 62A to 62C provide for the directing of trespassers to leave land and remove their vehicles/caravans when there is a relevant caravan site in the local authority area and it is managed by a relevant site manager.
- Under s 62F, police officers in England and Wales must have regard to the Home Office statutory guidance 'Unauthorised encampments: a summary of available powers' when exercising any of those functions conferred on them within ss 60C to 62E and regulations under s 67 relating to the retention of vehicles seized under s 62(1) or s 62C(3).

Explanatory notes

For the purpose of s 60C:

- 'damage' includes:
  - (a) damage to the land;
  - (b) damage to any property on the land not belonging to the persons trespassing;
  - (c) damage to the environment (including excessive noise, smells, litter, or deposits of waste);
- 'disruption' includes an interference with:
  - (a) a person's ability to access any services or facilities located on the land or otherwise make lawful use of the land; or
  - (b) a supply of water, energy, or fuel;
- 'distress' means distress caused by:
  - (a) the use of threatening, abusive, or insulting words or behaviour, or disorderly behaviour; or
  - (b) the display of any writing, sign, or other visible representation that is threatening, abusive, or insulting.

E&S

Summary — 6 months

51 weeks' imprisonment and/or a fine

7.17.2 **Violent entry to premises**

Section 6 creates the offences of using or threatening violence to secure entry to premises.

Offences

Subject to the following provisions of this section, any person who, without lawful authority, uses or threatens violence for the purpose of securing entry into any premises for himself or for any other person is guilty of an offence, provided that—

(a) there is someone present on those premises at the time who is opposed to the entry which the violence is intended to secure; and
(b) the person using or threatening the violence knows that is the case.

Criminal Law Act 1977, s 6(1)

PNLD H2270, H2290

Points to prove

✓ without lawful authority
✓ used/threatened violence
✓ to secure entrance into premises
✓ knowing someone present on the premises opposed that entry

Meanings

Premises

Any building, part of a building under separate occupation (eg flat), land ancillary to a building, and the site comprising any building(s) together with any land ancillary thereto.

Provisions of this section

Section 6(1) does not apply to a **displaced residential occupier** or a **protected intending occupier** of the relevant premises or a person acting on behalf of such an occupier. If the defendant produces sufficient evidence that they are, or were acting on behalf of, such an occupier they will be presumed to be so unless the prosecution proves the contrary.

Displaced residential occupier

Subject to the following **exception**, any person who was occupying any premises as a residence immediately before being excluded from occupation by anyone who entered those premises, or any **access** to those premises, as a **trespasser** is a displaced residential occupier of the premises so long as they continue to be excluded from occupation of the premises by the original trespasser or by any subsequent trespasser.

Exception

A person who was occupying the relevant premises as a trespasser immediately before being excluded from occupation shall not be a displaced residential occupier of the premises.

Access

Means, in relation to any premises, any part of any site or building within which those premises are situated that constitutes an ordinary means of access to those premises (whether or not that is its sole or primary use).

Trespasser

Someone who wrongfully enters onto someone else's premises.

Protected intending occupier

This is extensively defined in s 12A but, in brief, means someone who has made a formal declaration to a commissioner of oaths that they were due to move into the affected premises.

Explanatory notes

- Anyone who enters, or is on or in occupation of, any premises under a title derived from a trespasser, or by a licence or consent given by a trespasser or by a person deriving title from a trespasser, will themselves be treated as a trespasser (whether or not they would be a trespasser apart from this provision).
- The fact that a person has an interest in, or right to possession or occupation of, the premises does not, for s 6(1), constitute lawful authority for the use or threat of violence by them or anyone else to secure entry into those premises.

Related case

Wakolo v DPP [2012] EWHC 611 (Admin) This case involved a married couple who had separated and both were co-owners of the matrimonial home. The defendant, W, who had previously left the home, attempted to gain entry to the house but was refused admittance by their wife. Consequently, W used force to gain entry and was convicted of s 6(1) and (5). W appealed and it was held that an individual who was the freeholder of a matrimonial property, from which they had not been formally excluded and which was occupied by their estranged wife, was not a protected intending occupier under the Criminal Law Act 1977, s 12A. W could not avail themselves of a defence under s 6(1A) and could be convicted of the use of violence to gain entry to a property the front door of which they had damaged.

Practical considerations

- It is immaterial whether the violence is directed against a person or property and whether the violent entry is to acquire possession of the premises.
- A person who, by virtue of the definition of 'displaced residential occupier', is a displaced residential occupier of any premises is also deemed to be a displaced residential occupier of any access to those premises.
- A person on premises as a trespasser does not cease to be a trespasser under this legislation by being allowed time to leave there, nor does a person cease to be a displaced residential occupier of any premises because of any such allowance of time to a trespasser.
- Proceed with care where squatting appears to have lasted for a long time. It is possible for a squatter (someone who possesses premises without the lawful consent of the owner) to gain legal title if they have held the property for twelve years adversely but without disturbance or legal attempts to repossess it.

E&S

Summary

None

6 months' imprisonment and/or a fine

7.17.3 Adverse occupation of residential premises

Section 7 creates an offence of failing to leave residential premises once the lawful occupiers have gained legitimate entry.

Offences

Subject to the provisions of this section and section 12A(9), any person who is on any premises as a trespasser after having entered as such is guilty of an offence if he fails to leave those premises on being required to do so by or on behalf of—

(a) a displaced residential occupier of the premises; or

(b) an individual who is a protected intending occupier of the premises.

Criminal Law Act 1977, s 7(1)

PNLD H1180

7.17.3 **Adverse occupation of residential premises**

Points to prove

- ✓ on premises
- ✓ as a trespasser
- ✓ having entered as such
- ✓ failed to leave when required
- ✓ by displaced residential/protected intending occupier

Meanings

Premises (see 7.17.2)

Trespasser

Someone who wrongfully enters onto someone else's premises.

Displaced residential occupier (see 7.17.2)

Protected intending occupier (see 7.17.2)

Explanatory note

- A reference to any premises includes a reference to any access to them, whether or not the access itself constitutes premises.

Defences

7(2) It is a defence for the accused to prove that he believed that the person requiring him to leave the premises was not a displaced residential occupier or protected intending occupier of the premises or a person acting on their behalf.

(3) It is a defence for the accused to prove that—

(a) the premises in question are, or form part of, premises used mainly for non-residential purposes; and

(b) he was not on any part of the premises used wholly or mainly for residential purposes.

12A(9) Where the accused was requested to leave the premises by a person claiming to be or to act on behalf of a protected intending occupier of the premises—

(a) it shall be a defence for the accused to prove that, although asked to do so by the accused at the time the accused was requested to leave, that person failed at that time to produce to the accused such a statement as is referred to in section 12A(2)(d) or section 12A(4)(d) or such a certificate as is referred to in section 12A(6)(d); and

(b) any document purporting to be a document under section 12A(6)(d) will be received in evidence and, unless the contrary is proved, will be determined to have been issued by or on behalf of the authority stated in the certificate.

Criminal Law Act 1977, ss 7 and 12A

Practical considerations

- Officers wishing to apply these provisions in an operational situation should make themselves conversant with the following terms: displaced residential occupier, squatters, and protected intending occupier (see **7.17.2**).
- A displaced residential occupier or a protected intending occupier (once they have completed the formalities) can use force (either personally or by others on their behalf) to break into the premises to regain possession. They can also demand that the premises be vacated and s 7 makes it an offence (subject to any defences) for the trespassers to remain.
- If the squatter is being evicted by a protected intending occupier (this does not apply to an eviction by a displaced residential occupier), they are entitled to see a copy of the statement or certificate which must be held by the person making the eviction. They have a statutory defence if the certificate is not produced.

E&S

Summary

None

6 months' imprisonment and/or a fine

7.17.4 Aggravated trespass on land

Section 68 of the Criminal Justice and Public Order Act 1994 makes it an offence for a trespasser to disrupt or obstruct any lawful activity taking place on that land or adjoining land.

Offence

A person commits the offence of aggravated trespass if he trespasses on land and, in relation to any lawful activity which persons are engaging in or are about to engage in on that or adjoining land, does there anything which is intended by him to have the effect—

(a) of intimidating those persons or any of them so as to deter them or any of them from engaging in that activity,
(b) of obstructing that activity, OR
(c) of disrupting that activity.

Criminal Justice and Public Order Act 1994, s 68(1)

PNLD H6320, H6321

7.17.4 Aggravated trespass on land

> **Points to prove**
>
> ✓ date and location
> ✓ having trespassed on land
> ✓ in relation to lawful activity
> ✓ which persons were engaged in/about to engage in
> ✓ on that/adjoining land
> ✓ did an act intended to
> ✓ obstruct/disrupt that activity, or
> ✓ intimidate persons, or
> ✓ so as to deter them from engaging in that activity

Meanings

Land

Includes any building but, in this section, land does not include a highway unless it is a footpath, bridleway, or byway open to all traffic within the meaning of Part 3 of the Wildlife and Countryside Act 1981, is a restricted byway within the meaning of Part 2 of the Countryside and Rights of Way Act 2000, or is a cycle track under the Highways Act 1980 or the Cycle Tracks Act 1984.

Trespasser

Is someone who goes on to land without an invitation of any sort and whose presence is either unknown to the lawful occupier of the land or is known but objected to by them in a practical way (eg if a landowner allowed local people to take a shortcut across their land and did not try to stop them, in time they would no longer be trespassers. If they put up signs or gates to stop the practice, but it continued despite those efforts, then the people crossing the land would continue to be trespassers indefinitely).

Explanatory notes

- Activity on any occasion on the part of a person or persons on land is lawful for the purposes of this section if they may engage in the activity on the land on that occasion without committing an offence or trespassing on the land.
- Section 69 of the Criminal Justice and Public Order Act 1994 empowers the senior police officer present at the scene, if they reasonably believe:
  (a) that a person is committing, has committed, or intends to commit the offence of aggravated trespass on land; or
  (b) that two or more persons are trespassing on land and are present there with the common purpose of intimidating persons so as to deter them from engaging in a lawful activity or of obstructing or disrupting a lawful activity,

  to direct that person to leave the land and it is an offence if they fail to do so or enter again as a trespasser within the period of three months beginning with the day on which the direction was given.

Related cases

DPP v Bailey and others [2022] EWHC 3302 (Admin) In this case, B and others took part in a protest on the site of the largest dairy in the UK. The protest lasted for seventeen hours and was organised by Animal Rebellion. The court held that a prosecution for an offence of aggravated trespass under s 68 does not require the prosecution to prove that the defendant either knew or was reckless as to whether they were trespassing. Trespass is a legal concept derived from the law of tort, the meaning of which is well settled; and proof of the civil wrong requires no mental element. That did not make the offence one of strict liability, since intention was required to be proved with respect to the various blameworthy effects needed for the aggravated element of the offence, and that mitigated any potential unfairness.

DPP v Cuciurean [2022] EWHC 736 (Admin) The prosecution successfully appealed against the acquittal of a protester's conviction for aggravated trespass as there was no general principle that the prosecution must prove that a conviction would be a proportionate interference with a defendant's rights under Arts 10 and 11 ECHR.

DPP v Tilly and others [2001] EWHC Admin 821 The persons engaged in the lawful activity must be present at the time of the trespass for an offence under s 68. The legislation was clearly designed to deal with a situation in which people were intimidated or could not get on with what they were entitled to do.

Capon and others v DPP [1998] QBD In this case, three people were peacefully videoing a fox hunt. The senior police officer at the scene had a genuine belief that an obstruction of lawful activity would occur if the suspected persons remained on the land in question. The officer gave a direction to leave under s 69 of the Act which was lawful even if no actual offence of aggravated trespass had been committed, since the prerequisite for a direction was a reasonable belief on the part of the officer, not the actual commission of the offence.

Summary 6 months

3 months' imprisonment and/or a fine

7.17.5 Causing serious disruption by locking-on

These offences under the Public Order Act 2023 deal with the protest tactics of individuals who cause serious disruption by attaching themselves to others, objects, or land, as well as going equipped to commit the offence.

7.17.5 Causing serious disruption by locking-on

Offences

1(1) A person commits an offence if—
  (a) they—
    (i) attach themselves to another person, to an object or to land,
    (ii) attach a person to another person, to an object or to land, or
    (iii) attach an object to another object or to land,
  (b) that act causes, or is capable of causing, serious disruption to—
    (i) two or more individuals, or
    (ii) an organisation,
    in a place other than a dwelling, and
  (c) they intend that act to have a consequence mentioned in paragraph (b) or are reckless as to whether it will have such a consequence.

2(1) A person commits an offence if they have an object with them in a place other than a dwelling with the intention that it may be used in the course of or in connection with the commission by any person of an offence under section 1(1) (offence of locking on).

Public Order Act 2023, ss 1 and 2

PNLD H101308, H101309

Points to prove

s 1(1) offence

✓ attached
✓ yourself to another person object/land OR
✓ a person to another person/object/land OR
✓ a an object to another object/land
✓ in a place other than a dwelling
✓ with that act causing or being capable of causing serious disruption to
✓ two or more individuals OR an organisation
✓ intending/being reckless to the act causing or being capable of causing serious disruption

s 2(1) offence

✓ had an object with you
✓ in a place other than a dwelling
✓ with the intention that it may be used in the course of/in connection with
✓ the commission by any person of an offence under s 1(1) of the Public Order Act 2023

Meanings

Dwelling

A building or structure which is used as a dwelling, or a part of a building or structure, if the part is used as a dwelling, and includes any yard, garden, grounds, garage, or outhouse belonging to and used with a dwelling.

Serious disruption

Defined in s 34 of the Act, serious disruption means where the individuals or the organisation:

(a) are by way of physical obstruction prevented, or hindered to more than a minor degree, from carrying out:
  - (i) their day-to-day activities (including in particular the making of a journey),
  - (ii) construction or maintenance works, or
  - (iii) activities related to such works,

(b) are prevented from making or receiving, or suffer a delay that is more than minor to the making or receiving of, a delivery of a time-sensitive product (*see s 34(2)*), or

(c) are prevented from accessing, or suffer a disruption that is more than minor to the accessing of, any essential goods or any essential service.

Explanatory notes

- It is a defence for a person charged with an offence under subsection (1) to prove that they had a reasonable excuse for the act mentioned in para (a) of that subsection.
- Public Order Act 2023 stop and search powers (see **7.17.9**).

Summary | 6 months

s 1(1) offence

6 months' or 51 weeks' imprisonment and/or a fine

s 2(1) offence

Fine

7.17.6 Causing serious disruption by tunnelling or being present in a tunnel

Offences

3(1) A person commits an offence if—
 (a) they create, or participate in the creation of, a tunnel,
 (b) the creation or existence of the tunnel causes, or is capable of causing, serious disruption to—
  (i) two or more individuals, or
  (ii) an organisation,
 in a place other than a dwelling, and
 (c) they intend the creation or existence of the tunnel to have a consequence mentioned in paragraph (b) or are reckless as to whether its creation or existence will have such a consequence.

4(1) A person commits an offence if—
 (a) they are present in a relevant tunnel having entered it after the coming into force of this section,
 (b) their presence in the tunnel causes, or is capable of causing, serious disruption to—
  (i) two or more individuals, or
  (ii) an organisation,
 in a place other than a dwelling, and
 (c) they intend their presence in the tunnel to have a consequence mentioned in paragraph (b) or are reckless as to whether their presence there will have such a consequence.

5(1) A person commits an offence if they have an object with them in a place other than a dwelling with the intention that it may be used in the course of or in connection with the commission by any person of an offence under section 3(1) or 4(1) (offences relating to tunnelling).

Public Order Act 2023, ss 3 to 5

PNLD H101311, H101312, H101314

Points to prove

s 3(1) offence

✓ created/participated in the creation of a tunnel
✓ with the creation/existence of the tunnel
✓ causing/being capable of causing serious disruption to
✓ two or more individuals OR an organisation
✓ in a place other than a dwelling and
✓ intending/being reckless that the creation/existence of the tunnel
✓ caused or being capable of causing serious disruption

s 4(1) offence

- ✓ being present in a relevant tunnel
- ✓ their presence causing or being capable of causing serious disruption
- ✓ to two or more individuals OR an organisation
- ✓ in a place other than a dwelling and
- ✓ intending/being reckless that their presence in the tunnel
- ✓ was capable of causing serious disruption

s 5(1) offence

- ✓ had an object with them
- ✓ in a place other than a dwelling
- ✓ with the intention that it may be used in the course of/in connection with
- ✓ the commission by any person of an offence under s 3(1)/4(1) of the Public Order Act 2023

Meanings

Dwelling (see **7.17.5**)

Serious disruption (see **7.17.5**)

Tunnel

Defined in s 3(5)(a) of the Act:

(a) a tunnel means an excavation that extends beneath land, whether or not:
  (i) it is big enough to permit the entry or passage of an individual, or
  (ii) it leads to a particular destination;
(b) an excavation which is created with the intention that it will become or connect with a tunnel is to be treated as a tunnel, whether or not:
  (i) any tunnel with which it is intended to connect has already been created, or
  (ii) it is big enough to permit the entry or passage of an individual.

Relevant tunnel

For the purposes of s 4, a relevant tunnel means a tunnel which was created for the purposes of, or in connection with, a protest (and it does not matter whether an offence has been committed under s 3 in relation to the creation of the tunnel).

Explanatory notes

- Under s 3(2), it is a defence for a person charged with an offence under s 3(1) to prove that they had a reasonable excuse for creating, or participating in the creation of, the tunnel.
- The creation of an excavation includes the extension or enlargement of an excavation and the alteration of a natural or artificial underground feature.
- The burden of proof for the defence in s 3(2) and s 4(2) is placed on the defendant as the facts as to whether they have a reasonable excuse will be within their knowledge. The prosecution will still need to prove all the elements of the offence to the criminal standard of proof. Although not explicitly set out, the standard to which the defendant will be required to prove the defence is a balance of probabilities.
- For the s 4 offence, it is a defence for a person charged with an offence under subsection (1) to prove that they had a reasonable excuse for their presence in the tunnel.
- Section 3 and s 4 offences do not apply in relation to a tunnel if or to the extent that it is in or under a dwelling.
- For both s 3 and s 4 offences, it is without prejudice that a person is to be treated as having a reasonable excuse if the creation of the tunnel, or being present in a tunnel, was authorised by a person with an interest in land which entitled them to authorise its creation.
- Public Order Act 2023 stop and search powers (see **7.17.9**).

s 3(1) and s 4(1) offences

Either way None

Summary: 6/12 months' imprisonment and/or a fine

Indictment: 3 years' imprisonment and/or a fine

s 5(1) offence

Summary 6 months

Summary: 6 months' or 51 weeks' imprisonment and/or a fine

7.17.7 Obstruction etc of major transport works

Section 6 of the Public Order Act 2023 provides for the obstruction etc of major transport works.

Offence

A person commits an offence if the person—
(a) obstructs the undertaker or a person acting under the authority of the undertaker—
  (i) in setting out the lines of any major transport works,
  (ii) in constructing or maintaining any major transport works, or
  (iii) in taking any steps that are reasonably necessary for the purposes of facilitating, or in connection with, the construction or maintenance of any major transport works, or
(b) interferes with, moves or removes any apparatus which—
  (i) relates to the construction or maintenance of any major transport works, and
  (ii) belongs to a person within subsection (5).

Public Order Act 2023, s 6(1)

PNLD H101315, H101316

Points to prove

s 6(1)(a) offence

✓ obstructed the undertaker/person acting under the authority of the undertaker in setting out the lines OR constructing or maintaining of any major transport works OR
✓ in taking any steps reasonably necessary for the purpose of facilitating/in connection with the construction/maintenance of any major transport works

s 6(1)(b) offence

✓ interfered with/moved/removed
✓ any apparatus relating to the construction/maintenance of major transport works and belonging to the undertaker/person acting under the authority of the undertaker/statutory undertaker/person acting under the authority of a statutory undertaker

Meanings

Major transport works (s 6(6))

(a) works in England and Wales—
  (i) relating to transport infrastructure, and
  (ii) the construction of which is authorised directly by an Act of Parliament, or
(b) works the construction of which comprises development within subsection (7) that has been granted development consent by an order under section 114 of the Planning Act 2008.

7.17.7 **Obstruction etc of major transport works**

Undertaker

(a) A person who is authorised by or under the Act (whether as a result of being appointed the nominated undertaker for the purposes of the Act or otherwise) to construct or maintain any of the works.

(b) In relation to major transport works within subsection (6)(b), means a person who is constructing or maintaining any of the works (whether as a result of being the undertaker for the purposes of the order granting development consent or otherwise).

Associated development

Has the same meaning as in the Planning Act 2008 (see s 115 of that Act).

Development

Has the same meaning as in the Planning Act 2008 (see s 32 of that Act).

Development consent

Has the same meaning as in the Planning Act 2008 (see s 31 of that Act).

England

Includes the English inshore region within the meaning of the Marine and Coastal Access Act 2009 (see s 322 of that Act).

Maintain

Includes inspect, repair, adjust, alter, remove, reconstruct, and replace, and 'maintenance' is to be construed accordingly.

Nationally significant infrastructure project

Has the same meaning as in the Planning Act 2008 (see s 14(1) of that Act).

Statutory undertaker

A person who is, or who is deemed to be, a statutory undertaker for the purposes of any provision of Part 11 of the Town and Country Planning Act 1990.

Trade dispute

Has the same meaning as in Part 4 of the Trade Union and Labour Relations (Consolidation) Act 1992, except that s 218 of that Act is to be read as if:

(a) it made provision corresponding to s 244(4) of that Act; and

(b) in subsection (5), the definition of worker included any person falling within para (b) of the definition of worker in s 244(5) of that Act.

Explanatory notes

- The following persons are within this subsection:
  - ✦ the undertaker;
  - ✦ a person acting under the authority of the undertaker;

  - ✦ a statutory undertaker;
  - ✦ a person acting under the authority of a statutory undertaker.
- Section 6(2) provides a defence for a person charged with an offence under subsection (1) to prove that they had a reasonable excuse for the act mentioned in para (a) or (b) of that subsection, or the act mentioned in para (a) or (b) of that subsection was done wholly or mainly in contemplation or furtherance of a trade dispute.
- Development is within this subsection if:
  - ✦ it is or forms part of a nationally significant infrastructure project within any of paras (h) to (l) of s 14(1) of the Planning Act 2008;
  - ✦ it is or forms part of a project (or proposed project) in the field of transport in relation to which a direction has been given under s 35(1) of that Act (directions in relation to projects of national significance) by the Secretary of State; or
  - ✦ it is associated development in relation to development within para (a) or (b).
- Public Order Act 2023 stop and search powers (see **7.17.9**).

SSS

Summary   6 months

Imprisonment for a term not exceeding the maximum term for summary offences, to a fine, or to both

7.17.8 Interference with national infrastructure

Section 7 of the Public Order Act 2023 creates the offence of interfering with use or operation of key national infrastructure.

Offence

A person commits an offence if—

(a) they do an act which interferes with the use or operation of any key national infrastructure in England and Wales, and

(b) they intend that act to interfere with the use or operation of such infrastructure or are reckless as to whether it will do so.

Public Order Act 2023, s 7(1)

PNLD H101310

7.17.8 Interference with national infrastructure

Points to prove

✓ did an act that interfered with the use/operation of any key national infrastructure in England and Wales and
✓ intended/were reckless that the act would interfere with the use/operation of such infrastructure

Meanings

Key national infrastructure

Road transport infrastructure, rail infrastructure, air transport infrastructure, harbour infrastructure, downstream oil infrastructure, downstream gas infrastructure, onshore oil and gas exploration and production infrastructure, onshore electricity generation infrastructure, or newspaper printing infrastructure.

England (see **7.17.7**)

Trade dispute (see **7.17.7**)

Wales

Includes the Welsh inshore region within the meaning of the Marine and Coastal Access Act 2009 (see s 322 of that Act).

Explanatory notes

- Section 7(2) provides a defence for a person charged with an offence under subsection (1) to prove that they had a reasonable excuse for the act mentioned in para (a) of that subsection, or the act mentioned in para (a) of that subsection was done wholly or mainly in contemplation or furtherance of a trade dispute.
- For the purposes of subsection (1), a person's act interferes with the use or operation of key national infrastructure if it prevents the infrastructure from being used or operated to any extent for any of its intended purposes.
- The cases in which infrastructure is prevented from being used or operated for any of its intended purposes include where its use or operation for any of those purposes is significantly delayed.
- Public Order Act 2023 stop and search powers (see **7.17.9**).

SSS

Either way

None

Summary: maximum 6/12 months' imprisonment and/or a fine

Indictment: maximum 12 months' imprisonment and/or a fine

7.17.9 Powers to stop and search without suspicion

Section 11 of the Public Order Act 2023 provides for powers to stop and search persons or vehicles for objects made, adapted, or intended for use in connection with specified protest-related offences.

Powers

This section applies if a police officer of or above the rank of inspector reasonably believes—

(a) that any of the following offences may be committed in any locality within the officer's police area—

(i) an offence under section 137 of the Highways Act 1980 (wilful obstruction) involving activity which causes or is capable of causing serious disruption to two or more individuals or to an organisation [see **10.21.1**];

(ii) an offence under section 78 of the Police, Crime, Sentencing and Courts Act 2022 (intentionally or recklessly causing public nuisance) [see **7.13.3**];

(iii) an offence under section 1 (offence of locking on) [see **7.17.5**];

(iv) an offence under section 3 (offence of causing serious disruption by tunnelling) [see **7.17.6**];

(v) an offence under section 4 (offence of causing serious disruption by being present in a tunnel) [see **7.17.6**];

(vi) an offence under section 6 (obstruction etc of major transport works) [see **7.17.7**];

(vii) an offence under section 7 (interference with use or operation of key national infrastructure), [see **7.17.8**] or

(b) that persons are carrying prohibited objects in any locality within the officer's police area.

Public Order Act 2023, s 11

Meanings

Prohibited object

An object which is made or adapted for use in the course of or in connection with an offence within subsection (1)(a) or is intended by the person having it with them for such use by them or by some other person, and for the purposes of this section a person carries a prohibited object if they have it in their possession.

Specified

Means specified in an authorisation under this section.

Vehicle

Includes a caravan as defined in s 29(1) of the Caravan Sites and Control of Development Act 1960.

Explanatory notes

- This section makes provision for a senior police officer to provide an authorisation within a specific locality for a specified period, allowing constables in uniform to stop and search persons or vehicles for an object made, adapted, or intended for use in the course of or in connection with a specified protest-related offence being the offences listed in subsection (1).
- If it appears to a police officer of or above the rank of superintendent that it is necessary to do so to prevent the commission of offences within subsection (1)(a) or the carrying of prohibited objects, the officer may direct that the authorisation is to continue in force for a further period not exceeding twenty-four hours.
- This section confers on any constable in uniform power:
  - ✦ to stop any person and search them or anything carried by them for a prohibited object;
  - ✦ to stop any vehicle and search the vehicle, its driver, and any passenger for a prohibited object.
- A constable may, in the exercise of these powers, stop any person or vehicle and make any search the constable thinks fit whether or not the constable has any grounds for suspecting that the person or vehicle is carrying a prohibited object.
- If in the course of a search under this section, a constable discovers an object which the constable has reasonable grounds for suspecting to be a prohibited object, the constable may seize it.

Practical considerations

- Section 12 makes further provisions regarding authorisations and directions under this section. For example, where an inspector gives an authorisation under s 11, they must inform an officer of or above the rank of superintendent as soon as it is practicable to do so (s 12(1)).
- In accordance with PACE Code A (g) para 2.43 , an inspector who gives an authorisation must communicate their decision to the public as soon as possible and where it is operationally beneficial to do so. This information must include the reason, time limit, and geographical location of the authorisation.
- An authorisation under s 11 must be given in writing, signed by the officer giving it, specify the grounds on which it was given, and specify the locality in which it is in force and the period during which powers under the section are exercisable (s 12(2)).
- A direction of a superintendent under s 11(5) must be given in writing or, where it is not practicable to do so due to operational circumstances, it can be given verbally and be recorded in writing as soon as it is practicable.

- Section 13 provides further provisions about searches under s 11 including that a person searched or who has their vehicle searched under s 11 is entitled to obtain a written statement from the officer that the person was searched and/or the vehicle was stopped. This must be requested within twelve months.
- Section 14 creates an offence relating to obstruction of a search under this section.

Links to alternative subjects and offences

1.3.2 **PACE power to search and detain** 22
2.1.1 **Common assault—battery** 53
2.8 **Domestic Abuse** 125
3.3 **Burglary/Aggravated Burglary** 145
4.4 **Criminal Damage** 193
4.6 **Threats to Destroy or Damage Property** 203
4.7 **Custody/Control of Articles with Intent to Damage** 206
Appendix 1 **Human Rights** 839

7.18 Football/Sporting Event Offences/Banning Orders

At designated sporting events and grounds, the Sporting Events (Control of Alcohol) Act 1985 deals with police powers and offences in connection with alcohol, articles capable of causing injury, flares, and other articles; whereas at designated football matches, the Football (Offences) Act 1991 deals with offences such as throwing missiles, indecent/racist chanting, or going onto the pitch, and the Football Spectators Act 1989 controls admission through football banning orders.

7.18.1 Possess alcohol/article or drunk at sporting event

Section 7 of the Sporting Events (Control of Alcohol) Act 1985 provides the police with powers of entry, stop, and search in connection with the Act.

Offences

(1) A person who has alcohol or an article to which this section applies in his possession—
- (a) at any time during the period of a designated sporting event when he is in any area of a designated sports ground from which the event may be directly viewed, or
- (b) while entering or trying to enter a designated sports ground at any time during the period of a designated sporting event at that ground,

is guilty of an offence.

(2) A person who is drunk in a designated sports ground at any time during the period of a designated sporting event at that ground or is drunk while entering or trying to enter such a ground at any time during the period of a designated sporting event at that ground is guilty of an offence.

Sporting Events (Control of Alcohol) Act 1985, s 2

PNLD H1764 to H1770, H2213 to H2215, H2170, H2171

Points to prove

s 2(1)(a) offence

- ✓ possessed
- ✓ alcohol/article to which s 2 applies
- ✓ during period of designated sporting event
- ✓ in area of designated sports ground
- ✓ with a direct view of the event

s 2(1)(b) offence

- ✓ possessed
- ✓ alcohol/article to which s 2 applies
- ✓ while entering/trying to enter
- ✓ a designated sports ground
- ✓ during period of designated sporting event

s 2(2) offence

- ✓ drunk
- ✓ in/while entering/trying to enter
- ✓ a designated sports ground
- ✓ during period of a designated sporting event

Powers

(1) A constable may, at any time during the period of a designated sporting event at any designated sports ground, enter any part of the ground for the purpose of enforcing the provisions of this Act.

(2) A constable may search a person he has reasonable grounds to suspect is committing or has committed an offence under this Act.

(3) A constable may stop a public service vehicle (within the meaning of section 1 of this Act) or a motor vehicle to which section 1A of this Act applies and may search such a vehicle or a railway passenger vehicle if he has reasonable grounds to suspect that an offence under that section is being or has been committed in respect of the vehicle.

Sporting Events (Control of Alcohol) Act 1985, s 7

Meanings

Alcohol (see **9.1.1**)

Article to which s 2 applies

Applies to any article capable of causing injury to a person struck by it, being:

- a bottle, can, or other portable container (including such an article when crushed or broken) which is for holding any drink and, when empty, is normally discarded or returned/recovered by, the supplier; or
- part of any of the above articles;
- but does not apply to anything that holds medicinal/veterinary products.

Designated sporting event

Is a sporting event or proposed sporting event for the time being designated, or of a class designated, by order made by the Secretary of State, and the order may apply to events or proposed events outside GB as well as those in England and Wales.

Period of a designated sporting event

This is the period beginning two hours before the start of the event or (if earlier) two hours before the time at which it is advertised to start and ending one hour after the end of the event.

Designated sports ground

Means any place used (wholly or partly) for sporting events where accommodation is provided for spectators and for the time being designated, or of a class designated, by order made by the Secretary of State. Such an order may include the outer limit of any designated sports ground.

Drunk (see **7.2.1**)

Offence under this Act (see '**Practical considerations**')

Public service vehicle (PSV)

Means a motor vehicle (other than a tramcar) used for carrying passengers for hire or reward, and either adapted to carry more than eight passengers or, not so adapted, which in the course of business carries passengers at separate fares.

Motor vehicle

Means a mechanically propelled vehicle intended or adapted for use on roads.

Explanatory notes

- Article 2 of the Sports Grounds and Sporting Events (Designation) Order 2005 designates the classes of sports grounds in Sch 1 and sporting events in Sch 2 with regards to offences under the 1985 Act:
  - ✦ Sch 1 refers to any sports ground in England and Wales;
  - ✦ Sch 2 lists sporting events—FA matches at sports grounds, being within or outside England and Wales, in which one or both of the participating teams represents a club which is for the time being a member (whether a full or associate member) of the:
    - Football League;
    - Football Association Premier League;
    - Football Conference National Division;
    - Scottish Professional Football League;
    - Welsh Premier League;
    - whose home ground is situated outside England and Wales; or
    - represents a country or territory;

- ✦ FA matches in competition for the FA Cup (other than in a preliminary or qualifying round).
- Whilst this Act was aimed primarily at football matches, it can also apply to other sporting events.

Practical considerations

- Offences under this Act are s 2 (above), and:
  - ✦ s 1—where a vehicle, being a PSV or train, is mainly used for carrying passengers for the whole or part of a journey to or from a designated sporting event, then if the operator/hirer or their servant/agent knowingly causes/permits alcohol to be carried on the vehicle they will commit an offence. An offence is also committed if a person is drunk or in possession of alcohol on the vehicle.
  - ✦ s 1A—where a motor vehicle, which is not a PSV but is adapted to carry more than eight passengers, is mainly used for carrying two or more passengers for the whole or part of a journey to or from a designated sporting event, then a person who knowingly causes/permits alcohol to be carried on the motor vehicle is guilty of an offence if they are the driver, if not the driver but are the keeper or their servant/agent or a person to whom it is made available (by hire, loan, or otherwise) by its keeper or their servant/agent. An offence is also committed if a person is drunk or in possession of alcohol on the motor vehicle.
  - ✦ s 2A—this offence replicates the s 2(1) offence but instead of alcohol or connected receptacle it applies to flares, fireworks, or an article/substance that emits smoke or visible gas (eg distress flares, fog signals, or pellets/capsules used for testing pipes or as fumigators).
- Consider CPS charging standards and guidance for these offences.
- A constable may, at any time during the period of a designated sporting event at any designated sports ground, enter any part of the ground for the purpose of enforcing the provisions of this Act.
- A constable may search a person they have reasonable grounds to suspect is committing or has committed an offence under this Act, all of which are summary offences.

Summary

6 months

s 2(1) offence

3 months' imprisonment and/or a level 3 fine

s 2(2) offence

Level 2 fine

7.18.2 Throw object—designated football match/football banning orders

Offences

It is an offence for a person at a designated football match to throw anything at or towards—

(a) the playing area, or any area adjacent to the playing area to which spectators are not generally admitted, or

(b) any area in which spectators or other persons are or may be present,

without lawful authority or lawful excuse (which shall be for him to prove).

Football (Offences) Act 1991, s 2

PNLD H2740, H3475, H4236

Points to prove

✓ while at a designated football match
✓ without lawful authority/excuse
✓ threw missile/object
✓ at/towards

s 2(a) offence

✓ first four 'Points to prove' (above)
✓ the playing area/area adjacent to playing area
✓ where spectators not generally admitted

s 2(b) offence

✓ first four 'Points to prove' (above)
✓ an area where spectators/other persons
✓ were/may be present

Meaning of designated football match

Means an association football match designated, or of a description designated, for the purposes of this Act by order of the Secretary of State.

Explanatory notes

- Article 3 of the Football (Offences) (Designation of Football Matches) Order 2004 provides the definition of a designated match for the purposes of s 1(1) of the Football (Offences) Act 1991.
  - ✦ A designated match is an association football match in which one or both of the participating teams represents a club which is for the time a member (whether a full or associate member) of the Football League, the Football Association Premier League, the Football Conference, the Football Association Women's Super League, the Football Association Women's Championship, or the

Scottish Professional Football League or the Welsh Premier League, or whose home ground is for the time being situated outside England and Wales, or represents a country or territory.
  - A designated match is an association football match in competition for the FA Cup (other than in a preliminary or qualifying round).
- Offences under this Act can only be committed in England and Wales. The Act covers acts done within a period of two hours before the start of the match (or two hours before the advertised start, if earlier) and ending one hour after the end of the match. Offences could also apply where the match is cancelled, if it has been advertised to start at a particular time on a particular day, in which case it will apply within a period beginning two hours before and ending one hour after the advertised starting times.

Practical considerations

- Offences under this Act are **s 2** (above), **and**:
  - s 3—it is an offence to engage or take part in **chanting** of an indecent or **racialist nature** at a designated football match. For this purpose:
    - chanting means the repeated uttering of any words or sounds (whether alone or in concert with one or more others); and
    - of a racialist nature means consisting of or including matter which is threatening, abusive, or insulting to a person by reason of their colour, race, nationality (including citizenship), or ethnic or national origins;
  - s 4—it is an offence for a person at a designated football match to go onto the playing area, or any area adjacent to the playing area to which spectators are not generally admitted, without lawful authority or lawful excuse (which shall be for them to prove).
- The act of throwing the missile/object constitutes the s 2 offence. There is no need to prove that it was directed at anyone or that anyone was likely to be alarmed or distressed by it.
- Be aware of 'ticket touting' offences under s 166 of the Criminal Justice and Public Order Act 1994 where it is an offence for an unauthorised person to sell a ticket for a designated football match or otherwise to dispose of such a ticket to another person.

Football banning orders

- The Football Spectators Act 1989 controls the admission of spectators to designated football matches by means of a national membership scheme. It also provides for the safety of spectators at such matches. In addition, it empowers the courts to make orders imposing restrictions on persons convicted of certain offences (banning orders) for the purpose of preventing violence or disorder at or in connection with both designated and regulated football matches.

Meanings

Banning order

An order made by the court which:

(a) in relation to regulated football matches in the UK, prohibits the person who is subject to the order from entering any premises for the purpose of attending such matches, and
(b) in relation to regulated football matches outside the UK, requires that person to report at a police station in accordance with this Part.

Regulated football match

An association football match (whether in the UK or elsewhere) which is a prescribed match or a match of a prescribed description.

See also reg 3 of the Football Spectators (Prescription) Order 2022 which widens this definition of a regulated football match.

Regulated football organisation

An organisation (whether in the UK or elsewhere) which:

(a) relates to association football; and
(b) is a prescribed organisation or an organisation of a prescribed description.

See also regs 4 and 5 of the Football Spectators (Prescription) Order 2022 which further define regulation football organisations.

- Section 14A of the 1989 Act applies where a person (the offender) is convicted of a **relevant offence**. Then if the court is satisfied that there are reasonable grounds to believe that making a banning order would help to prevent violence or disorder at or in connection with any regulated football matches, it must make such an order in respect of the offender.
- Schedule 1 to the 1989 Act provides the list of **relevant offences** in relation to applications for banning orders:
  - ✦ any offence under s 14J(1), 19(6), 20(10), or 21C(2) of the Football Spectators Act 1989;
  - ✦ s 2 or 2A offence under the Sporting Events (Control of Alcohol) Act 1985 (alcohol, containers, and fireworks) (see **7.18.1**);
  - ✦ any offence under the Football (Offences) Act 1991;
  - ✦ any offence under s 166 of the Criminal Justice and Public Order Act 1994 (sale of tickets by unauthorised persons) which relates to tickets for a football match;
  - ✦ any of the following offences committed during a period relevant to a designated football match while the accused was at any premises or was entering/leaving or trying to enter/leave the premises:
    - ▪ under s 4, 4A (see **7.7**), or 5 (see **7.8**) of the Public Order Act 1986 (fear or provocation of violence, or harassment, alarm, or distress) or ss 17 to 29 (see **7.9**) of that Act (racial hatred);

  - the use or threat of violence (threatening behaviour or another public order offence) by the accused towards another person (see **2.1**) or property (see **4.4**);
  - the use, carrying, or possession of an offensive weapon (see **8.9**) or a firearm (see **8.1**);
- any of the following offences committed while the accused was on a journey to or from a designated football match, being an offence which the court declares related to football matches:
  - under s 12 of the Licensing Act 1872 (drunk in a highway or public place) (see **7.2.2**);
  - under s 91(1) of the Criminal Justice Act 1967 (drunk and disorderly in a public place) (see **7.2.1**);
  - under s 1 of the Sporting Events (Control of Alcohol) Act 1985, (alcohol on coaches or trains to or from sporting events) (see **7.18.1**);
  - under s 4, 4A (see **7.7**), or 5 (see **7.8**) of the Public Order Act 1986 (fear or provocation of violence, or harassment, alarm, or distress) or ss 17 to 29 (see **7.9**) of that Act (racial hatred);
  - under s 4 (see **10.10.1**), 5 (see **10.11.1**), or 5A (see **10.11.2**) of the Road Traffic Act 1988 (drive while unfit through drink or drugs, while over the alcohol prescribed limit, or above the drugs specified limit);
  - the use or threat of violence by the accused towards another person (see **2.1**) or property (see **4.4**);
  - the use, carrying, or possession of an offensive weapon (see **8.9**) or a firearm (see **8.1**);
- any of the following offences, which do not apply to any of the above circumstances but were committed during a period relevant to a designated football match, and the court declares that the offence related to that match or to that match and any other football match which took place during that period:
  - under s 4, 4A (see **7.7**), or 5 (see **7.8**) of the Public Order Act 1986 (fear or provocation of violence, or harassment, alarm, or distress);
  - the use or threat of violence by the accused towards another person (see **2.1**) or property (see **4.4**);
  - the use, carrying, or possession of an offensive weapon (see **8.9**) or a firearm (see **8.1**);
  - any offence under any provision of Part 3 or 3A of the Public Order Act 1986 (hatred by reference to race etc).

Paragraph 4(2) of Sch 1 provides that for the purposes of this Schedule each of the following periods is 'relevant to' a football match to which this Schedule applies:

(a) in the case of a match which takes place on the day on which it is advertised to take place, the period—
   (i) beginning 24 hours before whichever is the earlier of the start of the match and the time at which it was advertised to start; and
   (ii) ending 24 hours after it ends;

(b) in the case of a match which does not take place on the day on which it was advertised to take place, the period—
  (i) beginning 24 hours before the time at which it was advertised to start on that day; and
  (ii) ending 24 hours after that time.

Practical considerations

Note that football banning orders are not a punishment and, therefore, do not contravene Art 7 of the Human Rights Act 1998—'no punishment without law' (*Gough and another v CC Derbyshire; R (Miller) v Leeds Magistrates' Court; Lilley v DPP*, The Times, 18 July 2001 and 10 April 2002).

Summary

6 months

Level 3 fine

Links to alternative subjects and offences

2.1 **Assault (Common/Actual Bodily Harm)** 53
4.4 **Criminal Damage** 193
4.6 **Threats to Destroy or Damage Property** 203
8.1 **'Section 1 Firearms' Offences** 507
8.9 **Offensive Weapons and Crossbows** 572
9.2 **Drunkenness on Licensed Premises** 633
10.10 **Drive/Attempt to Drive/in Charge of Vehicle While Unfit** 705
10.11 **Drive/Attempt to Drive/in Charge While Over the Prescribed/Specified Limit** 712
Appendix 1 **Human Rights** 839

Chapter 8

Firearms, Fireworks, and Weapons

8.1 'Section 1 Firearms' Offences

The Firearms Act 1968 provides various offences connected with firearms, air weapons, shotguns, and associated ammunition.

8.1.1 Possessing s 1 firearm/ammunition without certificate

This offence involves being in possession of a firearm/ammunition without a valid firearm certificate. Any weapon or ammunition applicable to s 1 is commonly known as a 'section 1 firearm/ammunition'.

Offences

Subject to any exemption under this Act, it is an offence for a person—
(a) to have in his possession, or to purchase or acquire, a firearm to which this section applies without holding a firearm certificate in force at the time, or otherwise than as authorised by such a certificate;
(b) to have in his possession, or to purchase or acquire, any ammunition to which this section applies without holding a firearm certificate in force at the time, or otherwise than as authorised by such a certificate, or in quantities in excess of those so authorised.

Firearms Act 1968, s 1(1)

PNLD H489, H491, H2246, H2248

Points to prove

✓ possessed/purchased/acquired
✓ s 1 firearm/ammunition

8.1.1 **Possessing s 1 firearm/ammunition without certificate**

✓ without/not authorised by/in quantities exceeding those authorised by
✓ a firearms certificate

Meanings

Exemptions

This includes: antique firearms; rifles loaned on private land; carriers, auctioneers, and warehousemen; Crown servants; police; BTP; Civil Nuclear Constabulary; armed forces; athletics and other approved activities; museums; police permits; registered firearms dealers; rifle and pistol clubs; ship and aircraft equipment; licensed slaughterers; theatres and cinemas; Northern Ireland firearms certificate holder; visiting forces; visitors' permits.

Possession

This has a wide meaning. The term has two distinct elements:

- *The mental element*: whereby the defendant must know of the existence of the firearm but cannot claim ignorance that it was technically 'a firearm'.
- *The practical element*: this term is broader than actual physical possession; a person can 'possess' a firearm in a house or premises under their control, even though they are not at the premises. Similarly, the same firearm could be 'possessed' by two people at the same time, such as the firearm's lawful owner and also its custodian who keeps the firearm at their home (see **5.2.1** notes on '**constructive possession**' of drugs).

Purchase

This is not defined and should be given its natural meaning.

Acquire

Means hire, accept as a gift, or borrow.

Firearm to which s 1 applies

This section applies to every **firearm** except:

- normal shotguns (see **8.2.1** for description);
- normal air weapons (see **8.7.2** for description).

Firearm

Means:

(a) a lethal barrelled weapon;
(b) a prohibited weapon;
(c) a relevant component part in relation to a lethal barrelled weapon or prohibited weapon;
(d) an accessory to a lethal barrelled weapon or a prohibited weapon where the accessory is designed or adapted to diminish the noise or flash by firing the weapon.

Lethal barrelled weapon

Means a barrelled weapon of any description from which a shot, bullet, or other missile, with kinetic energy of more than one joule at the muzzle of the weapon, can be discharged.

Shot, bullet, or other missile

These terms are not defined and should be given their natural meaning:
- 'shot' usually means round pellets;
- 'bullet' is normally discharged from a weapon with a rifled barrel;
- 'missile' is a more general term—darts and pellets have been held to be missiles.

Prohibited weapons

- Prohibited weapons and ammunition require an authority from the Secretary of State and the descriptions of such weapons are listed under s 5. The list includes weapons such as: machine guns; self-loading or pump-action rifled guns (other than a 0.22 rifle); rocket launchers; air weapons with self-contained gas cartridge system; grenades; any weapon of whatever description designed or adapted for the discharge of any noxious liquid, gas, or other thing, such as CS spray, stun guns, and conducted energy devices (CED).
- Any written authority granted will have conditions imposed so as not to endanger the public safety or the peace.
- A person commits an offence under s 5 if, without an authority from the Secretary of State, they possess, purchase or acquire, manufacture, sell, or transfer any prohibited weapon or ammunition.
- Failure to comply with any condition imposed by this authority is also an offence under s 5(5).
- The Secretary of State may revoke an authority by notice in writing. Failure to return the authority within twenty-one days is an offence under s 5(6).
- The Anti-social Behaviour, Crime and Policing Act 2014, s 108, inserted s 5(2A) so that an offence will be committed if, without authority, a person manufactures; sells or transfers; possesses, purchases, or acquires for sale or transfer, any prohibited weapon, device, or prohibited ammunition. This offence carries a sentence of life imprisonment if a person manufactures, distributes, or possesses for distribution any prohibited weapons or ammunition. HOC 9/2014 provides further details.
- The Offensive Weapons Act 2019, s 54, made further changes to s 5 prohibited weapons, which inserted any rifle with a chamber from which empty cartridge cases are extracted using propellant gas (see **8.7.3**) (other than a rifle which is chambered for 0.22 rim-fire cartridges); secondly, prohibiting devices commonly known as 'bump stocks', namely, one that is designed or adapted so that:
  (a) it is capable of forming part of or being added to a self-loading lethal barrelled weapon (as defined in s 57(1B) and (2A)); and

(b) if it forms part of or is added to such a weapon, it increases the rate of fire of the weapon by using the recoil from the weapon to generate repeated pressure on the trigger.

Component part

Each of the following items is a relevant component part in relation to a lethal barrelled weapon or a prohibited weapon as defined in s 57(1D) but only where the item is capable of being used as part of a lethal barrelled weapon or a prohibited weapon, including:

(a) a barrel, chamber, or cylinder;
(b) a frame, body, or receiver;
(c) a breech block, bolt, or other mechanism for containing the pressure of discharge at the rear of a chamber.

Accessory

This is given its natural meaning and includes such accessories as a silencer or flash eliminator.

Firearm certificate

Means a certificate granted by a chief officer of police in respect of any firearm or ammunition to which s 1 applies.

Ammunition to which s 1 applies

This section applies to any **ammunition** for any firearm, except the following articles, namely:

- cartridges containing five or more shot, none of which exceeds 0.36 inch in diameter;
- ammunition for an air gun, air rifle, or air pistol; and
- blank cartridges not more than one inch in diameter.

Ammunition

Means ammunition—being any shot, bullet, or other missile—for any firearm and includes grenades, bombs, and other like missiles, whether capable of use with a firearm or not, and also includes prohibited ammunition.

Explanatory notes

- This is an offence of strict liability.
- A telescopic laser/night sight is **not** a component part or accessory that requires a firearm certificate.
- Whether a silencer or flash eliminator can be an accessory will be a question of fact to be determined in all the circumstances (ie whether it could be used with that firearm and did the defendant have it with them for that purpose). It is the accessory that must be 'so designed or adapted', not the weapon.
- Blank cartridges are cases with primer (small explosive charge at the end of the cartridge) and gunpowder; or primed cartridges (as blank but without the gunpowder) both able to be used in a firearm and producing an explosive effect when fired. It is considered that blank

cartridges are included under the general term 'ammunition'. However, in accordance with s 1(4), blank cartridges not more than one inch in diameter, measured immediately in front of the rim or cannelure of the base of the cartridge, are exempt from the certification procedure.
- It is a summary offence under s 35 of the Violent Crime Reduction Act 2006 for a person to sell or purchase a cap-type primer designed for use in metallic ammunition for a firearm being either:
  - ✦ a primer to which this section applies;
  - ✦ an empty cartridge case incorporating such a primer;

  unless that person: is a registered firearms dealer; it is their trade or business; produces a certificate authorising possession; is in His Majesty's Services and entitled to do so; or shows that they are entitled by virtue of any enactment.
- An airsoft gun, being a barrelled weapon of any description which is designed to discharge only a small plastic missile (see s 57A of the Firearms Act 1968) is not regarded as a firearm for the purposes of this Act.
- Section 58(2) of the Firearms Act 1968 exempts firearms regarded as antique from most of the controls under the Act. This includes being able to possess a firearm without a firearms certificate and to trade in them without being registered with the police as a firearms dealer. Section 58 also provides a definition of an antique firearm: see also the Antique Firearms Regulations 2021.

Defences

There is no statutory defence as it is an offence of strict liability.

Related cases

Jenkins V DPP [2020] EWHC 1307 (Admin) A stun gun being placed in the glove compartment of the defendant's vehicle which was then driven, showed a degree of control and amounted to 'possession'.

R v Heddell [2016] EWCA Crim 443 An imitation firearm could still be a prohibited firearm where it was readily convertible without the use of specialist knowledge or skills.

R v Deyemi and Edwards [2007] All ER 369, CA The defendants were in possession of an electrical stun gun which discharged electricity through electrodes (a prohibited weapon under s 5(1)(b)). In their defence, the defendants said that they believed it was a torch. It was held that offences under ss 1 and 5 are strict liability.

R v Steele [1993] Crim LR 298 Conviction for possession of a firearm was safe where the defendant's denial of the knowledge of the contents of a bag in their possession was not a valid defence; possession of a firearm without a certificate is an absolute offence. The judge ruled that 'the fact that the defendant had custody of the holdall for only a matter of a minute or did not know or could not reasonably have been expected to know that it contained a firearm would afford no defence'.

Moore v Gooderham [1960] 3 All ER 575, QBD This case considered what constituted a lethal barrelled weapon. It was held that the test to be applied was: 'Is this a weapon which, however misused, may cause injury from which death may result?' If the answer is 'Yes' the weapon should be classed as a 'lethal barrelled weapon'.

Practical considerations

- The prosecution need only prove knowledge of the existence of the item, as opposed to its nature. Similarly, there is no onus to prove that the defendant knew that the article was a firearm.
- In practice, forensic testing will determine whether weapons are lethal or not. The main characteristic that is measured is the muzzle velocity (the speed at which the projectile leaves the barrel).
- Certain imitation or replica firearms may be s 1 firearms (see **8.1.4**).
- A s 1 firearm can only be possessed by a firearms certificate holder or some other lawful authority such as a registered firearms dealer, member of the armed forces, or police officer.
- If someone had a silencer in their possession with no evidence linking it to a suitable weapon, possession alone is unlikely to be an offence.
- All repeating shotguns holding more than two cartridges (eg pump-action and revolver shotguns) are 's 1 firearms'.

SSS E&S

Either way

None

Summary: 6/12 months' imprisonment and/or a fine

Indictment: 5 years' imprisonment and/or a fine (where the offence is committed in the aggravated form within the meaning of s 4(4) of the Act, maximum 7 years' imprisonment and/or a fine)

8.1.2 Aggravated s 1 offences/registered firearms dealers

The offences of possessing, purchasing, or acquiring a s 1 firearm carry a greater punishment if they are aggravated by the shotgun barrel being less than 24 inches long (creating a 'sawn-off' shotgun) or illegally converting anything having the appearance of a firearm into a s 1 firearm.

Offences

(1) Subject to this section [see '**Defences**'], it is an offence to shorten the barrel of a shotgun to a length less than 24 inches.

(3) It is an offence for a person other than a registered firearms dealer to convert into a firearm anything, which though having the appearance of being a firearm, is so constructed as to be incapable of discharging any missile through its barrel.

(4) A person who commits an offence under section 1 of this Act by having in his possession, or purchasing or acquiring, a shotgun which has been shortened contrary to subsection (1) above or a firearm which has been converted as mentioned in subsection (3) above (whether by a registered firearms dealer or not), without holding a firearm certificate authorising him to have it in his possession, or to purchase or acquire it, shall be treated for the purposes of provisions of this Act relating to the punishment of offences as committing that offence in an aggravated form.

Firearms Act 1968, s 4

PNLD H1786, H1787, H2220, H2262, H1785, H2079

Points to prove

- ✓ possessed/purchased/acquired
- ✓ a shortened shotgun barrel (to length less than 24 inches) or a thing converted into a firearm
- ✓ without holding/not authorised by
- ✓ a firearm certificate

Meanings

Registered

Means registered, as a **firearms dealer**, under s 33 of this Act; and references to 'the register', 'registration', and a 'certificate of registration' shall be construed accordingly, except in s 40.

Firearms dealer

Means a person who, by way of trade or business:

- manufactures, sells, transfers, repairs, tests, or proves firearms, or ammunition to which s 1 of this Act applies, or shotguns; or
- sells or transfers air weapons.

Explanatory notes

- This offence could apply to weapons such as starting pistols or imitation firearms which have been converted to s 1 firearms.
- A shotgun which has a barrel shortened to less than 24 inches becomes a s 1 firearm. The length of the barrel is determined by measuring from the muzzle to the point at which the charge is exploded on firing the cartridge.

Defences

It is not an offence under subsection (1) above for a registered firearms dealer to shorten the barrel of a shotgun for the sole purpose of replacing a defective part of the barrel so as to produce a barrel not less than 24 inches in length.

Firearms Act 1968, s 4(2)

Practical considerations

- Section 3(1) makes it an offence, if by way of trade or business, a person:
  - ✦ manufactures, sells, transfers, repairs, tests, or proves any firearm or ammunition to which s 1 of this Act applies, or a shotgun;
  - ✦ exposes for sale or transfer, or has in their possession for sale, transfer, repair, test, or proof any such firearm or ammunition, or a shotgun; or
  - ✦ sells or transfers an air weapon, exposes such a weapon for sale or transfer, or has such a weapon in their possession for sale or transfer;

  without being registered under this Act as a firearms dealer.
- Consider confiscation of cash and property for the s 3(1) offence (above), as this is given as a 'criminal lifestyle' offence under Sch 2 to the Proceeds of Crime Act 2002 (see **5.5** for details).
- Section 32 of the Violent Crime Reduction Act 2006 makes it a summary offence to sell air weapons by way of trade or business other than face-to-face to an individual who is not a registered firearms dealer. This allows an air weapon to be sent from one registered firearms dealer to another to make the final transfer in person to the buyer. Guidance is given on ss 31 and 32 in HOC 31/2007.

SSS E&S

Either way

None

Summary: 6/12 months' imprisonment and/or a fine

Indictment: 7 years' imprisonment and/or a fine

8.1.3 Restrictions on s 1 firearms/ ammunition to under 14 years

Sections 22(2) and 24(2) of the Firearms Act 1968 place tight restrictions on persons under the age of 14 years from possessing, or receiving as gifts or on loan, any s 1 firearm/ammunition.

Offences

Possession by under 14

It is an offence for a person under the age of fourteen to have in his possession any firearm or ammunition to which section 1 of this Act applies, except in circumstances where under section 11(1), (3) or (4) of this Act or section 15 of the Firearms (Amendment) Act 1988 he is entitled to have possession of it without holding a firearm certificate.

Firearms Act 1968, s 22(2)

Make gift, lend, or part with possession to under 14

It is an offence—

(a) to make a gift of or lend any firearm or ammunition to which section 1 of this Act applies to a person under the age of 14; or

(b) to part with the possession of any such firearm or ammunition to a person under that age, except in circumstances where that person is entitled under section 11(1), (3) or (4) of this Act or section 15 of the Firearms (Amendment) Act 1988 to have possession thereof without holding a firearm certificate.

Firearms Act 1968, s 24(2)

PNLD H505, H541, H512, H573, H574

Points to prove

Possess

✓ being a person under the age of 14 years
✓ possessed
✓ any s 1 firearm or ammunition

Make gift/lend/part with possession

✓ make a gift/lend/part with possession
✓ a s 1 firearm or ammunition
✓ to a person under the age of 14 years

Meanings

Possession

This has a wide meaning (see **8.1.1**).

Section 1 firearm or ammunition (see **8.1.1**)

Section 15 of the Firearms (Amendment) Act 1988

This provides the mechanism for the creation of approved rifle and **muzzle-loading pistol** clubs where members can, if they wish, use such weapons without being the holder of a firearm certificate.

Muzzle-loading pistol

Means a pistol designed to be loaded at the muzzle end of the barrel or chambered with a loose charge (such as gun powder) and a separate ball (or other missile).

Explanatory notes

- These restrictions are in addition to those imposed on persons under 18 and 15 years of age.
- Both offences can be committed anywhere and not just in a public place.

- The 1968 Act s **11 exceptions**, applicable to both offences are:
  - ✦ a person carrying a firearm or ammunition belonging to another person holding a certificate under this Act may, without themselves holding such a certificate, have in their possession that firearm or ammunition under instructions from, and for the use of, that other person for sporting purposes only; but where the person carrying the firearm or ammunition is under the age of 18, this subsection applies only if the other person is of or over the age of 18 (see s 11(1)).
  - ✦ a person conducting or carrying on a miniature rifle range (whether for a rifle club or otherwise) or shooting gallery at which no firearms are used other than air weapons or miniature rifles not exceeding 0.23 inch calibre, may possess, purchase, or acquire such miniature rifles and ammunition suitable for that purpose; and any person using such rifles/ammunition at such a range or gallery (see s 11(4)).
- Section 11A of the Firearms Act 1968 provides additional provisions for the authorised lending and possession of firearms for hunting.
- Any firearm or ammunition found on a person for these offences may be confiscated by the court.

Defences

Both offences

The s 11 exceptions (see '**Explanatory notes**' above) may apply.

Section 24(2) offence

Under s 24(5), having reasonable grounds to believe that the person was 14 years of age or over (see **8.7.1**).

SSS

Summary

48 months (consent of DPP required after 6 months)

6 months' imprisonment and/or a fine

8.1.4 Imitation/replica firearm—convertible to s 1 firearm

Section 1 of the Firearms Act 1982 controls imitation firearms and, subject to conditions, brings them within the scope of s 1 of the Firearms Act 1968.

> This Act applies to an imitation firearm if it—
> (a) has the appearance of being a firearm to which section 1 of the 1968 Act (firearms requiring a certificate) applies; and

(b) is so constructed or adapted as to be readily convertible into a firearm to which that section applies.

Firearms Act 1982, s 1(1)

Points to prove

✓ possessed/purchased/acquired
✓ an imitation firearm
✓ having the appearance of a s 1 firearm AND
✓ is constructed/adapted so as to be readily converted into a s 1 firearm
✓ without holding a firearms certificate

Meanings

Imitation firearm (see **8.3.3**)

Section 1 firearm (see **8.1.1**)

Certificate (see **8.1.1**)

Readily convertible into a firearm

Section 1(6) states that an imitation firearm shall be regarded as readily convertible into a firearm to which s 1 of the 1968 Act applies if:

(a) it can be so converted without any special skill on the part of the person converting it in the construction or adaptation of firearms of any description; and
(b) the work involved in converting it does not require equipment or tools other than such as are in common use by persons carrying out works of construction and maintenance in their own homes.

Explanatory notes

- A readily convertible imitation firearm that can be turned into a s 1 firearm will require a firearms certificate.
- The Firearms Act 1982, s 1 was enacted because some 'replica' weapons could be converted into s 1 working firearms with no specialist skill/tools.
- Excepting s 4(3) and (4), ss 16 to 20, and s 47, the provisions of the 1968 Act shall apply in relation to an imitation firearm to which this Act applies as it applies to a 's 1 firearm'.
- Apart from excepted air weapons, component parts, and accessories, any expression given a meaning for the purposes of the 1968 Act has the same meaning in this Act.

Defences

It shall be a defence for the accused to show that he did not know and had no reason to suspect that the imitation firearm was so constructed or adapted as to be readily convertible into a firearm to which section 1 of that Act applies.

Firearms Act 1982, s 1(5)

SSS E&S

Either way None

Summary: 6/12 months' imprisonment and/or a fine

Indictment: 5 years' imprisonment and/or a fine

Aggravated offence (see **8.1.2**): 7 years' imprisonment and/or a fine

8.1.5 Failing to comply with firearm certificate conditions

Offence

It is an offence for a person to fail to comply with a condition subject to which a firearm certificate is held by him.

Firearms Act 1968, s 1(2)

PNLD H2120

Points to prove

✓ failed to comply with condition
✓ subject to which firearm certificate is held

Meaning of firearm certificate (see 8.1.1)

Explanatory notes

- Section 27(2) of the 1968 Act stipulates that a firearm certificate shall be in the prescribed form and shall specify the **conditions** subject to which it is held. Those conditions are set out in the Firearms Rules 1998 (SI 1941/1998) and HOC 41/1998, with prescribed forms under HOC 16/2013.
- A statutory **condition** under the Firearms (Amendment) Act 1988, s 14 also imposes a duty on auctioneers, carriers, or warehousemen to take reasonable care of the custody of firearms and/or ammunition which they have in their possession without holding a certificate; being an offence if they fail to keep them in safe custody or fail to notify any loss or theft forthwith to the police.

Related cases

DPP v Houghton-Brown [2010] EWHC 3527 (Admin) Leaving a firearm loaded under a pile of clothing on the back seat of a car while it was parked on a city street can be considered reasonable steps taken to ensure the safe custody of the firearm.

Hall v Cotton [1976] 3 WLR 681, QBD The defendant owned two shotguns and held a shotgun certificate, took the guns to a friend's house for safe keeping, and then went on holiday. The police checked the guns some six weeks later. It was held that the defendant remained in possession of the firearms even though there was no physical control of them while they were at the friend's house. The friend had custodial possession of the guns without a certificate as they had been 'transferred' to their possession.

Summary

48 months

6 months' imprisonment and/or a fine

Links to alternative subjects and offences

2.3.2 **Wounding or grievous bodily harm—with intent** 82
2.5 **Threats to Kill** 97
2.7 **Sudden and Unexplained Deaths** 109
5.5 **Proceeds of Crime** 270
Appendix 4 **Firearms Offences Relating to Age** 857

8.2 Shotgun Offences

The Firearms Act 1968 provides various offences connected with firearms, associated ammunition, air weapons, and shotguns.

8.2.1 Shotgun without a certificate

Section 2 of the Firearms Act 1968 creates the offence of possessing, purchasing, or acquiring a shotgun when not being the holder of a relevant certificate.

Offences

Subject to any exemption under this Act, it is an offence for a person to have in his possession or to purchase or acquire a shotgun without holding a certificate under this Act authorising him to possess shotguns.

Firearms Act 1968, s 2(1)

PNLD H2176, H2180

Points to prove

✓ possessed/purchased/acquired
✓ a shotgun
✓ without a certificate

Meanings

Exemptions (see **8.1.1**)

Possession (see **8.1.1**)

Purchase (see **8.1.1**)

Acquire (see **8.1.1**)

Shotgun

Means a smooth-bore gun (not being an air gun) which:

- has a barrel not less than 24 inches in length and does not have any barrel with a bore exceeding 2 inches in diameter;
- either has no magazine or has a non-detachable magazine incapable of holding more than two cartridges; **and**
- is not a **revolver** gun.

Revolver

In relation to a smooth-bore gun, means a gun containing a series of chambers which revolve when the gun is fired.

Shotgun certificate

Means a certificate granted by a chief officer of police under this Act authorising a person to possess shotguns.

Explanatory notes

- The length of the barrel of a firearm is measured from the muzzle to the point at which the charge is exploded on firing, in the case of a shotgun that length must not be less than 24 inches, otherwise it becomes a s 1 firearm (see **8.1.2**).
- Some antique shotguns may be classed as an 'antique firearm' and thus be exempt from shotgun offences. However, if 'modern' cartridges can be bought and fired using an antique shotgun it cannot be exempt. This exemption does not cover a modern replica of an antique weapon.
- For a full definition of antique firearms, see s 58 of the Firearms Act 1968 and the Antique Firearms Regulations 2021.
- An auctioneer cannot sell shotguns without either being a registered firearms dealer or obtaining a police permit.
- A person may, without holding a shotgun certificate, use a shotgun at a time and place approved for shooting at artificial targets by the chief officer of police for the area in which the place is situated (s 11(6)).

Practical considerations

- All repeating shotguns holding more than two cartridges (eg pump-action and revolver shotguns) are s 1 firearms.
- Offences may be committed in relation to persons under 15 years where they have an assembled shotgun with them or for a person to give them a shotgun/ammunition as a gift (see **8.2.2**).
- Any offence involving a shotgun that has an illegally shortened barrel (less than 24 inches), being a 'sawn-off' shotgun, will be an 'aggravated offence' (see **8.1.2**) carrying a greater penalty. It will also make the shotgun a s 1 firearm.
- A shotgun is deemed to be loaded if there is a cartridge in the barrel or approved magazine that can feed the cartridge into the barrel by manual or automatic means.
- A shotgun adapted to have a magazine must bear a mark on the magazine showing approval by the Secretary of State.
- 'Shotgun' includes any component part and any accessory for a shotgun designed or adapted to diminish the noise or flash caused by firing the gun.

SSS E&S

Either way

None

Summary: 6/12 months' imprisonment and/or a fine

Indictment: 5 years' imprisonment and/or a fine

8.2.2 Shotgun restrictions to under 15 years

Sections 22(3) and 24(3) of the Firearms Act 1968 impose shotgun restrictions relating to persons under 15.

Offences

Under 15 have with them

It is an offence for a person under the age of fifteen to have with him an assembled shotgun, except while under the supervision of a person of or over the age of twenty one, or while the shotgun is so covered with a securely fastened gun cover that it cannot be fired.

Firearms Act 1968, s 22(3)

Make gift to under 15

It is an offence to make a gift of a shotgun or ammunition for a shotgun to a person under the age of fifteen.

Firearms Act 1968, s 24(3)

PNLD H506, H514

Points to prove

Have with them

✓ person under 15
✓ had with them
✓ assembled shotgun

Make gift

✓ made a gift of
✓ shotgun/ammunition for a shotgun
✓ to a person under 15

Meanings

With him (see **8.3.6**)

Shotgun (see **8.2.1**)

Defence for person making gift (see s 24(5), **8.7.1**)

Practical considerations

- Offences in relation to air weapons/firearms are imposed on persons under 18 years (see **8.7.1** and **8.7.2**).
- Both ss 22(3) and 24(3) offences can be committed anywhere and not just in a public place.

- A court can order the destruction of any shotgun and ammunition to which this offence relates.
- Restrictions also apply to persons under 14 years in relation to s 1 firearms (see **8.1.3**).

SSS

Summary

6 months

Level 3 fine

8.2.3 Fail to comply with shotgun certificate conditions

Section 2 of the Firearms Act 1968 creates an offence of failing to comply with a condition imposed by a shotgun certificate.

Offences

It is an offence for a person to fail to comply with a condition subject to which a shotgun certificate is held by him.

Firearms Act 1968, s 2(2)

PNLD H2119

Points to prove

✓ failed to comply with condition
✓ subject to which shotgun certificate is held

Meaning of shotgun certificate (see 8.2.1)

Practical considerations

- Regarding public safety, the two main **conditions** applying to shotgun certificate holders are the failure to keep the shotgun(s) and/or cartridges in safe custody or in failing to notify any loss forthwith to the police.
- Under s 28(1), a chief officer of police has to be satisfied that the applicant can be permitted to possess a shotgun without danger to the public safety or to the peace.
- Section 28(1A) states that no certificate shall be granted or renewed if the chief officer of police has reason to believe that the applicant is prohibited from possessing a shotgun **or** does not have a good reason for possessing, purchasing, or acquiring one. However, a

certificate can be extended for a period of eight weeks beginning with the day after the day at the end of which the certificate was due to expire, allowing time for the chief officer to make a decision.

- It is an offence, under s 28A(7), to knowingly or recklessly make a false statement for the purpose of procuring the grant or renewal of a certificate.
- There is a presumption in favour of granting unless the police can prove any of the exemptions.
- The certificate must contain a description of the weapon including identity numbers.

Summary 48 months

6 months' imprisonment and/or a fine

Links to alternative subjects and offences

2.3.2 **Wounding or grievous bodily harm—with intent** 82
2.5 **Threats to Kill** 97
Appendix 4 **Firearms Offences Relating to Age** 857

8.3 Criminal Use of Firearms

There is a raft of legislation which was put in place to try and curb possession of firearms by criminals: some of these measures are discussed below.

8.3.1 Ban on possession by convicted person

Section 21 of the Firearms Act 1968 creates an offence for the possession of any firearm or ammunition by convicted criminals. The section first provides for three types of ban: total; five years from date of release; and while under a licence, order, or binding-over condition.

Lengths of ban

Total ban

A person who has been sentenced to custody for life or preventive detention, imprisonment, or corrective training for a term of three years or more, or to youth custody or detention in a young offender institution for such a term, shall not **at any time** have a firearm or ammunition in their possession—s 21(1).

Five years

- A person who has been sentenced to imprisonment for a term of three months or more but less than three years, or to youth custody or detention in a young offender institution for such a term, or who has been subject to a secure training order or a detention and training order, shall not at any time before the expiration of the period of five years from **the date of release** have a **firearm** or **ammunition** in their **possession**—s 21(2).
- Where a person has been sentenced to imprisonment, or detention in a young offender institution for a term of three months or more, and the sentence is suspended under s 189 of the Criminal Justice Act 2003, or s 264 or 277 of the Sentencing Code, the person shall not have a firearm or ammunition in their possession at any time during the period of five years beginning with the second day after the date on which the sentence is passed—s 21(2C).

Other bans

A person who:

- being the holder of a licence issued for the detention of children and young persons convicted of serious crime but enables them to be discharged on licence by the Secretary of State; or

- is subject of a recognizance to keep the peace or be of good behaviour, a condition of which is that they shall not possess, use, or carry a firearm, or is subject to a community order containing a requirement that they shall not possess, use, or carry a firearm,

shall not at any time during which they hold the licence or are so subject or have been so ordained, have a firearm or ammunition in their possession—s 21(3).

Offences

Possess whilst banned

It is an offence for a person to contravene any of the foregoing provisions of this section [*contravene any of the above bans*].

Firearms Act 1968, s 21(4)

Sell/transfer/repair/test/prove for banned person

It is an offence for a person to sell or transfer a firearm or ammunition to, or to repair, test or prove a firearm or ammunition for, a person whom he knows or has reasonable ground for believing to be prohibited by this section from having a firearm or ammunition in his possession.

Firearms Act 1968, s 21(5)

PNLD H9753, H9754, H9756, H18704, H2208, H2219

Points to prove

Possess whilst banned

- ✓ being person sentenced to
- ✓ imprisonment/youth custody/detention in YOI/detention and training order/secure training order/suspended sentence or other sentence subject to s 21(3)
- ✓ for a term of [period]
- ✓ possessed a firearm and/or ammunition namely [description]
- ✓ while banned/before the expiration of ban

Sell/transfer/repair/test/prove for banned person

- ✓ sell/transfer OR repair/test/prove
- ✓ firearm or ammunition for
- ✓ a person
- ✓ prohibited by s 21 from possessing

Meanings

Date of release

Details vary and are as follows:

- normal sentence—actual date a prisoner leaves prison;
- part imprisonment and part suspended sentence—date of release from prison;

- a 'secure training order' or 'detention and training order' whichever is the latest of the following:
  - ✦ actual date of release;
  - ✦ date the person was released from the order because of a breach;
  - ✦ date halfway through the total period of the order.

Possession (see **8.1.1**)

Firearm or ammunition (see **8.1.1**)

Practical considerations

- A person given a suspended sentence of three months or more imprisonment will be subject to a five-year ban under s 21(2C).
- Where there are several short sentences, it is the total sentence that counts.
- Anyone who is banned by these provisions can apply to the Crown Court under s 21(6) for removal of the ban.
- Do not confuse the terms 'firearm' or 'ammunition' with 's 1 firearms or ammunition'. This section includes **all** firearms including air weapons and shotguns.
- If it is an air weapon, it must be proved that it can discharge a shot or missile and that it is a lethal barrelled weapon, capable of causing injury from which death could result.

SSS E&S

Either way

None

Summary: 6/12 months' imprisonment and/or a fine

Indictment: 5 years' imprisonment and/or a fine

8.3.2 Possession with intent to endanger life

Section 16 of the Firearms Act 1968 creates the offence of possession of a firearm or ammunition with intent to endanger life.

Offences

It is an offence for a person to have in his possession any firearm or ammunition with intent by means thereof to endanger life or to enable another person by means thereof to endanger life, whether any injury has been caused or not.

Firearms Act 1968, s 16

PNLD H1763, H2218, H2212, H2224

8.3.2 **Possession with intent to endanger life**

Points to prove

✓ possessed firearm/ammunition
✓ with intent
✓ to endanger life/enable another to endanger life thereby

Meanings

Possession (see **8.1.1**)

Firearm or ammunition

Includes all firearms and ammunition (see **8.1.1**).

Intent (see **4.1.2**)

Endanger life

Life need not actually be endangered, although if there is danger to life this may assist in proving intent. There is no need to prove any harm or injury to the victim.

Explanatory note

- The intention to endanger life need not be immediate, but it must result from the firearm/ammunition (eg if the defendant possesses the firearm or ammunition but intends to endanger life some other way, say by arson, this offence is **not** committed).

Related cases

R v Salih [2007] EWCA Crim 2750 The law would be seriously impaired if a person who reasonably thought that, at some point, they may be unlawfully attacked, was allowed to carry a weapon. However, if a person carrying a firearm or offensive weapon is at that time in fear of an imminent attack and is carrying the weapon for self-protection against an explicit and specific threat then that might be a different matter.

R v El-hakkaoui [1975] 2 All ER 146 It is an offence under s 16 for a person (in the UK) to have in their possession a firearm/ammunition with intent to endanger the life of people outside the UK.

Practical considerations

- The offence of possession for another to endanger life requires the firearm to be specifically held intending that the other should endanger life with it. If the firearm/ammunition is simply held for someone known to be involved in crime, that will be insufficient for this offence.
- Consider the alternative offences of possession:
  - with intent to cause fear of violence (which covers a wider set of circumstances) (see **8.3.3**);
  - at the time of committing/being arrested for a relevant offence (see **8.3.5**).

SSS E&S

Indictable

None

Life imprisonment and/or a fine

8.3.3 Possession with intent to cause fear of violence

Section 16A of the Firearms Act 1968 creates an offence of possessing a firearm (or imitation firearm) with intent to cause others to fear unlawful violence being used against them.

Offences

It is an offence for a person to have in his possession any firearm or imitation firearm with intent—
(a) by means thereof to cause; or
(b) to enable another person by means thereof to cause
any person to believe that unlawful violence will be used against him or another person.

Firearms Act 1968, s 16A

PNLD H1162, H1163, H1215, H1164

Points to prove

- ✓ had in your possession
- ✓ a firearm/imitation firearm
- ✓ with intent
- ✓ to cause/enable another to cause
- ✓ any person
- ✓ to believe unlawful violence will be used
- ✓ against them or another person

Meanings

Possession (see **8.1.1**)

Firearm

Means all firearms, not just s 1 firearms (see **8.1.1**).

Imitation firearm

Means any thing that has the appearance of being a firearm (other than appearance of a prohibited weapon under s 5(1)(b) for discharge of any noxious liquid, gas, or other thing) whether or not it is capable of discharging any shot, bullet, or other missile.

Intent (see **4.1.2**)

Unlawful violence

Means the unlawful exercise of physical force so as to cause injury.

Related case

R v Rahman and Others [2023] EWCA Crim 1177 The defendants in this case were wrongly charged on one count. The possession of ammunition with intent to cause fear of violence is not an offence; therefore, the defendants could not conspire to commit such an offence.

Practical considerations

- The offence can be committed anywhere and does not require intent to commit any specific criminal offence.
- It does not matter if the weapon is an imitation, inoperative, or unloaded. (The scope of the offence under s 16 requires possession of a firearm or ammunition with intent to endanger life.)
- Violence is not defined by the statute so its ordinary meaning should apply. A dictionary meaning is 'the exercise of physical force so as to cause injury to a person'. The violence has to be 'unlawful' (eg a police officer pointing a firearm to subdue an armed suspect in the course of a lawful arrest would not commit the offence). Actual violence does not need to be committed, merely a genuine belief by a victim that such violence would be used.

SSS E&S

Indictable None

10 years' imprisonment and/or a fine

8.3.4 Using a firearm to resist or prevent a lawful arrest

Section 17(1) of the Firearms Act 1968 creates the offence of using a firearm or imitation firearm to resist or prevent a lawful arrest.

Offences

It is an offence for a person to make or attempt to make any use whatsoever of a firearm or imitation firearm with intent to resist or prevent the lawful arrest or detention of himself or another person.

Firearms Act 1968, s 17(1)

PNLD H2285, H2293

Points to prove

- ✓ made/attempted to make use
- ✓ of a firearm/an imitation firearm
- ✓ with intent
- ✓ to resist/prevent lawful arrest/detention
- ✓ of self/another

Meanings

Firearm

The definition of firearms for this offence is taken from s 57 and means all firearms except prohibited weapons or relevant component parts in relation to lethal barrelled weapons or prohibited weapons.

Imitation firearm (see **8.3.3**)

Intent (see **4.1.2**)

Explanatory note

- It has to be proved that the firearm was being used intentionally to resist/prevent the lawful arrest of the offender or another person.

SSS E&S

Indictable None

Life imprisonment and/or a fine

8.3.5 Possession at time of committing/being arrested

Section 17(2) of the Firearms Act 1968 makes it an offence to be in possession of a firearm or imitation firearm at the time of arrest for certain specified offences.

Offences

If a person at the time of his committing or being arrested for an offence specified in schedule 1 to this Act, has in his possession a firearm or imitation firearm he shall be guilty of an offence under this subsection unless he shows that he had it in his possession for a lawful object.

Firearms Act 1968, s 17(2)

8.3.5 Possession at time of committing/being arrested

PNLD H1750, H1751, H2201, H2204, H2203, H2202, H2231, H2206

Points to prove

✓ at the time of being arrested for/committing
✓ a Sch 1 offence
✓ possessed firearm/imitation firearm

Meanings

Schedule 1 offences

- Criminal Damage Act 1971, s 1—damage; damage with intent to endanger life; arson.
- Offences Against the Person Act 1861—
  - s 20—wounding/GBH;
  - s 21—criminal intent choke/strangle;
  - s 22—criminal use of stupefying drugs;
  - s 30—laying explosive to building, etc;
  - s 32—endangering persons by tampering with railway;
  - s 38—assault with intent to resist lawful arrest;
  - s 47—assault occasioning actual bodily harm.
- Child Abduction Act 1984, Part 1—abduction of children.
- Theft Act 1968—burglary; blackmail; theft: robbery; taking of motor vehicles.
- Police Act 1996—assaulting/impeding a police officer.
- Criminal Justice Act 1991—assault prisoner custody officer.
- Criminal Justice and Public Order Act 1994—assault secure training centre custody officer.
- Criminal Justice and Courts Act 2015—assault secure college custody officer.
- Sexual Offences Act 2003:
  - s 1—rape;
  - s 2—assault by penetration;
  - s 4—cause person to engage in sexual activity involving penetration;
  - s 5—rape of a child under 13;
  - s 6—assault of a child under 13 by penetration;
  - s 8—cause/incite child under 13 to engage in sexual activity involving penetration;
  - s 30—sexual activity with a mentally disordered person involving penetration;
  - s 31—cause/incite mentally disordered person to engage in penetrative sexual activity.
- Aiding and abetting any of the Sch 1 offences.
- Attempting to commit any of the Sch 1 offences.

Possession (see **8.1.1**)

Firearm (see **8.3.4**)

Imitation firearm (see **8.3.3**)

Defences

Proving possession of the firearm or imitation firearm for a lawful reason or purpose.

Explanatory note

- There is no need to prove any use or intended use of the firearm. Possession of it may be completely unconnected with the other offence committed by the person or for which they are arrested.

Related case

R v Nelson [2000] All ER (D) 206 When the defendant is arrested for a 'relevant' Sch 1 offence, there is no need to prove the Sch 1 offence itself.

SSS E&S

Indictable   None

Life imprisonment and/or a fine

8.3.6 Carrying firearm—criminal intent/resist arrest

Section 18 of the Firearms Act 1968 makes it an offence to carry a firearm or imitation firearm with criminal intent or to resist/prevent arrest.

Offences

It is an offence for a person to have with him a firearm or imitation firearm with intent to commit an indictable offence, or to resist arrest or prevent the arrest of another, in either case while he has the firearm or imitation firearm with him.

Firearms Act 1968, s 18 (1)

PNLD H1706, H1707, H1708, H1709, H2142, H1710

Points to prove

- ✓ had with them
- ✓ a firearm/imitation firearm
- ✓ with intent
- ✓ to commit an indictable offence/resist arrest/prevent the arrest of another

Meanings

Has with him

This is a narrower definition than 'possession' (see **8.1.1**). Here there is a need to prove:

- a knowledge of the existence of the article;
- that the article was 'to hand and ready for use' (eg it might be hidden a few feet away: it does not have to be physically on the defendant's person).

Firearm (see **8.3.3**)

Imitation firearm (see **8.3.3**)

Intent (see **4.1.2**)

Indictable offence

This includes either way offences.

Related cases

R v Duhaney, R v Stoddart (1998) 2 Cr App R 25 Mere possession of a firearm is not sufficient for an offence under s 18 to be made out, there must be intent to commit an indictable offence.

R v Pawlicki and Swindell [1992] 3 All ER 903 'Has with him' means a closer relation with an item than possession. The exact distance between a criminal and their gun should not be the main factor—the accessibility of the gun should be judged in common-sense terms in the context of criminals embarking on a joint enterprise to commit an indictable offence.

Practical considerations

- Proof that the defendant had a firearm or imitation firearm with them and intended to commit the offence, or to resist or prevent arrest, is evidence that they intended to have it with them while doing so.
- Consider 'possess firearm with intent to cause the fear of unlawful violence' (see **8.3.3**) which has a much wider scope.

SSS E&S

Indictable

None

Life imprisonment and/or a fine

8.3.7 Using person to mind a firearm/weapon

Section 28 of the Violent Crime Reduction Act 2006 makes it an offence to use another person to look after, hide, or transport a dangerous weapon, subject to an agreement that it will be available when required for an unlawful purpose.

Offences

(1) A person is guilty of an offence if—
  (a) he uses another to look after, hide or transport a dangerous weapon for him; and
  (b) he does so under arrangements or in circumstances that facilitate, or are intended to facilitate, the weapon's being available to him for an unlawful purpose.

Violent Crime Reduction Act 2006, s 28

PNLD H8714, H8715

Points to prove

- ✓ uses another person to
- ✓ look after/hide/transport
- ✓ dangerous weapon and
- ✓ under arrangements made or facilitation agreed/intended
- ✓ the weapon is made available
- ✓ for an unlawful purpose

Meanings

Dangerous weapon (s 28(3))

In this section, 'dangerous weapon' means:

(a) a firearm (see **8.1.1**) **other than** an air weapon or a component part of, or accessory to, an air weapon (see **8.1.2**); or
(b) a weapon to which s 141 (see **8.9.3**) or s 141A (see **8.10.2**) of the Criminal Justice Act 1988 applies (specified offensive weapons, knives, and bladed weapons).

Available for an unlawful purpose (s 28(2))

For the purposes of this section, the cases in which a dangerous weapon is to be regarded as available to a person for an unlawful purpose include any case where:

(a) the weapon is available for them to take possession of it at a time and place; **and**

(b) their possession of the weapon at that time and place would constitute, or be likely to involve or to lead to, the commission by them of an offence.

Practical considerations

Section 70 of the Sentencing Act 2020 sets out how a court must treat as an aggravating factor the fact that the s 28 offence of using someone to mind a weapon was committed by an adult using a minor to look after, hide, or transport the weapon.

E&S

Indictable None

4 to 10 years' imprisonment and/or a fine (details given in s 29)

Links to alternative subjects and offences

2.3.2 **Wounding or grievous bodily harm—with intent** 82
2.5 **Threats to Kill** 97
2.7 **Sudden and Unexplained Deaths** 109
Appendix 4 **Firearms Offences Relating to Age** 857

8.4 Trespassing with Firearms

The Firearms Act 1968 provides various offences connected with firearms, air weapons, shotguns, and associated ammunition. Some such offences involve trespassing.

8.4.1 Trespass with any firearm in a building

Section 20 of the Firearms Act 1968 creates two offences of trespassing with firearms, one of which is concerned with trespass in buildings.

Offences

A person commits an offence if, while he has a firearm or imitation firearm with him, he enters or is in any building or part of a building as a trespasser and without reasonable excuse (the proof whereof lies on him).

Firearms Act 1968, s 20(1)

PNLD H483, H496, H497, H498

Points to prove

✓ had with them
✓ firearm/imitation firearm
✓ entered or was in
✓ building/part of building
✓ as a trespasser
✓ without reasonable excuse

Meanings

Firearm (see 8.3.3)

Imitation firearm (see 8.3.3)

Has with him (see 8.3.6)

Explanatory notes

- A firearm in these circumstances means any firearm—shotgun, air weapon, prohibited weapon, and s 1 firearm.
- The terms 'enters', 'building', 'part of a building', and 'trespasser' should be interpreted as terms used in legislation/case law relating to burglary (see 3.3.1).

Defence

Reasonable excuse (the burden of proof lies with the defendant). This defence could include saving life/property or self-defence (eg the police carrying out a planned firearms operation).

Practical considerations

- In order to prove a trespass, it must be shown that the defendant knew that they were a trespasser or were reckless as to whether the facts existed which made them a trespasser.
- It is important to note that although this is an either way offence if the weapon is an air weapon or imitation firearm, it is triable summarily only.
- The burden of proof lies with the defendant if they claim to have a reasonable excuse. Whether an excuse is reasonable would be for the court to decide having considered all the circumstances.
- Unless it is an imitation, there needs to be some evidence that the weapon is a firearm. It is immaterial whether or not the firearm is loaded or whether the individual has ammunition with them.
- Consider the offences of aggravated burglary (see **3.3.2**) or attempt aggravated burglary (see **4.1.1**) (especially if an imitation or air weapon is used—greater penalty).

SSS E&S

Either way | None

Summary: 6/12 months' imprisonment and/or a fine
Indictment: 7 years' imprisonment and/or a fine

Air weapons/imitation firearms

Summary | 48 months

48 months and/or a fine for an imitation firearm, 6 months' imprisonment and/or a fine for an air weapon

8.4.2 Trespass with firearm on land

Section 20(2) of the Firearms Act 1968 creates an offence of trespass with a firearm on land.

Offences

A person commits an offence if, while he has a firearm or imitation firearm with him, he enters or is on any land as a trespasser and without reasonable excuse (the proof whereof lies on him).

Firearms Act 1968, s 20(2)

PNLD H485, H499, H500, H501

Points to prove

- ✓ had with them
- ✓ firearm/imitation firearm
- ✓ entered/was on land
- ✓ as a trespasser
- ✓ without reasonable excuse

Meanings

Firearm (see **8.3.3**)

Imitation firearm (see **8.3.3**)

Has with him (see **8.3.6**)

Land

This includes land covered with water.

Trespass (see **3.3.1**)

Explanatory note

- A firearm in these circumstances means any firearm—shotgun, air weapon, prohibited weapon, and s 1 firearm.

Defence

Reasonable excuse (see **8.4.1**).

Practical considerations

- In order to prove a trespass, it must be shown that the defendant knew that they were a trespasser or were reckless as to whether the facts existed which made them a trespasser.
- If a defence of reasonable excuse is claimed, the burden of proof lies with the defendant.
- Unless it is an imitation firearm, there needs to be some evidence that the weapon is 'a firearm'.

8.4.2 **Trespass with firearm on land**

SSS

Summary

48 months for imitation firearms

3 months' imprisonment and/or a level 4 fine

Links to alternative subjects and offences

2.3.2 **Wounding or grievous bodily harm—with intent** 82
2.5 **Threats to Kill** 97
3.3 **Burglary/Aggravated Burglary** 145
Appendix 4 **Firearms Offences Relating to Age** 857

8.5 **Possess Firearm or Imitation Firearm in a Public Place**

Section 19 of the Firearms Act 1968 provides various offences relating to the possession of shotguns, air weapons, firearms, and imitation firearms in a public place.

Offences

A person commits an offence if, without lawful authority or reasonable excuse (the proof whereof lies on him) he has with him in a public place—

(a) a loaded shotgun,
(b) an air weapon (whether loaded or not),
(c) any other firearm (whether loaded or not) together with ammunition suitable for use in that firearm, or
(d) an imitation firearm.

Firearms Act 1968, s 19

PNLD **H494, H4711, H4712, H8732**

Points to prove

✓ without lawful authority/reasonable excuse
✓ had with you in a public place
✓ firearm (together with suitable ammunition) OR
✓ loaded shotgun OR
✓ loaded/unloaded air weapon OR
✓ an imitation firearm

Meanings

Has with him (see **8.3.6**)

Public place

This includes any highway and any other premises or place to which at the material time the public have or are permitted to have access, whether on payment or otherwise.

Loaded

Means if there is ammunition in the chamber or barrel or in any magazine or other device which is in such a position that the ammunition can be fed into the chamber or barrel by the manual or automatic operation of some part of the gun or weapon (s 57(6)(b)).

Shotgun (see **8.2.1**)

Air weapon (see **8.7.2**)

Other firearm (see **8.1.1**)

Imitation firearm (see **8.3.3**)

Explanatory notes

In this offence, the requirement for whether or not the weapons are loaded varies:

- the requirement for a loaded weapon only applies to shotguns;
- for air weapons, there is no need to have ammunition for them;
- for other firearms, the defendant must have ammunition suitable for use with that firearm.

Defences

Having lawful authority or reasonable excuse (the burden of proof lies with the defendant). This defence could include saving life/property or self-defence (eg the police carrying out a planned firearms operation). Whether an excuse is reasonable would be for the court to decide having considered all the circumstances.

Related cases

R v Harrison [1996] 1 Cr App R 138 During a robbery, one of the robbers had a loaded sawn-off shotgun which the other knew nothing about. On police arrival, the other offender took possession of the gun and it was held that only the knowledge of the fact of possession was needed to prove an offence under s 19 rather than the nature or quality of what was possessed. Once the prosecution has shown that a person had the shotgun, the fact that it was loaded makes it a breach of the section.

R v Jones [1995] QB 235 It was held in this case that a firearms certificate does not give the holder a defence of 'lawful authority' against a charge under s 19.

R v Morris and King (1984) 79 Cr App Rep 104 The key word in these definitions is 'appearance'. The test is whether the thing looked like a firearm at the time when the defendant had it with them. It is ultimately for the jury to decide, what a witness believed about the object, and/or any admissions made by the defendant as to their reason for carrying it.

Practical considerations

- The requirement of the weapon being loaded applies only to shotguns. If the person has with them some other firearm they need only have suitable ammunition with them to commit the offence.
- A valid shotgun certificate does not give the person lawful authority to have with them a loaded shotgun in a public place. A certificate for a firearm and ammunition is not in itself lawful authority.

- Section 161 of the Highways Act 1980 deals with the offence of discharging any firearm within 50 feet from the centre of a highway (see **8.8.7**).
- Section 28 of the Town Police Clauses Act 1847 deals with the offence of reckless discharge of a firearm in the street to the annoyance or danger of residents or passengers (see **8.8.8**).
- The 'guilty knowledge' that the prosecution must prove is knowledge of existence of the firearm, not the nature and quality of the weapon.
- The prosecution must prove that the firearm is 'to hand and able to be used'.
- With an imitation firearm, the key issue is whether it looked like a firearm at the time of the offence. It is for the jury to decide on the circumstances of each case.
- Imitation or replica weapons that can be converted into working firearms will be classed as s 1 firearms (see **8.1.4**).
- Unless it is an imitation firearm, there needs to be some evidence that the weapon is a firearm (see **8.1.1**).

SSS E&S

In the case of possession of a loaded shotgun in a public place, or possession of a loaded/unloaded firearm and suitable ammunition in public place

Either way None

Summary: 6/12 months' imprisonment and/or a fine

Indictment: 7 years' imprisonment and/or a fine

In the case of possession of an imitation firearm in a public place

Either way 4 years

Summary: 6/12 months' imprisonment and/or a fine

Indictment: 12 months' imprisonment and/or a fine

In the case of possession of a loaded/unloaded air weapon in a public place

Summary 6 months

6 months' imprisonment and/or a fine

Links to alternative subjects and offences

2.3.2 **Wounding or grievous bodily harm—with intent** 82
2.5 **Threats to Kill** 97
3.2 **Robbery** 140
Appendix 4 **Firearms Offences Relating to Age** 857

8.6 Police Powers—Firearms

The Firearms Act 1968 provides various offences and powers connected with firearms, air weapons, shotguns, and associated ammunition.

8.6.1 Requirement to hand over firearm/ammunition

Section 47 of the Firearms Act 1968 deals with police powers to stop and search for firearms and provides an offence for failure to do so.

> **Police stop and search powers**
>
> A constable may require any person whom he has reasonable cause to suspect—
>
> (a) of having a firearm, with or without ammunition, with him in a public place; or
>
> (b) to be committing or about to commit, elsewhere than in a public place, an offence relevant for the purposes of this section,
>
> to hand over the firearm or any ammunition for examination by the constable.
>
> Firearms Act 1968, s 47(1)

Meanings

Reasonable cause to suspect

There must be objective grounds for the suspicion based on facts, information, or intelligence that are relevant to the likelihood of finding the article(s) (see **1.3.2**).

Firearm/ammunition (see **8.1.1**)

Has with him (see **8.3.6**)

Public place (see **8.5**)

Relevant offence

This refers to s 18 and s 20 offences, being either having a firearm or imitation firearm:

- with intent to commit an indictable offence, or to resist arrest, or prevent the arrest of another (see **8.3.6**);
- with them and entering either a building, or part of a building, or land as a trespasser (see **8.4**).

Offences

It is an offence for a person having a firearm or ammunition with him to fail to hand it over when required to do so by a constable under subsection (1) above.

Firearms Act 1968, s 47(2)

PNLD H2122, H2123

Points to prove

✓ failed to hand over
✓ a firearm/ammunition for a firearm
✓ which you had with you
✓ when required to do so by a constable

Section 47 of the Firearms Act 1968 also provides qualified powers to search both people and vehicles for firearms and detain them for that purpose.

Police search and detain powers

Person

If a constable has reasonable cause to suspect a person of having a firearm with him in a public place, or to be committing or about to commit elsewhere than in a public place an offence relevant for the purposes of this section, the constable may search that person and may detain him for the purpose of doing so.

Firearms Act 1968, s 47(3)

Vehicle

If a constable has reasonable cause to suspect that there is a firearm in a vehicle in a public place, or that a vehicle is being or is about to be used in connection with the commission of an offence relevant for the purposes of this section elsewhere than in a public place, he may search the vehicle and for that purpose require the person driving or in control of it to stop it.

Firearms Act 1968, s 47(4)

Explanatory notes

- In exercising these powers, s 47(5) also gives a constable power to enter any place.
- The police also have the power to demand the production of shotgun or firearm certificates (see **8.6.2**).
- The power to stop the vehicle is not restricted to a constable in uniform.

- Officers should ensure that the stop and search procedures comply with PACE and the relevant Code (see **1.3**).
- With regard to premises, a search warrant will have to be obtained under s 46 (see **8.6.3**).

SSS

Summary

48 months

3 months' imprisonment and/or a level 4 fine

8.6.2 Police powers—firearms/shotgun certificates

Section 48 of the Firearms Act 1968 gives a constable power to demand from a person they believe to be in possession of a s 1 firearm/ammunition or shotgun the production of a valid certificate or European pass or to show that they are exempt.

Production of certificate

A constable may demand, from any person whom he believes to be in possession of a firearm or ammunition to which section 1 of this Act applies, or of a shotgun, the production of his firearm certificate or, as the case may be, his shotgun certificate.

Firearms Act 1968, s 48(1)

Meanings

Believes

This is a more stringent requirement than 'suspects' and requires stronger grounds.

Section 1 firearm/ammunition (see **8.1.1**)

Firearm certificate (see **8.1.1**)

Shotgun (see **8.2.1**)

Shotgun certificate (see **8.2.1**)

Seize/detain weapon and require details

If a person upon whom a demand is made fails to produce the certificate, or to permit the constable to read it, or to show that he is entitled by virtue of this Act to have the firearm, ammunition or shotgun in his possession without holding a certificate, the constable may seize and detain the firearm, ammunition or shotgun and may require the person to declare to him immediately his name and address.

Firearms Act 1968, s 48(2)

Offences

If under this section a person is required to declare to a constable his name and address, it is an offence for him to refuse to declare it or to fail to give his true name and address.

Firearms Act 1968, s 48(3)

PNLD H4336, H4342, H4374, H4381

Points to prove

- ✓ having possession
- ✓ of a firearm/shotgun
- ✓ failed/refused
- ✓ to divulge
- ✓ when required by a constable
- ✓ their name and address

Explanatory notes

- A firearm certificate also includes a Northern Ireland Certificate.
- As the requirement is to declare 'immediately' their name and address, it is taken that the demand to produce a valid certificate/document or show exemption and (if applicable) the subsequent seizure of the firearm, ammunition, or shotgun will also follow the same immediacy.

SSS

Summary

6 months

Level 3 fine

8.6.3 Premises search warrant

Section 46 of the Firearms Act 1968 deals with the issue of premises search warrants for firearms and authorities attached thereto.

Granting of warrant

If a justice of the peace is satisfied by information on oath that there is reasonable ground for suspecting—

(a) that an offence relevant for the purposes of this section has been, is being, or is about to be committed; or
(b) that, in connection with a firearm or ammunition, there is a danger to the public safety or to the peace,

he may grant a warrant for any of the purposes mentioned in subsection (2) below.

Firearms Act 1968, s 46(1)

Meanings

Relevant offences

All offences under this Act except an offence under s 22(3) (unsupervised 15-year-old possessing shotgun—see **8.2.3**) or an offence relating specifically to air weapons.

Purposes of warrant

A warrant under this section may authorise a constable or civilian officer—

(a) to enter at any time any premises or place named in the warrant, if necessary by force, and to search the premises or place and every person found there;
(b) to seize and detain anything which he may find on the premises or place, or on any such person, in respect of which or in connection with which he has reasonable ground for suspecting—
   (i) that an offence **relevant** for the purposes of this section has been, is being or is about to be committed; or
   (ii) that in connection with a firearm, imitation firearm, or ammunition, there is a danger to the public safety or to the peace.

Firearms Act 1968, s 46(2)

Offences

It is an offence for any person intentionally to obstruct a constable or civilian officer in the exercise of his powers under this section.

Firearms Act 1968, s 46(5)

PNLD H1259

Points to prove

✓ intentionally obstruct
✓ constable/civilian officer
✓ whilst exercising their powers under s 46

Meaning of civilian officer

Means a person employed by a police authority or the Corporation of the City of London who is under the direction and control of a chief officer of police.

Explanatory notes

- Ensure that the application and execution of the warrant complies with PACE and the COP (see **1.5**).
- In some forces, inspections of gun clubs and other routine firearms enquiries are performed by police staff rather than police officers.

SSS

Summary

48 months

6 months' imprisonment and/or a fine

8.7 Firearms, Air Weapons, Imitation Firearms—Age Restrictions

The Firearms Act 1968 provides various offences connected with firearms, imitation firearms, air weapons, shotguns, and associated ammunition. Invariably restrictions are in place as to the age of the person involved.

8.7.1 Purchase/hire or supply by/to under 18

Sections 22(1) and 24(1) of the Firearms Act 1968 prohibit purchase/hire or supply (sell or let on hire) of any firearm or ammunition by or to a person under 18 years of age.

Offences

Purchase/hire by under 18

It is an offence for a person under the age of 18 to purchase or hire any firearm or ammunition.

Firearms Act 1968, s 22(1)

Supplier (sell/hire) to under 18

It is an offence to sell or let on hire any firearm or ammunition to a person under the age of 18.

Firearms Act 1968, s 24(1)

PNLD H6921, H6923, H6924, H6925, H6927, H6929, H6931, H8719, H8721

Points to prove

Purchase/hire

✓ being a person under the age of 18
✓ purchased/hired
✓ any firearm/ammunition

Supplier (sell/hire)

✓ sold/let on hire, either
✓ any firearm/ammunition
✓ to a person under the age of 18

Meanings

Air weapons and air pellets/darts (see **8.7.2**)

Shotguns and cartridges (see **8.2.1**)

Section 1/other firearms or ammunition (see **8.1.1**)

Defence for supplier under s 24

In proceedings for an offence under any provision of this section it is a defence to prove that the person charged with the offence believed the other person to be of or over the age mentioned in that provision and had reasonable ground for the belief.

Firearms Act 1968, s 24(5)

Practical considerations

- Further prohibitions on minors possessing, acquiring, or being supplied with firearms and/or ammunition are given in other s 22 and s 24 offences:
  - ✦ **section 1 firearms/ammunition (under 14)**—possessing, making a gift of, lending, or parting with possession (see **8.1.3**);
  - ✦ **shotgun/cartridges (under 15)**—having an assembled shotgun without being supervised (by a person aged 21 years or over) or securely fastened in a gun cover or making a gift of a shotgun or cartridges to such person (see **8.2.2**);
  - ✦ **air weapons/ammunition (under 18)**—having, making a gift of, or parting with possession (see **8.7.2**).
- It is an offence under s 24A for a person under 18 to purchase or to be sold an imitation firearm (see **8.7.5**).

SSS

Summary

48 months (6 months if air weapon/ammunition)

6 months' imprisonment and/or a fine (a fine if shotgun/air weapon)

8.7.2 Air weapons—further offences (others)/under 18 restrictions

The Firearms Act 1968 provides exceptions for young people to possess air weapons but generally it is an offence for a person under 18 to have with them, or be given, an air weapon or ammunition for an air weapon.

Possess, make gift, or part with possession

Offences

Under 18 have with them

Subject to section 23, it is an offence for a person under the age of 18 to have with him an air weapon or ammunition for an air weapon.

Firearms Act 1968, s 22(4)

Make gift/part with possession to under 18

It is an offence—

(a) to make a gift of an air weapon or ammunition for an air weapon to a person under the age of 18; or

(b) to part with the possession of an air weapon or ammunition for an air weapon to a person under the age of 18 except where by virtue of section 23 of this Act the person is not prohibited from having it with him.

Firearms Act 1968, s 24(4)

PNLD H9310, H9311, H9312, H9313

Points to prove

Have with them

✓ being under 18 years of age
✓ had with them
✓ an air weapon or ammunition for an air weapon

Make a gift

✓ made a gift
✓ of an air weapon/ammunition for an air weapon
✓ to a person under the age of 18

Part with possession (not s 23 excepted)

✓ parted with possession
✓ of an air weapon/ammunition for an air weapon
✓ to a person under the age of 18
✓ being prohibited from having possession

Meanings

Section 23 (see '**Fire missile beyond premises**' below)

Has with him (see **8.3.6**)

Air weapon

Most air weapons are firearms but not s 1 firearms (see **8.1.1**). Part of the definition of a s 1 firearm (s 1(3)(b) of the Firearms Act 1968) relates to every firearm, except air weapons: 'an air weapon that is to say, an air rifle, air gun or air pistol which does not fall within s 5(1) [*being a prohibited weapon—having compressed gas cartridge system*] and which is not of a type declared by rules [*sets the power levels at which an air weapon becomes a s 1 firearm*] made by the Secretary of State under s 53 of this Act to be specially dangerous'.

Defences

Sections 22(4) and 24(4)(b)

Consider s 23 (see '**Fire missile beyond premises**' section).

Section 24

Consider s 24(5) (see **8.7.1**).

Fire missile beyond premises

Offences

Fire missile beyond premises (any age)

A person commits an offence if—

(a) he has with him an air weapon on any premises; and
(b) he uses it for firing a missile beyond those premises.

Firearms Act 1968, s 21A(1)

PNLD H8723

Section 23 exceptions and supervisor offence

(1) It is not an offence under section 22(4) of this Act for a person to have with him an air weapon or ammunition while he is under the supervision of a person of or over the age of 21; but where a person has with him an air weapon on any premises in circumstances where he would be prohibited from having it with him but for this subsection, it is an offence for the person under whose supervision he is to allow him to use it for firing any missile beyond those premises.

(1A) In proceedings against a person for an offence under subsection (1) it shall be a defence for him to show that the only premises into or across which the missile was fired were premises the occupier of which had consented to the firing of the missile (whether specifically or by way of a general consent).

(2) It is not an offence under section 22(4) of this Act for a person to have with him an air weapon or ammunition at the time when—
    (a) being a member of a rifle club or miniature rifle club for the time being approved by the Secretary of State for the purposes of this section or section 15 of the Firearms (Amendment) Act 1988, he is engaged as such a member in or in connection with target shooting; or

(b) he is using the weapon or ammunition at a shooting gallery where the only firearms used are either air weapons or miniature rifles not exceeding 0.23 inch calibre.

(3) It is not an offence under section 22(4) of this Act for a person of or over the age of 14 to have with him an air weapon or ammunition on private premises with the consent of the occupier.

Firearms Act 1968, s 23

PNLD H10095

Points to prove

s 21A(1) offence (anyone)

✓ had with them on premises
✓ an air weapon
✓ which they used for firing missile(s)
✓ beyond those premises

s 23(1) offence (supervisor)

✓ being person 21 or over
✓ supervising person under 18 who had an air weapon
✓ on premises (specify)
✓ allowed them to fire a missile beyond those premises

Defences

Offences under s 23(1) or s 21A(1)

It shall be a defence for him to show that the only premises into or across which the missile was fired were premises the occupier of which had consented to the firing of the missile (whether specifically or by way of a general consent).

Firearms Act 1968, ss 23(1A) and 21A(2)

Fail to prevent under 18 from having air weapon

Offences

It is an offence for a person in possession of an air weapon to fail to take reasonable precautions to prevent any person under the age of 18 from having the weapon with him.

Firearms Act 1968, s 24ZA(1)

PNLD H7054

Points to prove

✓ having possession of air weapon
✓ failed to prevent person under 18
✓ from having air weapon

Defences

(2) Subsection (1) does not apply where by virtue of section 23 [*above*] of this Act the person under the age of 18 is not prohibited from having the weapon with him.
(3) In proceedings for an offence under subsection (1) it is a defence to show that the person charged with the offence—
  (a) believed the other person to be aged eighteen or over; and
  (b) had reasonable ground for that belief.
(4) For the purposes of this section a person shall be taken to have shown the matters specified in subsection (3) if—
  (a) sufficient evidence of those matters is adduced to raise an issue with respect to them; and
  (b) the contrary is not proved beyond a reasonable doubt.

Firearms Act 1968, s 24ZA

Explanatory notes

- Section 24ZA makes it an offence for the person in possession of the air weapon to fail to take reasonable precautions to prevent a person under the age of 18 from gaining unauthorised access to it. HOC 4/2011 provides guidance and further details on this offence.
- HOC 31/2007 provides guidance in relation to air weapons as to: raising the age limits to 18; firing air weapons beyond premises; sales or transfer to be only through a registered firearms dealer by 'face-to-face' transactions (see **8.1.2**).
- As 'air gun', 'air rifle', and 'air pistol' are not defined in the Firearms Act 1968, each case will have to be considered on its own facts and the article in question. As to whether a weapon falls into these categories, the court will have to be aware of the following:
  - an 'air gun' is generally a weapon that has an unrifled barrel;
  - an 'air rifle' is a weapon that does have a rifled barrel; and
  - an 'air pistol' is a weapon designed to be fired by using one hand and having the appearance of a pistol;
  - any air rifle, air gun, or air pistol which uses, or is designed or adapted for use with, a self-contained gas cartridge system (see also **8.7.3**);
  - air weapons using or designed/adapted for use with a self-contained compressed gas cartridge system will be prohibited weapons (see **8.7.3**).
- An air weapon is deemed to be loaded if there is ammunition in the chamber or barrel.

Practical considerations

- The prosecution has to prove that the air weapon was a lethal barrelled weapon capable of discharging a shot or missile.
- In practice, forensic testing will determine whether weapons are lethal or not. The main characteristic which is measured is the muzzle velocity (the speed at which the projectile leaves the barrel).
- An air weapon normally fires a projectile by compressed air/gases and is a firearm, namely 'a lethal barrelled weapon of any description from which any shot, bullet, or other missile can be discharged' (do not confuse a 'firearm' with the narrower definition of a s 1 firearm).
- Certain air weapons can be subject to the prohibition under rules denoting them as especially dangerous.
- Air weapons using, or designed/adapted for use with, a self-contained compressed gas cartridge system will be prohibited weapons (**8.7.3**).
- Application may be made to the court for a confiscation order in relation to a seized air weapon or ammunition.
- For police powers relating to firearms/ammunition, see **8.6**.
- Normally it is an offence for a person under 18 years to have an air weapon and/or ammunition anywhere. However, a young person may possess one if accompanied by someone of or over 21 years of age.
- On premises, the person under 18 years old is allowed to fire the weapon but the missiles must not go beyond those premises—otherwise an offence is committed by the supervisor (subject to defence). Furthermore, the user (who must be at least 14 years old) may have with them an air weapon or ammunition on private premises with permission of the occupier.
- Section 21A(1) (above) makes it an offence for **any person** to use an air weapon on premises which fires a missile beyond those premises, although it is a defence if the occupier of the premises into or across which the missile was fired had consented.
- Under s 19, it is an offence for a person to have with them in a public place an air weapon (loaded or not) or imitation firearm without lawful authority or reasonable excuse (see **8.5**).

Summary

6 months

Level 3 fine

8.7.3 Air weapons deemed prohibited weapons

Any person who has with him any air rifle, air gun, or air pistol that uses, or is designed or adapted for use with, a self-contained compressed gas cartridge system (SCGC) will be in possession of a prohibited weapon under s 5(1)(af) of the Firearms Act 1968 (see **8.1.1**).

Explanatory notes

- Weapons that use a CO_2 bulb system are not affected because CO_2 bulbs do not contain a projectile and are not therefore self-contained.
- A CO_2 bulb system that gives a pressure less than 12 ft/lbs on air rifles or 6 ft/lbs on air pistols is not restricted, but over that pressure they become s 1 firearms.
- If the air weapon contains a brass cartridge system and uses a self-contained gas cartridge system that can be converted to fire conventional ammunition, say, then this would make it a prohibited weapon under s 5(1)(af).
- If the weapon comes under s 5(1)(af), then it cannot be possessed, purchased, acquired, manufactured, sold, or transferred without written authority from the Secretary of State. However, under special arrangements, a person might have been granted permission to possess such a weapon under the terms of a firearms certificate.
- Further details on this matter are given in HOC 1/2004.
- Under s 5(1)(ag), any rifle with a chamber from which empty cartridge cases are extracted using:
  - ✦ energy from propellant gas; or
  - ✦ energy imparted to a spring or other energy storage device by propellant gas;

  other than a rifle which is chambered for 0.22 rim-fire cartridges, is a weapon subject to general prohibition; note that possession is not yet an offence for this weapon as a number of compensation and surrender arrangements must be followed before the prohibition on possession can be in force.

8.7.4 'BB guns'

BB guns derived their name from guns that fired ball bearings by different methods such as compressed air or an electrical system, some even firing 4.5 mm lead shot. Such weapons would almost certainly be firearms for the purposes of s 1(3) (see **8.1.1**).

If the method of propulsion is a self-contained compressed gas cartridge, the BB gun may be a prohibited weapon (see **8.7.3**). However, most gas BB guns do not have cartridges: the built-in gas container is recharged by an external aerosol, which is not the same thing.

A more common and readily available BB gun is designed to fire plastic or aluminium pellets which may be too powerful to be officially classed as a toy. These are unlikely to be lethal barrelled weapons (see **8.1.1**) because they are usually too low-powered to be 'lethal'. This type of BB gun will normally have a power rating of about 0.06 ft/lbs. Compare this to a BSA Airsporter 0.22 air rifle that has a power rating of 10.07 ft/lbs (150 times more powerful).

If required, forensic testing of the BB gun can ascertain its power rating, categorise the gun, and say whether or not it is lethal.

As some BB guns closely resemble other firearms, if one is being used in a public place, consider the offence of possession of an imitation firearm in a public place (see **8.5**).

8.7.5 Under 18—sell/buy an imitation firearm

Section 24A of the Firearms Act 1968 makes it an offence to sell an imitation firearm to a person under the age of 18 or for a young person under the age of 18 to purchase one.

Offences

(1) It is an offence for a person under the age of 18 to purchase an imitation firearm.
(2) It is an offence to sell an imitation firearm to a person under the age of 18.

Firearms Act 1968, s 24A

PNLD H8730, H8731

Points to prove

s 24A(1) under 18 purchase

✓ being a person under 18 years of age
✓ purchased an imitation firearm

s 24A(2) sell to under 18

✓ sold an imitation firearm
✓ to a person under 18 years of age

Meaning of imitation firearm

Means any thing which has the appearance of being a firearm whether or not it is capable of discharging any shot, bullet, or other missile.

Explanatory note

- Imitation firearms have been increasingly misused to threaten and intimidate others. Although offences and controls exist relating to imitation firearms, s 24A seeks to tackle the problem at source by restricting the sale of imitation firearms.

Defence for seller

In proceedings for an offence under subsection (2) it is a defence to show that the person charged with the offence—
(a) believed the other person to be aged eighteen or over; and
(b) had reasonable ground for that belief.

Firearms Act 1968, s 24A(3)

Practical considerations

- The onus is on the prosecution to show that the seller did not take sufficient steps (eg producing ID) to establish that the purchaser was 18 or over.
- Also consider s 36 of the Violent Crime Reduction Act 2006 which makes it an offence to manufacture, import, or sell a realistic imitation firearm.
- The Violent Crime Reduction Act 2006 (Realistic Imitation Firearms) Regulations 2007 (SI 2606/2007) provide defences, burden of proof, details on historical re-enactments, size, and colours of imitation firearms. HOC 31/2007 gives guidance on ss 36 to 41 (realistic imitation firearms and supplying to those aged under 18).

Summary | 48 months

6 months' imprisonment and/or a fine

Links to alternative subjects and offences

2.1.2 **Assault occasioning actual bodily harm** 56
2.3.2 **Wounding or grievous bodily harm—with intent** 82
4.4 **Criminal Damage** 193
4.7 **Custody/Control of Articles with Intent to Damage** 206
7 **Public Disorder/Nuisance** 351
Appendix 4 **Firearms Offences Relating to Age** 857

8.8 Fireworks

The Fireworks Regulations 2004 and the Pyrotechnic Articles (Safety) Regulations 2015 give firework prohibitions that are enforced by the Fireworks Act 2003 and the Consumer Protection Act 1987 respectively. The Highways Act 1980 and the Town Police Clauses Act 1847 also provide for offences involving fireworks in a street or highway.

8.8.1 Categories of fireworks

There are different categories of fireworks in relation to supply or possession offences. Category 1, 2, and 3 fireworks are considered suitable for use by the public: whereas a Category 4 firework is only for use by people with specialist knowledge.

Category 1 fireworks present a very low hazard, negligible noise level, and are intended for use in confined areas: including fireworks which are intended for use inside domestic buildings (Indoor Fireworks). These are innocuous fireworks (eg cap, cracker snap, novelty match, party popper, serpent, sparkler, or throw-down).

Category 2 fireworks present a low hazard and low noise level and are intended for outdoor use in confined areas (Garden Fireworks). They normally require a minimum spectator distance of 5 metres.

Category 3 fireworks present a medium hazard, are intended for outdoor use in large open areas, and the noise level is not considered harmful to human health (Display Fireworks). They normally require a minimum spectator distance of 25 metres.

Category 4 fireworks present a high hazard, are intended for use only by people with specialist knowledge and have a noise level that is not considered harmful to human health (Fireworks for professional use). The general public is prohibited from possessing these fireworks.

Firework means a **pyrotechnic article** intended for entertainment purposes.

Pyrotechnic article means any article containing explosive substances or an explosive mixture of substances designed to produce heat, light, sound, gas, or smoke or a combination of such effects through self-sustained, exothermic chemical reactions.

8.8.2 Under 18 years—possessing 'adult' fireworks

Offences

Any person who contravenes a prohibition imposed by fireworks regulations is guilty of an offence.

Fireworks Act 2003, s 11(1)

PNLD H6243

Points to prove

✓ breached a reg 4 prohibition, namely
✓ being a person under the age of 18
✓ in a public place
✓ possessing an adult firework

Prohibition

Subject to regulation 6 below, no person under the age of eighteen years shall possess an adult firework in a public place.

Fireworks Regulations 2004, reg 4(1)

Meanings

Regulation 6

- Regulations 4 and 5 shall not prohibit the possession of any firework by any person who is employed by/in trade or business as:
  - ✦ professional organiser or operator of firework displays;
  - ✦ manufacture of fireworks or assemblies;
  - ✦ supply of fireworks or assemblies;
  - ✦ local authority/government department/forces of the Crown for use at a firework display or national public celebration/ commemorative event;
  - ✦ special effects in the theatre, on film, or on television;
  - ✦ acting on behalf of and for purposes of exercising enforcement powers of local authority or enforcement body;
  - ✦ government department use for research or investigations;
  - ✦ supplier of goods designed and intended for use in conjunction with fireworks or assemblies for testing and safety purposes.
  - ✦ naval, military, or air force for use at firework displays at that establishment or at a national public celebration or national commemorative event.

Adult firework

Means any firework, except Category 1 Indoor Fireworks (see **8.8.1**).

Public place

Includes any place to which at the material time the public have or are permitted access, whether on payment or otherwise.

Explanatory note

- Those people listed in reg 6 (above) are exempted from liability for this offence and are not prohibited from possession.

Practical considerations

- Any breach of the prohibitions in the Fireworks Regulations 2004 is a criminal offence under the Fireworks Act 2003, s 11(1).
- Consider stop, search, and seizure powers under s 1(8B) of PACE (see **1.3.1**).

SSS

Summary　　12 months

6 months' imprisonment and/or a fine

8.8.3 Ban on possession of Category 4 fireworks

Offences

Any person who contravenes a prohibition imposed by fireworks regulations is guilty of an offence.

Fireworks Act 2003, s 11(1)

PNLD H6244

Points to prove

✓ breached a reg 5 prohibition, namely
✓ possessed a Category 4 firework
✓ when not exempt from such possession

Prohibition

Subject to regulation 6, no person shall possess a Category 4 firework.

Fireworks Regulations 2004, reg 5

Explanatory notes

- Those people listed in reg 6 (see **8.8.2**) are exempted from liability for this offence and are not prohibited from possession.
- Unless exempted by reg 6, this prohibits a person of any age from possessing **anywhere** a Category 4 firework and an offence will be committed by that person if they breach that regulation.

Practical considerations

- Any breach of the prohibitions in the Fireworks Regulations 2004 is a criminal offence under s 11(1) of the Fireworks Act 2003.
- Consider issuing a PND for this offence (see **7.1.1**).
- Consider stop, search, and seizure powers under s 1(8B) of PACE (see **1.3**).
- Category 4 fireworks are for use by individuals with specialist knowledge only (see **8.8.1**).

SSS PND

Summary

12 months

6 months' imprisonment and/or a fine

8.8.4 Use firework after 11 p.m.

Offences

Any person who contravenes a prohibition imposed by fireworks regulations is guilty of an offence.

Fireworks Act 2003, s 11(1)

PNLD H6245

Points to prove

✓ breached a reg 7(1) prohibition, namely
✓ used an adult firework
✓ during night hours on a time and date not exempt from the prohibition on use

Prohibition

Subject to paragraph (2) [*exception*] below, no person shall use an adult firework during night hours.

Fireworks Regulations 2004, reg 7(1)

Meanings

Exception (reg 7(2))

Regulation 7(1) above shall not prohibit the use of a firework:
(a) during a permitted fireworks night; or
(b) by any person who is employed by a local authority and who uses the firework in question:
  (i) for the purposes of putting on a firework display by that local authority; or
  (ii) at a national public celebration or a national commemorative event.

Adult firework (see **8.8.2**)

Night hours

Means the period beginning at 11 p.m. and ending at 7 a.m. the following day.

Permitted fireworks night

Means a period beginning at 11 p.m.:
- on the first day of the Chinese New Year and ending at 1 a.m. the following day;
- and ending at midnight on 5 November;
- on the day of Diwali and ending at 1 a.m. the following day;
- on 31 December and ending at 1 a.m. the following day.

Explanatory notes

- This prohibits the use of a firework (except Category 1 Indoor Fireworks) (see **8.8.1**) after 11 p.m. and an offence being committed by that person if they breach that regulation.
- Exceptions are New Year's Eve, Diwali, Chinese New Year, Bonfire Night, or the local authority putting on a firework display.
- This offence is not restricted to a public place and will be committed if a person breaches this prohibition in their own private garden/land.

Practical considerations

- A breach of this prohibition is a criminal offence under s 11(1) of the Fireworks Act 2003, for which a PND can be issued (see **7.1.1**).
- Consider stop, search, and seizure powers under s 1(8B) of PACE (see **1.3**).

SSS **PND**

Summary

12 months

6 months' imprisonment and/or a fine

8.8.5 Supply of fireworks and pyrotechnic article offences

The Pyrotechnic Articles (Safety) Regulations 2015 creates prohibitions on the supply of various categories of Christmas crackers, fireworks, and pyrotechnic articles to people under the age of 12, 16, or 18 years.

Regulation 31 states that an **economic operator** must not make a **pyrotechnic article** available on the market in the UK to a person younger than the following minimum age limits:

(a) for a Christmas cracker, 12 years;
(b) for a category F1 firework other than a Christmas cracker, 16 years;
(c) for a category F2 firework or a category F3 firework, 18 years;
(d) for a category T1 theatrical pyrotechnic article, 18 years;
(e) for a category P1 other pyrotechnic article, 18 years.

Regulation 62 provides the offences that can be committed by an economic operator or conformity assessment body, including failing to comply with a notice, intentionally obstruct an enforcing authority/HMRC, provide false misleading statement/information/document/record, and purporting to exercise powers under these regulations when not authorised to do so.

Meanings

Economic operator

A manufacturer, importer, or distributor.

Christmas cracker

A paper or foil tube, crimped at each end, enclosing novelties, and with one or more snaps running along the length of the tube.

Pyrotechnic article (see **8.8.1**)

Category F1, F2 and F3 fireworks (see **8.8.1**)

Category T1 theatrical pyrotechnic articles

Theatrical pyrotechnic articles which present a low hazard.

Category P1 other pyrotechnic articles

Pyrotechnic articles, other than fireworks and theatrical pyrotechnic articles, which present a low hazard.

Defence

Regulation 64 provides a defence of due diligence for a person to show that they took all reasonable steps and exercised all due diligence to avoid committing the offence. It also sets out the circumstances when they may not rely on this defence.

Practical considerations

- Breaching the prohibitions under these regulations is an offence under reg 62. None of the supply offences are subject to the PND procedure.

SSS

For offences under reg 62

Category 1, 2, or 3 fireworks: Summary

Other pyrotechnic articles: Either way

Category 1, 2, or 3 fireworks: 12 months

Other pyrotechnic articles: None

Category 1, 2, or 3 fireworks offences: 3 months' imprisonment and/or a fine

Other pyrotechnic articles:
Summary: 3 months' imprisonment and/or a fine
Indictment: 2 years' imprisonment and/or a fine

8.8.6 Throwing fireworks

Section 80 of the Explosives Act 1875 creates various offences relating to throwing, casting, or firing any fireworks in a public place.

Offences

If any person throw, cast, or fire any fireworks in or into any highway, street, thoroughfare, or public place, he shall be guilty of an offence.

Explosives Act 1875, s 80

PNLD H1367

Points to prove

✓ throw/cast/fire
✓ a firework/fireworks
✓ in/into a highway/street/thoroughfare/public place

Practical considerations

- Consider issuing a PND for this offence—'**Throwing fireworks in a thoroughfare**' (see **7.1.1**).

SSS PND

Summary

6 months

Fine

8.8.7 Causing danger in the highway

Section 161 of the Highways Act 1980 creates various offences relating to causing danger on the highway.

Offences

If a person without lawful authority or excuse—

(a) lights any fire on or over a highway which consists of or comprises a carriageway; or

(b) discharges any firearm or firework within 50 feet of the centre of such a highway,

and in consequence a user of the highway is injured, interrupted or endangered, that person is guilty of an offence.

Highways Act 1980, s 161(2)

PNLD **H1689, H1690, H2107**

Points to prove

✓ without lawful authority/excuse
✓ lit a fire on/over a highway, OR
✓ discharged a firework or firearm within 50 ft of centre of highway
✓ as a result, user injured/interrupted/endangered

Meanings

Highway (see **10.1.1**)

Carriageway

Means a way constituting or comprised in a highway, being a way (other than a cycle track) over which the public have a right of way for the passage of vehicles.

Summary

6 months

Level 3 fine

8.8.8 Discharging firearm/missile or throwing fireworks

Section 28 of the Town Police Clauses Act 1847 creates numerous offences.

Offences

Every person who in any street, to the obstruction, annoyance, or danger of the residents or passengers, who wantonly discharges any firearm or missile or throws or sets fire to a firework commits an offence.

Town Police Clauses Act 1847, s 28

PNLD H1359, H1360, H1076, H1357

Points to prove

✓ in street
✓ wantonly
✓ **discharges firearm/missile OR**
✓ threw/set fire to a firework
✓ to the obstruction/annoyance/danger of residents/passengers

Meaning of street

Street includes any road, square, court, alley, thoroughfare, or public passage.

Explanatory notes

- None of the Town Police Clauses Act offences are complete unless it can be proved that they would obstruct, annoy, or cause danger to any residents or passengers.

Related case

Mantle v Jordan [1897] 1 QB 248 The Town Police Clauses Act offences can only be committed in the street, but the annoyance may be to 'residents', meaning the occupiers of houses in the street, although the residents might not be in the street at the time.

Summary

6 months

14 days' imprisonment or a level 3 fine

8.8.9 Possession of pyrotechnic articles at musical events

The Policing and Crime Act 2017 and the Possession of Pyrotechnic Articles at Musical Events Regulations 2017 together create offences relating specifically to musical events.

Offence

It is an offence for a person to have a pyrotechnic article in his or her possession at any time when the person is—
(a) at a place where a qualifying musical event is being held, or
(b) at any other place that is being used by a person responsible for the organisation of a qualifying musical event for the purpose of—
  (i) regulating entry to, or departure from, the event, or
  (ii) providing sleeping or other facilities for those attending the event.

Policing and Crime Act 2017, s 134(1)

PNLD H18814

Points to prove

✓ possessed a pyrotechnic article
✓ when at a place where qualifying musical event held OR
✓ when at a place used for entry to/departure from the event/providing facilities for those attending

Meanings

Pyrotechnic article

Pyrotechnic article (see **8.8.1**) means an article that contains explosive substances, or an explosive mixture of substances, designed to produce heat, light, sound, gas, or smoke, or a combination of such effects, through self-sustained exothermic chemical reactions, other than a match or article/description as specified in regulations made by the Secretary of State.

Qualifying musical event

An event at which one or more live musical performances take place and which is specified, or of a description specified, in regulations made by statutory instrument by the Secretary of State.

Premises licence

Has the meaning given in s 11 of the Licensing Act 2003.

The provision of regulated entertainment

Has the meaning given in Sch 1(2) to the Licensing Act 2003.

Explanatory notes

- This offence does not apply to a person responsible for organising the event (organiser) or a person who has the article in their possession with the consent of the organiser.
- A qualifying musical event applies to an event that is provided for members of the public or a section of the public on premises which have a premises licence that authorises regulated entertainment in the form of a performance of live music.

Summary

6 months

3 months' imprisonment and/or a level 3 fine

Links to alternative subjects and offences

2.1 **Assault (Common/Actual Bodily Harm)** 53
4.4 **Criminal Damage** 193
4.5.2 **Arson** 200
7.1 **Penalty Notices for Disorder** 351
7.3 **Breach of the Peace** 362
7.7 **Intentional Harassment, Alarm, or Distress** 376
7.13 **Anti-Social Behaviour** 435
7.15.1 **Dispersal powers** 456

8.9 Offensive Weapons and Crossbows

Possession of or threatening with offensive weapons in a public place, the manufacture and sale of offensive weapons, trespassing with a weapon of offence, and offences involving crossbows form a key part of operational policing.

8.9.1 Offensive weapons in public place—possess/threaten

The Prevention of Crime Act 1953 deals with offences regarding possession of or threatening with offensive weapons in a public place.

Offences

Possess

1(1) Any person who without lawful authority or reasonable excuse, the proof whereof shall lie on him, has with him in any public place any offensive weapon shall be guilty of an offence.

Threaten

1A(1) A person is guilty of an offence if that person—
- (a) has an offensive weapon with him or her in a public place,
- (b) unlawfully and intentionally threatens another person ('A') with the weapon, and
- (c) does so in such a way that a reasonable person ('B') who was exposed to the same threat as A would think that there was an immediate risk of physical harm to B.

Prevention of Crime Act 1953, ss 1(1) and 1A(1)

PNLD H486, H20300

Points to prove

Possess (s 1(1))

✓ without lawful authority/reasonable excuse
✓ had with them
✓ in a public place
✓ an offensive weapon

> ***Threaten (s 1A(1))***
> ✓ had with them an offensive weapon in a public place
> ✓ unlawfully and intentionally threaten another person with the weapon
> ✓ in such a way that a reasonable person exposed to the same threat would think there was an immediate risk of physical harm to them

Meanings

Has with him (see **8.3.6**)

Public place

Includes any highway and any other premises or place to which at the material time the public have or are permitted to have access, whether on payment or otherwise.

Offensive weapon

Means any article **made** or **adapted** for use for causing injury to the person or **intended** by the person having it with them for such use by them or by some other person.

Intentionally (see **4.1.2**)

Explanatory notes

- Within the meaning of 'offensive weapon', particular terms used and case law have provided meanings to those terms as follows:
  - **'made'** includes articles that have been specifically created for the purpose of causing injury, and includes knuckledusters, flick knives, butterfly knives, sword sticks, truncheons, daggers, bayonets, and rice flails. All of these items are generally classed as offensive weapons per se ('by themselves');
  - **'adapted'** consists of articles that have generally been altered in some way with the intention of causing injury, such as smashing a bottle to make the broken end into a weapon for causing injury;
  - **'intended'** these can be otherwise inoffensive articles that the defendant proposes to use to cause injury to a person, such as a bunch of keys held in the fist with the keys projecting through the fingers (making it an impromptu knuckleduster).
- The primary aim of the s 1 possession offence is the **carrying** of such weapons rather than their **use** in the heat of the moment.
- The Offensive Weapons Act 2019 amended the s 1A offence to include an objective element—whether a reasonable person exposed to the same threat would think there was an immediate risk of physical harm.

Defences

Possess (s 1)

Lawful authority

This extends to people such as an on-duty police officer with a baton.

Reasonable excuse

Whether an excuse is reasonable is for the court to decide having heard all the circumstances. These could include:

- people carrying the tools of their trade (eg hammer/saw by a carpenter or filleting knife by a fishmonger);
- self-defence—if there is an imminent threat, this defence may be available.

Threaten (s 1A)

The use of the weapon must be unlawful; this allows the person to raise relevant defences such as self-defence, defence of others or of property, and prevention of crime.

Related cases

Garry v Crown Prosecution Service [2019] EWHC 636 (Admin) The carrying of a butterfly knife (an offensive weapon per se) for an innocent purpose, namely, for use as a work tool, in a public place, did not amount to a reasonable excuse for the purpose of s 1(1) of the Prevention of Crime Act 1953. Where the item is offensive per se and other items might do just as well for the innocent purpose, the innocent purpose did not equate to reasonableness: 'conclusive proof of a habit of using the weapon for work might prompt review of whether that use were reasonable: the wedding planner supplies a sword for cake-cutting, the chef tenderises meat using knuckle dusters'.

R v Tucker [2016] EWCA Crim 13 The defendant was aware of an affray taking place outside their flat and, in anger, they went out with a cricket bat with the intent to injure another person. While the offence of possessing an offensive weapon does not occur where it is used in the heat of the moment (see the case of *Ohlson v Hylton* below as an example), it was held in this case that where a person introduces an article into a public place to use it offensively there, this would be an offence under s 1 of the Act.

DPP v Christof [2015] EWHC 4096 (Admin) The defendant had a belt buckle in the form of a knuckleduster that could be detached from the belt. The defendant was charged with the s 1 offence but acquitted on the basis that it was being used as a belt buckle and the fact that the belt had to be disassembled in order to use it as a weapon negated the idea that it was a weapon at all. On appeal by the DPP, the court held that the item in question appeared to have unusual features for a knuckleduster and it was possible that it had been made or designed for the purpose of causing injury, even though it was being put to another use. If it was a fashion item that was widely worn, then those who wore them needed to know that they were potentially at risk of prosecution.

Ohlson v Hylton [1975] 2 All ER 490, QBD and **R v Veasey [1999] Crim LR 158, CA** The defendant was a carpenter who was on their way home from work carrying tools in a bag. As the defendant was trying to get onto a Tube train, they got involved in an argument with another passenger. A scuffle ensued and the two of them fell over. The defendant took a hammer from a bag and hit the other person with it. The defendant was convicted of assault but acquitted of possession of an offensive weapon. It was held that the acquittal was correct. If the defendant seized a weapon for 'instant use' on the victim or grabbed something innocuous (like a hammer or snooker cue) in the heat of the moment, then the 'weapon' was not carried unlawfully with prior intent.

Practical considerations

- For further information regarding this offence, see MOJ Circular 8/2012.
- If a person is found not guilty of the s 1A (threaten) offence (whether on indictment or not), but it is proved that the person committed the s 1 (possess) offence, then they may be convicted of the s 1 offence.
- Consider stop, search, and seizure powers under s 1 of PACE (see **1.3**).
- For the s 1 possession offence, where an article is 'made' or 'adapted' to cause injury (offensive per se), the prosecution does not need to prove intent to cause injury as merely having it with them is sufficient.
- The 'intended' use requires an element of intent to use the article to cause injury, which must be proved. An instant use of an innocent article will need proof of a prior intent otherwise no offence is committed, either by possessing or threatening with the weapon.
- Upon conviction, the court may make an order for the forfeiture or disposal of any weapon in respect of which the offence was committed.
- If appropriate, consider the offence of possession of a blade/pointed article in a public place (see **8.10.6**) or on school/further education premises (see **8.10.7**).
- There is a need to prove a knowledge of the existence of the article and that the article is 'to hand and ready for use' (eg it may be hidden a few feet away; it does not have to be physically on the defendant's person).
- The burden of proof for lawful authority or reasonable excuse lies with the accused and it is for the prosecution to disprove it (*R v Archbold* [2007] EWCA Crim 2137).

SSS E&S

Either way

None

Summary: 6/12 months' imprisonment and/or a fine

Indictment: 4 years' imprisonment and/or a fine

8.9.2 Offensive weapons—threaten in private

This offence concerns threatening someone with an offensive weapon etc in a private place.

Offence

A person ('A') commits an offence if—
(a) while A is in a private place, A unlawfully and intentionally threatens another person ('B') with an article or substance to which this subsection applies, and
(b) A does so in such a way that there is an immediate risk of serious physical harm to B.

Offensive Weapons Act 2019, s 52(1)

PNLD H20294

Points to prove

- ✓ unlawfully and intentionally
- ✓ threatened another person with
- ✓ an offensive weapon within the meaning of s 1 of the Prevention of Crime Act 1953 OR
- ✓ an article to which s 139 of the Criminal Justice Act 1988 applies OR
- ✓ a corrosive substance
- ✓ in a private place
- ✓ in a way that there is an immediate risk of serious physical harm to that person

Meanings

Article or substance to which this subsection applies

Means:
- an offensive weapon within the meaning of s 1 of the Prevention of Crime Act 1953;
- an article to which s 139 of the Criminal Justice Act 1988 (offence of having article with blade or point in public place) applies; or
- a corrosive substance.

Corrosive substance (see **8.11.3**)

Private place

For an offensive weapon/article, this means:
- a place other than a:
  - ✦ public place;
  - ✦ place which is part of school premises; or
  - ✦ place which is part of further education premises.

For a corrosive substance, this means:
- a place other than a public place.

Public place

Includes any place to which, at the time in question, the public have or are permitted to have access, whether on payment or otherwise.

School premises (see **8.10.7**)

Further education premises (see **8.10.7**)

Explanatory note

- The Offensive Weapons Act 2019 amended s 1 of PACE to include a corrosive substance in relation to which a person has committed, or is committing or is going to commit, an offence under s 6 (having a corrosive substance in a public place) (see **8.11.3**).

Practical considerations

- Section 53 of the Offensive Weapons Act 2019 outlines further entry and search powers for any premises and any person for a corrosive substance if they have reasonable grounds for suspecting that an offences (as it applies to corrosive substances) has or is being committed.

SSS E&S

Either way

None

Summary: 6/12 months' imprisonment and/or a fine
Indictment: 4 years' imprisonment and/or a fine

8.9.3 Offensive weapons—provide/trade/manufacture/possess in private

Transferring ownership, trading in, importing, manufacturing, or possessing private certain offensive weapons is an offence.

Offences

(1) Any person who manufactures, sells or hires or offers for sale or hire, exposes or has in his possession for the purpose of sale or hire, or lends or gives to any other person, a weapon to which this section applies shall be guilty of an offence.

> (1A) Any person who possesses a weapon to which this section applies in private is guilty of an offence.
>
> Criminal Justice Act 1988, s 141

PNLD H1728 to H1733, H20299

Points to prove

Provide/trade/manufacture/import (s 141(1))

✓ manufactured/sold/hired/lent/gave OR
✓ possessed/exposed/offered
✓ for sale/hire
✓ an offensive weapon

Possess (s 141(1A))

✓ possessed in private
✓ an offensive weapon

Meanings

Weapon to which s 141 applies

These are specified in the Schedule to the Criminal Justice Act 1988 (Offensive Weapons) Order 1988 (see **8.9.4**).

Private

Means in any place other than a public place, school premises, further education premises, or a prison.

School premises (see **8.10.7**)

Further education premises (see **8.10.7**)

Explanatory notes

- The importation of weapons to which s 141 applies is prohibited.
- Some will also fall into the category of being a bladed/pointed article (see **8.10**).
- See also a warrant to search for and a power to stop/search/seize these weapons (see **8.12**).
- It is an offence to lend, give, or trade in flick or gravity knives (see **8.10.2**).
- This section does not apply to any weapons subject to the Firearms Act 1968 (see **8.1**) or crossbows (see **8.9.6**).
- Consider the offence of using another person to look after, hide, or transport a firearm, offensive/bladed weapon, or knife so that it will be available when required for an unlawful purpose (see **8.3.7**).
- The Offensive Weapons Act 2019 inserted the additional offence to possess in private.

Defences

Both offences

If it can be shown that their conduct was only for the purposes of:

- functions carried out on behalf of the Crown or of a visiting force;
- making the weapon available to a museum or gallery;
- making the weapon available for the purposes specified in s 141(11B).
- making the weapon available for the purposes of use for religious reasons (see '**Explanatory notes**' for further defences in relation to curved swords and those of Sikh faith).

Section 141(1A) offence

If the weapon possessed:

- is of historical importance;
- for educational purposes;
- is in their capacity as the operator of, or as a person acting on behalf of, a museum or gallery.

Defence notes

- A person acting on behalf of a **museum or gallery** can use the above defence if they had reasonable grounds to believe that the person to whom they lent or hired it would use it only for cultural, artistic, or educational purposes. The defence will only apply if the **museum or gallery** does not distribute profits.
- **Museum or gallery** includes any institution which has as its purpose, or one of its purposes, the preservation, display, and interpretation of material of historical, artistic, or scientific interest, and gives the public access to it.
- The purposes under s 141(11B) are for theatrical performances and rehearsals for such performances or for the production of films or television programmes.
- An antique weapon is exempt (more than 100 years old).

SSS

Summary

6 months

51 weeks' imprisonment and/or a fine

8.9.4 The Criminal Justice Act 1988 (Offensive Weapons) Order 1988

This Order provides a list of weapons where their sale, hire, offering for sale/hire, exposing, importation, and possession in private is prohibited.

8.9.4 Criminal Justice Act 1988 (Offensive Weapons) Order 1988

The Order excludes antique weapons and provides that a weapon is an antique if it was manufactured more than 100 years before the date of any offence alleged to have been committed in respect of that weapon.

This list only applies to s 141 offences (see **8.9.3**) and is not a list of all offensive weapons per se: knuckleduster; sword stick; butterfly knife; death star; belt buckle knife; hollow kubotan (cylinder holding sharp spikes); push dagger; kusari (rope, cord, wire, or chain with hooked knife, sickle, hard weight or hand grip fastened at one end); foot or hand claw; blowpipe; telescopic truncheon; baton; stealth knife (non-metallic); disguised knife (blade or sharp point concealed within an everyday object such as a comb, brush, writing instrument, cigarette lighter, key, lipstick, or telephone); cyclone/spiral knife, various types of zombie knives, and a sword with a curved blade.

Explanatory notes

- There are exceptions even if the weapon is on this list.
- The list given above is not an exhaustive or descriptive list, it just gives an idea of the type of weapons included in this Order.
- Stealth knives are non-metallic hunting or stiletto knives, made of a range of materials, such as nylon zytel or high-impact plastic. Although they look like conventional knives, they are difficult to detect by security apparatus. Their design and construction mean that their possession in public may be an offence under:
  - s 1(1) of the Prevention of Crime Act 1953 (**8.9.1**); or
  - s 139(1) of the Criminal Justice Act 1988 (**8.10**).
- The Weapons Amendment Order 2008 (SI 973/2008) added a sword with a curved blade of 50 cm or over in length to the list, the length of the blade being measured in a straight line from the top of the handle to the tip of the blade. It is a defence if a person can show that:
  - the sword was made in Japan before 1954 or at any other time using traditional Japanese methods of forging swords; and
  - an organisation requires the use of the weapon for a permitted activity (historical re-enactment or a sporting activity) and that public liability insurance was in force which indemnified those taking part in the activity.
- The Offensive Weapons Act 2019 added zombie knives and cyclone knives to the Order.
- The Offensive Weapons Act 2019 added further defences to the Order in regard to curved swords. It is a defence for those of Sikh faith to present curved swords to another at a religious ceremony or other ceremonial event and a defence for possession is also available for a Sikh for the purposes of presenting the sword and for the recipients (whether a Sikh or non-Sikh) to possess a sword presented to them. A Sikh means a follower of the Sikh religion. A further defence for possession of curved swords is also available if the person possessed the weapon for religious reasons only.

8.9.5 Trespassing with weapon of offence

Section 8 of the Criminal Law Act 1977 creates the offence of 'trespassing with a weapon of offence'.

Offences

A person who is on any premises as a trespasser, after having entered as such, is guilty of an offence if, without lawful authority or reasonable excuse, he has with him on the premises any weapon of offence.

Criminal Law Act 1977, s 8(1)

PNLD H2287

Points to prove

✓ on premises as trespasser
✓ having entered as such
✓ had weapon of offence
✓ without lawful authority or reasonable excuse

Meanings

Premises

This consists of any:

- building/part of a building (under separate occupation);
- land adjacent to and used/intended for use in connection with a building;
- site comprising any building(s) together with ancillary land;
- fixed structure; and
- moveable structure, vehicle, or vessel designed or adapted for residential purposes.

Trespasser (see **3.3.1**)

Has with him (see **8.3.6**)

Weapon of offence (see **3.3.2**)

Practical considerations

- This offence is worth bearing in mind if the carrying of offensive weapons in a public place/school premises or aggravated burglary does not apply.
- Consider stop, search, and seizure powers under s 1 of PACE (see **1.3**).
- Entry must have been as a trespasser—it does not extend to a person who has entered lawfully and later becomes a trespasser (eg being asked to leave by the occupier).

Summary

6 months

3 months' imprisonment and/or a fine

8.9.6 Crossbows

Crossbows are extremely accurate weapons and potentially as lethal as a firearm. This legislation creates offences in relation to persons under 18 years possessing, hiring, or purchasing crossbows.

Sell, purchase, or hire crossbow

Offences

Sell/hire to under 18

A person who sells or lets on hire a **crossbow** or part of a crossbow to a person under the age of 18 is guilty of an offence unless he believes him to be 18 years of age or older and has reasonable grounds for that belief.

Crossbows Act 1987, s 1

Purchase/hire by under 18

A person under the age of 18 who buys or hires a crossbow, or a part of a crossbow is guilty of an offence.

Crossbows Act 1987, s 2

PNLD H8734 to H8737, H8738 to H8741

Points to prove

Sell/hire (s 1)

✓ sold/let on hire or sold/let on hire part(s) of
✓ a crossbow
✓ to person under 18 years of age

Purchase/hire (s 2)

✓ person under 18 years of age
✓ hired/purchased or purchased/hired part(s) of
✓ a crossbow

Meaning of crossbow

Does not apply to crossbows with a draw weight of less than 1.4 kg.

Defences (sell/hire)

Reasonable grounds to believe that the person is 18 years or older.

Practical considerations

- Proof required of age (eg ID card or birth certificate).
- Only applies to crossbows of a certain strength, having a draw weight of 1.4 kg or over.
- The draw weight limit is very low and can be determined by the forensic testing; only toys will be excluded by this definition.

Summary 6 months

Sell/hire (s 1)
6 months' imprisonment and/or a fine

Purchase/hire (s 2)
Level 3 fine

Under 18—possess a crossbow

Offences

A person under the age of 18 who has with him—
(a) a crossbow which is capable of discharging a missile, or
(b) parts of a crossbow which together (and without any other parts) can be assembled to form a crossbow capable of discharging a missile,
is guilty of an offence, unless he is under the supervision of a person who is 21 years of age or older.

Crossbows Act 1987, s 3

PNLD H8742, H8743

Points to prove

- ✓ being under the age of 18
- ✓ had with them
- ✓ a crossbow/crossbow parts (able to form a crossbow)
- ✓ capable of discharging a missile
- ✓ without supervision of person age 21 or over

Meanings

Has with him (see 8.3.6)

Crossbow (see s 1 above)

Explanatory notes

- This offence can be committed anywhere and not just in public.
- No offence will be committed if under supervision of person age 21 or over.

8.9.6 Crossbows

Practical considerations (see also ss 1 and 2 above)

- The legislation allows a person of 18 or over to possess a crossbow in public in certain circumstances. However, such possession may fall foul of the law on offensive weapons and the bolts might also fall within the provisions of s 139 of the Criminal Justice Act 1988 (pointed article/blades).

SSS

Summary

6 months

Level 3 fine

Crossbows—search and seizure powers

Section 4 of the Crossbows Act 1987 gives police officers quite wide powers of search, detention, seizure, and entry onto land if a person under 18 years is unsupervised and is in possession of a crossbow/parts.

Powers

(1) If a constable suspects with reasonable cause that a person is committing or has committed an offence under section 3, the constable may—
   (a) search that person for a crossbow or part of a crossbow;
   (b) search any vehicle, or anything in or on a vehicle, in or on which the constable suspects with reasonable cause there is a crossbow, or part of a crossbow, connected with the offence.

(2) A constable may detain a person or vehicle for the purpose of a search under subsection (1).

(3) A constable may seize and retain for the purpose of proceedings for an offence under this Act anything discovered by him in the course of a search under subsection (1) which appears to him to be a crossbow or part of a crossbow.

(4) For the purpose of exercising the powers conferred by this section a constable may enter any land other than a dwelling-house.

Crossbows Act 1987, s 4

Explanatory notes

- A constable may detain a person or vehicle for the search.
- A constable may seize and retain anything found during the search which appears to be a crossbow or part of a crossbow.
- In exercising this power, a constable may enter on any land **other than** a dwelling house.

Practical considerations (see also ss 1, 2, and 3 above)

- Consider powers under s 1 of PACE and ensure compliance with the PACE Codes procedures relating to stop and searches (see **1.3**).

Links to alternative subjects and offences

2.1.2 **Assault occasioning actual bodily harm** 56
2.3.2 **Wounding or grievous bodily harm—with intent** 82
2.5 **Threats to Kill** 97
3.3 **Burglary/Aggravated Burglary** 145
4.4 **Criminal Damage** 193
4.7 **Custody/Control of Articles with Intent to Damage** 206
7.6 **Fear or Provocation of Violence** 373
7.10 **Racially/Religiously Aggravated Offences** 390

8.10 Bladed Articles/Knives Offences

The Criminal Justice Act 1988 deals with offences of having knives/bladed articles in a public place or on school premises, and sale to persons under 18 years.

8.10.1 Possession of bladed/pointed article in public place

Section 139 of the Criminal Justice Act 1988 creates an offence of having a bladed or pointed article in a public place.

Offences

Subject to subsections (4) and (5) [see '**Defences**'] below, any person who has an article to which this section applies with him in a public place shall be guilty of an offence.

Criminal Justice Act 1988, s 139(1)

PNLD H8776

Points to prove

✓ had with them
✓ without good reason/lawful authority
✓ an article being bladed/sharply pointed
✓ in a public place

Meanings

Article

Applies to any article which has a **blade** or is sharply pointed, including a folding pocket knife if the cutting edge of the blade exceeds 3 inches (7.62 cm).

Blade

Examples of this will be the blade of a knife, sword.

Has with him (see **8.3.6**)

Public place

Includes any place to which at the material time the public have or are permitted access, whether on payment or otherwise.

Explanatory notes

- A folding pocket knife does not include a lock knife, regardless of the blade length (*Harris v DPP* [1993] 1 WLR 82, QBD).
- Possession of a multi-tool incorporating a prohibited blade/pointed article is capable of being an offence under this section, even if there are other tools on the instrument that may be of practical use (such as a bottle-opener). It is for the defendant to show that they had good reason for possession (*R v Giles* [2003] EWCA Crim 1287).

Defences

(4) It shall be a defence for a person charged with an offence under this section to prove that he had good reason or lawful authority for having the article with him in a public place.

(5) Without prejudice to the generality of subsection (4) above, it shall be a defence for a person charged with an offence under this section to prove that he had the article with him—

(a) for use at work;

(b) for religious reasons; or

(c) as part of any national costume.

Criminal Justice Act 1988, s 139

Defence notes

The burden of proof is with the defendant to show good reason or lawful authority for having the blade/pointed article with them. Examples of s 139(5) could be:

- **for use at work**—fishmonger, carpet fitter, chef;
- **for religious reasons**—members of the Sikh religion having a kirpan;
- **as part of a national costume**—the skean dhu in Highland dress.

Related cases

R v Hamer [2023] EWCA Crim 516 In this case, H was made the subject of a Knife Crime Prevention Order (see **8.13**) which prohibited them from carrying a knife or bladed article in any public place. However, at a later time CCTV captured them on a public road being in possession of a lock-knife in a box and then handing it to a teenager. Convictions for having a bladed article in public and breach of a knife crime prevention order were safe where, although the two charges arose from the same conduct, the two offences were legally distinct and could both be prosecuted.

R v Szewczyk [2019] EWCA Crim 1811 This case involved the defendant carrying two kitchen knives in a public place. It was held that under s 139 the relevant articles need not be inherently offensive or carried with any offensive intent, but must just conform to the description in the section of the legislation. If a person had with them, even just for a short time, a bladed article, that proved the actus reus of the offence under that Act; then the burden of showing that they had good reason or lawful authority fell upon them.

R v D [2019] EWCA Crim 45 A foldable cut-throat razor with a blade length of 2 inches could not properly be regarded as a pocketknife for the purposes of s 139.

Sharma v DPP [2018] EWHC 3330 (Admin) A blade capable of being locked, however weakly, was not a folding pocket knife when a further process was required to undo the handle and unfold and rotate the blade back into place, as it was not immediately foldable by simply applying pressure to the blade.

R v Henderson [2016] EWCA Crim 965 The defendant was in a private flat and kept a knife in a car parked in a public place. In determining whether the weapon was *'with him'* for the purpose of s 139, the court should bear in mind that: possession of an article is a wider concept than that of a person *'having an article with him'* but is broader than 'carrying' an article; the proximity between the person and the weapon; whether the weapon was immediately available; accessibility of the weapon; the context of the criminal enterprise embarked upon; and the purpose of the legislation. It was held in this case that there was no evidence that the knife was 'immediately available' to the defendant who had not shortly left or was to shortly to return to the car and the knife was not linked in any way to their presence in the flat.

R v Clancy [2012] EWCA Crim 8 An accused's state of mind should not be entirely disregarded when considering 'good reason' in relation to possession of a bladed or pointed article in a public place.

R v Cleaver [2011] EWCA Crim 983 The landing of a block of flats to which access was controlled by an intercom system was not a 'public place' and the offence was not committed.

Practical considerations

- Consider stop, search, and seizure powers under s 1(8A) of PACE (see **1.3**).
- Consider s 139AA if offences relate to threats made when in possession of articles/offensive weapons in public or on school premises (see **8.10.6**).
- Sections 52 to 55A of the Courts Act 2003 give a court security officer powers to search, exclude, remove, or restrain person(s) in a court building with regard to an article/knife in their possession, including seizing any article or knife found by that officer.

SSS E&S

Either way

None

Summary: 6/12 months' imprisonment and/or a fine

Indictment: 4 years' imprisonment and/or a fine

8.10.2 Sale of knives/blades to persons under 18

Section 141A of the Criminal Justice Act 1988 creates the offence of selling knives or certain articles with a blade or point to people under the age of 18.

Offences

Any person who sells to a person under the age of 18 years an article to which this section applies shall be guilty of an offence.

Criminal Justice Act 1988, s 141A(1)

PNLD H8733

Points to prove

✓ sold to person under 18 years
✓ knife/axe/knife blade/razor blade or
✓ bladed, sharply pointed article being made/adapted for use for causing injury

Meanings

Article to which this section applies

Subject to **subsection (3)** below, this section applies to:

(a) any knife, knife blade, or razor blade;
(b) any axe; and
(c) any other article which has a blade, or which is sharply pointed, and which is made or adapted for use for causing injury to the person.

Subsection (3)

This section does not apply to any article described in:

(a) s 1 of the Restriction of Offensive Weapons Act 1959 (see **8.10.5**); or
(b) an order made by the Secretary of State under this section.

Explanatory notes

- Section 1 of the Restriction of Offensive Weapons Act 1959 makes possessing, lending, giving, or trading of flick or gravity knives a summary offence (see **8.10.5**).
- The Offensive Weapons Act amended the offence to include weapons given in the Criminal Justice Act 1988 (Offensive Weapons) Order 1988 such as knuckledusters, sword sticks, and belt daggers (see **8.9.4**) thus closing the legal gap created by the defences which would permit, in some circumstances, the sale of these weapons to an under 18.

8.10.2 **Sale of knives/blades to persons under 18**

- The Criminal Justice Act 1988 (Offensive Weapons) (Exemption) Order 1996 states that this section does not apply to:
  - ✦ folding pocket knives if the cutting edge of the blade does not exceed 7.62 cm (3 inches);
  - ✦ razor blades permanently enclosed in a cartridge or housing where less than 2 mm of any blade is protruding.

Defence

To prove that they took all reasonable precautions and exercised all due diligence to avoid the commission of the offence.

Criminal Justice Act 1988, s 141A(4)

Defence for remote sales

The Offensive Weapons Act 2019 inserts a new defence at s 141B of the Criminal Justice Act 1988 in relation to remote sales (where the seller was not in the presence of the buyer at the time of the sale, ie online). It will be a defence as long as the seller as a minimum prove they have met the conditions outlined in s 141B. These include age-verification software being used, clearly marking packaging, all reasonable precautions/due diligence being exercised, and not delivering to a locker.

The seller is said **not to be in the presence of the buyer at the time of sale** if:

(a) where the seller is an individual, the seller or a person acting on the seller's behalf was not in the presence of the buyer at that time;

(b) where the seller is not an individual, a person acting on the seller's behalf was not in the presence of the buyer at that time.

Meaning of locker (see **8.10.3**)

Practical considerations

- Reasonable precautions go beyond appearance or enquiring about the age of the purchaser, such as proving age by ID card.
- Consider the offence of using another person to look after, hide, or transport a firearm, offensive/bladed weapon, or knife so that it will be available when required for an unlawful purpose (see **8.3.7**).

SSS

Summary

6 months

6 months' imprisonment and/or a fine

8.10.3 Deliver bladed product to residential premises/locker

Offences

(1) This section applies if—
- (a) a person ('the seller') sells a bladed product to another person ('the buyer'), and
- (b) the seller and the buyer are not in each other's presence at the time of the sale.

(2) The seller commits an offence if, for the purposes of supplying the bladed product to the buyer, the seller delivers the bladed product, or arranges for its delivery, to residential premises.

(3) The seller commits an offence if, for the purposes of supplying the bladed product to the buyer, the seller delivers the bladed product, or arranges for its delivery, to a locker.

Offensive Weapons Act 2019, s 38

PNLD H20291, H20442

Points to prove

- ✓ sold a bladed product to a person
- ✓ whilst not in each other's presence at the time of sale
- ✓ for the purposes of supplying the bladed product
- ✓ delivered/arranged delivery of the bladed product
- ✓ to a residential premises/locker

Meanings

Bladed product

Bladed product means an article which:

- is or has a blade, and
- is capable of causing a serious injury to a person which involves cutting that person's skin.

It does not include an article described in:

- s 1 of the Restriction of Offensive Weapons Act 1959; or
- an order made by the Secretary of State.

See s 41 of the Offensive Weapons Act 2019.

Residential premises

Means premises used solely for residential purposes and not where a person carries on a business from the premises.

Locker

Means a lockable container to which a bladed product is delivered with a view to collection by the buyer or a person acting on behalf of the buyer.

8.10.3 **Deliver bladed product to residential premises/locker**

Not in each other's presence at the time of the sale

Means:

- where A is an individual, A or a person acting on behalf of A is not in the presence of B at that time;
- where A is not an individual, a person acting on behalf of A is not in the presence of B at that time.

Explanatory notes

- Section 1 of the Restriction of Offensive Weapons Act 1959 makes possessing, lending, giving, or trading of flick or gravity knives a summary offence (see **8.10.5**).
- Where a person carries on a business from their home address, they will be able to receive delivery of bladed products as it is not 'residential premises' for the purposes of this section.

Defences

(1) It is a defence for a person charged with an offence under section 38 to prove that they took all reasonable precautions and exercised all due diligence to avoid the commission of the offence.

(2) It is a defence for a person ('the seller') charged with an offence under section 38(2) of delivering a bladed product to residential premises to prove that—

(a) at the time the offence is alleged to have been committed, the seller had procedures in place which were likely to ensure that any bladed product delivered by the seller to residential premises would be delivered into the hands of a person aged 18 or over, and

(b) the seller took all reasonable precautions and exercised all due diligence to ensure that the product to which the charge relates would be delivered into the hands of a person aged 18 or over.

(3) It is a defence for a person ('the seller') charged with an offence under section 38(2) of arranging for the delivery of a bladed product to residential premises to prove that—

(a) the arrangement required the person with whom it was made to have procedures in place which were likely to ensure that any bladed products delivered to residential premises pursuant to the arrangement would be delivered into the hands of a person aged 18 or over, and

(b) the seller took all reasonable precautions and exercised all due diligence to ensure that the product to which the charge relates would be delivered into the hands of a person aged 18 or over.

(4) It is a defence for a person charged with an offence under section 38 to prove that the bladed product was designed or manufactured for the buyer in accordance with specifications provided by the buyer.

(5) It is a defence for a person charged with an offence under section 38 to prove that—

(a) the bladed product was adapted for the buyer before its delivery in accordance with specifications provided by the buyer, and

(b) the adaptations were made to enable or facilitate the use of the product by the buyer or its use for a particular purpose.

(6) It is a defence for a person charged with an offence under section 38 to prove that they reasonably believed that the buyer bought the bladed product for use for relevant sporting purposes or for the purposes of historical re-enactment.

Offensive Weapons Act 2019, s 40

Summary

6 months

6 months' imprisonment and/or a fine

8.10.4 Deliver bladed product/article to under 18

Offences

39(1) This section applies if—

(a) a person ('the seller') sells a bladed product to another person ('the buyer'),

(b) the seller and the buyer are not in each other's presence at the time of the sale and the seller is within the United Kingdom at that time,

(c) before the sale, the seller entered into an arrangement with a person who is a body corporate by which the person agreed to deliver bladed products for the seller,

(d) that person was aware when they entered into the arrangement that it covered the delivery of bladed products, and

(e) that person delivers the bladed product to residential premises pursuant to that arrangement.

(6) The person mentioned in subsection (1)(e) commits an offence if, when they deliver the bladed product, they do not deliver it into the hands of a person aged 18 or over.

42(1) This section applies if—

(a) a person ('the seller') sells a bladed article to another person ('the buyer'),

(b) the seller and the buyer are not in each other's presence at the time of the sale and the seller is outside the United Kingdom at that time,

(c) before the sale, the seller entered into an arrangement with a person who is a body corporate by which the person agreed to deliver bladed articles for the seller,

(d) that person was aware when they entered into the arrangement that it covered the delivery of bladed articles, and

(e) that person delivers the bladed article pursuant to that arrangement.

(4) The person mentioned in s 1(e) commits an offence if, when they deliver the bladed article, they do not deliver it into the hands of a person aged 18 or over.

Offensive Weapons Act 2019, ss 39 and 42

PNLD H20292, H20293

Points to prove

s 39 offence

✓ a seller within the UK at that time
✓ sold a bladed product to another whilst not in each other's presence at the time of sale
✓ prior to the sale the seller entered into an arrangement with a body corporate
✓ being fully aware bladed products were being delivered
✓ agreed to deliver bladed products
✓ delivered a bladed product
✓ to a residential premises
✓ into the hands of
✓ a person under the age of 18

s 42 offence

✓ a seller outside the UK at that time
✓ sold a bladed article to a person
✓ whilst not in each other's presence at the time of sale
✓ prior to the sale the seller entered into an arrangement with a body corporate
✓ agreed to deliver bladed articles
✓ delivered a bladed article
✓ into the hands of
✓ a person under the age of 18

Meanings

Bladed product (see **8.10.3**)

Bladed article (see **8.10.3**)

Not in each other's presence (see **8.10.3**)

Explanatory notes

- Section 39 applies to a delivery company which has entered into an arrangement to deliver bladed products for a sale carried out remotely by a UK-based seller. An offence is committed when they deliver the bladed product to a residential premises to a person who is under 18.

- Section 42 applies to a delivery company which has entered into a delivery arrangement to deliver bladed articles for a sale that is carried out remotely by a seller who is outside the UK. An offence is committed when they deliver the bladed product to a person who is under 18.

Defence

It is a defence for a person to prove that they took all reasonable precautions and exercised all due diligence to avoid the commission of the offence.

Summary

6 months

Fine

8.10.5 Possess, manufacture, sell, hire, or lend dangerous weapons

Section 1 of the Restriction of Offensive Weapons Act 1959 creates offences in connection with the manufacture, sale, hire, or importation of certain dangerous weapons, such as flick or gravity knives.

Offences

1(1) Any person who manufactures, sells or hires, or offers for sale or hire or exposes or has in his possession for the purpose of sale or hire, or lends or gives to any other person—

(a) any knife which has a blade which opens automatically—

(i) from the closed position to the fully opened position, or

(ii) from a partially opened position to the fully opened position, by manual pressure applied to a button, spring or other device in or attached to the knife, and which is sometimes known as a 'flick knife' or 'flick gun'; or

(b) any knife which has a blade which is released from the handle or sheath thereof by the force of gravity or the application of centrifugal force and which, when released, is locked in place by means of a button, spring, lever, or other device, sometimes known as a 'gravity knife',

shall be guilty of an offence.

1(1A) Any person who possesses any knife of a kind described in subsection (1) is guilty of an offence.

Restriction of Offensive Weapons Act 1959, s 1(1), (1A)

PNLD H20295, H20296

Points to prove

Manufacture, sell, hire, or lend (s 1(1))

✓ manufacture/sold/hired OR
✓ offered for sale OR
✓ exposed/possessed for the purpose of sale/hire OR
✓ loaned/gave
✓ to any other person
✓ a flick knife/gun or gravity knife

Possess (s 1(1A))

✓ possessed
✓ a flick knife/gun or gravity knife

Explanatory notes

The importation of any knife of a kind described in subsection (1) is prohibited.

A lock knife is not a gravity knife. A gravity knife should not be confused with a lock knife. Lock knife means a knife which is similar to a folding pocket knife, in that there is a spring holding the blade closed and it has to be prised open. However, a lock knife has a mechanism which locks the blade in position when fully extended. The blade cannot then be closed without that mechanism being released.

Defences

Section 1(1) offence

- It is a defence if a person can show that the conduct was only for the purposes of making the knife available to a museum or gallery. Furthermore, if an operator or person acting on behalf of museum or gallery is charged with lending or hiring, it is a defence if they had reasonable grounds for believing that the person would use it only for cultural, artistic, or educational purposes.

Section 1(1A) offence

- It is a defence if the weapon possessed is in their capacity as operator of or a person acting on behalf of a museum or gallery.

Practical considerations

- See also s 141 of the Criminal Justice Act 1988 which provides separate restrictions for the sale of other martial arts weapons and knives.
- Where an object has all the characteristics of a flick knife, it does not cease to be one because it also has a secondary characteristic as a lighter.
- Possession of a flick knife in a public place is an offence under s 1 of the Prevention of Crime Act 1953 (see **8.9.1**).

- A 'museum or gallery' includes any institution, if it does not distribute profits, and which has as its purpose, or one of its purposes, the preservation, display, and interpretation of material of historical, artistic, or scientific interest and gives the public access to it.

SSS E&S

Summary 6 months

Summary: 6 months' imprisonment and/or a fine for s 1(1) offence

Summary: 51 weeks' imprisonment and/or a fine for s 1(1A) offence

8.10.6 Threaten with article in public place/school/further education premises

Section 139AA of the Criminal Justice Act 1988 creates the offence of threatening another person with an article in a public place or on school premises, where a reasonable person would believe there to be an immediate risk of serious physical harm to them.

Offences

(1) A person is guilty of an offence if that person—
- (a) has an article to which this section applies with him or her in a public place or on school premises,
- (b) unlawfully and intentionally threatens another person with the article, and
- (c) does so in such a way that a reasonable person ('B') who was exposed to the same threat as A would think that there was an immediate risk of physical harm to B.

(1A) A person is guilty of an offence if that person—
- (a) has an article to which this section applies with them on further education premises,
- (b) unlawfully and intentionally threatens another person ('A') with the article, and
- (c) does so in such a way that a reasonable person ('B') who was exposed to the same threat as A would think that there was an immediate risk of physical harm to B.

Criminal Justice Act 1988, s 139AA(1), (1A)

PNLD H20302, H20304, H20305, H20843, H20847

8.10.6 Threaten with article in public place etc

Points to prove

✓ had with them
✓ a bladed/sharp-pointed article
✓ in a public place/on school/further education premises
✓ unlawfully and intentionally threatened another person with it
✓ in such a way that a reasonable person exposed to the same threat would think there was an immediate risk of physical harm to them

Meanings

Article to which this section applies

Article in a public place means:

- an article to which s 139 applies (see **8.10.1**).

Article on school premises means:

- an article to which s 139 applies (see **8.10.1**);
- an offensive weapon within the meaning of s 1 of the Prevention of Crime Act 1953 (see **8.9.1**).

Public place (see **8.10.1**)

School premises (see **8.10.7**)

Further education premises (see **8.10.7**)

Intentionally (see **4.1.2**)

Explanatory notes

- The meaning of an article will depend on whether it occurs in a public place or on school/further education premises.
- If a person is found not guilty of an offence under this section (whether on indictment or not), but it is proved that the person committed an offence under s 139 (see **8.10.1**) or s 139A (see **8.10.7**), then the person may be convicted of that offence.
- The Offensive Weapons Act 2019 amended the offence to include an objective element—whether a reasonable person exposed to the same threat would think there was an immediate risk of physical harm.

Defences

The use of the weapon must be unlawful, so this allows the person to raise relevant defences such as self-defence, defence of others or of property, and prevention of crime.

Practical considerations

- For further information regarding this offence, see MOJ Circular 008/2012.

- Consider the offence of possessing article/weapon on school premises (see **8.10.7**) and causing/permitting a nuisance/disturbance on school premises (see **8.10.8**).
- There is a specific police power under s 139B to enter and search school premises regarding s 139A and s 139AA offences (see **8.12.2**).
- Consider stop, search, and seizure powers under s 1(8A) of PACE (see **1.3**).

SSS E&S

Either way

None

Summary: 6/12 months' imprisonment and/or a fine

Indictment: 4 years' imprisonment and/or a fine

8.10.7 Possess weapon/blade/sharp point on school/further education premises

Section 139A of the Criminal Justice Act 1988 creates the offence of possessing an article with a blade or sharp point, or an offensive weapon, on school or further education premises.

Offences

(1) Any person who has an article to which section 139 of this Act applies with him on school premises or further education premises shall be guilty of an offence.

(2) Any person who has an offensive weapon within the meaning of section 1 of the Prevention of Crime Act 1953 with him on school premises or further education premises shall be guilty of an offence.

Criminal Justice Act 1988, s 139A

PNLD H20297, H20298

Points to prove

- ✓ without good reason/lawful authority
- ✓ had with them
- ✓ on school/further education premises
- ✓ an article with a blade/sharply pointed OR
- ✓ a folding pocket knife with blade cutting edge exceeding 7.62 m (3 inches) OR
- ✓ offensive weapon

Meanings

Has with him (see **8.3.6**)

School premises

Means land used for the purposes of a **school**, excluding any land occupied solely as a dwelling by a person employed at the school.

School (Education Act 1996, s 4)

Means an educational institution which is outside the further or higher education sector and is an institution for providing:

(a) primary education;
(b) secondary education; or
(c) both primary and secondary education;

whether or not the institution also provides further education.

An alternative provision Academy is also a school.

Further education premises

Means land used solely for the purposes of an institution within the further education sector or a 16 to 19 Academy.

Further education sector (Further and Higher Education Act 1992, s 91)

References to institutions are to institutions conducted by further education corporations, designated institutions, and sixth form colleges.

16 to 19 Academy (Academies Act 2010, s 1B)

An institution meets these requirements if it is principally concerned with providing full-time or part-time education suitable to the requirements of persons over compulsory school age but under 19.

Article (see **8.10.1**)

Offensive weapon (see **8.9.1**)

Explanatory notes

- School/further education premises can include open land, such as playing fields or schoolyards. However, dwellings occupied within the premises by employees, such as caretakers' or wardens' houses, are outside the scope of this section.
- The offence applies to both publicly maintained and independent schools.
- This offence can be committed at any time of the day or night, during term time or holidays; it does not have to be during school hours.
- Many schools/further education premises do not allow access to the general public outside or even during school hours: so these offences

cover the situation where such weapons are carried on school premises that are not public places.

Defences

(3) It shall be a defence for a person charged with an offence under subsection (1) or (2) above to prove that he had good reason or lawful authority for having the article or weapon with him on the premises in question.

(4) Without prejudice to the generality of subsection (3) above, it shall be a defence for a person charged with an offence under subsection (1) or (2) above to prove that he had the article or weapon in question with him—
- (a) for use at work,
- (b) for educational purposes,
- (c) for religious reasons, or
- (d) as part of any national costume.

Criminal Justice Act 1988, s 139A

Practical considerations

- If threats are used when in possession of the article or offensive weapon, then consider the s 139AA offence (see **8.10.6**).
- Consider the offence of causing/permitting a nuisance/disturbance on school premises and power to remove offenders (see **8.10.8**).
- Section 139B gives the police power to enter and search school premises in connection with the s 139A and s 139AA offences (see **8.12.2**).
- Consider powers given to teachers at schools and members of staff at higher education establishments (see **8.10.8**).

SSS E&S

Either way

None

Summary: 6/12 months' imprisonment and/or a fine

Indictment: 4 years' imprisonment and/or a fine

8.10.8 Nuisance/disturbance/powers at school premises

Section 547 of the Education Act 1996 creates the offence of causing a nuisance or disturbance on school premises and provides the police with a power to remove offenders.

Offences

Any person who without lawful authority is present on premises to which this section applies and causes or permits nuisance or disturbance to the annoyance of persons who lawfully use those premises (whether or not any such persons are present at the time) is guilty of an offence.

Education Act 1996, s 547(1)

PNLD **H1687, H2099**

Points to prove

- ✓ without lawful authority
- ✓ was present on premises of local authority maintained/ grant-maintained school/an Academy that is not an independent school
- ✓ and caused/permitted a nuisance/disturbance
- ✓ to the annoyance of persons lawfully using those premises

Power to remove offenders

If a police constable, or an authorised person (of appropriate authority) has reasonable cause to suspect that any person is committing or has committed an offence under this section, he may remove him from the premises in question.

Education Act 1996, s 547(3)

Explanatory notes

- **Premises** includes playgrounds, playing fields, and other premises for outdoor recreation of any:
  - ✦ school maintained by a local authority;
  - ✦ special school not so maintained;
  - ✦ independent school; and
  - ✦ an alternative provision Academy (that is not an independent school).
- **Premises** also applies to those provided by the local education authority and used wholly or mainly in connection with instruction or leadership in sporting, recreational, or outdoor activities.
- Note that a 16 to 19 Academy is not a school.

School staff members' powers

- Education acts give school teachers and members of staff at higher education premises various powers.
- Section 93 of the Education and Inspections Act 2006 gives members of staff powers to restrain pupils to prevent the pupil

from: committing an offence; causing personal injury/damage to another pupil or personal property; or engaging in any behaviour prejudicial to the maintenance of good order and discipline at the school.

- In England, ss 550ZA and 550ZB of the Education Act 1996 allow the head teacher or authorised member of staff to use reasonable force to search a pupil if they have reasonable grounds to suspect that the pupil has a prohibited item in their possession. A prohibited item is a bladed article/knife (see **8.10.1**); offensive weapon (see **8.9.1**); alcohol (see **9.1.1**); controlled drugs (see **5.2.1**); stolen goods (see **3.5**); an article likely to be used to commit an offence or cause personal injury or damage to property; an article as specified in regulations; and any item which the school rules identify as an item for which a search may be made.
- The Schools (Specification and Disposal of Articles) Regulations 2012 (SI 951/2012) list further items that are prohibited under s 550ZA. They are tobacco and cigarette papers, fireworks, and a pornographic image.
- The above regulations and s 550ZC give power to seize and retain, and give directions as to disposal of, any prohibited items found.
- In Wales, s 550AA of the 1996 Act applies and only allows a search of pupils for a bladed article/knife or an offensive weapon. It also provides conditions for such a search, together with powers to seize and retain, and directions as to dispose of any such items found.
- Similar powers exist under the Further and Higher Education Act 1992:
    - ✦ under s 85A, a person who is causing a nuisance or disturbance on higher educational premises will commit an offence. The Act also gives a constable or authorised person power to remove such a person from those premises;
    - ✦ in England, ss 550ZA and 550ZB of the Education Act 1996 allow the head teacher or authorised member of staff to use reasonable force to search a pupil if they have reasonable grounds to suspect that the pupil has a prohibited item in their possession. Section 550ZC gives power to seize, retain, and dispose of any prohibited items found;
    - ✦ in Wales, s 85B of the 1992 Act applies and only allows staff to search for weapons as given in s 550AA above. Section 85B also gives power to seize, retain, and dispose of such items found.

Summary

6 months

Level 2 fine

Links to alternative subjects and offences

2.1 Assault (Common/Actual Bodily Harm) ... 53
2.3.2 Wounding or grievous bodily harm—with intent ... 82
2.5 Threats to Kill ... 97
4.4 Criminal Damage ... 193
4.7 Custody/Control of Articles with Intent to Damage ... 206
7.6 Fear or Provocation of Violence ... 373
7.10 Racially/Religiously Aggravated Offences ... 390

8.11 Corrosives

The use of corrosive products and other acids as a weapon is of significant concern given the life-changing injuries that the products can cause. The Offensive Weapons Act 2019 prohibits the delivery, purchase, and possession of such products to persons under 18 years and the delivery to residential premises and lockers.

8.11.1 Sell/deliver corrosive products to under 18

Offences

Sell to under 18

A person commits an offence if they sell a corrosive product to a person who is under the age of 18.

Offensive Weapons Act 2019, s 1(1)

Deliver to under 18

(1) This section applies if—
- (a) a person ('the seller') sells a corrosive product to another person ('the buyer'),
- (b) the seller and the buyer are not in each other's presence at the time of the sale and the seller is outside the United Kingdom at that time,
- (c) before the sale, the seller entered into an arrangement with a person who is a body corporate by which the person agreed to deliver corrosive products for the seller,
- (d) that person was aware when they entered into the arrangement that it covered the delivery of corrosive products, and
- (e) that person delivers the corrosive product pursuant to that arrangement.

(4) The person mentioned in subsection (1)(e) commits an offence if, when they deliver the corrosive product, they do not deliver it into the hands of a person aged 18 or over.

Offensive Weapons Act 2019, s 4

PNLD H20282, H20284

Points to prove

Sell to under 18

- ✓ sold to a person
- ✓ under 18 years of age
- ✓ a corrosive product

8.11.1 **Sell/deliver corrosive products to under 18**

Deliver to under 18
✓ being a body corporate ✓ having made an arrangement to deliver a corrosive product ✓ for a seller who, when outside the UK, had sold that corrosive product to another person whilst not in that person's presence ✓ being aware upon entering the arrangement that it covered the delivery of corrosive products ✓ delivered the corrosive product into the hands of a person under the age of 18

Meanings

Corrosive product

Means a substance listed in Sch 1 to the Act or any products which contain a substance listed in the Schedule with concentration limits higher than the limits set out for that substance in the schedule.

Not in each other's presence at the time of the sale (see **8.10.3**)

Explanatory note

- The delivery offence applies to a delivery company which entered into an arrangement with a seller outside the UK to deliver corrosive products. An offence is committed when they deliver the corrosive substance to a person who is under 18. The offence applies to both individuals and companies.

Defences

- It is a defence if a person can prove that they took all reasonable precautions and exercised all due diligence to avoid the commission of the offence.
- It is a further defence in relation to remote sales (where the seller was not in the presence of the buyer at the time of the sale, ie online) as long as the seller as a minimum proved they met the conditions outlined in s 2. These include age-verification software being used, clearly marking packaging, all reasonable precautions/due diligence being exercised, and not delivering to a locker.
- A seller is said not to be in the presence of the buyer at the time of sale where:
  - ✦ the seller is an individual, the seller or a person acting on the seller's behalf was not in the presence of the buyer at that time;
  - ✦ the seller is not an individual, a person acting on the seller's behalf was not in the presence of the buyer at that time.

Summary 6 months

Sell

51 weeks' imprisonment and/or a fine

Deliver

Fine

8.11.2 Deliver/arrange delivery to residential premises/locker

Offences

(2) The seller commits an offence if, for the purposes of supplying the corrosive product to the buyer, the seller delivers the product, or arranges for its delivery, to residential premises.
(3) The seller commits an offence if, for the purposes of supplying the corrosive product to the buyer, the seller delivers the product, or arranges for its delivery, to a locker.

Offensive Weapons Act 2019, s 3

PNLD H20283, H20441

Points to prove

✓ sold a corrosive product to a person whilst not in each other's presence at the time of sale
✓ for the purposes of supplying the corrosive product to the person
✓ delivered/arranged delivery of
✓ a corrosive product
✓ to a residential premises/locker

Meanings

Corrosive product (see **8.11.1**)

Not in each other's presence at the time of sale (see **8.10.3**)

Residential premises (see **8.10.3**)

Locker (see **8.10.3**)

Explanatory note

- Where a person carries on a business from a premises, it is not considered a residential premises, meaning those who require corrosive products for business will be able to request delivery.

Summary | 6 months

6 months' imprisonment and/or a fine

8.11.3 Possess a corrosive substance in a public place

Offences

A person commits an offence if they have a corrosive substance with them in a public place.

Offensive Weapons Act 2019, s 6

PNLD H20285

Points to prove

- ✓ without good reason or lawful authority
- ✓ had with them
- ✓ a corrosive substance
- ✓ in a public place

Meanings

Corrosive substance

Means a substance which is capable of burning human skin by corrosion.

Public place

Includes any place to which, at the time in question, the public have or are permitted access, whether on payment or otherwise.

Defences

It will be a defence if a person has good reason or lawful authority which will include for use at work.

Practical considerations

- Consider stop, search, and seizure powers under s 1(8AA) of PACE (see **1.3**).

Either way | None

Summary: 6/12 months' imprisonment and/or a fine

Indictment: 4 years' imprisonment and/or a fine

8.12 Stop and Search Powers—Knives and Weapons

The Criminal Justice Act 1988 deals with premises search warrants and stop and search powers for school premises.

8.12.1 Search warrant for premises

Section 142 of the Criminal Justice Act 1988 creates a search power in respect of premises.

Grounds for issue of warrant

(1) If on an application made by a constable a justice of the peace is satisfied that there are reasonable grounds for believing—
  (a) that there are on premises specified in the application—
    (i) knives such as are mentioned in section 1(1) of the Restriction of Offensive Weapons Act 1959 [see **8.10.5**]; or
    (ii) weapons to which section 141 applies; and
  (b) that an offence under section 1 of the Restriction of Offensive Weapons Act 1959 or section 141 above has been or is being committed in relation to them; and
  (c) that any of the conditions specified in subsection (3) below applies,

he may issue a warrant authorising a constable to enter and search the premises.

Criminal Justice Act 1988, s 142(1)

Meaning of conditions

The conditions relate to any of the following, in that:
- it is not practicable to communicate with any person entitled to grant entry to the premises or grant access to the knives or weapons to which the application relates;
- entry to the premises will not be granted unless a warrant is produced;
- the purpose of a search may be frustrated or seriously prejudiced unless a constable arriving at the premises can secure immediate entry to them.

Explanatory notes

- The Restriction of Offensive Weapons Act 1959 refers to any flick knife, flick gun, or gravity knife (see 8.10.5).
- Weapons under s 141 are listed in the Offensive Weapons Order 1988 (see **8.9.3** and **8.9.4**).

- A constable may seize and retain anything for which a search has been authorised under s 142(1) above.

8.12.2 Powers for article/weapon on school/further education premises

Section 139B of the Criminal Justice Act 1988 provides a power of entry to school or further education premises to search for offensive weapons or articles with a blade or sharp point, and to seize/retain any weapon/article found.

Enter and search

A constable may enter school premises or further education premises and search those premises and any person on those premises for—
(a) any article to which section 139 of this Act applies, or
(b) any offensive weapon within the meaning of section 1 of the Prevention of Crime Act 1953,
if he has reasonable grounds for suspecting that an offence under section 139A or 139AA of this Act is being, or has been, committed.

Criminal Justice Act 1988, s 139B(1)

Seize and retain

If, in the course of a search under this section, a constable discovers an article or weapon which he has reasonable grounds for suspecting to be an article or weapon of a kind described in subsection (1) above, he may seize and retain it.

Criminal Justice Act 1988, s 139B(2)

Explanatory notes

- A constable may use reasonable force, if necessary, in the exercise of the power of entry conferred by this section.
- This power is available where there are reasonable grounds to suspect that an offence under s 139A (see **8.10.7**) and s 139AA (see **8.10.6**) is being or has been committed.
- An article under s 139 is a bladed/sharply pointed article (see **8.10.1**).
- For offensive weapon under the Prevention of Crime Act 1953, s 1, see **8.9.1**.

Practical considerations

- Powers under s 139B are additional to entry and search powers under s 17 of PACE (see **1.4.2**).
- If a large number of people are involved, causing fear of a serious public order situation, then consider stop and search powers under the Criminal Justice and Public Order Act 1994, s 60 (see **8.12.3**).
- Consider the offence and power to remove a person who causes or permits a nuisance or disturbance on school premises (see **8.10.8**).

8.12.3 Stop and search—serious violence/offensive weapon

Section 60 of the Criminal Justice and Public Order Act 1994 allows senior police officers to authorise constables to stop and search people or vehicles in a specific area either where a serious public order problem is likely to arise or has taken place or where people are carrying offensive weapons or sharp-pointed blades. An offence will be committed if that person fails to comply with a constable's requirements.

Authorisation

(1) If a police officer of or above the rank of inspector reasonably believes—
(a) that incidents involving serious violence may take place in any locality in his police area, and that it is expedient to give an authorisation under this section to prevent their occurrence,
(aa) that—
(i) an incident involving serious violence has taken place in England and Wales in his police area;
(ii) a dangerous instrument or offensive weapon used in the incident is being carried in any locality in his police area by a person; and
(iii) it is expedient to give an authorisation under this section to find the instrument or weapon; or
(b) that persons are carrying dangerous instruments or offensive weapons in any locality in his police area without good reason,
he may give an authorisation that the powers conferred by this section are to be exercisable at any place within that locality for a specified period not exceeding 24 hours.

Criminal Justice and Public Order Act 1994, s 60(1)

Explanatory notes

- Home Office guidance for the 'Best Use of Stop and Search Scheme' contains important changes to the use of this power in particular with regard to the rank of officer who can give an authorisation and the length of time the authorisation lasts for. This is a voluntary scheme to which all forces have signed up; however, the legislation has not yet been amended.
- Where a serious violent incident has occurred, and the weapon used in the incident is believed to still be in the locality, this power assists in locating the weapon used and in apprehending the offender before they leave the area or disperse.
- If an authorisation has been given orally under s 60(1)(aa), it needs to be in writing as soon as practicable. Authorisations made under s 60(1)(a) or (b) will still need to be made in writing.

8.12.3 **Stop and search—serious violence/offensive weapon**

- If an inspector gives an authorisation under s 60(1) (forces participating in the scheme will limit the maximum duration of the initial authorisation to fifteen hours), they must, as soon as practicable, inform an officer of or above the rank of chief superintendent.
- In accordance with PACE Code A (b) para 2.14C, an inspector who gives an authorisation under s 60 must communicate their decision to the public as soon as possible and where it is operationally beneficial to do so. This information must include the reason, time limit, and geographical location of the authorisation.
- If it appears to an officer of or above the rank of chief superintendent that it is expedient to do so, they may direct that the authorisation shall continue being in force for a further twenty-four hours. This shall be recorded in writing as soon as practicable.
- Any authorisation shall be in writing signed by the officer giving it and shall specify the grounds, locality, and the period during which the powers are exercisable.
- PACE Code A, specifically paras 2.12–2.18, must be adhered to when utilising this stop and search power.

Power to stop and search pedestrian/vehicle

(4) This section confers on any constable in uniform power—
  (a) to stop any pedestrian and search him or anything carried by him for offensive weapons or dangerous instruments;
  (b) to stop any vehicle and search the vehicle, its driver and any passenger for offensive weapons or dangerous instruments.

(5) A constable may, in the exercise of the powers conferred by subsection (4) above, stop any person or vehicle and make any search he thinks fit whether or not he has any grounds for suspecting that the person or vehicle is carrying weapons or articles of that kind.

Criminal Justice and Public Order Act 1994, s 60

Power to seize

If in the course of such a search under this section a constable discovers a dangerous instrument or an article which he has reasonable grounds for suspecting to be an offensive weapon, he may seize it.

Criminal Justice and Public Order Act 1994, s 60(6)

Offences

A person who fails to stop, or to stop a vehicle, when required to do so by a constable in the exercise of his powers under this section commits an offence.

Criminal Justice and Public Order Act 1994, s 60(8)

PNLD H348, H352

Points to prove

✓ failed to stop (person) or vehicle
✓ when required to do so
✓ by a constable in uniform
✓ in exercising powers of stop/search

Meanings

Offensive weapon (see **8.9.1**)

For incidents involving serious violence under s 60(1)(aa)(i), this means any article made or adapted for use for causing injury to any person or intended for such use and includes any article used in the incident to cause or threaten injury to any person or otherwise to intimidate.

Dangerous instrument

Means instruments which have a blade or are sharply pointed.

Vehicle

This has its natural meaning (see **1.3.2**) and includes a caravan.

Explanatory notes

- Once a written authority has been given for searches, under s 60(5) a constable can stop any person/vehicle or make any search that they think fit, whether or not there are grounds for suspecting that the person or vehicle is carrying weapons or articles.
- Ensure compliance with paras 2.12–2.18 of Code A in relation to searches of persons and vehicles under s 60. Persons involved are entitled to a written statement as to being stopped and/or searched under s 60 if they apply within twelve months.
- A person carries a dangerous instrument or an offensive weapon if they have it in their physical possession.

Related cases

R (on the application of Roberts) v Commissioner of Police for the Metropolis [2015] UKSC 79 It was held in this case that the use of force when exercising a power under s 60 was compatible with ECHR Arts 5 (right to liberty and security) and 8 (right to respect for private and family life) (see **Appendix 1**).

R (on the application of Laporte) v CC of Gloucestershire [2006] UKHL 55 (see **7.3 'Related cases'** for further details).

Practical considerations

- Apart from BTP, only inspectors and superintendents from Home Office forces may authorise these powers to be exercised, although officers from other police forces (RMP, Civil Nuclear Constabulary) may be involved in such searches.

8.12.3 Stop and search—serious violence/offensive weapon

- With the necessary modifications, s 60 also applies to ships, aircraft, and hovercraft as it applies to vehicles.
- Powers conferred by s 60 are in addition to and do not derogate from any other statutory powers.
- Where a s 60 authority is in force, then s 60AA can be utilised, whereby any items, masks, or disguises which are used in order to conceal identity can be removed and seized. An offence will be committed if a person fails to remove an item worn by them when required to do so by a constable under s 60AA(7).

E&S

Summary — 6 months

1 month's imprisonment and/or a level 3 fine

8.13 Serious Violence Reduction Orders

New provisions in the Sentencing Act 2020 provide for the courts to be able to make Serious Violence Reduction Orders (SVROs) in respect of offenders convicted of offences where a knife or offensive weapon was used or was present. The police have additional stop and search powers to target individuals subject to the orders.

This power applies to pilot forces only, beginning 19 April 2023 (Merseyside, Thames Valley, Sussex, and West Midlands) and where an SVRO is in effect against a person. Such searches remain under the scope of PACE Code A until 23.59hrs on 17 July 2025 (see Annex G of Code A). This period covers the twenty-four-month pilot period plus an additional six-month transitional period.

Power

The Sentencing Act 2020 provides the police with a power to search a person subject to a serious violence reduction order to ascertain whether the offender has a bladed article or offensive weapon with them, and to detain the person for the purpose of carrying out that search, provided that such person is in a public place.

Sentencing Act 2020, s 342E

Offences

Where a serious violence reduction order is in effect, the offender commits an offence if the offender—

(a) fails without reasonable excuse to do anything the offender is required to do by the order,
(b) without reasonable excuse does anything the offender is prohibited from doing by the order,
(c) notifies to the police, in purported compliance with the order, any information which the offender knows to be false,
(d) tells a constable that they are not subject to a serious violence reduction order, or
(e) intentionally obstructs a constable in the exercise of any power conferred by section 342E.

Sentencing Act 2020, s 342G(1)

PNLD H101118, H101121, H101123, H101122

Points to prove

- ✓ date and location
- ✓ without reasonable excuse failed to do something required by a serious violence reduction order OR
- ✓ notified the police false information OR
- ✓ intentionally obstructed a constable in the exercise of a power conferred by section 342E OR
- ✓ told a constable you were not subject to an order

Meaning of serious violence reduction order

An order made in respect of an offender that imposes on the offender a requirement to notify the information to the police within the period of three days beginning with the day on which the order takes effect.

That information is:

- the offender's name on the day that the notification is given and, where the offender uses one or more other names on that day, each of those names;
- the offender's home address on that day; and
- the address of any other premises at which, on that day, the offender regularly resides or stays.

The offender must notify the police within three days of using a name not previously notified, changing their home address, or where deciding to live at any premises not previously notified for one month or longer.

This also includes the requirements and prohibitions, if any, specified in regulations made by the Secretary of State for the purposes of this section.

Explanatory notes

- SVROs are intended to deter those offenders from carrying weapons as there is a greater likelihood of being caught and brought to justice.
- The six-month transitional period allows for SVROs which take effect before the end of the pilot period to remain 'live' for six months after the end of the pilot, but it will not be possible to apply for new SVROs or renew existing SVROs once the pilot period ends. This allows courts to issue an SVRO on the last day of the pilot for the minimum duration of the order (six months).
- Applications for SVROs can currently only be made to courts sitting at a place which is within the pilot areas.
- A constable may search the offender for the purpose of ascertaining whether the offender has a bladed article or an offensive weapon with them and detain the offender for the purpose of carrying out the search (see PACE Code of Practice A, Annex G).

- A constable may seize anything that the constable finds in the course of the search if the constable reasonably suspects it to be a bladed article or an offensive weapon.
- A constable may use reasonable force, if necessary, for the purpose of exercising a power conferred by this section.
- Grounds for making an order under s 342A state that the offender must be aged 18 years or above and the court must be satisfied on the balance of probabilities that a bladed article or offensive weapon was used by or was with the offender when the offence was committed; or another person who committed the offence used or had with them a bladed article or offensive weapon in the commission of the offence and the offender knew or ought to have known that this would be the case.

Practical considerations

- Notifications requirements under s 342(B) mean that the offender must notify the police in a police area where the offender lives; consequently, this could be a non-pilot force. (See 'Serious Violence Reduction Orders (Pilot) Guidance for Non-Pilot Forces'.)
- Section 342F and the Sentencing Act 2020 (Serious Violence Reduction Orders: Retention and Disposal of Seized Items) Regulations 2022 make provision for the retention, safe-keeping, disposal, and destruction of items seized under s 342E(4).
- For other powers to search for offensive weapons, consider:
  - ✦ s 1 of PACE which allows an officer to search someone if they have reasonable grounds to suspect that the person is carrying a knife to commit an offence or carrying an offensive weapon (see **1.3.2**);
  - ✦ s 60 of the Criminal Justice and Public Order 1994 Act which allows a constable, on the authorisation of an officer of the rank of inspector or above, where serious violence is anticipated, to search anybody, without suspicion, to see if the person is carrying an offensive weapon or dangerous implement (see **8.12.3**); and
  - ✦ Part 2 of the Offensive Weapons Act 2019, 'Knife Crime Prevention Orders' (a pilot scheme currently restricted to the Metropolitan Police District: S2826) applies to adults and children aged 12 or over. It allows a court to impose specific requirements or restrictions, for example prohibiting a person from being in a certain place, associating with particular people, or undertaking certain activities.

Either way

None

Summary: maximum 6/12 months' imprisonment and/or a fine

Indictment: maximum 2 years' imprisonment and/or a fine

Links to alternative subjects and offences

1.3 **Stop and Search Powers** 22
2.1 **Assault (Common/Actual Bodily Harm)** 53
2.3.2 **Wounding or grievous bodily harm—with intent** 82
4.4 **Criminal Damage** 193
4.7 **Custody/Control of Articles with Intent to Damage** 206
7.4 **Riot and Violent Disorder** 365
7.5 **Affray** 370
7.6 **Fear or Provocation of Violence** 373
7.8 **Threatening/Abusive Words/Behaviour** 380
7.10 **Racially/Religiously Aggravated Offences** 390
Appendix 1 **Human Rights** 839

Chapter 9
Alcohol and Licensing

9.1 Alcohol Restrictions on Persons under 16/18

The sale and supply of alcohol is regulated by the Licensing Act 2003 which creates several offences relating to children, young people, alcohol, drunkenness, and disorderly conduct.

The following offences protect children both on and off licensed premises; some of them apply anywhere and are not restricted to licensed premises.

9.1.1 Unaccompanied children prohibited from certain premises

It is an offence to admit children under 16 to certain categories of relevant premises if they are not accompanied by an adult or allow them to be on these premises between midnight and 5 a.m., and those premises are open for the supply of alcohol for consumption therein.

Offences

A person to whom subsection (3) applies commits an offence if—

(a) knowing that relevant premises are within subsection (4), he allows an unaccompanied child to be on the premises at a time when they are open for the purposes of being used for the supply of alcohol for consumption there, or

(b) he allows an unaccompanied child to be on relevant premises at a time between the hours of midnight and 5 a.m. when the premises are open for the purposes of being used for the supply of alcohol for consumption there.

Licensing Act 2003, s 145(1)

PNLD H5462, H5463, H5467, H5468

Points to prove

✓ being a person to whom subsection (3) applies
✓ knowing they were relevant premises
✓ allowed an unaccompanied child to be on premises
✓ when open **or** open between midnight and 5 a.m.
✓ when used for supplying alcohol for consumption therein

Meanings

Person to whom subsection (3) applies

Any person who:

- works at the premises in a capacity, whether paid or unpaid, which authorises them to request the unaccompanied child to leave the premises;
- in the case of licensed premises, is the holder of a premises licence in respect of the premises, and the designated premises supervisor (if any) under such a licence;
- in the case of premises in respect of which a club premises certificate has effect, is any member or officer of the club which holds the certificate who is present on the premises in a capacity which enables them to make such a request;
- in the case of premises which may be used for a permitted temporary activity by virtue of Part 5, is the premises user in relation to the temporary event notice in question.

Relevant premises (s 159)

Means premises that:

- are licensed; or
- have a club premises certificate in force; or
- may be used for a permitted temporary activity (under Part 5).

Relevant premises within subsection 4 (s 145(4))

Means relevant premises that are:

- exclusively or primarily used for the supply of alcohol for consumption on the premises; or
- open for the purposes of the supply of alcohol for consumption on the premises by virtue of Part 5 (permitted temporary activities) and, at the time the temporary event notice has effect, they are exclusively or primarily used for such supplies.

Child (s 145(2))

Means an individual aged under 16.

Alcohol (s 191)

Means spirits, wine, beer, cider, or any other fermented, distilled, or spirituous liquor (in any state), but does **not** include:

- alcohol which is of a strength not exceeding 0.5 per cent at the time of the sale or supply in question;

- perfume;
- flavouring essences recognised by Commissioners of Customs and Excise as not being intended for consumption as or with dutiable alcoholic liquor;
- aromatic flavouring essence commonly known as Angostura bitters;
- alcohol which is, or is included in, a medicinal product, or a veterinary medicinal product;
- denatured alcohol;
- methyl alcohol;
- naphtha; or
- alcohol contained in liqueur confectionery.

Unaccompanied

Means not in the company of an individual aged 18 or over.

Supply of alcohol

Means the sale by retail of alcohol, or the supply of alcohol by or on behalf of a club to, or to the order of, a member of the club.

Explanatory note

- No offence is committed if the unaccompanied child is on the premises solely for the purpose of passing to or from some other place to or from which there is no other convenient means of access or exit (s 145(5)).

Defences—s 145(6) and (8)

- Where the defendant by reason of their own conduct;
- believed that the unaccompanied child was aged 16 or over or that an individual accompanying the child was aged 18 or over; and
  - ✦ either:
    - ▪ had taken all reasonable steps to establish the individual's age; or
    - ▪ nobody could reasonably have suspected from the individual's appearance that they were aged under 16 or, as the case may be, under 18.
- That the conduct was by the act or default of some other person and the defendant exercised all due diligence to avoid committing it.

Defence notes

- A person is treated as having 'taken all reasonable steps' to establish an individual's age if:
  - ✦ they asked the individual for evidence of their age; and
  - ✦ the evidence would have convinced a reasonable person (s 145(6)).
- This defence will fail if the prosecution proves that the evidence of age was such that no reasonable person would have been convinced

by it—for example, if the proof of age was either an obvious forgery or clearly belonged to another person.
- The defence also applies in situations where the child looks exceptionally old for their age.

Practical considerations

- Age to be confirmed by ID card, driving licence, or similar document.

Summary

12 months

Level 3 fine

9.1.2 Sale of alcohol to person under 18

The sale of alcohol to a person under 18 anywhere is an offence.

Offences

A person commits an offence if he sells alcohol to an individual aged under 18.

Licensing Act 2003, s 146(1)

PNLD H5472

Points to prove

✓ sold alcohol
✓ to person under the age of 18

Meaning of alcohol (see 9.1.1)

Explanatory notes

- Similar offences apply where a club supplies alcohol to persons under 18 by itself or on its behalf (s 146(2)) or where a person supplies to persons under 18 on behalf of the club (s 146(3)).
- The sale of alcohol to children is an offence, not only if it occurs on relevant licensed premises, but **anywhere**.

Defences—s 146(4) and (6)

- Where a defendant by reason of their own conduct:
  - believed that the individual was aged 18 or over, and either:
    - they had taken all reasonable steps to establish the individual's age; or

- nobody could reasonably have suspected from the individual's appearance that they were aged under 18.
- That the offence was committed by the act or default of some other person and that the defendant exercised all due diligence to avoid committing it.

Defence notes

- For 'having taken all reasonable steps', see **9.1.1 'Defence notes'**.
- The second part of the defence could be where the actual sale was made by a barman and the manager had exercised all due diligence to avoid this offence being committed.

Practical considerations

- Age to be confirmed by ID card, driving licence, or similar document.
- This offence can be dealt with by PND (see **7.1.1**).

Issue for s 146(1), (3) offences only (**not** s 146(2) club offences)

E&S

Summary

12 months

Fine

9.1.3 Allowing the sale of alcohol to children

Offences

A person to whom subsection (2) applies commits an offence if he knowingly allows the sale of alcohol on relevant premises to an individual aged under 18.

Licensing Act 2003, s 147(1)

PNLD H5477, H5478

Points to prove

- ✓ being person to whom subsection (2) applies
- ✓ on relevant premises
- ✓ knowingly allowed the sale of alcohol
- ✓ to a person under the age of 18

9.1.3 Allowing the sale of alcohol to children

Meanings

Person to whom subsection (2) applies

Any person who works at the premises in a capacity, whether paid or unpaid, which authorises them to prevent the sale.

Knowingly

Means having knowledge; an awareness, informed, consciously, intentionally, or an understanding.

Alcohol (see **9.1.1**)

Relevant premises (see **9.1.1**)

Explanatory notes

- There are no statutory defences to this offence. The mental element 'knowingly' applies only to allowing the sale; it does not require knowledge that the individual was under 18. The prosecution need only prove that the individual was under 18.
- Similar offences apply under s 147(3) where an employee or member/officer of a club fails to prevent supply on relevant premises by or on behalf of the club to a member/individual who is aged under 18.

Practical considerations

- Age to be confirmed by ID card, driving licence, or similar document.
- **Persistently selling alcohol to children (under 18)**: a summary offence will be committed under s 147A if on two or more different occasions, within a period of three consecutive months, alcohol is unlawfully sold on the same premises to an individual aged under 18.
- The following procedural requirements under s 147A also apply:
  - ✦ The premises must be either licensed premises or authorised premises for a permitted temporary activity by virtue of Part 5, and the offender must hold the premises licence or be the named premises user for a temporary event notice.
  - ✦ The same sale may not be counted as different offences for this purpose.
- Section 147B provides that if the holder of a premises licence is convicted of a s 147A offence for sales on those premises, the court may order that the premises licence is suspended for a period not exceeding three months.
- A closure notice for persistently selling alcohol to children under 18 can be issued (see **9.3.3**).

Summary

12 months

Fine

9.1.4 Purchase of alcohol by or on behalf of person under 18

Offences are committed by a person under 18, or a person on behalf of the under-18, who purchases or attempts to purchase alcohol anywhere. Similarly, it is an offence for a person to buy or attempt to buy alcohol for consumption by a person who is under 18 on licensed premises.

Offences

(1)(a) An individual aged under 18 commits an offence if he buys or attempts to buy alcohol.

(3)(a) A person commits an offence if he buys or attempts to buy alcohol on behalf of an individual aged under 18.

(4)(a) A person commits an offence if he buys or attempts to buy alcohol for consumption on relevant premises by an individual aged under 18.

Licensing Act 2003, s 149

PNLD H5487, H5491, H5495

Points to prove

s 149(1)(a) offence

✓ being a person under the age of 18
✓ bought **or** attempted to buy alcohol

s 149(3)(a) offence

✓ bought **or** attempted to buy alcohol
✓ on behalf of individual under the age of 18

s 149(4)(a) offence

✓ bought **or** attempted to buy alcohol
✓ for consumption on relevant premises
✓ by an individual under the age of 18

Meanings

Alcohol (see **9.1.1**)

Relevant premises (see **9.1.1**)

Explanatory notes

- Offences in s 149(1)(a) and s 149(3)(a) may be committed **anywhere**.
- '**On behalf of**' does not mean that the purchase must be instigated by the child; the alcohol need only be bought for a child.
- Section 149(2) states that the s 149(1) offence does not apply to an individual aged under 18 who buys or attempts to buy the alcohol

at the request of a constable or a weights and measures inspector who is acting in the course of their duty. This exception allows test-purchasing operations to take place (see **9.3.1**).

- Similarly, s 149(5) states that a s 149(4) offence does not apply if:
  - ✦ the relevant person is aged 18 or over;
  - ✦ the individual is aged 16 or 17;
  - ✦ the alcohol is beer, wine, or cider;
  - ✦ its purchase or supply is for consumption at a **table meal** on **relevant premises**; and
  - ✦ the individual is accompanied at the meal by an individual aged 18 or over.
- **Table meal** means a meal eaten by a person seated at a table or at a counter or other structure which serves the purpose of a table and is not used for the service of refreshments for consumption by persons not seated at a table or structure serving the purpose of a table.
- Bar snacks do not amount to a table meal.
- Similar offences apply to clubs under s 149(1)(b), (3)(b), and (4)(b) respectively, where a member of a club is supplied with alcohol by or on behalf of that club for:
  - ✦ that member (being under 18) as a result of their act, default, or attempts to do so;
  - ✦ an individual aged under 18 as a result of their making, or attempting to make, such arrangements; and
  - ✦ consumption on relevant premises by an individual aged under 18 by their act, default, or attempts to do so.

Defences—s 149(6)

Section 149(3) and (4) offences only

The defendant had no reason to suspect that the individual was aged under 18.

Related cases (on test purchases, see **9.3.1**)

Practical considerations

- Consider issuing a PND for the s 149(3)(a) and (4) offences (see **7.1.1**), but not the s 149(1) offence as PNDs can no longer be issued to a person under 18.

E&S **s 149(3)(a) and (4) only**

Summary

12 months

s 149(1) offence: Level 3 fine

s 149(3) and s 149(4) offences: Fine

9.1.5 Consumption of alcohol by person under 18

Persons aged under 18 are not allowed to consume alcohol on relevant premises.

Offences

(1) An individual under 18 commits an offence if he knowingly consumes alcohol on relevant premises.
(2) A person to whom subsection (3) applies commits an offence if he knowingly allows the consumption of alcohol on relevant premises by an individual aged under 18.

Licensing Act 2003, s 150

PNLD H5499, H5500, H5501

Points to prove

s 150(1) offence

✓ being an individual under the age of 18
✓ knowingly consumed alcohol on relevant premises

s 150(2) offence

✓ knowingly allowed the consumption of alcohol
✓ on relevant premises
✓ by an individual under the age of 18
✓ at a time when you are present in a capacity which enabled you to prevent it

Meanings

Knowingly (see **9.1.3**)

Alcohol (see **9.1.1**)

Relevant premises (see **9.1.1**)

Person to whom subsection (3) applies

This subsection applies:

(a) to a person who works at the premises in a capacity, whether paid or unpaid, which authorises them to prevent the consumption; and
(b) where the alcohol was supplied by a club to or to the order of a member of the club, to any member or officer of the club who

is present at the premises at the time of the consumption in a capacity which enables them to prevent it.

Explanatory notes

- The s 150(1) knowingly consumed offence will not be committed if the individual inadvertently consumes alcohol, for example if the drink is spiked.
- Section 150(4) states that the s 150(1) and (2) offences do not apply if:
  - ✦ the individual is aged 16 or 17;
  - ✦ the alcohol is beer, wine, or cider;
  - ✦ its consumption is at a **table meal** on relevant premises; and
  - ✦ the individual is accompanied at the meal by an individual aged 18 or over.
- Both offences under s 150(1) and (2) also apply to clubs.

Practical considerations

- Knowledge must be proved for both offences, either to 'knowingly' consume or to 'knowingly' allow consumption of the alcohol.
- Age to be proved by ID card, driving licence, or similar documentation.
- Consider issuing a PND for the s 150(2) offence (see **7.1.1**), but not the s 150(1) offence as PNDs cannot be issued to a person under 18.

E&S **s 150(2) only**

Summary

12 months

s 150(1) offence: Level 3 fine
s 150(2) offence: Fine

9.1.6 Delivering alcohol to person under 18

It is an offence for certain people to deliver or allow delivery of alcohol to a person under 18.

Offences

(1) A person who works on relevant premises in any capacity, whether paid or unpaid, commits an offence if he knowingly delivers to an individual aged under 18—
  (a) alcohol sold on the premises, or

(b) alcohol supplied on the premises by or on behalf of a club to or to the order of a member of the club.

(2) A person to whom subsection (3) applies commits an offence if he knowingly allows anybody else to deliver to a person under 18 alcohol sold on relevant premises.

Licensing Act 2003, s 151

PNLD H5502, H5503, H5504

Points to prove

s 151(1) offence

✓ being a person who worked in a capacity, whether unpaid or paid
✓ on relevant premises
✓ knowingly delivered to an individual under the age of 18
✓ alcohol sold on those premises OR
✓ supplied on those premises (by or on behalf of a club/order of member)

s 151(2) offence

✓ being a person to whom subsection (3) applies
✓ on relevant club premises with the authority to prevent it
✓ knowingly allowed another person to deliver
✓ to an individual under the age of 18
✓ alcohol sold on those premises

Meanings

Relevant premises (see **9.1.1**)

Knowingly (see **9.1.3**)

Alcohol (see **9.1.1**)

Person to whom subsection (3) applies

Any person who works on the premises in a capacity, whether paid or unpaid, which authorises them to prevent the delivery of the alcohol.

Explanatory notes

- Offences in this section cover various situations; for example, under s 151(1)(a) a child takes delivery of a consignment of alcohol bought by a parent from an off-licence (unless the defence applies); or a person authorises a delivery of that sort under s 151(2).
- An offence similar to s 151(2) is to knowingly allow somebody else to deliver alcohol supplied by a club under s 151(4).

Defences—s 151(6)

Subsections (1), (2) and (4) do not apply where—

(a) the alcohol is delivered at a place where the buyer or, as the case may be, person supplied lives or works, or

(b) the individual aged under 18 works on the relevant premises in a capacity, whether paid or unpaid, which involves the delivery of alcohol, or

(c) the alcohol is sold or supplied for consumption on the relevant premises.

Licensing Act 2003, s 151(6)

Defence notes

This covers cases where, for example, a child answers the door and signs for the delivery of an order for the house or where a 16-year-old office worker is sent to collect an order for their employer.

Practical considerations

- Knowledge must be proved for all the offences, either to 'knowingly' (see **9.1.3**) deliver or to 'knowingly' allow anybody else to deliver the alcohol.
- Age to be proved by ID card, driving licence, or similar document.
- Consider issuing a PND for these offences (see **7.1.1**).

E&S

Summary | 12 months

Fine

9.1.7 Sending person under 18 to obtain alcohol

A person under 18 must not be sent to obtain alcohol.

Offences

A person commits an offence if he knowingly sends an individual aged under 18 to obtain—

(a) alcohol sold or to be sold on relevant premises for consumption off the premises, or

(b) alcohol supplied or to be supplied by or on behalf of a club to or to the order of a member of the club for such consumption.

Licensing Act 2003, s 152(1)

PNLD H5507, H5508

Points to prove

- ✓ knowingly sent an individual under the age of 18
- ✓ to obtain alcohol
- ✓ sold/to be sold on relevant premises OR
- ✓ supplied/to be supplied (by/on behalf of club/order of member)
- ✓ for consumption off those premises

Meanings

Knowingly (see **9.1.3**)

Alcohol (see **9.1.1**)

Relevant premises (see **9.1.1**)

Explanatory notes

- Section 152(3) allows an individual under 18 to work on the relevant premises in a capacity (whether paid or unpaid) that involves delivery of alcohol.
- Similarly, s 152(4) states that no offence will be committed if an individual aged under 18 is sent by a constable or a weights and measures inspector who is acting in the course of their duty. This exception allows test-purchasing operations to take place (see **9.3.1**).

Related cases (on test purchases, see 9.3.1)

Practical considerations

- This offence covers, for example, circumstances where a parent sends their child (being under 18) to an off-licence to buy and collect alcohol for them.
- Knowledge must be proved as to 'knowingly' send an individual aged under 18 to obtain alcohol sold or supplied from the relevant premises.
- It is an offence under s 153 to knowingly allow a person under 18 to sell or, in the case of a club, to supply alcohol unless each sale or supply is approved by a responsible person.
- Selling liqueur confectionery/chocolates to children under 16 is not an offence.

9.1.7 **Sending person under 18 to obtain alcohol**

Summary

12 months

Fine

Links to alternative subjects and offences

7.1 **Penalty Notices for Disorder** 351
7.2 **Drunkenness in Public Places** 358
11.1.4 **Powers to search for and seize alcohol and tobacco** 787

9.2 Drunkenness on Licensed Premises

The Licensing Act 2003 creates several offences relating to alcohol and offences concerning drunkenness and disorderly conduct.

9.2.1 Sale of alcohol to person who is drunk

It is an offence to sell or attempt to sell alcohol to a person who is drunk, or to allow alcohol to be sold to such a person, on relevant premises.

Offences

A person to whom subsection (2) applies commits an offence if, on relevant premises, he knowingly—
(a) sells or attempts to sell alcohol to a person who is drunk, or
(b) allows alcohol to be sold to such a person.

Licensing Act 2003, s 141(1)

PNLD H5437 to H5442

Points to prove

- ✓ person to whom subsection (2) applies
- ✓ knowingly sold/attempted to sell/allowed sale of alcohol
- ✓ on relevant premises to a person who was drunk

Meanings

Person to whom subsection (2) applies

- Any person who works at the premises in a capacity, whether paid or unpaid, which gives them authority to sell the alcohol concerned.
- In the case of licensed premises, to the holder of a premises licence in respect of the premises, and the designated premises supervisor (if any) under such a licence.

Relevant premises (see 9.1.1)

Knowingly (see 9.1.3)

Alcohol (see 9.1.1)

Drunk (see 7.2.1)

Explanatory notes

- In each case, drunkenness will be a question of fact for the court to decide.
- It is also an offence, under s 141(3), to supply alcohol by or on behalf of a club or to the order of a member of the club to a person who is drunk.

Practical considerations

- If the person is under 18 consider offences under s 145 (see **9.1.1**).
- Knowledge must be proved as to 'knowingly' sell, attempt to sell, or allow to be sold alcohol to a person who is drunk.
- This offence can be dealt with by PND (see **7.1.1**).
- Details of the licence holder and/or the designated premises supervisor should be clearly displayed in the premises.
- Under s 142, it is also an offence to knowingly obtain or attempt to obtain alcohol on relevant premises for consumption on those premises by a person who is drunk.

E&S

Summary | 12 months

Level 3 fine

9.2.2 Failure to leave licensed premises

People who are drunk or disorderly may be requested to leave certain premises and commit an offence if they fail to do so.

Offences

A person who is drunk or disorderly commits an offence if, without reasonable excuse—

(a) he fails to leave relevant premises when requested to do so by a constable or by a person to whom subsection (2) applies, or

(b) he enters or attempts to enter relevant premises after a constable or a person to whom subsection (2) applies has requested him not to enter.

Licensing Act 2003, s 143(1)

PNLD H5454, H5455, H5456

Points to prove

- ✓ without reasonable excuse while drunk or disorderly
- ✓ failed to comply with request
- ✓ by a constable or a person to whom subsection (2) applies
- ✓ to leave **or** not to enter/attempt to enter relevant premises

Meanings

Drunk (see **7.2.1**)

Disorderly (see **7.2.1**)

Relevant premises (see **9.1.1**)

Person to whom subsection (2) applies

- Any person who works at the premises in a capacity, whether paid or unpaid, which authorises them to make such a request.
- In the case of licensed premises, to the holder of a premises licence in respect of the premises, and the designated premises supervisor (if any) under such a licence.

Explanatory notes

- An offence may not be committed if the person has a reasonable excuse, for example if they are physically prevented by serious disability or injury from leaving the premises.
- Apart from licensed premises, this offence also applies to clubs and premises being used for a permitted temporary activity.
- Whether a person is drunk and/or disorderly will be a question of fact for the court to decide.

Practical considerations

- On being requested to do so by the appropriate person, a constable must help to expel from relevant premises a person who is drunk/disorderly or help to prevent such a person from entering relevant premises.
- Consider either drunk and disorderly in a public place (see **7.2.1**) or drunk on licensed premises/public place (see **7.2.2**)—both can be dealt with by PND (see **7.1.1**).

Summary | 12 months

Level 1 fine

9.2.3 Allowing disorderly conduct on licensed premises

It is also an offence to knowingly allow disorderly conduct on relevant premises.

Offences

A person to whom subsection (2) applies commits an offence if he knowingly allows disorderly conduct on relevant premises.

Licensing Act 2003, s 140(1)

PNLD H5432, H5433, H5435

Points to prove

✓ being a person to whom subsection (2) applies
✓ knowingly allowed disorderly conduct on relevant premises

Meanings

Person to whom subsection (2) applies

- Any person who works at the premises in a capacity, whether paid or unpaid, which authorises them to prevent the conduct.
- In licensed premises, clubs, or permitted temporary activity, the same persons as given in s 145(3) (see **9.1.1**).

Knowingly (see **9.1.3**)

Disorderly (see **7.2.1**)

Relevant premises (see **9.1.1**)

Explanatory note

- Apart from licensed premises, this offence also applies to clubs and premises which may be used for a permitted temporary activity.

Summary — 12 months

Level 3 fine

Links to alternative subjects and offences

7.1 **Penalty Notices for Disorder** 351
7.2 **Drunkenness in Public Places** 358

7.3 **Breach of the Peace** 362
7.8 **Threatening/Abusive Words/Behaviour** 380
7.13 **Anti-Social Behaviour** 435
7.15.1 **Dispersal powers** 456
11.1.4 **Powers to search for and seize alcohol and tobacco** 787

9.3 Powers to Enter/Close Licensed Premises and Test Purchases

The Licensing Act 2003 provides a variety of offences relating to alcohol and powers to enter/close licensed premises/clubs and allows test purchases.

9.3.1 Test purchases

Sections 149 and 152 allow the police and trading standards officers to use individuals under 18 to make test purchases to ascertain if such individuals can buy or be supplied with alcohol from on/off-licensed premises, certified club premises, or premises used for a permitted temporary activity without any offences being committed.

Authorities

149(2) But subsection (1) [see **9.1.4**] does not apply where the individual buys or attempts to buy the alcohol at the request of—

(a) a constable, or

(b) a weights and measures inspector, who is acting in the course of his duty.

152(4) Subsection (1) [see **9.1.7**] also does not apply where the individual aged under 18 is sent by—

(a) a constable, or

(b) a weights and measures inspector, who is acting in the course of his duty.

Licensing Act 2003, ss 149(2) and 152(4)

Explanatory note

- This statutory authority allows test-purchasing operations to establish whether licensees and staff working in relevant licensed premises are complying with the prohibition on the sale/supply of alcohol to individuals aged under 18.

Related cases

R v Loosely/A-G's Reference (No 3 of 2000) [2001] UKHL 53 This was a case of entrapment; police officers must not instigate or incite the commission of an offence. To do this would also amount to a breach of Art 6 ECHR (see **Appendix 1**). But if the police do no more than what an ordinary customer would do, this will not generally be subject to successful challenge.

DPP v Marshall [1988] 3 All ER 683, QBD Police officers in plain clothes bought four cans of lager and a bottle of wine from the defendant's shop which was licensed to sell liquor by the case but not in individual containers. It was argued that evidence should be excluded under s 78 of PACE as the officers had not revealed the fact that they were police at the time of the purchase and this was unfair. It was held that evidence of police officers had been wrongly excluded; it had not been shown that the evidence would have had an adverse effect on the proceedings.

Practical considerations

- Consider the protection of children engaged in such operations.
- Assess the reliability of their evidence.

9.3.2 Powers to enter licensed premises and clubs

The Licensing Act 2003 contains provisions dealing with powers of entry to investigate licensable activities or immigration offences:

- Section 179(1) gives power to a constable or an authorised person to enter premises if they have reason to believe that they are being, or are about to be, used for a licensable activity, in order to see whether the activity is being carried on in accordance with the authorisation. However, this does not apply to clubs unless there is other authorisation apart from a club premises licence.
- Similarly, under s 180(1) a constable may enter and search any premises in respect of which they have **reason to believe** that an offence under the Licensing Act has been, is being, or is about to be committed. A constable exercising a power conferred by this section may, if necessary, use reasonable force.
- Section 97(1) allows a constable to enter and search club premises if they have reasonable cause to believe that an offence under s 4(3)(a), (b), or (c) of the Misuse of Drugs Act 1971 (supplying or offering to supply, or being concerned in supplying or making an offer to supply, a controlled drug) has been, is being, or is about to be, committed there (see **5.1.1**), or that an offence under s 5(1) or (2) of the Psychoactive Substances Act 2016 (supplying, or offering to supply, a psychoactive substance) (see **5.3.5**) has been, is being, or is about to be committed there, or that there is likely to be a breach of the peace (see **7.3**). A constable exercising a power conferred by this section may, if necessary, use reasonable force.

Meanings

Authorisation

- A premises licence;
- a club premises certificate; or
- a temporary event notice in respect of which the conditions of s 98(2) to (4) are satisfied.

Authorised person

- An officer of the licensing authority in whose area the premises are situated; or
- if the premises are situated in the area of more than one licensing authority, an officer of any of those authorities, authorised for the purposes of this Act.

Explanatory notes

- It is not necessary to obtain a warrant.
- Police have lawful authority to require production of a premises licence, club premises certificate, or temporary event notice.
- The police may lawfully enter premises to inspect them before a licence or certificate is granted.

9.3.3 **Police powers—closure notice**

Where an offence of persistently selling alcohol to children (under 18) has been committed under s 147A (see **9.1.3**), a closure notice can be issued by a superintendent (or above) to close the premises.

Closure notice

A relevant officer may give a notice under section 169A(1) (a 'closure notice') applying to any premises if—

(a) there is evidence that a person ('the offender') has committed an offence under section 147A in relation to those premises;

(b) the relevant officer considers that the evidence is such that, if the offender were prosecuted for the offence, there would be a realistic prospect of his being convicted; and

(c) the offender is still, at the time when the notice is given, the holder of a premises licence in respect of those premises, or one of the holders of such a licence.

Licensing Act 2003, s 169A(1)

Meaning of relevant officer

Means a police officer of the rank of superintendent or above or an appointed inspector of weights and measures.

Explanatory notes

- The closure notice will:
  - ✦ prohibit sale of alcohol on the premises, for at least 48 hours but no more than 336 hours; and
  - ✦ if accepted, will discharge all criminal liability in respect of the s 147A offence (see **9.1.3**).
- A closure notice must:
  - ✦ be in the form as prescribed by regulations;
  - ✦ specify the premises and circumstances surrounding the offence;
  - ✦ specify the length of the period during which it is proposed that sales of alcohol should be prohibited on those premises and when that period would begin if the prohibition is accepted;
  - ✦ explain the consequences/penalties of the prohibition and any sale of alcohol on the premises during the period for which it is in force;
  - ✦ explain the rights of that person; and how those rights may be exercised.

Practical considerations

- The period specified for which it is proposed that sales of alcohol should be prohibited on those premises must be at least must be at least 48 hours but not more than 336 hours; and the time specified as the time from which that period would begin must be not less than 14 days after the date of the service of the closure notice.
- Service of the closure notice may be served on the premises by a constable or trading standards officer to a person having control/ responsibility for the premises, and only when licensable activities are being carried on there. A copy must be served on the licence holder of the premises.
- A closure notice must not be given more than three months after the s 147A offence.
- No more than one closure notice may be given in respect of offences relating to the same sales; nor may such a notice be given in respect of an offence in respect of which a prosecution has already been brought.
- Section 169B prescribes other matters when a closure notice has been issued:
  - ✦ no proceedings may be brought for the s 147A offence or any **related offence** at any time before the time when the prohibition proposed by the notice would take effect;
  - ✦ if the premises' licence holder accepts the proposed prohibition in the manner specified in the notice then that prohibition takes effect (as specified) and no proceedings may be brought against that person for the alleged offence or any related offence;
  - ✦ **'related offence'** means an offence under s 146 (see **9.1.2**) or s 147 (see **9.1.3**) in respect of any of the sales to which the alleged offence relates.

Links to alternative subjects and offences

5.4.2 Occupier/manager permits drug use on premises 266
7.2 Drunkenness in Public Places 358
7.6 Fear or Provocation of Violence 373
7.8 Threatening/Abusive Words/Behaviour 380
7.13 Anti-Social Behaviour 435
11.1.4 Powers to search for and seize alcohol and tobacco 787

9.4 Public Spaces Protection Order—Alcohol Restrictions

9.4.1 Power to require person to cease drinking alcohol

Powers

(1) This section applies where a constable or an authorised person reasonably believes that a person (P)—
  (a) is or has been consuming alcohol in breach of a prohibition in a public spaces protection order or an expedited order, or
  (b) intends to consume alcohol in circumstances in which doing so would be a breach of such a prohibition.

(2) The constable or authorised person may require P—
  (a) not to consume, in breach of the order, alcohol or anything which the constable or authorised person reasonably believes to be alcohol;
  (b) to surrender anything in P's possession which is, or which the constable or authorised person reasonably believes to be, alcohol or a container for alcohol.

Anti-social Behaviour, Crime and Policing Act 2014, s 63

Meanings

Authorised person

Means a person authorised for the purposes of this section by the local authority that made the public spaces protection order.

Alcohol (see **9.1.1**)

Public spaces protection order (PSPO) (see **7.15.2**)

Explanatory notes

- A requirement imposed by a constable or an authorised person as per the legislation is not valid if they are asked by P to show evidence of their authorisation and they fail to do so.
- Local authorities are responsible for making a PSPO and will have to be satisfied, on reasonable grounds, that activities in a public space: have had or will be likely to have a detrimental effect on the quality of life of those in the locality; it is, or is likely to be, persistent or continuing in nature, such as to make the activities unreasonable; and the order justifies the restrictions imposed (see **7.15.2**).

- The person must be informed that failure to comply with the officer's request, without reasonable excuse, is an offence (see **9.4.2**).
- A prohibition in a PSPO on consuming alcohol does not apply to:
  - ✦ premises (other than council-operated) which have a premises licence or club premises certificate for the supply of alcohol; or
  - ✦ a place within the curtilage of those premises;
  - ✦ a place where the sale of alcohol is for the time being authorised by a temporary event notice or was so authorised within the last thirty minutes;
  - ✦ a place where facilities/activities relating to the sale/consumption of alcohol are permitted by a permission granted under s 115E of the Highways Act 1980.
- A constable or an authorised person may dispose of anything surrendered to them under s 63(2)(b) in such manner as they consider appropriate.
- Consider using the power to confiscate alcohol from people under 18 years of age (see **9.5**).

9.4.2 **Failure to comply with alcohol requirements**

Example of constable's requirement

'This is a restricted area in a public place, and I have reason to believe that you are/have been consuming or intend to consume alcohol in breach of a prohibition in a public spaces protection order. I require you to stop drinking and give me the container from which you are/have been drinking and any other containers (sealed or unsealed). I must inform you that failure to comply with my request, without reasonable excuse, is an offence.'

Offences

A person who fails without reasonable excuse to comply with a requirement imposed on him or her under subsection 63(2) [see **9.4.1**] commits an offence.

Anti-social Behaviour, Crime and Policing Act 2014, s 63(6)

PNLD H11455

Points to prove

✓ failed without reasonable excuse
✓ to comply with a requirement
✓ imposed by a constable/authorised person
✓ to not consume/surrender alcohol
✓ consumption of which would breach prohibition in a public spaces protection order

Practical considerations

- A constable or an authorised person who imposes the requirement shall inform the person concerned that failing without reasonable excuse to comply with the requirement is an offence.
- A chief officer of police may confer powers for a CSO or CSV to search a person for alcohol or a container for alcohol if after a requirement to surrender alcohol or a container is made under s 63(2) the person fails to comply with the requirement. The CSO or CSV must reasonably believe that the person has alcohol or a container for alcohol in their possession (see **11.1.4**).
- The seizure and disposal of alcohol in both sealed and unsealed containers is allowed, although officers should follow their own force orders or LA procedure in relation to disposal.
- Consider issuing a FPN under s 68 for this offence (see **7.15.2**).

E&S

Summary

6 months

Level 2 fine

Links to alternative subjects and offences

7.1 **Penalty Notices for Disorder** 351
7.2 **Drunkenness in Public Places** 358
7.3 **Breach of the Peace** 362
7.6 **Fear or Provocation of Violence** 373
7.8 **Threatening/Abusive Words/Behaviour** 380
7.13 **Anti-Social Behaviour** 435
11.1.4 **Powers to search for and seize alcohol and tobacco** 787

9.5 Alcohol in Public Place (under 18)—Offences/ Confiscation

The Confiscation of Alcohol (Young Persons) Act 1997 allows the police to confiscate alcohol from people under 18 years in certain public places, with a failure to comply offence, while s 30 of the Policing and Crime Act 2009 makes it an offence for a person under 18 to persistently possess alcohol in a public place.

9.5.1 Offences/confiscation of alcohol (under 18)

Power

(1) Where a constable reasonably suspects that a person in a relevant place is in possession of alcohol and that either—
  (a) he is under the age of 18; or
  (b) he intends that any of the alcohol should be consumed by a person under the age of 18 in that or any other relevant place; or
  (c) a person under the age of 18 who is, or has recently been, with him has recently consumed alcohol in that or any other relevant place, the constable may require him to surrender anything in his possession which is, or which the constable reasonably believes to be, alcohol or a container for alcohol.

(1AA) A constable who imposes a requirement on a person under subsection (1) shall also require him to state his name and address.

Confiscation of Alcohol (Young Persons) Act 1997, s 1(1) and (1AA)

Offences

(3) A person who fails without reasonable excuse to comply with a requirement imposed on him under subsection (1) or (1AA) commits an offence.

Confiscation of Alcohol (Young Persons) Act 1997, s 1(3)

PNLD H16

Points to prove

- ✓ without reasonable excuse
- ✓ failed to comply with requirement
- ✓ imposed by constable
- ✓ to surrender
- ✓ alcohol/suspected alcohol OR a container for such
- ✓ in their possession
- ✓ and/or state their name and address

Meanings

Relevant place

Means any **public place**, other than **licensed premises**; or any place, other than a public place, to which the person has unlawfully gained access.

Licensed premises

Means premises which may by virtue of Part 3 or 5 of the Licensing Act 2003 (premises licence; permitted temporary activity) be used for the **supply of alcohol**.

Supply of alcohol (see **9.1.1**)

Public place

For this purpose, a place is a public place if at the material time the public or any section of the public has access to it, on payment or otherwise, as of right or by virtue of express or implied permission.

Possession

At common law possession is defined as **actual** or **potential** physical control and an intention to possess. In practice, visible or external signs of possession, which can be demonstrated to a court, must support the two conditions above (*Jowett's Dictionary of English Law*).

Alcohol (see **9.1.1**)

Recently

Defined by the *Oxford English Dictionary* as 'lately' or 'comparatively near to the present time'.

Explanatory notes

- Officers can seize sealed and open containers, as well as the alcohol they hold, and dispose of both in an appropriate manner. Where a young person has, for example, a sealed six-pack under their arm, officers should still consider who sold it, and whether there are any child welfare issues, and act as appropriate.

- A constable may dispose of anything surrendered in such manner as they consider appropriate.
- When imposing a requirement to surrender, a constable must inform the person of the suspicion and that failing without reasonable excuse to comply with the requirement as to surrender of alcohol and/or to state their name and address is an offence.

Example of officer's requirement

'I have reason to suspect that you are in possession of alcohol and that either you are under 18 years of age or you intend that any of the alcohol will be consumed or it has recently been consumed by a person under 18 in this or any other relevant place. (If applicable) You must stop drinking immediately. I require you to give me that can/bottle/plastic cup, etc and to give me your name and address. I must warn you that failure to comply with my requirements is an offence.'

Practical considerations

- A constable imposing a requirement under s 1(1) may, if the constable reasonably suspects that person to be under the age of 16, remove that person to their place of residence or a place of safety.
- Officers should follow their own force orders in relation to disposal.
- A chief officer of police may confer powers for a CSO or CSV to have the same powers as a police constable under this section (other than the arrest power) (see **11.1.4**).

Summary

6 months

Level 2 fine

9.5.2 Persistently possess alcohol in public (under 18)

Offences

A person under the age of 18 is guilty of an offence if, without reasonable excuse, the person is in possession of alcohol in any relevant place on 3 or more occasions within a period of 12 consecutive months.

Policing and Crime Act 2009, s 30(1)

PNLD H10152

Points to prove

✓ person under 18
✓ without reasonable excuse
✓ in possession of alcohol
✓ **in any** relevant place
✓ on three or more occasions
✓ within a twelve-month (consecutive) period

Meanings

Possession (see **9.5.1**)

Alcohol (see **9.1.1**)

Relevant place

Means any public place, other than **excluded premises** or any place, other than a **public place**, to which the person has unlawfully gained access.

Excluded premises

Means premises which may by virtue of the Licensing Act 2003:
- Part 3 or 5 (premises licence or permitted temporary activity) should be used for the supply of alcohol;
- Part 4 (club premises certificate) should be used for the supply of alcohol to members or guests.

Public place (see **9.5.1**)

Explanatory note

- This offence only applies to people under the age of 18 if they possess alcohol in a relevant public place and this has occurred on three or more occasions within a twelve-month period.

Summary

6 months

Level 2 fine

Links to alternative subjects and offences

7.1 **Penalty Notices for Disorder** 351
7.2 **Drunkenness in Public Places** 358
7.3 **Breach of the Peace** 362

9.5.2 **Persistently possess alcohol in public (under 18)**

7.8 **Threatening/Abusive Words/Behaviour** 380
7.13 **Anti-Social Behaviour** 435
7.15.1 **Dispersal powers** 456
11.1.4 **Powers to search for and seize alcohol and tobacco** 787

Chapter 10
Road Traffic

10.1 Meanings: Roads, Public Places, Vehicles, and Drives

10.1.1 Roads

The term 'road' has many meanings within various pieces of legislation.

Meaning of road

Any (length of) highway and any other road to which the public has access and includes bridges over which a road passes (Road Traffic Act 1988, s 192(1)).

Explanatory notes

- 'Road' includes public highways, footpaths, and bridleways maintained by government agencies or local authorities.
- The term 'public road' in the Vehicle Excise and Registration Act 1994 means a road repairable at public expense.
- The physical nature of a road provides a defined or definable route, or way to which the general public has legal access, being a route allowing travel between two places.
- A field used for parking at an agricultural show was held not to be a road as it had no definable way.
- A privately-owned hotel forecourt used as a shortcut between two streets is a road.
- Walking or driving must take place on the road and such walking or driving must be lawful.

Related cases

Hallett v DPP [2011] EWHC 488 (Admin) Residents were responsible for maintaining a 'service road' to their homes but it had no barriers or 'private road' signs in place. It was held that actual use of the road by the public must be evidenced for it to be a public road.

Sadiku v DPP [2000] RTR 155, QBD A paved area used as a thoroughfare by pedestrians can be a road.

Cutter v Eagle Star Insurance Company Ltd [1998] 4 All ER 417, HL and **Clarke v Kato and others [1998] 4 All ER 417, HL** Designated parking bays in a car park will not be a road but a definable route with direction arrows and lane markings, etc may be.

Practical considerations

- In instances of real doubt, the courts have to decide on a case-by-case basis.
- Public access alone is not sufficient to make a place a road; similarly, some form of private use will not necessarily prevent it from being a road.
- Most important road traffic legislation relates to 'public places' as well—this is a wider and different definition that should be considered in each case (see **10.1.2**).
- The footway (pavement), lay-by, or verge is normally part of the road.
- The mode of transport is not relevant and such travellers may be on foot, riding on animals, or in a vehicle.

10.1.2 **Public place**

Meaning of public place

A place is a public place if those people who are admitted are members of the general public (not members of some special or particular class of the public) and admission is with the express or implied permission of the owner of the land. This remains a question of fact to be judged on a case-by-case basis.

Explanatory notes

- Whether a place to which the public have limited, or restricted, access is a public place is a question of fact and degree in each case.
- The time at which the place was being used is important in dealing with 'public place' considerations. The car park of a public house may be a public place during licensing hours but may not be so outside those hours.
- An off-road parking bay adjacent to a highway with no physical impediment between the bay and the road is a public place.

Related cases

Richardson v DPP [2019] EWHC 428 (Admin) It was held that the conviction was not safe where there was insufficient evidence to prove that the car park was a public place within the meaning of s 4(2) of the Road Traffic Act 1988. There had to be evidence that the public actually used the car park lawfully. In this case, there was no evidence of any use of the car park by the public; nor was there evidence excluding the possibility that the appellant had parked in the private areas of the car park.

Cowan v DPP [2013] EWHC 192 (Admin) No evidence was provided for the court to conclude that a university campus was a public place so it was unable to convict for an offence of driving a motor vehicle while OPL.

R v Spence [1999] Crim LR 975, CA A company car park in an industrial estate, used by employees, customers, and visitors on business, but not the general public, was held not to be a public place.

10.1.3 **Vehicles/motor vehicles/ mechanically propelled vehicles**

Meaning of vehicles

General

The *Oxford English Dictionary* defines a 'vehicle' as a conveyance, usually with wheels, for transporting people, goods, etc; a car, cart, truck, carriage, sledge, etc; any means of carriage or transport; a receptacle in which something is placed in order to be moved.

For vehicle excise duty purposes

For the provisions contained in the Vehicle Excise and Registration Act 1994, 'vehicle' means:

- a mechanically propelled vehicle; or
- any thing (whether or not it is a vehicle) that has been, but has ceased to be, a mechanically propelled vehicle.

Vehicle Excise and Registration Act 1994, s 1(1B)

Explanatory notes

The above definitions of 'vehicle' should not be confused with the meaning of 'motor vehicle' or 'mechanically propelled vehicle'.

- Motor vehicle **means:**
  - ✦ subject to s 20 of the Chronically Sick and Disabled Persons Act 1970 (which makes special provision about invalid carriages), a **mechanically propelled vehicle** intended or adapted for use on roads (Road Traffic Act 1988, s 185);
  - ✦ any mechanically propelled vehicle, whether or not it is intended or **adapted for use on a road** (Police Reform Act 2002, s 59).
- **Mechanically propelled vehicle**—this is not legally defined but it has a wider meaning than 'motor vehicle' as a mechanically propelled vehicle does not have to be 'intended or adapted for use on a road'. It means a vehicle which can be propelled by mechanical

means and would include electric or steam-powered vehicles. Whether it is a mechanically propelled vehicle will have to be determined by the court.
- **Adapted for use on a road** means fit and apt for use on a road.
- A sidecar is part of a motor vehicle when attached to a motorbike and is not a trailer (Road Traffic Act 1988, s 186(1)).
- Conversely, the semi-trailer of an articulated vehicle is a trailer and not part of the towing vehicle (Road Traffic Act 1988, s 187(1)).
- An articulated bus ('bendy bus') should be treated as one vehicle (Road Traffic Act 1988, s 187(2)).
- A hovercraft is a motor vehicle (Road Traffic Act 1988, s 188).

Electric scooters

Regulation 33 of the Road Vehicles (Registration and Licensing) Regulations 2002 creates provisions for nil (vehicle excise) licences and this includes electric scooters so long as they fall within certain criteria. An electric scooter means a vehicle which:
(a) is fitted with an electric motor with a maximum continuous power rating not exceeding 500 watts;
(b) is not fitted with pedals that are capable of propelling the vehicle;
(c) has two wheels, one front and one rear, aligned along the direction of travel;
(d) is designed to carry no more than one person;
(e) has a maximum weight, excluding the driver, not exceeding 55 kgs;
(f) has a maximum design speed not exceeding 15.5 mph [25 km/h];
(g) has a means of directional control through the use of handlebars which are mechanically linked to the steered wheel;
(h) has a means of controlling the speed through hand controls; and
(i) has a power control that defaults to the 'off' position.

Road Vehicles (Registration and Licensing) Regulations 2002, reg 33(1A)

Related cases

DPP v King [2008] EWHC 447 (Admin) A 'City Mantis' electric scooter that looked like a bicycle, except that it did not have any pedals or other means of manual propulsion and was capable of speeds up to 10 mph, was held to be a motor vehicle.

CC of North Yorkshire Police v Saddington [2001] Crim LR 41, QBD A 'Go-Ped' (which resembles a child's scooter with an engine) has been held to be a motor vehicle. Despite a warning on it that it was not intended for use on a road, the correct test would be whether a reasonable person would say that one of its uses would be some general use on a road.

CC of Avon and Somerset v Fleming [1987] RTR 378 The test for whether a vehicle is a motor vehicle for the purposes of what is now s 185 is whether a reasonable person, looking at the vehicle, would say that its general use encompassed possible general road use; the particular use to which a particular person put it is irrelevant. A vehicle originally manufactured for use on a road could cease to be a motor vehicle for the purposes of s 185 if it were subsequently altered, but only if such alterations were very substantial.

Thomas v Hooper [1986] RTR 1, QBD A vehicle may no longer be a motor vehicle if none of the normal vehicular controls are operative.

Burns v Currell [1963] 2 All ER 297, QBD When deciding whether one of the uses of a vehicle would be on a road, a 'reasonable person' test should be applied to the vehicle and not the intentions of the specific user at the time it was stopped.

Practical considerations

- What was the vehicle intended for and to what use is it currently being put?
- The onus of proving that a motor vehicle remained a mechanically propelled vehicle lies with the prosecution.
- Pedestrian-controlled mowing machines, other pedestrian-controlled vehicles, and electrically assisted pedal cycles approved by the Secretary of State are **not** motor vehicles (Road Traffic Act 1988, s 189).
- It is a matter of fact and degree for the court to decide whether or not a vehicle is a motor vehicle or mechanically propelled vehicle at the time of a specific incident.
- In such cases, include evidence of the characteristics of the vehicle, which may be a photograph if appropriate.

10.1.4 **Drives/driving**

Meaning of drives/driving

- The statutory definition of a 'driver'—where a separate person acts as a steersman of a motor vehicle—includes (except for the purposes of s 1 of this Act) that person as well as any other person engaged in the driving of the vehicle, and 'drive' is to be interpreted accordingly (Road Traffic Act 1988, s 192(1)).
- Case law provides matters to consider but the principal test is:
  - 'the essence of driving is the use of the driver's controls for the purpose of directing the movement of the car however the movement is produced' (*R v MacDonagh* [1974] 2 All ER 257).
- Whether or not a person was driving is ultimately a matter of fact and degree. It is for the court or jury to decide on the facts in each case (*Edkins v Knowles* [1973] 2 All ER 503, QBD).

Explanatory notes

- The vehicle does not have to be moving. A driver is still driving until they have completed the normal operations, such as applying the handbrake, that occur at the end of a journey.
- A vehicle may halt temporarily such as at traffic lights, so consider:
  - ✦ What was the purpose of the stop?
  - ✦ How long was the vehicle stopped?
  - ✦ Did the driver get out of the vehicle?
- It is also possible for two people to be driving the same vehicle.

Related cases

Avery v CPS [2011] EWHC 2388 (Admin) A car driven on a private driveway collided with a parked car on the adjacent road, with the collision being caused by the protruding boot of the car. It was held that although the tyres of the car remained on private land and only part of the car (the boot) encroached onto the road, the driver was still found to have driven the vehicle 'on' a road.

Cawthorn v DPP [2000] RTR 45, QBD A driver left their vehicle for a few minutes, set the handbrake, and switched on the hazard warning lights, but the passenger released the handbrake. The vehicle rolled down a hill and hit a brick wall. It was held that this intervening act did not make that person the driver, as the passenger did not have sufficient control to fulfil the definition of driving. The defendant still remained the driver until the journey was complete or someone else had taken over the driving. Whether someone was a driver at any particular time was a question of fact for the court or jury to decide.

DPP v Hastings (1993) 158 JP 118, QBD A passenger snatching the wheel momentarily is not a 'driver' because that action does not constitute the act of driving.

Burgoyne v Phillips [1983] RTR 49, QBD The fact that the steering was momentarily locked did not prevent the defendant from 'driving' the car.

McQuaid v Anderton [1980] 3 All ER 540, QBD Steering a car being towed can be 'driving'. The essence of 'driving' was the use of the driver's controls in order to direct the movement of the car, the method of propulsion being irrelevant.

Tyler v Whatmore [1976] RTR 83, QBD Two people can be driving a vehicle at the same time. The defendant (the front seat passenger) was leaning across steering the car whilst the other driver manipulated the controls. In this case, neither person had full control of both the brakes and the steering and, although the passenger could not control the propulsion, there was some control over the handbrake and ignition system.

Practical considerations

- As a general rule, there are three elements to driving:
  - control of the steering; *and*
  - control of the propulsion; *and*
  - the actions of the person must fall within the everyday meaning of driving.

10.2 Powers to Stop/Direct Vehicles and Pedestrians

The Road Traffic Act 1988 provides various powers to stop vehicles and offences of drivers neglecting or refusing to comply with traffic directions given by a police constable.

10.2.1 Drivers to comply with traffic directions

Section 35 of the Road Traffic Act 1988 provides for drivers who refuse or neglect to comply with traffic directions given by a police constable.

Offences

(1) Where a constable or traffic officer is for the time being engaged in the regulation of traffic in a road, a person driving or propelling a vehicle who neglects or refuses—
  (a) to stop the vehicle; or
  (b) to make it proceed in, or keep to, a particular line of traffic, when directed to do so by the constable in the exercise of his duty or the traffic officer (as the case may be) is guilty of an offence.

(2) Where—
  (a) a traffic survey of any description is being carried out on or in the vicinity of a road, and
  (b) a constable or traffic officer gives a person driving or propelling a vehicle a direction—
    (i) to stop the vehicle,
    (ii) to make it proceed in, or keep to, a particular line of traffic, or
    (iii) to proceed to a particular point on or near the road on which the vehicle is being driven or propelled,

  being a direction given for the purposes of the survey (but not a direction requiring any person to provide any information for the purposes of a traffic survey),
  the person is guilty of an offence if he neglects or refuses to comply with the direction.

Road Traffic Act 1988, s 35

PNLD H2501, H2502, H3001, H3017, H3022

Points to prove

s 35(1) offence

✓ constable or traffic officer
✓ engaged in the regulation of traffic in a road
✓ driver/rider of vehicle neglected/refused
✓ to stop vehicle/proceed/keep to particular line of traffic
✓ as directed

s 35(2) offence

✓ traffic survey on/in vicinity of a road
✓ driver/rider of vehicle
✓ refused/failed/neglected to comply
✓ with directions given by constable or traffic officer
✓ for purposes of the survey

Meanings

Traffic officer

Person designated under the Traffic Management Act 2004, s 2.

Road (see **10.1.1**)

Driving (see **10.1.4**)

Vehicle (see **10.1.3**)

Explanatory notes

- The constable/traffic officer must be engaged in the regulation of traffic and acting in the execution of their duty.
- A constable may direct a person to disobey a traffic sign if it is reasonably necessary for the protection of life.
- The prosecution needs to show that the given signal was obvious and should have been evident to the motorist, not that the motorist saw it.
- Any direction in connection with a traffic survey must not cause undue delay to a person who indicates that they are unwilling to give information for the survey.

Practical considerations

- Offences under s 35 are not confined to mechanically propelled vehicles.
- Stop does not automatically mean the driver must remain stationary until signalled to proceed, unless the direction was to remain stationary.
- Notice of intended prosecution (NIP) to be issued (see **10.5**).
- Consider issuing a TFPN (see **10.4.1**).

TFPN

Summary 6 months

Level 3 fine

If committed in a motor vehicle

Discretionary disqualification and obligatory endorsement of 3 penalty points

10.2.2 Directions to pedestrians

Section 37 of the Road Traffic Act 1988 empowers a constable in uniform or traffic officer engaged in the direction of vehicular traffic on a road to also direct a pedestrian walking along or across the carriageway to stop.

Offences

Where a constable in uniform or traffic officer is for the time being engaged in the regulation of vehicular traffic in a road, a person on foot who proceeds across or along the carriageway in contravention of a direction to stop given by the constable in the execution of his duty or the traffic officer (as the case may be), either to persons on foot or to persons on foot and other traffic, is guilty of an offence.

Road Traffic Act 1988, s 37

PNLD **H4913**

Points to prove

- ✓ being a pedestrian proceeded along/across carriageway
- ✓ contravened direction of constable or traffic officer
- ✓ engaged in direction of vehicular traffic on a road

Meanings

Traffic officer (see **10.2.1**)

Road (see **10.1**)

Practical considerations

- A pedestrian breaching s 37 may be required to give their name and address.
- Whether or not a constable is in uniform at the relevant time is a question of fact. In the absence of evidence, a court may assume that a constable acting under this section was wearing uniform at the time.

Summary

6 months

Level 3 fine

10.2.3 Police powers to stop a vehicle on a road

Section 163 of the Road Traffic Act 1988 empowers a police constable in uniform or a traffic officer to stop a mechanically propelled vehicle on a road.

Offences

(1) A person driving a mechanically propelled vehicle on a road must stop the vehicle on being required to do so by a constable in uniform or a traffic officer.
(2) A person riding a cycle on a road must stop the cycle on being required to do so by a constable in uniform or a traffic officer.
(3) If a person fails to comply with this section, he is guilty of an offence.

Road Traffic Act 1988, s 163

PNLD H4, H8761

Points to prove

✓ drove mechanically propelled vehicle/rode cycle
✓ on a road
✓ required by constable or traffic officer
✓ to stop the vehicle/cycle
✓ failed to do so

Meanings

Driving (see **10.1.4**)

Mechanically propelled vehicle (see **10.1.3**)

Road (see **10.1.1**)

Traffic officer (see **10.2.1**)

Explanatory notes

- 'Mechanically propelled vehicle' is not defined in the Act and is a matter of fact and degree to be decided by the court (see **10.1.3**).

10.2.3 Police powers to stop a vehicle on a road

- Plain-clothed police officers can use the common law to stop vehicles they reasonably believe to be involved in crime (eg a stolen car) (*R (on the application of Rutherford) v IPCC* [2010] EWHC 2881 (Admin)).

Practical considerations

- Consider issuing a traffic fixed penalty notice (TFPN) (see **10.4.1**).

E&S TFPN

Summary | 6 months

Fine level 5 (level 3 fine if a cycle)

10.3 Fail to Comply with Traffic Signs

Section 36 of the Road Traffic Act 1988 creates an offence of failing to comply with certain traffic signs.

> **Offences**
>
> Where a traffic sign, being a sign—
> (a) of the prescribed size, colour and type, or
> (b) of another character authorised by the Secretary of State under the provisions in that behalf of the Road Traffic Regulation Act 1984,
>
> has been lawfully placed on or near a road, a person driving or propelling a vehicle who fails to comply with the indication given by the sign is guilty of an offence.
>
> Road Traffic Act 1988, s 36(1)

PNLD H19108

Points to prove

- ✓ authorised traffic sign lawfully placed
- ✓ on or near a road
- ✓ driver/rider of vehicle on that road
- ✓ failed to comply with the direction of that sign

Meanings

Traffic sign

As given in the Traffic Signs Regulations and General Directions 2016.

Lawfully placed

A sign will not be lawfully placed unless it indicates a statutory prohibition, restriction, or requirement or a provision of the Traffic Acts specifically states that it is a sign to which this section applies.

Road (see **10.1.1**)

Driving (see **10.1.4**)

Vehicle see **10.1.3**)

Explanatory notes

- Some of the traffic signs to which this section applies are: double white line markings; box junction markings; traffic lights (including temporary traffic lights at roadworks); 'stop' sign (including manually operated at roadworks); flashing red 'stop' lights on motorways or automatic tram/railway crossing; no entry sign; give way sign; directional arrow; keep left/right sign; bus/cycle/tramcar route sign; weight/height restriction sign.

- This section applies to traffic survey signs and emergency traffic signs put out by police (eg football matches, processions).
- A single dotted white line in the centre of the road separating two carriageways does not fall into this section.
- Failure by the driver to see the traffic sign is not a defence except in very limited situations (see *Coombes v DPP* [2006] EWHC 3263 (Admin)) and will generally be evidence to support an offence of driving without due care and attention (see **10.6**).

Defences

This section creates absolute offences except for the possible defences of mechanical defect, automatism, or not seen due to badly located signage.

Defence notes

- 'Automatism' has been defined as 'the involuntary movement of a person's body or limbs' and its source or cause must be something of which the driver was unaware or something that they could not reasonably be expected to foresee.
- In very limited situations, where a driver fails to see the sign (see *Coombes v DPP* [2006] EWHC 3263 (Admin)).

Related cases

R v McKay (2015) unreported, CA The defence of automatism was not available to an offender who had induced a state of automatism through taking drink or drugs.

A-G's Reference (No 2 of 1992) [1993] 4 All ER 683, CA Driving without awareness (such as falling asleep) is not a case where automatism can be used as a defence.

Practical considerations

- Traffic signs placed on or near a road are deemed to be of the correct specification and to have been lawfully placed unless the contrary is proved.
- A stop sign at a junction indicates that a vehicle must at least momentarily stop at the stop line and not merely slow down.
- Section 87 of the Road Traffic Regulation Act 1984 exempts fire, ambulance responding to an emergency for NHS ambulance service, and police vehicles from speed limits if observance would hinder the use of the vehicle for the purpose it was being used for on that occasion. The Deregulation Act 2015 amended s 87 to include

providing a response to an emergency at the request of an NHS ambulance service.

- Consider issuing a TFPN (see **10.4.1**).
- Is the contravention evidence of a more serious offence (eg dangerous driving, driving without due care and attention)?
- A notice of intended prosecution (NIP) must be served for offences of failing to comply with some types of traffic signs (see **10.5**). Parking, bus lane use, and certain other moving-traffic contraventions are increasingly being enforced by local traffic authorities which have sought and been granted civil enforcement powers.

TFPN NIP

Summary

6 months

Level 3 fine

Discretionary disqualification, obligatory endorsement—3 penalty points

10.4 Traffic Fixed Penalty Notices

Traffic fixed penalty notices (TFPNs) and procedures with regard to road traffic offences are covered by ss 51 to 90 of the Road Traffic Offenders Act 1988.

10.4.1 Traffic fixed penalty notices

Section 54 of the Act allows a constable in uniform who has reason to believe that a person they find is committing or has committed a fixed penalty offence to then issue a TFPN in respect of the offence.

Offences

A person is guilty of an offence if he removes or interferes with any notice fixed to a vehicle under this section, unless he does so by or under the authority of the driver or person in charge of the vehicle or the person liable for the fixed penalty offence in question.

Road Traffic Offenders Act 1988, s 62(2)

A person who, in a response to a notice to owner, provides a statement which is false in a material particular and does so recklessly or knowing it to be false in that particular is guilty of an offence.

Road Traffic Offenders Act 1988, s 67

PNLD H20055

Points to prove

s 62(2) offence

✓ without authority of driver/person in charge or liable for TFPN
✓ removed/interfered with TFPN fixed to vehicle

s 67 offence

✓ in response to notice to owner
✓ provided false statement
✓ recklessly/knowing it to be false

Meaning of 'traffic fixed penalty notice'

Means a notice offering the opportunity of the discharge of any liability to conviction of the offence to which the notice relates by payment of a fixed penalty in accordance with Part 3 of this Act.

Explanatory notes

- TFPNs apply where a constable in uniform believes that a person is committing or has committed a **relevant offence** (see below) and may be issued either at the time of the offence or at a police station.
- If the offence involves obligatory endorsement, the constable may only issue a TFPN if the offender is not liable to disqualification under s 35—the 'totting up' procedure.
- The obligation on drivers to surrender their driving licence before they can accept a fixed penalty notice or a conditional offer, or before they attend a court hearing for a road traffic offence, has been removed.
- A fixed penalty notice must give details of the identification information (as defined in s 69(3D)) that may be required under s 69 where the notice relates to an offence involving obligatory endorsement.
- A TFPN must give details of the offence, **suspended enforcement period**, penalty payable, and how it should be paid.
- '**Suspended enforcement period**' means the period following the date of the offence during which no proceedings will be brought against the offender.
- Where the penalty has not been paid or a hearing elected during the suspended enforcement period, the penalty plus 50 per cent may be registered against them.
- If the licence holder is liable to disqualification under the 'totting up' (see **10.13**) system, the fixed-penalty clerk must forward the licence on to the chief officer of police who may commence proceedings. Where such proceedings are commenced, any action already taken (eg registration as a fine) is void.
- At the end of the suspended enforcement period, if the penalty has not been paid or a hearing requested by the driver at the relevant time, a notice to owner may be served on the owner.
- A notice to owner must include particulars as to the offence, TFPN issued, response time allowed (minimum twenty-one days), penalty if it is not paid, requesting a hearing.
- If the person on whom the notice to owner was served was not the owner of the vehicle at the time of the offence and provides a statutory statement of ownership to that effect, they are not liable for the fine registered against them.
- If a notice to owner has been served, proceedings may not be brought against anybody else in relation to that offence unless they are identified as the driver at the relevant time in a statutory statement of facts.

Relevant offences

Schedule 3 to this Act lists the TFPN offences:

Highways Act 1835

s 72—Driving/cycling on footway.

10.4.1 Traffic fixed penalty notices

Transport Act 1968

s 96(11)—Contravened drivers' hours.
s 96(11A)—Contravened periods of driving.
s 97(1)—Contravened recording equipment regulations.
s 97ZA(1) and (2)—Using vehicle in contravention of requirements relating to installation, use, or repair or recording equipment in accordance with the European Agreement Concerning the Work of Crews of Vehicles Engaged in International Road Transport (AETR).
s 98(4)—Contravened drivers' hours written records regulations.
s 99(4)—Fail to produce records/obstruction.
s 99ZD(1)—Fail to comply with requirements/obstruction.
s 99C—Fail to comply with prohibition/direction.

Road Traffic (Foreign Vehicles) Act 1972

s 3(1)—Drive foreign GV or PSV in contravention of prohibition.

Greater London Council (General Powers) Act 1974

s 15—Parking vehicles on footways, verges, other related offences.

Highways Act 1980

s 137—Obstruction of highway committed in respect of a vehicle.

Public Passenger Vehicles Act 1981

s 12(5)—Use PSV on road without PSV operator's licence.

Road Traffic Regulation Act 1984

s 5(1)—Traffic regulation order outside Greater London.
s 8(1)—Traffic regulation order in Greater London.
s 11—Breach of experimental traffic order.
s 13—Breach of experimental traffic scheme.
s 16(1)—Temporary prohibition or restriction.
s 17(4)—Wrongful use of special road.
s 18(3)—One-way traffic order on trunk road.
s 20(5)—Prohibition/restriction of driving on certain classes of road.
s 25(5)—Breach of pedestrian crossing regulations, except offence in respect of moving motor vehicle, other than contravention of regs 23, 24, 25, and 26 of the Zebra, Pelican and Puffin Pedestrian Crossings Regulations and General Directions 1997.
s 29(3)—Street playground order.
s 35A(1)—Local authority parking place on a road.
s 47(1)—Parking place designation order.
s 53(5)—Parking place designation order under s 53(1)(a).
s 53(6)—Designation order authorised parking on road without charge.
s 88(7)—Minimum speed limit.
s 89(1)—Speeding.

Road Transport (International Passenger Services) Regulations 1984

reg 19(1)—Use vehicle for carriage of passengers without authorisation/certificate.
reg 19(2)—Use vehicle for carriage of passengers without passenger waybill.

Road Traffic Act 1988

s 3—Driving mechanically propelled vehicle on a road/public place without due care and attention, or reasonable consideration.
s 14—Seat belt regulations.
s 15(2)—Restriction re children in front of vehicles.
s 15(4)—Restriction re children in rear of vehicles.
s 16—Crash helmet regulations re motorcycle rider/passenger.
s 18(3)—Breach use of eye protector regulations on motorcycles.
s 19—Parking heavy commercial vehicle on verge/footway.
s 22—Leave vehicle in dangerous position.
s 23—Unlawfully carry passenger on motorcycle.
s 24—Carry more than one person on pedal cycle.
s 34—Drive mechanically propelled vehicle elsewhere than on road.
s 35—Fail to comply with traffic directions.
s 36—Fail to comply with prescribed traffic signs (see 10.3).
s 40A—Use vehicle where condition, purpose used, passengers carried, load involves danger of injury.
s 41A—Breach of requirements re brakes, steering-gear, or tyres.
s 41B—Breach of weight requirement re goods and passenger vehicles.
s 41D—Breach of requirements re control, view of road, or use hand held device.
s 42—Breach of other construction and use regulations.
s 47—Using vehicle without a test certificate.
s 71(1)—Contravened prohibition order or fail comply order.
s 87(1)—Drive vehicle otherwise than in accordance with licence.
s 143—Using a motor vehicle without insurance.
s 163—Fail to stop vehicle when required by officer in uniform.
s 172—Failed to give information re driver of motor vehicle.

Road Traffic Offenders Act 1988

s 90D(6)—Drive in contravention of prohibition or fail to comply direction.

Goods Vehicles (Community Authorisations) Regulations 1992

reg 3—Use goods vehicle without community authorisation.
reg 7—Use vehicle contravening regulations under community authorisation.

10.4.1 Traffic fixed penalty notices

Vehicle Excise and Registration Act 1994

s 34—Use trade licence for unauthorised purposes/circumstances.
s 42—Driving/keeping vehicle without required registration mark.
s 43—Drive/keep vehicle with registration mark obscured.
s 43C—Offence of using an incorrectly registered vehicle.
s 59—Fail to affix prescribed registration mark to vehicle.

Goods Vehicles (Licensing of Operators) Act 1995

s 2(5)—Use GV on road for carriage of goods—no operator's licence.

Public Service Vehicles (Community Licences) Regulations 1999

reg 3—Use PSV on road without community licence.
reg 7—Use PSV under community licence—contravened licence conditions.

Road Transport (Passenger Vehicles Cabotage) Regulations 1999

reg 3—Using vehicle on road for UK cabotage operations—no EC licence.
reg 4—Using vehicle on road for UK cabotage operations—no control document.
reg 7(1)—Fail to produce EC licence when requested.
reg 7(3)—Failed to produce control document when requested.

Vehicle Drivers (Certificates of Professional Competence) Regulations 2007

reg 11(7)—Driver of relevant vehicle failed to produce evidence/document.

Practical considerations

- Consider the seriousness of the offence. There is no obligation to issue a TFPN—it is at the discretion of the constable.
- Is the fixed penalty scheme appropriate?
- Is the offence endorsable—if so, is the offender with the vehicle?
- Only a non-endorsable TFPN may be attached to a vehicle.
- Is the offender liable to disqualification under the totting up system?

Summary

s 62 offence

6 months

s 67 offence

If statutory declaration is made, 6 months from date of declaration, up to a maximum of 3 years from the original offence. In all other cases—6 months.

s 62 offence
Level 2 fine

s 67 offence
Fine not exceeding level 5

10.4.2 Control of vehicle and use of hand-held device

Offences

A person who contravenes or fails to comply with a construction and use requirement—

(a) as to not driving a motor vehicle in a position which does not give proper control or a full view of the road and traffic ahead, or not causing or permitting the driving of a motor vehicle by another person in such a position, or

(b) as to not driving or supervising the driving of a motor vehicle while using a hand-held mobile telephone or other hand-held interactive communication device, or not causing or permitting the driving of a motor vehicle by another person using such a telephone or other device,

is guilty of an offence.

Road Traffic Act 1988, s 41D

PNLD **H100578 to H100580, H18725**

Points to prove

s 41D(a) offence

✓ contravened/failed to comply with requirement
✓ by driving a motor vehicle on a road
✓ without proper control of vehicle or full view or
✓ caused/permitted the above offences

s 41D(b) offence

✓ contravened/failed to comply with requirement
✓ being the driver/driving supervisor
✓ of a motor vehicle on a road
✓ **used hand-held** mobile/similar device **or**
✓ caused/permitted above offence

Meaning of 'construction and use requirement'

Means requirement imposed by regulations made under s 41 of the Road Traffic Act 1988, being mainly the Road Vehicles (Construction and Use) Regulations 1986.

Explanatory notes

- Not being in a position to have proper control of the vehicle or a full view of the road and traffic ahead comes under reg 104 of the Road Vehicles (Construction and Use) Regulations 1986.
- Using a hand-held mobile telephone or similar device comes under reg 110 of the Road Vehicles (Construction and Use) Regulations 1986.

Related cases

R v Barreto [2019] EWHC 2044 (Admin) The meaning of the word 'using' in s 41D and reg 110 was confined to the use of hand-held devices falling within reg 110(4) for interactive communication functions. That meant that the prohibition did not extend to the use of all functions of hand-held mobile phones while driving, but only the making and receiving of calls or performing any other interactive communication functions. (However, as the court noted, this is not a green light for people to make films or photographs as they drive, since doing so may be cogent evidence of careless driving and possibly of dangerous driving.) Note that reg 110 has subsequently been amended. It now includes a list of what 'using' includes—see below.

Bendt v CPS [2022] EWHC 502 (Admin) It was held that a conviction was safe where a driver who had used their mobile telephone to change the music being listened to via Bluetooth connectivity over their car's sound system was found to be performing an interactive communication function with another device; the communication did not have to be with another person.

Practical considerations

- These offences provide for obligatory endorsement and disqualification (at the court's discretion).
- A two-way radio which performs an interactive communication function by transmitting and receiving data is not a device under reg 110.
- Regulation 110(5) states that a person does not contravene this regulation if:
  - ✦ they are using the telephone or device to call the police, fire, ambulance, or other emergency service on 112 or 999;
  - ✦ they are acting in response to a genuine emergency; and
  - ✦ it is unsafe or impracticable for them to cease driving in order to make the call.

- Regulation 110(5A) provides that a person does not contravene a provision of this regulation if, at the time of the alleged contravention:
  - ✦ that person is using the mobile telephone or other device only to perform a remote controlled parking function of the motor vehicle; and
  - ✦ that mobile telephone or other device only enables the motor vehicle to move where the following conditions are satisfied:
    - ▪ there is continuous activation of the remote control application of the telephone or device by the driver;
    - ▪ the signal between the motor vehicle and the telephone or the motor vehicle and the device, as appropriate, is maintained; and
    - ▪ the distance between the motor vehicle and the telephone or the motor vehicle and the device, as appropriate, is not more than 6 metres.
- Regulation 110(5B) provides that a person does not contravene a provision of this regulation if at the time of the alleged contravention:
  - ✦ that person is using the mobile telephone or other device to make a contactless payment;
  - ✦ for a good or service which is received at the same time as, or after, the contactless payment is made; and
  - ✦ the motor vehicle is stationary.

Regulation 110(6) states that for the purposes of reg 110:

- A mobile telephone or other device is to be treated as hand-held if it is, or must be, held at some point while being used.
- A person who supervises the holder of a provisional licence must be at least 21 years of age and hold a full EC/EEA licence for that type of vehicle (including manual or automatic).
- The word **using** includes the following:
  - ✦ illuminating the screen;
  - ✦ checking the time;
  - ✦ checking notifications;
  - ✦ unlocking the device;
  - ✦ making, receiving, or rejecting a telephone or internet-based call;
  - ✦ sending, receiving, or uploading oral or written content;
  - ✦ sending, receiving, or uploading a photo or video;
  - ✦ utilising camera, video, or sound-recording functionality;
  - ✦ drafting any text;
  - ✦ accessing any stored data such as documents, books, audio files, photos, videos, films, playlists, notes, or messages;
  - ✦ accessing an application;
  - ✦ accessing the internet.

10.4.3 **Graduated fixed penalties**

TFPN

Summary

6 months

Level 4 fine for goods vehicle or vehicle carrying more than eight passengers

Level 3 fine in any other case

Discretionary disqualification. Obligatory endorsement—3 penalty points for an offence under s 41D(a) and 6 penalty points for an offence under s 41D(b)

10.4.3 Graduated fixed penalties, penalty deposits, and immobilisation

The Road Safety Act 2006 introduced the graduated fixed penalty scheme, roadside deposits, and vehicle immobilisation.

Schedule 2 to the Fixed Penalty Order 2000 lists the graduated fixed penalties and graduates the level of specified fixed penalties based on the seriousness of the offending. It increases the level of fine for some offences to above the default amount (£100 endorsable and £50 non-endorsable). Initially, these graduated fixed penalties only apply to specific offences relating to commercial and PSV vehicles.

Any officer appointed by their force or a DVSA officer will have responsibility for dealing with graduated fixed penalties.

Roadside deposits

The Road Traffic Offenders Act 1988, ss 90A to 90D provide enforcement powers under what is termed the 'roadside deposit scheme'.

Offences

A person who—
(a) drives a vehicle in contravention of a prohibition under this section,
(b) causes or permits a vehicle to be driven in contravention of such a prohibition, or
(c) fails to comply within a reasonable time with a direction under subsection (5) above, is guilty of an offence.

Road Traffic Offenders Act 1988, s 90D(6)

PNLD H8707 to H8710

Points to prove

✓ drives a vehicle or causes/permits vehicle to be driven
✓ in contravention of a prohibition OR
✓ fails to comply within a reasonable time with a direction under s 90D(5)

Meanings

Prohibition

(1) This section applies where a person on whom a financial penalty deposit requirement is imposed does not make an immediate payment of the appropriate amount in accordance with section 90B(1) of this Act (and any order made under it).
(2) The constable or vehicle examiner by whom the requirement was imposed may prohibit the driving on a road of any vehicle of which the person was in charge at the time of the offence by giving to the person notice in writing of the prohibition.
(3) The prohibition—
  (a) shall come into force as soon as the notice is given, and
  (b) shall continue in force until the happening of whichever of the events in subsection (4) below occurs first.
(4) Those events are—
  (a) the person making a payment of the appropriate amount in accordance with section 90B(1) of this Act (and any order made under it) at any time during the relevant period,
  (b) (where a fixed penalty notice was given, or a conditional offer handed, to the person in respect of the offence) payment of the fixed penalty,
  (c) the person being convicted or acquitted of the offence,
  (d) the person being informed that he is not to be prosecuted for the offence, and
  (e) the coming to an end of the prosecution period.

Direction

(5) A constable or vehicle examiner may by direction in writing require the person to remove the vehicle to which the prohibition relates (and, if it is a motor vehicle drawing a trailer, also to remove the trailer) to such place and subject to such conditions as are specified in the direction; and the prohibition does not apply to the removal of the vehicle (or trailer) in accordance with the direction.

Road Traffic Offenders Act 1988, s 90D

Explanatory notes

• Section 90A gives a constable in uniform or a vehicle examiner power to require the payment of a deposit from a person whom they believe is committing or has committed an offence in relation to a motor vehicle and who is unable to provide a satisfactory address in the UK at which they can be found. Furthermore, the police officer or vehicle examiner must also believe that the person, the offence, and the circumstances in which the offence is committed are of a description specified by order made by the Secretary of State.

- Under s 90B, a financial penalty deposit, of an amount specified by order, can be paid to the constable or examiner. That person must then be given either a fixed penalty notice or written notice as to proposed court proceedings for the offence.
- The specified amounts are:
  - when it is a TFPN, the amount of that fixed penalty;
  - in other cases, it is a maximum of £500 per offence, to a maximum of £1,500 per vehicle stoppage.
- Once payment is made, s 90C stipulates that the person must be issued with a written receipt and notice outlining the process that applies through the various provisions of s 90C.
- If the driver does not contest the roadside deposit within twenty-eight days, then the deposit is paid into court and that is the end of the matter. Alternatively, should the driver contest and the court decide in their favour or if the case did not go to court within a year (or less than this if a shorter prosecution period applies), then the deposit will be refunded with the relevant interest. Similarly, if the court decided against them, the deposit will be retained to be offset against all, or part, of the fine imposed.
- Under s 90D, if a person does not make an immediate roadside deposit payment of the appropriate amount, the constable or vehicle examiner may then give the person a prohibition notice which prohibits the moving of the vehicle, though the vehicle/trailer may be moved to a specified place by way of a written direction.
- This prohibition will remain in force until one of the following occurs:
  - payment of the appropriate amount, during the relevant period;
  - payment of the fixed penalty notice;
  - conviction or acquittal of the offence;
  - driver informed that they will not be prosecuted; or
  - the prosecution period has expired.

Practical considerations

- This legislation provides enforcement powers against both UK and non-UK drivers who do not have a satisfactory UK address and were previously able to avoid payment of fixed penalties and prosecution as a result. It applies to both fixed penalty offences and other traffic offences.
- Enforcement of this scheme is through prohibition notices and vehicle immobilisation, removal, and disposal powers.
- Under the Road Safety (Immobilisation, Removal and Disposal of Vehicles) Regulations 2009 a vehicle may be immobilised when the vehicle is being driven:

- ✦ whilst unfit for service or overloaded;
- ✦ in contravention of the drivers' hours rules;
- ✦ in contravention of international transport requirements;
- ✦ by a person who has failed to pay the financial penalty deposit.

- Immobilisation will physically prevent a prohibition being disregarded but the vehicle cannot be immobilised simply because it appears that the driver is likely to abscond.
- Therefore, where a driver does not make a payment under the roadside deposit scheme, the prohibition and immobilisation powers can be applied by the enforcement officer until the prohibition requirements are satisfied or, in cases of offenders who do not have a reliable UK address, until a deposit is paid or the case is settled in court.
- Prior to this scheme, prohibitions were usually imposed for breaches of drivers' hours or when the vehicle was not roadworthy.
- Payment will normally be made by cash or debit cards as payment by credit cards can be cancelled prior to the transfer taking place.

TFPN (including graduated TFPN)

Summary 6 months

Fine

Discretionary disqualification

10.5 Notice of Intended Prosecution

Section 1 of the Road Traffic Offenders Act 1988 requires a notice of intended prosecution to be given to a defendant for certain offences.

Requirement

Subject to section 2 of this Act, a person shall not be convicted of an offence to which this section applies unless—

(a) he was warned at the time the offence was committed that the question of prosecuting him for one or other of the offences to which this section applies would be taken into consideration, or

(b) within 14 days of the commission of the offence a summons for the offence was served on him, or

(c) within 14 days of the commission of the offence a notice of the intended prosecution specifying the nature of the alleged offence and the time and place where it is alleged to have been committed, was—

   (i) in the case of an offence under section 28 or 29 of the Road Traffic Act 1988 (cycling offences) [see **10.12**], served on him,

   (ii) in the case of any other offence, served on him or on the person, if any, registered as the keeper of the vehicle at the time of the commission of the offence.

Road Traffic Offenders Act 1988, s 1(1)

Meanings

Subject to section 2

This section will not apply if:

- at the time of the offence or immediately after it, the vehicle concerned was involved in an accident;
- a fixed penalty notice or a notice under the fixed penalty scheme requiring production of the defendant's licence and counterpart at a police station is issued (see **10.4**).

Within 14 days

Means the notice must be posted to reach the defendant within fourteen days of the offence.

Explanatory notes

- Notices of intended prosecution (NIPs) may be served personally or by registered post, recorded delivery, or first-class post to the defendant's last known address.
- A NIP sent by registered post or recorded delivery is deemed served if addressed to the defendant at their last known address even if it is returned undelivered or not received by them for some other reason.

- Requirements of s 1 are met unless the contrary is proved or if the defendant is charged and given a copy of the charge within fourteen days of the commission of the offence.
- A NIP posted the day after the offence which failed to arrive within the fourteen days, was good service; whereas one sent by recorded delivery on the fourteenth day was deemed not 'served'.
- Failure to comply with s 1 is not a bar to conviction if the name and address of the defendant or the registered keeper could not be ascertained with due diligence in time to comply, or that the accused's conduct contributed to the failure.
- If an alternative verdict is returned by the court and the alternative offence requires a NIP, this is not a bar to conviction providing the original offence did not require a NIP.

Related cases

R v Pledge [2019] EWCA Crim 912 A conviction was safe where the officer issuing the NIP had acted with reasonable diligence to ascertain the name and address of the registered keeper.

R v Myers [2007] EWCA Crim 599 There must be a causal link between a traffic offence and the accident, otherwise the driver requires serving with a NIP.

Relevant offences

Schedule 1 to the Road Traffic Offenders Act 1988 lists the offences for which a NIP is required under s 1, being:

Road Traffic Regulation Act 1984

s 16—Contravene speed restriction at road works.
s 17(4)—Contravene motorway speed limit.
s 88(7)—Contravene minimum speed limit.
s 89(1)—Exceeding speed limit.

Road Traffic Act 1988

s 2—Dangerous driving.
s 3—Careless, and inconsiderate, driving.
s 22—Leaving vehicles in dangerous position.
s 28—Dangerous cycling.
s 29—Careless, and inconsiderate, cycling.
s 35—Failing to comply with traffic directions.
s 36—Failing to comply with traffic signs prescribed under s 36 (see **10.3**).

Practical considerations

- If the offence arises out of an accident of which the driver may not be aware, a NIP is required (*Bentley v Dickinson* [1983] RTR 356).
- No NIP is required if a TFPN (see **10.4**) is issued.
- A NIP is also required for those who aid/abet the commission of relevant offences.

10.6 Driving without Due Care and Attention

Section 3 of the Road Traffic Act 1988 relates to the offence of driving without due care and attention or without reasonable consideration for other users of the road or public place. Section 168 requires a person alleged to have committed this offence to give their details to any person having reasonable grounds for obtaining them.

10.6.1 Driving without due care and attention

> **Offences**
>
> If a person drives a mechanically propelled vehicle on a road or other public place without due care and attention, or without reasonable consideration for other persons using the road or public place, he is guilty of an offence.
>
> Road Traffic Act 1988, s 3

PNLD H8757, H8758

> **Points to prove**
>
> ✓ drove mechanically propelled vehicle
> ✓ on road/other public place
> ✓ without due care and attention/reasonable consideration for other road users

Meanings

Drives (see 10.1.4)

Mechanically propelled vehicle (see 10.1.3)

Road (s 192) (see 10.1.1)

Public place (see 10.1.2)

Driving without due care and attention or reasonable consideration (careless driving)

(1) This section has effect for the purposes of sections 2B, 2C, 3 and 3A.

(2) A person is to be regarded as driving without due care and attention if (and only if) the way he drives falls below what would be expected of a competent and careful driver. But this subsection does not apply where subsection (2B) applies.

(2A) Subsection (2B) applies where a designated person—
(a) is driving for police purposes (subject to subsections (2E) and (2F)), and
(b) has undertaken prescribed training.

(2B) The designated person is to be regarded as driving without due care and attention if (and only if) the way the person drives falls below what would be expected of a competent and careful constable who has undertaken the same prescribed training.

(2C) In subsections (2A) and (2B) designated person means—
(a) a constable,
(b) a member of staff appointed by the chief officer of police of a police force in England and Wales,
(c) a member of staff appointed by a local policing body and employed to assist a police force in England and Wales . . .

(3) In determining for the purposes of subsection (2) or (2B) above what would be expected of a careful and competent driver or constable (as the case may be) in a particular case, regard shall be had not only to the circumstances of which he could be expected to be aware but also to any circumstances shown to have been within the knowledge of the accused.

(4) A person is to be regarded as driving without reasonable consideration for other persons only if those persons are inconvenienced by his driving.

Road Traffic Act 1988, s 3ZA

Explanatory notes

- The Road Traffic Act 1988 (Police Driving: Prescribed Training) Regulations 2023 make provisions for 'prescribed training'.
- Breaching certain road traffic regulations (eg crossing central white lines without explanation) can be enough to prove this offence.
- Section 168 of the Road Traffic Act 1988 empowers the obtaining of the defendant's name and address (see **10.6.2**).
- Riding a pedal cycle without due care and attention is an offence under s 29 (see **10.12.2**).

Defences

The defences of automatism, unconsciousness and sudden illness, duress, sudden mechanical defect, assisting in the arrest of offenders, and taking part in an authorised motoring event may be used.

Defence notes

- 'Automatism' means an affliction which overcomes the driver and causes them to lose control of the vehicle. It must be sudden and something that they were unaware of and could not reasonably be expected to foresee.
- 'Unconsciousness and sudden illness' applies if a driver is rendered unconscious and unable to control the vehicle. For example, a blow to the head or sudden and unforeseen epileptic fit may cause this.
- The defence of 'duress' may be split into two parts—duress by threat or duress of necessity (of circumstances).
  - For duress by threat to apply, a person cannot deliberately put themselves in a position where they are likely to be subject to threats and, if they can escape the duress by escaping the threats, they must do so.
- 'Sudden mechanical defect' applies if a sudden and unexpected defect in the motor vehicle causes the driver to totally lose control. It does not apply to a defect already known to the driver or one that could be easily discovered with reasonable prudence.
- The defence of 'assisting in the arrest of offenders' may be available to a driver if their driving, though careless or inconsiderate, amounted to reasonable force assisting in the arrest of an offender (see **1.2**).
- Section 13A(1) states that a person shall not be guilty of an offence under s 1, 1A, 2, 2B, or 3 of this Act by virtue of driving a vehicle in a public place other than a road if they show that they were driving in accordance with an authorisation for a motoring event given under regulations made by the Secretary of State (currently the Motor Vehicles (Off Road Events) Regulations 1995 (SI 1371/1995)).

Related cases

Jones v Crown Prosecution Service [2019] EWHC 2826 (Admin) The condition of the driver was relevant and admissible to prove the offences of careless driving or of causing death by careless driving, but it did not determine whether the driving had been careless.

R v McKay (2015) unreported CA (see **10.3**).

DPP v Harris [1994] 158 JP 896, QBD A detective constable driving an unmarked police car was covertly following a vehicle carrying suspects planning to commit an armed robbery when the defendant went through a red traffic light and collided with another vehicle. It was held that care due in these circumstances would involve edging slowly forwards, being prepared to stop if required. For the defence of 'necessity', it would be necessary to show that actions were reasonable and proportionate in the light of a threat of death or serious injury.

Practical considerations

- This offence requires a NIP to be served (see **10.5**).
- This offence can be dealt with by TFPN (see **10.4.1**).

- Although there is no special standard for emergency vehicles, the courts have made it clear that public safety must be paramount (see '**Related cases**' above).
- This section creates two offences and it is bad for duplicity to charge both of them as alternatives.
- Other persons using the road include other drivers, passengers, pedestrians, or cyclists.
- Section 38(7) of the Road Traffic Act 1988 states that failure to observe a provision of the Highway Code shall not render that person liable to criminal proceedings, but any such failure may be relied upon by any party to any proceedings (civil or criminal) as tending to establish or negate any liability which is in question in those proceedings.
- Consider CPS guidance on prosecuting cases of bad driving.
- In s 3ZA, the statutory meaning of driving without due or reasonable consideration for others also applies to s 3A (death by careless driving when under influence) (see **10.8.2**) and s 2B (death by careless driving) (see **10.8.3**).

TFPN £100 and licence endorsed with 3 penalty points

Summary 6 months

Fine

Discretionary disqualification, obligatory endorsement—3 to 9 penalty points

10.6.2 Request details after reckless, careless, or inconsiderate driving or cycling

Offences

Any of the following persons—

(a) the driver of a mechanically propelled vehicle who is alleged to have committed an offence under section 2 or 3 of this Act, or

(b) the rider of a cycle who is alleged to have committed an offence under section 28 or 29 of this Act,

who refuses, on being so required by any person having reasonable ground for so requiring, to give his name and address, or gives a false name and address, is guilty of an offence.

Road Traffic Act 1988, s 168

PNLD H3260, H3261, H3383, H3384

10.6.2 Request details after inconsiderate driving or cycling

Points to prove

- ✓ driver of mechanically propelled vehicle/rider of cycle
- ✓ commits offence under ss 2/3 or 28/29 of RTA 1988
- ✓ when required by person having reasonable grounds
- ✓ refused to give name and address/gave false details

Meanings

Mechanically propelled vehicle (see **10.1.3**)

Driver (see **10.1.4**)

Explanatory notes

Above offences applicable to this section are:

- dangerous driving, s 2 (see **10.7.1**);
- driving without due care and attention/without reasonable consideration, s 3 (see **10.6.1**);
- ss 28 and 29 involve similar offences to above but riding pedal cycles (see **10.12**).

Summary

6 months

Level 3 fine

10.7 Dangerous Driving/Cause Serious Injury

10.7.1 Dangerous driving

Section 2 of the Road Traffic Act 1988 relates to dangerous driving.

Offences

A person who drives a mechanically propelled vehicle dangerously on a road or other public place is guilty of an offence.

Road Traffic Act 1988, s 2

PNLD H12

Points to prove

✓ being driver of a mechanically propelled vehicle
✓ drove dangerously
✓ on a road/other public place

Meanings

Drives (see **10.1.4**)

Mechanically propelled vehicle (see **10.1.3**)

Dangerous driving (s 2A)

For the purposes of ss 1, 1A, and 2, a person is regarded as driving dangerously if the way they drive falls far below what would be expected of a competent and careful driver and it would be obvious to a competent and careful driver that driving in that way would be dangerous. This subsection does not apply where the designated person is driving for police purposes and has undertaken prescribed training.

Road (s 192) (see **10.1.1**)

Public place (see **10.1.2**)

Explanatory notes

- The designated person (see **10.6.1**) is to be regarded as driving dangerously if the way the person drives falls far below what would be expected of a competent and careful constable who has undertaken the same prescribed training and it would be obvious to such a competent and careful constable that driving in that way would be dangerous.

- 'Dangerous' refers to danger either of injury to any person or serious damage to property.
- Consideration will be taken not only of the circumstances which a competent and careful driver could be expected to be aware of but also any circumstances shown to be within the defendant's knowledge.

Defences (see 10.6.1)

Related cases

DPP v Milton [2006] EWHC 242 (Admin) Excessive speed alone is insufficient for dangerous driving; the driving must be considered with all the circumstances.

R v Pleydell [2005] EWCA Crim 1447 Evidence that a driver had taken cocaine was, by itself, admissible as the defendant had driven dangerously because of being adversely affected by drugs.

R v Strong [1995] Crim LR 428, CA The danger is 'obvious' only if it can be seen or realised at first glance, or is evident to the competent or careful driver, or the defendant knew of it.

R v Woodward [1995] 3 All ER 79, CA Evidence of consumption of alcohol is admissible only where it is to the effect that the defendant had drunk so much of it as would adversely affect a driver.

R v Spurge [1961] 2 All ER 688, CA A driver aware of a mechanical defect, which caused the vehicle to be dangerous, could not use this defence.

Practical considerations

- This offence requires NIP to be served (see **10.5**).
- Consider CPS guidance on prosecuting cases of bad driving.
- A court may convict of an alternative offence under s 3 (see **10.6.1**).
- Forfeiture of the vehicle used may also be ordered.

E&S NIP

Either way

None

Summary: 6/12 months' imprisonment and/or a fine

Indictment: 2 years' imprisonment and/or a fine. Obligatory disqualification until test passed

Obligatory endorsement—3 to 11 penalty points (unless special reasons apply)

10.7.2 Cause serious injury by dangerous driving

Section 1A of the Road Traffic Act 1988 relates to causing serious injury by dangerous driving.

Offences

A person who causes serious injury to another person by driving a mechanically propelled vehicle dangerously on a road or other public place is guilty of an offence.

Road Traffic Act 1988, s 1A

PNLD H7232

Points to prove

- ✓ being driver of a mechanically propelled vehicle
- ✓ caused serious injury to another person
- ✓ by driving dangerously
- ✓ on a road/other public place

Meanings

Serious injury

In England and Wales, physical harm which amounts to grievous bodily harm for the purposes of the Offences Against the Person Act 1861—s 2C(2) of the Road Traffic Act 1988.

Physical harm which amounts to grievous bodily harm (see **2.3.1**)

Drives (see **10.1.4**)

Mechanically propelled vehicle (see **10.1.3**)

Driving dangerously (see **10.7.1**)

Road (s 192) (see **10.1.1**)

Public place (see **10.1.2**)

Defences (see 10.6.1)

Defence notes (see 10.6.1)

Related cases (see 10.7.1)

Practical considerations (see 10.7.1)

- A court may convict of an alternative offence under s 2 (see **10.7.1**) or s 3 (see **10.6.1**).
- For further information, see MOJ Circular 8/2012.

E&S

Either way — None

Summary: 6/12 months' imprisonment and/or a fine

Indictment: 5 years' imprisonment and/or a fine. Obligatory disqualification until test passed

Obligatory endorsement—3 to 11 penalty points (unless special reasons apply)

10.7.3 Causing serious injury by careless, or inconsiderate, driving

Section 2C of the Road Traffic Act 1988 provides for the offence of causing serious injury by careless, or inconsiderate, driving.

Offences

A person who causes serious injury to another person by driving a mechanically propelled vehicle on a road or other public place without due care and attention, or without reasonable consideration for other persons using the road or place, is guilty of an offence.

Road Traffic Act 1988, s 2C

PNLD H100722

Points to prove

- ✓ caused serious injury to another person
- ✓ by driving a mechanically propelled vehicle
- ✓ on a road/public place
- ✓ without due care and attention/reasonable consideration for others

Meanings

Serious injury (see **10.7.2**)

Another person (see **10.8.1**)

Driving (see **10.1.4**)

Mechanically propelled vehicle (see **10.1.3**)

Road (s 192) (see **10.1.1**)

Public place (see **10.1.2**)

Without due care and attention or reasonable consideration (see **10.6.1**)

Explanatory notes (see **10.6.1**)

Defences (see **10.6.1**)

Practical considerations (see also **10.6.1** and **10.8.2**)

- Ensure compliance with the law in relation to reporting road traffic collisions (RTCs) (see **10.9**).

E&S

Either way

None

Summary: 6/12 months' imprisonment and/or a fine

Obligatory disqualification and obligatory endorsement with 3 to 11 penalty points

Indictment: 2 years' imprisonment and/or a fine

Obligatory disqualification and obligatory endorsement with 3 to 11 penalty points

10.7.4 Wanton or furious driving

Section 35 of the Offences Against the Person Act 1861 provides for the offence of wanton or furious driving.

Offences

Whosoever, having the charge of any carriage or vehicle, shall by wanton or furious driving or racing, or other wilful misconduct, or by wilful neglect, do or cause to be done any bodily harm to any person whatsoever, shall be guilty of an offence.

Offences Against the Person Act 1861, s 35

10.7.4 Wanton or furious driving

PNLD H2503, H2504, H2505, H3007

Points to prove

✓ in charge of a carriage/vehicle
✓ by wanton/furious driving/racing or other wilful misconduct/neglect
✓ did/caused bodily harm to be done to another

Meanings

Vehicle (see **10.1.3**)

Wanton

Means without any lawful motive and being thoughtless as to the possible consequences.

Driving (see **10.1.4**)

Bodily harm (see **2.1.2**)

Explanatory note

- A person riding a pedal cycle in a wanton or furious manner resulting in injuries to another person may be convicted under this section.

Practical considerations

- This offence can be committed anywhere.
- Consider CPS guidance on prosecuting cases of bad driving.

E&S

Indictment

None

2 years' imprisonment

If a mechanically propelled vehicle—discretionary disqualification and obligatory endorsement of 3 to 9 penalty points

10.8 Fatal Road Traffic Collision Incidents

A driver involved in a fatal road traffic incident has the same obligations as a driver involved in any other reportable RTC (see **10.9**). Offences connected with deaths caused by road traffic incidents are found in s 1 (dangerous driving); s 2B (due care); s 3A (careless driving when under influence of drink or drugs); s 3ZB (no licence/insurance); and s 3ZC (disqualified).

10.8.1 Causing death by dangerous driving

Causing death by dangerous driving is an offence created by s 1 of the Road Traffic Act 1988.

> **Offences**
>
> A person who causes the death of another person by driving a mechanically propelled vehicle dangerously on a road or other public place is guilty of an offence.
>
> Road Traffic Act 1988, s 1

PNLD H100713

> **Points to prove**
>
> ✓ caused the death of another person
> ✓ by driving a mechanically propelled vehicle dangerously
> ✓ on a road/public place

Meanings

Another person

Means anybody, other than the defendant. It has been held to include a foetus in utero (still in the uterus) and subsequently born alive but who later dies of their injuries.

Driving (see **10.1.4**)

Mechanically propelled vehicle (see **10.1.3**)

Driven dangerously (see **10.7.1**)

Road (s 192) (see **10.1.1**)

Public place (see **10.1.2**)

Explanatory notes

- The death of the person concerned must be shown to have been caused in some way by the incident to which the charge relates.
- The cause of death does not need to be a substantial cause, but neither should it be a slight or trifling link. It will suffice if the driving was a cause of the death even though it was not the sole or even a substantial cause.
- A person charged with this offence may be convicted of the alternative offences of dangerous driving (see **10.7**), death by driving without due care (see **10.8.3**), or careless, and inconsiderate, driving (see **10.6**).

Defences (see 10.6.1)

Defence notes (see 10.6.1)

Related cases (see also 'Dangerous driving' cases 10.7.1)

R v Holder [2023] EWCA Crim 5 H, who was aged 17, was riding a stolen motor scooter with a 14-year-old friend as the pillion passenger. They were travelling at between 37 and 44 mph on a road with a 20 mph speed limit, when H lost control of the scooter and collided with a kerb, killing the passenger. It was held that the jury was entitled to consider the fact that the 14-year-old passenger was not wearing a helmet when determining the standard of a careful and competent driver under s 1 and s 2A of the Road Traffic Act 1988.

R v A [2020] EWCA Crim 407 It was held in this case that the law did not require that the particular circumstances in which a collision occurred should be foreseeable for a case of causing death by dangerous driving and causing serious injury by dangerous driving to be established. It was sufficient that the jury could properly conclude from the facts known to the accused that some form of collision could occur and that death or serious injury could be caused.

R v Bannister [2009] EWCA Crim 1571 Special skill, or lack of such skill, is an irrelevant circumstance when considering whether driving was dangerous.

R v Buono [2005] EWCA Crim 1313 In this case, a fatal collision had been caused by the defendant taking a bend in the middle of the road at excessive speed. Similar fact evidence was admitted showing the way the car had been driven earlier—swerving across the road and driving at excessive speed. Such evidence had considerable probative force, which undoubtedly outweighed any prejudice to the defendant.

Practical considerations

- This section applies to tramcars and trolley vehicles operating under a statutory power.

- If appropriate, consider manslaughter (see **2.7**) for this offence.
- Theoretically, two different drivers could cause the same death.
- Consider CPS guidance on prosecuting cases of bad driving.
- Consider seizing the vehicle as it may be forfeited. This will also ensure that the vehicle can be examined for any mechanical defect defences before eventual disposal.

E&S

Indictment

None

Life imprisonment

Obligatory disqualification until extended test passed

Obligatory endorsement—3 to 11 penalty points

10.8.2 Causing death by careless driving when under influence

Section 3A of the Road Traffic Act 1988 provides an offence of causing the death of another by careless driving when under the influence of drink or drugs or failing to provide or give permission for a specimen.

Offences

If a person causes the death of another person by driving a mechanically propelled vehicle on a road or other public place without due care and attention, or without reasonable consideration for other persons using the road or place, and—

(a) he is, at the time when he is driving, unfit to drive through drink or drugs, or

(b) he has consumed so much alcohol that the proportion of it in his breath, blood or urine at that time exceeds the prescribed limit, or

(ba) he has in his body a specified controlled drug and the proportion of it in his blood or urine at that time exceeds the specified limit for that drug, or

(c) he is, within 18 hours after that time, required to provide a specimen in pursuance of section 7 of this Act [see **10.11.2**], but without reasonable excuse fails to provide it, or

(d) he is required by a constable to give his permission for a laboratory test of a specimen of blood taken from him under section 7A of this Act [see **10.11.2**], but without reasonable excuse fails to do so,

he is guilty of an offence.

Road Traffic Act 1988, s 3A(1)

10.8.2 Causing death by careless driving when under influence

PNLD H100714, H100715, H100716, H100710, H100711, H100712

Points to prove

- ✓ caused the death of another person
- ✓ by driving a motor vehicle
- ✓ on a road/public place
- ✓ without due care or reasonable consideration for other road users and
- ✓ at the time of driving was unfit through drink/drugs OR
- ✓ was over the prescribed (alcohol) or specified (drugs) limit
- ✓ within eighteen hours of incident failed to provide specimen OR
- ✓ on being required failed to give permission to take specimen of blood

Meanings

Another person (see **10.8.1**)

Driving (see **10.1.4**)

Mechanically propelled vehicle (see **10.1.3**)

Road (s 192) (see **10.1.1**)

Public place (see **10.1.2**)

Without due care and attention or reasonable consideration (see **10.6.1**)

Unfit to drive

When the ability to drive properly is impaired.

Through drink or drugs (see **10.10**)

Exceeds the prescribed limit (alcohol) (see **10.11.1**)

Exceeds the specified limit (drugs) (see **10.11.2**)

Explanatory notes

- The careless or inconsiderate driving (see **10.6**) must be a cause of the death of another person, as must being under the influence of drink/drugs or failing to provide or give permission for a specimen.
- Section 3A(3) states that s 3A(1)(b), (ba), (c), and (d) do not apply to a mechanically propelled vehicle. They only apply to a motor vehicle (see **10.1.3**).
- It is not necessary for the intoxication to be a direct cause of the careless/inconsiderate driving.

- A person charged with this offence may be convicted of the alternative driving offences of careless and inconsiderate (see **10.6**), unfit through drink/drugs (see **10.10**), excess alcohol in breath/blood/urine (see **10.11.1**), while over the specified (drugs) limit in blood/urine (see **10.11.2**), or failing to provide a specimen (see **10.11.3**).

Defences (see **10.6.1**)

Defence notes (see 10.6.1)

Related case

R v Twigg [2019] EWCA Crim 1553 It was held that evidence of a blood sample was admissible even though it had been obtained unlawfully. The trial judge had been entitled not to exclude the evidence under s 78 of PACE where the defendant had lied about whether drugs had been taken.

Practical considerations

- Consider CPS driving offences charging standards.
- As with all fatal RTCs, protect and prevent contamination of the scene. Seize the vehicle as it may be forfeited.

E&S

Indictment

None

Life imprisonment and/or a fine

Obligatory disqualification until extended test passed

Obligatory endorsement—3 to 11 penalty points

10.8.3 Causing death by driving: disqualified driver

Section 3ZC of the Road Traffic Act 1988 provides for the offence of causing the death of another person by driving a motor vehicle on a road while at the time disqualified from driving.

Offences

A person is guilty of an offence under this section if he or she—

(a) causes the death of another person by driving a motor vehicle on a road, and

(b) at that time, is committing an offence under section 103(1)(b) of this Act (driving while disqualified).

Road Traffic Act 1988, s 3ZC

PNLD H12083

Points to prove

✓ caused the death of another person
✓ by driving a motor vehicle
✓ on a road
✓ whilst disqualified

Meanings

Another person (see **10.8.1**)

Driving (see **10.1.4**)

Motor vehicle (see **10.1.3**)

Road (s 192) (see **10.1.1**)

Explanatory note

- This offence is subject to a fatal RTC and committing an offence under s 103(1)(b) driving whilst disqualified (see **10.13.1**). It has effect only in relation to driving which occurs on or after 13 April 2015.

Practical considerations

- Consider CPS driving offences charging standards.
- Protect and prevent contamination of the scene. Consider CCTV, if available.
- This offence requires some element of fault by the driver that they caused the death of another person (*R v Hughes* [2013] UKSC 56, see **10.8.5**), not just driving a motor vehicle whilst disqualified.
- Annex A of MOJ Circular 1/2015 provides guidance on this matter.

E&S

Indictment

None

10 years' imprisonment and/or a fine

Obligatory disqualification until extended test passed

Obligatory endorsement—3 to 11 penalty points

10.8.4 Causing death by careless, or inconsiderate, driving

Section 2B of the Road Traffic Act 1988 provides for the offence of causing death by careless, or inconsiderate, driving.

Offences

A person who causes the death of another person by driving a mechanically propelled vehicle on a road or other public place without due care and attention, or without reasonable consideration for other persons using the road or place is guilty of an offence.

Road Traffic Act 1988, s 2B

PNLD H8562

Points to prove

✓ caused the death of another person
✓ by driving a mechanically propelled vehicle
✓ on a road/public place
✓ without due care and attention/reasonable consideration for others

Meanings

Another person (see **10.8.1**)

Driving (see **10.1.4**)

Mechanically propelled vehicle (see **10.1.3**)

Road (s 192) (see **10.1.1**)

Public place (see **10.1.2**)

Without due care and attention or reasonable consideration (see **10.6.1**)

Explanatory notes (see 10.6.1)

Defences (see 10.6.1)

Practical considerations (see also 10.6.1 and 10.8.2)

- This section may be an alternative verdict to an offence under:
  - ✦ s 1 (causing death by dangerous driving—see **10.8.1**);
  - ✦ s 3A (causing death by driving without due care when under the influence—see **10.8.2**).

- Ensure compliance with the law in relation to reporting RTCs (see **10.9**).

E&S

Either way

None

Summary: 6/12 months' imprisonment and/or a fine

Obligatory disqualification and obligatory endorsement with 3 to 11 penalty points

Indictment: 5 years' imprisonment and/or a fine

Obligatory disqualification and obligatory endorsement with 3 to 11 penalty points

10.8.5 Causing death by driving: no insurance or licence

Section 3ZB of the Road Traffic Act 1988 provides for the offence of causing the death of another person by driving a motor vehicle on a road otherwise than in accordance with a licence, or without insurance.

Offences

A person is guilty of an offence under this section if he causes the death of another person by driving a motor vehicle on a road and, at the time when he is driving, the circumstances are such that he is committing an offence under—

(a) section 87(1) of this Act (driving otherwise than in accordance with a licence), . . . , or

(c) section 143 of this Act (using motor vehicle while uninsured or unsecured against third party risks).

Road Traffic Act 1988, s 3ZB(a) and (c)

PNLD H8674

Points to prove

✓ caused the death of another person
✓ by driving a motor vehicle
✓ on a road
✓ without driving licence/insurance

Meanings

Another person (see **10.8.1**)

Driving (see **10.1.4**)

Motor vehicle (see **10.1.3**)

Road (s 192) (see **10.1.1**)

Explanatory notes

This offence is subject to a fatal RTC by **causing** the death by their driving and committing an offence under:

- s 87(1)—Driving otherwise than in accordance with a licence (see 10.14.1); or
- s 143—Using motor vehicle without insurance (see **10.16.1**).

Related case

R v Hughes [2013] UKSC 56 The s 3ZB offence requires at least some act or omission in respect of the control of the car. The act/omission must involve some element of fault, whether amounting to s 3 driving or not, and must contribute in more than a minimal way to the death but does not necessarily have to be the principal cause of death.

Practical considerations

- Consider CPS driving offences charging standards.
- Consider powers of seizure and removal under s 165A (see **10.16.6**).
- This offence requires some element of fault by the driver (*R v Hughes* [2013] UKSC 56) of causing the death.

E&S

Either way None

Summary: 6/12 months' imprisonment and/or a fine

Obligatory disqualification and obligatory endorsement with 3 to 11 penalty points

Indictment: 2 years' imprisonment and/or a fine

Obligatory disqualification and obligatory endorsement with 3 to 11 penalty points

10.9 Road Traffic Collisions

Section 170 of the Road Traffic Act 1988 imposes duties on the driver of a mechanically propelled vehicle involved in certain RTCs on a road or other public place.

10.9.1 Incidents to which applicable

Collisions which apply

If owing to the presence of a mechanically propelled vehicle on a road or other public place, an accident occurs by which—

(a) personal injury is caused to a person other than the driver of that mechanically propelled vehicle, or

(b) damage is caused—

  (i) to a vehicle other than that mechanically propelled vehicle or a trailer drawn by that mechanically propelled vehicle, or

  (ii) to an animal other than an animal in or on that mechanically propelled vehicle or a trailer drawn by that mechanically propelled vehicle, or

  (iii) to any other property constructed on, fixed to, growing in or otherwise forming part of the land on which the road or place in question is situated or land adjacent to such land.

Road Traffic Act 1988, s 170(1)

Meanings

Mechanically propelled vehicle (see **10.1.3**)

Road (s 192) (see **10.1.1**)

Public place (see **10.1.2**)

Accident

This is an unintended occurrence having an adverse physical result.

Injury

Includes any actual bodily harm and may well include nervous shock.

Driver (see **10.1.4**)

Animal

Means horse, cattle, ass, mule, sheep, pig, goat, or dog.

Practical considerations

- There must be some link between the presence of the vehicle and the occurrence of the accident.
- 'Vehicle', in respect of the other vehicle damaged, may include a pedal cycle.
- If attending a potential fatal RTC, see **10.8**.

10.9.2 **Duties of driver after accident**

Offences

(2) The driver of the mechanically propelled vehicle must stop and, if required to do so by any person having reasonable grounds for so requiring, give his name and address and also the name and address of the owner and the identification marks of the vehicle.

(3) If for any reason the driver of the mechanically propelled vehicle does not give his name and address under subsection (2) above, he must report the accident.

(4) A person who fails to comply with subsection (2) or (3) above is guilty of an offence.

Road Traffic Act 1988, s 170

PNLD H102, H103, H105

Points to prove

✓ being the driver of a mechanically propelled vehicle
✓ involved in a road traffic accident
✓ failed to stop AND
✓ on being requested by a person having grounds to do so
✓ failed to provide details, as required

Meanings

Driver (see **10.1.4**)

Mechanically propelled vehicle (see **10.1.3**)

Accident (see **10.9.1**)

Explanatory notes

- If the driver does not stop immediately, they must do so as soon as it is safe and convenient to do so.
- If personal injury is involved and the vehicle is a motor vehicle and the driver does not, at the time of the collision, produce evidence of insurance to a constable or some person having reasonable grounds

for requiring them to do so, they must report the collision and produce such evidence (see **10.9.3**).
- After stopping, the driver must remain there long enough to enable them, if required, to furnish the relevant information.

Related cases

DPP v Hay [2005] EWHC 1395 (Admin) The defendant was driving a vehicle involved in an accident and was taken to hospital without exchanging details or reporting the collision to the police and, subsequently, failed to report the accident after being discharged. It was held that the defendant failed to comply with s 170 even though the police observed the collision.

DPP v McCarthy [1999] RTR 323, DC The requirement to give a name and address has a wider meaning than just the driver's home address. An address needs to be somewhere where a person can be contacted.

Practical considerations

- The driver does not commit this offence if they are unaware that the RTC has occurred.
- These two subsections create two separate offences (failing to stop and give information **and** failing to report). Therefore, the driver may be charged with either one or both. A further offence may be committed in a s 170(1)(a) injury accident where the driver fails to comply with s 170(5) (see **10.9.3**).
- The scene of the RTC is the place in the road or public place where the collision occurs.

Summary　　6 months

6 months' imprisonment and/or a fine not exceeding level 5

Discretionary disqualification and obligatory endorsement with 5 to 10 penalty points

10.9.3 Duty of driver to report the incident

Section 170 provides for the obligation and a subsequent offence where a reportable RTC occurs.

Offences

(5) If, in a case where this section applies by virtue of subsection (1)(a) above [*injury*, see **10.9.1**], the driver of a motor vehicle does not at the time of the accident produce such a certificate of insurance or security, or other evidence, as is mentioned in section 165(2)(a) of this Act—

(a) to a constable, or

(b) to some person who, having reasonable grounds for so doing, has required him to produce it,

the driver must report the accident and produce such a certificate or other evidence.

(7) A person who fails to comply with a duty under subsection (5) above is guilty of an offence.

Road Traffic Act 1988, s 170

PNLD H3131

Points to prove

✓ being driver of a motor vehicle
✓ involved in a relevant road traffic accident
✓ did not at the time of the accident
✓ produce to a constable/person with grounds for requiring
✓ relevant evidence of insurance OR
✓ failed to report the accident and produce relevant insurance

Meanings

Driver (see **10.1.4**)

Motor vehicle (see **10.1.3**)

Accident (see **10.9.1**)

Insurance/security (see **10.16.1**)

For s 165(2)(a) (see **10.16.5**)

Explanatory notes

- To comply with the requirement to produce the relevant proof of insurance, s 170(6) states that the driver must do so at a police station or to a constable, which must be done as soon as is reasonably practicable and, in any case, within twenty-four hours of it occurring.

10.9.3 **Duty of driver to report the incident**

- A person will not be convicted of this offence only because they failed to produce the relevant insurance document if, within seven days following the accident, it is produced at a police station specified by them at the time they reported the accident.
- The obligation to report the accident includes where there is nobody else about to whom the driver can give the details (eg damage to street furnishings).

Practical considerations

- Note that whereas s 170(2) and (3) create offences in relation to a mechanically propelled vehicle, this offence is in relation to the use of a motor vehicle.
- This requirement does not apply to an invalid carriage.
- 'At a police station' means the motorist should report it in person at a police station or to a constable; a report by telephone will not suffice.

Summary

6 months

Fine not exceeding level 3

Discretionary disqualification and obligatory endorsement with 5 to 10 penalty points

10.10 Drive/Attempt to Drive/ in Charge of Vehicle While Unfit through Drink/Drugs

10.10.1 Drive while unfit drink/drugs

Section 4 of the Road Traffic Act 1988 provides for the offences of driving, attempting to drive, and being in charge of a mechanically propelled vehicle on a road or public place while unfit through drink or drugs.

Offences

(1) A person who, when driving or attempting to drive a mechanically propelled vehicle on a road or other public place, is unfit to drive through drink or drugs is guilty of an offence.

(2) Without prejudice to subsection (1) above, a person who, when in charge of a mechanically propelled vehicle which is on a road or other public place, is unfit to drive through drink or drugs is guilty of an offence.

Road Traffic Act 1988, s 4

PNLD H15, H19, H26, H42, H43, H44

Points to prove

s 4(1) offence

✓ drove/attempted to drive
✓ a mechanically propelled vehicle
✓ on a road/other public place
✓ when unfit to drive through drink/drugs

s 4(2) offence

✓ in charge of a mechanically propelled vehicle
✓ on a road/public place
✓ being unfit to drive through drink/drugs

Meanings

Driving (see 10.1.4)

Mechanically propelled vehicle (see 10.1.3)

Road (s 192) (see 10.1.1)

Public place (see 10.1.2)

In charge

There is no legislation or test for what constitutes 'in charge' for the purposes of being in charge of a vehicle under s 4, s 5, or s 5A (see **10.11**), but a close connection between the defendant and control of the vehicle is required.

Explanatory notes

- A person is **unfit to drive** properly if their ability is for the time being impaired.
- It needs to be ascertained whether the person is in charge of the vehicle by virtue of being the owner, lawful possessor, or recent driver.
- Factors that need to be considered in establishing whether the person was in charge include:
  - ✦ Who is the registered keeper of the vehicle; who is insured to drive it; where were the other insured drivers (if any)?
  - ✦ What were their immediate and future intended movements?
  - ✦ If away from their home/accommodation, how did they propose to return without driving?
  - ✦ How had the vehicle got to where it was; when did they last drive it; are they in possession of a key which fits the ignition?
  - ✦ What was their position in relation to the car; were they in the vehicle; if not how far away were they?
  - ✦ Was anyone else in or around the vehicle; what were they doing at the relevant time?
  - ✦ Is there evidence of an intention to take control of the vehicle?
  - ✦ When and where had they been drinking; time of last drink; what had they been doing since then?
- The evidence of a doctor who examines the defendant at the request of the police is admissible even if they had to persuade the defendant to allow the examination.

Defences

For the purposes of subsection (2) above, a person shall be deemed not to have been in charge of a mechanically propelled vehicle if he proves that at the material time the circumstances were such that there was no likelihood of his driving it so long as he remained unfit to drive through drink or drugs.

Road Traffic Act 1988, s 4(3)

Defence notes

- In the case of *Sheldrake v DPP (A-G's Reference No 4 of 2002)* [2005] 1 Cr App R 28, it was held that the burden of proof should remain on the defendant, to be decided on the balance of probabilities. This imposition did not contravene the presumption of innocence and was compatible with the ECHR.

- The court, in determining whether there was a likelihood of a person driving whilst still unfit through drink or drugs, should disregard any injury to them and any damage to the vehicle (ie it is not the practical possibility of the person being able to drive the vehicle that is relevant here, but rather the possibility of that person driving at all while still impaired).

Practical considerations

- A charge under this section, which uses both the alternatives of 'drink or drugs', is not bad for duplicity.
- The CPS is unlikely to take the case forward unless there is evidence that the suspect was likely to drive whilst under the influence of drink/drugs. Similarly, if in charge, ensure that the s 4(3) defence can be countered if raised.
- This section applies to trolley vehicles operated under statutory powers but not to tramcars.
- An indictment containing a charge under s 1 of the Road Traffic Act 1988 (see **10.8**) should not include a charge under this section as this section is triable summarily only.
- A non-expert witness may give evidence of the defendant's condition but not of their fitness to drive.

E&S

Summary | 6 months

s 4(1) offence
6 months' imprisonment and/or a fine

Obligatory disqualification

Obligatory endorsement—3 to 11 penalty points

s 4(2) offence
3 months' imprisonment and/or a level 4 fine
Discretionary disqualification, obligatory endorsement—10 penalty points

10.10.2 **Preliminary test powers**

Section 6 of the Road Traffic Act 1988 provides for the requiring of preliminary tests for alcohol, impairment, or drugs to drivers of motor vehicles. Sections 6A to 6C relate to the specific tests, whilst s 6D provides a power of arrest and s 6E a power of entry.

Offences

A person commits an offence if without reasonable excuse he fails to cooperate with a preliminary test in pursuance of a requirement imposed under this section.

Road Traffic Act 1988, s 6(6)

PNLD H5623

Points to prove

✓ without reasonable excuse
✓ failed to cooperate with a preliminary test
✓ when required under this section

Meanings

Fails

Fail includes refuse.

Preliminary test

This refers to any of the tests described in ss 6A to 6C and means a preliminary test of breath/impairment or for drugs.

Hospital

An institution which provides medical or surgical treatment for in-patients or out-patients.

Requirements

Under s 6(1)–(5), a constable may require a person to cooperate with any one or more preliminary tests administered to them by that constable or another constable, if the constable reasonably suspects that:

- they are driving, attempting to drive, or are in charge of a motor vehicle on a road or other public place and have alcohol or a drug in their body or are under the influence of a drug; **or**
- they had been driving, attempting to drive, or in charge of a motor vehicle on a road or other public place while having alcohol or a drug in their body, or while unfit to drive because of a drug, and still have alcohol or a drug in their body or are still under the influence of a drug; **or**
- they are or have been driving, attempting to drive, or in charge of a motor vehicle on a road or other public place and have committed a **traffic offence** while the vehicle was in motion; or
- an accident has occurred owing to the presence of a motor vehicle on a road or other public place and a constable reasonably believes that they were driving, attempting to drive, or in charge of the vehicle at the time of the accident.

Traffic offence

Means an offence under the Public Passenger Vehicles Act 1981, Part 2 (ss 6 to 29); Road Traffic Regulation Act 1984; Road Traffic Offenders Act 1988 (except Part 3—fixed penalties); or Road Traffic Act 1988 (except Part 5—driving instruction).

Explanatory notes

- Only a constable in uniform may administer a preliminary test, except if it relates to an accident under s 6(5).
- A preliminary breath test (s 6A) is a procedure by which the person taking the test provides a specimen of breath (using a device approved by the Secretary of State) to ascertain whether the proportion of alcohol in their breath or blood is likely to exceed the prescribed limit.
- For a preliminary impairment test (s 6B), the constable requesting it observes the person taking it performing tasks specified by the constable and makes any observations of the person's physical state as they think are expedient. The constable shall have regard to the code of practice issued by the Secretary of State which governs preliminary impairment tests.
- For a preliminary drug test (s 6C), a specimen of sweat or saliva is obtained (using a device approved by the Secretary of State) to ascertain whether the person tested has a drug in their body; if so, whether it is a specified controlled drug; if it is, whether the proportion of it in their blood or urine is likely to exceed the specified limit for that drug. Up to three preliminary drug tests may be administered at or near the place where the test requirement is imposed or if expedient at a specified police station.
- A person will not be required at random to provide a specimen of breath for a breath test.
- An asthma sufferer who is incapable of providing a sample has a duty to inform the officer requiring it.
- A person who refuses (without good cause) to take a test is deemed to have failed to take it.
- Section 9 of the Road Traffic Act 1988 provides procedures for taking breath tests or blood or urine specimens from patients in hospitals.

Power of arrest

(1) A constable may arrest a person without warrant if as a result of a preliminary breath test or preliminary drug test the constable reasonably suspects that—

(a) the proportion of alcohol in that person's breath or blood exceeds the prescribed limit, or

(b) the person has a specified controlled drug in his body and the proportion of it in the person's blood or urine exceeds the specified limit for that drug.

> (2) A constable may arrest a person without warrant if—
> (a) the person fails to co-operate with a preliminary test in pursuance of a requirement imposed under s 6, and
> (b) the constable reasonably suspects that the person has alcohol or a drug in his body or is under the influence of a drug.
>
> Road Traffic Act 1988, s 6D

> **Power of entry (after injury accident)**
>
> A constable may enter any place (using reasonable force if necessary) for the purpose of—
> (a) imposing a requirement by virtue of section 6(5) following an accident in a case where the constable reasonably suspects that the accident involved injury of any person, or
> (b) arresting a person under section 6D following an accident in a case where the constable reasonably suspects that the accident involved injury of any person.
>
> Road Traffic Act 1988, s 6E(1)

Related cases

DPP v Wilson [2009] EWHC 1988 (Admin) The defendant provided a positive breath test at hospital following an RTC and was arrested. The doctor consented to blood being taken and the result confirmed that the defendant was OPL. It was argued that the arrest was unlawful per s 6D(3) and, consequently, the blood result could not be used as evidence. It was held that the fact that an arrest is prohibited does not prevent the blood and breath test procedures; provided they are taken in accordance with statutory requirements, they remain valid.

Gearing v DPP [2008] EWHC 1695 (Admin) There is clear conflict between s 58 of PACE as to consulting a solicitor and requirements under the 1988 Act. What is important is the public interest of evidential testing as soon as possible with safeguards accompanying the procedure itself.

Hollingsworth v Howard [1974] RTR 58 In this case, a motorist had been injured in an accident. On the way to hospital in an ambulance, a constable requested a breath test which was positive. It was held that in this case the constable's discretion justified the ambulance breath test which had not been made 'at a hospital' and accordingly the driver should be convicted (see ss 6 and 6A of the Road Traffic Act 1988).

Practical considerations

- A constable can arrest a person under s 6D(1A) if specimens of breath have been provided under s 7 (see **10.11.3**) and the constable imposing the requirement has reasonable cause to believe that the approved device used for analysis did not produce a reliable result.

- A preliminary breath test requested because a constable suspects that a person has alcohol or a drug in their body or is under the influence of a drug may only be given at or near the place where it is requested.
- Following an RTC, a preliminary breath, impairment, or drugs test may be given at or near the place where it is requested or, if the constable requesting it thinks it expedient, at a police station specified by them.
- Only a constable approved by their chief officer may give a preliminary impairment test, which must satisfy the codes of practice.
- A person arrested under the above powers may, instead of being taken to a police station, be detained at or near the place where the preliminary test was, or would have been, administered, to impose a requirement there under s 7 on them (see **10.11.3**).
- A person may not be arrested under s 6D(3) while at a hospital as a patient.
- A constable may enter any place (by reasonable force if necessary) to impose a requirement by virtue of an RTC having occurred, or to arrest a person under s 6D following an RTC, where they reasonably suspect that such RTC involved injury to a person.
- If a motorist supplies enough breath for the device to give a reading, they cannot be said to have failed to cooperate.
- Evidential specimens can be obtained at the roadside.

E&S

Summary

6 months

Level 3 fine

Discretionary disqualification, obligatory endorsement—4 penalty points

10.11 Drive/Attempt to Drive/in Charge While Over the Prescribed/Specified Limit

10.11.1 Drive motor vehicle while over the prescribed (alcohol) limit

Section 5 of the Road Traffic Act 1988 provides the offences of driving, attempting to drive, and being in charge of a motor vehicle on a road or public place while over the prescribed limit of alcohol in blood, breath, or urine.

Offences

If a person—
(a) drives or attempts to drive a motor vehicle on a road or other public place, or
(b) is in charge of a motor vehicle on a road or other public place,
after consuming so much alcohol that the proportion of it in his breath, blood or urine exceeds the prescribed limit he is guilty of an offence.

Road Traffic Act 1988, s 5(1)

PNLD H21, H25, H34

Points to prove

- ✓ drove/attempted to drive/in charge of motor vehicle
- ✓ on a road/public place
- ✓ proportion of alcohol in blood/breath/urine exceeded prescribed limit

Meanings

Drive (see 10.1.4)

Motor vehicle (see 10.1.3)

Road (s 192) (see 10.1.1)

Public place (see 10.1.2)

In charge (see 10.10.1)

Consuming

With regard to alcohol primarily means by mouth but can include other means of ingesting it into the blood, breath, or urine.

Prescribed limit

For driving offences, the limits are:
- 35 microgrammes of alcohol in 100 millilitres of breath;
- 80 milligrammes of alcohol in 100 millilitres of blood;
- 107 milligrammes of alcohol in 100 millilitres of urine.

Power of arrest (see **10.10.2**)

Explanatory notes

- Be aware of the powers to administer a preliminary breath test (see **10.10.2**).
- Being so hopelessly drunk that a person is incapable of driving a motor vehicle is not a defence to this offence.
- If the offence is under s 5(1)(b), then it needs to be ascertained whether the person is in charge of the vehicle (see '**Explanatory notes**', **10.10.1**).
- Evidence of the proportion of alcohol at the time of driving other than that provided by the specimen is admissible.
- Where it is established that the defendant was driving and has given a positive sample, it is assumed that the amount of alcohol at the time of the alleged offence is not less than the specimen provided.

Defence—being in charge

It is a defence for a person charged with an offence under subsection (1)(b) above to prove that at the time he is alleged to have committed the offence the circumstances were such that there was no likelihood of his driving the vehicle whilst the proportion of alcohol in his breath, blood or urine remained likely to exceed the prescribed limit.

Road Traffic Act 1988, s 5(2)

Defence notes (see also 10.10.1)

- The burden of proof is on the defendant.
- In determining whether there was any likelihood of them driving, the court may ignore any injury to them or damage to the vehicle.

Related cases (see also 10.1.4 and 10.10 cases)

Croitoru v CPS [2016] EWHC 1645 (Admin) The rider of a mechanically propelled invalid carriage was charged and convicted with the s 5 offence. The carriage was exempt from being classified as a motor vehicle under s 20 of the Chronically Sick and Disabled Persons Act

1970, however, drunk driving was not included in these exemptions so the conviction was upheld.

CPS v Thompson [2007] EWHC 1841 (Admin) The police found the defendant asleep and intoxicated in a car but they stated that there was no intention of driving. The defendant was arrested and a subsequent breath sample showed over the prescribed limit. The defendant was acquitted but the prosecution appealed. It was held that by merely focusing on the evidence given by the defendant (no intention of driving until they felt alright) the court had failed to focus sufficiently on the wording of s 5(2) when considering whether the defendant had satisfied the defence. The court's conclusion that the defendant had no intention of driving at the time they got into the vehicle, or when the police had awoken them, did not meet the statutory test and s 5(2) is not primarily concerned with the person's intentions.

DPP v Mullally [2006] EWHC 3448 (Admin) The defendant, acting in fear for a sister who had been assaulted, drove a car to the sister's house while over the prescribed limit and then called the police. When the police arrived, the defendant drove away. Once a defence of duress is raised, the burden of proof rests upon the prosecution to dispel the evidence. The court must consider:

- Were they forced to act as they did because of a genuine belief that death or serious injury would result if they had not acted in that manner?
- Would a sober person of reasonable firmness have been forced into acting in the same way?

The court held in this case that the defendant had a genuine fear but the response to that genuine fear had not been reasonable and they had not been entitled to drive away after the police had arrived at the sister's house.

DPP v Janman [2004] EWHC 101 (Admin) An individual supervising a learner driver was in charge of a motor vehicle for the purposes of drink driving legislation and would be convicted under s 5 of the Road Traffic Act 1988.

Kennedy v DPP [2002] EWHC 2297 (Admin) Where the matter under investigation was a suspected offence contrary to s 5, public interest required that the obtaining of the breath specimen part of the investigation could not be delayed to any significant extent in order to enable a suspect to take legal advice.

DPP v H [1997] 1 WLR 1406, QBD Insanity cannot be used as a defence against a s 5 offence as there is no requirement for any intent; the offence is one of strict liability.

Lafferty v DPP [1995] Crim LR 430, QBD In a claim that the intoximeter reading was inaccurate, the court may consider evidence of the roadside breath test.

DPP v Johnson (1994) 158 JP 891, QBD The 'consumption' of alcohol may be by injection.

Sharpe v DPP (1994) 158 JP, QBD If an officer is a trespasser at the time of the screening test it may invalidate the procedure.

DPP v Wilson [1991] Crim LR 441, QBD An officer is entitled to form an opinion that a driver has been drinking from information from an anonymous caller.

Practical considerations

- The CPS is unlikely to take the case forward unless there is evidence of a likelihood of driving whilst under the influence of drink or drugs. Similarly, if in charge, ensure that the s 5(2) defence can be countered if raised.
- A person acting as a supervisor of a provisional licence holder is 'in charge' of the vehicle and can commit that offence under this section.
- 'Lacing' a person's drink without their knowledge may constitute an offence of aiding and abetting the commission of an offence under this section if there is proof that the intent was to bring about the offence.
- Be aware of the 'Hip Flask Defence' (where the suspect claims to have had an alcoholic drink since driving but before providing a specimen). Ascertain the amount drunk and inform the laboratory so the appropriate calculations can be made.
- A power of entry is available for the provision of a preliminary test in cases which involve an injury accident. Reasonable force may be used to effect entry under s 6E or carry out a preliminary test and arrest a person under s 6D (see **10.10.2**).

Summary 6 months

s 5(1)(a) offence
6 months' imprisonment and/or a fine not exceeding level 5 on the standard scale

Obligatory disqualification, obligatory endorsement—3 to 11 penalty points

s 5(1)(b) offence
3 months' imprisonment and/or a level 4 fine

Discretionary disqualification, obligatory endorsement—10 penalty points

10.11.2 Drive motor vehicle while over the specified (drugs) limit

Section 5A of the Road Traffic Act 1988 provides the offences of driving, attempting to drive, and being in charge of a motor vehicle on a road or public place while over the specified limit of a specified controlled drug in blood or urine.

Offences

(1) This section applies where a person ('D')—
  (a) drives or attempts to drive a motor vehicle on a road or other public place, or
  (b) is in charge of a motor vehicle on a road or other public place,
  and there is in D's body a specified controlled drug.
(2) D is guilty of an offence if the proportion of the drug in D's blood or urine exceeds the specified limit for that drug.

Road Traffic Act 1988, s 5A

PNLD H10926 to H10929

Points to prove

✓ drove/attempted to drive/in charge of motor vehicle
✓ on a road/public place
✓ proportion of specified controlled drug in blood/urine
✓ exceeded specified limit for that drug

Meanings

Drive (see **10.1.4**)

Motor vehicle (see **10.1.3**)

Road (s 192) (see **10.1.1**)

Public place (see **10.1.2**)

In charge (see **10.10.1**)

Specified

Means specified in regulations made by the Secretary of State.

Controlled drug (see **5.1.1**)

Specified controlled drug/limit

The Drug Driving (Specified Limits) Regulations 2014, reg 2 (SI 2868/2014) provides for the limits for various drugs.

Explanatory notes

- Officers can screen for specified drugs at the roadside by using an approved device under s 6C (see **10.10.2**).
- If the offence is under s 5A(1)(b), then it needs to be ascertained whether the person is in charge of the vehicle (see '**Explanatory notes**', **10.10.1**).

- The s 5A offence makes it easier for police to detect and prosecute drug-drivers, being an offence to drive/attempt to drive or being in charge while over the limit for drugs (as specified), as it is for drink driving over the prescribed limit (see **10.11.1**).
- There is no requirement to provide proof of impairment for this offence. Under s 5A(2), the defendant is guilty of the offence if the proportion of the drug in their blood or urine exceeds the specified limit for that drug.

Power of arrest (see 10.10.2)

Defences

(3) It is a defence for a person ('D') charged with an offence under this section to show that—
  (a) the specified controlled drug had been prescribed or supplied to D for medical or dental purposes,
  (b) D took the drug in accordance with any directions given by the person by whom the drug was prescribed or supplied, and with any accompanying instructions (so far as consistent with any such directions) given by the manufacturer or distributor of the drug, and
  (c) D's possession of the drug immediately before taking it was not unlawful under section 5(1) of the Misuse of Drugs Act 1971 (restriction of possession of controlled drugs) because of an exemption in regulations made under section 7 of that Act (authorisation of activities otherwise unlawful under foregoing provisions).

(4) The defence in subsection (3) is not available if D's actions were—
  (a) contrary to any advice, given by the person by whom the drug was prescribed or supplied, about the amount of time that should elapse between taking the drug and driving a motor vehicle, or
  (b) contrary to any accompanying instructions about that matter (so far as consistent with any such advice) given by the manufacturer or distributor of the drug.

(5) If evidence is adduced that is sufficient to raise an issue with respect to the defence in subsection (3), the court must assume that the defence is satisfied unless the prosecution proves beyond reasonable doubt that it is not.

(6) It is a defence for a person ('D') charged with an offence by virtue of subsection (1)(b) to prove that at the time D is alleged to have committed the offence the circumstances were such that there was no likelihood of D driving the vehicle whilst the proportion of the specified controlled drug in D's blood or urine remained likely to exceed the specified limit for that drug.

(7) The court may, in determining whether there was such a likelihood, disregard any injury to D and any damage to the vehicle.

Road Traffic Act 1988, s 5A

10.11.2 **Over the specified (drugs) limit**

Defence notes (see also **10.10.1**)

- The burden of proof is on the defendant to show that the drug had been prescribed or supplied to them for medical or dental purposes, was taken as directed, and they complied with the accompanying instructions; but this defence is not available if their actions were contrary to the advice or instructions given.
- If there is sufficient evidence to show a valid defence under s 5A(3), then the prosecution would have to prove beyond reasonable doubt that this is not the case.
- It is a defence for a person charged with the s 5A(1)(b) offence that the circumstances were such that there was no likelihood of them driving the vehicle whilst over the specified limit for that drug. In determining whether there was any likelihood of them driving, the court may ignore any injury to them or damage to the vehicle.

Related cases (see **10.1.4**, **10.10**, and **10.11** cases)

Practical considerations

- The CPS is unlikely to take the case forward unless there is evidence of a likelihood of driving whilst under the influence of drink or drugs. Similarly, ensure that the s 5A(3)–(7) defences are considered and can be countered if raised.
- A person acting as a supervisor of a provisional licence holder is 'in charge' of the vehicle and can commit that offence under this section.
- The s 5A offence will work alongside the existing s 4 offence (see **10.10.1**) of being unfit through drink or drugs, which will continue to be used for drugs which are not specified controlled or prescribed drugs.
- Limits are set at very low levels for the illegal drugs including cocaine, cannabis, ecstasy, and ketamine; while some legally prescribed drugs, including Diazepam and methadone, are included as certain strong medication can affect people's ability to drive safely.
- As s 5A sets limits for specified legal drugs, it is vital that anyone taking prescribed medication reads the instructions carefully and keeps to the prescribed dosage. If anyone is unsure as to whether their medication affects their ability to drive, they should obtain advice from a doctor or pharmacist.
- A power of entry is available for the provision of a preliminary test in cases involving an injury accident. Reasonable force may be used to effect entry under s 6E or carry out a preliminary test and arrest a person under s 6D (see **10.10.2**).

Summary

6 months

s 5A(1)(a) offence

51 weeks' imprisonment and/or a level 5 fine

Obligatory disqualification, obligatory endorsement—3 to 11 penalty points

s 5A(1)(b) offence

51 weeks' imprisonment and/or a level 4 fine

Discretionary disqualification, obligatory endorsement—10 penalty points

10.11.3 **Provision of specimens for analysis**

Section 7 of the Road Traffic Act 1988 deals with the provision of evidential specimens and s 7A details the provisions in relation to the taking of specimens of blood from persons incapable of consenting.

Offences

A person who, without reasonable excuse, fails to provide a specimen when required to do so in pursuance of this section is guilty of an offence.

Road Traffic Act 1988, s 7(6)

PNLD H10942, H10974

Points to prove

- ✓ without reasonable excuse
- ✓ failed/refused to provide specimen
- ✓ when lawfully required to do so

Meanings

Fails (see **10.10.2**)

Specimen

Specimens taken under s 7 may consist of two specimens of breath for analysis by an approved device (alcohol) or a specimen of blood or urine for laboratory analysis (alcohol or drugs).

Explanatory notes

Specimens may be required from a person suspected of having committed an offence under:

- s 3A—Causing death by careless driving when under influence of drink or drugs (see **10.8.2**);
- s 4—Driving, attempting to drive, or being in charge, when under influence of drink or drugs (see **10.10.1**);
- s 5—Driving, attempting to drive, or being in charge of a motor vehicle with alcohol concentration above prescribed limit (see **10.11.1**);
- s 5A—Driving, attempting to drive, or being in charge of a motor vehicle with specified controlled drug being over specified limit (see **10.11.2**).

Related cases

Miller v DPP [2018] EWHC 262 (Admin) The defendant was a person who had learning difficulties and was autistic, and for whom appropriate adults had been called on in the past. On this occasion, **no** appropriate adult had been requested. The defendant refused to provide a specimen and was charged and convicted of the s 7 offence. On appeal, the case was returned to the magistrates' court to acquit.

DPP v Camp [2017] EWHC 3119 (Admin) Self-induced intoxication does not amount to a reasonable excuse for failing to provide a specimen of breath for analysis under s 7(6) of the Road Traffic Act 1988.

CPS v Chalupa [2009] EWHC 3082 (Admin) Only in exceptional circumstances (where a solicitor is readily available) could a breath test be delayed allowing an individual to take legal advice as there is a public interest requirement that a test be undertaken promptly.

DPP v Baldwin [2000] RTR 314, QBD The purpose of the requirement to provide a specimen of urine one hour after the first specimen is to give the motorist a finite time. If this period is extended, that extension does not make any findings inadmissible.

DPP v Furby [2000] RTR 181, QBD A medical condition of which a person is unaware cannot later be used as an excuse for failing to provide the required sample.

R v Epping Justices, ex parte Quy [1998] RTR 158 A conviction for driving with excess alcohol in the defendant's breath was quashed when a fear of needles was capable of amounting to a medical reason.

Francis v DPP [1997] RTR 113, QBD A request can be legitimately made of a mentally unstable person if they understand what is happening. (However, note the case of **Miller v DPP** above.)

Hague v DPP [1997] RTR 146, QBD Breath samples were taken on an intoximeter machine. The officer believed the machine to be faulty and requested blood or urine, which was refused. The machine was examined and found to be working correctly so the readings were still admissible.

DPP v Coyle [1996] RTR 287, CA It is not necessary to wait for the intoximeter machine to 'time out' before a suspect's refusal or failure to give a sample of breath will be complete.

DPP v Wythe [1996] RTR 137, QBD If a medical reason is put forward by the suspect, the final decision as to whether blood can be taken is for the doctor.

Wade v DPP [1996] RTR 177, QBD A defendant on medication may have a medical reason for not providing a specimen of blood.

DPP v Garrett [1995] RTR 302, QBD Where the blood sample procedure was flawed, but the sample was not taken and used, it did not affect the request for a urine sample.

DPP v Nesbitt and Duffy [1995] 1 Cr App R 38 Where a request for blood or urine is made at a hospital, the required warnings must explain the procedures in full, with reasons, and state the consequences of failing to comply.

DPP v Smith, The Times, 1 June 1994, QBD A defendant cannot insist that blood should be taken by their own GP.

Practical considerations

- On requiring a person to provide a specimen under this section, a constable **must** warn them that failure to provide it may render them liable to prosecution.
- A requirement for a specimen of breath can only be made at a police station, a hospital, or at or near a place where a relevant breath test has been given to the person concerned or would have been so given but for their failure to cooperate.
- Section 9 of the Road Traffic Act 1988 states that while a person is at a hospital as a patient they shall not be required to cooperate with a preliminary test or to provide a specimen under s 7 of this Act unless the medical practitioner in immediate charge of their case has been notified of the proposal to make the requirement, and:
  - ◆ if the requirement is then made, it shall be for cooperation with a test administered or for the provision of a specimen at the hospital; but
  - ◆ if the medical practitioner objects on the ground specified in subsection (2), the requirement shall not be made.
- The constable requiring the breath sample must be in uniform or have imposed a requirement on the defendant to cooperate with a breath test as a result of an accident.
- Where a requirement has been imposed for a person to cooperate with a relevant breath test at any place, the constable may remain at or near there to impose a requirement under this section.
- If a requirement is made for two samples of breath for analysis by an approved device at a place other than a police station, it may revert to being made at a police station if a device or reliable device is not available there, or it is not practicable to use one there, or the constable making the previous requirement believes that the device has not produced a reliable result.
- Under this section, a requirement for a specimen of blood or urine can only be made at a police station or a hospital (for the definition of a hospital, see **10.10.2**).

10.11.3 **Provision of specimens for analysis**

- A requirement for a sample of blood or urine can be made at a police station unless: the constable requiring it believes that for medical reasons it cannot or should not be made; specimens of breath have not been provided elsewhere and an approved device is not available there; an approved device has been used but the constable believes the result to be unreliable; the constable believes, following a preliminary drugs test, that the defendant has a drug in their body; or, if the offence is under s 3A, 4, or 5A of the Act and the constable has been informed by a medical practitioner that the person's condition might be due to some drug.
- The above requirement may be made even if the defendant has been required to supply two specimens of breath.
- If a specimen other than breath is required, the question as to whether it is blood or urine (and, if it is blood, who will take it) will be decided by the constable making the requirement.
- If a medical or health care practitioner thinks that, for medical reasons, blood cannot or should not be taken the requirement will not be made. A urine sample may then be required instead.
- A specimen of urine must be provided within an hour of its being required and after the provision of a previous such specimen.
- In cases involving a failure to provide breath, consider retaining the mouthpiece as a possible exhibit.
- If a person is involved in a traffic accident and their medical condition prevents them from giving consent, then s 7A(1) allows taking a blood specimen from that person—providing blood could have been requested under s 7.
- If blood has been taken by a 'police medical or health care practitioner' under s 7A(1), then under s 7A(5) a constable must require the person to give permission for a laboratory test of the blood specimen taken, and warn that failure to give this permission may render them liable to prosecution under s 7A(6).
- **Section 7A(6) offence**—a person who, without reasonable excuse, fails to give their permission for a laboratory test of a specimen of blood taken from them under this section is guilty of a summary offence.

Summary 6 months

Failing to provide specimen for analysis—vehicle driver

6 months' imprisonment and/or a fine not exceeding level 5

Obligatory disqualification, obligatory endorsement—3 to 11 penalty points

Fail to provide specimen—person in charge of vehicle

3 months' imprisonment and/or a level 4 fine

Discretionary disqualification, obligatory endorsement—10 penalty points

10.12 **Pedal Cycle Offences**

Sections 28, 29, and 30 of the Road Traffic Act 1988 provide similar offences for cyclists to those contained in ss 1, 2, and 3 for motorists. Additionally, there is the offence of driving or cycling on a footpath under s 72 of the Highways Act 1835.

10.12.1 **Dangerous cycling**

Section 28 creates an offence of dangerous cycling on a road.

> **Offences**
>
> A person who rides a cycle on a road dangerously is guilty of an offence.
>
> Road Traffic Act 1988, s 28(1)

PNLD H3388

> **Points to prove**
>
> ✓ rode a cycle
> ✓ on a road
> ✓ dangerously

Meanings

Cycle

Means a bicycle, a tricycle, or a cycle having four or more wheels, not being in any case a motor vehicle.

Road (s 192) (see **10.1.1**)

Dangerously

A person is to be regarded as riding dangerously if and only if:
- the way that they ride falls far below what would be expected of a competent and careful cyclist; **and**
- it would be obvious to a competent and careful cyclist that riding in that way would be dangerous.

Explanatory notes

- The term 'danger' refers to danger either of injury to any person or of serious damage to property.
- To determine what would be obvious to a competent and careful cyclist in a particular case, regard shall be had not only to the

circumstances of which they could be expected to be aware but also to any shown to have been within their knowledge.
- A person may be convicted of the alternative offence of careless, and inconsiderate, cycling (see **10.12.2**).

Practical considerations

- NIP to be issued (see **10.5**).
- This offence must be on a road—it does not extend to a public place.
- Section 168 empowers obtaining of the cyclist's name and address (see **10.6.2**).
- Section 163 of the Road Traffic Act 1988 empowers a police constable in uniform to stop a cycle on a road. A person who fails to stop the cycle will be guilty of an offence (see **10.2.3**).
- Where a cyclist persistently causes anti-social behaviour, consider provisions under the Anti-social Behaviour, Crime and Policing Act 2014 for injunctions, criminal behaviour orders, dispersal powers, and public spaces protection orders (see **7.13**).

NIP

Summary

6 months

Level 4 fine

10.12.2 Careless, and inconsiderate, cycling

Section 29 creates an offence of cycling on a road without due care and attention or without reasonable consideration for other road users.

Offences

If a person rides a cycle on a road without due care and attention, or without reasonable consideration for other persons using the road, he is guilty of an offence.

Road Traffic Act 1988, s 29

PNLD H2511, H3011

Points to prove

✓ rode a cycle
✓ on a road
✓ without due care and attention/reasonable consideration for other road users

Meanings

Cycle (see 10.12.1)

Road (s 192) (see 10.1.1)

Without due care and attention

Means that their cycling falls below the level of care, skill, and attention that would have been exercised by a competent and careful cyclist.

Without reasonable consideration

Requires other persons to be inconvenienced by the defendant's cycling.

Practical considerations (see 10.12.1)

Summary

6 months

Level 3 fine

10.12.3 Cycling when under the influence of drink or drugs

Section 30 creates an offence of cycling on a road or public place while unfit through drink or drugs.

> **Offences**
>
> A person who, when riding a cycle on a road or other public place, is unfit to ride through drink or drugs (that is to say, is under the influence of drink or a drug to such an extent as to be incapable of having proper control of the cycle) is guilty of an offence.
>
> Road Traffic Act 1988, s 30(1)

PNLD H3013

Points to prove

- ✓ rode a cycle
- ✓ on a road/other public place
- ✓ while unfit to ride through drink/drugs

Meanings

Road (s 192) (see 10.1.1)

Public place (see 10.1.2)

Practical considerations

- As there is no power to require a specimen of breath, blood, or urine, other methods of calculating the extent to which the defendant is under the influence of drink or drugs need to be used.
- Section 163 of the Road Traffic Act 1988 empowers a police constable in uniform to stop a cycle on a road. A person who fails to stop the cycle will be guilty of an offence (see **10.12.1**).
- This offence does not extend to being in charge of a cycle as it would with other forms of transport.
- A bicycle or tricycle is a carriage under the Licensing Act 1872. Therefore, consider the offence of being drunk in charge of a carriage on any highway or other public place under s 12 of that Act (see **7.2.2**).

Summary

6 months

Level 3 fine

10.12.4 Riding or driving on the footpath

Section 72 of the Highways Act 1835 creates an offence of wilfully riding or driving on the footpath.

Offences

If any person shall wilfully ride upon any footpath or causeway by the side of any road, made or set apart for the use or accommodation of foot passengers; or shall wilfully lead or drive any horse, ass, sheep, mule, swine, cattle or carriage of any description, or any truck or sledge, upon any such footpath or causeway or tether any horse, ass, mule, swine or cattle on any highway so as to suffer or permit the tethered animal to be thereon, he shall be guilty of an offence.

Highways Act 1835, s 72

PNLD H4105

Points to prove

✓ wilfully rode/drove/led/tethered
✓ carriage of any description, truck, sledge, or animal (as described)
✓ upon a footpath/causeway
✓ by the side of a road
✓ made/set apart
✓ for the use/accommodation of foot passengers

Meanings

Wilfully

'Wilful' under this section means 'purposely'.

Footpath

A footpath is part of a highway if it is beside a road.

Carriage of any description

This includes bicycles, tricycles, motor vehicles, and trailers.

Explanatory notes

- Section 72 applies not only to the riding of bicycles or tricycles on the footpath/causeway but also to the riding/driving of motor vehicles/trailers/truck/sledge and leading/tethering any animals as described.
- A Segway is a 'carriage' for the purposes of s 72 (*Coates v CPS* [2011] EWHC 2032 (Admin)).
- This offence requires proof of wilfully riding, driving a carriage, or leading/tethering animals as specified.
- Proceedings may be instituted by anyone.
- Consider issuing a TFPN for driving or cycling on the footway (see **10.4.1**).

TFPN

Summary

6 months

Level 2 fine

10.13 Driving While Disqualified/Cause Serious Injury

10.13.1 Obtain licence/drive on a road—while disqualified

Section 103 of the Road Traffic Act 1988 creates the offences of obtaining a driving licence while disqualified from driving and driving a motor vehicle on a road while so disqualified.

Offences

A person is guilty of an offence if, while disqualified for holding or obtaining a licence, he—
(a) obtains a licence, or
(b) drives a motor vehicle on a road.

Road Traffic Act 1988, s 103(1)

PNLD H66, H3258

Points to prove

✓ while disqualified for holding/obtaining a licence
✓ obtained a licence/drove a motor vehicle on a road

Meanings

Disqualified

Means disqualified for holding or obtaining a licence and, where the disqualification relates only to vehicles of a particular class, a licence to drive vehicles of that particular class.

Licence (see **10.14.1**)

Drives (see **10.1.4**)

Motor vehicle

This is defined by s 185 (see **10.1.3**).

Road (s 192) (see **10.1.1**)

Explanatory notes

- An under-age driver (unless disqualified by the court) should be charged with the offence of 'driving otherwise than in accordance with a licence' (see **10.14.1**).
- Subsection (1)(b) does not apply to a person disqualified for obtaining a licence authorising them to drive a motor vehicle of a specific class while they hold another licence to drive that class of vehicle.
- Such a person is disqualified for obtaining such a licence even if the licence held is suspended (s 102).
- Disqualification given in England and Wales applies to all of GB, even if the defendant holds a foreign or international driving licence or permit or service driving licence.
- A driver disqualified in a foreign country would not be guilty of this offence but may be guilty of driving without a licence.
- Disqualification by a court is usually for a specified period as punishment for a road traffic offence.
- If penalty points imposed by the court, together with any to be taken into account on that occasion, total twelve or more (the 'totting up' system) the court must, other than in exceptional circumstances, disqualify the defendant for at least a **minimum period** (Road Traffic Offenders Act 1988, s 35).
- **Minimum period** is six months if no previous disqualification, one year if one such period is to be taken into account, and two years if two or more such periods are taken into account.
- The court may order a driver to be disqualified until they pass a driving test. Such driver may not drive during the disqualification period; after this period, they can only drive on a provisional licence. Thereafter, if they fail to comply with the provisional licence conditions they may be guilty of driving whilst disqualified. Disqualification will only come to an end after they have passed the driving test.

Related cases (see also **10.1.4** cases)

Pattison v DPP [2005] EWHC 2938 (Admin) The prosecution must prove that the defendant was a disqualified driver. Identification of the defendant as the person convicted in court may be established by admission, fingerprints, or by a person in court at time of conviction.

DPP v Barker [2004] EWHC 2502 (Admin) If a person was disqualified until they had passed a driving test, the burden of proof was on the driver to show that they had a provisional licence and were driving in accordance with the licence conditions.

Practical considerations

- This offence is committed only if the defendant drives a motor vehicle of a class that is subject to the disqualification, although a disqualification by order of the court will not normally be limited to a particular class of vehicle.
- A licence obtained by a disqualified person is not valid.
- Proving beyond reasonable doubt that the person named on the certified court extract is the accused is an essential element of the prosecution case, although there is no prescribed way in which identity must be proved.
- Proof that the defendant knew of the disqualification is not necessary.
- A person is disqualified for holding or obtaining a licence to drive a certain class of motor vehicle if they are under the age stipulated for that class (s 101), but the offence would be contrary to s 87(1) (see **10.14.1**).

Summary

Normally 6 months but no more than 3 years after the offence

s 103(1)(a) offence

Level 3 fine

s 103(1)(b) offence

6 months' imprisonment and/or a fine not exceeding level 5

Discretionary disqualification, obligatory endorsement—6 penalty points

10.13.2 Causing serious injury by driving: disqualified driver

Section 3ZD of the Road Traffic Act 1988 provides for the offence of causing the serious injury of another person by driving a motor vehicle on a road and at the time being disqualified from driving.

Offences

(1) A person is guilty of an offence under this section if he or she—
- (a) causes serious injury to another person by driving a motor vehicle on a road and,
- (b) at that time, is committing an offence under section 103(1)(b) of this Act (driving while disqualified).

Road Traffic Act 1988, s 3ZD

PNLD H12084

Points to prove

✓ caused the serious injury of another person
✓ by driving a motor vehicle
✓ on a road
✓ whilst disqualified

Meanings

Physical harm which amounts to grievous bodily harm (see **2.3.1**)

Another person (see **10.8.1**)

Driving (see **10.1.4**)

Motor vehicle (see **10.1.3**)

Road (s 192) (see **10.1.1**)

Explanatory note

- This offence is subject to driving a motor vehicle on a road and **causing** serious injury to another person whilst disqualified from driving under s 103(1)(b) (see **10.13.1**). It has effect only in relation to driving which occurs on or after 13 April 2015.

Practical considerations

- Consider CPS driving offences charging standards.
- Consider drive disqualification offence matters (see **10.13.1**).
- This offence requires some element of fault by the driver for causing the death of another person (*R v Hughes* [2013] UKSC 56; see **10.8.5**), not just driving a motor vehicle whilst disqualified.
- Annex A of MOJ Circular 1/2015 provides further guidance on this offence.

Summary None

Summary: 6/12 months' imprisonment and/or a fine

Obligatory disqualification

Obligatory endorsement—3 to 11 penalty points

Indictment: 4 years' imprisonment and/or a fine

Obligatory disqualification

Obligatory endorsement—3 to 11 penalty points

10.14 Driving Not in Accordance with a Driving Licence

Section 87 of the Road Traffic Act 1988 requires all people driving a motor vehicle on a road to hold a driving licence for that class of vehicle and to comply with any conditions attached to it.

10.14.1 Drive motor vehicle of a class not authorised

Offences

(1) It is an offence for a person to drive on a road a motor vehicle of any class otherwise than in accordance with a licence authorising him to drive a motor vehicle of that class.

(2) It is an offence for a person to cause or permit another person to drive on a road a motor vehicle of any class otherwise than in accordance with a licence authorising that other person to drive a motor vehicle of that class.

Road Traffic Act 1988, s 87

PNLD H31, H7223, H7224, H9420

Points to prove

s 87(1) offence

✓ drove motor vehicle
✓ on a road
✓ otherwise than in accordance with licence
✓ authorising driving of that class of vehicle

s 87(2) offence

✓ caused/permitted
✓ another person to commit s 87(1) offence

Meanings

Drive (see 10.1.4)

Road (s 192) (see 10.1.1)

Motor vehicle (see 10.1.3)

Cause

Means involving some degree of control or dominance by or some express mandate from the causer. It also requires some positive action and knowledge by the defendant (*Price v Cromack* [1975] 1 WLR 988).

Permit

Is less direct or explicit than 'causing' and involves leave or licence to do something. Permission can be express or inferred. A person cannot permit a vehicle to be used unless they are in a position to forbid and no one can permit what they cannot control.

Licence

Means a licence to drive a motor vehicle under Part 3 of the Road Traffic Act 1988 or a community licence.

Community licence

Means a document issued by an EEA state by authority of the EEA state authorising the holder to drive a motor vehicle.

Full licence

Means a licence other than a **provisional licence**.

Provisional licence

Means a licence issued to enable an applicant to drive motor vehicles with a view to passing a test of competence to drive.

Explanatory notes

- The holder of a Convention driving permit, a domestic driving licence/permit issued by a country outside the UK, or a British Forces driving permit who is resident outside the UK may drive any class of vehicle specified in the permit or licence for twelve months.
- A person who is an EU citizen and holds a driving licence or permit issued in another EU country may drive on that licence or permit in this country in accordance with that licence or permit. They would not need to exchange the licence or permit for a UK licence no matter how long they stayed here. A person could drive in GB for only twelve months if they got their EU licence by exchanging a non-EU licence.
- Under s 88, a person who has held a driver's licence, a Community licence, a Northern Ireland licence, a British external licence, a British Forces licence, or an exchangeable licence may, in certain circumstances, still drive a relevant vehicle even if the licence and its counterpart have been surrendered or revoked. This includes where a qualifying application has been received at DVLA or their licence to drive that class of vehicle and its counterpart has been revoked or surrendered for renewal; was granted in or contains an error; or for

amendment of a requirement or the holder's name and address. A new reg 80A has been included in the Motor Vehicles (Driving Licences) Regulations 1999. It provides that individuals who have entry clearance or permission to stay under the Appendix Ukraine Scheme to the Immigration Rules (Ukraine Family Scheme, Homes for Ukraine Sponsorship Scheme, and Ukraine Extension Scheme), and are holders of licences issued in Ukraine authorising the driving of a vehicle of a class included in category A (motorcycle) and category B (car), are authorised to drive such vehicles on their Ukrainian driving licence in GB for up to three years after becoming resident.

- A new reg 80B has been included in the Motor Vehicles (Driving Licences) Regulations 1999. It applies to individuals who become resident in GB and who are holders of an EEA licence which had been issued in exchange for a licence or a Northern Ireland licence that was issued on or after 1 January 2021 authorising the driving of any class of motor vehicle. These individuals are authorised, after becoming resident, to rely on their EEA licence to drive in GB any class of motor vehicle as authorised by their EEA licence, for as long as they are authorised to do so by their EEA licence.

Practical considerations

- Where a person is charged with driving without a licence, the burden of proving that they have a licence is with that person (*John v Humphreys* [1955] 1 All ER 793, QBD).
- The police have powers to seize and remove a motor vehicle if the driver has no driving licence or there is no insurance in force for the vehicle (see **10.16.6**).
- It is an offence for a person not to produce their driving licence (see **10.16.4**).
- A TFPN can be issued for the s 87(1) offence (see **10.4**).
- This offence includes circumstances where the driver is driving under age.
- The classes of vehicles which a licence holder is authorised by it to drive are stated on the licence itself.
- A licence is valid only when it is used in accordance with its conditions of use.

TFPN

Summary

6 months

s 87(1) offence

Level 3 fine. Discretionary disqualification, obligatory endorsement—3 to 6 penalty points

s 87(2) offence

Level 3 fine

10.15 Drive with Defective Eyesight

Section 96 of the Road Traffic Act 1988 creates an offence of driving with defective eyesight.

Offences

Drive with uncorrected defective eyesight

(1) If a person drives a motor vehicle on a road while his eyesight is such (whether through a defect which cannot be or one which is not for the time being sufficiently corrected) that he cannot comply with any requirement as to eyesight prescribed under this Part of this Act for the purposes of tests of competence to drive, he is guilty of an offence.

Refuse to submit to eyesight test

(2) A constable having reason to suspect that a person driving a motor vehicle may be guilty of an offence under subsection (1) above may require him to submit to a test for the purpose of ascertaining whether, using no other means of correction than he used at the time of driving, he can comply with the requirement concerned.

(3) If that person refuses to submit to the test he is guilty of an offence.

Road Traffic Act 1988, s 96

PNLD H3028, H17087

Points to prove

s 96(1) offence

✓ drove a motor vehicle
✓ on a road
✓ while unable to meet eyesight requirements

s 96(3) offence

✓ being the driver of a motor vehicle
✓ on a road
✓ and being required to take eyesight test
✓ by a constable under s 96(2)
✓ refused to take such test

Meanings

Drives (see **10.1.4**)

Motor vehicle (see **10.1.3**)

Road (s 192) (see **10.1.1**)

Explanatory notes

- This section creates two offences:
    - ✦ driving with defective eyesight;
    - ✦ refusing to submit to an eyesight test.
- The **requirement** as to **eyesight prescribed** can be found in reg 72 of the Motor Vehicles (Driving Licences) Regulations 1999. This requires a person to be able to read, in good light (with visual aids if used), a number plate on a vehicle containing characters of the **prescribed size**.
- **Prescribed size** means characters which are 79 mm high and 50 mm wide.
- The distance from which the number plate should be read is 20 metres, but for a category K vehicle (eg mowing machine and pedestrian-controlled vehicle) it is 12 metres.
- Spectacles or contact lenses may be used for the test if they were wearing them while driving.
- For the purposes of this offence, it does not matter whether the defect is one that can be corrected or not. The important matter is the state of the defendant's eyesight at the time they were driving.
- Knowledge of the defect by the defendant is not necessary, although this may be used in mitigation if the defendant has suffered a gradual and unnoticed deterioration in their eyesight.
- However, under s 92(1) any person holding or applying for a licence has a duty to inform the DVLA of any prescribed disability likely to cause the driving of a vehicle by them in accordance with the licence to be a source of danger to the public. This includes a 'prospective' disability such as a condition that does not at the time amount to a relevant disability but which is likely to deteriorate to that level in the course of time.

Practical considerations

- The degree by which the defendant's eyesight fails to meet the requirement is particularly relevant as this will reflect the degree of risk taken or danger created by them.
- The more severe the defect, the more difficult it will be for the defendant to mitigate the offence.
- Depending on the problem the person has with their eyesight, they may be under a legal obligation to inform the DVLA under the provisions of s 92(1).

Summary

6 months

Level 3 fine

Discretionary disqualification, obligatory endorsement—
3 penalty points

10.16 Vehicle Document Offences and Seizure of Vehicles

10.16.1 No insurance (use, cause, or permit)

Section 143 of the Road Traffic Act 1988 requires the user of a motor vehicle to be insured or secured against third party risks.

Offences

(1) Subject to the provisions of this Part of this Act—
   (a) a person must not use a motor vehicle on a road or other public place unless there is in force in relation to the use of the vehicle by that person such a policy of insurance or such a security in respect of third party risks as complies with the requirements of this Part of this Act, and
   (b) a person must not cause or permit any other person to use a motor vehicle on a road or other public place unless there is in force in relation to the use of the vehicle by that other person such a policy of insurance or such a security in respect of third party risks as complies with the requirements of this Part of this Act.

(2) If a person acts in contravention of subsection (1) above he is guilty of an offence.

Road Traffic Act 1988, s 143

PNLD H33, H47, H48

Points to prove

✓ used/caused/permitted another to use
✓ motor vehicle
✓ on a road/public place
✓ without insurance/security for third party risks

Meanings

Use

Means the driver of a vehicle, the driver's employer while it is being used for their business, the vehicle owner if they are in it while somebody else is driving it, or the steersman of a broken-down vehicle which is being towed.

10.16.1 **No insurance (use, cause, or permit)**

Motor vehicle (see **10.1.3**)

Road (s 192) (see **10.1.1**)

Public place (see **10.1.2**)

Policy of insurance

This includes a cover note.

Security

This section does not apply to a vehicle owned by a person who has deposited and keeps deposited with the Accountant General of the Senior Courts the sum of £500,000 at a time when the vehicle is being driven under the owner's control.

Cause (see **10.14.1**)

Permit (see **10.14.1**)

Explanatory notes

- This section does not apply to invalid carriages.
- Section 144 states that s 143 does not apply to:
  - ✦ a vehicle owned by a county or county district council, Broads Authority, City of London Common/Borough Council, National Park Authority, Inner London Education Authority, London Fire and Emergency Planning Authority, joint (local government) waste authorities, or a joint authority, or a joint board or committee which includes member representatives of such council—at a time when the vehicle is being driven under the owner's control;
  - ✦ a vehicle owned by a local policing body when it is being driven under the owner's control, or a vehicle being driven for police purposes by or under the direction of a constable, by civilian staff of a police force or a member of staff of the police and crime commissioner's/Mayor's office (within the meaning of Part 1 of the Police Reform and Social Responsibility Act 2011);
  - ✦ a vehicle being driven to or from a place for the purposes of salvage under the Merchant Shipping Act 1995;
  - ✦ a vehicle owned by a health service body or Local Health Board—at a time when the vehicle is being driven under the owner's control;
  - ✦ an ambulance owned by an NHS Trust or Foundation Trust at a time when the vehicle is being driven under the owner's control;
  - ✦ a vehicle made available to a person, body, or local authority under s 12 or s 80 of the National Health Service Act 2006 (s 10 or s 38 of the National Health Service (Wales) Act 2006) while being used in accordance with the terms under which it was made available;
  - ✦ a vehicle owned by the Care Quality Commission, at a time when the vehicle is being driven under the owner's control.

- Section 144(2)(b), on its plain and ordinary meaning, exempts a police officer on duty using their own vehicle for police purposes from the requirement for third party insurance (*Jones v Chief Constable of Bedfordshire* [1987] RTR 332).

Defences

A person charged with using a motor vehicle in contravention of this section shall not be convicted if he proves—

(a) that the vehicle did not belong to him and was not in his possession under a contract of hiring or of loan,

(b) that he was using the vehicle in the course of his employment, and

(c) that he neither knew nor had reason to believe that there was not in force in relation to the vehicle such a policy of insurance or security as is mentioned in subsection (1) above.

Road Traffic Act 1988, s 143(3)

Related cases

DPP v Hay [2005] EWHC 1395 (Admin) It is for the defendant to show that there was in force a policy of insurance, once it has been proved that they used the motor vehicle on a road or public place.

Pumbien v Vines [1996] Crim LR 124, QBD A vehicle left on a road for several months, such that it could not be moved due to mechanical and/or brake faults, is still at the disposal of the owner and so requires insurance (and test certificate). This prevents, for example, an individual deliberately locking up the brakes to avoid their responsibilities.

Practical considerations

- Read the conditions on the insurance very carefully as they may, for example, cover a person who is not a current driving licence holder. Similarly, a valid insurance certificate may not cover that person for the vehicle being used or for that particular purpose.
- A TFPN for the s 143(1)(a) 'using' offence can be issued (see **10.4**).
- The policy must be issued by an authorised insurer (eg a member of the Motor Insurers' Bureau).
- It is an offence to fail to produce insurance (see **10.16.5**).
- The motor vehicle can be seized if no insurance is in force for the vehicle (see **10.16.6**).

TFPN s 143(1)(a) offence only

Summary 36 months

Fine not exceeding level 5

Discretionary disqualification, obligatory endorsement—6 to 8 penalty points

10.16.2 No insurance (registered keeper)

Section 144A makes it an offence to keep a registered vehicle which is not insured or secured against third party risks.

Offences

If a motor vehicle registered under the Vehicle Excise and Registration Act 1994 does not meet the insurance requirements, the person in whose name the vehicle is registered is guilty of an offence.

Road Traffic Act 1988, s 144A(1)

PNLD H8704

Points to prove

✓ person in whose name a motor vehicle is registered
✓ failed to ensure
✓ insurance requirements met for vehicle

Meanings

Motor vehicle (see **10.1.3**)

Registered

Means a vehicle registered with the Secretary of State under s 21 of the Vehicle Excise and Registration Act 1994.

Insurance requirements

A vehicle meets the insurance requirements if:

- covered by a **policy of insurance** or **security** in respect of third party risks as complies with the requirements of Part 6 of this Act; **and**
- **either** of the following conditions is satisfied:
  - ✦ **first condition** is that the policy or certificate of insurance or security identifies the vehicle by its registration mark as a vehicle covered by the policy or security;
  - ✦ **second condition** is that the vehicle is covered by the policy or security, which covers any vehicle, or vehicle of a particular description, the owner being named in that policy or certificate of insurance or security, and the vehicle is owned by that person.

Policy of insurance (see **10.16.1**)

Security (see **10.16.1**)

Explanatory notes

- For the purposes of this section, a vehicle is covered by a policy of insurance or security if the policy of insurance or security is in force in relation to the use of the vehicle.
- Section 144B provides exceptions for either the registered keeper or owner of the vehicle regarding the s 144A offence under the following conditions:
  - ✦ owns the vehicle and a security is in force or most of the exceptions to s 144 apply (see **10.16.1** 'Explanatory notes');
  - ✦ owns the vehicle with the intention that it should be used for the purposes of salvage under the Merchant Shipping Act 1995 or for NHS or social care purposes;
  - ✦ not keeping the vehicle, required details provided;
  - ✦ keeping the vehicle but not used on a road/public place, required details provided;
  - ✦ vehicle stolen before the relevant time, not recovered, and the theft reported as required;
  - ✦ keeping the vehicle, no VEL in force on or since 31 January 1998 and not used or kept on a road after that date.

Practical considerations

- The Motor Vehicles (Insurance Requirements) (Immobilisation, Removal and Disposal) Regulations 2011 (SI 1120/2011) provide for the immobilisation and/or removal of uninsured vehicles found stationary on roads and other public places.
- Sections 144A to 144D of this Act give DVLA and the MIB, which administers the Motor Insurance Database, powers to deal with registered keepers of vehicles that are taxed but not insured, through the introduction of Continuous Insurance Enforcement (CIE).
- Where a vehicle is taxed but uninsured, the MIB will issue an 'Insurance Advisory Letter' to the registered keeper advising them as follows:
  - ✦ if not insured, insure immediately;
  - ✦ if insured, contact insurance provider immediately to check that the Motor Insurance Database has been correctly updated;
  - ✦ send a SORN to DVLA so the vehicle is not included in CIE;
  - ✦ if they no longer have the vehicle, notify DVLA in writing.
- If the keeper fails to act and the vehicle remains taxed but not insured, DVLA will issue a £100 fixed penalty notice to the keeper (reduced to £50 if paid within twenty-one days).
- These sections only apply to GB (vehicles registered in Northern Ireland, Channel Islands, and Isle of Man are excluded as they have their own registration authorities).

10.16.3 **No test certificate**

TFPN

Summary

6 months

Level 3 fine

Fixed penalty ticket: £100

Note: A fixed penalty notice for this offence shall be treated as having been paid if the amount of £50 is paid before the end of the period of twenty-one days following the date the notice is given.

10.16.3 No test certificate

Section 47 creates an offence relating to motor vehicles over three years old being on a road without a valid test certificate in force, and s 53 creates a similar offence for goods vehicles over twelve months old.

Offences

Motor vehicle

A person who uses on a road at any time, or causes or permits to be so used, a motor vehicle to which this section applies, and as respects which no test certificate has been issued within the appropriate period before that time, is guilty of an offence.

Road Traffic Act 1988, s 47(1)

PNLD H35, H69, H70

Points to prove

- ✓ used/caused to use/permitted to use
- ✓ a motor vehicle to which s 47 applies
- ✓ on a road
- ✓ without a valid test certificate

Meanings

Uses (see **10.16.1**)

Road (see **10.1.1**)

Causes (see **10.14.1**)

Permits (see **10.14.1**)

Motor vehicles to which section 47 applies

Motor vehicles (see **10.1.3**) (not being goods vehicles) which have been registered under the Vehicles Excise and Registration Act 1994 for not less than three years or were manufactured at least three years ago and have been used on roads (whether in GB or elsewhere) before being so registered.

Appropriate period

Means a period of twelve months or shorter as may be prescribed.

Related case

Pumbien v Vines [1996] Crim LR 124, QBD (see **10.16.1**).

Practical considerations

- Vehicles exempted from a s 47 test certificate are vehicles:
  - being driven to a pre-arranged test;
  - being tested by an authorised examiner;
  - where a test certificate is refused, vehicles:
    - being driven from the test;
    - being delivered by pre-arranged delivery to or from a place where work is to be or has been done to remedy the defects;
    - delivering or towing to a place to be scrapped;
  - being removed under a statutory power;
  - being tested by a motor trader under a trade licence;
  - that are imported and that are being driven from entry port to the owner's residence;
  - detained/seized by police and HMRC;
  - exempt from testing by order under s 44 (see below).
- Vehicles exempted from testing are described in reg 6(1) of the Motor Vehicles (Tests) Regulations 1981, being: vehicles that are temporarily in GB (not exceeding twelve months); manufactured before 1 January 1960; proceeding to a port for export; used on a public road only to travel between land in occupation of the vehicle keeper not exceeding an aggregate of 6 miles per calendar week; provided for police purposes by a police authority and maintained in approved workshops; provided for NCA; heavy locomotive; light locomotive; motor tractor; track laying vehicle; goods vehicle exceeding 3,500 kg design gross weight (subject to goods vehicle testing); articulated vehicle not being an articulated bus; works truck; pedestrian-controlled vehicle; invalid carriage not exceeding 306 kg unladen weight (510 kg unladen weight if supplied by NHS); visiting forces' or imported Armed Forces' vehicles; current Northern Ireland test certificate; electrically propelled goods vehicle not exceeding 3,500 kg design gross weight; licensed hackney carriage or private hire car which undergoes testing by the local authority; agricultural motor vehicle; street cleansing, refuse, and gully cleaning vehicle

constructed and not merely adapted, being either a three-wheeled vehicle or maximum design speed of 20 mph, or inside track width less than 810 mm; tramcar and trolley vehicles.

- The date of manufacture is taken to be the last day of the year in which its final assembly is completed.
- Consider issuing a TFPN for a motor vehicle s 47 offence (see **10.4**).
- A TFPN **cannot** be issued for a goods vehicle, s 53 offence.

TFPN s 47(1) offence

Summary

6 months

s 47(1) offence

Level 3 fine. Level 4 if vehicle adapted to carry more than eight passengers

s 53(2) offence

Level 4 fine

10.16.4 Fail to produce driving licence

Section 164 empowers a constable or vehicle examiner to require production of a driving licence and a certificate of completion of a motorcycle course.

Offences

If a person required under the preceding provisions of this section to produce a licence or state his date of birth or to produce his certificate of completion of a training course for motorcyclists fails to do so he is, subject to subsections (7) to (8A) [see '**Defences**'], guilty of an offence.

Road Traffic Act 1988, s 164(6)

PNLD H38, H3269

Points to prove

✓ when required by a constable/vehicle examiner
✓ failed to state date of birth or produce driving licence, motorcycle training certificate

Meanings

Required to produce

Any of the following persons—

(a) driving a motor vehicle on a road,

(b) whom a police constable or vehicle examiner has reasonable cause to believe to have been the driver of a motor vehicle at a time when an accident occurred owing to its presence on a road,
(c) whom a constable or vehicle examiner has reasonable cause to believe to have committed an offence in relation to the use of a motor vehicle on a road, or
(d) a person—
  (i) who supervises the holder of a **provisional licence** while the holder is driving a motor vehicle on a road, or
  (ii) whom a constable or vehicle examiner has reasonable cause to believe was supervising the holder of a provisional licence while driving, at a time when an accident occurred owing to the presence of the vehicle on a road or at a time when an offence is suspected of having been committed by the holder of the provisional licence in relation to the use of the vehicle on a road,

must, on being so required by a constable or vehicle examiner, produce his licence for examination, so as to enable the constable or vehicle examiner to ascertain the name and address of the holder of the licence, the date of issue, and the authority by which they were issued.

Road Traffic Act 1988, s 164(1)

State date of birth (s 164(2))

A person required by a constable under s 164(1) to produce their licence must in **prescribed circumstances**, on being required by the constable, state their date of birth.

Prescribed circumstances

The circumstances in which a constable may require a person's date of birth are given in reg 83(1) of the Motor Vehicles (Driving Licences) Regulations 1999. Where the person:

- fails to produce their licence for immediate examination;
- produces a licence which the constable suspects was not granted to that person, was granted to them in error, or contains an alteration in particulars entered on the licence made with intent to deceive or where the driver number has been altered, removed, or defaced; or
- is a supervisor under s 164(1)(d) and the constable suspects they are under 21 years of age.

Provisional licence (see **10.14**)

Explanatory notes

Other preceding provisions for failing to produce offences under s 164(6) are:

- s 164(3): where a licence has been revoked by the Secretary of State, a constable may require its production and, if it is produced, may seize it and deliver it to the Secretary of State;

- s 164(4): if a constable reasonably believes that a licence holder, or any other person, has knowingly made a false statement to obtain a licence, they may require the holder to produce it to them;
- s 164(4A): where a provisional licence is produced by a motorcyclist and a constable reasonably believes that the holder was not riding the motorcycle as part of an approved training course, the constable may require production of their certificate of completion of a training course for motorcyclists;
- s 164(5): if a person has been required to produce their licence to a court and fails to do so, a constable may require them to produce it and, when it is produced, may seize it and deliver to the court.

Defences

(7) Subsection (6) [see '**Offences**'] above does not apply where a person required on any occasion under the proceeding provisions of this section to produce a licence—
  (a) produces on that occasion a current receipt for the licence issued under section 56 of the Road Traffic Offenders Act 1988 and, if required to do so, produces the licence in person immediately on its return at a police station that was specified on that occasion, or
  (b) within 7 days after that occasion produces such a receipt in person at a police station that was specified by him on that occasion and, if required to do so, produces the licence in person immediately on its return at a police station.

(8) In proceedings against any person for the offence of failing to produce a licence it shall be a defence for him to show that—
  (a) within 7 days after the production of his licence was required he produced it in person at a police station that was specified by him at the time its production was required, or
  (b) he produced it in person there as soon as was reasonably practicable, or
  (c) it was not reasonably practicable for him to produce it there before the day on which the proceedings were commenced.

(8A) Subsection (8) above shall apply in relation to a certificate of completion of a training course for motorcyclists as it applies in relation to a licence.

Road Traffic Act 1988, s 164

Practical considerations

- Since 8 June 2015, the driving licence paper counterpart has no longer been issued with driving licences. Endorsements will no longer be entered onto counterparts as they will be entered onto a person's electronic driving record maintained by the DVLA. GB licence holders will no longer be required to retain or produce the paper counterpart.

Summary

6 months

Level 3 fine

10.16.5 Fail to provide details or produce vehicle documents

Section 165 empowers a constable or vehicle examiner to require production of insurance and vehicle test documents.

Requirements

Any of the following persons—
(a) driving a motor vehicle (other than an invalid carriage) on a road, or
(b) whom a constable or vehicle examiner has reasonable cause to believe to have been the driver of a motor vehicle (other than an invalid carriage) at a time when an accident occurred owing to its presence on a road or other public place, or
(c) whom a constable or vehicle examiner has reasonable cause to believe to have committed an offence in relation to the use on a road of a motor vehicle (other than an invalid carriage),

must, on being so required by a constable or vehicle examiner, give his name and address and the name and address of the owner of the vehicle and produce the following documents for examination.

Road Traffic Act 1988, s 165(1)

Offences

Subject to subsection (4) [see '**Defences**'], a person who fails to comply with a requirement under subsection (1) is guilty of an offence.

Road Traffic Act 1988, s 165(3)

PNLD H46, H63, H64, H836, H837

Points to prove

- ✓ being a person falling under s 165(1)
- ✓ failed when required by a constable/vehicle examiner
- ✓ to give name and address or name and address of vehicle owner AND/OR
- ✓ produce for inspection a test certificate or goods vehicle test certificate or certificate of insurance or certificate of security

10.16.5 **Fail to provide details or produce vehicle documents**

Meanings

Owner

In relation to a vehicle which is the subject of a hiring agreement, this includes each party to the agreement.

Documents (s 165(2))

The documents specified in subsection (1) are:

- a relevant certificate of insurance or certificate of security;
- a test certificate required by s 47; and
- a plating certificate or goods vehicle test certificate required by s 53.

Explanatory notes

- Under s 165(5), a supervisor of a provisional licence holder must, on being required by a constable/vehicle examiner, give their name and address and the name and address of the owner of the vehicle.
- If the supervisor fails to comply with the name and address requirements, then under s 165(6) they will commit an offence.

Defences

A person shall not be convicted of an offence under subsection (3) by reason only of failure to produce any certificate or other evidence in proceedings against him for the offence if he shows that—

(a) within 7 days after the date on which the production of the certificate or other evidence was required it was produced at a police station that was specified by him at the time when its production was required, or

(b) it was produced there as soon as was reasonably practicable, or

(c) it was not reasonably practicable for it to be produced there before the day on which the proceedings were commenced,

and for the purposes of this subsection the laying of the information shall be treated as the commencement of the proceedings.

Road Traffic Act 1988, s 165(4)

Practical considerations

- In the above defence, the question of whether a defendant produced documents 'as soon as was reasonably practicable' will be a question of fact for the court to decide in each case.

Summary

6 months

Level 3 fine

10.16.6 Seize and remove motor vehicle (no insurance/driving licence)

Section 165A empowers a constable to seize and remove a motor vehicle which they believe is being used without a driving licence or insurance.

Powers

Seizure conditions

Under s 165A, a constable may seize a motor vehicle under this section if any of the following sections apply:

- s 164, on being required by a constable in uniform to produce their licence for examination (see **10.16.3**), a person fails to do so, and the constable reasonably believes that they are or were driving without a licence (see **10.14**);
- s 165, on being required by a constable in uniform to produce evidence of insurance, a person fails to do so (see **10.16.4**) and the constable reasonably believes that the vehicle was being driven without such insurance (see **10.16.1**);
- s 163, on being required by a constable in uniform to stop a vehicle, the driver fails to do so (see **10.2.3**) or fails to do so long enough for the constable to make appropriate enquiries, and the constable reasonably believes that they are or were driving without a licence or insurance.

Removal

The Road Traffic Act 1988 (Retention and Disposal of Seized Motor Vehicles) Regulations 2005, made under s 165B, specifically provide for the retention, safe keeping, and disposal by the police or persons authorised by them of vehicles seized under s 165A.

Explanatory notes

- Before seizing the motor vehicle, the driver or person appearing to be the driver must be warned of the consequences of failure to immediately produce their driving licence, or provide evidence of insurance, unless circumstances make it impracticable to give the warning.
- If the vehicle fails to stop or drives off and cannot be seized immediately, it may be seized at any time within twenty-four hours of the original incident.
- To seize the vehicle, a constable may enter any premises (except a private **dwelling house**) on which they reasonably believe the vehicle to be. If necessary, reasonable force may be used in the exercise of this power.
- A **dwelling house** does not include a garage or other structure occupied with the dwelling house or land belonging to it.

Related case

Pryor v CC of Greater Manchester Police [2011] EWCA Civ 749 In this case, the defendant lent their motor vehicle to another person with written authority. Although the other person's insurance policy allowed them to drive a car not owned by them (with consent of the owner), the police still seized the car under s 165A for no insurance as PNC showed no current keeper and no insurance in force. The defendant was awarded damages for wrongful interference with their car as the police had failed to establish grounds for seizure.

Practical considerations

- In this section, motor vehicle does not include an invalid carriage.
- A constable must be in uniform and may use reasonable force, if necessary, to exercise these powers.
- The police are under a duty to ensure the retention and safe keeping of a seized vehicle until it is released to the owner or otherwise disposed of under the 2005 Regulations (see '**Removal**' above).
- Regulation 4 of the 2005 Regulations states that when the vehicle is seized, a seizure notice shall be given to the driver of the seized vehicle unless the circumstances make it impracticable to do so. It also gives the procedure to follow in respect of seized vehicles. The Regulations have been amended to enable police officers to electronically serve notices of seizure or removal of vehicles.
- Where practicable, a seizure notice must be given to the registered keeper and the owner.

10.17 Seat Belts

Section 14 of the Road Traffic Act 1988 relates to the wearing of seat belts in motor vehicles by adults and s 15 by children.

10.17.1 Seat belts—adults

Section 14 empowers the Secretary of State to make regulations requiring, subject to such exemptions as may be prescribed, persons who are driving or riding in motor vehicles on a road to wear seat belts of such description as may be prescribed.

Offences

A person who drives or rides in a motor vehicle in contravention of regulations under this section is guilty of an offence; but notwithstanding any enactment or rule of law, no person other than the person actually committing the contravention is guilty of an offence by reason of the contravention.

Road Traffic Act 1988, s 14(3)

PNLD H9957, H9965, H9966

Points to prove

✓ drove/rode in a motor vehicle
✓ contravened regulations made under s 14

Meanings

Drives (see **10.1.4**)

Motor vehicle

Defined by s 185 (see **10.1.3**), **but** for s 14 or s 15(1) **does not include** a motorcycle (with or without a sidecar).

Exemptions

Regulation 6 of the above regulations gives exemptions from reg 5 requirements to:

- a person holding a medical certificate;
- a driver/passenger in a motor vehicle constructed or adapted for carrying goods, being on a journey which does not exceed 50 metres used for delivery or collection;
- a driver of a vehicle performing a manoeuvre including reversing;

- a qualified driver supervising a provisional licence holder who is performing a manoeuvre including reversing;
- a driving test examiner conducting a test of competence to drive and wearing a seat belt would endanger the examiner or any other person;
- a person driving or riding in a vehicle being used for fire and rescue authority, police, or NCA purposes, or for carrying a person in lawful custody;
- a person riding in a motor ambulance while they are providing medical attention or treatment to a patient which cannot be delayed;
- a driver of a licensed taxi used for seeking hire, answering a call for hire, or carrying a passenger for hire or a driver of a private hire vehicle used to carry a passenger for hire;
- a person riding in a vehicle used on trade plates to investigate or remedy a fault in the vehicle;
- a disabled person wearing a disabled person's belt;
- a person riding in a vehicle taking part in a procession organised by or on behalf of the Crown;
- a person driving a vehicle if the driver's seat is not provided with an adult belt;
- a person riding in the front/rear of a vehicle if no adult belt is available for them;
- a person riding in a small or large bus which is:
  - ✦ being used to provide a local service in a built-up area; or
  - ✦ constructed or adapted for the carriage of standing passengers and on which the operator permits standing.

Explanatory notes

- Regulation 47(1) of the Road Vehicles (Construction and Use) Regulations 1986 stipulates that seat belts are required to be fitted to a motor vehicle to which reg 46 applies.
- Regulation 46 applies to a motor vehicle which is not an **excepted vehicle** and includes:
  - ✦ a bus first used on or after 1 April 1982;
  - ✦ a wheeled motor car first used on or after 1 January 1965;
  - ✦ a three-wheeled motorcycle having an unladen weight exceeding 255 kg, first used on or after 1 September 1970;
  - ✦ a pedestrian-controlled vehicle;
  - ✦ a vehicle used on roads outside GB (being driven from the port of entry to the place of residence of the owner or driver.
- The holder of a medical certificate cannot rely on the reg 5 exception unless they produce the certificate to the constable at the time of being reported for summons, or produce it within seven days or as soon as practicable after being reported at a police station specified by them, or where it is not so produced it is not reasonably practicable to produce it there before the commencement of proceedings.

Practical considerations

- Consider issuing a TFPN for this offence (see **10.4**).
- Each passenger is responsible for wearing a seat belt and liable for the s 14(3) offence, except passengers under the age of 14 years (see **10.17.2**) where the responsibility is then with the driver.
- Regulation 5 above does not apply where there is no adult seat belt available in that part of the vehicle.

TFPN

Summary

6 months

Level 2 fine

10.17.2 Seat belts—children

Section 15 creates offences concerning the wearing of seat belts by children in motor vehicles.

Offences

Seated in front

(1) Except as provided by regulations, where a child under the age of 14 years is in the front of a motor vehicle, a person must not without reasonable excuse drive the vehicle on a road unless the child is wearing a seat belt in conformity with regulations.

(1A) Where—
- (a) a child is in the front of a motor vehicle other than a bus,
- (b) the child is in a rear-facing child restraining device, and
- (c) the passenger seat where the child is placed is protected by a front air bag,

a person must not without reasonable excuse drive the vehicle on a road unless the air bag is deactivated.

(2) It is an offence for a person to drive a motor vehicle in contravention of subsection (1) or (1A) above.

Seated in rear

(3) Except as provided by regulations, where—
- (a) a child under the age of three years is in the rear of a motor vehicle, or
- (b) a child of or over that age but under the age of fourteen years is in the rear of a motor vehicle and any seat belt is fitted in the rear of that vehicle,

a person must not without reasonable excuse drive the vehicle on a road unless the child is wearing a seat belt in conformity with regulations.

(3A) Except as provided by regulations, where—

(a) a child who is under the age of 12 years and less than 150 cm in height is in the rear of a passenger car,

(b) no seat belt is fitted in the rear of the passenger car, and

(c) a seat in the front of the passenger car is provided with a seat belt but is not occupied by any person,

a person must not without reasonable excuse drive the passenger car on a road.

(3) It is an offence for a person to drive a motor vehicle in contravention of subsection (3) or (3A) above.

Road Traffic Act 1988, s 15

PNLD H9958, H9964, H9967, H9968, H9969

Points to prove

s 15(2) offence (seated in front)

✓ without reasonable excuse
✓ drove a motor vehicle
✓ on a road
✓ child under 14 years
✓ in the front of the vehicle
✓ not wearing a seat belt OR
✓ in a rear-facing restraining device and front airbag not deactivated

s 15(4) offence (seated in rear)

✓ per first four points of s 15(2)
✓ in the rear of the vehicle
✓ a child under the age of 3 years OR aged 3 years to 13 years
✓ not wearing a fitted seat belt OR
✓ motor vehicle was a passenger car
✓ child under 12 years and less than 150 cm tall
✓ with no rear seat belt fitted and
✓ a front seat (with belt) was available

Meanings

Motor vehicle (see **10.17.1**)

Road (see **10.1.1**)

Seat belt

This includes any description of restraining device for a child.

Bus

Means a motor vehicle that:

- has at least four wheels;
- is constructed or adapted for the carriage of passengers;

- has more than eight seats in addition to the driver's seat; and
- has a maximum design speed exceeding 25 kilometres per hour.

Passenger car

Means a motor vehicle which:

- is constructed or adapted for use for the carriage of passengers and is not a goods vehicle;
- has no more than eight seats in addition to the driver's seat;
- has four or more wheels;
- has a maximum design speed exceeding 25 kilometres per hour; and
- has a **maximum laden weight** not exceeding 3.5 tonnes.

Maximum laden weight

In relation to a vehicle or combination of vehicles means:

- in respect of which a gross weight not to be exceeded in GB is specified in construction and use requirements, **that weight**;
- in respect of which **no such weight is specified** in construction and use requirements, the weight which the vehicle, or combination of vehicles, is designed or adapted not to exceed when in normal use and travelling on a road laden.

Regulations (seated in front)

Means the Motor Vehicles (Wearing of Seat Belts by Children in Front Seats) Regulations 1993. Regulation 5 describes the belt or restraint to be worn.

Small child

A child under the age of 12 years and under 135 cm in height.

Large child

Is a child who is not a small child.

Explanatory notes

- The concept of a small child and a large child has been added by the above regulations. This has resulted in the lowering of the height from 150 cm down to 135 cm for a small child. This only affects the type of restraint that a small child should wear.
- Sections 15(3) and 15(3A) rear seat prohibitions do not apply to:
  - ✦ a child for whom there is a medical certificate;
  - ✦ a small child aged **under 3 years** who is riding in a licensed taxi or licensed hire car if no appropriate seat belt is available for them in the front or rear of the vehicle;
  - ✦ a small child aged **3 years or more** who is riding in a licensed taxi, a licensed hire car, or a small bus and wearing an adult belt if an appropriate seat belt is not available for them in the front or rear of the vehicle;
  - ✦ a small child aged **3 years or more** who is wearing an adult belt and riding in a passenger car or light goods vehicle where the use

of child restraints by the child occupants of two seats in the rear of the vehicle prevents the use of an appropriate seat belt for that child and no appropriate seat belt is available for them in the front of the vehicle;
  - a small child riding in a vehicle being used for the purposes of the police, security, or emergency services to enable the proper performance of their duty;
  - a small child aged **3 years or more** who is wearing an adult belt and who, because of an unexpected necessity, is travelling a short distance in a passenger car or light goods vehicle in which no appropriate seat belt is available for them; or
  - a disabled child who is wearing a disabled person's belt or whose disability makes it impracticable to wear a seat belt where a disabled person's belt is unavailable to them.
- Prohibitions in s 15(1) do not apply to:
  - a small child aged **3 years or more** who is riding in a bus and is wearing an adult belt if an appropriate seat belt is not available for them in the front or rear of the vehicle;
  - a child for whom there is a medical certificate;
  - a disabled child who is wearing a disabled person's belt;
  - a child riding in a bus which is being used to provide a local service in a built-up area or which is constructed/adapted for the carriage of standing passengers and on which the operator permits standing; or
  - a large child if no appropriate seat belt is available for them in the front of the vehicle.
- The driver of a motor vehicle has the same opportunity to produce a medical certificate for a child not wearing a seat belt as an adult (see **10.17.1**).

Practical considerations

- Consider issuing a TFPN for this offence (see **10.4**).
- The seat belt must be appropriate for a child of a particular weight and height travelling in a particular vehicle.
- A seat is regarded as provided with child restraint if the child restraint is:
  - fixed in such a position that it can be worn by an occupier of that seat; or
  - elsewhere in or on the vehicle but could readily be fixed in such a position without the aid of tools and is not being worn by a child for whom it is appropriate and who is occupying another seat.
- A seat belt is considered appropriate in relation to:
  - **a small child**, if it is a child restraint of a description prescribed for their height and weight by reg 5;
  - **a large child**, if it is a child restraint of a description prescribed for their height and weight by reg 5 or an adult belt; or
  - a person aged 14 years or more, if it is an adult belt.
- In relation to ages and height, subject to exceptions/requirements:

- **a child aged under 3** must travel in front or rear in an appropriate baby/child seat:
  - an approved seat and selected according to weight;
  - where a rear-facing baby seat is in the front seat, the airbag has to be deactivated;
- **a child aged 3 to 11 and under 135 cm**, in rear using appropriate child seat, booster seat, or booster cushion;
- **a child aged 12 to 13 or under 12 but over 135 cm**, in front or rear using adult seat belt, if no suitable child restraint is available;
- **a child aged 14 and over**, adult regulations apply (see **10.17.1**).

TFPN

Summary

6 months

s 15(2) offence

Level 2 fine

s 15(4) offence

Level 2 fine

10.18 Motorcycle—No Crash Helmet/Eye Protectors

Section 16 of the Road Traffic Act 1988 empowers the Secretary of State to make regulations concerning the wearing of crash helmets by motorcyclists and an offence of breaching such regulations.

Offences

A person who drives or rides on a motor cycle in contravention of regulations under this section is guilty of an offence; but not withstanding any enactment or rule of law no person other than the person actually committing the contravention is guilty of an offence by reason of the contravention unless the person actually committing the contravention is a child under the age of 16 years.

Road Traffic Act 1988, s 16(4)

PNLD H110

Points to prove

✓ drove/rode on motorcycle
✓ contravened regulations under s 16

Meanings

Drives (see **10.1.4**)

Motorcycle

Means a **mechanically propelled vehicle**, not being an invalid carriage, having less than four wheels and the unladen weight does not exceed 410 kg.

Mechanically propelled vehicle (see **10.1.3**)

Regulations

Every person driving or riding (otherwise than in a sidecar) on a **motor bicycle** when on a **road** shall wear protective headgear (Motor Cycles (Protective Helmets) Regulations 1998, reg 4).

Road (see **10.1.1**)

Explanatory notes

- '**Motor bicycle**' means a two-wheeled **motorcycle**, whether or not having a sidecar attached, although where the distance measured between the centre of the area of contact with the road surface of any two wheels of a motorcycle is less than 460 mm, those wheels are counted as one wheel.

- This section does not include people riding in a sidecar or people of the Sikh religion while wearing a turban.
- A British Standards mark must be on the helmet.
- Regulation 4 does not apply to a mowing machine or if propelled by a person on foot.
- If the vehicle is being propelled by 'scooter' style (eg the rider sitting astride the machine and propelling it by pushing on the ground with their foot/feet), then a helmet should be worn.
- **Eye protectors offence**—Motor Cycles (Eye Protectors) Regulations 1999, reg 4 creates an offence under s 18(3) of not wearing approved eye protectors. Each person driving or riding on a motor bicycle (otherwise than in a sidecar) is required to wear eye protectors of a prescribed type.

Related case

DPP v Parker [2005] RTR 16 A motorcycle fitted with enhanced safety features (eg a roof) does not negate the requirement to wear protective headgear.

Practical considerations

- In general, the rider of a quad bike would not be required to wear a crash helmet.
- Consider issuing a TFPN for these offences (see **10.4**).
- Any helmet worn must be securely fastened using straps or other means of fastening provided.
- If the helmet has a chin cup, it must have an additional strap to fit under the jaw.
- Eye protectors/visors marked 'Daytime Use' or bearing a symbol of the same meaning should only be used in daytime.
- Visors that transmit less than 50 per cent of visible light cannot be legally used on the road.

TFPN

Summary 6 months

Level 2 fine

10.19 Improper Use of Trade Plates

The Vehicle Excise and Registration Act 1994 provides for the registration and excise duty payable in respect of motor vehicles. Section 34 relates to offences committed in relation to trade licences.

Offences

A person holding a trade licence or trade licences is guilty of an offence if he—

(a) uses at any one time on a public road a greater number of vehicles (not being vehicles for which vehicle licences are for the time being in force) than he is authorised to use by virtue of the trade licence or licences,

(b) uses a vehicle (not being a vehicle for which a vehicle licence is for the time being in force) on a public road for any purpose other than a purpose which has been prescribed under section 12(2) (b), or

(c) uses the trade licence, or any of the trade licences, for the purposes of keeping on a public road in any circumstances other than circumstances which have been prescribed under section 12(1)(c) a vehicle which is not being used on that road.

Vehicle Excise and Registration Act 1994, s 34(1)

PNLD H787, H782, H786

Points to prove

s 34(1)(a) offence

- ✓ being the holder of trade licence(s)
- ✓ used on a public road
- ✓ by virtue of that licence
- ✓ more vehicles than authorised by the licence

s 34(1)(b) offence

- ✓ being the holder of trade licence(s)
- ✓ used a vehicle on a public road
- ✓ by virtue of that licence
- ✓ for purposes other than as prescribed in the licence

s 34(1)(c) offence

- ✓ being the holder of trade licence(s)
- ✓ kept a vehicle on a public road
- ✓ by virtue of that licence
- ✓ when the vehicle was not being used on that road

Meanings

Trade licence

Is a licence issued under s 11.

Uses (see **10.16.1**)

Public road (s 62)

Means a road repairable at public expense.

Road (s 192) (see **10.1.1**)

Vehicle (s 1(1B))

Means a mechanically propelled vehicle, or anything (whether or not it is a vehicle) that has been, but has ceased to be, a mechanically propelled vehicle.

Section 12(2)(b)

Regulations giving purposes for which the holder of a trade licence may use a vehicle under that licence.

Section 12(1)(c)

Holder of a trade licence is not entitled to keep any vehicle on a road if it is not being used on the road for the purposes prescribed by regulations.

Regulations

Currently these are the Road Vehicles (Registration and Licensing) Regulations 2002 (SI 2742/2002).

Explanatory notes

- A trade licence will only be issued to a motor trader (including a vehicle manufacturer), vehicle tester, or person intending to start a business as a motor trader or vehicle tester.
- Where the conviction is for a continuing offence, the offence will be taken as committed on the latest date to which the conviction relates.
- The trade licence holder who changes their name or the name and/ or address of their business must notify the Secretary of State and submit the licence for amendment.
- It is an offence under s 44 for a person to forge, fraudulently alter, or use, or fraudulently lend or allow to be used by another person, any trade plate.
- Nothing that can be mistaken for a trade plate should be displayed on a vehicle.

Practical considerations

- Consider issuing a TFPN (see **10.4.1**) for offences under s 34.
- A trade licence is valid only for vehicles temporarily in the possession of a motor trader (including a vehicle manufacturer) or vehicle tester in the course of their business.
- A trade licence only authorises the use of one vehicle at any one time under s 12(1)(a) but a person may hold more than one licence.
- A vehicle and semi-trailer superimposed thereon counts as only one vehicle.
- If a question arises as to the number of vehicles used, their character, weight or cubic capacity (cc) rating, the seating capacity, or the purpose for which they were being used, then s 53 places the burden of proof on the defendant.
- Section 29 creates the offence of using/keeping an unlicensed vehicle (including trade licence) on a public road (see **10.20.1**).

TFPN

Summary   36 months

Level 3 fine or 5 times VEL duty amount

10.20 Vehicle Excise/Trade Licences and Registration Marks/Documents

The Vehicle Excise and Registration Act 1994 offences include failing to fix a registration mark to a vehicle, or to produce a registration document, and using or keeping an unlicensed vehicle on a road or a vehicle bearing an obscured/misrepresented registration mark.

10.20.1 Using/keeping unlicensed vehicle

Section 29 creates the offence of using or keeping an unlicensed vehicle on a public road.

Offences

If a person uses, or keeps, a vehicle which is unlicensed he is guilty of an offence.

Vehicle Excise and Registration Act 1994, s 29(1)

PNLD H749, H751, H811

Points to prove

✓ used/kept a vehicle
✓ without VEL or trade licence being in force

Meanings

Uses (see **10.16.1**)

Vehicle (see **10.19**)

Unlicensed

If there is no vehicle licence or trade licence in force for vehicle.

Exempt vehicles (exempt from vehicle excise duty)

Applies to the following vehicles listed under Sch 2:
- certain historic vehicles constructed forty years or more ago;

- electrically assisted pedal cycles;
- vehicles not used or adapted for carrying a driver or passenger;
- emergency vehicles;
- disabled persons' vehicles;
- a vehicle on test;
- a vehicle travelling between parts of private land;
- a vehicle for export or imported by members of foreign armed forces;
- an off-road vehicle after notifying DVLA (SORN);
- tractor, light agricultural vehicle, agricultural engine;
- mowing machine;
- steam-powered vehicles;
- electrically propelled vehicle, trams, and snow ploughs.

Explanatory notes

- Various people can 'use' a vehicle, being the driver, the employer if the vehicle is being used for the employer's business, an owner being driven by another person while the owner is in the vehicle, or a steersman where a broken-down vehicle is being towed.
- Where a vehicle licence has expired and the vehicle is not to be used/kept on a road, the vehicle keeper must notify the Secretary of State.

Practical considerations

- All exempt vehicles require a nil licence except trams; electrically assisted pedal cycles; vehicles that do not carry a driver or passenger; vehicles going to, from, or taking a test of road worthiness or pollution; or vehicles which are zero-rated whilst awaiting export. It is an offence under s 43A to use/keep a vehicle that requires a nil licence without such licence.
- The burden of proof that the defendant was the keeper of the vehicle on the relevant day is on the prosecutor, but it is on the defendant to prove that a VEL was in force for the vehicle.
- Under s 53, the burden of proof is on the defendant if a question arises as to the character, weight, cubic capacity (cc) rating, or seating capacity of the vehicle or the purpose for which it was being used.

TFPN

Summary

6 months

Level 3 fine or 5 times the excise duty, whichever is greater

10.20.2 No registration mark on vehicle/fail to produce registration document

Section 42 relates to the fixing of the registration mark to a vehicle and creates an offence of failure to do so.

Offences

If a registration mark is not fixed on a vehicle as required by virtue of section 23, the relevant person is guilty of an offence.

Vehicle Excise and Registration Act 1994, s 42(1)

PNLD H7254, H7255, H7257

Points to prove

✓ drove/kept
✓ vehicle on a road
✓ registration mark not fixed to front/rear of vehicle as required

Meanings

Registration mark required by section 23(1)

A vehicle registered under s 21(1) shall be assigned a registration mark indicating the registered number of that vehicle.

Vehicle (see **10.19**)

Relevant person

Driver of vehicle or, if not being driven, the keeper.

Explanatory notes

- The Road Vehicles (Display of Registration Marks) Regulations 2001 govern how such marks must be displayed on vehicles first registered on or after 1 October 1938, such as the size, shape, and character of the lettering and the manner by which the registration marks are to be displayed and rendered easily distinguishable (whether by day or by night) (see **10.20.3**).
- A registration plate must be fixed to the rear of the vehicle or, if towing a trailer or trailers, the rear of the rearmost trailer, in a vertical position or, if that is not practicable, as close to vertical as possible and in such position that, in normal daylight, the characters are easily distinguishable.
- Similarly, except a motorcycle, a registration plate must be fixed to the front of the vehicle in a vertical position or, if that is not

practicable, as close to vertical as possible and in such position that, in normal daylight, the characters are easily distinguishable from every part of the relevant area.

Defences

(4) It is a defence for a person charged with an offence under subsection (1) to prove that—

(a) he had no reasonable opportunity to register the vehicle under this Act, and

(b) the vehicle was being driven for the purpose of being so registered.

(5) It is a defence for a person charged with an offence under subsection (1) in relation to a vehicle to which s 47 of the Road Traffic Act 1988 applies by virtue of subsection (2)(b) of that section (vehicles manufactured before the prescribed period and used before registration) to prove that he had no reasonable opportunity to register the vehicle under this Act and that the vehicle was being driven in accordance with subsection (6).

Vehicle Excise and Registration Act 1994, s 42

Defence notes

A vehicle is driven under s 42(6) if it is being driven for, or in connection with, examination under s 45 of the Road Traffic Act 1988 (MOT tests) in circumstances in which its use is exempted from s 47(1) of that Act by regulations.

Practical considerations

- Consider issuing a TFPN (see **10.4**).
- The Regulations concerning the displaying of registration marks do not apply to invalid vehicles or pedestrian-controlled vehicles.
- A motorcycle first registered on or after 1 September 2001 **must not** have a registration plate fixed to the front, and one first registered before that date does not need to have a front registration plate fixed to it.
- If an agricultural machine is towing a trailer, the registration plate on the rear of the trailer may show the registration mark of any similar machine owned by the keeper.

Produce registration document

- Section 28A of the Act makes it a summary offence if, when using (eg driver or keeper) a vehicle, they fail to produce the registration document for inspection on being so required by a constable or authorised person (authorised by the Secretary of State).
- Like other document production offences, s 28A does not apply if the registration document is produced at a police station specified by the person required to produce within seven days of the request or as soon as reasonably practicable.

TFPN

Summary

6 months

Level 3 fine

10.20.3 Obscured/misrepresented registration marks

Section 43 requires a registration plate fixed to a vehicle to be unobscured, easily distinguishable, and not be misrepresented.

Offences

If a registration mark fixed on a vehicle as required by virtue of section 23 is in any way—
(a) obscured, or
(b) rendered, or allowed to become, not easily distinguishable,
the relevant person is guilty of an offence.

Vehicle Excise and Registration Act 1994, s 43(1)

PNLD H788, H7258

Points to prove

✓ drove/kept
✓ vehicle on a road
✓ registration mark obscured/rendered/allowed to become indistinguishable

Meanings

Registration mark required by section 23 (see **10.20.2**)

The Road Vehicles (Display of Registration Marks) Regulations 2001 have been made under s 23.

Vehicle (see **10.19**)

Relevant person (see **10.20.2**)

Defences

It is a defence for a person charged with an offence under this section to prove that he took all steps which it was reasonably practicable to take to prevent the mark being obscured or rendered not easily distinguishable.

Vehicle Excise and Registration Act 1994, s 43(4)

Practical considerations

- Examples of this offence could be where the registration plate is obscured by the tow bar/ball, or covered by a pedal cycle rack, or is covered by dirt/mud and is allowed to remain there.
- Officers should use their discretion when dealing with this type of offence.
- The Vehicles (Crime) Act 2001 concerns the control of registration plate suppliers. It is an offence under s 28 of that Act to sell a plate where the registration mark is misrepresented. Prosecution to show that the supplier knew of the defective plate or was reckless as to the nature of the plate.
- DVLA has issued guidelines for tackling misrepresented number plates. Action should be considered where the number plate may be unreadable by ANPR, uses bolts/screws to change appearance of characters, has illegal font, looks foreign (on GB vehicle), is patterned or textured, has incorrectly spaced/sized characters, does not show plate supplier, displays illegal graphics, or appears offensive.
- Where s 43 offences are dealt with by TFPN (see **10.4**) or report for summons, photographic evidence should be obtained (where possible) and the driver issued with a DVLA form V796. Send an offence notification report form to DVLA, accompanied by photograph and details of plate supplier. DVLA will then take follow-up action, including revocation of registration mark for repeat offences or repeat use of misrepresented plates; but DVLA will take no action if it is dealt with by VDRS.
- The BS for number plates states that characters must be a 'Shade of Black'. 3D characters meet this description and are acceptable but patterns, such as stripes, are not allowed. Plates with 3D characters must comply with other BS requirements.
- If a vehicle is liable for vehicle excise duty or is an exempt vehicle that requires a nil licence to be in force (see **10.20.1**), s 43C makes it a summary offence to use such a vehicle on a public road/place if the keeper details are incorrect or not recorded in the DVLA vehicle register. A TFPN can be issued for this offence (see **10.4.1**).

TFPN

Summary

6 months

Level 3 fine

10.21 Obstruction of the Road/Footpath

Obstruction of a road is catered for by the Highways Act 1980 and the Road Vehicles (Construction and Use) Regulations 1986.

10.21.1 Wilful obstruction of the highway

Section 137 of the Highways Act 1980 provides an offence of wilful obstruction of the highway.

Offences

If a person, without lawful authority or excuse, in any way wilfully obstructs the free passage along a highway he is guilty of an offence and liable to imprisonment for a term not exceeding 51 weeks or a fine or both.

Highways Act 1980, s 137(1)

PNLD H100652, H100653

Points to prove

- ✓ without lawful authority/excuse
- ✓ wilfully obstructed
- ✓ free passage of the highway

Meanings

Person

Includes a body corporate.

Wilfully

Means purposefully, deliberately.

Highway

Means the whole or part of a highway other than a ferry or waterway. Where a highway passes over a bridge or through a tunnel, that bridge or tunnel is taken to be part of the highway.

Explanatory notes

- Stopping someone from using the highway by fear alone is insufficient to commit obstruction: there should be some physical obstruction.
- The highway does not need to be completely blocked, only made less convenient or roomy.
- If a person is convicted under s 137 and the obstruction is continuing, the court may, instead of or in addition to imposing any punishment, order them to remove it within a fixed period under s 137ZA. Failure to comply with this order, without reasonable excuse, will be an offence.
- For Public Order Act 2023 stop and search powers relevant for this offence, see **7.17.9**.

Related cases

DPP v Ziegler and others [2021] UKSC 23 In this case, as part of a protest outside an arms fair, Z and others argued that they had a lawful excuse for obstructing the highway. Reliance was placed on their rights under Art 10 ECHR (the right to freedom of expression) and Art 11 ECHR (right to freedom of peaceful assembly). It was held that deliberate physically obstructive conduct by protesters was capable of constituting a lawful excuse for the purposes of s 137 of the Highways Act 1980, where the impact of the deliberate obstruction on other highway users was more than *de minimis*, and prevented them, or was capable of preventing them, from passing along the highway.

R v Buchanan v Crown Prosecution Service [2018] EWHC 1773 (Admin) The defendant and others protested outside the Home Office in London. The actions put themselves and others at significant risk of serious injury and created a risk of damage being caused to property. It was held that the defendant was entitled to protest from the pavement but once they moved the protest into the highway, Art 11 was no longer relevant; their rights under Art 10 (see **Appendix 1**) remained but were still subject to restrictions.

Nagy v Weston [1965] 1 All ER 78, QBD The test for determining whether a particular use of the highway amounts to an obstruction is, if in the particular circumstances, such use is unreasonable. Circumstances would include duration, position of the obstruction, its purpose, and whether it caused an actual or potential obstruction.

Practical considerations

- Consider whether the obstruction is wilful or deliberate (as opposed to accidental) or without lawful excuse.
- If a motor vehicle is involved, consider issuing a TFPN (see **10.4**).
- If it can be proved the obstruction was with the consent or connivance of an officer of a body corporate, then the person may have committed the offence as well as the body corporate.

- Duration and extent of the obstruction are important considerations.
- The Town Police Clauses Act 1847, s 28 obstruction offences have been repealed by the Deregulation Act 2015, Sch 23.

TFPN

Summary

6 months

Maximum 51 weeks' imprisonment and/or a level 3 fine

10.21.2 Builders' skips on the highway

Section 139 of the Highways Act 1980 controls the use of builders' skips deposited on the highway.

Offences

(3) If a builder's skip is deposited on a highway without a permission granted under this section, the owner of the skip is, subject to subsection (6) below, guilty of an offence.

(4) Where a builder's skip has been deposited on a highway in accordance with a permission granted under this section, the owner of the skip shall secure—

(a) that the skip is properly lighted during the hours of darkness and, where regulations made by the Secretary of State under this section require it to be marked in accordance with the regulations (whether with reflecting or fluorescent material or otherwise), that it is so marked;

(b) that the skip is clearly and indelibly marked with the owner's name and with his telephone number or address;

(c) that the skip is removed as soon as practicable after it has been filled;

(d) that each of the conditions subject to which that permission was granted is complied with;

and, if he fails to do so, he is, subject to subsection (6) below, guilty of an offence.

Highways Act 1980, s 139

PNLD H3010, H9366

Points to prove

s 139(3) offence

✓ deposited builder's skip on a highway
✓ without permission under s 139

10.21.2 **Builders' skips on the highway**

> ***s 139(4) offence***
>
> ✓ owner of a builder's skip
> ✓ deposited skip on a highway
> ✓ with a permission granted under s 139
> ✓ failed to secure that the skip was
> ✓ properly lighted during the hours of darkness OR
> ✓ clearly and indelibly marked with owner's details OR
> ✓ removed as soon as practicable after being filled OR
> ✓ not complying with each of the conditions

Meanings

Builder's skip

Means a container designed to be carried on a road vehicle and to be placed on a highway or other land for the storage of builders' materials or for the removal and disposal of builders' rubble, household waste, and other rubbish or earth.

Highway (see **10.21.1**)

Owner

In relation to a builder's skip which is the subject of a hiring agreement, being an agreement for a hiring of not less than one month, or which is the subject of a hire-purchase agreement, means the person in possession of the skip under that agreement.

Hours of darkness

Half an hour after sunset and half an hour before sunrise.

Power to move skip

Under s 140, the highways authority or a constable in uniform may require the owner of a skip to remove or reposition it or cause it to be so removed or repositioned themselves. This applies even though it has been deposited with a permission granted under s 139.

Explanatory notes

- A permission under s 139 authorises a person to whom it is granted to deposit, or cause to be deposited, a skip on a highway specified therein.
- Such permission may be granted unconditionally or with specified conditions such as: siting of skip; its dimensions; manner in which it must be marked to be visible to oncoming traffic; care and disposal of contents; way in which it must be lighted or guarded; and its removal at the expiry of the permission.
- Permission must be in writing and blanket permission is not allowed (*York City Council v Poller* [1976] RTR 37).

- Nothing in this section authorises the creation of a nuisance or a danger to users of the highway or imposes on a highway authority granting permission any liability for any injury caused, damage, or loss resulting from the presence on a highway of a skip to which the permission relates.

Defences

(6) In any proceedings for an offence under this section it is a defence, subject to subsection (7) below, for the person charged to prove that the commission of the offence was due to the act or default of another person and that he took all reasonable precautions and exercised all due diligence to avoid the commission of such an offence by himself or any person under his control.

(7) A person charged with an offence under this section is not, without leave of the court, entitled to rely on the defence provided by subsection (6) above unless, within a period ending 7 clear days before the hearing, he has served on the prosecutor a notice in writing giving such information identifying or assisting in the identification of that other person as was then in his possession.

(8) Where any person is charged with an offence under any other enactment for failing to secure that a builder's skip which has been deposited on a highway in accordance with a permission granted under this section was properly lighted during the hours of darkness, it is a defence for the person charged to prove that the commission of the offence was due to the act or default of another person and that he took all reasonable precautions and exercised all due diligence to avoid the commission of such an offence by himself or any person under his control.

(9) Where a person is charged with obstructing, or interrupting any user of, a highway by depositing a builder's skip on it, it is a defence for the person charged to prove that the skip was deposited on it in accordance with a permission granted under this section and either—

   (a) that each of the requirements of subsection (4) above had been complied with; or

   (b) that the commission of any offence under that subsection was due to the act or default of another person and that he took all reasonable precautions and exercised all due diligence to avoid the commission of such an offence by himself or any person under his control.

Highways Act 1980, s 139

Practical considerations

- If a person commits an offence under s 139 because of an act or default of another person, that other person is guilty of the offence and may be charged with and convicted of the offence whether or not proceedings are taken against the first-mentioned person.

- Requirement for a skip to be moved must be made face to face (*R v Worthing Justices, ex parte Waste Management Ltd* (1988) 152 JP 362, DC).

Summary

6 months

Level 3 fine

10.21.3 Cause injury/danger/annoyance on the highway

Section 161 of the Highways Act 1980 creates various offences that relate to causing danger on a highway, including annoyance by playing games on the highway.

Offences

(1) If a person, without lawful authority or excuse, deposits any thing whatsoever on a highway in consequence of which a user of the highway is injured or endangered, that person is guilty of an offence.

(2) [See **8.8.7**]

(3) If a person plays at football or any other game on a highway to the annoyance of a user of the highway he is guilty of an offence.

(4) If a person, without lawful authority or excuse, allows any filth, dirt, lime or other offensive matter or thing to run or flow on to a highway from any adjoining premises, he is guilty of an offence.

Highways Act 1980, s 161

PNLD **H4035, H4094, H15474**

Points to prove

s 161(1) offence

✓ without lawful authority/excuse
✓ deposits any thing whatsoever on a highway
✓ thus injuring/endangering user of the highway

s 161(3) offence

✓ played football/a game on a highway
✓ thus annoying a user of the highway

s 161(4) offence

✓ without lawful authority/excuse
✓ allowed any filth, dirt, lime, or other offensive matter or thing
✓ to run or flow on to a highway
✓ from any adjoining premises

Meaning of highway (see 10.21.1)

Explanatory notes

- The s 161(2) offences relate to lighting any fire on/over a highway or discharging any firearm or firework within 50 feet of the centre of a highway and are dealt with in **8.5** and **8.8.7**.
- Section 161A creates another offence of lighting a fire on any land (not part of a highway/carriageway) and as a result the user of any highway being injured, interrupted, or endangered by smoke from that fire.
- Any rope, wire, or other apparatus placed across a highway so as to cause danger to users of the highway is an offence under s 162, unless adequate warning has been given of this danger.
- The s 161(3) offence is very wide and covers all types of 'game'. For example, a mock hunt with a man dressed as a stag being chased by people in fancy dress and with trumpets has been held to be a game (*Pappin v Maynard* (1863) 27 JP 745).

Summary

6 months

s 161(1) offence

Level 3 fine

s 161(3) and (4) offences

Level 1 fine

10.21.4 Unnecessary obstruction

Regulation 103 of the Road Vehicles (Construction and Use) Regulations 1986 creates an offence of causing an unnecessary obstruction.

Offences

No person in charge of a motor vehicle or trailer shall cause or permit the vehicle to stand on a road so as to cause any unnecessary obstruction of the road.

Road Vehicles (Construction and Use) Regulations 1986, reg 103

PNLD H213, H214, H10847

> **Points to prove**
>
> ✓ in charge of a motor vehicle/trailer
> ✓ caused/permitted vehicle
> ✓ to stand on a road
> ✓ so causing an unnecessary obstruction on road

Meanings

Motor vehicle (see **10.1.3**)

Mechanically propelled vehicle intended or adapted for use on roads.

Trailer

Vehicle drawn by a motor vehicle but does not apply to any part of an articulated bus.

Road

Includes the footpath.

Explanatory notes

- A motor vehicle left on a road for an unreasonable time may be an unreasonable obstruction.
- Consider the use to which the highway was being put by the vehicle causing the obstruction. The highway is intended as a means of transit not a store (*Nelmes v Rhys Howells Transport Ltd* [1977] RTR 266).
- Where a motorist parks their vehicle on one side of the road and the subsequent parking of vehicles on the opposite side of the road causes an obstruction, no offence under this regulation was committed by the parking of the original vehicle (*Langham v Crisp* [1975] Crim LR 652).

Related case

Carey v CC of Avon and Somerset [1995] RTR 405, CA The purpose of the Removal and Disposal of Vehicles Regulations 1986 is to clear the road of an 'obstruction' as a matter of urgency even if no one is really at fault. They do not apply to s 137 of the Highways Act 1980 and reg 103 of the Road Vehicles (Construction and Use) Regulations 1986 which relate to obstruction of the highway without a lawful excuse and constitute an unreasonable use of the highway.

Practical consideration

- Consider the offence of wilfully obstructing the free passage of the highway, without lawful authority or excuse, under s 137(1) of the

Highways Act 1980 (see **10.21.1**). A TFPN can be issued for this offence (see **10.4.1**).

TFPN

Summary

6 months

Level 4 fine if goods vehicle or a vehicle adapted to carry more than eight passengers. Level 3 fine in any other case

10.22 **Off-Road Driving**

Section 34 of the Road Traffic Act 1988 prohibits the driving of motor vehicles elsewhere than on a road.

> **Offences**
>
> Subject to the provisions of this section, if without lawful authority a person drives a mechanically propelled vehicle—
> (a) on to or upon any common land, moorland or land of any other description, not being land forming part of a road, or
> (b) on any road being a footpath, bridleway or restricted byway, he is guilty of an offence.
>
> Road Traffic Act 1988, s 34(1)

PNLD **H117, H363**

> **Points to prove**
>
> ✓ without lawful authority
> ✓ drove a mechanically propelled vehicle
> ✓ on to/upon common land/moorland/land
> ✓ not being land forming part of a road or
> ✓ on a road being a footpath/bridleway/restricted byway

Meanings

Drives (see **10.1.4**)

Mechanically propelled vehicle (see **10.1.3**)

Excluding a pedestrian-controlled vehicle, a pedestrian-controlled mowing machine, or an electrically assisted pedal cycle.

Common land

Land that is:
- subject to '**rights of common**' whether those rights are exercisable at all times or only during limited periods; and
- waste land of a manor not subject to 'rights of common'.

Rights of common

These include:
- rights of sole or several vesture, or herbage (rights to take vegetation or flowers from the land);
- rights of sole or several pasture (allowing animals to be put out to pasture on the land);
- cattlegates and beastgates (a particular right, mainly existing in northern England, to graze an animal on common land).

They do not include rights held for a term of years or from year to year.

Road (see **10.1.1**)

Footpath

Means a highway over which the public have a right of way on foot only, not being a footway.

Bridleway

A way over which the public have the following, but no other, rights of way: a right of way on foot and a right of way on horseback, or leading a horse, with or without a right to drive animals of any description along the way.

Restricted byway

A way over which the public have restricted byway rights within the meaning of Part 2 of the Countryside and Rights of Way Act 2000, with or without a right to drive animals of any description along the way, but no other rights of way.

Explanatory notes

- A way shown in a definitive map and statement as a footpath, bridleway, or restricted byway is taken to be so unless the contrary is shown.
- Nothing in s 34 prejudices the rights of the public over commons and waste lands, or any by-laws applying to any land, or affects the law of trespass to land, or any right or remedy to which a person may by law be entitled in respect of any such trespass, or in particular confers a right to park a vehicle on any land.
- It is not an offence under s 34 to drive on any land within 15 yards of a road for the purpose only of parking the vehicle on that land (s 34(3)).
- Police powers concerning the stopping, seizure, and removal of a motor vehicle that is used in contravention of s 34, which is causing, or likely to cause, alarm, distress, or annoyance to members of the public can be used under s 59 of the Police Reform Act 2002 (see **7.14**).

Defences

(2A) It is not an offence under this section for a person with an interest in land, or a visitor to any land, to drive a mechanically propelled vehicle on a road if, immediately before the commencement of section 47(2) of the Countryside and Rights of Way Act 2000, the road was—
- (a) shown in a definitive map and statement as a road used as a public path, and
- (b) in use for obtaining access to the land by the driving of mechanically propelled vehicles by a person with an interest in the land or by visitors to the land.

> (3) It is not an offence under this section to drive a mechanically propelled vehicle on land within 15 yards of a road, being a road on which a motor vehicle may legally be driven, for the purpose only of parking the vehicle on that land.
> (4) A person shall not be convicted of an offence under this section with respect to a vehicle if he proves to the satisfaction of the court that it was driven in contravention of this section for the purpose of saving life or extinguishing fire or meeting any other like emergency.
>
> Road Traffic Act 1988, s 34

Practical considerations

- **Interest in land** includes any estate in land and any right over land (whether exercisable by virtue of the ownership of an estate or interest in the land or by virtue of a licence or agreement) and, in particular, includes rights of common and sporting rights.
- Consider issuing a TFPN (see **10.4**).
- Unlike ss 35 and 36 of the RTA 1988, a NIP is not required for an offence contrary to s 34.
- A power of entry to premises to exercise the powers of seizure and removal of the motor vehicle is granted by s 59 of the Police Reform Act 2002. Reasonable force may be used, if necessary, to stop, seize, or remove the motor vehicle or for the power of entry (see **7.14**).
- **Immobilise vehicles left on land**: s 54 of the Protection of Freedoms Act 2012 provides that a person commits an offence if without lawful authority they immobilise a motor vehicle by attaching an immobilising device (eg wheel clamp) or move or restrict the movement of such a vehicle by any means, intending to prevent or inhibit the removal of the vehicle by a person otherwise entitled to remove it.
- The restriction of movement of the vehicle offence does not apply to a lawfully erected fixed barrier in place at the time of parking. In this section, 'motor vehicle' means a mechanically propelled vehicle or a vehicle designed or adapted for towing by a mechanically propelled vehicle.

TFPN

Summary

6 months

Level 3 fine

Chapter 11
General: Patrol

11.1 Police Powers for Civilian Staff and Volunteers

Section 38(6B) of the Police Reform Act 2002 (the exercise of police powers etc by civilians) allows for the designation of a person as a community support officer (CSO) or a community support volunteer (CSV).

Powers

The powers and duties that may be conferred or imposed on a person designated under s 38 are:

(a) any power or duty of a constable, other than a power or duty specified in Part 1 of Sch 3B (excluded powers and duties) (see **11.1.1**);

(b) where the person is designated as a CSO or a CSV, any power or duty that is described in Sch 3C as a power or duty of a CSO or CSV.

Police Reform Act 2002, s 38(6B)

Schedule 3C sets out the powers and duties that may be conferred or imposed on a designated CSO or CSV and include:

- issue fixed penalty notices (see **11.1.2**);
- require names and addresses (see **11.1.3**);
- search for and seize alcohol and tobacco (see **11.1.4**);
- seize and detain in relation to controlled drugs (see **11.1.5**);
- seize and detain in relation to psychoactive substances (see **11.1.6**);
- detain pending arrival of a constable etc (see **11.1.7**);
- search individuals detained (see **11.1.8**);
- powers re persons detained in relation to park trading offences (see **11.1.9**);
- powers in relation to road traffic (see **11.1.10**);
- power to use reasonable force (see **11.1.11**).

Meanings

CSO

A person designated by a chief officer of police as a community support officer under s 38.

CSV

A person designated by a chief officer of police as a community support volunteer under s 38.

The relevant police area

In relation to a CSO or CSV, means the police area for which the police force in question is maintained.

Explanatory notes

- The chief officer of police of any police force may designate a **relevant employee** as either or both of the following: a CSO or a policing support officer; or designate a **police volunteer** as either a CSV or a policing support volunteer.
- A chief officer of police shall not designate a person under this section unless they are satisfied that that person is a suitable person to carry out the functions for the purposes of which they are designated; are capable of effectively carrying out those functions; and have received adequate training in the carrying out of those functions and in the exercise and performance of the powers and duties to be conferred on them by virtue of the designation.
- **Any** power or duty of a constable that is conferred or imposed on a person designated under this section by a chief officer of police of a police force may be exercised or performed by the person in the area of that police force, and in any cases or circumstances in which it could be exercised or performed by a constable who is a member of that force.
- A designation under this section may provide that any power or duty of a constable that is conferred or imposed by the designation may be exercised or performed by the person designated in such areas outside the area of the police force in question as are specified in the designation (as well as within the area of the police force); only in such parts of the area of that police force as are specified in the designation; and only in cases or circumstances so specified.
- Failing to comply with a power which has been conferred or designated (under Sch 3C (see **11.1.11**)) on a CSO or a CSV and executed by the CSO or CSV is a summary offence.

11.1.1 Schedule 3B—designations under s 38

Part 1 of Sch 3B to the Police Reform Act 2002 lists the powers and duties (the 'core' powers that constables are afforded) that a person designated under s 38 (civilian staff and volunteers) cannot be given and hence is titled 'excluded powers and duties of constables'. These are:

1. Any power or duty of a constable to make an arrest.
2. Any power or duty of a constable to stop and search an individual or a vehicle or other thing.
3. The power of a constable under s 36(4) of PACE to perform the functions of a custody officer at a designated police station if a custody officer is not readily available to perform them.

3A. The power of a constable under s 55(6) of PACE to conduct an intimate search if an officer of at least the rank of inspector considers under s 55(5) of that Act that an intimate search by a suitably qualified person is not practicable.

4. Any power that is exercisable only by a constable of a particular rank.
5. Any power of a constable under:
   (a) the Terrorism Act 2000 (except for cordons—see **11.1.11**);
   (b) the Terrorism Act 2006;
   (c) the Counter-Terrorism Act 2008;
   (d) the Terrorism Prevention and Investigation Measures Act 2011;
   (e) the Counter-Terrorism and Security Act 2015.
6. Any power of a constable under the National Security Act 2023.
7. The power of a constable to make an application on behalf of the Commissioner of Police of the Metropolis under s 19 or 21 of the Investigatory Powers Act 2016 (applications for warrants under Chapter 1 of Part 2 of that Act).

Apart from the powers and duties listed above, any power or duty of a constable may be conferred or imposed on a person designated under s 38 and the statutory provisions are to be interpreted in a way to ensure the power works as intended—see Part 2 of Sch 3B:

Part 2 Application of legislation

Section 8(1) of Sch 3B, Part 2 of the Police Reform Act 2002 states that where a power or duty of a constable is conferred or imposed on a person designated under s 38:

(a) a reference to a constable (however expressed) in legislation relating to the power or duty includes a reference to the person designated under s 38;

(b) a reference in legislation to anything done in the exercise or purported exercise of the power, or in the performance or purported performance of the duty, includes a reference to anything done in the exercise or purported exercise of the power, or the performance or purported performance of the duty, by the person designated under s 38.

Schedule 3C—designations under s 38—additional powers and duties

Schedule 3C lists the powers that can be given to a person designated as a CSO or a CSV under s 38. Such powers may be given in their full extent or only in cases or circumstances described by the chief officer in the designation. These powers and duties are additional and/or differ to those of a constable. There are powers which a constable has which cannot be designated to a CSO or a CSV and, similarly, there are powers that can be designated to a CSO or CSV that a constable does not have.

Additional powers that can be designated to a CSO or a CSV are listed in what follows.

11.1.2 Powers to issue fixed penalty notices etc

Paragraph 2 of Sch 3C provides for powers to issue fixed penalty notices as follows:

- **Litter**: a CSO or CSV has the power of an authorised officer of a litter authority to give a notice under s 88 of the Environmental Protection Act 1990 (fixed penalty notices in respect of **litter**) in relation to an individual whom the CSO or CSV has reason to believe has committed an offence under s 87 of that Act at a place within the relevant police area (see **7.16.2**).
- **Graffiti or fly-posting**: a CSO or CSV has the power of an authorised officer of a local authority to give a notice under s 43(1) of the Anti-social Behaviour Act 2003 (penalty notices in respect of **graffiti or fly-posting**) in relation to an individual whom the CSO or CSV has reason to believe has committed an offence that is a relevant offence for the purposes of s 43(1) at a place within the relevant police area.
- **Offence under s 38(1) of the London Local Authorities Act 1990**: a CSO or CSV designated under s 38 by the Commissioner of Police of the Metropolis has the power of an authorised officer of a borough council to give a notice under s 15 of the London Local Authorities Act 2004 in relation to an individual whom the CSO or CSV has reason to believe has committed an offence under **s 38(1) of the London Local Authorities Act 1990**.
- **Unlicensed street trading**: a CSO or CSV designated under s 38 by the Commissioner of Police for the City of London has the power of an authorised officer of a borough council to give a notice under s 15 of the London Local Authorities Act 2004 in relation to an individual whom the CSO or CSV has reason to believe has committed an offence under s 27(1) of the City of Westminster Act 1999 (**unlicensed street trading**).
- **Offence against a listed byelaw**: a CSO or CSV has the power of an authorised officer of an authority to give a notice under s 237A of the Local Government Act 1972 or under s 12 of the Local Government Byelaws (Wales) Act 2012 (fixed penalty notices in relation to offences against certain byelaws) in relation to an individual whom the CSO or CSV has reason to believe has committed an **offence against a listed byelaw** at a place within the relevant police area.

Explanatory notes

- A byelaw is a 'listed byelaw' for the purposes of Police Reform Act 2002, Sch 3C, para 2(5) if, at the time the CSO or CSV gives the notice:
  - ✦ it is a byelaw to which s 237A of the Local Government Act 1972 or to which s 12 of the Local Government Byelaws (Wales) Act 2012 (fixed penalty notices in relation to offences against certain byelaws) applies; and
  - ✦ the chief officer of police for the relevant police area and the authority that made the byelaw have agreed to include it in a list of byelaws kept for the purposes of sub-para (5).
- The chief officer of police for the relevant police area must publish the list of byelaws kept for the purposes of sub-para (5) in such a way as to bring it to the attention of members of the public in localities where the byelaws in the list apply.

11.1.3 Powers to require the names and addresses

Paragraph 3 of Sch 3C provides for powers to require the names and addresses of persons believed to have committed a relevant offence.

Power

A CSO or CSV may require a person to give his or her name and address if the CSO or CSV has reason to believe that—

(a) the person has committed a relevant offence in the relevant police area, or

(b) the person has committed a relevant licensing offence (whether or not in the relevant police area).

Police Reform Act 2002, Sch 3C para 3(1)

Meanings

Relevant offence

Means any of the following offences:

(a) an offence in respect of which the CSO or CSV is authorised to give a penalty notice (whether in consequence of para 2 of this Schedule or in consequence of provision included in their designation in reliance on s 38(6B)(a));

(b) an offence under s 3 or 4 of the Vagrancy Act 1824;

(c) an offence committed in a specified park which by virtue of s 2 of the Parks Regulation (Amendment) Act 1926 is an offence against the Parks Regulation Act 1872;

(d) an offence under s 39 of the Anti-social Behaviour, Crime and Policing Act 2014 (see **7.15.1**);
(e) an offence under a listed byelaw;
(f) an offence the commission of which appears to the CSO or CSV to have caused:
 (i) injury, alarm, or distress to any other person; or
 (ii) the loss of, or any damage to, any other person's property.

Relevant licensing offence

Means an offence under any of the following provisions of the Licensing Act 2003:

(a) s 141 (sale of alcohol to a person who is drunk) (otherwise than by virtue of subsection (2)(c) or (3) of that section) (see **9.2.1**);
(b) s 142 (knowingly obtain or attempt to obtain alcohol on relevant premises for consumption on those premises by a person who is drunk) (see **9.2.1**);
(c) s 146(1) (sale of alcohol to a person under 18) (see **9.1.2**);
(d) s 149(1)(a), (3)(a), or (4)(a) (purchase of alcohol by or on behalf of person under 18) (see **9.1.4**);
(e) s 150(1) (consumption of alcohol by person under 18 on relevant premises) (see **9.1.5**);
(f) s 150(2) (allows consumption of alcohol on relevant premises by individual aged under 18) (otherwise than by virtue of subsection (3)(b) of that section) (see **9.1.5**);
(g) s 152(1) (sending person under 18 to obtain alcohol) (excluding para (b)) (see **9.1.7**).

Listed byelaw

A byelaw is a 'listed byelaw' for the purposes of sub-para (3)(e) if, at the time the CSO or CSV requires a person to give their name and address:

(a) it is a byelaw which has been made by a relevant body with authority to make byelaws for any place within the relevant police area; and
(b) it is included in the list of byelaws published for the purposes of this paragraph by the chief officer of police for the relevant police area.

Explanatory notes

- In the case of a relevant offence that is an offence under a listed byelaw (see sub-paras (3)(e) and (5)), the power to impose a requirement under sub-para (1) is exercisable only in a place to which the byelaw relates.
- In relation to an offence in respect of which the CSO or CSV is authorised to give a penalty notice under s 444A of the Education Act 1996 (penalty notice in respect of failure to secure regular attendance at school of registered pupil), sub-para (1)(a) of this paragraph has effect as if the words 'in the relevant police area' were omitted.

11.1.4 Powers to search for and seize alcohol and tobacco

Paragraph 4 of Sch 3C allows for search and seizure of alcohol or containers for alcohol and tobacco or cigarette papers. Failure to consent to being searched is an offence.

- **Paragraph 4(1)**: a CSO or CSV may search a person for alcohol or a container for alcohol if:
  - (a) the CSO or CSV has (in consequence of provision included in their designation in reliance on s 38(6B)(a)) imposed a requirement on a person to surrender alcohol or a container for alcohol under s 63(2) of the Anti-social Behaviour, Crime and Policing Act 2014 (see **9.4.1**) or under s 1 of the Confiscation of Alcohol (Young Persons) Act 1997 (see **9.5.1**);
  - (b) the person has failed to comply with the requirement; and
  - (c) the CSO or CSV reasonably believes that the person has alcohol or a container for alcohol in their possession.
- **Paragraph 4(2)**: a CSO or CSV may search a person for tobacco or cigarette papers where:
  - (a) the CSO or CSV has (in consequence of provision included in their designation in reliance on s 38(6B)(a)) sought to seize the tobacco or cigarette papers under s 7(3) of the Children and Young Persons Act 1933 (seizure of tobacco from young persons) (see '**Explanatory notes**' below);
  - (b) the person from whom the CSO or CSV sought to seize the item has failed to surrender it; and
  - (c) the CSO or CSV reasonably believes that the person has it in their possession.
- **Paragraph 4(3)**: the power to search under sub-para (1) or (2):
  - (a) is to do so only to the extent that is reasonably required for the purpose of discovering whatever the CSO or CSV is searching for; and
  - (b) does not authorise the CSO or CSV to require a person to remove any of their clothing in public other than an outer coat, jacket, or gloves.
- **Paragraph 4(5)**: a CSO or CSV who proposes to exercise a power to search a person under sub-para (1) or (2) must inform them that failing without reasonable excuse to consent to being searched is an offence.
- **Paragraph 4(6)**: if the person in question fails to consent to being searched, the CSO or CSV may require them to give the CSO or CSV their name and address.
- **Paragraph 4(7)**: if on searching the person the CSO or CSV discovers what they are searching for, the CSO or CSV may seize it and dispose of it.

Explanatory notes

Section 7(3) of the Children and Young Persons Act 1933 provides that it shall be the duty of a constable and of a park-keeper being in uniform to seize any tobacco or cigarette papers in the possession of any person apparently under the age of 16 years whom they find smoking in any street or public place, and any tobacco or cigarette papers so seized shall be disposed of, if seized by a constable, in such manner as the local policing body may direct, and if seized by a park-keeper, in such manner as the authority or person by whom they were appointed may direct.

11.1.5 Powers to seize and detain—controlled drugs

Paragraph 5 of Sch 3C provides for powers to seize and detain controlled drugs and makes it an offence for a person to fail to give their name and address when required under this paragraph.

- **Paragraph 5(1)**: a CSO or CSV may exercise the powers conferred by sub-para (2) or (3) in the relevant police area.
- **Paragraph 5(2)**: if the CSO or CSV:
  - (a) finds a controlled drug in a person's possession (whether or not the CSO or CSV finds it in the course of searching the person in the exercise of a power or duty conferred or imposed by their designation under s 38); and
  - (b) reasonably believes that it is unlawful for the person to be in possession of it;

  the CSO or CSV may seize it and retain it.
- **Paragraph 5(3)**: if the CSO or CSV:
  - (a) either:
    - (i) finds a controlled drug in a person's possession (as mentioned in sub-para (2)(a)); or
    - (ii) reasonably believes that a person is in possession of a controlled drug; and
  - (b) reasonably believes that it is unlawful for the person to be in possession of it;

  the CSO or CSV may require the person to give the CSO or CSV their name and address.
- **Paragraph 5(4)**: if, in exercise of the power conferred by sub-para (2), the CSO or CSV seizes and retains a controlled drug, the CSO or CSV must:
  - (a) if the person from whom it was seized maintains that they were lawfully in possession of it, tell the person where enquiries about its recovery may be made; and
  - (b) comply with a constable's instructions about what to do with it.

Meaning of controlled drug

The same meaning as in the Misuse of Drugs Act 1971 (see **5.1.1**).

11.1.6 Powers to seize and detain—psychoactive substances

Paragraph 6 of Sch 3C allows for seizure and detention of psychoactive substances (see **5.3.2**) and makes it an offence for a person not to give their name and address when required under this paragraph.

- **Paragraph 6(1)**: a CSO or CSV may exercise the powers conferred by sub-para (2) or (3) in the relevant police area.
- **Paragraph 6(2)**: if the CSO or CSV:
  - (a) finds a psychoactive substance in a person's possession (whether or not the CSO or CSV finds it in the course of searching the person in the exercise of a power or duty conferred or imposed by their designation under s 38); and
  - (b) reasonably believes that it is unlawful for the person to be in possession of it;

  the CSO or CSV may seize it and retain it.
- **Paragraph 6(3)**: if the CSO or CSV:
  - (a) either:
    - (i) finds a psychoactive substance in a person's possession (as mentioned in sub-para (2)(a)); or
    - (ii) reasonably believes that a person is in possession of a psychoactive substance; and
  - (b) reasonably believes that it is unlawful for the person to be in possession of it;

  the CSO or CSV may require the person to give the CSO or CSV their name and address.
- **Paragraph 6(4)**: if, in exercise of the power conferred by sub-para (2), the CSO or CSV seizes and retains a psychoactive substance, the CSO or CSV must:
  - (a) if the person from whom it was seized maintains that they were lawfully in possession of it:
    - (i) tell the person where enquiries about its recovery may be made; and
    - (ii) explain the effect of ss 49 to 51 and 53 of the Psychoactive Substances Act 2016 (retention and disposal of items); and
  - (b) comply with a constable's instructions about what to do with it.
- **Paragraph 6(5)**: any substance seized in exercise of the power conferred by sub-para (2) is to be treated for the purposes of ss 49 to 53 of the Psychoactive Substances Act 2016 as if it had been seized by a police or customs officer under s 36 of that Act.
- Section 50 of the Psychoactive Substances Act 2016 (power of police, etc to dispose of seized psychoactive substances) applies in relation to any such substance as if the reference in subsection (1)(b) to the police or customs officer who seized it were a reference to the CSO or CSV who seized it.
- **Paragraph 6(7)**: in this paragraph, police or customs officer and psychoactive substance have the same meaning as in the Psychoactive Substances Act 2016.

11.1.7 Powers to detain pending arrival of a constable etc

Paragraph 7 of Sch 3C makes provision for the detention of persons while waiting for the arrival of a constable and creates offences of making off.

Power

A CSO or CSV may require a person to wait with the CSO or CSV, for a period not exceeding 30 minutes, for the arrival of a constable where—

(a) the CSO or CSV has required the person to give his or her name and address (whether in consequence of paragraph 3, 4(6), 5(3) or 6(3) or in consequence of provision included in his or her designation in reliance on section 38(6B)(a)), and

(b) either—

  (i) the person has failed to comply with the requirement, or

  (ii) the CSO or CSV has reasonable grounds for suspecting that the person has given a name or address that is false or inaccurate.

Police Reform Act 2002, Sch 3C para 7(1)

Explanatory notes

- **Paragraph 7(2)**: sub-para (1) does not apply if the requirement to give a name and address was imposed in connection with a relevant licensing offence mentioned in para 3(4)(a), (c), or (f) which the CSO or CSV believes to have been committed on licensed premises (within the meaning of the Licensing Act 2003).
- **Paragraph 7(3)**: a CSO or CSV may require a person to wait with the CSO or CSV, for a period not exceeding 30 minutes, for the arrival of a constable where:
  (a) the CSO or CSV has reason to believe that the person is committing an offence under s 3 (begging in a public place) or s 4 (lodging outdoors) of the Vagrancy Act 1824;
  (b) the CSO or CSV requires the person to stop doing whatever gives rise to that belief; and
  (c) the person fails to stop as required.
- **Paragraph 7(4)**: a person who has been required under sub-para (1) or (3) to wait with a CSO or CSV may, if requested to do so, elect that (instead of waiting) they will accompany the CSO or CSV to a police station in the relevant police area.
- **Paragraph 7(5)**: where the person does not elect to accompany the CSO or CSV to the police station, and the constable arrives within the period of 30 minutes, the CSO or CSV is under a duty to remain with the person and the constable until the CSO or CSV has transferred control of the person to the constable.
- **Paragraph 7(6)**: where the person does elect to accompany the CSO or CSV to the police station:

(a) the CSO or CSV is under a duty to remain at the police station until the CSO or CSV has transferred control of the person to the custody officer there;
(b) until control is transferred, the CSO or CSV is treated for all purposes as having the person in their lawful custody; and
(c) for so long as the CSO or CSV remains at the police station or in its immediate vicinity (whether before control of the person is transferred or afterwards), the CSO or CSV is under a duty to prevent the person's escape and to assist in keeping the person under control.

11.1.8 Powers to search etc—individuals detained

Powers and duties that may be conferred or imposed on a CSO or CSV as provided for in s 38(6B)(b).

- **Paragraph 8(1)**: a CSO or CSV may exercise the powers set out in sub-paras (2) and (3) in relation to a person whom the CSO or CSV has required to wait for the arrival of a constable under para 7(1) or (3) (whether or not that person makes an election under para 7(4)).
- **Paragraph 8(2)**: if the CSO or CSV has reasonable grounds for believing that the person may present a danger to themselves or to others, the CSO or CSV may search the person.
- **Paragraph 8(3)**: if the CSO or CSV has reasonable grounds for believing that the person may have concealed on them anything which might be used to assist in escaping from lawful custody, the CSO or CSV may search the person for that thing.
- **Paragraph 8(4)**: the power conferred by sub-para (2) or (3):
  (a) does not authorise a CSO or CSV to require a person to remove any of their clothing in public other than an outer coat, jacket, or gloves;
  (b) does authorise a search of a person's mouth.
- **Paragraph 8(5)**: a CSO or CSV searching a person under sub-para (2) may seize and retain anything that is found if the CSO or CSV has reasonable grounds for believing that the person searched might use it to cause physical injury to themselves or to any other person.
- **Paragraph 8(6)**: a CSO or CSV searching a person under sub-para (3) may seize and retain anything that is found, other than an item subject to legal privilege, if the CSO or CSV has reasonable grounds for believing that the person might use it to assist in escaping from lawful custody.
- **Paragraph 8(7)**: if a CSO or CSV seizes or retains anything under sub-para (5) or (6), the CSO or CSV must:
  (a) tell the person from whom it was seized where enquiries about its recovery may be made; and
  (b) comply with a constable's instructions about what to do with it.

11.1.9 Persons detained for park trading offences

Powers and duties that may be conferred or imposed on a CSO or CSV as provided for in s 38(6B)(b).

- **Paragraph 9(1)**: if a CSO or CSV reasonably suspects that a person required to wait for the arrival of a constable under para 7(1) has committed a park trading offence, the CSO or CSV may take possession of anything of a non-perishable nature which:
  - (a) the person has in their possession or under their control; and
  - (b) the CSO or CSV reasonably believes to have been used in the commission of the offence.
- **Paragraph 9(2)**: the CSO or CSV may retain possession of the thing in question for a period not exceeding 30 minutes unless the person makes an election under para 7(4), in which case the CSO or CSV may retain possession of the thing in question until they are able to transfer control of it to a constable.
- **Paragraph 9(3)**: in this paragraph, park trading offence means an offence committed in a specified park which is a park trading offence for the purposes of the Royal Parks (Trading) Act 2000.

Meaning of specified park

The same meaning as in s 162 of the Serious Organised Crime and Police Act 2005 and includes a park, garden, recreation ground, open space, or other land in the metropolitan police district.

11.1.10 Road traffic powers

Powers and duties that may be conferred or imposed on a CSO or CSV as provided for in s 38(6B)(b). Paragraph 10 provides for powers in relation to the removal of abandoned vehicles.

- Paragraph 10 of Sch 3C states that a CSO or CSV has in the relevant police area the powers conferred on persons designated by regulations under s 99 of the Road Traffic Regulation Act 1984 (**removal of abandoned vehicles**).

11.1.11 Power to use reasonable force

Paragraph 11 of Sch 3C provides for the use of reasonable force when exercising powers under para 7 or 8.

Paragraph 11: a CSO or CSV has power to use reasonable force:

(a) to prevent a person whom the CSO or CSV has required under para 7(1) or (3) (see **11.1.7**) to wait for a constable from making off, or to keep the person under control, at any time while the person is subject to the requirement;

(b) where such a person elects under para 7(4) to accompany a CSO or CSV to a police station, to prevent the person from making off, or to keep the person under control, while the person is accompanying the CSO or CSV to the police station;

(c) where a CSO or CSV is fulfilling a duty imposed under para 7(5) or (6), to prevent the person from making off (or escaping) and to keep them under control;

(d) where a CSO or CSV is exercising a power conferred by para 8 (see **11.1.8**).

Explanatory notes

- PACE Codes of Practice have to be observed by designated officers when exercising powers (see s 67(9A) of PACE).
- Special constables—designated officers should be distinguished from special constables who have much wider policing powers and different terms of employment; see the Special Constables Regulations 1965.
  - ✦ Section 54(3)(ba) and (g) of the Firearms Act 1968 make it clear that police civilian volunteers do not need a certificate or authorisation in order to carry a defensive spray.
  - ✦ Guidance on relevant experience and qualifications appropriate for a person to have before being designated as a CSV or policing support volunteer, and the training that should be undertaken, may be issued by the College of Policing (see s 53F of the Police Act 1996).
  - ✦ Volunteers designated as CSVs or policing support volunteers are within the definition of individuals serving with the police and are subject to the police complaints system set out in Part 2 of the Police Reform Act 2002 (see s 12(7)(d) of the Police Reform Act 2002).
- Section 38(7A): a relevant employee authorised or required to do anything by virtue of a designation under this section:
  (a) shall not be authorised or required by virtue of that designation to engage in any conduct otherwise than in the course of that employment; and
  (b) shall be so authorised or required subject to such restrictions and conditions (if any) as may be specified in their designation.
- Where any power exercisable by any person in reliance on their designation under this section is a power which, in the case of its exercise by a constable, includes or is supplemented by a **power to use reasonable force**, any person exercising that power in reliance on that designation shall have the same entitlement as a constable to use reasonable force (Police Reform Act 2002, s 38(8)).
- Where any power exercisable by any person in reliance on their designation under s 38 includes power to use force to enter any premises, that power **shall not** be exercisable by that person except:

   (a) in the company, and under the supervision, of a constable; or
   (b) for the purpose of saving life or limb or preventing serious damage to property (Police Reform Act 2002, s 38(9)).
- Section 38(9A): the chief officer of police of a police force must ensure that no person designated by the chief officer under this section is authorised to use a firearm, within the meaning given by s 57(1) of the Firearms Act 1968, in carrying out functions for the purposes of the designation.
- Section 38(9B): however, subsection (9A) does not apply to:
   (a) the use of a weapon, designed or adapted for the discharge of either of the following substances, for the purpose of discharging either of those substances:
      (i) the substance, commonly known as CS spray, that is produced by the use of 2-chlorobenzalmalononitrile;
      (ii) the substance, commonly known as PAVA spray, that is produced by the use of pelargonic acid vanillylamide;
   (b) the use of a weapon for a purpose specified in regulations made by the Secretary of State;
   (c) the use of a weapon of a description specified in regulations made by the Secretary of State, whether generally or for a purpose so specified

Practical considerations

- Section 46 of the Police Reform Act 2002 makes it an offence to assault/resist/obstruct a designated or accredited person in execution of their duty (see **2.2.5**).
  (See PNLD **H18929 to H18932**.)
- It is an offence for a person to fail to comply with any powers exercised under Sch 3C paras 3 to 9 inclusive.

Summary

6 months

Level 3 fine

Links to alternative subjects and offences

2.2.5 **Assault etc, a designated or accredited person in execution of duty** 70
5.3.3 **Psychoactive substances** 257
7.1 **Penalty Notices for Disorder** 351
7.2 **Drunkenness in Public Places** 358
7.8 **Threatening/Abusive Words/Behaviour** 380
7.13 **Anti-Social Behaviour** 435
7.14 **Vehicles Causing Annoyance** 451

7.16 **Community/Environmental Protection** 465
8.8 **Fireworks** 561
9.1 **Alcohol Restrictions on Persons under 16/18** 619
9.2 **Drunkenness on Licensed Premises** 633
9.5 **Alcohol in Public Place (under 18)—Offences/Confiscation** 646
10.2 **Powers to Stop/Direct Vehicles and Pedestrians** 658

11.2 Mental Health Act—Removal etc of Mentally Disordered Persons without a Warrant

The Mental Health Act 1983 provides for police powers to act in respect of people experiencing a mental health crisis for the purposes of ensuring their care and safety.

A person experiencing a mental health crisis should receive the best possible care at the earliest possible point. The legal changes to the Mental Health Act 1983 introduced by the Policing and Crime Act 2017 are intended to improve immediate service responses to people who need urgent help with their mental health in cases where police officers are the first to respond.

Powers

(1) If a person appears to a constable to be suffering from mental disorder and to be in immediate need of care or control, the constable may, if he thinks it necessary to do so in the interests of that person or for the protection of other persons—
  (a) remove the person to a place of safety within the meaning of section 135, or
  (b) if the person is already at a place of safety within the meaning of that section, keep the person at that place or remove the person to another place of safety.

(1A) The power of a constable under subsection (1) may be exercised where the mentally disordered person is at any place, other than—
  (a) any house, flat or room where that person, or any other person, is living, or
  (b) any yard, garden, garage or outhouse that is used in connection with the house, flat or room, other than one that is also used in connection with one or more other houses, flats or rooms.

(1B) For the purpose of exercising the power under subsection (1), a constable may enter any place where the power may be exercised, if need be by force.

(1C) Before deciding to remove a person to, or to keep a person at, a place of safety under subsection (1), the constable must, if it is practicable to do so, consult—
  (a) a registered medical practitioner,
  (b) a registered nurse,
  (c) an approved mental health professional, or
  (d) a person of a description specified in regulations made by the Secretary of State.

Mental Health Act 1983, s 136

Permitted period of detention

Under s 136(2), a person removed to, or kept at, a place of safety under this section may be detained there for a period not exceeding the **permitted period of detention** for the purpose of enabling them to be examined by a registered medical practitioner and to be interviewed by an approved mental health professional and of making any necessary arrangements for their treatment or care.

Section 136(2A) states that the permitted period of detention means:

(a) the period of **24 hours** beginning with—
  (i) in a case where the person is removed to a place of safety, the time when the person arrives at that place;
  (ii) in a case where the person is kept at a place of safety, the time when the constable decides to keep the person at that place; or
(b) where an authorisation is given in relation to the person under s 136B, that period of 24 hours and such further period as is specified in the authorisation.

Under s 136(3), a constable, an approved mental health professional, or a person authorised by either of them for the purposes of this subsection may, before the end of the permitted period of detention mentioned in subsection (2) above, take a person detained in a place of safety under that subsection to one or more other places of safety.

Under s 136(4), a person taken to a place of safety under subsection (3) above may be detained there for a purpose mentioned in subsection (2) above for a period ending no later than the end of the permitted period of detention mentioned in that subsection.

Protective search powers

(3) Where a person is detained under section 136(2) or (4), a constable may search the person, at any time while the person is so detained, if the constable has reasonable grounds for believing that the person—
  (a) may present a danger to himself or herself or to others, and
  (b) is concealing on his or her person an item that could be used to cause physical injury to himself or herself or to others.
(4) The power to search conferred by subsection (1) or (3) is only a power to search to the extent that is reasonably required for the purpose of discovering the item that the constable believes the person to be concealing.
(5) The power to search conferred by subsection (1) or (3)—
  (a) does not authorise a constable to require a person to remove any of his or her clothing other than an outer coat, jacket or gloves, but
  (b) does authorise a search of a person's mouth.
(6) A constable searching a person in the exercise of the power to search conferred by subsection (1) or (3) may seize and retain anything found, if he or she has reasonable grounds for believing that the

person searched might use it to cause physical injury to himself or herself or to others.

(7) The power to search a person conferred by subsection (1) or (3) does not affect any other power to search the person.

Mental Health Act 1983, s 136C

Use of police stations as places of safety

- Section 136A(1): a **child** may not, in the exercise of a power to which this section applies, be removed to, kept at, or taken to a place of safety that is a police station.
- Section 136A(2): the Secretary of State may by regulations:
  - (a) provide that **an adult** may be removed to, kept at, or taken to a place of safety that is a police station, in the exercise of a power to which this section applies, only in circumstances specified in the regulations;
  - (b) make provision about how adults removed to, kept at, or taken to a police station, in the exercise of a power to which this section applies, are to be treated while at the police station, including provision for review of their detention.
- The power to which this section applies includes the power under s 136(3) where a constable, an approved mental health professional, or a person authorised by either of them for the purposes of this subsection may, before the end of the permitted period of detention mentioned in subsection (2) (**see earlier**), take a person detained in a place of safety under that subsection to one or more other places of safety.

Meanings

Child

A person aged under 18.

Adult

A person aged 18 or over.

Mental disorder

Means any disorder or disability of the mind, and 'mentally disordered' shall be construed accordingly.

Place of safety

Section 135(6) states that a place of safety means residential accommodation provided by a local social services authority under Part 1 of the Care Act 2014, a hospital as defined by this Act, a police station, an **independent hospital** or **care home** for mentally disordered persons, or any other suitable place.

(a) A house, flat, or room where a person is living **may not** be regarded as a suitable place unless:
   (i) if the person believed to be suffering from a mental disorder is the sole occupier of the place, that person agrees to the use of the place as a place of safety;
   (ii) if the person believed to be suffering from a mental disorder is an occupier of the place but not the sole occupier, both that person and one of the other occupiers agree to the use of the place as a place of safety;
   (iii) if the person believed to be suffering from a mental disorder is not an occupier of the place, both that person and the occupier (or, if more than one, one of the occupiers) agree to the use of the place as a place of safety.

(b) A place other than (i), (ii), and (iii) above may not be regarded as a suitable place unless a person who appears to the constable exercising powers under this section to be responsible for the management of the place agrees to its use as a place of safety.

Approved mental health professional

Means a person approved under s 114(1) by any local social services authority.

Care home/independent hospital

These have the same meaning as in ss 2 and 3 of the Care Standards Act 2000.

Explanatory notes

- The protective search powers under s 136C(1) also apply where a warrant is issued under s 135.
- While s 136A(1) prevents the use of police stations as place of safety in any circumstances where the person is under 18, s 136A(2) allows the Secretary of State to make regulations to restrict circumstances in which police cells may be used as a place of safety for persons aged 18 and over. The prohibition in s 136A(1) means that children must not be removed to any part of a police station as a place of safety under this Act.
- The powers under s 136(1) apply to any public or private place other than dwellings. Public or private place would therefore include private work premises, schools, rooftops of commercial or business buildings, on railway lines, in hospital emergency departments, schools, non-residential parts of residential buildings with restricted entry, and police custody. A place of safety could not be a private room in a care or a residential home where a person lives.
- Although s 136(1) requires that a constable consults with a health care professional before taking a person into detention, it may not always be practicable. The reasons include:
    - ✦ the time it is likely to carry out the consultation;

- ✦ whether the person appearing to suffer from a mental disorder is likely to remain cooperative and present during the time taken to undertake the consultation; and
- ✦ whether it is safe to undertake a consultation or whether the behaviour of the person requires immediate action in the interests of safety.

The Home Office guidance (October 2017) for the 'changes to police powers and places of safety provisions in the Mental Health Act 1983' provides more detail on places of safety and advice on welfare for persons detained at police stations.

Practical considerations

- The Mental Health Act 1983: Codes of Practice (England) (last updated 31 October 2017): Chapter 16 of the Code is the most relevant for the police and relates to police powers and places of safety. The Code of Practice issued under s 118 of the Mental Health Act 1983 provides guidance to professionals on how to carry out their responsibilities under the Act. It guides patients, their families, and carers on their rights and has been revised reflecting the changes in legislation, case law, policy, and professional practice since its last revision in 2008. Although the Code remains in force, the revised legislation under the Policing and Crime Act 2017 will mean that parts of the Code will require updating in due course.
- When a person is detained under this section, an ambulance should be requested to transport the person, accompanied by a police officer, to the place of safety.
- Although the maximum period of detention is twenty-four hours, this can be extended if a doctor certifies that an extension of up to twelve hours is necessary.
- Section 135 deals with an application for a warrant on suspicion that a person is suffering from a mental disorder and has been, or is being, ill-treated, neglected, or kept otherwise than under proper control, in any place or being unable to care for themselves, is living alone in any such place. The warrant may authorise any constable to enter the place, if need be by force in order to take that person to a place of safety.
- A person cannot be deemed to be suffering from mental disorder by reason only of their promiscuity, immoral conduct, sexual deviancy, or dependence on alcohol or drugs.
- If an offence has also been committed, the PACE powers of arrest (or other relevant power to arrest) could be considered.
- Legality of detention issues:
  - ✦ People removed from public places under s 136 should be assessed as soon as possible. If that assessment is to take place in a police station, an approved mental health professional and registered medical practitioner **must** be called to carry out the interview and examination (PACE Code C para 3.16). Once interviewed, examined, and suitable arrangements made for their treatment or care, they can no longer be lawfully detained under s 136.

- The person should not be released until they have been assessed by an approved mental health professional and the registered medical practitioner.
- If the decision has been made that the person is not 'mentally disordered', admittance for treatment can only be effected with that person's consent.

11.3 Illegal Entry into the UK/Identity Documents/Illegal Entry by Deception

Legislation relating to immigration is vast. However, three major aspects potentially affect policing and include: illegal entry into the UK, illegal entry by deception, and assisting and harbouring an illegal immigrant.

11.3.1 Illegal entry into the UK

Section 24 of the Immigration Act 1971 creates offences in relation to illegal entry and other associated offences.

Offences

24(A1) A person who knowingly enters the United Kingdom in breach of a deportation order.

24(B1) A person who—
- (a) requires leave to enter the United Kingdom under this Act, and
- (b) knowingly enters the United Kingdom without such leave.

24(C1) A person who—
- (a) has only a limited leave to enter or remain in the United Kingdom, and
- (b) knowingly remains beyond the time limited by the leave.

24(D1) A person who—
- (a) requires entry clearance under the immigration rules, and
- (b) knowingly arrives in the United Kingdom without a valid entry clearance.

Immigration Act 1971, s 24(A1) to (D1)

PNLD **H100693, H100694, H100695, H100696**

Offences

A person who is not a British citizen shall be guilty of an offence in any of the following cases—
- (a) and (aa) [*repealed*]
- (b) if, having only a limited leave to enter or remain in the United Kingdom, he knowingly fails to observe a condition of the leave;
- (c) if, having lawfully entered the United Kingdom without leave by virtue of section 8(1) above, he remains without leave beyond the time allowed by section 8(1);

(d) if, without reasonable excuse, he fails to comply with any requirement imposed on him under Schedule 2 to this Act to report to a medical officer of health, or to attend, or submit to a test or examination, as required by such an officer;
(e) [*omitted*]
(f) if he disembarks in the United Kingdom from a ship or aircraft after being placed on board under Schedule 2 or 3 to this Act with a view to his removal from the United Kingdom;
(g) if he embarks in contravention of a restriction imposed by or under an Order in Council under section 3(7) of this Act;
(h) if the person is on immigration bail within the meaning of Schedule 10 to the Immigration Act 2016 and, without reasonable excuse, the person breaches a bail condition within the meaning of that Schedule.

Immigration Act 1971, s 24(1)

PNLD H580, H4039, H4069, H4046, H4065, H4071, H18905

Points to prove

For ss 24 (A1) to (D1)

✓ date and location
✓ being subject to a deportation order, entered the UK or
✓ being a person who required leave to enter UK, knowingly entered the UK without that leave or
✓ being a person subject to limited leave to enter/remain in UK, knowingly remained beyond the date allowed by the leave or
✓ being a person who needed entry clearance under the immigration rules, knowingly arrived in the UK without a valid entry clearance

Explanatory notes

- A person commits an offence under subsection (C1) on the day when they first know that the time limited by the leave has expired and continues to commit it throughout any period during which they remain in the UK thereafter; but that person shall not be prosecuted under that provision more than once in respect of the same limited leave.
- Section 24B creates a summary offence if a person works in circumstances where they have not been granted leave to enter or remain, the leave to enter or remain is invalid, has ceased to have effect, or is subject to a condition preventing them from doing that kind of work, and at the time they know or have reasonable cause to believe that they are disqualified from working by reason of immigration status. Where a person has been arrested for an offence under this section, there is a power to search business premises without a warrant. Wages paid to illegal workers could be recoverable under the Proceeds of Crime Act 2002 (see **5.5**).

Related case

R v Uxbridge Magistrates' Court, ex parte Sorani, Adimi and Kaziu [1999] 4 All ER 529, QBD Provides guidance on the prosecution of asylum seekers as illegal immigrants.

Practical considerations

- Illegal entrants should not be prosecuted for offences of illegal entry or travelling on false documents if they are claiming political asylum, arriving directly from a place where they were in danger, present themselves immediately, and show good reason for their entry. This is in line with the UN Convention relating to refugee status and was followed in the case of *R v Uxbridge Magistrates' Court, ex p Sorani, Adimi and Kaziu* [1999] 4 All ER 529, QBD. This only applies to offences relating to asylum seekers who face charges relating to illegal entry and the use of false travel documents; they are still subject to prosecution for other offences in the usual way.
- Section 25D provides that where a person has been arrested for assisting in illegal entry or any of the following offences:
  - ✦ s 25—to assist a non-EU citizen to breach the immigration laws of a member state of the European Union or the UK, that is, to assist illegal entry or to harbour illegal immigrants;
  - ✦ s 25A—to help an asylum-seeker to enter the UK where this is done for gain;

  then any vehicle, ship, or aircraft used when committing these offences may be seized and detained by a police constable or senior immigration officer, pending a court order for their forfeiture.
- Consider confiscation of cash and property for the s 25 or 25A of the Immigration Act 1971 (assisting unlawful immigration) offences. These and other people trafficking offences are given as 'criminal lifestyle' offences under Sch 2 to the Proceeds of Crime Act 2002 (see **5.5** for details).

Offences under s 24(A1) to (D1)

Either way

None

Section 24(A1)

Summary: 6/12 months' imprisonment and/or a fine

Indictment: maximum 5 years' imprisonment and/or a fine

Section 24(B1), (C1), and (D1)

Summary: 6/12 months' imprisonment and/or a fine

Indictment: maximum 4 years' imprisonment and/or a fine

Offences under s 24(1)

Summary

6 months or 36 months when exceeding time limits

Six months' imprisonment and/or a level 5 fine

11.3.2 Identity documents

- Section 4 of the Identity Documents Act 2010 makes it an indictable offence for a person with an improper intention to have in their possession or control an **identity document** that is false, improperly obtained, or relates to someone else.
- Section 6 of the Identity Documents Act 2010 makes it an 'either way' offence for a person, without reasonable excuse, to have in their possession or control an **identity document** that is false, improperly obtained, relates to someone else, or any apparatus/ article which, to their knowledge, is specially designed or adapted for the making of false identity documents.
- An **identity document** means any document that is or purports to be an immigration document, UK passport, passport for a country or territory outside the UK, a document that can be used instead of a passport, UK driving licence, or driving licence for a country or territory outside the UK.
- HOC 4/2010 provides guidance on the entry, search, and seizure powers, relating to nationality or identity documents, which are available to a constable or the UKBA under ss 44 to 47 of the UK Borders Act 2007.

Powers relating to passports

- Schedule 8 to the Anti-social Behaviour, Crime and Policing Act 2014 provides search powers in relation to passports and if required to seize and retain the passport/travel document.
- HOC 4/2014 provides guidance for the police and immigration and customs officials in applying these powers at ports; and for the police to seize/retain passports that have been cancelled by the Secretary of State where a person is suspected of involvement in activities contrary to the public interest.

Powers of search and seizure at ports (para 2)

- An **examining officer** may exercise any of the following powers in the case of a person at a **port** whom the officer believes to be there in connection with entering or leaving GB or Northern Ireland or travelling by air within GB or Northern Ireland. The powers are to:
    - ✦ require the person to hand over all travel documents in their possession for inspection by the officer;

  - search for travel documents, and take possession to inspect any found by the officer;
  - (subject to para 4) retain any **travel document** taken from the person, while its validity is checked or which the examining officer believes to be **invalid**.
- To search for travel documents, the officer has a power to search:
  - the person;
  - anything that the person has with them;
  - any vehicle in which the examining officer believes the person to have been travelling or to be about to travel.
- An examining officer may:
  - stop a person or vehicle and, if necessary, use reasonable force for the purposes of exercising the above powers;
  - authorise a person to carry out a search on behalf of the officer.
- An examining officer, other than a constable, in exercising the above powers has the same powers of arrest (without warrant) as a constable in relation to offences under s 4 or 6 of the Identity Documents Act 2010 (above).

Meanings

Examining officer

Means a constable, immigration officer, or a general customs official.

Port

Means:
- an airport, sea port, hoverport, heliport;
- a railway station where passenger trains go to/from places outside the UK; or
- any other place at which a person is able, or attempting, to get on or off any craft, vessel, or vehicle in connection with entering or leaving GB or Northern Ireland.

Travel document

Means anything that is, or appears to be, a passport or other document which has been issued by or for HM Government, or the government of another state, and enables or facilitates travel from one state to another.

Invalid travel document

A travel document is invalid if: it has been cancelled or expired; it was not issued by the government or authority by which it purports to have been issued; or it has undergone an unauthorised alteration.

Constable's search and seizure powers (para 3)

- A constable may exercise any of the below powers, at a place that is not a port, if the constable reasonably believes that a person is in possession of a passport which:
  - was issued by or for HM Government; and

    - has been cancelled by the Secretary of State on the basis that the person to whom it was issued has or may have been, or will or may become, involved in activities so undesirable that it is contrary to the public interest for the person to have access to passport facilities.
- The powers are to:
    - require the person to hand over all travel documents in their possession for inspection by the constable;
    - search for travel documents and to take possession of any that the constable finds;
    - inspect any travel document taken from the person and to retain it while its validity is checked;
    - (subject to para 4) retain any travel document taken that the constable believes to be invalid.
- The power to search for travel documents is a power to search:
    - the person;
    - anything that the person has with them;
    - any vehicle in which the constable believes the person has travelled in or is about to travel;
    - any premises on which the constable is lawfully present.
- A constable may:
    - if necessary, use reasonable force for the purpose of exercising the above powers;
    - authorise a person to carry out the above search powers on the constable's behalf.

Retention or return of documents seized (para 4)

- If a travel document is retained under para 2(2)(c), 3(3)(c), or 3A(2)(c) while its validity is checked, the checking must be carried out as soon as possible.
- If such a travel document is valid, or is invalid only because it has expired, it must be returned to the person straight away.
- A travel document taken under para 2, 3, or 3A must be returned to the person before the end of the period of seven days beginning with the day on which it was taken, unless during that period it is established that the document is invalid for some reason other than expiry.
- A requirement to return an expired travel document does not apply where the officer concerned reasonably believes that the person from whom they took the document (as the case may be), to whom it was issued, or some other person intends to use it for purposes for which it is no longer valid.
- A requirement to return a travel document has effect subject to any provision not in this Schedule under which the document may be lawfully retained.

Schedule 8 offences (para 5)

- A person who is required under para 2(2)(a) or 3(3)(a) to hand over all travel documents in their possession commits an offence if they fail without reasonable excuse to do so.

- A person who intentionally obstructs, or seeks to frustrate, the exercise of a power of search under para 2, 3, or 3A, or the exercise of a power of entry under para 3A, commits an offence.

Illegal entry/passports

SSS

Summary

6 months

6 months' imprisonment and/or a fine

Identity documents

E&S

s 4 Indictable; s 6 Either way

None

s 4 offence

Indictment: 10 years' imprisonment and/or a fine

s 6 offence

Summary: 6/12 months' imprisonment and/or a fine

Indictment: 2 years' imprisonment and/or a fine

11.3.3 Illegal entry by deception

Offences

A person who is not a British citizen is guilty of an offence if, by means which include deception by him—

(a) he obtains or seeks to obtain—

(i) leave to enter or remain in the United Kingdom; or

(ii) an ETA [electronic travel authorisation]; or

(b) he secures or seeks to secure the avoidance, postponement or revocation of enforcement action against him.

Immigration Act 1971, s 24A(1)

PNLD **H100756, H3448**

Points to prove

✓ not being a British citizen
✓ by means including deception
✓ obtained/sought to obtain leave to enter/remain in UK/an ETA OR
✓ secured/sought to secure the avoidance/postponement/revocation of enforcement action

Meaning of enforcement action

Enforcement action in relation to a person means:

- the giving of directions for their removal from the UK ('directions') under Sch 2 to this Act or s 10 of the Immigration and Asylum Act 1999;
- the making of a deportation order under s 5 of this Act; or
- the removal from the UK in consequence of directions or a deportation order.

E&S

Either way   None

Summary: 6/12 months' imprisonment and/or a fine

Indictment: 2 years' imprisonment and/or a fine

11.4 Wasting Police Time

This section considers two aspects of taking up police resources on false pretences: those of wasting police time and of carrying out a bomb hoax.

11.4.1 Wasting police time

Section 5(2) of the Criminal Law Act 1967 creates the offence of the wasteful employment of the police by making false reports.

Offences

Where a person causes any wasteful employment of the police by knowingly making to any person a false report tending to show that an offence has been committed or to give rise to apprehension for the safety of any persons or property or tending to show that he has information material to any police inquiry, he shall be guilty of an offence.

Criminal Law Act 1967, s 5(2)

PNLD H2080

Points to prove

- ✓ knowingly caused
- ✓ wasteful employment of police
- ✓ by false report
- ✓ that offence committed OR
- ✓ giving apprehension for safety of persons/property OR
- ✓ that had information material to police enquiry

Explanatory note

- 'Giving rise to apprehension for safety of any persons or property' could apply where a person falsely reports a house fire in order to commit a burglary or a mother falsely reports that their child is missing in an attempt to get their estranged husband back.

Practical considerations

- Consent of the DPP is required before commencing a prosecution.
- If suitable, consider issuing a PND (see **7.1.1**).
- Decisions to prosecute are often inconsistent and may bear no relation to the number of hours wasted on the investigation.
- Consider other similar offences such as hoax bomb calls (see **11.4.2**) or false messages (see **7.12**).

PND

Summary

6 months

6 months' imprisonment and/or a level 4 fine

11.4.2 Bomb and terrorist-type hoaxes

Bomb hoaxes

Section 51 of the Criminal Law Act 1977 concerns bomb hoaxes.

Offences

(1) A person who—
   (a) places any **article** in any place whatever; or
   (b) dispatches any article by post, rail or any other means whatever of sending things from one place to another,

   with the **intention** (in either case) of inducing in some other person a belief that it is likely to explode or ignite and thereby cause personal injury or damage to property is guilty of an offence.

(2) A person who communicates any information which he knows or believes to be false to another person with the intention of inducing in him or any other person a false belief that a bomb or other thing liable to explode or ignite is present in any place or location whatever is guilty of an offence.

Criminal Law Act 1977, s 51

PNLD H2056, H2057, H2102

Points to prove

s 51(1) offence

✓ placed in any place or dispatched by post/rail/other means of sending things
✓ an article
✓ with intent
✓ to induce in another the belief
✓ that the article
✓ was likely to explode/ignite
✓ and cause personal injury/damage to property

s 51(2) offence

✓ communicated
✓ information to another person
✓ knew/believed to be false

✓ with intent
✓ of inducing a false belief in that person/any other person
✓ that bomb/thing was in place or location and
✓ was liable to explode/ignite at that place/location

Meanings

Article

This includes substance.

Intention (see **4.1.2**)

Person

It is not necessary to have any particular person in mind as the person in whom they intend to induce the belief in question.

Explanatory notes

- Section 51(1) concerns the placing or dispatching of articles with the intention that people believe that they are bombs or explosive devices; whereas s 51(2) concerns people who communicate false information intending others to believe there is a bomb or explosive device likely to explode.
- This section does not require a specific place or location to be given.
- For a person to be guilty of an offence under subsection (1) or (2) above, it is not necessary for them to have any particular person in mind as the person in whom they intend to induce the belief mentioned in that subsection.

Related case

R v Webb [1995] 27 LS Gaz R 31, CA The hoax message does not have to give a specific place or location.

Terrorist-type hoaxes

Section 114 of the Anti-terrorism, Crime and Security Act 2001 has created a similar offence for biological, chemical, and nuclear hoaxes. These include actions such as sending powders or liquids through the post and claiming that they are harmful.

Offences

(1) A person is guilty of an offence if he—
  (a) places any substance or other thing in any place; or
  (b) sends any substance or other thing from one place to another (by post, rail or any other means whatever);

with the intention of inducing in a person anywhere in the world a belief that it is likely to be (or contain) a noxious substance or other noxious thing and thereby endanger human life or create a serious risk to human health.

(2) A person is guilty of an offence if he communicates any information which he knows or believes to be false with the intention of inducing in a person anywhere in the world a belief that a noxious substance or other noxious thing is likely to be present (whether at the time the information is communicated or later) in any place and thereby endanger human life or create a serious risk to human health.

Anti-terrorism, Crime and Security Act 2001, s 114

PNLD H4770, H4771, H4772

Points to prove

s 114(1) offence

✓ placed OR sent
✓ a substance/thing
✓ Intending
✓ to induce in a person
✓ a belief that it is likely to be/contain a noxious substance/thing
✓ and thereby endanger human life/create a serious risk to human health

s 114(2) offence

✓ communicated information
✓ knew/believed to be false
✓ Intending
✓ to induce in a person
✓ anywhere in the world
✓ a belief that a noxious substance/thing
✓ was likely to be present in any place
✓ thereby endanger human life/create a serious risk to human health

Meanings

Substance

Includes any biological agent and any other natural or artificial substance (whatever its form, origin, or method of production).

Intention (see **4.1.2**)

Person (see '**Bomb hoaxes**' above)

Practical considerations

- A related offence is food contamination contrary to s 38 of the Public Order Act 1986. It is an offence under s 38(1) to intend to cause alarm, injury, or loss by contamination of or interference with **goods**, or by making it appear that goods have been contaminated or interfered with, in a place where goods of that description are consumed, used, sold, or otherwise supplied. It is also an offence under s 38(2) to make threats or claims relating to s 38(1) or to possess materials under s 38(3) with a view to committing a s 38(1) offence.

- Section 38 concerns 'consumer terrorism' which could involve animal rights activists or an individual trying to blackmail a manufacturer or supermarket chain. **Goods** includes substances whether natural or manufactured and whether or not incorporated in or mixed with other goods.
- The court should be made aware of the disruptions and anxiety caused by the hoax.
- How much time and expense were wasted by the hoax?

SSS E&S

Either way

None

Summary: 6/12 months' imprisonment and/or a fine

Indictment: 7 years' imprisonment and/or a fine

Links to alternative subjects and offences

2.5 **Threats to Kill** ... 97
4.6 **Threats to Destroy or Damage Property** ... 203
7.1 **Penalty Notices for Disorder** ... 351
7.6 **Fear or Provocation of Violence** ... 373
7.8 **Threatening/Abusive Words/Behaviour** ... 380
7.12 **Communications Causing Distress, Anxiety, or Serious Harm** ... 418
8.12 **Stop and Search Powers—Knives and Weapons** ... 609

11.5 Supplying Tobacco

11.5.1 Supplying butane lighter refills and tobacco

The Cigarette Lighter Refill (Safety) Regulations 1999 (SI 1844/1999) make it an offence to supply butane lighter refills to people under 18. The Children and Young Persons Act 1933 makes it an offence to sell tobacco or cigarette papers to a person under 18, with a power to search and seize from people under 16 found smoking in a street or public place.

Offences

No person shall supply any cigarette lighter refill canister containing butane or a substance with butane as a constituent part to any person under the age of 18 years.

Cigarette Lighter Refill (Safety) Regulations 1999, reg 2

PNLD H3403

Points to prove

✓ supplied
✓ cigarette lighter refill canister containing butane/substance with butane
✓ as a constituent part to a person aged under 18 years

Explanatory notes

- These Regulations prohibit the supply of cigarette lighter refill canisters containing butane to persons under the age of 18.
- Contravention of these Regulations is an offence under s 12(5) of the Consumer Protection Act 1987.

Defences

It shall be a defence for that person to show that he took all reasonable steps and exercised all due diligence to avoid committing the offence.

Consumer Protection Act 1987, s 39(1)

Possession of tobacco or cigarette papers

- Section 7 of the Children and Young Persons Act 1933 makes it an offence to sell to a person under the age of 18 any tobacco or cigarette papers, whether for their own use or not. It is a defence for the seller to prove that they took all reasonable precautions and exercised all due diligence to avoid committing the offence.

- A power of seizure exists but there is an anomaly in that it only applies to a person who appears to be under 16. A constable in uniform can seize any tobacco or cigarette papers from a person who appears to be under 16 whom they find smoking in any street or public place and can dispose of any seized tobacco or cigarette papers as directed by the police authority.
- CSOs and CSVs have conferred powers to seize tobacco or cigarette papers from any person who appears to be under 16 whom they find smoking in any street or public place. CSOs and CSVs have an additional power to search if they reasonably believe the person has tobacco/cigarette papers in their possession (see **11.1.4** and **9.5.1**).
- Section 91 of the Children and Families Act 2014 makes it an offence to purchase tobacco, nicotine products, etc on behalf of persons under 18 (so-called 'proxy purchasing').

Summary

6 months

Butane refills: 6 months' imprisonment and/or a fine

Tobacco: Level 4 fine

Links to alternative subjects and offences

7.3 **Breach of the Peace** ... 362
7.8 **Threatening/Abusive Words/Behaviour** ... 380
7.13 **Anti-Social Behaviour** ... 435
7.15.1 **Dispersal powers** ... 456

11.6 Animal Welfare and Control of Dogs

The Animal Welfare Act 2006 is discussed in the first subject area, and the remaining topics deal with dangerous dogs, orders for their control, and guard dogs. The Act provides several offences that are intended to prevent harm and distress to animals.

11.6.1 Unnecessary suffering

Offences

(1) A person commits an offence if—
   (a) an act of his, or a failure of his to act, causes an **animal** to suffer,
   (b) he knew, or ought reasonably to have known, that the act, or failure to act, would have that effect or be likely to do so,
   (c) the animal is a **protected animal,** and
   (d) the **suffering** is unnecessary.

(2) A person commits an offence if—
   (a) he is **responsible** for an animal,
   (b) an act, or failure to act, of another person causes the animal to suffer,
   (c) he permitted that to happen or failed to take such steps (whether by way of supervising the other person or otherwise) as were reasonable in all the circumstances to prevent that happening, and
   (d) the suffering is unnecessary.

Animal Welfare Act 2006, s 4

PNLD H22911, H22912

Points to prove

s 4(1) offence

- ✓ did an act/failed to act
- ✓ that caused a protected animal to suffer
- ✓ knowing/ought to have known by this act/failure to act
- ✓ caused/was likely to cause this suffering and
- ✓ the suffering is unnecessary

s 4(2) offence

- ✓ being responsible for an animal where
- ✓ another person did an act/failed to act
- ✓ that caused the animal to suffer

> ✓ permitted/failed to prevent this suffering happening
> ✓ it caused/was likely to cause this suffering and
> ✓ the suffering is unnecessary

Meanings

Animal

Means a vertebrate other than man. It does not apply to an animal while in a foetal or embryonic form.

Protected animal

An animal if it is:
- of a kind which is commonly domesticated in the British Islands;
- under the control of man whether permanent or temporary; or
- not living in a wild state.

Suffering

Means physical or mental suffering.

Responsible

A person is responsible for an animal:
- whether on a permanent or temporary basis;
- when they are in charge of it;
- when they own it;
- when they have actual care and control of a person under the age of 16 who is responsible for it.

Relevant officer

For the purposes of s 4(3A), a constable, a person (other than a constable) who has the powers of a constable, is otherwise employed for police purposes, or is engaged to provide services for police purposes; or a prisoner custody officer within the meaning of Part 4 of the Criminal Justice Act 1991.

Explanatory notes

- An offence under s 4(1) would only be committed through a failure to act if that failure to act causes unnecessary suffering. An example would be a dog owner who fails to feed their pet which then starves as a result. However, a person who encounters a starving dog in public and chooses not to act is unlikely to be guilty of the offence as their failure to act is not the cause of the animal's suffering.
- In determining for the purposes of s 4(1) whether suffering is unnecessary in a case where it was caused by conduct for the purpose of protecting a person, property, or another animal, the fact that the conduct was for that purpose is to be disregarded if:
  - ✦ the animal was under the control of a relevant officer at the time of the conduct (being a constable or a person (other than a constable) who has the powers of a constable or is otherwise

employed for police purposes or is engaged to provide services for police purposes);
  - it was being used by that officer at that time, in the course of the officer's duties, in a way that was reasonable in all the circumstances; and
  - that officer is not the defendant.
- In circumstances where a relevant officer is not on duty but they are still in control of a protected animal (including a service animal), a defendant will not be able to rely on the arguments in s 4(3)(c)(i) and (ii); however, the common law defence of self-defence will still be available to them.
- Matters to consider whether suffering is unnecessary include:
  - Could it have been avoided or reduced?
  - Was there compliance with legislation/licence/code of practice?
  - Was it for a legitimate purpose, such as benefiting the animal or protecting a person, property, or another animal?
  - Was it proportionate to the purpose of the conduct concerned?
  - Was the conduct that of a reasonably competent and humane person?
- This section does not apply to the destruction of an animal in an appropriate and humane manner.

Related cases

Riley and others v CPS [2016] EWHC 2513 (Admin) In this case, it was held that partners in a business could not be liable for events in their absence where there was no allegation of a systematic failure or a proper joint charge.

RSPCA v Colchester Magistrates' Court and others [2015] EWHC 1418 (Admin) A search under a warrant may only be a search to the extent required for the purpose for which the warrant was issued unless 'expressly' relying upon s 19 PACE powers of general seizure (see **1.4.4**).

11.6.2 **Offences involving animals fighting**

Offences

(1) A person commits an offence if they:
  (a) cause an **animal fight** to take place, or attempt to do so;
  (b) knowingly receive money for admission to an animal fight;
  (c) knowingly publicise a proposed animal fight;
  (d) provide information about an animal fight to another with the intention of enabling or encouraging attendance at the fight;
  (e) make or accept a bet on the outcome of an animal fight, or on the likelihood of anything occurring or not occurring in the course of an animal fight;
  (f) take part in an animal fight;

(g) have in their possession anything designed or adapted for use in connection with an animal fight with the intention of its being so used;
(h) keep or train an animal for use for or in connection with an animal fight;
(i) keep any premises for use for an animal fight.

(2) A person commits an offence if, without lawful authority or reasonable excuse, they are present at an animal fight.

Animal Welfare Act 2006, s 8

PNLD H22926, H22923, H22928, H22931, H22932, H22925

Points to prove

s 8(1) offence

- ✓ date and location
- ✓ caused/attempted to cause an animal fight to take place or
- ✓ knowingly receives money for admission to an animal fight or
- ✓ knowingly publicises a proposed animal fight or
- ✓ provides information about an animal fight to another with the intention of enabling or encouraging attendance at the fight or
- ✓ made/accepted a bet on the outcome of an animal fight or the likelihood of something occurring/not occurring in the course of that animal fight or
- ✓ took part in an animal fight or
- ✓ possess a thing designed/adapted for use in connection with an animal fight with intention of its being so used or
- ✓ kept/trained an animal for use in connection with an animal fight or
- ✓ kept premises for use for an animal fight

s 8(2) offence

- ✓ date and location
- ✓ without lawful authority or reasonable excuse, is present at an animal fight

Meanings

Animal (see **11.6.1**)

Animal fight

Means an occasion on which a protected animal is placed with an animal, or with a human, for the purpose of fighting, wrestling, or baiting.

Premises

Includes any place and, in particular, includes:

(a) any vehicle, vessel, aircraft, or hovercraft;
(b) any tent or movable structure.

Related cases

Wright v Reading Crown Court [2017] EWHC 2643 (Admin) A person could commit an offence under s 8 if they kept or trained an animal for use in connection with an animal fight, through an agent.

RSPCA v McCormick and others [2016] EWHC 928 (Admin) If a fight or intended fight was to fall within the meaning of s 8 of the Act, it could not be the by-product of a chance meeting but had to be a contrived or artificial creation specifically for the purpose of a fight during which the other animal had no natural means of escape. An animal must be under some degree of control and not wild. While this section is aimed at animal fights that are organised or controlled, the payment of money does not have to be involved; however, if it was, it would be an aggravating factor.

Practical considerations

- Section 22(1) gives a constable power to seize any animal that appears to have been involved in fighting where an offence under s 8 has been committed.
- Section 18 gives a constable powers to take such steps as appear to be immediately necessary to alleviate a protected animal's suffering. It is an offence to intentionally obstruct a person exercising the s 18 powers.
- Section 19 allows a constable to enter premises (except a part which is used as a private dwelling) to search for a protected animal in order to exercise their s 18 power, having a reasonable belief that the animal is on the premises and is suffering or likely to suffer. A constable may use reasonable force to gain entry but only if it appears that entry is required before a warrant can be obtained (under s 23) and executed.
- In accordance with s 17(1)(c)(v) of PACE, a constable has the power to enter and search premises for the purpose of arresting a person for an offence under s 8(1) and (2).
- Section 54 states that a constable in uniform may stop and detain a vehicle for the purpose of entering and searching it in the exercise of a search power conferred under:
  - s 19 for a protected animal believed to be suffering; or
  - s 22 for an animal believed to be involved in fighting under s 8.
- A vehicle may be detained for as long as is reasonably required to permit a search or inspection to be carried out (including the exercise of any related power under this Act) either at the place where the vehicle was first detained or nearby.
- Section 17(1)(c)(v) of PACE (see **1.4.2**) gives further power to a constable in order to enter and search premises for the purpose of arresting a person for offences under ss 4, 5, 6(1) and (2), 7, and 8(1) and (2) of this Act.

Applies to s 4 and s 8 offences

E&S

Either way

Maximum of 3 years from date of offence, **but** 6 months from date on which evidence which the prosecutor thinks is sufficient to justify the proceedings comes to their knowledge.

Summary: 6/12 months' imprisonment and/or a fine

Indictment: imprisonment for a term not exceeding 5 years, or to a fine, or to both.

11.6.3 Dangerous dogs not under control

The Dangerous Dogs Act 1991 imposes restrictions on keeping dogs which are a danger to the public and creates offences relating to a dog being dangerously out of control.

Offences

If a dog is dangerously out of control in any place in England or Wales (whether or not a public place)—

(a) the owner; and

(b) if different, the person for the time being in charge of the dog, is guilty of an offence, or, if the dog while so out of control injures any person or assistance dog, an aggravated offence, under this subsection.

Dangerous Dogs Act 1991, s 3(1)

PNLD **H11472 to H11475**

Points to prove

Standard offence

✓ owner/person in charge of dog
✓ dangerously out of control
✓ in any place

Aggravated offence

✓ while out of control caused injury to any person or assistance dog

Meanings

Dangerously out of control

Means when there are grounds for reasonable apprehension that the dog will injure any person or **assistance dog**, whether or not it actually does so.

Public place

Means any street, road, or other place (whether or not it is enclosed) to which the public have or are permitted to have access, whether for payment or otherwise, including the common parts of a building containing two or more separate dwellings.

Owner

Where a dog is owned by a person who is under 16, any reference to its owner shall include a reference to the head of the household, if any, of which that person is a member.

Assistance dog

Means a dog which has been trained:
- to guide a blind person;
- to assist a deaf person;
- by a prescribed charity to assist a disabled person with a disability that consists of epilepsy or otherwise affects their mobility, manual dexterity, physical coordination, or ability to lift, carry, or otherwise move everyday objects;
- to assist a disabled person who has a disability of a prescribed kind (not given above) and the dog is of a prescribed category.

Explanatory notes

- The offence extends to not just a public place, or a private place where the dog is not permitted to be, but to all places including private property.
- The exemptions given in ss 3(1A) and (1B) (see '**Defences**') cover cases where a dog becomes dangerously out of control when a trespasser is inside, or is in the process of entering, a building that is a place where a person lives. It does not matter whether the person was a trespasser; if the owner is in the building when the dog becomes out of control and believes that the person is a trespasser, that is sufficient.
- People who live in buildings which serve a dual purpose as a place of residence and a place of work (eg a shopkeeper and their family who live above the shop) can rely on the defence of self-defence given in s 76(8B) of the Criminal Justice and Immigration Act 2008 (see **1.2**) regardless of which part of the building they were in when they were confronted by an intruder, providing that there is an internal means of access between the two parts of the building.

Defences

(1A) A person ('D') is not guilty of an offence under subsection (1) in a case which is a householder case.

(1B) For the purposes of subsection (1A) 'a householder case' is a case where—

(a) the dog is dangerously out of control while in or partly in a building, or part of a building, that is a dwelling or is forces accommodation (or is both), and

(b) at that time—
(i) the person in relation to whom the dog is dangerously out of control ('V') is in, or is entering, the building or part as a trespasser, or
(ii) D (if present at that time) believed V to be in, or entering, the building or part as a trespasser.

Section 76(8B) to (8F) of the Criminal Justice and Immigration Act 2008 (use of force at place of residence) [see **1.2**] apply for the purposes of this subsection as they apply for the purposes of subsection (8A) of that section (and for those purposes the reference in section 76(8D) to subsection (8A)(d) is to be read as if it were a reference to paragraph (b)(ii) of this subsection).

(2) In proceedings for an offence under subsection (1) above against a person who is the owner of a dog, but was not at the material time in charge of it, it shall be a defence for the accused to prove that the dog was, at the material time, in the charge of a person whom he reasonably believed to be a fit and proper person to be in charge of it.

Dangerous Dogs Act 1991, s 3

Destruction and disqualification orders

(1) Where a person is convicted of an offence under section 1 or 3(1) above the court—
(a) may order the destruction of any dog in respect of which the offence was committed and, subject to subsection (1A) below, shall do so in the case of an offence under section 1 or an aggravated offence under section 3(1) above; and
(b) may order the offender to be disqualified, for such period as the court thinks fit, for having custody of a dog.

(1A) Nothing in subsection (1)(a) above shall require the court to order the destruction of a dog if the court is satisfied that the dog would not constitute a danger to public safety.

(1B) For the purposes of subsection (1A)(a), when deciding whether a dog would constitute a danger to public safety, the court—
(a) must consider—
(i) the temperament of the dog and its past behaviour, and
(ii) whether the owner of the dog, or the person for the time being in charge of it, is a fit and proper person to be in charge of the dog, and
(b) may consider any other relevant circumstances.

Dangerous Dogs Act 1991, s 4

Related cases (see also 11.6.5)

R (on the application of Andrews) v Chief Constable of Thames Valley [2022] EWHC 887 (Admin) By reference to the seizure of a dog under s 5 of the Dangerous Dogs Act 1991, an officer may reasonably conclude that a dog is dangerously out of control on the grounds of the officer's knowledge of evidence of the dog's conduct on previous occasions. This is notwithstanding that the dog appears calm at the point of seizure and is held securely on a lead.

Royal Mail Group Ltd v Watson [2021] EWHC 2098 (Admin) A Royal Mail postal worker who was bitten on the finger by a dog after they failed to use a postal peg to push mail through a letterbox was not a trespasser for the purposes of the Dangerous Dogs Act 1991. The failure to adhere to the Royal Mail requirement to use a postal peg was irrelevant, since what the worker had done by putting their fingers briefly through the letterbox did not exceed the invitation by the householder implicit in a letterbox. Further, any lack of due diligence on the part of an injured person did not give rise to a defence and was irrelevant to causation. That was because the offence was one of strict liability in the sense that liability follows where the dog bites someone and, immediately before doing so, the dog is dangerously out of control in the sense that the dog is shown to be acting in a way that gives grounds for reasonable apprehension that it will injure someone.

L v CPS [2010] EWHC 341 (Admin) The defendant took their dog into a public place and asked the co-defendant to take the dog's lead. The co-defendant released the dog and shouted, 'Get him', and the dog attacked and injured the victim. Although the co-defendant took physical control of the dog, the defendant remained 'in charge'. They had been in charge of the dog during the whole incident, both before and after the co-defendant had taken physical control. The defendant would have remained in control of the dog if, for example, it was let off its lead in a park, and there was no reason why they did not remain in charge even where, for a short period, they put the dog under another's physical control. The defendant could have taken control of the dog at any time because the dog reacted to their commands and, if they had given such commands, they would have been able to control it.

R v Gedminintaite and Collier [2008] EWCA Crim 814 The defendant owned two Rottweiler dogs and with the assistance of another person was taking them for a walk. During the walk, the dog that was under the control of the other person bit a child. It was held that the behaviour of the dog, and the fact that the defendant had no proper control over it, was sufficient evidence that the dog was dangerously out of control in a public place.

R v Bezzina; R v Codling; R v Elvin [1994] 3 All ER 964, CA It was held that the s 3(1) offence imposes strict liability as no 'mens rea' is required on the part of the owner or handler of dogs.

Practical considerations

- In considering whether a dog is dangerously out of control, references to a dog injuring a person or assistance dog, or there being grounds for reasonable apprehension that it will do so, do not include references to any case in which the dog is being used for a lawful purpose by a constable or a person in the service of the Crown.

- An order under s 2 of the Dogs Act 1871 (order on complaint that a dog is dangerous and not kept under proper control) (see **11.6.4**) may be made whether or not the dog is shown to have injured any person; and may specify measures for keeping the dog under proper control whether by muzzling, keeping on a lead, excluding it from specified places, requiring it to be neutered, or otherwise.
- If animals are injured, apart from an assistance dog, consider using powers under s 2 of the 1871 Act (see **11.6.4**).
- Section 1 of the Dogs (Protection of Livestock) Act 1953 provides an offence for the owner (person in charge) of a dog that has worried livestock on agricultural land. This could be attacking or chasing livestock or being at large in a field or enclosure in which there are sheep. Any dog found under such circumstances (without an owner/ person in charge on any land) may be seized and detained by a police officer under s 2 of that Act.

Standard offence

Summary　　6 months

6 months' imprisonment and/or a fine

Aggravated offence

E&S

Either way　　None

Summary: 6/12 months' imprisonment and/or a fine

Indictment: If a person dies as a result of being injured: 14 years' imprisonment and/or a fine

Where a person is injured: 5 years' imprisonment and/or a fine

Where an assistance dog is injured/dies: 3 years' imprisonment and/or a fine

11.6.4 **Dog control orders**

Section 2 of the Dogs Act 1871 allows magistrates' courts to make orders in respect of dangerous dogs.

Complaint

Any court of summary jurisdiction may hear a complaint that a dog is dangerous and not kept under proper control, and if satisfied that it is dangerous, may order that it be kept under proper control by the owner, or destroyed.

Dogs Act 1871, s 2

PNLD H569

Meanings

Dangerous

Is not limited to meaning dangerous to people. It could include other animals.

Proper control

Proper control is also a question of fact for the court. If a dog is kept under proper control, an order cannot be made in respect of it.

Explanatory notes

The expression '**dangerous**' will be a question of fact for the courts to determine. It includes:

- being dangerous to livestock, birds, and other dogs (*Briscoe v Shattock* [1999] 1 WLR 432, QBD);
- however, a dog that killed two pet rabbits on only one occasion was held not to be dangerous as it was in the nature of dogs to chase and kill other small animals;
- a dog could be dangerous on private property to which people have a right of access.

Practical considerations

- Where a court orders a dog to be destroyed, it may appoint a person to undertake the seizure and destruction and require any person with custody to deliver it up, and in addition may disqualify the owner from having custody of a dog under s 1 of the Dangerous Dogs Act 1989 or under s 4(1)(b) of the 1991 Act.
- In a statement of complaint, the victim must identify the dog. It is usually necessary for the victim to then identify the dog in the presence of the owner and the investigating officer. Any injuries should be examined by the officer and described in both their statement and that of the victim. This is a complaint rather than an offence but it is advisable to interview the owner under the provisions of PACE.
- If there has been a genuine transfer of ownership of the dog, an order can only be made against the new owner.

11.6.5 Restrictions on dangerous dog breeds

The Dangerous Dogs Act 1991 imposed restrictions on keeping dogs that are a danger to the public. Section 1 created offences relating to dogs bred for fighting.

Offences

(2) No person shall—
  (a) breed, or breed from, a dog to which this section applies;
  (b) sell or exchange such a dog or offer, advertise or expose such a dog for sale or exchange;
  (c) make or offer to make a gift of such a dog or advertise or expose such a dog as a gift;
  (d) allow such a dog of which he is the owner or for the time being in charge, to be in a public place without being muzzled and kept on a lead; or
  (e) abandon such a dog of which he is the owner or, being the owner or for the time being in charge of such a dog, allow it to stray.

(3) No person shall have any dog to which this section applies in his possession or custody except—
  (a) in pursuance of the power of seizure; or
  (b) in accordance with an order for its destruction under the subsequent provisions of this Act.

(7) Any person who contravenes this section is guilty of an offence (penalty see below) except that a person who publishes an advertisement in contravention of subsection (2)(b) or (c)—
  (a) shall not on being convicted be liable to imprisonment if he shows that he published the advertisement to the order of someone else and did not himself devise it; and
  (b) shall not be convicted if, in addition, he shows that he did not know and had no reasonable cause to suspect that it related to a dog to which this section applies.

Dangerous Dogs Act 1991, s 1

PNLD H2747, H2749, H2755, H2756, H4244 to H4251

Points to prove

s 1(2) offence

✓ breed from/sell/exchange/offer/advertise/make a gift of OR
✓ allow in public place without muzzle and kept on lead OR
✓ abandon/allow to stray
✓ a fighting dog (as defined in s 1(1))

s 1(3) offence

✓ had in possession/custody
✓ a fighting dog (as defined in s 1(1))

Meanings

Dog to which this section applies

- Any dog of:
  (a) the type known as the **pit bull terrier**;
  (b) the type known as the **Japanese tosa**; and

(c) any dog of any type designated for the purposes of this section by an order of the Secretary of State, being a type appearing to him to be bred for fighting or to have the characteristics of a type bred for that purpose.

Dangerous Dogs Act 1991, s 1(1)

- SI 1743/1991 added three more dogs to s 1(1) above:
  - the type known as the **XL Bully**;
  - the type known as the **Dogo Argentino**; and
  - the type known as the **Fila Braziliero**.

Advertise

This includes any means of bringing a matter to the attention of the public.

Public place (see **11.6.3**)

Defences

The above does not apply to dogs being used for lawful purposes by a constable or any other person in the service of the Crown, such as dogs being used by the police, prison service, military police, and Customs & Excise.

Related cases (see also 11.6.3)

R v Haringey Magistrates' Court, ex parte Cragg (1996) 161 JP 61, QBD and **R v Trafford Magistrates' Court, ex parte Riley (1996) 160 JP 418, QBD** These two cases were concerned with dog destruction orders. It was held that where the owner of a dog is known, the owner must be informed of any court proceedings which may result in an order for destruction of the dog. The court suggested that had the owner been present during the proceedings against a friend, they may have been able to convince the court to come to a different decision. Even though the legislation makes no provision for informing the owner of such proceedings, not giving them this opportunity is against the rules of natural justice.

DPP v Kellet (1994) 158 JP 1138, QBD A dangerous dog wandered into a public place because the defendant was drunk and had left their front door open. It was held that voluntary intoxication is not a defence.

Bates v DPP (1993) 157 JP 1004, QBD An unmuzzled pit bull terrier was found loose in the back of a car and the defendant was convicted under s 1(2)(d). It was held that a dog in a vehicle may be deemed to be in a public place if the vehicle itself is in a public place.

Practical considerations

- From 31 January 2024, the type of dog known as the XL Bully is designated for the purposes of this section as being a type appearing to the Secretary of State to be bred for fighting or to have the characteristics of a type bred for that purpose.

- Where a dog is owned by a person who is less than 16 years old, any reference to its owner in s 1(2)(d) or (e) or 3 shall include a reference to the head of the household, if any, of which that person is a member (see s 6).
- The Dangerous Dogs (Exemption Schemes and Miscellaneous Provisions) (England and Wales) Order 2023 provides an exemption from the prohibition in s 1(3) of the Dangerous Dogs Act 1991 where the Secretary of State has issued a certificate of exemption in relation to dogs of the type known as XL Bully.
- The Dangerous Dogs Exemption Schemes (England and Wales) Order 2015 (SI 138/2015) states that the prohibition in s 1(3) of the Act shall not apply if the Agency (DEFRA) has issued a certificate of exemption in respect of a dog.
- A certificate of exemption can be issued by DEFRA (see **Appendix 2**) if it is satisfied that: a court has determined that the dog is not a danger to public safety and the person is a fit and proper person to be in charge of the dog; a court has made the dog subject to a contingent destruction order under s 4A; and that the dog has been neutered, microchipped, and third party insurance is in force regarding death or bodily injury to any person caused by the dog.
- For further guidance on this Act, see HOC 29/1997.
- The word '**type**' has a wider meaning than '**breed**' in that behavioural characteristics can also be considered: *Brock v DPP* [1993] 4 All ER 491, QBD.
- If it is alleged that a dog is of a type to which this section applies, it is presumed to be so until the owner proves to the contrary. If there is any doubt, the dog may be seized and taken to kennels where the owner may have it examined at their own expense.
- DEFRA (see **Appendix 2**) has guidance on its website to help police and local authorities enforce dangerous dog laws more effectively and crack down on irresponsible dog owners. It provides:
  - ✦ an outline and explanation of current law;
  - ✦ best practice for the main enforcement authorities;
  - ✦ guidance on identifying pit bull terrier-type dogs; and
  - ✦ local initiatives.

Summary | 6 months

6 months' imprisonment and/or a fine

11.6.6 Guard dogs

The Guard Dogs Act 1975 was introduced to regulate the use of guard dogs.

Offences

1(1) A person shall not use or permit the use of a guard dog at any premises unless a person ('the handler') who is capable of controlling the dog is present on the premises, and the dog is under the control of the handler at all times while being so used, except while it is secured so that it is not at liberty to go freely about the premises.

(2) The handler of a guard dog shall keep the dog under his control at all times while it is being used as a guard dog at any premises, except—

(a) while another handler has control over the dog; or

(b) while the dog is secured so that it is not at liberty to go freely about the premises.

(3) A person shall not use or permit the use of a guard dog at any premises unless a notice containing a warning that a guard dog is present is clearly exhibited at each entrance to the premises.

5(1) A person who contravenes section 1 or 2 of this Act shall be guilty of an offence.

Guard Dogs Act 1975, ss 1 and 5

PNLD **H571, H572, H593, H2745, H4243**

Points to prove

s 1(1) offence

- ✓ use/permit the use of
- ✓ a guard dog(s)
- ✓ on premises without a capable controller present and not under control
- ✓ of handler at all times

s 1(2) offence

- ✓ handler of guard dogs(s) fail
- ✓ to keep dog
- ✓ under control at all times
- ✓ on premises

s 1(3) offence

- ✓ use/permit the use of
- ✓ a guard dog(s)
- ✓ on premises
- ✓ when warning notice(s) that a guard dog was present
- ✓ was/were not clearly exhibited at each entrance

Meanings

Guard dog

Means a dog which is being used to protect premises, or property kept on the premises, or a person guarding the premises or such property.

Premises

Means land other than **agricultural land** and land within the curtilage of a dwelling house; and buildings, including parts of buildings, other than dwelling houses.

Agricultural land (see **11.6.3**)

Section 2

This states that a person shall not keep a dog at guard dog kennels unless a licence under s 3 is held in respect of the kennels.

Related case

Hobson v Gledhill [1978] 1 All ER 945, QBD It was held in this case that the handler is not required to be on the premises whilst the dog is properly secured. Whether a dog is secured so that it is not at liberty to go freely about the premises will depend on the facts of each case.

Summary

6 months

Fine

11.7 **Unmanned Aircraft (Drones)**

Popularly known as drones, but also referred to as remotely piloted aircraft systems or unmanned aerial vehicles, these vehicles come in a variety of shapes and sizes, ranging from hand-held types to large aircraft.

Just like any other aircraft, an unmanned aircraft must always be flown in a safe manner, both with respect to other aircraft in the air and to people and properties on the ground.

The problems associated with the use of drones have become more common when they are flown near to airliners or when used to deliver tobacco, drugs, mobile phones, etc to prisons. The Air Navigation Order 2016 aims to prevent such use.

11.7.1 **Unmanned aircraft—permission for certain flights**

The Air Navigation Order 2016 provides for permission required for certain flights of unmanned aircraft systems (UAS) and contains offences for flying or causing/permitting an aircraft to be flown without such permission.

Permission

(1) If the permission that is required under paragraph (4) of this article for a flight, or a part of a flight, by an unmanned aircraft has not been obtained—
   (a) the UAS operator must not cause or permit the unmanned aircraft to be flown on that flight or that part of the flight, and
   (b) the remote pilot must not fly the unmanned aircraft on that flight or that part of that flight.

(4) Subject to paragraph (4A), permission for a flight, or a part of a flight, by an unmanned aircraft in the flight restriction zone of a protected aerodrome is required—
   (a) from any air traffic control unit at the protected aerodrome, if the flight, or the part of the flight, takes place during the operational hours of the air traffic control unit;
   (b) from any flight information service unit at the protected aerodrome, if the flight, or the part of the flight, takes place during the operational hours of the flight information service unit and either—
      (i) there is no air traffic control unit at the protected aerodrome, or
      (ii) the flight, or the part of the flight, takes place outside the operational hours of the air traffic control unit at the protected aerodrome;

> (c) from the operator of the protected aerodrome, if—
> (i) there is neither an air traffic control unit nor a flight information service unit at the protected aerodrome, or
> (ii) the flight, or the part of the flight, takes place outside the operational hours of any such unit or units at the protected aerodrome.
>
> (4A) Permission is not required under paragraph (4) for a flight, or a part of a flight, by an unmanned aircraft subject to certification.
>
> Air Navigation Order 2016, art 94A

PNLD H22343, H22344

Points to prove

art 94A(1)(a) and (b) and (4) and art 265(6)

- ✓ date and location
- ✓ UAS operator/remote pilot of an unmanned aircraft
- ✓ caused or permitted that aircraft to be flown/flew that aircraft
- ✓ in the flight restriction zone of a protected aerodrome
- ✓ when permission had not been obtained from
- ✓ the air traffic control unit at the protected aerodrome, if the flight, or the part of the flight, took place during the operational hours of the air traffic control unit OR
- ✓ the flight information service unit at the protected aerodrome if the flight, or the part of the flight, took place during the operational hours of the flight information service unit and there was no air traffic control unit at the protected aerodrome or the flight, or the part of the flight, took place outside the operational hours of the air traffic control unit at the protected aerodrome OR
- ✓ the operator of the protected aerodrome, if there was neither an air traffic control unit nor a flight information service unit at the protected aerodrome OR
- ✓ the flight, or the part of the flight, took place outside the operational hours of any such unit

Meanings

Flight and to fly

Have the meanings respectively assigned to them by art 3.

Remote pilot

Means an individual responsible for safely conducting the flight of an unmanned aircraft by operating its flight controls either manually or, when the unmanned aircraft flies automatically, by monitoring its course and remaining able to intervene and change the course at any time.

Unmanned aircraft system (UAS)

An unmanned aircraft and the equipment to control it remotely.

Unmanned aircraft system operator

Any legal or natural person operating or intending to operate one or more UAS.

Operational hours

In relation to an air traffic control unit or flight information service unit, means the operational hours:

(a) notified in relation to the unit; or
(b) set out in the UK military Aeronautical Information Publication (AIP) in relation to the unit.

Protected aerodrome

(a) an EASA (European Aviation Safety Agency) certified aerodrome;
(b) a government aerodrome;
(c) a national licensed aerodrome; or
(d) an aerodrome that is prescribed, or of a description prescribed, for the purposes of this paragraph.

Explanatory note

- More detailed information related to 'flight restriction zones' is contained in art 94A(7).

Practical considerations

- Article 265B of the Air Navigation Order 2016 provides for offences in relation to remote pilots relating to breaches of the European Commission implementing Regulation (EU) 2019/947 Rules and Procedures for the operation of unmanned aircraft (see PNLD **D45738** and web link at **Appendix 2**).
- The rules and procedures in Art 4 of the Commission Regulation relate to the operation of unmanned aircraft and provide that the remote pilot:
  - ensures that the unmanned aircraft has a maximum take-off mass of less than 25 kg;
  - ensures that the unmanned aircraft is kept at a safe distance from people and that it is not flown over assemblies of people;
  - keeps the unmanned aircraft in visual line of sight at all times except when flying in follow-me mode or when using an unmanned aircraft observer;
  - maintains the unmanned aircraft during flight within 120 metres from the closest point of the surface of the earth, except when overflying an obstacle;
  - during flight, the unmanned aircraft does not carry dangerous goods and does not drop any material.
- Other articles of the Commission Regulation provide rules for remote pilot competencies (Art 8) and ages (Art 9).

- Also consider the offences in arts 240 and 241 of the Air Navigation Order 2016 (endangering safety of an aircraft and endangering safety of any person or property) and under s 1 of the Aviation and Maritime Security Act 1990 (endangering safety at aerodromes).
- The Air Traffic Management and Unmanned Aircraft Act 2021 provides police powers relating to requirements and offences in the Air Navigation Order 2016.
- In particular, s 13 and Sch 8 outline general powers of police officers which include the power to:
  - ✦ require an unmanned aircraft to be grounded;
  - ✦ stop and search persons or vehicles;
  - ✦ use reasonable force if necessary.
- Schedule 8 amends s 93 of the Police Act 1997 which provides that authorisation can be given by a public authority listed in that section to interfere with property and wireless telegraphy. Such authorisations may be given where the authoriser believes it is necessary for the action specified to be taken to prevent or detect the use of an unmanned aircraft in the commission of a relevant offence, and that taking such action is proportionate to what the action seeks to achieve.
- Schedule 8 amends s 94 of the Police Act 1997 to include authorisations in the absence of the usual authorising officer, in urgent cases, in respect of a prison authorisation.
- Section 14 of and Sch 9 to the Act provide that a police officer may require a:
  - ✦ remote pilot to provide evidence of competency (para 1(2));
  - ✦ remote pilot to provide information as to the identity of the person or persons who are or were the UAS operator for the flight, or the person or persons who made the unmanned aircraft (UA) available to the remote pilot (para 2(2));
  - ✦ UAS operator to provide evidence of registration (para 3(2));
  - ✦ UAS operator to provide information as to the identity of the person or persons who are or were the remote pilot or remote pilots of the flight (para 4(2));
  - ✦ person to provide information, documentation, or evidence that is of a 'specified description' (para 5(2));
  - ✦ person to provide evidence of a 'relevant consent' for a flight to take place (para 6(2)).
- Schedule 9 to the Act also outlines the power of a constable to require evidence of an 'Air Navigation Order (ANO) exemption' for a flight to take place (para 7(2)) and to inspect the UA if they consider it would assist in determining whether a power conferred by paras 1 to 7 of Sch 9 is exercisable (para 8(1)).
- Paragraph 9 makes it an offence to provide false or misleading information.

Summary   6 months

Level 4 fine for offences under arts 94A(1) and (4) and 265B(6)

11.8 Shining or Directing a Laser Beam Towards a Vehicle or Aircraft

This Act creates new offences of shining or directing a laser beam towards a vehicle or air traffic facility; and for connected purposes.

Offence

A person commits an offence if—

(a) the person shines or directs a laser beam towards a vehicle which is moving or ready to move, and

(b) the laser beam dazzles or distracts, or is likely to dazzle or distract, a person with control of the vehicle.

Laser Misuse (Vehicles) Act 2018, s 1(1)

PNLD H19374

Points to prove

✓ date and location
✓ without reasonable excuse
✓ shone/directed a laser beam towards a vehicle
✓ which was moving or ready to move AND
✓ the laser beam dazzled/distracted or was likely to have dazzled/distracted
✓ a person with control of the vehicle

Meanings

Aircraft

Means any vehicle used for travel by air.

Laser beam

Means a beam of coherent light produced by a device of any kind.

Vehicle

Means any vehicle used for travel by land, water, or air.

Vessel

Includes any ship or boat, or any other description of vessel used in navigation.

Defence

It is a defence to show—

(a) that the person had a reasonable excuse for shining or directing the laser beam towards the vehicle, or

(b) that the person—

  (i) did not intend to shine or direct the laser beam towards the vehicle, and

  (ii) exercised all due diligence and took all reasonable precautions to avoid doing so.

Laser Misuse (Vehicles) Act 2018, s 1(2)

Explanatory notes

- A person is taken to have shown a fact mentioned in subsection (2) (see '**Defences**') if sufficient evidence is adduced to raise an issue with respect to it **and** the contrary is not proved beyond reasonable doubt.
- Section 2 of the Act provides a similar offence in relation to laser misuse and air traffic services.
- A mechanically propelled vehicle which is not moving or ready to move but whose engine or motor is running is to be treated for the purposes of subsection (1)(a) as ready to move.
- 'Moving or ready to move' is intended to capture any journey made by an aircraft, vessel, or other vehicle, including land-based journeys and taxiing by aircraft, and both voyages and short journeys made by vessels. It would also cover when a vehicle is about to move and a temporary stop such as a car stopped at traffic lights or a train stopping at a station.
- The intention of subsection (2) is to provide a defence which can be relied on by persons who, eg, when in distress, shine or direct a laser beam at a rescue vehicle to get its attention or who accidentally shine or direct a laser beam towards a vehicle when using a laser for a legitimate reason.

Either way

None

Summary: 6/12 months' imprisonment and/or a fine

Indictment: 5 years' imprisonment and/or a fine

Appendix 1
Human Rights

The Human Rights Act 1998 affects operational policing, legislation, court decisions, and encompasses the fundamental rights and freedoms contained in the ECHR. These are set out in Arts 2 to 12 and 14 of the Convention and a summary is provided below. Note that for Arts 9, 10, and 11, no restrictions shall be placed on the exercise of these rights other than such as are prescribed by law.

Article 2 Right to life

1. Everyone's right to life shall be protected by law. No one shall be deprived of his life intentionally save in the execution of a sentence of a court following his conviction of a crime for which this penalty is provided by law.
2. Deprivation of life shall not be regarded as inflicted in contravention of this Article when it results from the use of force which is no more than absolutely necessary:
   (a) in defence of any person from unlawful violence;
   (b) in order to effect a lawful arrest or to prevent the escape of a person lawfully detained;
   (c) in action lawfully taken for the purpose of quelling a riot or insurrection.

Article 3 Prohibition of torture

No one shall be subjected to torture or to inhuman or degrading treatment or punishment.

Article 4 Prohibition of slavery and forced labour

1. No one shall be held in slavery or servitude.
2. No one shall be required to perform forced or compulsory labour.
3. For the purpose of this Article the term 'forced or compulsory labour' shall not include:
   (a) any work required to be done in the ordinary course of detention imposed according to the provisions of Article 5 of this Convention or during conditional release from such detention;
   (b) any service of a military character or, in case of conscientious objectors in countries where they are recognised, service exacted instead of compulsory military service;

(c) any service exacted in case of an emergency or calamity threatening the life or well-being of the community;

(d) any work or service which forms part of normal civic obligations.

Article 5 Right to liberty and security

1. Everyone has the right to liberty and security of person. No one shall be deprived of his liberty save in the following cases and in accordance with a procedure prescribed by law:
   (a) the lawful detention of a person after conviction by a competent court;
   (b) the lawful arrest or detention of a person for non-compliance with the lawful order of a court or in order to secure the fulfilment of any obligation prescribed by law;
   (c) the lawful arrest or detention of a person effected for the purpose of bringing him before the competent legal authority on reasonable suspicion of having committed an offence or when it is reasonably considered necessary to prevent his committing an offence or fleeing after having done so;
   (d) the detention of a minor by lawful order for the purpose of educational supervision or his lawful detention for the purpose of bringing him before the competent legal authority;
   (e) the lawful detention of persons for the prevention of the spreading of infectious diseases, of persons of unsound mind, alcoholics or drug addicts or vagrants;
   (f) the lawful arrest or detention of a person to prevent his effecting an unauthorised entry into the country or of a person against whom action is being taken with a view to deportation or extradition.
2. Everyone who is arrested shall be informed promptly, in a language which he understands, of the reasons for his arrest and of any charge against him.
3. Everyone arrested or detained in accordance with the provisions of paragraph 1(c) of this Article shall be brought promptly before a judge or other officer authorised by law to exercise judicial power and shall be entitled to trial within a reasonable time or to release pending trial. Release may be conditioned by guarantees to appear for trial.
4. Everyone who is deprived of his liberty by arrest or detention shall be entitled to take proceedings by which the lawfulness of his detention shall be decided speedily by a court and his release ordered if the detention is not lawful.
5. Everyone who has been the victim of arrest or detention in contravention of the provisions of this Article shall have an enforceable right to compensation.

Article 6 Right to a fair trial

1. In the determination of his civil rights and obligations or of any criminal charge against him, everyone is entitled to a fair and public hearing within a reasonable time by an independent and impartial tribunal established by law. Judgment shall be pronounced publicly but the press and public may be excluded for all or part of the trial in the interest of morals, public order or national security in a democratic society, where the interests of juveniles or the protection of the private life of the parties so require, or to the extent strictly necessary in the opinion of the court in special circumstances where publicity would prejudice the interests of justice.
2. Everyone charged with a criminal offence shall be presumed innocent until proved guilty according to law.
3. Everyone charged with a criminal offence has the following minimum rights:
   (a) to be informed promptly, in a language which he understands and in detail, of the nature and cause of the accusation against him;
   (b) to have adequate time and facilities for the preparation of his defence;
   (c) to defend himself in person or through legal assistance of his own choosing or, if he has not sufficient means to pay for legal assistance, to be given it free when the interests of justice so require;
   (d) to examine or have examined witnesses against him and to obtain the attendance and examination of witnesses on his behalf under the same conditions as witnesses against him;
   (e) to have the free assistance of an interpreter if he cannot understand or speak the language used in court.

Article 7 No punishment without law

1. No one shall be held guilty of any criminal offence on account of any act or omission which did not constitute a criminal offence under national or international law at the time when it was committed. Nor shall a heavier penalty be imposed than the one that was applicable at the time the criminal offence was committed.

...

Article 8 Right to respect for private and family life

1. Everyone has the right to respect for his private and family life, his home and his correspondence.
2. There shall be no interference by a public authority with the exercise of this right except such as is in accordance with the law

and is necessary in a democratic society in the interests of national security, public safety or the economic well-being of the country, for the prevention of disorder or crime, for the protection of health or morals, or for the protection of the rights and freedoms of others.

Article 9 Freedom of thought, conscience, and religion

1. Everyone has the right to freedom of thought, conscience, and religion; this right includes freedom to change his religion or belief and freedom, either alone or in community with others and in public or private, to manifest his religion or belief, in worship, teaching, practice, and observance.
2. Freedom to manifest one's religion or beliefs shall be subject only to such limitations as are prescribed by law and are necessary in a democratic society in the interests of public safety, for the protection of public order, health or morals, or for the protection of the rights and freedoms of others.

Article 10 Freedom of expression

1. Everyone has the right to freedom of expression. This right shall include freedom to hold opinions and to receive and impart information and ideas without interference by public authority and regardless of frontiers. This Article shall not prevent States from requiring the licensing of broadcasting, television or cinema enterprises.
2. The exercise of these freedoms, since it carries with it duties and responsibilities, may be subject to such formalities, conditions, restrictions or penalties as are prescribed by law and are necessary in a democratic society, in the interests of national security, territorial integrity or public safety, for the prevention of disorder or crime, for the protection of health or morals, for the protection of the reputation or rights of others, for preventing the disclosure of information received in confidence, or for maintaining the authority and impartiality of the judiciary.

Article 11 Freedom of assembly and association

1. Everyone has the right to freedom of peaceful assembly and to freedom of association with others, including the right to form and to join trade unions for the protection of his interests.
2. No restrictions shall be placed on the exercise of these rights other than such as are prescribed by law and are necessary in a democratic society in the interests of national security or public safety, for the prevention of disorder or crime, for the protection of health or morals or for the protection of the rights and freedoms or others. This Article shall not prevent the imposition of lawful

restrictions on the exercise of these rights by members of the armed forces, of the police or of administration of the State.

...

Article 12 Right to marry

Men and women of marriageable age have the right to marry and to found a family, according to the national laws governing the exercise of this right.

...

Article 14 Prohibition of discrimination

The enjoyment of the rights and freedoms set forth in this Convention shall be secured without discrimination on any ground such as sex, race, colour, language, religion, political or other opinion, national or social origin, association with a national minority, property, birth or other status.

Appendix 2
Useful Contacts and Links

ACPO (see **NPCC**)

Alcohol Concern

http://www.alcoholconcern.org.uk
Telephone: 020 7566 9800
Helpline (Drinkline): 0300 123 1110

Ask the police FAQ (**a PNLD official police resource**)

https://www.askthe.police.uk

British Association of Women Police

https://www.bawp.org

CEOP (**Child Exploitation and Online Protection Centre**)

http://www.ceop.police.uk

Child sex offender disclosure scheme guidance

https://www.gov.uk/government/publications/child-sex-offender-disclosure-scheme-guidance

Childline

http://www.childline.org.uk
Telephone: 0800 1111

Citizens Advice Bureau (**provides local links**)

http://www.citizensadvice.org.uk

College of Policing

https://www.college.police.uk

CPS (**Crown Prosecution Service**)

https://www.cps.gov.uk

Crime Stoppers

http://www.crimestoppers-uk.org
Telephone: 0800 555 111

DEFRA (Department for Environment, Food and Rural Affairs)

https://www.gov.uk/government/organisations/department-for-environment-food-rural-affairs

Department for Transport (see **Transport**)

Disclosure and Barring Service (DBS)

https://www.gov.uk/government/organisations/disclosure-and-barring-service/
Telephone: 03000 200 190

Domestic abuse (see **National Domestic Violence Helpline**)

Drones (see **Unmanned aerial vehicles**)

DVLA (Driver and Vehicle Licensing Agency)

https://www.gov.uk/government/organisations/driver-and-vehiclelicensing-agency

DVSA (Driver and Vehicle Standards Agency)

https://www.gov.uk/government/organisations/driver-and-vehicle-standards-agency

Equality and Human Rights Commission (EHRC)

http://www.equalityhumanrights.com
Telephone: 0808 800 0082

Forced Marriage Unit (see **Honour Network for victim support**)

https://www.gov.uk/guidance/forced-marriage
Telephone: 020 7008 5000

Foreign & Commonwealth Office

https://www.gov.uk/government/organisations/foreign-commonwealth-off ice

Galop (LGBT+ Victims and Survivors of Abuse and Violence)

http://www.galop.org.uk
Telephone: 0800 999 5428

GMB (Union)

http://www.gmb.org.uk

Gov.uk (Driving licence categories/ages/rules)

Categories: https://www.gov.uk/driving-licence-categories
Ages: https://www.nidirect.gov.uk/articles/minimum-ages-you-can-ride-or-drive-vehicles

Gov.uk (Government official information)

https://www.gov.uk

Hate crime (Stop Hate UK)

http://www.stophateuk.org
Telephone: 0113 293 5100

Highways Agency

https://nationalhighways.co.uk
Telephone: 0300 123 5000

HM Prison Service

https://www.gov.uk/government/organisations/hm-prison-service
Telephone: 0300 047 6325

HMCTS (His Majesty's Courts & Tribunals Service)

https://www.gov.uk/government/organisations/hm-courts-and-tribun als-service

HMICFRS (His Majesty's Inspectorate of Constabulary and Fire & Rescue Services)

https://www.justiceinspectorates.gov.uk/hmicfrs/
Telephone: 0300 071 3217

HMRC (HM Revenue & Customs)

https://www.gov.uk/government/organisations/hm-revenue-customs

Home Office

http://www.gov.uk/government/organisations/home-off ice
Telephone: 020 7035 4848

Honour Network (honour violence and forced marriages)

http://www.karmanirvana.org.uk
Telephone: 0800 5999 247

Hope for Justice (human trafficking and slavery)

https://hopeforjustice.org
Telephone: HQ at 0300 008 8000 and 0300 008 0055 for press and media enquiries

HSE (Health and Safety Executive)

http://www.hse.gov.uk

Health and safety issues: 0300 003 1647

Building safety: 0300 790 6787

Appendix 2: Useful Contacts and Links

Identity and Passport Service (agency of the Home Office)

https://www.gov.uk/government/organisations/hm-passport-office
Passport advice: 0300 222 0000

Information Commissioner (data protection/freedom of information)

http://www.ico.org.uk
Telephone: 0303 123 1113

Intellectual Property Office

http://www.gov.uk/government/organisations/intellectual-property-office
Telephone: 0300 300 2000

International Police Association

http://www.ipa-uk.org
Telephone: 0115 981 3638

IOPC (Independent Office for Police Conduct)

https://www.policeconduct.gov.uk

Law Society

http://www.lawsociety.org.uk

Practice Advice Service: 020 7320 5675

Anti-money laundering helpline: 020 7320 9544

Legislation

http://www.legislation.gov.uk/

Mental illness advice (SANE)

http://www.sane.org.uk
Telephone: 020 3805 1790
Helpline: 0300 304 7000

MIB (Motor Insurers' Bureau)

http://www.mib.org.uk

Ministry of Justice

https://www.gov.uk/government/organisations/ministry-of-justice
Telephone: 020 3334 3555

Missing persons (National Crime Agency—Missing Persons Unit)

http://missingpersons.police.uk
Telephone: 0800 234 6034

Missing persons (National Missing Persons Helpline)

https://www.missingpeople.org.uk
Telephone: Freephone: 116 000

National Black Police Association

https://www.nationalbpa.com

National Domestic Violence Helpline (men)

http://www.mankind.org.uk
Telephone: 01823 334244

National Domestic Violence Helpline (women and children)

http://www.womensaid.org.uk
Online live chat for advice available via this link

National Stalking Helpline

https://www.suzylamplugh.org/Pages/Category/national-stalking-helpline
Telephone (Support): 0808 802 0300

NCA (National Crime Agency)

http://www.nationalcrimeagency.gov.uk
Telephone: 0370 496 7622

NPCC (National Police Chiefs' Council—formerly ACPO)

http://www.npcc.police.uk

NSPCC (National Society for Prevention of Cruelty to Children)

https://www.nspcc.org.uk
Help for adults concerning a child: 0808 800 5000
ChildLine: 0800 1111

Parliament

http://www.parliament.uk

Penalty notices for disorder: guidance for police officers

https://www.gov.uk/government/publications/penalty-notices-for-disorder-guidance-for-police-officers

PNLD (Ask the police FAQ database)

https://www.askthe.police.uk

PNLD (Police National Legal Database)

http://www.pnld.co.uk
email: pnld@westyorkshire.pnn.police.uk
Telephone: 01924 294086

Appendix 2: Useful Contacts and Links

Police Federation

http://www.polfed.org
Telephone: 01372 352000

Police Superintendents' Association

http://www.policesupers.com
Telephone: 0118 984 4005

POSH (Professionals Online Safety Helpline)

http://swgfl.org.uk/about/UK-Safer-Internet-Centre/Professionals-Online-Safety-Helpline

Racist and Religious Hate Crime—Prosecution Guidance

https://www.cps.gov.uk/legal-guidance/racist-and-religious-hate-crime-prosecution-guidance

Rape Crisis (England and Wales)

http://www.rapecrisis.org.uk
Telephone: 0808 500 2222

Revenue & Customs (see HMRC)

RNID (Royal National Institute for Deaf)

https://rnid.org.uk
Telephone: 0808 808 0123

RSPB (Royal Society for the Protection of Birds)

https://www.rspb.org.uk
Telephone: 01767 693 680

RSPCA (Royal Society for the Prevention of Cruelty to Animals)

http://www.rspca.org.uk
Telephone: 0300 1234 999

Samaritans (organisation)

http://www.samaritans.org
Telephone: 116 123

Sentencing Council (Sentencing Guidelines)

http://www.sentencingcouncil.org.uk

Sexual Offences Act 2003 (Guidance on Part 2 of the Act)

https://assets.publishing.service.gov.uk/government/uploads/system/uploads/attachment_data/file/1120422/Guidance_on_part_2_of_the_sexual_offencesact2003_FINAL.pdf

Stonewall (**lesbian, gay, and bisexual charity**)

https://www.stonewall.org.uk

Trading Standards (**Chartered trading standards institute**)

http://www.tradingstandards.uk

Transport (**Department for Transport**)

https://www.gov.uk/government/organisations/department-for-transport
Telephone: 0300 330 3000

Unmanned aerial vehicles (**UAVs**)

https://www.caa.co.uk/uk-regulations/
https://eur-lex.europa.eu/legal-content/EN/TXT/?uri=CELEX:32019R0947

Victim Support

https://www.victimsupport.org.uk
Telephone: 0808 1689 111

VIPER® Video Identification Parade Electronic Recording

http://www.viper.police.uk
Telephone: 01274 373880

VOSA (see **DVSA**)

Youth Justice Board

https://www.gov.uk/government/organisations/youth-justice-board-for-england-and-wales

Note: All listed online resources accessed and verified on 26 June 2024.

Appendix 3

Traffic Data—Vehicle Categories and Minimum Ages

Motorcycles and three- or four-wheeled light vehicles

Minimum age		
Category	**Description**	**Minimum age**
AM	**Mopeds**—Two or three-wheel vehicles with a maximum design speed over 25 km/h but not more than 45 km/h. **Light Quadricycles**—With a mass in running order of not more than 425 kg, not including the mass of the batteries in the case of electric vehicles, whose maximum design speed is over 25 km/h and not more than 45 km/h	16*
A1	**Motorcycles** • A motorcycle with a cylinder capacity not exceeding 125cc, of a power not exceeding 11 kW and with a power/weight ratio not exceeding 0.1 kW per kg. • A motor tricycle with a power not exceeding 15 kW.	17*
A2	A motorcycle of a power not exceeding 35 kW and with a power/weight ratio not exceeding 0.2 kW/kg and not derived from a vehicle of more than double its power.	19*
A	• A motorcycle of a power exceeding 35 kW or with a power to weight ratio exceeding 0.2 kW per kg. • A motorcycle of a power not exceeding 35 kW with a power to weight ratio not exceeding 0.2 kW per kg and derived from a vehicle of more than double its power. • A motor tricycle with a power exceeding 15 kW.	24 (21 via Progressive Access)

* Will usually have to have passed Compulsory Basic Training (CBT) before riding a moped/motorcycle on the road.

Other categories

Category	Description	Minimum age
F	Agricultural tractors.	17*
K	Ride-on mowers and pedestrian-controlled vehicles excluding pedestrian-controlled mowers.	16
P	Moped—A motor vehicle with fewer than four wheels with a maximum design speed exceeding 45 km/h but not exceeding 50 km/h and which, if propelled by an internal combustion engine, has a cylinder capacity not exceeding 50cc.	16
Q	Moped—A motor vehicle with fewer than four wheels which, if propelled by an internal combustion engine, has a cylinder capacity not exceeding 50cc and, if not equipped with pedals by means of which the vehicle is capable of being propelled, has a maximum design speed not exceeding 25 km/h.	16

* Age 16 for tractors less than 2.45 m wide pulling trailers less than 2.45 m wide with two wheels, or four close-coupled.

Cars or light vans, with and without trailers

Category	Description	Minimum age
B	• Motor vehicles with a MAM not exceeding 3,500 kg, designed and constructed for the carriage of no more than eight passengers in addition to the driver with a trailer up to 750 kg. • As category B but with a trailer weighing more than 750 kg. The total weight of the vehicle and trailer cannot weigh more than 3,500 kg.	17*
B auto	As category B with automatic transmission.	17*
BE	Combinations of vehicles consisting of a vehicle in category B and a trailer, where the combination does not come within category B, and the MAM of the trailer or semi-trailer does not exceed 3,500 kg.	17

* Age 16 if currently receiving a Disability Living Allowance at the higher rate (mobility component).

Appendix 3: Traffic Data—Vehicle Categories and Minimum Ages

These tables contain public sector information licensed under the Open Government Licence v3.0 and are a summary of the data provided for guidance only—more information regarding other categories and relevant ages is available online at <https://www.gov.uk/driving-licence-categories> and <https://www.nidirect.gov.uk/articles/minimum-ages-you-can-ride-or-drive-vehicles> (accessed on 26 June 2024).

Appendix 4

Firearms Offences Relating to Age

Any firearm/ammunition

- Purchase or hire any firearm or ammunition (see **8.7.1**).
- Sell or let on hire any firearm or ammunition (see **8.7.1**).

'Section 1 firearm/ammunition'

- Purchase or hire s 1 firearm/ammunition (see **8.7.1**).
- Sell or let on hire or hire s 1 firearm/ammunition (see **8.7.1**).

Shotgun/cartridges

- Purchase or hire shotgun/cartridges (see **8.7.1**).
- Sell or let on hire or hire shotgun/cartridges (see **8.7.1**).

Air weapon/ammunition

- Purchase or hire an air weapon or ammunition for an air weapon (see **8.7.1**).
- Sell or let on hire or hire an air weapon or ammunition for an air weapon (see **8.7.1**).
- Make a gift of an air weapon or ammunition for an air weapon (see **8.7.2**).
- Part with possession of an air weapon or ammunition for an air weapon *subject to exceptions below* (see **8.7.2**).
- Have an air weapon or ammunition for an air weapon (see **8.7.2**), *except if*:
    - ✦ that person is under the supervision of a person of or over the age of 21;
    - ✦ member of approved rifle clubs;
    - ✦ using at authorised shooting galleries (not exceeding 0.23 inch calibre);
    - ✦ that person has attained the age of 14 and is on private premises with the consent of the occupier, and is under the supervision of a person of or over the age of 21, but it is an offence for the supervisor to allow them to fire any missiles beyond those premises—subject to defence (see **8.7.2**).

Imitation firearm

- Purchase an imitation firearm (see **8.7.5**).
- Sell an imitation firearm (see **8.7.5**).

Under 15 offences (shotgun/cartridges)

- Have an assembled shotgun except while under the supervision of a person of or over the age of 21, or while the shotgun is so covered with a securely fastened gun cover that it cannot be fired (see **8.2.2**).
- Make a gift of a shotgun or ammunition for a shotgun to a person under the age of 15 (see **8.2.2**).

Under 14 offences ('s 1 firearm/ammunition')

- Possess s 1 firearm or ammunition (see **8.1.3**), except for:
  - ✦ use of a certificate holder, being under their instructions, and for sporting purposes only;
  - ✦ a person conducting or carrying on a miniature rifle or shooting gallery for air weapons or miniature rifles not exceeding 0.23 inch calibre; or using such rifles/ammunition at such a range or gallery.
- Part with possession of a s 1 firearm or ammunition to a person under 14, subject to above exceptions (see **8.1.3**).
- Make a gift of or lend s 1 firearm or ammunition to a person under 14 (see **8.1.3**).

Appendix 5
Religious Dates/Events

Advisory notes: These dates are provided for guidance purposes only. Some dates may vary as the festivals are guided by the lunar calendar and some local customs may also vary the date. The religions are listed alphabetically.

	2024	2025
Baha'I		
World Religion Day	21 January 2024	19 January 2025
Naw-Rúz (New Year)	20 March 2024	20 March 2025
First Day of Ridvan	21 April 2024	21 April 2025
Last Day of Ridvan	2 May 2024	3 May 2025
Declaration of the Báb	24 May 2024	22 May 2025
Ascension of Baha'u'llah	29 May 2024	29 May 2025
Martyrdom of the Báb	9 July 2024	9 July 2025
Birth of the Báb	2 November 2024	22 October 2025
Birth of Baha'u'llah	3 November 2024	23 October 2025
Day of the Covenant	25 November 2024	25 November 2025
Ascension of 'Abdu'l-Baha	27 November 2024	27 November 2025
Buddhist		
Mahayana Buddhist New Year	25 January 2024	14 January 2025
Parinirvana Day	15 February 2024	15 February 2025
Nirvana Day (alternative date)	15 February 2024	15 February 2025
Magha Puja Day	24 February 2024	12 February 2025
Therevadin Buddhist New Year	24 April 2024	13 April 2025
Wesak (Buddha Day)	22 May 2024	12 May 2025
Asalha (Puja Day)	21 July 2024	10 July 2025
Obon (Ulambana)	15 August 2024	15 August 2025
Bodhi Day (Rohatsu)	8 December 2024	8 December 2025

Appendix 5: Religious Dates/Events

	2024	2025
Catholic		
Mary Mother of God	1 January 2024	1 January 2025
Blessing of the Animals (Hispanic)	17 January 2024	17 January 2025
Corpus Christi	30 May 2024	19 June 2025
Sacred Heart of Jesus	7 June 2024	27 June 2025
St Benedict Day	11 July 2024	11 July 2025
Assumption of Blessed Virgin Mary	15 August 2024	15 August 2025
St Francis' Day	4 October 2024	4 October 2025
All Souls' Day	2 November 2024	2 November 2025
Immaculate Conception of Mary	8 December 2024	8 December 2025
Feast Day—Our Lady of Guadalupe	12 December 2024	12 December 2025
Feast of the Holy Family	29 December 2024	28 December 2025
Chinese		
Lunar New Year	10 January 2024	29 February 2025
Christian		
Twelfth Night	5 January 2024	5 January 2025
Epiphany	6 January 2024	6 January 2025
Shrove Tuesday	13 February 2024	4 March 2025
Ash Wednesday (Lent begins)	14 February 2024	5 March 2025
St David's Day	1 March 2024	1 March 2025
St Patrick's Day	17 March 2024	17 March 2025
Palm Sunday	24 March 2024	13 April 2025
Maundy Thursday	28 March 2024	17 April 2025
Good Friday	29 March 2024	18 April 2025
Easter Day	31 March 2024	20 April 2025
St George's Day	23 April 2024	23 April 2025
Ascension Day	9 May 2024	29 May 2025
Whit Sunday (Pentecost)	19 May 2024	8 June 2025
Trinity Sunday	26 May 2024	15 June 2025

	2024	2025
Lammas	1 August 2024	1 August 2025
All Hallows Eve	31 October 2024	31 October 2025
St Andrew's Day	30 November 2024	30 November 2025
Advent Sunday	1 December 2024	30 November 2025
Christmas Day	25 December 2024	25 December 2025
Hindu		
Vasant Panchami (Saraswati's Day)	14 February 2024	2 February 2025
Maha Shivaratri	8 March 2024	26 February 2025
Holi	25 March 2024	14 March 2025
New Year	9 April 2024	29 April 2025
Ramayana Begins	9 April 2024	5 April 2025
Ramanavami	17 April 2024	6 April 2025
Hanuman Jayanti	26 April 2024	12 April 2025
Guru Purnima	21 July 2024	10 July 2025
Raksha Bandhan	19 August 2024	9 August 2025
Krishna Janmashtami	26 August 2024	16 August 2025
Ganesa Chaturthi	7 September 2024	27 August 2025
Navaratri first Day	3 October 2024	22 September 2025
Dasera	12 October 2024	2 October 2025
Navaratri Ends	12 October 2024	1 October 2025
Diwali (Deepavali)	31 October 2024	20 October 2025
Islam		
Lailat Al-Isra wa Al-Miraj (Ascension to Heaven)	7 February 2024	27 January 2025
Lailat al Bara'ah (Night of Emancipation)	25 February 2024	14 February 2025
Commencement of Ramadhan (Fasting)	10 March 2024	28 February 2025
Laylat el qadr	6 April 2024	27 March 2025
Eid Al-Fitr (Completion of Fasting)	10 April 2024	30 March 2025
Waqf al Arafa (Hajj—Pilgrimage Day)	16 June 2024	6 June 2025

	2024	2025
Eid-al-Addha (Day of Sacrifice)	17 June 2024	7 June 2025
Muharram (Islamic New Year)	6 July 2024	6 July 2025
Day of Ashura	17 July 2024	5 July 2025
Mawlid-al-Nabi (Birth of Prophet)	16 September 2024	5 September 2025

Jehovah's Witness

Lord's Evening Meal	24 March 2024	12 April 2025

Jewish

Notes: All Jewish holidays commence/start on the evening before the actual day specified, as the Jewish day actually begins at sunset on the previous night.

Rosh Chodesh Sh'vat	11 January 2024	29 January 2025
Tu B'Shvat	25 January 2024	13 February 2025
Shabbat Shekalim	9 March 2024	1 March 2025
Rosh Chodesh Adar	9–11 March 2024	27 February–1 March 2025
Shabbat Zachor	23 March 2024	7 March 2025
Ta'anit Esther	21 March 2024	13 March 2025
Purim	24 March 2024	14 March 2025
Shushan Purim	25 March 2024	15 March 2025
Shabbat Parah	30 March 2024	22 March 2025
Shabbat HaChodesh	6 April 2024	29 March 2025
Rosh Chodesh Nisan	9 April 2024	29 March 2025
Shabbat HaGadol	20 April 2024	12 April 2025
Ta'anit Bechorot	22 April 2024	12 April 2025
Pesach	23 April 2024	12 April 2025
Yom HaShoah	6 May 2024	23 April 2025
Yom HaZikaron	24–25 May 2024	29–30 April 2025
Lag B'Omer	26 May 2024	25 May 2025
Yom Yerushalayim	5 June 2024	25 May 2025
Rosh Chodesh Iyyar	7–9 May 2024	27–29 May 2025
Rosh Chodesh Sivan	7 June 2024	27 May 2025
Yom HaAtzma'ut	13–14 May 2024	30 April–1 May 2025

	2024	2025
Shavuot	11–13 June 2024	1–3 June 2025
Rosh Chodesh Tamuz	5–7 July 2024	25–27 June 2025
Tzom Tammuz	23 July 2024	13 July 2025
Rosh Chodesh Av	5 August 2024	25 July 2025
Shabbat Chazon	10 August 2024	1 August 2025
Tish'a B'Av	13 August 2024	2 August 2025
Shabbat Nachamu	17 August 2024	8 August 2025
Rosh Chodesh Elul	2–4 September 2024	23–25 August 2025
Rosh Hashana	2–4 October 2024	22–24 September 2025
Tzom Gedaliah	6 October 2024	25 September 2025
Shabbat Shuva	5 October 2024	26 September 2025
Yom Kippur	12 October 2024	1 October 2025
Sukkot	16–23 October 2024	6–13 October 2025
Shmini Atzeret	24 October 2024	13 October 2025
Simchat Torah	25 October 2024	14 October 2025
Rosh Chodesh Cheshvan	31 October–2 November 2024	21–23 October 2025
Rosh Chodesh Kislev	30 November–2 December 2024	20–21 November 2025
Chanukah	25 December 2024–2 January 2025	14–22 December 2025
Sikh		
Birthday of Guru Gobind Singh Ji	20 January 2024	27 December 2025
Maghi	13 January 2024	14 January 2025
Hola Mohalla	27 March 2024	14 March 2025
Baisakhi (Vaisakhi)	13 April 2024	14 April 2025
Martyrdom of Guru Arjan Dev Ji	16 June 2024	30 May 2025
Installation of Scriptures as Guru Granth	20 October 2024	20 October 2025
Diwali (Deepavali)	1 November 2024	20 October 2025
Martyrdom of Guru Tegh Bahadur Ji	24 November 2024	24 November 2025
Birthday of Guru Nanak Dev Ji	15 November 2024	5 November 2025

Index

abandoned dangerous dogs, 11.6.5
abandoned vehicles, 7.16.3
abatement notices, 7.16.1
abduction of child *see* **child abduction**
abortion, 2.7.6
abstracting electricity, 3.4
abuse of position, fraud by, 3.8.1, 3.8.4
abusive words or behavior *see* **threatening or abusive words or behaviour**
accelerants, 4.5.2
accessory to commission of offence, 4.1.4
accredited person
assault, 2.2.5
meaning, 2.2.5
obstruction, 2.2.5
acid *see* **corrosive substances**
actual bodily harm, assault occasioning, 2.1, 2.1.2
body mutilation, consent to, 2.1.2
chastisement, reasonable, 2.1.2
consent, 2.1.2
definition, 2.1.2
maliciously administering poison with intent, 2.1.3
psychiatric harm, 2.1.2
racially or religiously aggravated, 2.1.2
sadomasochism, 2.1.2
self-defence, 2.1.2
sport, 2.1.2
surgery, 2.1.2
wounding and grievous bodily harm, 2.3.1
administering substance with intent to commit a sexual offence, 6.10
adverse occupation of residential premises, 7.17.3
advertising
prostitution, placing of adverts in telephone boxes and, 6.11.1
aerosol paints to children, sale of, 4.7.2
affray, 7.5
conduct, meaning of, 7.5
defences, 7.5
domestic violence, 7.5
evidence, 7.5
intent, 7.5
offensive weapons or knives, stop and search for, 7.5
petrol bombs, possession of, 7.5
reasonable firmness, persons of, 7.5
stop and search, 7.5
threatens, definition of, 7.5
violence, definition of, 7.5
age of criminal responsibility, 2.7.1
aggravated burglary, 3.3.2
aggravated firearms offences, 8.1.2, 8.2.1
aggravated trespass, 7.17.4
land, meaning of, 7.17.4
police powers, 7.17.4
trespassers, meaning of, 7.17.4
aggravated vehicle-taking, 4.3.2
accidents, meaning of, 4.3.2
damage, meaning of, 4.3.2
dangerously, meaning of, 4.3.2
defences, 4.3.2
passengers, 4.3.2
recovery of vehicle, 4.3.2
agricultural machines towing trailers, registration marks and, 10.20.2
aiding, abetting, counselling, procuring, or suborning, 4.1.1
drink or drugs, driving or attempting to drive/in charge of vehicles whilst unfit through, 10.10.1
knowledge, 4.1.3
meaning of aid, abet, counsel, and procure, 4.1.3
air weapons
18, persons under, 8.7.1, 8.7.2
21, supervision by person over, 8.7.2
age restrictions, 8.7–8.7.4
air gun, definition, 8.7.2
air pistol, definition, 8.7.2
air rifle, definition, 8.7.2
ammunition, 8.7.2
BB (ball bearing) guns, 8.7.4
certificates, 8.7.3
clubs, 8.7.2
confiscation orders, 8.7.2
consent to firing, 8.7.2
convicted persons, bans on possession by, 8.3.1
dealers, 8.1.2, 8.7.2
defences, 8.7.1, 8.7.2
evidence, 8.7.2
face-to-face transactions, sale or transfer through, 8.7.2
firearms dealers, 8.1.2, 8.7.2
gas cartridge systems, with, 8.7.2, 8.7.3, 8.7.4
gifts, 8.7.1, 8.7.2
has with him, meaning of, 8.3.6
hire, 8.7.1
Home Office Circular 31/2007, 8.7.2
Home Office Circular 4/2011, 8.7.2

air weapons (*cont.*)
lethal barrelled weapon, as, 8.7.2, 8.7.4
loaded, meaning of, 8.7.2
meaning, 8.7.2
missile fired beyond premises, 8.7.2
prohibited weapons, deemed as, 8.7.3
public place, 8.7.2
purchase, 8.7.1
rifle clubs, 8.7.2
section 1 firearms, 8.1.1, 8.7.2
shooting galleries, 8.7.2
supervision, 8.7.2
supply, 8.7.1
aircraft
illegal entry, 11.3.1
shining light or laser towards, 11.8
alarm *see* **harassment, alarm, or distress**
alcohol
careless driving when under the influence of drink or drugs, causing death by, 10.8.2
cycling, 10.12.3
driving or attempting to drive mechanically propelled vehicles whilst unfit through drink or drugs, 10.10–10.10.1
drunk and disorderly in public places, 7.2–7.2.2
drunk and incapable, 7.2.2
highway, drunk on a, 7.2.2
licensed premises, drunkenness on, 9.2–9.2.3
persistently possess alcohol in a public place (under 18), 9.5.2
possession at sporting events, 7.18.1
prescribed alcohol limit, drive or attempt to drive/in charge of motor vehicle whilst over, 10.11–10.11.1, 10.11.3
PSPOs, 7.15.2
rape, 6.1.1
riot, 7.4.1
search for in motor vehicle en route to sporting event, 7.18.1
spiking drinks, 6.10, 10.11.1
stalking, 7.11.4
substance with intent to commit a sexual offence, administering a, 6.10
see also **children and alcohol**
alcohol restrictions in area subject to PSPO, 9.4.1–9.4.2
authorisation, 9.4.1
cease drinking alcohol, power to require to, 9.4.1
constable's requirements, examples of, 9.4.1, 9.4.2
CSOs, 9.4.2, 9.5.1
CSVs, 9.4.2, 9.5.1
detrimental effect of quality of life, 9.4.1
failure to comply with requirements, 9.4.2
local authority areas, 9.4.1
seizure and disposal, 9.4.2
ambulance services, obstruction of, 2.2.7
ammunition
age restrictions, 8.7.1
air weapons, 8.7.2
bullets, 8.1.1, 8.6.2
convicted person, ban on possession by, 8.3.1
endanger life, possession with intent to, 8.3.2
hand over, requirement to, 8.6.1
Home Office Circular 12/2010, 8.7.1
loaded, meaning of, 8.5
manufacture or distribution without authority, 8.1.1
meaning, 8.1.1
possession without a certificate, 8.1.1, 8.1.3
purchase, supply, or hire, 8.7.1
section 1, 8.1.1
shotgun offences, 8.2.1
ancient monuments, 4.4
animal welfare, 11.6.1
animals
criminal damage, 4.4
entry, powers of, 1.4.2
fighting, offences involving, 11.6.2
horses, 4.3.1
livestock worrying, 11.6.3
protected animals, meaning of, 11.6.1
responsible person, meaning of, 11.6.1
saving, 1.4.2
threats to, 7.11.2
unnecessary suffering, 11.6.1
wild animals, 3.1.1, 4.4
see also **dangerous dogs**; **dogs**
annoyance
fireworks, 8.8.8
off-road driving, 10.22
vehicles, 7.14–7.14.2
see also **anti-social behaviour**; **harassment**; **harassment, alarm, or distress**
anti-social behaviour, 7.13–7.13.5
abandoned vehicles, 7.16.3
anti-social behaviour orders (ASBOs), 7.13.1
anti-social manner—fail to give name and address, 7.13.2
applicants for injunctions, 7.13.1
civil proceedings, 7.13.1
dispersal powers, 7.15.1
dumping vehicles, 7.16.3
false alarms of fire, 7.12.7
fly tipping, 7.16.3
harassment, alarm, or distress, 7.13.1

housing related, 7.13.1
illegal conduct, 7.13.3
injunctions, breach of, 7.13.1
injunctions, power to grant, 7.13.1
litter, 7.16.2
meaning, 7.13.1, 7.13.2
name and address, failure to give, 7.13.2
NHS premises, causing nuisance/ disturbance on, 7.13.5
penalty notices for disorder, 7.1.2
powers of arrest, 7.13.1
premises, closure of, 7.13.4
public nuisance, 7.13.3
standard of proof, 7.13.1
unauthorised dumping or abandoning vehicles, 7.16.3
vehicles causing annoyance, 7.14–7.14.2

antique firearms and weapons, 8.1.4, 8.2.1, 8.7.5, 8.9.3

approved device, analysis by
intoximeter faulty, 10.11.3
intoximeter 'time out', 10.11.3

arms trafficking, criminal lifestyle offences, 5.5

arranged and forced marriage, difference between, 4.11.2

arrest, 7.6
appropriate adult, 1.1.2
assault with intent to resist or prevent lawful arrest, 2.2.1
breach of the peace, 7.3
cautions, 1.1.2
CSOs and CSVs, 11.1.1
detention, 2.2.2
drink or drugs, driving/attempting to drive/in charge of vehicle whilst unfit through, 10.10.2
due care and attention, driving without, 10.6.1
entry, powers of, 1.4.2
fear or provocation of violence, 7.6
firearms, 8.3.2, 8.3.4–8.3.6
further offences, 1.1.4
grievous bodily harm, 2.3.2
harassment, alarm, or distress, 7.11.7
illegal entry, 11.3.1
imitation firearms, 8.3.4, 8.3.5, 8.3.6
indictable offences, meaning of, 1.1.5
information to be given on arrest, 1.1.2
injunctions, 2.8, 7.13.1
not at police station, 1.1.3
PACE Codes, 1.1.2
penalty notices for disorder, 7.1.2
plain clothes officers, 2.2.2
police stations, 1.1.3
powers of arrest, 1.1
prescribed alcohol limit, drive or attempt to drive/in charge of motor vehicle whilst over, 10.11.1
release prior to arrival at police station, 1.1.4
resisting or preventing lawful, 2.2.1, 8.3.4
searches, 1.4.1, 1.4.3, 1.5.1
violent entry to premises, 7.17.2
warrant, without
  breach of injunction, 7.13.1
  constables, 1.1.1
  other persons, 1.1.5
wounding and grievous bodily harm, 2.3.2

arrest, assault with intent to resist or prevent lawful
firearms, 8.3.4
intention, meaning of, 2.2.1
mistake, 2.2.1

arson, 4.5.1, 4.5.2
accelerants, 4.5.2
criminal damage, 4.4, 4.5.2
defences, 4.5.2
intent, 4.5.2
preservation and packaging of accelerants, 4.5.2
recklessness, 4.5.2
separate activities, 4.5.2
smoke damage, 4.5.2

articles of police uniforms
impersonation, 2.2.4
possession or wearing, offence of, 2.2.4

articles with intent to damage, possessing, 4.7.1
anything, meaning of, 4.7.1
cause, meaning of, 4.7.1
custody or control, meaning of, 4.7.1
defence, 4.7.1
going equipped, 4.7.1
intention, 4.7.1
permit, meaning of, 4.7.1

articulated (bendy) bus, 10.1.3

artist's composites or likenesses, 1.4

assault, 2.1–2.5
accredited person, assaulting or wilfully obstructing an, 2.2.5
actual bodily harm, occasioning, 2.1, 2.1.2, 2.3.1
arrest, with intent to resist or prevent lawful, 2.2.1
assault, sport, 2.1.2
battery, 2.1, 2.1.1
certificates of dismissal, 2.1.1
chastisement, reasonable, 2.1.2
common assault, 2.1–2.1.1
consent, 2.1.2
constables
  execution of their duty, assault in the, 2.2.2
  obstruction or resisting a constable, 2.2.3
defences to assault, 2.1.2

assault (*cont.*)
definition, 2.1.1
designated or accredited person, assaulting or wilfully obstructing a, 2.2.5
discipline, 2.1.2
duplicity, charges dismissed for, 2.1.1
emergency workers, 2.2.6
forced marriages, 4.11
grievous bodily harm, 2.3–2.3.2
lawful correction, 2.1.2
lawful sports, 2.1.2
maliciously administering poison with intent, 2.1.3
obstructing or resisting a constable in the execution of their duty, 2.2.3
occasioning actual bodily harm, 2.1, 2.1.2
plain clothes officers, 2.2.2
practical considerations, 2.1.1
preventing lawful arrest, 2.2.1
racially or religiously aggravated, 2.1.1, 7.10.2
recklessness, 2.1.1
resisting arrest, 2.2.1
self-defence, 2.1.2
sexual offence, commit an offence with intent to commit a, 6.10
threats, 2.1.1, 2.5
touching, 2.1.1
using reasonable force, 2.1.2
words alone, 2.1.1
wounding, 2.3–2.3.2
assist a crime *see* **encourage or assist a crime**
asylum seekers, 11.3.1
attempts, 4.1.1
beginning of offence, 4.1.1
criminal damage, 4.1.1
drink or drugs, driving or attempting to drive/in charge of vehicles whilst unfit through, 10.10–10.10.1
drugs, producing or supplying controlled, 5.1.1
impossibility, 4.1.1
intent distinguished from, 4.1.1
murder, 2.7.1, 4.1.1
offences, 4.1.1
perverting the course of justice, 4.8.2
preparatory, acts which are more than merely, 4.1.1
tests, 4.1.1
auctioneers, firearms and, 8.1.5, 8.2.1
automatism, 10.3, 10.6.1
axes, 8.10.2

bail
breach of the peace, 7.3
penalty notices for disorder, 7.1.2
police, 7.1.2
bailiffs, 7.3
ball bearing (BB) guns, 8.7.4
bar snacks, 9.1.4
batons, 8.9.4
battery, 2.1, 2.1.1, 2.4.1
bayonets, 8.9.1
BB guns, 8.7.4
beaches, litter and, 7.16.2
belt buckle knives, 8.9.4
belt daggers, 8.10.2
bendy buses, 10.1.3
bicycles *see* **pedal cycles**
bilking, 3.7
binding over, 7.3
birth certificates
change of gender, 6.2.1
birth, concealment of, 2.7.6
blackmail, 3.2.2, 7.12.1
criminal lifestyle offences, 5.5
defences, 3.2.2
menaces, meaning of, 3.2.2
sexual offence, commit an offence with intent to commit, 6.10
bladed articles/knives, 8.10–8.10.8
affray, 7.5
age, proof of, 8.10.2
article, meaning of, 8.10.1, 8.10.2, 8.10.7
axes, 8.10.2
belt buckle knives, 8.9.4
blade, meaning of, 8.10.1
bottle openers, 8.10.1
burden of proof, 8.10.1
butterfly knives, 8.9.1, 8.9.4
court building, 8.10.1
daggers, 8.9.1
defences, 8.10.1–8.10.7
delivery to person under 18, 8.10.4
delivery to residential premises/ locker, 8.10.3
disguised, 8.9.4
due diligence, 8.10.2
entry, powers of, 8.12.2
flick guns, 8.10.2, 8.12.1
flick knives, 8.9.1, 8.9.3, 8.10.2, 8.10.5, 8.12.1
folding knives, 8.10.1, 8.10.2
further or higher education, places of, 8.10.6, 8.10.7
gravity knives, 8.9.3, 8.10.2, 8.10.5, 8.12.1
has with him, meaning of, 8.10.1
identification, 8.10.2
kitchen knives, 8.10.1
knowledge, 8.10.1
lawful authority, 8.10.1, 8.10.8
list of weapons, 8.9.1
lock knives, 8.10.1
locker, delivery to, 8.10.3

manufacture, 8.9.3
multi-tools, possession of, 8.10.1
national costume, 8.10.1
nuisance or disturbance on school premises, 8.10.8
police powers, 8.12–8.12.3
possession
further education premises, on, 8.10.7
public place, in, 8.10.1
school premises, on, 8.10.7
precautions, 8.10.2
provision, 8.9.3
public order, 8.12.2
public place
meaning of, 8.9.1, 8.10.1
possession, in, 8.10.1
razor blades, 8.10.2
religion, 8.10.1
remote sales, 8.10.2
retention, 8.12.1, 8.12.2
sale to persons under 18, 8.10.2
school premises, 8.10.1, 8.10.7
entry, powers of, 8.12.2
lawful authority to be on, 8.10.7
meaning of, 8.10.7, 8.10.8
nuisance or disturbance on, 8.10.7, 8.10.8, 8.12.2
remove people from, power to, 8.10.7, 8.10.8
seizure, 8.10.7, 8.12.2
threaten with article in, 8.10.6
screwdrivers, 8.10.1
search warrants
conditions, 8.12.1
grounds for issue of, 8.12.1
use of force, 8.12.2
seizure, 8.10.1, 8.10.7, 8.12.1, 8.12.2
serious violence reduction orders, 8.13
Sikhs, 8.10.1
skean dhu in Highland dress, 8.10.1
stealth knives, 8.9.4
stop and search, 1.3.2, 7.5, 8.10.1, 8.10.7, 8.12.2
threaten with article in public place/ school premises, 8.10.6
trade, 8.9.3
use of force, 8.12.2
vehicles, stop and search of, 8.10.1, 8.10.7, 8.12.2
work, use at, 8.10.1
blank cartridges, 8.1.1
blood samples, 10.8.2, 10.11.3
fear of needles, 10.11.3
blowpipes, 8.9.4
body mutilation, consent to, 2.1.2
bombs and explosives
affray, 7.5
articles with intent to make people believe they are bombs, placing or dispatching, 11.4.2
hoax bomb calls, 11.4.1–11.4.2
petrol bombs, possession of, 7.5
wasting police time, 11.4.1–11.4.2
bored barrels, 8.1.4
bottle openers, 8.10.1
bottles, broken, 8.9.1
breach of the peace, 7.3
arrest, 7.3
bail, 7.3
bailiffs, 7.3
binding over, 7.3
complaint, 7.3
court powers, 7.3
detention, 7.3
domestic abuse, 2.8
ECHR, 7.3
entry, right of, 1.4.2, 2.8, 7.3
freedom of expression, 7.3
magistrates, 7.3
meaning, 7.3
obstruction, 2.2.3
recognisances, entering into, 7.3
breath tests
analysis, 10.11.3
drink or drugs, driving/attempting to drive/in charge of vehicle whilst unfit through, 10.10.2
mouthpiece as exhibit, retention of, 10.11.3
prescribed alcohol limit, drive or attempt to drive/in charge of motor vehicle whilst over, 10.11.1
roadside tests, 10.11.1
bridges, 10.1.1
bridleways, 10.1.1, 10.22
British Transport Police
assault of constable in execution of duty, 2.2.2
impersonation of constables, 2.2.4
broadcasting
networks, improper use of, 7.12.2
television decoders, use of, 3.9
builders' skips on the highway, obstruction by, 10.21.2
builders' skip, meaning of, 10.21.2
conditions, 10.21.2
defences, 10.21.2
hire, 10.21.2
hours of darkness, 10.21.2
move or reposition skip, power to require owner to, 10.21.2
nuisance, 10.21.2
other persons, acts or default of, 10.21.2
owners, meaning of, 10.21.2
permission, 10.21.2
bulk material, 1.4.4, 1.5.1, 1.5.4
bullets, 8.1.1

burden of proof
bladed articles/knives, 8.10.1
drink or drugs, driving or attempting to drive/in charge of vehicles whilst unfit through, 10.10.1
driving motor vehicle of class not authorised, 10.14.1
driving on road whilst disqualified, 10.13.1
evidential burden, 7.8
fair trials, 7.8
firearms, 8.4.1, 8.4.2, 8.5
possession with intent to supply a controlled drug, 5.2.2
prescribed alcohol limit, drive or attempt to drive/in charge of motor vehicle whilst over, 10.11.1
specified drugs limit, drive or attempt to drive/in charge of motor vehicle whilst over, 10.11.2
threatening or abusive words or behaviour, 7.8
unlicensed vehicles, using or keeping, 10.20.1
vehicles, 10.1.3
burglary, 3.3–3.3.2
aggravated, 3.3.2
building, meaning of, 3.3.1
caravans, 3.3.1
entry, 3.3.1
explosives, 3.3.2
firearms, 3.3.1, 3.3.2
has with him, meaning of, 3.3.2
imitation firearms, 3.3.1, 3.3.2
intention, 3.3.1
lookouts, 3.3.1
trespassers, 3.3.1
use of force, 3.3.1
weapon of offence, 3.3.2
buses
'bendy', 10.1.3
children, 10.17.2
improper use of bus lanes, 10.3
seat belts, 10.17.1, 10.17.2
butane lighter refills to young people, supply of, 11.5.1
butterfly knives, 8.9.1, 8.9.4
byelaws, offences against
fixed penalty notices, 11.1.2

cannabis
classification, 5.3.1
cultivate, 5.3.1
defences, 5.3.1
equipment used at cannabis farms, 5.3.1
hydroponic equipment, supplying, 5.3.1
licences, 5.3.1
meaning, 5.3.1
medical necessity, defence of, 5.3.1
penalty notices for disorder, 7.1.2
possession of, 5.2.1
premises, permitting use of drug on, 5.4.2
production or supply of drugs, 5.1.1
car parks, 10.1.1, 10.1.2
caravans
burglary, 3.3.1
trespass and, 7.17.1
care workers, ill-treatment or neglect by, 4.10
health care, 4.10
meaning of care worker, 4.10
paid work, 4.10
prison officers, 4.10
social care, 4.10
careless driving when under the influence of drink or drugs, causing death by, 10.8.2
careless or inconsiderate cycling, 10.12.2
due care and attention, cycling without, 10.12.2
name and address requirement, 10.6.2
reasonable consideration of other road users, 10.12.2
careless or inconsiderate driving
causing death by, 10.8.4
causing serious injury, 10.7.3
causing serious disruption
locking-on, 7.17.5
obstruction of major transport works, 7.17.7
tunnelling of being present in a tunnel, 7.17.6
causing serious injury
by careless or inconsiderate driving, 10.7.3
by driving, disqualified driver, 10.13.2
fault element, 10.13.2
serious injury, meaning of, 10.13.2
cautions
arrest, on, 1.1.2
drink or drugs, driving or attempting to drive/in charge of vehicles whilst unfit through, 10.10.2
certificates
air weapons, 8.7.3
ammunition, 8.6.2
club premises certificates, 9.1.1
firearms, 8.1.1, 8.1.3, 8.1.5, 8.6.1, 8.6.2
motorcycle training certificate, failure to produce, 10.16.4
seat belts, medical certificates and, 10.17.1, 10.17.2
shotgun offences, 8.2.1, 8.2.3, 8.6.2
test certificates, 10.16.3
charity shop, theft of items left outside, 3.1.1

chastisement, reasonable, 2.1.2, 2.4.1
child abduction, 2.6.3
Child Abduction Warning Notices, 2.6.3
child arrangement orders, 2.6.3
consent, meaning of appropriate, 2.6.3
defences, 2.6.3
detains, meaning of, 2.6.3
ECHR agreements, 2.6.3
lawful control, removal from, 2.6.3
other persons, meaning of, 2.6.3
persons connected, meaning of, 2.6.3
sends, meaning of, 2.6.3
takes, meaning of, 2.6.3
Child Abduction Warning Notices, 2.6.3
child arrangement orders, 2.4.2, 2.6.3
child cruelty
corporal punishment, 2.1.2, 2.4.1
death of vulnerable adult or child, causing or allowing the, 2.7.4
guardians, meaning of, 2.4.1
ill-treated, meaning of, 2.4.1
legal guardians, meaning of, 2.4.1
manslaughter, 2.4.1
neglect, 2.4.1
parental responsibility, 2.4.1
police protection, 2.4.1
reasonable chastisement, 2.1.2, 2.4.1
child destruction, 2.7.6
child or vulnerable adult, death of or physical harm to, 2.7.4
child, meaning of, 2.7.4
cot or accidental deaths, 2.7.4
same household, meaning of members of, 2.7.4
serious physical harm, 2.7.4
unlawful act, meaning of, 2.7.4
vulnerable adult, meaning of, 2.7.4
child sex offences
arranges, meaning of, 6.5.4
arranging or facilitating, 6.5.4
criminal lifestyle offences, 5.5
defence, 6.5.4
evidence, 6.5.4
facilitates, meaning of, 6.5.4
grooming, meeting a child through, 6.5.5
healthcare workers, provision of condoms by, 6.5.4
indecent photographs/images, 6.6.1–6.6.2
paedophile hunter, evidence of, 6.5.5
proceeds of crime, 5.5
procurement of child, 6.5.4
rape of child under 13, 6.1.2
sexual activity, cause or incite child to engage in, 6.5.1
sexual activity with a child, 6.4
sexual communication with a child, 6.5.6
sexual exploitation, child *see* **child sexual exploitation offences**
touching, sexual assault by, 6.3.2
Child Sex Offender (CSO) disclosure scheme, 6.5.4
child sexual exploitation offences, 5.5, 6.5–6.5.6
arrange/facilitate commission of a child sex offence, 6.5.4
cause or incite child under 13 to engage in sexual activity, 6.5.3
cause or incite child under 16 to engage in sexual activity, 6.5.1
Home Office Circular 8/2015 on, 6.5.1
hotels, use for, 6.5.1
meeting a child following sexual grooming, 6.5.5
paedophile manuals, possession of, 6.5.1
paying for sexual services of a child, 6.5.2
payment, 6.5.1
prostitution, 6.11.1
sexual communication with a child, 6.5.6
sexual exploitation, meaning of, 6.5.1
children *see* **children and alcohol; children and young persons; school premises**
children and alcohol
16, persons aged under, 9.1.1, 9.1.4, 9.1.5
18, persons under, 9.1.2, 9.1.3, 9.1.4, 9.1.5, 9.1.6, 9.1.7
age, evidence of, 9.1.1, 9.1.2, 9.1.3, 9.1.5, 9.1.6
alcohol, meaning of, 9.1.1
bar snacks, 9.1.4
charge of a child, drunk in, 7.2.2
child, meaning of, 9.1.1
club premises certificates, 9.1.1
confiscation of alcohol, 9.5.1
consumption of alcohol by children, 9.1.5
delivery of alcohol to children, 9.1.6
drunk in charge of a child, 7.2.2
excluded premises, meaning of, 9.5.2
from certain premises of, 9.1.1
knowledge
knowingly consumes, meaning of, 9.1.5
sending child to obtain alcohol, 9.1.7
'shutting one's eyes' knowledge, 9.1.3
spiked drinks, 9.1.5
licensing, 9.1–9.1.7

children and alcohol (*cont.*)
persistently possess alcohol in a public place, 9.5.2
premises
closure notices, 9.1.3, 9.3.3
club premises certificates, 9.1.1
employees, 9.1.7
permitted temporary activities, 9.1.1
relevant, meaning of, 9.1.1
unaccompanied children from certain, prohibition of, 9.1.1
purchase of alcohol by and on behalf of person under 18, 9.1.4
relevant place, meaning of, 9.5.2
sale of alcohol to children, 9.1.2
16, under, 9.1.1
18, under, 9.1.2, 9.1.3
allowing the, 9.1.3
knowledge, 9.1.3
persistently selling, 9.1.3
sending child to obtain alcohol, 9.1.7
spiked drinks, 9.1.5
supply of alcohol, 9.1.1
table meals, 9.1.4
consumption of alcohol by children, 9.1.4, 9.1.5
meaning of, 9.1.4
temporary activities, permitted, 9.1.1
test purchases, 9.1.4, 9.1.7
unaccompanied children, prohibition
working on premises, persons under 18, 9.1.7
children and young persons
abduction, 2.6.3
aerosol paints, sale of, 4.7.2
age of criminal responsibility, 2.7.1
air weapons, 8.7.1, 8.7.2
assault occasioning actual bodily harm, 2.1.2
birth, concealment of, 2.7.6
bladed articles/knives
delivery of, 8.10.4
sale of, 8.10.2
butane lighter refills to young people, supply of, 11.5.1
chastisement, reasonable, 2.1.2, 2.4.1
child cruelty, 2.1.2, 2.4.1
child destruction, 2.7.6
child, meaning of, 2.4.1
cigarette papers, selling/supplying, 11.5.1
concealment of birth, 2.7.6
corrosive substances, sale/delivery of, 8.11.1
crossbows, 8.9.6
cruelty, 2.1.2, 2.4.1
death by dangerous driving, causing, 10.8.1
death of vulnerable adult or child, causing or allowing the, 2.7.4
destruction, 2.7.6
discipline, 2.1.2, 2.4.1, 2.6.1
dispersal powers, 7.15.1
disqualified, driving whilst, 10.13.1
false imprisonment, 2.6.1
firearms, 8.1.3, App 4
fireworks, 8.8.2, 8.8.5
forced marriage, 4.11
infanticide, 2.7.6
kidnapping, 2.6.2
Local Safeguarding Children Board, establishment of, 2.4.2
mentally disordered people, removal without warrant of, 11.2
miscarriage, causing a, 2.5
murder, 2.7.1
parental responsibility, 2.4.1
penalty notices for disorder, 7.1.2
police protection, taking into, 2.4.1, 2.4.2
possession of prohibited image of, 6.6.2
procurement of child, 6.5.4
protection of, 2.4.1, 2.4.2
seat belts, 10.17.1, 10.17.2
sexual exploitation, 5.5
suffocation or over-laying of infant under 3 years, 2.7.5
unborn children, causing death by dangerous driving and, 10.8.1
young person, meaning of, 2.4.1
see also **child sex offences; children and alcohol**
Christmas crackers, 8.8.5
cigarette papers, selling/supplying to person under 18, 11.5.1
Civil Nuclear Constabulary
assault of constable in execution of duty, 2.2.2
claw, foot or hand, 8.9.4
clippers, 6.11.1
closure of licensed premises
children, selling alcohol to, 9.1.3, 9.3.3
closure notices
disorder/nuisance, 7.13.4
form, 9.3.3
selling alcohol to minors and, 9.3.3
service, 9.3.3
police powers, 9.3.3
closure of premises (nuisance/disorder), 5.4.2, 7.13.4
anti-social behaviour, nuisance/disorder, 7.13.4
authorisation/authorised persons, 7.13.4
cancellation notices, 7.13.4
closure notice, meaning of, 7.13.4
closure order, meaning of, 7.13.4
consultation, 7.13.4
defences, 7.13.4

duration of closure notice, 7.13.4
enforcement, 7.13.4
entry, powers of, 7.13.4
grounds, 7.13.4
permitting drugs use on premises, 5.4.2
requirements, 7.13.4
service, 7.13.4

clubs
air weapons, 8.7.2
children and alcohol, 9.1.1
club premises certificates, 9.1.1
club premises licences, 9.3.2
entry, powers of, 9.3.2
firearms, 8.1.3, 8.6.3
inspection, 8.6.3
rifle and muzzle loading, 8.1.3

coastguard, obstruction of, 2.2.7
codes *see* **PACE and codes**
coercive and controlling behaviour, 2.8
collisions, 10.8–10.8.5, 10.9–10.9.3
common assault, 2.1–2.1.1
common land, 10.22
communications causing distress, anxiety, or serious harm, 7.12–7.12.7
broadcasting, 7.12.2
defence, 7.12.1
demands, reasonable grounds for making, 7.12.1
distress and anxiety, intent to cause, 7.12.1, 7.12.2
electronic communications, 7.12.1, 7.12.2
electronic public communications networks, improper use of, 7.12.2
emails, faxes, and text messages, 7.12.1
encouraging or assisting serious self-harm, 7.12.6
evidence, 7.12.1
Facebook, 7.12.1
false alarms of fire, 7.12.7
forwarding messages created by others, 7.12.3, 7.12.6
grossly offensive, meaning of, 7.12.1
harassment, 7.12.1
hyperlinks, 7.12.3, 7.12.5, 7.12.6
intention, 7.12.1, 7.12.2
internet service providers, 7.12.3, 7.12.5
menacing, meaning of, 7.12.2
obscene telephone calls, 7.12.2
OFCOM, 7.12.2
penalty notices for disorder, 7.12.2, 7.12.7
persistently, meaning of, 7.12.2
private networks, 7.12.2
psychiatric injury, 7.12.2
public electronic communications network, definition of, 7.12.2
public nuisance, 7.12.2
sending communications threatening death or serious harm, 7.12.4
sending false communications with intent to cause harm, 7.12.3
sending letters with intent to cause distress and anxiety, 7.12.1
sending or showing flashing images electronically, 7.12.5
silent telephone calls, 7.12.2
social media, 7.12.1
telephone calls, 7.12.2
telephone messages, 7.12.1
terrorism, 7.12.2
threats, 7.12.2
X (formerly known as Twitter), 7.12.1

Community licences, 10.14.1
community protection notices (CPN), 7.16.1
appeals, 7.16.1
detrimental effect on quality of life, 7.16.1
forfeiture of items, 7.16.1
remedial actions, 7.16.1
requirements, 7.16.1
written warnings, 7.16.1

community support officers (CSOs)
additional powers and duties, 11.1.1
alcohol, confiscation of, 9.5.1
application of legislation, 11.1.1
arrest, 11.1.1
byelaws, 11.1.3
confiscation of alcohol from young persons, 9.5.1
custody officers, 11.1.1
cycling on footpath, 10.12.4
designation as, 11.1.1
detention pending arrival of constable, 11.1.7
directions to pedestrians, 10.2.2
dispersal powers, 7.15.1
entry, powers of
saving life or limb or serious damage to property, 1.4.2
failure to comply with, 11.1
failure to comply with alcohol requirements, 9.4.2
false alarm of fire, 7.12.7
fixed penalty notices, 11.1.2
improper use of public communications network, 7.12.2
licensing offences, 11.1.3
meaning, 11.1
names and addresses, power to require, 11.1.3
Official Secrets Act, and, 11.1.1
park trading offences, 11.1.9
penalty notices for disorder, 7.1.2, 7.12.2, 7.12.7
powers, 11.1
powers not able to be given to, 11.1.1

community support officers (CSOs) (*cont.*)
psychoactive substances, 5.3.6, 11.1.6
relevant police area, 11.1
restricted designations, 11.1.1
road traffic powers, 11.1.10
search and seizure of alcohol and tobacco, 11.1.4
search of individuals detained, 11.1.8
seizure and detention
controlled drugs, 5.4.1, 11.1.5
psychoactive substances, 11.1.6
stop and search, 11.1.1
terrorist offences, 11.1.1
tobacco, confiscation of, 11.5.1
Traffic Fixed Penalty Notices, 10.12.4
transitional provisions, 11.1
use of reasonable force, 11.1.11
warrants, 11.1.1
community support volunteers (CSVs)
additional powers and duties, 11.1.1
alcohol, confiscation of, 9.5.1
application of legislation, 11.1.1
arrest, 11.1.1
byelaws, 11.1.3
confiscation of alcohol from young persons, 9.5.1
custody officers, 11.1.1
designation as, 11.1.1
detention pending arrival of constable, 11.1.7
dispersal powers, 7.15.1
entry, powers of
saving life or limb or serious damage to property, 1.4.2
failure to comply with, 11.1
failure to comply with alcohol requirements, 9.4.2
fixed penalty notices, 11.1.2
licensing offences, 11.1.3
meaning, 11.1
names and addresses, power to require, 11.1.3
Official Secrets Act, and, 11.1.1
park trading offences, 11.1.9
penalty notices for disorder, 7.1.2
powers, 11.1
powers not able to be given to, 11.1.1
psychoactive substances, 5.3.6, 11.1.6
relevant police area, 11.1
restricted designations, 11.1.1
road traffic powers, 11.1.10
search and seizure of alcohol and tobacco, 11.1.4
search of individuals detained, 11.1.8
seizure and detention
controlled drugs, 5.4.1, 11.1.5
psychoactive substances, 11.1.6
stop and search, 11.1.1
terrorist offences, 11.1.1
tobacco, confiscation of, 11.5.1
transitional provisions, 11.1
use of reasonable force, 11.1.11
warrants, 11.1.1
computer misuse, 4.12–4.12.2
data protection, 4.12.1
personal data, 4.12.1
unauthorised access to computer material, 4.12.1
unauthorised access with intent to commit further offence, 4.12.2
computerised information, seizure, 1.4.4
concealment of birth, 2.7.6
condoms, healthcare workers providing, 6.5.4
confiscate alcohol, power to, 9.5–9.5.1
18, persons under, 9.5.1
containers, seizure of, 9.5.1
CSOs and CSVs, 9.5.1
disposal, 9.5.1
example of officer's requirement, 9.5.1
failure to surrender alcohol, 9.5.1
licensed premises, meaning of, 9.5.1
possession, meaning of, 9.5.1
public place, 9.5.1
recently, meaning of, 9.5.1
relevant place, meaning of, 9.5.1
seizure, 9.5.1
surrender alcohol, requirement to, 9.5.1
confiscation
air weapons, 8.7.2
alcohol, 9.5–9.5.1
controlled dugs on premises, permitting, 5.4.2
criminal lifestyle offences, 5.4.2, 5.5
see also **seizure**
confiscation orders, 5.5
confiscation proceedings, 5.5
consideration, driving without reasonable, 10.6.1
conspiracy, 7.13.3
consumer terrorism, 11.4.2
contacts, useful, App 2
contempt, 7.11.7
control, loss of, murder, 2.7.1
controlled drugs *see* **drugs**
convention driving permits, 10.14.1
conveyance, taking *see* **taking a conveyance without owner's consent (TWOC)**
corporal punishment, 2.1.2, 2.4.1
corporate manslaughter, 2.7.2, 2.7.3
deaths in custody, 2.7.3
directors, senior managers, and other individuals, liability of, 2.7.3
employees, 2.7.3
gross breach, 2.7.3
organisations to which s 1 applies, 2.7.3

prosecution, consent to, 2.7.3
correction, lawful, 2.1.2
corrosive substances
deliver or arrange delivery to residential premises or locker, 8.11.2
grievous bodily harm, using with intent to cause, 2.3.3
meaning, 8.11.1
possess in public place, 8.11.3
sell/deliver to persons under 18, 8.11.1
threatening with in private, 8.9.2
cot or accidental deaths, 2.7.4
cottaging, 6.9
counterfeiting, criminal lifestyle offences, 5.5
credit cards, fraud and, 3.8.2, 3.9
crime, encouraging, assisting or accessory to commit, 4.1.4
accessory to offence, 4.1.4
capable of encouraging or assisting, 4.1.4
defences, 4.1.4
does, an act, 4.1.4
encouraging or assisting commission of an offence, 4.1.4
meanings, 4.1.4
crime scenes, managing
corporate manslaughter, 2.7.3
death, causing by driving when disqualified, 10.8.3
death by dangerous driving, causing, 10.8.1
death by driving without insurance or licence, 10.8.5
drink or drugs, causing death by careless driving when under the influence of, 10.8.2
rape, 6.1.1
sexual exploitation offences, child, 6.5.1, 6.5.3
touching, sexual assault by, 6.3.1–6.3.2
criminal behaviour orders, 7.1.1
criminal damage, 4.4
aggression, crimes of, 4.4
ancient monuments, 4.4
arson, 4.4, 4.5.2
attempts, 4.1.1
belonging to another, meaning of, 4.4
cleaning, cost of, 4.4
damaged, meaning of, 4.4
defences, 4.4
destroy or damage property, threats to, 4.6
destroyed, meaning of, 4.4
entry, powers of, 1.4.2
intent, 4.4
lawful excuse, 4.4
life or property, protection of, 4.4
obstruction, 4.4
penalty notices for disorder, 7.1.2
property, meaning of, 4.4
protests, 4.4
racially or religiously aggravated, 4.4, 7.10.3
reckless, meaning of, 4.4
separate activities, 4.4
stop and search, 1.3.5
threats, 4.6
wild plants and creatures, 4.4
criminal lifestyle
criteria, 5.5
offences, 5.5
tests, 5.5
criminal lifestyle offences, 5.5
attempts, 4.1.1
blackmail, 3.2.2
child sex offence, arrange/ facilitate, 6.5.4
drugs, 5.2.2, 5.4.2
encourage or assist a crime, 4.1.4
trafficking, 11.3.1
crossbows
18, persons under, 8.9.6
age, proof of, 8.9.6
detention, 8.9.6
draw weight limit, 8.9.6
entry, powers of, 8.9.6
hire, 8.9.6
meaning, 8.9.6
possession, 8.9.6
purchase, 8.9.6
sale, 8.9.6
search and seizure, 8.9.6
vehicles, search of, 8.9.6
crowbars, 1.3.5
cruelty
animals, 11.6.1
children, to, 2.1.2, 2.4.1
curved swords, 8.9.4
custody, deaths in, 2.7.3
custody officers
assaults on, 2.2.6
CSOs and CSVs as, 11.1.1
cutting-agents, drug, 5.1.2
cyber-flashing, 6.7.2
cycles *see* **motor cycles; pedal cycle**
cyclone knives, 8.9.4

daggers, 8.9.1
damage to property *see* **criminal damage**
damages, 2.6.1, 7.11.7
dangerous cycling, 10.12.1
careful and competent cyclist, 10.12.1
cycle, meaning of, 10.12.1
dangerously, meaning of, 10.12.1
notice of intended prosecution, 10.12.1

dangerous dogs, 11.6.3–11.6.5
abandoning, 11.6.5
assistance dogs, 11.6.3
behavioural characteristics, 11.6.5
breeding, prohibition on, 11.6.5
breeds of dog, list of, 11.6.5
certificates of exemption, 11.6.5
control orders, 11.6.4
council housing, common areas around, 11.6.5
dangerous, meaning of, 11.6.4
dangerously out of control, meaning of, 11.6.3
defences, 11.6.5
destruction of dogs, 11.6.3, 11.6.4, 11.6.5
disqualification orders, 11.6.3, 11.6.4
fighting dogs, 11.6.5
identification
of dogs, 11.6.4
of owners, 11.6.5
intoxication as defence, voluntary, 11.6.5
livestock, worrying, 11.6.3
magistrates' courts, 11.6.4
neutering, 11.6.3
owner, meaning of, 11.6.3
private property, on, 11.6.3, 11.6.4
proper control, meaning of, 11.6.4
public places, meaning of, 11.6.3, 11.6.5
restrictions on dangerous dog breeds, 11.6.5
sale or exchange, 11.6.5
seizure, 11.6.4, 11.6.5
vehicles, dogs in, 11.6.5
XL Bully breed, 11.6.5
dangerous driving, 10.7–10.7.4
alcohol, evidence of consumption of, 10.7.1
alternative offences, conviction of, 10.7.1
carried in or attached to vehicle, 10.7.1
competent and careful driver standard, 10.7.1
dangerous vehicles, 10.7.1
dangerously, meaning of, 10.7.1
defences, 10.7.1
drugs, evidence of consumption, 10.7.1
forfeiture of vehicle, 10.7.1
injury, cause serious, 10.7.2
mechanical defects, 10.7.1
name and address
failure to give or giving false, 10.6.2
requirement to give, 10.7.1
notice of intended prosecution, 10.7.1
obvious dangers, 10.7.1
pedal cycles, 10.7.1
public place, definition of, 10.7.1
road, definition of, 10.7.1
speed, 10.7.1
wanton or furious driving, 10.7.4
see also **death by dangerous driving, causing**
dangerous weapons
possess, manufacture, sale, hire, or importation of, 8.10.5
see also **offensive weapons**
date of birth, requirement to give, 10.16.4
date rape drugs, 6.1.1, 6.10
death by careless or inconsiderate driving, causing, 10.8.4
death by dangerous driving, causing, 10.8.1
another, meaning of, 10.8.1
blood samples, 10.8.2
crime scene management, 10.8.1
defences, 10.8.1
evidence, 10.8.1
mechanical defects, 10.8.1
more than one driver, 10.8.1
seizure of vehicle, 10.8.1
substantial cause, 10.8.1
tramcars and trolley vehicles, 10.8.1
unborn children, 10.8.1
death, causing by driving when disqualified, 10.8.3
fault, 10.8.3
MOJ Circular 1/2015 guidance, 10.8.3
death, causing by driving when without insurance, or class of licence, 10.8.5
another, meaning of, 10.8.5
crime scene, management of, 10.8.5
evidence, 10.8.5
seizure of vehicle, 10.8.5
death caused by road traffic collisions, 10.8–10.8.5
death of vulnerable adult or child, causing or allowing the, 2.7.4
death stars, 8.9.4
deaths in custody, corporate manslaughter, 2.7.3
decency, outraging public, 6.7.4, 6.9
deception
impersonation of constable, 2.2.4
kidnapping, 2.6.2
rape, 6.1.1
decoders, use of television, 3.9
delivering alcohol to children, 9.1.6
demonstrations
criminal damage, 4.4
false imprisonment, 2.6.1
obstruction by, 10.21.1
stop and search organised protest groups, 1.3.2
threatening or abusive words or behaviour, 7.8
deportation orders, 11.3.1, 11.3.3

designated persons
assault, 2.2.5
excluded and special procedure material, access to, 1.5.4
investigating officers, 1.5.1, 1.5.4
meaning, 2.2.5
obstruction, 2.2.5
police protection, taking into, 2.4.2
search warrants, 1.5.1
seizure, 1.5.1
see also **community support officers**
destroy or damage property, threats to, 4.6
destruction of dogs, 11.6.3, 11.6.4, 11.6.5
detention
aircraft, ships, and vehicles, 11.3.1
arrest, 2.2.2
breach of the peace, 7.3
child abduction, 2.6.3
controlled drugs, 5.4.1
crossbows, 8.9.6
CSOs and CSVs, by, 11.1.7
firearms, 8.6.1, 8.6.2
fireworks, 8.8.2, 8.8.3, 8.8.4
illegal entry, 11.3.1
mentally disordered people, 11.2
stop and search, 1.3.2, 1.3.4
diminished responsibility, 2.7.1, 2.7.2
dinghies on trailers, 4.3.1
directions to leave *see* **dispersal powers**
disabilities, persons with
invalid carriages *see* **invalid carriages**
mental disabilities *see* **mental disabilities, persons with**
seat belts, 10.17.1, 10.17.2
disclose information, failing to
fraud, 3.8.1, 3.8.3
legal duty, meaning of, 3.8.3
life insurance, 3.8.3
meanings, 3.8.3
discrimination, App 1
dishonesty
fraud, 3.9
handling stolen goods, 3.5
services, obtaining, 3.9
theft, 3.1.1
disorderly conduct in licensed premises, allowing, 9.2.3
dispersal powers, 7.15.1
anti-social behaviour, 7.15.1
authorisations, requirements for, 7.15.1
crime or disorder, 7.15.1
CSOs and CSVs, 7.15.1
directions to exclude, 7.15.1
directions to surrender property, 7.15.1
duration, 7.15.1
ECHR rights, 7.15.1
harassment, alarm, or distress, 7.15.1
peaceful picketing, 7.15.1
persons under 16 to residence/place of safety, returning, 7.15.1
public place, meaning of, 7.15.1
public processions, 7.15.1
publicity no longer required, 7.15.1
residence, removal to place of, 7.15.1
vehicles causing annoyance, 7.14.1
written notices, 7.15.1
disqualification from owning dogs, 11.6.3, 11.6.4
disqualified, driving whilst, 10.13–10.13.1
causing serious injury by driving, 10.13.2
class of vehicle, 10.13.1
death by driving, causing, 10.8.3
disqualified, meaning of, 10.13.1
driving test, until driver passes, 10.13.1
foreign licences, 10.13.1
identification, 10.13.1
minimum period, 10.13.1
obtain licence/drive on road, 10.13.1
penalty points, 10.13.1
previous disqualification period, 10.13.1
provisional licences, 10.13.1
totting up, 10.13.1
underage drivers, 10.13.1
disruption, causing serious
locking-on, 7.17.5
tunnelling of being present in a tunnel, 7.17.6
distress *see* **harassment, alarm, or distress**
dogs, 11.6–11.6.6
control orders, 11.6.4
dangerous dogs *see* **dangerous dogs**
disqualification from owning, 11.6.3, 11.6.4
guard dogs, 11.6.6
livestock, worrying, 11.6.3
PSPOs, 7.15.2
domestic abuse, 2.8
affray, 7.5
breach of the peace, powers of entry for, 2.8
civil actions, 2.8
coercive behaviour, 2.8
controlling behaviour, 2.8
Domestic Violence Protection Notice (DVPN), 2.8
Domestic Violence Protection Order (DVPO), 2.8
entry, power of, 2.8
injunctions with power of arrest, 2.8
meaning, 2.8
PACE and codes, 2.8
personally connected, 2.8
relative, meaning of, 2.8

Domestic Violence Protection Notice (DVPN), 2.8
Domestic Violence Protection Order (DVPO), 2.8
downloading indecent photographs/ images, 6.6.1
drink driving
careless driving when under the influence of drink or drugs, causing death by, 10.8.2
cycling, 10.12.3
driving or attempting to drive mechanically propelled vehicles whilst unfit, 10.10–10.10.1
drink or drugs, causing death by careless driving when under the influence of
another person, meaning of, 10.8.1, 10.8.2
defences, 10.8.2
drink or drugs, meaning of through, 10.8.2
prescribed/specified limit, exceeds the, 10.8.2
scene, management of, 10.8.2
scrapped, preventing cars being, 10.8.2
specimen, failure to provide, 10.8.2
unfit to drive, meaning of, 10.8.2
drink or drugs, cycling whilst under the influence of, 10.12.3
drink or drugs, driving/attempting to drive/in charge of vehicle whilst unfit through, 10.10–10.10.1
aiding and abetting charge where driver cannot be identified, 10.10.1
arrest, powers of, 10.10.2
breath tests, preliminary, 10.10.2
burden of proof, 10.10.1
cautions, 10.10.2
dangerous driving, 10.7.1
defences, 10.10
doctors, evidence of, 10.10.1
drugs test, preliminary, 10.10.2
entry, powers of, 10.10.2
hospital patients, 10.10.2
identified, where driver cannot be, 10.10.1
impairment tests, preliminary, 10.10.2
innocence, presumption of, 10.10.1
likelihood of driving, 10.10.1
manslaughter, 10.10.1
medical examinations, consent to, 10.10.1
person in charge, establishing, 10.10.1
preliminary tests, 10.10.2
arrest for failure to cooperate with, 10.10.2
code of practice, 10.10.2
samples, persons incapable of providing, 10.10.2
tests
fails to cooperate, 10.10.2
power to administer, 10.10.2
preliminary, 10.10.2
refusal to cooperate, 10.10.2
traffic offences, meaning of, 10.10.2
tram cars, 10.10.1
trolley vehicles, 10.10.1
witnesses, 10.10.1
drives and driving, meaning of, 10.1.4
more than one person driving, 10.1.4
steering, 10.1.4
steering wheel, temporarily grabbing the, 10.1.4
temporary stops, 10.1.4
driving licence, counterpart or motorcycle training certificate, failure to produce
date of birth, requirement to give, 10.16.4
defences, 10.16.4
false statements, 10.16.4
provisional licence holders, 10.16.4
seizure, 10.16.4
driving licence, driving not in accordance with a, 10.14–10.14.1
ages for holding or obtaining licence, minimum, 10.14.1
burden of proof, 10.13.1, 10.14.1
cause, meaning of, 10.14.1
class of vehicle not authorised by licence, 10.14.1
Community licence, 10.14.1
convention driving permits, 10.14.1
fixed penalty scheme, 10.14.1
invalid carriages, 10.14.1
medium-sized vehicles, 10.14.1
military purposes, vehicles used for, 10.14.1
mopeds, 10.14.1
motorcycles, 10.14.1
permit, meaning of, 10.14.1
production of licence, 10.14.1
provisional licences, 10.14.1
seizure of vehicle, 10.14.1
small vehicles, 10.14.1
tractors, 10.14.1
driving licences
accordance with licence, driving not in, 10.14–10.14.1
counterparts no longer issued, 10.16.4
disqualified, driving whilst, 10.13.1
EEA driving licences, 10.14.1
electronic driving record, DVLA, 10.16.4
endorsements, 10.16.4
failure to produce, 10.16.4
foreign licences, 10.13.1
nil licence for exempt vehicle, failure to have, 10.20.1

production of, 10.4.1, 10.16.4
provisional licences, 10.11.1, 10.13.1, 10.16.4, 10.17.1
seizure, 10.16.4
Traffic Fixed Penalty Notices, 10.4.1
Ukrainian driving licences, 10.14.1
vehicles, seizure of, 10.14.1, 10.16.6
driving offences
causing serious injury by driving, disqualified driver, 10.13.2
collisions, 10.8–10.8.5, 10.9–10.9.3
consideration, driving without reasonable, 10.6.1
CSOs and CSVs, powers of, 11.1.10
death by dangerous driving, causing, 10.8.1
disqualified, driving whilst, 10.13
drink or drugs, causing death by careless driving when under the influence of, 10.8.2
drink or drugs, cycling whilst under the influence of, 10.12.3
drives and driving, meaning of, 10.1.4
driving licence, driving not in accordance with a, 10.14–10.14.1
due care and attention, driving without, 10.6.1–10.6.2
eyesight, driving with defective, 10.15
fatal road traffic collision incidents, 10.8–10.8.5
footpath, driving on the, 10.12.4
hand-held devices, control of vehicle and use of, 10.4.2
information, duty of driver to stop and give, 10.9.2
insurance
goods vehicle test certificate, failure to produce, 10.16.3
plating certificate, failure to produce, 10.16.3
proof of, 10.9.2, 10.9.3
registered keeper without, 10.16.2
test certificate, failure to produce, 10.16.3
user of vehicle without, 10.16.1
mechanically propelled vehicles whilst unfit through drugs or drink, driving or attempting to drive, 10.10–10.10.1
mobile phones or hand-held devices, control of vehicle and use of, 10.4.2
off-road driving, 10.22
prescribed/specified limit, 10.11.1
prescribed/specified limit, drive or attempt to drive/in charge of motor vehicle whilst over, 10.11–10.11.3
reasonable consideration, driving without, 10.6.1
reckless, careless, or inconsiderate driving or cycling, 10.6.2
registration documents, 10.20.2
report incidents, duty of driver to, 10.9.2, 10.9.3
seat belts, 10.17–10.17.2
underage drivers, 10.13.1
see also **dangerous driving; driving licences; vehicles**
drones, 11.7
permission for certain flights, 11.7.1
drug cutting, 5.1.2
drug search powers *see* **search powers for controlled drugs**
drugs
anabolic steroids and human growth hormones, 5.2.1
articles to administer or prepare, supply, or offer of, 5.1.2
carriers, 5.1.1
classification of, 5.1.1, 5.2.1, 5.3.1
CSOs and CSVs, seizure and detention by, 5.4.1, 11.1.5
customs and excise, 5.1.1
date rape drugs, 6.1.1, 6.10
drink or drugs, causing death by careless driving when under the influence of, 10.8.2
drink or drugs, cycling whilst under the influence of, 10.12.3
driving or attempting to drive mechanically propelled vehicles whilst unfit through, 10.10–10.10.1
drug-cutting, 5.1.2
drug-cutting agents, 5.1.2
fake drugs, 5.1.1
glue, sniffing, 7.2.1
legal highs *see* **psychoactive substances**
magic mushrooms, 5.1.2
occupiers or managers permitting drugs to be used on premises, 5.4.2
over-laying/suffocation of infant under 3 when under influence of, 2.7.5
possession, 5.1.1, 5.2.1–5.2.2
postal operators, 5.1.1
prescription drugs, supply of, 5.1.1
producing or supplying controlled, 5.1, 5.1.1, 5.1.2, 9.3.2
psychoactive substances *see* **psychoactive substances**
public places, 7.2.1
rape, 6.1.1, 6.10
searches, 5.1.1, 5.2.1, 5.2.2, 5.4.1, 5.4.2
seizure, 5.1.1, 5.2.1, 5.2.2
sniffing glue, 7.2.1
specified limit, driving over *see* **specified drugs limit, drive or attempt to drive/in charge of motor vehicle whilst over**

drugs (*cont.*)
suffocation or over-laying of infant under 3 when under influence of, 2.7.5
supply, 5.1, 5.1.2, 5.2.1, 9.3.2
temporary class, 5.1.1, 5.2.1
testing, 5.2.1, 5.3.3, 5.3.6, 10.10.2
testing kits, 5.2.1, 5.3.6
trafficking, 5.1.1
trafficking, proceeds of crime—lifestyle offences, 5.5
veterinary surgeons, supplied by, 5.1.1
see also **cannabis**
drugs, producing or supplying controlled, 5.1, 5.1.1, 5.1.2, 9.3.2
cannabis, cultivation of, 5.1.1, 5.3.1
classification of drugs, 5.1.1
controlled drug, meaning of, 5.1.1
defences, 5.1.1
drug-cutting agents, 5.1.2
entry, powers of, 9.3.2
fake drugs, 5.1.1
Home Office Circular 82/1980, 5.1.1
hydroponic equipment, supplying, 5.3.1
licensed premises, powers of entry to, 9.3.2
offers, 5.1.1
produce, meaning of, 5.1.1
school premises, 5.1.1
supply, meaning of, 5.1.1
supplying, meaning of, 5.1.1
test purchase officers, 5.1.1
drugs, supply or offer of articles or administering or preparing, 5.1.2
administration, meaning of, 5.1.2
defences, 5.1.2
opium use, 5.1.2
syringes, supply of, 5.1.2
drugs to be used on premises, occupiers or managers permitting, 5.4.2
closure notices, 5.4.2
confiscation of cash and property, 5.4.2
knowingly permits, 5.4.2
management, meaning of, 5.4.2
occupier, meaning of, 5.4.2
searches, 5.4.2
suffers, 5.4.2
drunk and disorderly in public places, 7.2–7.2.2
disorderly behaviour, meaning of, 7.2.1
drugs, 7.2.1
drunk, meaning of, 7.2.1
firearms, 7.2.2
glue, sniffing, 7.2.1
landings in blocks of flats, 7.2.1
public place, meaning of, 7.2.1
drunk and incapable, 7.2.2
drunk at sporting event, 7.18.1
drunk on a highway, 7.2.2
carriages, meaning of, 7.2.2
child, drunk in charge of a, 7.2.2
drunk and incapable, 7.2.2
incapable, meaning of, 7.2.2
licensed premises, residents in, 7.2.2
medical conditions giving appearance of, 7.2.2
motor vehicles, 7.2.2
penalties, 7.2.2
drunkenness on licensed premises, 9.2–9.2.3
display of licence, 9.2.1
drunk, meaning of, 9.2.1
failure to leave licensed premises, 9.2.2
knowledge, 9.2.1
Penalty Notice for Disorder, 9.2.1, 9.2.3
sale of alcohol to person who is drunk, 9.2.1
due care and attention, cycling without, 10.12.2
due care and attention, driving without, 10.6–10.6.2
arrest, assisting in, 10.6.1
automatism, 10.6.1
competent and careful drivers, 10.6.1
consideration, driving without, 10.6.1
cyclists, 10.6.1, 10.6.2
defences, 10.6.1
duress, 10.6.1
emergency vehicles, 10.6.1
footpath, mounting the, 10.6.1
mechanical defects, sudden, 10.6.1
mechanically propelled vehicles, 10.6.1
name and address
failure to give or giving false, 10.6.2
requirement to give, 10.6.2
necessity, 10.6.1
notice of intended prosecution, 10.6.1
objective test, 10.6.1
pedal cycles, 10.6.1
police drivers, 10.6.1
public place, definition of, 10.6.1
reasonable consideration, driving without, 10.6.1
road, meaning of, 10.6.1
unconscious and sudden illness, 10.6.1
dumping vehicles, 7.16.3
duress, driving without due care and attention under, 10.6.1

electric scooters, 10.1.3
electricity, abstracting, 3.4
electricity meters, causing to malfunction, 3.8.7
electronic communications
communications causing distress, anxiety, or serious harm, 7.12.1, 7.12.2
electronic communications network, meaning of, 7.12.1

electronic public communications networks, improper use, 7.12.2
emails, 6.6.1, 7.12.1
fraud, 3.8.2, 3.8.6
meaning of, 7.12.1
phishing, 3.8.2
seizure, 1.4.4
emails
attachments, 6.6.1
communications causing distress, anxiety, or serious harm, 7.12.1
deliberate opening of, 6.6.1
indecent photographs/images, 6.6.1
innocent opening of, 6.6.1
sexual communication with a child, 6.5.6
threats to kill, 2.5
emergencies
due care and attention, driving without, 10.6.1
obstruction or hindering of emergency workers and persons assisting, 2.2.7
seat belts, 10.17.1
traffic signs, 10.3
emergency workers, assaults on, 2.2.6
custodial institution, 2.2.6
custody officer, 2.2.6
fire fighters, 2.2.6
inchoate offences, 2.2.6
NHS bodies, persons working for, 2.2.6
NHS health services, 2.2.6
police, 2.2.6
prison officers, 2.2.6
rescue services, 2.2.6
emergency workers, obstruction and hindering of, 2.2.7
ambulance workers, 2.2.7
assisting, persons, 2.2.7
capacity for emergency workers, 2.2.7
circumstances of emergency, 2.2.7
coastguard, 2.2.7
Home Office Circular 3/2007, 2.2.7
lifeboats, 2.2.7
MOD fire fighters, 2.2.7
NHS bodies, persons working for, 2.2.7
persons assisting, 2.2.7
employees, corporate manslaughter and, 2.7.2, 2.7.3
encourage or assist a crime, 4.1.4
capable of encouraging or assisting, 4.1.4
defences of acting reasonably, 4.1.4
does an act, meaning of, 4.1.4
manslaughter, 2.7.2
serious self-harm, 7.12.6
suicide, 2.7.1, 2.7.2
endanger life, damage with intent to, 4.5.1
endanger life, intent to
abroad, possession of firearms, 8.3.2
ammunition, 8.3.2
defences, 4.5.1
firearms, 8.3.2
murder and manslaughter, 4.5.1
recklessness, 4.5.1
separate activities, 4.5.1
endorsements, 10.4.1, 10.16.4
enter licensed premises, power to
authorisation, 9.3.2
club premises licences, 9.3.2
drugs, supply of, 9.3.2
searches, 9.3.2
use of force, 9.3.2
entrance fee, watching sport without paying, 3.9
entrapment, 9.3.1
entry, powers of
animals, saving, 1.4.2
annoyance, vehicles causing, 7.14.1
arrest, 1.4.2
bladed articles/knives, 8.12.2
breach of the peace, 1.4.2, 2.8, 7.3
careless driving when under influence, causing death by, 10.8.2
conditions, 1.4.2
consumption of alcohol by person under 18, 9.1.5
crossbows, 8.9.6
CSOs and CSVs, 1.4.2
damage, to prevent, 1.4.2
dangerous driving, 10.7.1, 10.7.2
dangerous driving, causing death by, 10.8.1
delivering alcohol to person under 18, 9.1.6
domestic abuse, 2.8
drink or drugs, driving/attempting to drive/in charge of vehicle whilst unfit through, 10.10.2
driving while disqualified, causing death by, 10.8.3
drug search powers, 5.4.1
firearms, 8.6.1, 8.6.3
further education premises, 8.10.7, 8.10.8, 8.12.2
immediate pursuit, forced entry when in, 1.4.2
indictable offences, 1.4.2
licensing, 9.3.2
life, to save, 1.4.2
off-road driving, 10.22
offensive weapons, 8.12.1, 8.12.2
PACE and codes, 1.4.2
premises, closure of, 7.13.4
prescribed alcohol limit, drive/attempt to drive/in charge of vehicle whilst over, 10.11.1

entry, powers of (*cont.*)
purchase of alcohol by or on behalf of person under 18, 9.1.4
reasons for entry, 1.4.2
sale of alcohol to person who is drunk, 9.2.1
school premises, 8.10.7, 8.10.8, 8.12.2
searches
arrest, 1.4.1, 1.4.3
drugs, 5.4.1
extent of, 1.4.2
warrants, 1.5.1–1.5.3
seizure, 10.16.6
separate dwellings, 1.4.2
specified drugs limit, drive or attempt to drive/in charge of motor vehicle whilst over, 10.11.2
stopping vehicle on road, 10.2.3
use of force, 1.4.2, 10.11.1
vehicles
annoyance, causing, 7.14.1
seizure and removal of, 10.16.6
wanton or furious driving, 10.7.4
warrants
commitment, of, 1.4.2
firearms, 8.6.3
environmental protection *see* **community protection notices (CPN)**
equipment for drug-taking
search powers, 5.4.1
supply or offer of, 5.1.2, 5.2.2
escapes
searches for items used for, 1.4.1
seizure, 1.4.1
European Convention on Human Rights (ECHR), 7.3, App 1
excise duty, 10.19
excluded and special procedure material, access to
bulk material, seizure and examination of, 1.5.4
Crown Prosecution Service, 1.5.4
designated investigating officers, 1.5.4
excluded material, meaning of, 1.5.4
hospital records, 1.5.4
human tissue or tissue fluid, 1.5.4
journalistic material, 1.5.4
legal privilege, 1.5.4
PACE and codes, 1.5.4
personal records, 1.5.4
press photographs showing criminal acts, 1.5.4
procedure, 1.5.4
Schedule 1 applications, 1.5.4
search warrants, 1.5.1, 1.5.4
seizure, 1.5.4
special procedure material, meaning of, 1.5.4
execution of duty, assaulting or obstructing a constable in the, 2.2.2, 2.2.3
experts, 1.4.1, 1.5.3
explosives *see* **bombs and explosives**
exposure
intention, 6.7.1
streakers and naturists, 6.7.1
extreme pornographic images, 6.6.2
eyes
driving with defective eyesight, 10.15
eye protectors, motor cycles and, 10.18
eyesight, driving with defective, 10.15
eyesight test, refusal to submit to, 10.15
knowledge of defect, 10.15
licence applications, 10.15
number plate, ability to read, 10.15

Facebook
communications causing distress, anxiety, or serious harm, 7.12.1
failure to leave licensed premises, 9.2.2
failure to surrender alcohol, 9.5.1
fair trials, 7.8, App 1
fake drugs, 5.1.1
false alarms of fire, 7.12, 7.12.7
false imprisonment, 2.6.1
actus reus, 2.6.1
children, parental discipline and, 2.6.1
damages, 2.6.1
defences, 2.6.1
demonstrations, 2.6.1
forced marriages, 4.11
'kettling', 2.6.1
mens rea, 2.6.1
false messages *see* **communications causing distress, anxiety, or serious harm**
false reports, making, 11.4.1–11.4.2
false representations
conduct, by, 3.8.2
fraud, 3.8.1, 3.8.2
meanings, 3.8.2
fatal road traffic collision incidents, 10.8–10.8.5
causing death by careless or inconsiderate driving, 10.8.4
causing death by dangerous driving, causing, 10.8.1
causing death by driving when disqualified, 10.8.3
causing death by driving without insurance or licence, 10.8.5
drink or drugs, causing death by careless driving when under the influence of, 10.8.2
faxes with intent to cause distress or anxiety, sending, 7.12.1
fear or provocation of violence, 7.6
abusive, meaning of, 7.6
arrest, 7.6
defences, 7.6

display, meaning of, 7.6
distributes, meaning of, 7.6
firearms, 8.3.2, 8.3.3, 8.3.6
grievous bodily harm, 2.3.1
immediacy requirement, 7.6
inside a dwelling, 7.6
insulting, meaning of, 7.6
intent, 7.6
obstruction, 10.21.1
private, in, 7.6
racially or religiously aggravated offences, 7.6
rape, 6.1.1
robbery, 3.2.1
stalking, 7.11.4
threatening behaviour, 7.6
threatening, meaning of, 7.6
wounding and grievous bodily harm, 2.3.1
fighting offences involving animals
animal welfare offences, 11.6.2
dogs, 11.6.5
films, indecent photographs/images and, 6.6.1
fire, false alarms of, 7.12, 7.12.7
fire, rescue, and police vehicles, seat belts and, 10.17.1
fire and rescue services, assaults on, 2.2.6
firearms, 8.1–8.1.5
14, persons under, 8.1.3, 8.7.1, App 4
15, persons under, App 4
abroad, possession with intent to endanger life, 8.3.2
accessories, 8.1.1
acquire, meaning of, 8.1.1
age, 8.1.3, App 4
aggravated firearms offences, 8.1.2
ammunition
certificates, production of, 8.6.2
convicted person, ban on possession by, 8.3.1
endanger life, possession with intent to, 8.3.2
hand over, requirement to, 8.6.1
loaded, meaning of, 8.5
meaning, 8.1.1
possession without a certificate of, 8.1.1, 8.1.3
section 1, 8.1.1
antiques, 8.1.4
approved rifle and muzzle loading pistol clubs, 8.1.3
arrest
carrying firearm with criminal intent or resist, 8.3.6
endanger life, possession with intent to, 8.3.2
possession, 8.3.5
resisting or preventing lawful, 8.3.4, 8.3.6
auctioneers, 8.1.5
bans
convicted persons, possession by, 8.3.1
duration of, 8.3.1
sell, transfer, repair, test, prove, offence for banned person to, 8.3.1
total, 8.3.1
blank cartridges, 8.1.1
bored barrels, 8.1.4
buildings
meaning, 8.4.1
trespass with any firearm in, 8.4.1
bullets, 8.1.1
burden of proof, 8.4.1, 8.4.2, 8.5
burglary, 3.3.1, 3.3.2
carriers, 8.1.5
certificates
ammunition, 8.6.2
conditions, failure to comply with, 8.1.5
custody of, reasonable care with, 8.1.5
form of, 8.1.5
meaning, 8.1.1
Northern Ireland, 8.6.2
police powers, 8.6.1, 8.6.2
possession without, 8.1.1, 8.1.3
production of, 8.6.1, 8.6.2
civilian officers, meaning of, 8.6.3
clubs, 8.1.3, 8.6.3
component parts, 8.1.1, 8.1.4, 8.3.4, 8.3.5
convicted persons, ban on possession by, 8.3.1
criminal use of firearms, 8.3–8.3.7
date of release, meaning of, 8.3.1
dealers, 8.1.2
defences, 8.1.1, 8.1.3, 8.1.4, 8.3.5, 8.5
detention, 8.6.1, 8.6.2
discharging firearm to cause obstruction, annoyance or danger, 8.8.8
drunk on highway or in public place, 7.2.2
endanger life, possession with intent to, 8.3.2
entry, powers of, 8.6.1, 8.6.3
exemptions, 8.1.1
fear of violence, 8.3.2, 8.3.3, 8.3.6
flare launchers, 8.1.1
flash eliminators, 8.1.1, 8.3.4, 8.3.5
gifts, 8.1.3
gun clubs, 8.1.3, 8.6.3
hand over firearms or ammunition, requirement to, 8.6.1
has with him, meaning of, 8.3.6

firearms (*cont.*)
highway, discharging within 50 feet of, 8.5
hire, 8.7.1
Home Office Circular 12/2010, 8.7.1
inspection of gun clubs, 8.6.3
intent
criminal, 8.3.6
endanger life, to, 8.3.2
fear of violence, to cause, 8.3.3
knowledge, 8.1.1, 8.3.6, 8.4.2, 8.5
land, trespass with firearm on, 8.4.2
lawful authority, 8.5
lethal barrelled weapon, meaning of, 8.1.1
loaded, meaning of, 8.5
loans, 8.1.3
meaning, 8.1.1
mind firearm, using person to, 8.3.7
missiles, 8.1.1
muzzle loading and pistol clubs, 8.1.3
name and address, giving, 8.6.2
night sights, 8.1.1
Northern Ireland, 8.6.2
obstruction, 8.6.3
police powers, 8.6–8.6.3
possession
14, persons under, 8.1.3
abroad, intent to endanger life, 8.3.2
aggravated offences, 8.1.2
ammunition, 8.1.1, 8.1.3
arrested, at time of committing specific offence or being, 8.3.5
convicted persons, ban on, 8.3.1
endanger life, possession with intent to, 8.3.2
meaning of, 8.1.1, 8.1.3
mental element, 8.1.1
practical element, 8.1.1
public place, in a, 8.5
violence, with intent to cause, 8.3.3, 8.3.6
premises search warrants, 8.6.1, 8.6.3
pretending to have firearm, 8.3.5, 8.5
primed cartridges, 8.1.1
prohibited weapons, meaning of, 8.1.1
public place
highways or streets, 8.5, 8.7.2
meaning of, 8.5
possession in a, 8.5
stop and search, 8.6.1
pump-action shotguns, 8.1.1
purchase, 8.7.1
reasonable cause to suspect, meaning of, 8.6.1
reasonable excuse, 8.4.1, 8.4.2, 8.5
recklessness, 8.4.2
relevant offences, meaning of, 8.6.3
repeating shotguns, 8.1.1
replica firearms, 8.1.1, 8.1.4, 8.5
resisting arrest, 8.3.4, 8.3.6
revolvers, 8.2.1
rifle and muzzle loading clubs, 8.1.3
rifle ranges, 8.1.3
searches, 8.6.1, 8.6.3
section 1 offences, 8.1–8.1.5
seizure, 8.6.2, 8.6.3
self-defence, 8.3.2
sell, transfer, repair, test, prove, offence for banned person to, 8.3.1
shooting galleries, 8.1.3
shortened barrels, 8.1.2
shot, 8.1.1
shotgun offences, 8.2–8.2.3
signal pistol, 8.1.1
silencers, 8.1.1, 8.3.5
sport, 8.1.3
stop and search, 8.6.1
street, discharges firearms on, 8.5
stun guns, 8.1.1
supply, 8.7.1
telescopic sights, 8.1.1
trafficking, 5.5
trespassing
defences, 8.4.1, 8.4.2
firearms, with, 8.4–8.4.2
knowledge or recklessness, 8.4.2
land, on, 8.4.2
unlawful violence, meaning of, 8.3.3
using person to mind a firearm, 8.3.7
vehicles
public place as, 8.5
searches, 8.6.1
violence, fear of, 8.3.2, 8.3.3, 8.3.6
violence, with intent to cause, 8.3.3, 8.3.6
warehouses, 8.1.5
warrants
entry, powers of, 8.6.3
granting, 8.6.3
purposes of, 8.6.3
search, 8.6.3
seizure, 8.6.3
see also **air weapons**; **imitation firearms**
fireworks, 8.8–8.8.9
11pm, use after, 8.8.4
12, persons under, 8.8.5
16, persons under, 8.8.5
18, persons under, 8.8.2, 8.8.5
adult fireworks, meaning of, 8.8.2
annoyance, causing, 8.8.8
ban on Category 4 fireworks, 8.8.1, 8.8.3
carriageway, meaning of, 8.8.7
categories of, 8.8.1
Christmas crackers, 8.8.5
confined spaces outdoors, 8.8.1
danger on the highway, causing, 8.8.7
defence, 8.8.5

detention, 8.8.3, 8.8.4
displays, 8.8.1, 8.8.4
exemptions, 8.8.2, 8.8.3
highway, cast or fire any fireworks on the, 8.8.6
inside use, for, 8.8.1, 8.8.4, 8.8.5
meaning of, 8.8.1
night hours, meaning of, 8.8.4
night, use during the, 8.8.4
obstruct, annoy, or cause danger to residents or passengers, 8.8.8
organised displays, 8.8.1, 8.8.3
outdoor use, 8.8.1, 8.8.3, 8.8.4
penalty notices for disorder, 8.8.3, 8.8.4, 8.8.5, 8.8.6
permitted fireworks night, meaning of, 8.8.4
possession of Category 4 fireworks, ban on, 8.8.3
possession of pyrotechnic articles at musical events, 8.8.9
public place
adult fireworks in, possession of, 8.8.2
meaning of, 8.8.2
seizure, 8.8.2, 8.8.3, 8.8.4
pyrotechnic articles, 8.8.5
specialist use, 8.8.1, 8.8.3, 8.8.5
stop and search, 1.3.2, 1.3.5, 8.8.2, 8.8.3, 8.8.4
street, meaning of, 8.8.8
street, throw, cast, or fire any fireworks in the, 8.8.8
supply to persons under the age of 18, 8.8.5
Town Police Clauses Act 1847, 8.8.8
vehicles, stop, search, or detention of, 8.8.2, 8.8.3, 8.8.4
fixed penalty notices
abandoned vehicles, 7.16.3
alcohol, 9.4.2
community protection notices, 7.16.1
CSOs and CSVs, powers of, 11.1.2
litter, 7.16.2
notices of intended prosecutions, 10.5
see also **Traffic Fixed Penalty Notices**
flare launchers, 8.1.1
flash eliminators, 8.1.1, 8.3.4, 8.3.5
flick guns, 8.12.1
flick knives, 8.9.1, 8.9.3, 8.10.2, 8.10.5, 8.12.1
fly posting
fixed penalty notices, 11.1.2
fly tipping, 7.16.3
folded knives, 8.10.1, 8.10.2
food contamination or threats of food contamination, 11.4.2
foot claw, 8.9.4
football matches
alcohol, possession of, 7.18.1
banning orders, 7.18, 7.18.2
designated match, 7.18.2
racialist chanting, 7.18.2
regulated football match, 7.18.2
regulated football organisation, 7.18.2
relevant offences, list of, 7.18.2
throwing object, 7.18.2
ticket touting, 7.18.2
see also **sporting events**
footpaths
cycling on, 10.12.4
driving on the footpath, 10.12.4
meaning of, 10.22
mounting the footpath, 10.6.1
off-road driving, 10.22
riding on footpaths, 10.12.4
roads, as, 10.1.1
tethering animals, 10.12.4
wilfully, meaning of, 10.12.4
footways, 10.1.1
force *see* **use of force**
forced entry when in immediate pursuit, 1.4.2
forced marriages, 4.11–4.11.2
arranged marriages and, 4.11.2
capacity, lack of, 4.11.1
criminal offences, 4.11.1
domestic abuse and coercive behaviour, 2.8
Forced Marriage Unit, 4.11.2
Honour Network, 4.11.2
marriage, meaning of, 4.11.1
offences, 4.11.1
protection orders, 4.11.2
forecourts, roads as, 10.1.1
fraud, 2.6.2, 3.8–3.9
abuse of position, 3.8.1, 3.8.4
meanings, 3.8.4
omissions, 3.8.4
special relationships, existence of, 3.8.4
admissible evidence, 3.8.1, 3.8.5
articles for use in fraud, 3.8–3.8.7
making or supplying articles, 3.8.7
possession, 3.8.6
credit cards, 3.8.2, 3.9
decoders, use of television, 3.9
disclose information, failing to, 3.8.1, 3.8.3
legal duty, meaning of, 3.8.3
life insurance, 3.8.3
meanings, 3.8.3
dishonesty, 3.9
electronic means, fraud by, 3.8.2, 3.8.6
entrance fee, watching sport without paying, 3.9
evidence, 3.8.1, 3.8.5
false representation, 3.8.1, 3.8.2
conduct, by, 3.8.2
meanings, 3.8.2

fraud (*cont.*)
Fraud Act 2006, 3.8–3.8.7, 3.9
gain and loss, meaning of, 3.8.1
good faith, 3.8.3
intention, 3.8.1
life insurance, 3.8.3
obtaining services dishonestly, 3.9
omissions, 3.8.4, 3.9
phishing, 3.8.2
self-incrimination, privilege against, 3.8.5
special relationships, existence of, 3.8.4
spouses/civil partners, admissible evidence, 3.8.5
television decoders, use of, 3.9
freedom of assembly and association, 10.21.1, App 1
freedom of expression
breach of the peace, 7.3
harassment, alarm, and distress, 7.7
Human Rights Act 1998, App 1
obstruction, 10.21.1
religious hatred offences, 7.9.3
sexual orientation hatred offences, 7.9.3
freedom of thought, conscience and religion, App 1
furious driving, 10.7.4
further education premises
bladed articles/knives, 8.10.1, 8.10.6, 8.10.7, 8.12.2
offensive weapons, 8.9.2

games on highway, playing, 10.21.3
gang membership, indications of, 1.3.2
gang-related violence, 7.4.2
gardens or yards, restrictions on stop and search in, 1.3.2
gas cartridge systems, air weapons with, 8.7.2, 8.7.3, 8.7.4
GBH *see* **wounding and grievous bodily harm**
generalisations and stereotyping, stop and search and, 1.3.2
genitals, sending photograph or film of, 6.7.2
GHB, 6.1.1, 6.10
gloves for searches, using, 5.4.1
glue sniffing, 7.2.1
Go-Ped, 10.1.3
going equipped, 3.6
article, meaning of, 3.6
articles with intent to damage, possessing, 4.7.1
conveyance, taking a, 3.6
'has with him', meaning of, 3.6
place of abode, meaning of, 3.6
vehicles, interference with, 4.2.1
good faith, fraud and, 3.8.3
goods vehicles
seat belts, 10.17.1
test certificates for vehicles, 10.16.3
graduated fixed penalty scheme, 10.4.3
graffiti
fixed penalty notices, 11.1.2
racially aggravated criminal damage, 7.10.3
gravity knives, 8.9.3, 8.10.2, 8.10.5, 8.12.1
grievous bodily harm *see* **wounding and grievous bodily harm**
grooming, meeting a child through, 6.5.5
defences, 6.5.5
evidence, 6.5.5
has met or communicated, 6.5.5
meetings or travel, requirement for intent to have, 6.5.5
offences committed outside UK, 6.5.5
reasonable belief that child is over 16, 6.5.5
seizure, 6.5.5
single meeting, 6.5.5
gross negligence, manslaughter by, 2.7.2, 2.7.3
guard dogs, 11.6.6
handlers, presence of, 11.6.6
kennels, 11.6.6
meaning of, 11.6.6
premises, meaning of, 11.6.6
warning notices, 11.6.6
guardians, 2.4.1
gun clubs, 8.1.3, 8.6.3
gunpowder, using with intent to cause GBH, 2.3.3
guns *see* **firearms**

hand claw, 8.9.4
hand-held devices, control of vehicle and use of, 10.4.2
handling stolen goods, 3.5
arranges to do so, 3.5
assists, meaning of, 3.5
circumstantial evidence, 3.5
dishonesty, test for, 3.5
goods, meaning of, 3.5
knowing or believing, 3.5
possession, meaning of, 3.5
previous convictions, checking, 3.5
realisation, meaning of, 3.5
receives, meaning of, 3.5
recent possession, doctrine of, 3.5
retention, meaning of, 3.5
special evidence, 3.5
stolen abroad, 3.5
stolen goods, meaning of, 3.5
undertakes, meaning of, 3.5
harassment, 7.11–7.11.8
alarm and distress, and *see* **harassment, alarm, or distress**

animals, threats to, 7.11.2
arrest, 7.11.7
civil remedies, 7.11.7
company, by, 7.11.1
contempt, 7.11.7
course of conduct, 7.11.1, 7.11.2, 7.11.7
crime, prevention or detection of, 7.11.1, 7.11.2
damages, 7.11.7
defences, 7.11.1, 7.11.2, 7.11.7
direction, meaning of, 7.11.8
dwellings, meaning of, 7.11.8
evidence, 7.11.1
fear of violence, 7.11.2
home, in the, 7.11, 7.11.8
injunctions, 7.11.7
letters to cause distress and anxiety, sending, 7.12.1
meanings, 7.11.1
mental illness, 7.11.1
oral harassment, 7.11.1
racially or religiously aggravated, 7.10.4, 7.10.5, 7.11.1
reasonable excuse test, 7.11.7
reasonable person test, 7.11.1, 7.11.2
remedies, 7.11.1, 7.11.2, 7.11.6, 7.11.7
restraining orders, 7.11.1, 7.11.2, 7.11.6
stalking, 7.11, 7.11.1, 7.11.2
telephone, 7.11.1
vehicles causing annoyance, 7.14.1
violence
fear of, 7.11.2
where there is no violence, 7.11.1, 7.11.2
warnings, 7.11.1
witness statements, 7.11.1
writing, 7.11
harassment, alarm, or distress, 7.7
abusive, meaning of, 7.7
alarm, meaning of, 7.7
anti-social behaviour, 7.13.1
communications causing distress, anxiety, or serious harm, 7.12.1, 7.12.2
defences, 7.7
disorderly behaviour, meaning, 7.7
dispersal powers, 7.15.1
distress, meaning of, 7.7
freedom of expression, 7.7
harassment, meaning of, 7.7
insulting, meaning of, 7.7
intent, 7.7
naturists/nudity, 6.7.1
off-road driving, 10.22
police officers, 7.7
public or private places, 7.7
racially or religiously aggravated, 7.7
stalking, 7.11.4
threatening or abusive words or behaviour, 7.8
Health and Safety Executive (HSE), corporate manslaughter and, 2.7.3
health bodies, vehicles owned by, 10.16.1
healthcare workers
neglect or ill-treatment by *see* **care workers, ill-treatment or neglect by**
provision of condoms by, 6.5.4
provision of contraception, 6.5.1, 6.5.4
helplines
forced marriages, 4.11.2
Honour Network, 4.11.2
Highland dress, skean dhu in, 8.10.1
highways *see* **roads**
hip flask defence, 10.11.1
hire
air weapons, 8.7.1
ammunition, 8.7.1
builders' skips on the highway, obstruction by, 10.21.2
crossbows, 8.9.6
firearms, 8.7.1
taking a vehicle without consent, 4.3.1
hire purchase, 4.3.1
HIV
infecting through unprotected sexual intercourse, 2.3.1
hoax bomb calls, 11.4.1–11.4.2
home, harassment in the, 7.11, 7.11.8
Honour Network confidential helpline, 4.11.2
horses, 4.3.1
hospital patients, driving under the influence of drink or drugs and, 10.10.2
hospital records, 1.5.4
hovercrafts, 10.1.3
Human Rights Act 1998, 1.2, App 1
innocence, presumption of, 10.10.1
proportionality test, 1.2
use of force, 1.2
human tissue or tissue fluid, 1.5.4
human trafficking *see* **slavery and human trafficking**
hyperlinks, sending, 7.12.3, 7.12.5, 7.12.6
hypodermic needles, 5.4.1

identification
bladed articles/knives, 8.10.2
dangerous dogs
dogs, 11.6.4
owners, 11.6.5
disqualified, driving whilst, 10.13.1

identification (*cont.*)
drink or drugs, driving/attempting to drive/in charge of vehicle whilst unfit through, 10.10.1
penalty notices for disorder, 7.1.2
search warrants
accompanying persons, 1.5.3
slavery and human trafficking victims, 4.9.3
identity documents, 11.3.2
examining officer, 11.3.2
invalidity, 11.3.2
meaning of, 11.3.2
passports, powers relating to, 11.3.2
ports, meaning of, 11.3.2
retention or return of seized documents, 11.3.2
search and seizure, 11.3.2
travel documents, 11.3.2
illegal entry into the United Kingdom, 11.3–11.3.3
aircraft, vehicles, or ships
detention, 11.3.1
forfeiture of, 11.3.1
arrest, 11.3.1
assisting illegal entry, 11.3.1
asylum seekers, 11.3.1
deception, illegal entry by, 11.3.3
deportation orders, 11.3.1, 11.3.3
enforcement action, meaning of, 11.3.3
entry without entry clearance, 11.3.1
entry without leave to enter, 11.3.1
identity documents, 11.3.2
immigration bail, 11.3.1
medical tests and examinations, failure to comply with, 11.3.1
people trafficking, 11.3.1
remaining beyond limited leave to enter, 11.3.1
working when subject to immigration control, 11.3.1
ill-treatment, care worker by *see* **care workers, ill-treatment or neglect by**
images, extreme pornographic, 6.6.2
image of person under 18, possession of prohibited, 6.6.2
imitation firearms, 8.1.1, 8.1.4
18, sale or purchase by persons under, 8.7.1, 8.7.5
appearance of, 8.5
arrest, 8.3.4, 8.3.5, 8.3.6
bored barrels, 8.1.4
burglary, 3.3.1, 3.3.2
convertible, that are readily, 8.1.4
defences, 8.7.5
guidance, 8.7.5
meaning, 8.3.3, 8.7.5
public place, possession in a, 8.5
realistic firearms, meaning of, 8.7.5
sale or purchase by persons under 18, 8.7.1, 8.7.5
section 1 firearms, 8.1.1, 8.1.4
test for, 8.5
trespassing, 8.4.1
immediate pursuit, forced entry when in, 1.4.2
immigration *see* **illegal entry into the United Kingdom**
impairment tests, preliminary, 10.10.2
impersonating a constable, 2.2.4
inchoate offences, meaning of, 2.2.6
indecent exposure, 6.7.1
indecent photographs/images
18, persons under, 6.6.1, 6.6.2
audit chains, 6.6.2
child, of a, 6.6.1, 6.6.2
consent, 6.6.1, 6.6.2
defences, 6.6.1, 6.6.2
distribute, meaning of, 6.6.1
downloading, 6.6.1
email attachments
deliberate opening of, 6.6.1
innocent opening of, 6.6.1
evidence, 6.6.1
films, 6.6.1
forfeiture, 6.6.1, 6.6.2
intent, 6.6.1
internet, 6.6.1
knowledge, 6.6.2
make, meaning of, 6.6.1
married or in enduring family relationship with defendant, 6.6.1, 6.6.2
photograph, meaning of, 6.6.1
pseudo-photographs, meaning of, 6.6.1
seizure, 6.6.1, 6.6.2
sending photograph or film of genitals, 6.7.2
sexting, 6.6.1
sharing or threatening to share intimate photograph or film, 6.7.3
Trojan Horse virus defence, 6.6.1
video recordings, 6.6.1
industrial disputes, 7.15.1
infant death, overlaying and, 2.7.5
infanticide, 2.7.1, 2.7.6
infection, risk of, 5.4.1
information, duty of driver to stop and give
insurance, evidence of, 10.9.2
leaving the scene of an accident, 10.9.2
name and address, requirement to give, 10.9.2
report an accident, failure to, 10.9.2
road traffic collisions, 10.9.2
scene of accident, meaning of, 10.9.2
inhuman or degrading treatment, 1.2, App 1

injunctions
arrest, powers of, 2.8
domestic abuse, 2.8
harassment, 7.11.7
innocence, presumption of, 10.10.1
insanity, 2.7.1, 10.11.1
inspection
drug search powers, 5.4.1
gun clubs, 8.6.3
search warrants, 1.5.3
insurance
death, causing by driving when disqualified, 10.8.3
death, causing by driving when without insurance, or class of licence, 10.8.5
evidence of, 10.9.2, 10.9.3
failure to produce, 10.16.1, 10.16.5
fraud, 3.8.3
life insurance, fraud and, 3.8.3
use of vehicle without insurance, 10.16.1
Insurance Advisory Letter, 10.16.2
insurance, registered keeper of vehicle without, 10.16.2
exceptions, 10.16.2
fixed penalty procedure, 10.16.2
immobilisation and removal of vehicle, 10.16.2
registered, meaning of, 10.16.2
insurance, test certificate, plating certificate, or goods vehicle test certificate, failure to produce
defences, 10.16.5
name and address, requirement to give, 10.16.5
provisional drivers, supervisor's, 10.16.5
requirement, meaning of, 10.16.5
vehicle examiners, 10.16.5
insurance, user of vehicle without
Accountant General of Senior Courts, sums deposited with, 10.16.1
defences, 10.16.1
deposits with Accountant General, 10.16.1
failure to produce insurance, 10.16.1
fixed penalty procedure, 10.16.1
health bodies, vehicles owned by, 10.16.1
invalid carriages, 10.16.1
public authorities, vehicles owned by, 10.16.1
road, vehicles left on, 10.16.1
salvage, vehicle being driven to or from a place for, 10.16.1
seizure and removal of vehicle, 10.16.1, 10.16.5
use, meaning of, 10.16.1
valid insurer, 10.16.1
intellectual property
criminal lifestyle offences, 5.5
theft and, 3.1.1
intent
distinguished from attempts, 4.1.1
meaning of, 4.1.2
objective test, 4.1.2
proof of, 4.1.1, 4.1.2
strict liability, 4.1.2
subjective test, 4.1.2
interim orders
stalking prevention orders, 7.11.5
internet
indecent photographs/images, 6.6.1
phishing, 3.8.2
racial hatred offences, 7.9.2
internet service providers
communications offences, 7.12.3, 7.12.5
intimate photograph or film, sharing or threatening to share, 6.7.3
intimate searches, 5.4.1, 6.2.1
intimidation, 4.8–4.8.1
intoxication
careless driving when under the influence, causing death by, 10.8.2
cycling whilst under the influence of
dangerous dogs, 11.6.5
drink driving, 10.8.2, 10.10–10.10.2
drink or drugs, 10.12.3
drunk and disorderly in public places, 7.2–7.2.2
drunk and incapable, 7.2.2
drunk on a highway, 7.2.2
drunkenness on licensed premises, 9.2–9.2.3
riots, 7.4.1
sexual assault by touching, 6.3.1
spiking drinks, 6.10, 9.1.5, 10.11.1
intoximeter reading inaccurate, where, 10.11.1
invalid carriages
driving licence, minimum age for holding, 10.14.1
insurance, user of vehicle without, 10.16.1
pavements, used on, 10.1.3
registration marks on vehicles, 10.20.2
report incidents, duty of driver to, 10.9.3
vehicles, seizure of, 10.16.6
irritation or resentment, behaviour causing, 7.9.1

journalistic material, 1.5.4
jurors *see* **witnesses, victims or jurors intimidation of**

'kettling', 2.6.1
keys, bunch of, 8.9.1

khat, possessing, 5.3.2
Home Office Circular 11/2014, 5.3.2
PNDs for, 5.3.2, 7.1.2
kidnapping, 2.6.2
children, person's own, 2.6.2
consent, 2.6.2
deception, 2.6.2
defences, 2.6.2
deprivation of liberty, 2.6.2
forced marriages, 4.11
fraud, meaning of, 2.6.2
sexual offence, commit an offence with intent to commit, 6.10
spouses, 2.6.2
kirpan, 8.10.1
kitchen knives, 8.9.1
knife crime prevention orders, 8.13
knives *see* **bladed articles/knives**
knuckledusters, 8.9.1, 8.9.4, 8.10.2
kubotan, hollow, 8.9.4
kusari, 8.9.4

laced drinks, 6.1.1, 6.10, 9.1.5, 10.11.1
lasers
shining light or laser towards aircraft or vehicle, 11.8
lay-bys, 10.1.1
leaving the scene of an accident, 10.9.2
legal privilege
excluded and special procedure material, access to, 1.5.4
experts, 1.4.1
searches, 1.4.1, 1.4.3, 1.4.4
seizure, 1.4.1, 1.4.4
letters with intent to cause distress and anxiety, sending, 7.12.1
liberty and security, right to, App 1
licences *see* **driving licences; licensing; nil licence for exempt vehicles**
licensing, 9.1–9.5.2
children and alcohol, 9.1–9.1.7
disorderly conduct in licensed premises, allowing, 9.2.3
drunk on a highway, 7.2.2
drunkenness on licensed premises, 9.2–9.2.3
enter licensed premises, power to, 9.3.2
failure to leave licensed premises, 9.2.2
sale/supply of alcohol by under 18 persons, 9.1.7
test purchases, 9.3.1
life, damage with intent to endanger, 4.5.1
life or limb or serious damage to property
ammunition, possession of, 8.3.2
criminal damage, 4.4
entry to save, 1.4.2
firearms with intent to endanger life, possession of, 8.3.2
vehicles, power to stop, 10.2.1
life, right to, App 1
lifeboats, obstruction of, 2.2.7
lighter refills to young people, supply of, 11.5.1
litter, 7.16
anti-social behaviour, 7.16.2
beaches, 7.16.2
bins, removal or interference with, 7.16.2
community protection notices, 7.16.1
consent, 7.16.2
defences, 7.16.2
deposits, meaning of, 7.16.2
fixed penalty notices, 7.16.2, 11.1.2
keeper of vehicle, 7.16.2
litter authorities, meaning of, 7.16.2
meaning of, 7.16.2
notice boards, 7.16.2
place, meaning of, 7.16.2
livestock, dogs worrying, 11.6.3
Local Safeguarding Children Board, establishment of, 2.4.2
lock knives, 8.10.1
locker
deliver bladed articles to, 8.10.3
deliver corrosive substance to, 8.11.2
meaning, 8.10.3
locking-on, causing serious disruption by, 7.17.5
dwelling, meaning of, 7.17.5
key national infrastructure, 7.17.5
serious disruption, 7.17.5

magic mushrooms, 5.1.1
mailbags, robbery of, 3.2.1
making off without payment, 3.7
bilking, 3.7
defences, 3.7
defer payment, agreement to, 3.7
goods, meaning of, 3.7
intent, 3.7
payment on the spot, meaning of, 3.7
malice aforethought, 2.7.1
maliciously administering poison with intent, 2.1.3
manslaughter, 2.7.2
child cruelty, 2.4.1
corporate manslaughter, 2.7.2, 2.7.3
damage with intent to endanger life, 4.5.1
death by dangerous driving, 10.8.1
diminished responsibility, 2.7.2
grievous bodily harm, intent to cause, 2.7.2
gross negligence, 2.7.2, 2.7.3
involuntary, 2.7.2
malice, doctrine of transferred, 2.7.2
medical negligence, 2.7.2
mens rea, 2.7.2

suicide, encouraging or assisting, 2.7.2
unlawful act, 2.7.2
voluntary, 2.7.2
marriage, forced *see* **forced marriage**
marry, right to, App 1
medical examinations
consent to, 10.10.1
sexual assault by penetration, 6.2.1
medical necessity, drugs and, 5.3.1
medical negligence, 2.7.2
mental disabilities, persons with
forced marriage, 4.11.1
harassment, 7.11.1
insanity, 2.7.1, 10.11.1
mental illness, harassment by persons with, 7.11.1
murder, insanity and, 2.7.1
prescribed alcohol limit, drive or attempt to drive/in charge of motor vehicle whilst over, 10.11.1
sexual activity, 6.1.1
specimens, 10.11.3
see also **mentally disordered people in public places**
mental health professionals, 11.2
mentally disordered people, removal without warrant of, 11.2
alcohol dependence, 11.2
ambulance, use of, 11.2
approved mental health professionals, 11.2
assessment requirements, 11.2
care home, meaning of, 11.2
children, 11.2
drug dependence, 11.2
mental disorder, meaning of, 11.2
Mental Health Act 1983: Codes of Practice (England), 11.2
permitted period of detention, 11.2
place of safety, 11.2
promiscuity, 11.2
protective search powers, 11.2
public or private place, meaning of, 11.2
warrants, 11.2
messengers issuing threats, 4.8.1
meters, causing to malfunction, 3.8.7
military purposes, vehicles used for, 10.14.1
mind a weapon or firearm, using person to, 8.3.7
miscarriage, causing a, 2.5
missiles, 8.1.1
M'Naghten Rules, 2.7.1
mobile phones
control of vehicles, 10.4.2
money laundering, criminal lifestyle offences, 5.5
mopeds, 10.14.1
MOT tests, 10.20.2
motor cycle crash helmets/eye protectors, having no
British standard on helmet, 10.18
chin cups, 10.18
eye protectors, 10.18
fastening, 10.18
fixed penalty scheme, 10.18
motor bicycle, meaning of, 10.18
motor cycles, meaning of, 10.18
mowing machines, 10.18
scooter style, propelled, 10.18
Sikhs, 10.18
motor cycles
crash helmets/eye protectors, having no, 10.18
driving licence, minimum age for holding, 10.14.1
registration marks, 10.20.2
seat belts, 10.17.1
training certificate, failure to produce, 10.16.4
Motor Insurance Database, 10.16.2
motor vehicles *see* **driving offences; motor cycles; pedal cycles; taking a conveyance without owner's consent (TWOC); vehicles**
mounting the footpath, 10.6.1
mouth
drugs, searches for, 5.4.1
rape, 6.1.1
searches, 1.4.1, 5.4.1
mowing machines, 10.1.3, 10.18
multi-tools, possession of, 8.10.1
murder, 2.7.1
abroad, committed, 2.7.1
age of criminal responsibility, 2.7.1
cause and causation, 2.7.1
children, 2.7.1
creature in being, reasonable, 2.7.1
damage with intent to endanger life, 4.5.1
date of offence, 2.7.1
defences, 2.7.1
diminished responsibility, 2.7.1
grievous bodily harm, intent to cause, 2.7.1
infanticide, 2.7.1, 2.7.6
insanity, 2.7.1
intent, 2.7.1
intervening acts, 2.7.1
kills, meaning of, 2.7.1
lawful killing, meaning of, 2.7.1
loss of control, 2.7.1
malice aforethought, 2.7.1
medical treatment, intervening, 2.7.1
mens rea, 2.7.1
M'Naghten Rules, 2.7.1
motivation, 2.7.1
qualifying trigger, 2.7.1

murder (*cont.*)
Queen's peace, under the, 2.7.1
sound mind and discretion, 2.7.1
substantial test, 2.7.1
suicide pact, 2.7.1
transferred malice, doctrine of, 2.7.1
unlawfully, meaning of, 2.7.1
war, 2.7.1
museums, or galleries, gifts or loans of weapons to, 8.9.3
mushrooms, 3.1.1
magic mushrooms, 5.1.1
musical events, possession of pyrotechnic articles at, 8.8.9
mutilation, consent to body, 2.1.2

name and address, giving
anti-social behaviour, 7.13.2
CSOs and CSVs, powers of, 11.1.3
dangerous driving, 10.6.2, 10.7.1
due care and attention, driving without, 10.6, 10.6.2
false name and address, giving, 10.6.2
information, duty of driver to stop and give, 10.9.2
insurance, test certificate, plating certificate, or goods vehicle certificate, failure to produce, 10.16.5
reckless, careless, or inconsiderate driving or cycling, 10.6.2
serious violence reduction orders, 8.13
trade plates, 10.19
national costume, bladed articles/ knives and, 8.10.1
National Health Service
assaults on emergency workers, 2.2.6
National Health Service premises, causing nuisance/disturbance on, 7.13.5
anti-social behaviour, 7.13.5
authorised officer, meaning of, 7.13.5
hospital grounds, meaning of, 7.13.5
NHS premises, meaning of, 7.13.5
NHS staff member, meaning of, 7.13.5
person requires medical treatment, 7.13.5
power to remove, 7.13.5
reasonable excuse, 7.13.5
relevant NHS body, meaning of, 7.13.5
use of reasonable force, 7.13.5
vehicle, meaning of, 7.13.5
verbal aggression, 7.13.5
without reasonable excuse, 7.13.5
national infrastructure, key
interference with use or operation of, 7.17.8
locking-on, causing serious disruption by, 7.17.5
naturists, 6.7.1
necessity
cannabis, medical necessity, and, 5.3.1
driving without due care and attention, 10.6.1
needles, 5.1.2, 5.4.1
neglect, 2.4.1
care worker, by *see* **care workers, ill-treatment or neglect by**
negligence, manslaughter by gross, 2.7.2
night sights, 8.1.1
night use of fireworks, 8.8.4
nil licence for exempt vehicles
failure to have, 10.20.1
keeper details incorrect, 10.20.3
no punishment without law, App 1
non-fatal strangulation/ suffocation, 2.3.4
Northern Ireland, firearms and, 8.6.2
notices
dispersal powers, 7.15.1
guard dogs, 11.6.6
intended prosecution *see* **notices of intended prosecution**
PNDs *see* **penalty notices for disorder (PNDs)**
seizure, 1.4.4, 10.16.6
Traffic Fixed Penalty Notices, 10.2.3, 10.3, 10.4.1
see also **fixed penalty notices**
notices of intended prosecution, 10.5
dangerous cycling, 10.12.1
dangerous driving, 10.7.1, 10.7.2
due care and attention, driving without, 10.6.1
fixed penalty schemes, 10.5
relevant offences, list of, 10.5
service, 10.5
time limits, 10.5
traffic signs, failure to comply with, 10.3
vehicles, power to stop, 10.2.1
warnings, 10.5
noxious substances
maliciously administering poison with intent, 2.1.3
nuisance
builders' skips on the highway, obstruction by, 10.21.2
litter, 7.16.1
school premises, 8.10.8
see also **public nuisance**
number plate, ability to read, 10.15

obscene telephone calls, 7.12.2
obstructing or resisting a police officer in the execution of duty
assault, 2.2.3
execution of duty, in, 2.2.3, 2.2.5
positive acts, 2.2.3

resistance, meaning of, 2.2.3
wilful obstruction, 2.2.3
obstruction
bodies corporate, 10.21.1
builders' skips, 10.21.2
continuing obstructions, 10.21.1
criminal damage, 4.4
de minimis principle, 10.21.1
demonstrations, 10.21.1
drug search powers, 5.4.1
emergency workers and persons assisting, 2.2.7
endangering/injuring highway user, 10.21.3
fear, causing, 10.21.1
firearms, 8.6.3
fireworks, 8.8.8
fixed penalty schemes, 10.21.1, 10.21.4
games on highway, playing, 10.21.3
highway, wilful obstruction of the, 10.21.1
lawful excuse, 10.21.1
major transport works, 7.17.7
motor vehicles, 10.21.1, 10.21.4
parking, 10.21.4
proportionality of rights and interests, 10.21.1
remove obstruction, orders to, 10.21.1
roads, 10.21– 10.22
smoke on highway, 10.21.3
trailers, meaning of, 10.21.4
unnecessary obstruction, causing, 10.21.4
see also **obstructing or resisting a police officer**
obtaining services dishonestly, 3.9
occasioning actual bodily harm, assault, 2.1, 2.1.2
OFCOM, 7.12.2
off-road driving, 10.22
alarm, distress, or annoyance, causing, 10.22
bridleways, meaning of, 10.22
common land, meaning of, 10.22
defences, 10.22
entry, powers of, 10.22
fixed penalty procedure, 10.22
footpaths, meaning of, 10.22
interests in land, 10.22
meaning of, 10.22
parking, 10.22
restricted byways, meaning of, 10.22
stop, seizure, and removal of vehicle, 10.22
trespass, 10.22
use of force, 10.22
waste land, 10.22
offensive weapons, 8.9.1– 8.9.6
adapted, meaning of, 8.9.1
affray, 7.5
antiques, 8.9.3
carrying, 8.9.1
crossbows, 8.9.6
Crown, functions carried out on behalf of the, 8.9.3
dangerous instruments, meaning of, 8.12.3
defences, 8.9.1, 8.9.3
descriptions of, 2.3.1
entry, powers of, 8.12.1
flick knives, 8.10.5
gravity knives, 8.10.5
has with him, 8.9.1
hiring dangerous weapons, 8.10.5
imports, 8.9.3, 8.9.4
instant use, seizure of weapon for, 8.9.1
intention, 8.9.1
keys, bunch of, 8.9.1
kirpan, 8.10.1
knowledge, 8.9.1
knuckledusters, 8.9.1, 8.9.4, 8.10.2
kubotan, hollow, 8.9.4
kusari, 8.9.4
lawful authority, 8.9.1
lending dangerous weapons, 8.10.5
list of weapons, 8.9.4
made, meaning of, 8.9.1
manufacturing dangerous weapons, 8.10.5
meaning, 8.9.1, 8.9.3, 8.12.3
mind a weapon, using a person to, 8.3.7
museums, or galleries, gifts or loans to, 8.9.3
police powers, 8.12– 8.12.3
possession
dangerous weapons, 8.10.5
in private place, 8.9.3
in public place, 8.9.1
premises, meaning of, 8.9.5
provide, trade or manufacture, 8.9.3
public order, 8.12.2, 8.12.3
public place
meaning, 8.9.1
possession, in a, 8.9.1
school premises, 8.12.2
trespassing, 8.9.5
reasonable excuse, 8.9.1
remote sales, 8.10.2
retention, 8.12.1, 8.12.2
sale, hire, exposing, or importation, prohibition of, 8.9.4
sale of dangerous weapons, 8.10.5
school premises, 8.9.5, 8.10.1, 8.10.7
entry, powers of, 8.12.2
nuisance or disturbance on, 8.12.2
search warrants
conditions, 8.12.1

offensive weapons (*cont.*)
grounds for, 8.12.1
search premises, 8.12.1
seize, 8.9.1, 8.9.3, 8.9.5, 8.12.1, 8.12.2, 8.12.3
self-defence, 8.9.1
serious physical harm, meaning of, 8.9.1
serious violence, stop and search, 8.12.3
stop and search, 1.3.2, 7.5, 8.9.1, 8.9.3
affray, 7.5
authorisation, 8.12.3
reasonable grounds for suspicion, 8.12.3
serious violence, 8.12.3
theatrical/television performances, 8.9.3
threatening with, 8.9.1, 8.9.2
trespassing, 8.9.5
use of force, 8.12.2
using person to mind a weapon, 8.3.7
vehicles
meaning of, 8.12.3
stop and search of, 8.9.1, 8.9.5, 8.12.2, 8.12.3
violence
serious, 8.12.3
stop and search, 8.12.3
visiting forces, functions carried out on behalf of, 8.9.3
see also **bladed articles/knives; corrosive substances; firearms**
omissions
abuse of position, 3.8.4
fraud, 3.8.4, 3.9
online sales of offensive weapons, 8.10.2
outraging public decency, 6.7.4
balconies, 6.7.4
lewd, obscene, and disgusting, definition of, 6.7.4
public nuisance, 6.7.4
public place, meaning of, 6.7.4
reasonable person test, 6.7.4
sexual activity in a public lavatory, 6.9
over-laying/suffocation of infant under 3 years, 2.7.5
in bed/went to bed, meaning of, 2.7.5
prohibited drugs/drink, under influence of, 2.7.5

PACE and codes
domestic abuse, 2.8
entry, powers of, 1.4.2
excluded and special procedure material, access to, 1.5.4
searches, 1.4.1, 1.4.3, 1.5– 1.5.3
seizure, 1.4.4
stop and search, 1.3.2, 1.3.4, 1.3.5
use of force, 1.2
paints to children, sale of aerosol, 4.7.2
paraphernalia, 5.2.2, 5.4.1
parental responsibility, 2.4.1
park trading offences
CSOs and CSVs, powers of, 11.1.9
parking
obstruction, 10.21.4
off-road driving, 10.22
roads, car parks as, 10.1.1, 10.1.2
passports, powers relating to and illegal entry into UK, 11.3.2
patrol matters
dogs, 11.6– 11.6.6
forced marriages, 4.11
illegal entry into the UK, 11.3– 11.3.3
mentally disordered people, removal without warrant of, 11.2
wasting police time, 11.4– 11.4.2
paying for sexual services of a child, 6.5.2
online safety, 6.5.2
payment, meaning of, 6.5.2
paying for sexual services of a prostitute subject to exploitation, 6.11.3
exploitative conduct, meaning of, 6.11.3
gain, meaning of, 6.11.3
Home Office Circular 6/2010, 6.11.3
use of threats, 6.11.3
peace, breach of *see* **breach of the peace**
pedal cycles, 10.12– 10.12.4
careless and inconsiderate cycling, 10.12.2
dangerous cycling, 10.12.1
dangerous driving, 10.7.1
drink or drugs, cycling whilst under the influence of, 10.12.3
due care and attention, cycling without, 10.12.2
due care and attention, driving without, 10.6.1, 10.6.2
electrically assisted cycles, 10.1.3
footpath, riding on the, 10.12.4
road traffic collisions, 10.9.1
stop, power to, 10.2.3
taking or riding cycles, 4.3.1, 4.3.3
Traffic Fixed Penalty Notices, 10.4.1
wanton or furious driving, 10.7.4
pedestrians, directions to, 10.2.2
penalties *see* **fixed penalty notices; penalty notices for disorder (PNDs)**
penalty notices for disorder (PNDs), 3.1.1, 7.1– 7.1.2
arrest, 7.1.2

associated offences, 7.1.2
availability, 7.1.2
cannabis/khat possession, 5.3.1, 7.1.2
children under 18, 7.1.2
communications causing distress, anxiety, or serious harm, 7.12.2, 7.12.7
court hearing, requests for, 7.1.2
criminal damage, 7.1.2
criminal records, 7.1.2
CSOs and CSVs, powers of, 7.1.2, 7.12.2, 7.12.7
DBS check, disclosure under, 7.1.2
drunk and disorderly, 7.2.1
drunk on highway, 7.2.2
drunk on licensed premises, 9.2.3
educational course schemes, 7.1.2
false reports, 7.1.2
fines following failure to pay, 7.1.2
fireworks/throwing fireworks, 7.1.2, 8.8.3, 8.8.4, 8.8.5, 8.8.6
guidance for issuing, 7.1.2
identification, 7.1.2
issuing, 7.1.2
jointly committed offences, 7.1.2
nature of, 7.1.2
not appropriate, offenders for which PNDs, 7.1.2
nuisance calls, 7.1.2
offences, list of, 7.1.1
offences for which not appropriate, 7.1.2
pre-conditions, 7.1.2
retention of information on, 7.1.2
sale of alcohol to person who is drunk, 9.2.1
scheme, aim of, 7.1.2
shoplifting, 7.1.2
victims, 7.1.2
wasting police time, 7.1.2, 11.4.1

penalty points, 10.13.1
penetration *see* **sexual assault by penetration**
people trafficking, criminal lifestyle offences, 5.5
personal records, 1.5.4
perverting the course of justice, 4.8, 4.8.2
attempts, 4.8.2
documents, failure to produce, 4.8.2
evidence by unlawful means, producing, 4.8.2
inaction, deliberate, 4.8.2
positive acts, 4.8.2
petrol bombs, possession of, 7.5
phishing, 3.8.2
photographs, 1.3.4, 1.5.4
indecent *see* **indecent photographs/images**
sending photograph or film of genitals, 6.7.2
sharing or threatening to share intimate photograph or film, 6.7.3
place of safety
mentally disordered people, removal without warrant of, 11.2
plain clothes officers, 2.2.2
plants and creatures, wild, 3.1.1, 4.4
plating certificate or goods vehicle test certificate, failure to produce, 10.16.5
PNDs *see* **penalty notices for disorder (PNDs)**
poisoning, 6.10
maliciously administering poison with intent, 2.1.3
Police Community Support Officers *see* **Community Support Officers**
police protection, taking into, 2.4.1, 2.4.2
child, meaning of, 2.4.2
definition of police protection, 2.4.2
designated officers, duty of, 2.4.2
Home Office Circular 17/2008, 2.4.2
hospitals, meaning of, 2.4.2
Local Safeguarding Children Board, establishment of, 2.4.2
police stations, 2.4.2
reasons, 2.4.2
police stations
arrest at, 1.1.3
police protection, taking child into, 2.4.2
release prior to arrival at, 1.1.4
report incidents, duty of driver to, 10.9.3
pornography
extreme images, 6.6.2
ports, powers of search and seizure re illegal entry into UK, 11.3.2
possession of article of police uniform, 2.2.4
possession of a controlled drug, 5.2.1
cannabis, 5.2.1
defences, 5.2.1
general authority, 5.1.1
Home Office Circular 1/2009, 5.2.1
Home Office Circular 12/2011, 5.2.1
Home Office Circular 9/2012, 5.2.1
Home Office Circular 15/2012, 5.2.1
Home Office Circular 8/2014, 5.2.1
Home Office Circular 13/2014, 5.2.1
Home Office Circular 18/2018, 5.2.1
knowledge, lack of, 5.2.1
possession, meaning of, 5.2.1
temporary class drug, 5.2.1
testing, 5.2.1
possession of corrosive substance in public place, 8.11.3

possession of dangerous weapons, 8.10.5
possession with intent to supply a controlled drug, 5.2.2
burden of proof, 5.2.2
defences, 5.2.2
lifestyle and paraphernalia, 5.2.2
possession with intent to supply psychoactive substances, 5.3.6
possessions, right to peaceful enjoyment, App 1
postal packages or mail bags
robbery, 3.2.1
theft, 3.1.1
posters, racially or religiously insulting, 7.7
powers of arrest *see* **arrest**
powers of entry *see* **entry, powers of**
premises
adverse occupation of, 7.17.3
children and alcohol, 9.1.1
closure notices and orders, 5.4.2, 6.11.3, 7.13.4
club premises certificates, 9.1.1
firearms, premises search warrants and, 8.6.3
premises search warrants, firearms and, 8.6.3
trespass on premises/land, 7.17.1
unaccompanied children from certain premises, prohibition of, 9.1.1
violent entry to, 7.17.1, 7.17.2
see also **school premises**
premises, closure of *see* **closure of premises (nuisance/disorder)**
prescribed/specified limit, drive or attempt to drive/in charge of motor vehicle whilst over, 10.11– 10.11.3
alcohol, 10.11.1
anonymous callers, 10.11.1
arrest, 10.11.1
blood specimens, consent and, 10.11.3
breath tests, roadside, 10.11.1
burden of proof, 10.11.1
consuming, meaning of, 10.11.1
defences, 10.11.1
drugs, 10.11.2
duress, 10.11.1
entry, power of, 10.11.1
exhibit, retention of mouthpiece as, 10.11.3
hip flask defence, 10.11.1
insanity, 10.11.1
intoximeter reading inaccurate, where, 10.11.1
lacing drinks, 10.11.1
likelihood of driving, 10.11.1
mouthpiece as exhibit, retention of, 10.11.3
provisional licence holders, supervisors of, 10.11.1, 10.11.2
specimens, 10.11.1, 10.11.3
trespassers, where officers, 10.11.1
use of force, powers of entry and, 10.11.1
prescription drugs, 5.1.1
press photographs showing criminal acts, 1.5.4
presumption of innocence, 10.10.1
previous convictions
firearms, 8.3.1
handling stolen goods, 3.5
penalty notices for disorder, 7.1.2
stop and search, 1.3.2
prison officers, assaults on, 2.2.6
prisons
possession with intent to supply psychoactive substances, 5.3.6
private and family life, right to respect for, App 1
privilege
self-incrimination, privilege against, 3.8.5
see also **legal privilege**
proceeds of crime, 5.4.2, 5.5
confiscation orders, 5.5
confiscation proceedings, 5.5
criminal lifestyle criteria, 5.5
criminal lifestyle offences, 5.5
arms trafficking, 5.5
blackmail, 5.5
child sex, 5.5
counterfeiting, 5.5
directing terrorism, 5.5
drug trafficking, 5.5
inchoate offences, 5.5
intellectual property, 5.5
money laundering, 5.5
people trafficking, 5.5
prostitution, 5.5
criminal lifestyle tests, 5.5
procurement of child, 6.5.4
property damage *see* **criminal damage**
property unlawful to possess, stealing, 3.1.1
prosecutions *see* **notices of intended prosecution**
prostitution
criminal lifestyle offences, 5.5
loiter, meaning of, 6.11.1
to obtain services of a prostitute, 6.11.2
paying for sexual services of prostitute subject to exploitation, 6.11.3
persistently loitering, 6.11.1
persistently, meaning of, 6.11.1
placing of adverts in telephone boxes, 6.11.1

soliciting
meaning of, 6.11.1
persistent, 6.11.1
street or public place, in, 6.11.1
protests *see* **demonstrations**
provisional driving
disqualified, driving whilst, 10.13.1
driving motor vehicle of class not authorised, 10.14.1
prescribed alcohol limit drive or attempt to drive/in charge of motor vehicle whilst over, 10.11.1
seat belts, 10.17.1
provocation
murder, 2.7.1
see also **fear or provocation of violence**
psychiatric harm
actual bodily harm, assault occasioning, 2.1.2
communications causing distress, anxiety, or serious harm, 7.12.2
wounding and grievous bodily harm, 2.3.1
psychoactive substances, 5.3.3– 5.3.6
consumes, 5.3.4
CSOs and CSVs, powers of, 5.3.6, 11.1.6
disposal, 5.3.6
drug trafficking, 5.5
exempted substance, 5.3.4
meaning of psychoactive substance, 5.3.4
possession for personal use, 5.3.3
possession with intent to supply psychoactive substances, 5.3.6
producing psychoactive substances, 5.3.4
psychoactive effect, 5.3.4
supply of psychoactive substance/ offering to supply, 5.3.5
public authorities
insurance, user of vehicle without, 10.16.1
vehicles owned by, 10.16.1
public nuisance
alcohol restrictions, public spaces protection orders, 9.4
anti-social behaviour, 7.13.3
communications causing distress, anxiety, or serious harm, 7.12.2
conspiracy, 7.13.3
legal duty, 7.13.3
outraging public decency, 6.7.4
telephone calls, 7.13.3
public order
bladed articles/knives, 8.12.2, 8.12.3
directions to leave, 7.15.1
interference with use or operation of key national infrastructure, 7.17.8
offensive weapons, 8.12.2, 8.12.3
powers to stop and search without suspicion, 7.17.9
racially or religiously aggravated offences, 7.10.4
public places
car parks, 10.1.2
collection, meaning of, 3.1.2
corrosive substances, 8.11.3
defences, 3.1.2
directions to leave, 7.15.1
drunk and disorderly, 7.2– 7.2.2
due care and attention, driving without, 10.6.1
firearms, 8.5, 8.6.1, 8.7.2
fireworks, 8.8.2, 8.8.6
harassment, alarm, or distress, 7.7
mentally disordered people, 11.2
offensive weapons, 8.9.1, 8.9.5, 8.12.2
public access, 3.1.2
racial hatred offences, 7.9.1
removal of articles from, 3.1.2
roads, 10.1.2
threatened with article in, 8.10.6
public service vehicle
definition, 7.18.1
search of for alcohol when en route to sporting event, 7.18.1
public spaces protection orders (PSPOs), 7.15.2
alcohol/alcohol restrictions, 7.15.2, 9.4
anti-social behaviour, 7.15.2
challenging, 7.15.2
conditions, 7.15.2
consultation, 7.15.2
dogs, 7.15.2
duration, 7.15.2
local authorities, 7.15.2
meaning, 7.15.2
photographs, 7.15.2
public spaces, 7.15.2
publicity
dispersal powers, 7.15.1
pump-action shotguns, 8.1.1
purchase of alcohol by and on behalf of children, 9.1.4
push dagger, 8.9.4
pyrotechnics
possession at musical events, 8.8.9
supply of pyrotechnic articles, 8.8.5

Queen's peace, murder under the, 2.7.1
questioning
obstruction, 2.2.3
stop and search, 1.3.2

race, religion or appearance, stop and search and, 1.3.2
racial hatred offences, 7.9– 7.9.2
abusive, meaning of, 7.9.1
aggravated offences *see* **racially or religiously aggravated offences**
bodies corporate, 7.9.1
defences, 7.9.1, 7.9.2
display, meaning of, 7.9.1
display of written material, 7.9.1
distributes, meaning of, 7.9.3
distributing, showing, or playing a recording, 7.9.2
distributing written material, 7.9.3
dwelling, meaning of, 7.9.1
electronic form, material in, 7.9.2
forfeiture of material, 7.9.1
insulting, meaning of, 7.9.1
intention, 7.9.1
irritation or resentment, behaviour causing, 7.9.1
playing a performance, 7.9.2
possession of racially aggravated material, 7.9.2
public or private places, 7.9.1
publishing written material, 7.9.2
racial hatred, meaning of, 7.9.1
showing a recording, 7.9.3
threatening, abusive, and insulting words or behaviour, 7.9.1, 7.9.2
threatening, definition of, 7.9.1
written material, 7.9.1, 7.9.2
racialist chanting at football match, 7.18.2
racially or religiously aggravated offences, 7.10– 7.10.5
assault, 7.10.2
criminal damage, 4.4, 7.10.3
definition, 7.10.1
fear or provocation of violence, 7.6
graffiti, 7.10.3
grievous bodily harm, 2.3.1, 2.3.2
harassment, 7.7, 7.10.5, 7.11.1
harassment, alarm, or distress, 7.10.4
hostility, 7.10.1
membership, meaning of, 7.10.1
nationality, 7.10.1
police officers, against, 7.10.1
presumed, meaning of, 7.10.1
public order offences, 7.10.4
racial groups, 7.10.1
religious groups, 7.10.1
stalking, 7.10.5
strangulation, 2.3.4
suffocation, 2.3.4
threatening or abusive words or behaviour, 7.8
wounding and grievous bodily harm, 2.3.1, 2.3.2
see also **religious hatred offences**
racially or religiously insulting posters, 7.7
rape, 6.1– 6.1.2
alcohol, 6.1.1
capacity, 6.1.1
child under 13, 6.1.2
consent, 6.1.1
DPP guidance on, 6.1.1
CPS/police joint protocol, 6.1.1
crime scene, management of the, 6.1.1
deception, 6.1.1
defences, 6.1.1
drugs, 6.1.1
evidence, 6.1.1
freedom to agree, 6.1.1
gender
change of, 6.2.1
specificity of, 6.1.1
GHB (date rape drug), 6.1.1, 6.10
Home office Circular 1/2015 on, 6.1.1
intentionally, meaning of, 6.1.1
interview of defendant, 6.1.1
mental disorder, 6.1.1
mouth, penetration of the, 6.1.1
penetration, definition of, 6.1.1
personal characteristics of defendant, 6.1.1
presumptions, 6.1.1
reasonable belief, 6.1.1
relevant acts, 6.1.1
Rohypnol, 6.10
series of acts, 6.1.1
substances, administration of, 6.1.1
violence or fear of violence, 6.1.1
see also **sexual assault by penetration**
rape of child under 13
age of child, proof of, 6.1.2
consent, 6.1.2
intention, meaning of, 6.1.2
penetration, 6.1.2
razor blades, 8.10.2
reasonable chastisement, 2.1.2, 2.4.1
reasonable consideration, driving without, 10.6.1
recent possession, doctrine of, 3.5
reckless, careless, or inconsiderate driving or cycling
mechanically propelled vehicles, 10.6.2
name and address, failure to give or giving false, 10.6.2
recognisances, entering into, 7.3
registration documents, production of, 10.20.2
registration marks on vehicles
agricultural machines towing trailers, 10.20.2
defences, 10.20.2, 10.20.3
display, requirement to, 10.20.2

failure to fix, 10.20.2
fixed penalty notices, 10.20.3
invalid carriages, 10.20.2
misrepresented number plates, 10.20.3
MOT tests, 10.20.2
motorcycles, 10.20.2
obscured marks, 10.20.3
pedestrian controlled vehicles, 10.20.2
plates, 10.20.2
registration mark, meaning of, 10.20.2
relevant person, meaning of, 10.20.2
trailers, 10.20.2
religion
aggravated offences *see* **racially or religiously aggravated offences**
bladed articles/knives, 8.10.1
crash helmets, not wearing, 10.18
hatred offences *see* **religious hatred offences**
religious dates and events, App 5
Sikhs, 8.10.1, 10.18
religious hatred offences, 7.9.3
bodies corporate, 7.9.3
defence, 7.9.3
display of written material, 7.9.3
forfeiture, 7.9.3
freedom of expression, 7.9.3
Home Office Circular 29/2007, 7.9.3
religious hatred, meaning of, 7.9.3
threatening words or behaviour, 7.9.3
remote sales of offensive weapons, 8.10.2
removal of articles from places open to the public, 3.1.2
repeating shotguns, 8.1.1, 8.2.1
replica firearms, 8.1.1, 8.1.4, 8.5
report the incident, duty of driver to, 10.9.2, 10.9.3
information, duty of driver to stop and give, 10.9.2
insurance, production of proof of, 10.9.2, 10.9.3
invalid carriages, 10.9.3
police station, meaning of at the, 10.9.3
road traffic collisions, 10.9.3
resentment, behaviour causing, 7.9.1
residence, removal to place of, 7.15.1
restraining orders
duration of, 7.11.6
harassment, 7.11.1, 7.11.2, 7.11.6
Home Office Circular 17/2009, 7.11.6
reasonable excuse, without, 7.11.6
stalking, 7.11.3, 7.11.6
variation or discharge of, 7.11.6
revolvers, 8.2.1
rice flails, 8.9.1
riding cycles on the footpath, 10.12.4
rifle clubs, 8.1.3, 8.7.2
rifle ranges, 8.1.3
riots, 7.4.1
common purpose, meaning of, 7.4.1
defences, 7.4.1
drunkenness, 7.4.1
evidence, 7.4.1
intention, 7.4.1
intoxication, 7.4.1
present together, meaning of, 7.4.1
reasonable firmness, persons of, 7.4.1
stop and search, 7.4.1
violence, meaning of, 7.4.1
see also **violent disorder**
road traffic collisions, 10.9– 10.9.3
accident, meaning of, 10.9.1
animal, meaning of, 10.9.1
duties of driver after accident, 10.9.2, 10.9.3
incidents to which applicable, 10.9.1
injury, meaning of, 10.9.1
pedal cycles, 10.9.1
report the incident, duty of driver to, 10.9.2, 10.9.3
road traffic offences *see* **driving offences**
roads, 10.1– 10.1.2
access, 10.1.1
bridges, 10.1.1
bridleways, 10.1.1
car parks, 10.1.1, 10.1.2
drunk on a highway, 7.2.2
egress lanes at ferry ports, 10.1.2
firearms, discharging, 8.5
fireworks, 8.8.7
footpaths, 10.1.1
footways, 10.1.1
forecourts, 10.1.1
games on, playing, 10.21.3
lay-bys, 10.1.1
meaning of, 10.1.1, 10.6.1
obstruction, 10.21– 10.22
off-road parking bay, 10.1.2
paved areas used as thoroughfares, 10.1.1
private roads used by general public, 10.1.1
public access, 10.1.1, 10.1.2
public places
access, restricted, 10.1.2
meaning, 10.1.2
test for, 10.1.2
public roads, meaning of, 10.1.1
service road, 10.1.2
stop vehicle on roads, power to, 10.2.3
testing on roads, 10.2.3
university campus, on, 10.1.2
vehicles left on roads, 10.16.1
verges, 10.1.1
roadside deposit scheme, 10.4.3
direction, meaning of, 10.4.3
driver contest penalty, 10.4.3

roadside deposit scheme (*cont.*)
enforcement, 10.4.3
immobilisation of vehicle, 10.4.3
payment, 10.4.3
failure to make, 10.4.3
prohibition, meaning of, 10.4.3
prohibition notice, 10.4.3
receipt, 10.4.3
robbery, 3.2– 3.2.1
appropriation, 3.2.1
blackmail, 3.2.1
defences, 3.2.1
fear, 3.2.1
postal packages or mailbags, 3.2.1
stealing property which is unlawful to possess, 3.2.1
use of force, 3.2.1
Rohypnol, 6.10

sadomasochism, 2.1.2, 2.3.1
sale of alcohol to children, 9.1.2, 9.1.3
persistently selling, 9.1.3
salvage, vehicle being driven to or from a place for, 10.16.1
samples
blood, 10.8.2, 10.11.3
consent, 10.11.3
death by careless driving, causing, 10.8.2
failure to provide, 10.8.2, 10.11.3
fear of needles, 10.11.3
incapable of providing, person, 10.10.2
laboratory tests, 10.11.3
urine, 10.11.3
sawn-off shotguns, 8.1.2, 8.2.1
school, meaning of, 8.10.7
school premises
bladed articles/knives, 8.10.1, 8.10.6, 8.10.7, 8.12.2
entry, powers of, 8.10.7, 8.10.8, 8.12.2
lawful authority to be on, 8.10.7, 8.10.8
meaning of, 8.10.7, 8.10.8
nuisance or disturbances, 8.10.7, 8.10.8, 8.12.2
offensive weapons, 8.9.2, 8.9.5, 8.10.1, 8.10.7
remove people from, power to, 8.10.7, 8.10.8
school, meaning of, 8.10.7
searches, 8.10.7
seizure, 8.10.7, 8.12.2
school staff, powers, 8.10.8
scooters, 4.3.3
City Mantis, electric, 10.1.3
scrap metal, theft of, 3.1.1
screwdrivers, 8.10.1
search powers for controlled drugs
conceals, meaning of, 5.4.1
detention, 5.4.1
enter premises, power to, 5.4.1
equipment, drug abusers', 5.4.1
gloves, using, 5.4.1
grounds, 5.4.1
Home Office Circular 12/2011, 5.4.1
infection, risk of, 5.4.1
intimate searches, 5.4.1
mouth, searching the, 5.4.1
needles and syringes, avoiding, 5.4.1
obstructs, meaning of intentionally, 5.4.1
PACE and codes, 5.4.1
paraphernalia, 5.4.1
personal safety of officers, 5.4.1
reasonable excuse, without, 5.4.1
retention of property, 5.4.1
seizure, 5.4.1
stop and search persons, 5.4.1
use of force, 5.4.1
vehicles, 5.4.1
vessels, 5.4.1
warrants, 5.4.2
search warrants, 1.5– 1.5.3
accompanying persons
experts, 1.5.3
identification of, 1.5.3
all premises search warrants, 1.5.1, 1.5.2, 1.5.3
application procedure, 1.5.2
appropriate person, meaning of, 1.5.3
arrest, 1.5.1
bladed articles/knives, 8.12.1
conditions, 8.12.1
contents, 1.5.2
designated investigating officers, 1.5.1
entry, powers of, 1.5.1– 1.5.2
evidence, 1.5.1
excluded or special material, 1.5.1, 1.5.4
execution of search warrants, 1.5.3
notification requirements, 1.5.3
time for, 1.5.1, 1.5.3
experts, 1.5.3
firearms, 8.6.1, 8.6.3
grounds for issue of, 8.12.1
immigration, 1.5.1
indictable offences, 1.5.1
inspection, 1.5.3
multiple entries search warrants, 1.5.1, 1.5.2, 1.5.3
multiple occupancy premises, 1.5.2
notification requirements, 1.5.3
PACE and codes, 1.5– 1.5.3
premises search warrants, 1.5.1, 1.5.2, 1.5.3, 8.6.1, 8.6.3
seizure, 1.5.1, 1.5.3
serious violence reduction orders, 8.13

special procedure material, 1.5.1, 1.5.4
specific premises search warrants, 1.5.1, 1.5.2, 1.5.3
stalking, 7.11.3
sterile areas, moving persons to, 1.5.1
use of force, 8.12.2

searches
arrest
after, 1.4.3
upon, 1.4.1
bulk material, 1.4.4
careless driving when under influence, causing death by, 10.8.2
conditions, 1.4.3
consumption of alcohol by person under 18, 9.1.5
crossbows, 8.9.3, 8.9.6
CSOs and CSVs
search and seizure of alcohol and tobacco, 11.1.4
search of individuals detained, 11.1.8
stop and search, 11.1.1
dangerous driving, 10.7.1, 10.7.2, 10.8.1
delivering alcohol to person under 18, 9.1.6
driving whilst disqualified, causing death by, 10.8.3
drugs, 5.1.1, 5.2.1, 5.2.2, 5.3.3, 5.4.1, 5.4.2
entry, powers of, 1.4.1– 1.4.3, 9.3.2
escape from lawful custody, anything used to, 1.4.1
evidence relating to offences, 1.4.1, 1.4.3
firearms, 8.6.1, 8.6.3
identity documents, 11.3.2
illegal entry into UK, 11.3.1
indictable offences, 1.4.1, 1.4.3
intimate searches, 5.4.1, 6.2.1
legal privilege, 1.4.1, 1.4.3, 1.4.4
licensed premises, powers of entry and, 9.3.2
mouth, searches of, 1.4.1
occupied, meaning of, 1.4.3
offensive weapons, 8.9.1, 8.9.3
PACE and codes, 1.4.1, 1.4.3
person, meaning of, 1.4.1
premises, meaning of, 1.4.1
purchase of alcohol by or on behalf of person under 18, 9.1.4
reasonable grounds for suspicion, 1.4.1, 1.4.3
sale of alcohol to person who is drunk, 9.2.1
school premises, 8.10.7
seizure, 1.4.1, 1.4.3, 1.4.4, 1.5.1, 1.5.3
serious violence reduction orders, 8.13
stopping vehicle on road, 10.2.3
vehicles
crossbows, 8.9.6
firearms, 8.6.1
wanton or furious driving, 10.7.4
see also **search powers for controlled drugs; search warrants**

seat belts, 10.17– 10.17.2
adults, 10.17.1
age, 10.17.2
ambulances, 10.17.1
anchorage points, 10.17.1
buses, 10.17.1, 10.17.2
children, 10.17.1, 10.17.2
classic cars, 10.17.1
Crown, processions on behalf of the, 10.17.1
disabled persons, 10.17.1, 10.17.2
excepted vehicles, 10.17.1
exemptions, 10.17.1
fire, rescue, and police vehicles, 10.17.1
fitting requirements, 10.17.1
fixed penalty schemes, 10.17.1, 10.17.2
goods vehicles, 10.17.1
large children, 10.17.2
maximum laden weight, meaning of, 10.17.2
medical certificates, 10.17.1, 10.17.2
motorcycles, 10.17.1
passenger cars, meaning of, 10.17.2
provisional drivers, supervisors of, 10.17.1
responsibility for wearing, 10.17.1
reversing, 10.17.1
small children, 10.17.2
taxis, 10.17.1, 10.17.2
trade plates, 10.17.1

seizure
alcohol, 9.4.2
confiscation of, 9.5.1
animals involved in animal fight, 11.6.2
annoyance, vehicles causing, 7.14.1, 7.14.2
bladed articles/knives, 8.10.1, 8.10.7, 8.12.1, 8.12.2
bulk material, seizure of, 1.4.4, 1.5.4
cigarette papers from young people, 11.5.1
common law powers, 1.4.3
computerised information, 1.4.4
confiscation of alcohol, 9.5.1
crossbows, 8.9.6
CSOs and CSVs, powers of
alcohol and tobacco, 11.1.4
controlled drugs, 5.4.1, 11.1.5
psychoactive substances, 11.1.6

seizure (*cont.*)
dangerous dogs, 11.6.4, 11.6.5
designated investigating officers, 1.5.1
driving licence or counterpart, failure to produce, 10.16.4
drugs, 5.1.1, 5.2.1, 5.2.2, 5.3.3, 5.4.1
electronic information, 1.4.4
escape from lawful custody, anything used to, 1.4.1
evidence of offences, 1.4.1, 1.4.4
excluded and special procedure material, access to, 1.5.4
firearms, 8.6.2, 8.6.3
fireworks, 8.8.2, 8.8.3, 8.8.4
grooming, meeting a child through, 6.5.5
HM Customs and Revenue, 1.4.4
identity documents, 11.3.2
indecent photographs/images, 6.6.1, 6.6.2
insurance, user of vehicle without, 10.16.1
legal privilege, 1.4.1, 1.4.4
livestock, dogs worrying, 11.6.3
motorcycle training certificate, failure to produce, 10.16.4
notice, 1.4.4
off-road driving, 10.22
offensive weapons, 8.12.1, 8.12.2, 8.12.3
PACE and codes, 1.4.4
premises
meaning of, 1.4.1
power to seize from, 1.4.4
school premises, 8.12.2
reasonable grounds to believe, 1.4.1, 1.4.4
return, 1.4.4
school premises, 8.12.2
searches, 1.4.1, 1.4.3, 1.4.4, 1.5.1, 1.5.3
serious violence reduction orders, 8.13
stop and search, 1.3.2
tobacco from young people, 11.5.1
vehicles
annoyance, causing, 7.14.1, 7.14.2
death by careless driving when under death by driving when disqualified, 10.8.3
death by driving without insurance or licence, 10.8.5
influence, 10.8.2
insurance, without, 10.16.1
premises, as, 1.4.4
removal of, 10.16.6
seizure and removal of vehicles
annoyance, vehicles causing, 7.14.1, 7.14.2
driving licence, no, 10.16.6
driving motor vehicle of class not authorised, 10.14.1
entry, powers of, 10.16.6
insurance, no, 10.16.6
invalid carriages, 10.16.6
notices, 10.16.6
safekeeping, 10.16.6
use of force, 10.16.6
warnings, 10.16.6
self-defence
actual bodily harm, assault occasioning, 2.1.2
assault, 2.1.2
firearms, 8.3.2
offensive weapons, 8.9.1
threats to kill, 2.5
use of force, 1.2, 2.1.2
self-harm, encouraging or assisting serious, 7.12.6
self-incrimination, privilege against, 3.8.5
semi-trailers, 10.1.3
sending child to obtain alcohol, 9.1.7
sending communications threatening death or serious harm, 7.12.4
sending false communications with intent to cause harm, 7.12.3
sending letters with intent to cause distress and anxiety, 7.12.1
sending or showing flashing images electronically, 7.12.5
sending photograph or film of genitals, 6.7.2
serious violence reduction orders, 8.13
change of name or address, 8.13
failure to comply with order, 8.13
meaning, 8.13
notification requirements, 8.13
retention and disposal of seized items, 8.13
seizure, powers of, 8.13
stop and search, 8.13
use of reasonable force, 8.13
services dishonestly, obtaining, 3.9
servitude *see* **slavery and human trafficking**
sex education, 6.5.1
sex offences
exposure, 6.7.1
forced marriages, 4.11
paying for sexual services of a prostitute subject to exploitation, 6.11.3
prostitution, placing of adverts in telephone boxes and, 6.11.1
prostitution by persistently loitering, 6.11.1
sexual activity in a public lavatory, 6.9
sexual assault by penetration, 6.2– 6.2.2

sexual offence, commit an offence with intent to commit, 6.10
soliciting in the street or in public by prostitutes, 6.11.1
soliciting to obtain services of a prostitute, 6.11.2
substance with intent to commit a sexual offence, administering a, 6.10
touching, sexual assault by, 6.3– 6.3.2
trespass with intent to commit a sexual offence, 6.10
voyeurism, 6.7.5
see also **child sex offences; rape**
sexting, 6.6.1
sexual activity, cause or incite child under 16 to engage in, 6.5.1, 6.5.3
age 13, under, 6.5.1, 6.5.3
cause, meaning of, 6.5.1
closeness of defendant in age to victim, 6.5.1
crime scene, management of, 6.5.1, 6.5.3
evidence, 6.5.1, 6.5.3
incite, meaning of, 6.5.1
intention, meaning of, 6.5.1
reasonable belief, 6.5.1
specification of offence, 6.5.3
sexual activity in a public lavatory, 6.9
activity, meaning of, 6.9
cottaging, 6.9
intention, 6.9
outraging public decency, 6.9
sexual activity with a child, 6.4
age, discretion to prosecute where parties close in, 6.4
defences, 6.4
evidence, 6.4
public interest to prosecute, 6.4
reasonable belief that child was over 16, 6.4
touching, meaning of, 6.4
sexual activity with mentally disordered persons, 6.1.1
sexual assault by penetration, 6.2– 6.2.2
anything else, meaning of, 6.2.1
consent, 6.2.1
digital penetration, 6.2.1
evidence, 6.2.1, 6.2.2
intent, 6.2.1
intimate searches, 6.2.1
medical examinations, 6.2.1
part of his body, meaning of, 6.2.1
personal characteristics of defendant, 6.2.1
persons aged 13 or over, 6.2.1
persons aged under 13, 6.2.2
reasonable belief, 6.2.1
sexual communication with a child
chatrooms, 6.5.6
communication, 6.5.6
private networks, 6.5.6
sexual activity, 6.5.6
sexualised chat, 6.5.6
text messages, 6.5.6
sexual exploitation offences, child *see* **child sexual exploitation offences**
sexual harm prevention orders, 6.8, 6.8.1
breach, 6.8.1
duration, 6.8.1
not guilty by reason of insanity, 6.8.1
sexual harm, meaning of, 6.8.1
sexual, meaning of, 6.2.1
sexual offence, commit an offence with intent to commit a
evidence, 6.10
intention, 6.10
relevant sexual offence, meaning of, 6.10
sexual orientation hatred offences
body corporate, 7.9.3
defences, 7.9.3
display of written material, 7.9.3
forfeiture, 7.9.3
freedom of expression, 7.9.3
hatred on grounds of sexual orientation, meaning of, 7.9.3
Ministry of Justice Circular 5/ 2010, 7.9.3
sexual risk orders, 6.8, 6.8.2
breach, 6.8.2
conditions, 6.8.2
ships, illegal entry and, 11.3.1
shooting galleries, 8.1.3, 8.7.2
shoplifting
low value, 1.4.2, 3.1.1, 4.1.1
PNDs for, 7.1.2
shortened barrels, 8.1.2
shot, 8.1.1
shotgun offences, 8.2– 8.2.3
15, persons under, 8.2.1, 8.2.2, 8.7.1
acquire, meaning of, 8.2.1
aggravated offences, 8.2.1
antiques, 8.2.1
auctioneers, 8.2.1
barrels, length of, 8.2.1
borrowing, 8.2.1
cartridges, 8.2.1
certificates
borrowing shotgun, 8.2.1
conditions, failure to comply with, 8.2.3
meaning, 8.2.1
police powers, 8.6.2
without, 8.2.1
component parts, 8.2.1

shotgun offences (*cont.*)
defences, 8.2.2
gifts, 8.2.2, 8.7.1
loss, notification of, 8.2.3
magazines, 8.2.1
possession, 8.2.1, 8.2.2, 8.2.3
repeating shotguns, 8.2.1
safe custody, keeping in, 8.2.3
sale, 8.2.1
sawn-off shotguns, 8.1.2, 8.2.1
shortened barrels, 8.2.1
shotguns, meaning of, 8.2.1
targets, shooting, 8.2.1
sidecars, 10.1.3
signal pistol, 8.1.1
signs, failure to comply with traffic, 10.3
automatism, 10.3
defences, 10.3
directions to disobey, 10.2.1
drivers, 10.3
emergency traffic signs, 10.3
emergency vehicles, red traffic signs and, 10.3
fixed penalty scheme, 10.3
lawfully placed, 10.3
lines or marks on roads, 10.3
mechanical defects, 10.3
notice of intended prosecution, 10.3
red traffic signals, 10.3
speed limit, 10.3
stop signs, 10.3
traffic signs, meaning of, 10.3
traffic surveys, 10.3
Sikhs
bladed articles/knives, 8.10.1
crash helmets, not wearing, 10.18
silencers, 8.1.1, 8.3.5
silent telephone calls, 7.12.2
skean dhu in Highland dress, 8.10.1
skips *see* **builders' skips on the highway, obstruction by**
slavery and human trafficking, 4.9– 4.9.6, App 1
arranging or facilitating, 4.9.3
criminal lifestyle offences, 5.5
exploitation, 4.9, 4.9.3
Home Office Circular 24/2015, 4.9.2, 4.9.3
human trafficking, 4.9, 4.9.2, 4.9.3
Modern Slavery Act 2015, 4.9.1
paying for sexual services of prostitute subject to exploitation, 6.11.3
separate offences, 4.9.3
sexual and non-sexual exploitation, 4.9.3
slavery, servitude and forced or compulsory labour, 4.9.2
Slavery and Trafficking Prevention Orders, 4.9.4
supporting/protecting victims of human trafficking, 4.9, 4.9.1
suspected victims, duty to notify Home Office of, 4.9.6
travel, 4.9.3
victims
defence for, 4.9.5
identifying, 4.9.3
notification to Home Office, 4.9.6
vulnerable victims, 4.9.2
smoke damage, 4.5.2
smoke on highway, 10.21.3
sniffing glue, 7.2.1
social media
communications causing distress, anxiety, or serious harm, 7.12.1
soliciting in the street or in public by prostitutes
balconies or windows, 6.11.1
clippers, 6.11.1
court order to attend meetings, 6.11.1
doorways and entrances, 6.11.1
guidelines on, 6.11.1
loiter, meaning of, 6.11.1
notices in windows, 6.11.1
prostitute, meaning of, 6.11.1
public place, meaning of, 6.11.1
solicit, meaning of, 6.11.1
street, meaning of, 6.11.1
soliciting to obtain services of a prostitute, 6.11.2
payment, meaning of, 6.11.2
prostitute, meaning of, 6.11.2
special constables
impersonation, 2.2.4
uniform, possessing or wearing article of police, 2.2.4
special procedure material, access to, 1.5.4
specified drugs limit, drive or attempt to drive/in charge of motor vehicle whilst over, 10.11.2
drugs and specified limits, 10.11.2
illegal drugs, 10.11.2
legal drugs, 10.11.2
medical and dental purposes, drugs for, 10.11.2
preliminary tests, 10.11.2
proof of impairment, no requirement for, 10.11.2
roadside testing, 10.11.2
specimens for analysis, provision of
blood, 10.11.3
breath tests, 10.11.1, 10.11.3
careless driving when under the influence of drink or drugs, causing, 10.8.2
cycling whilst under the influence of drink or drugs, 10.12.3
drugs, 10.11.3

intoximeters, defects in, 10.11.1, 10.11.3
medical conditions, 10.11.3
mentally unstable persons, 10.11.3
prescribed alcohol limit, drive or attempt to drive/in charge of motor vehicle whilst over, 10.11.1, 10.11.3
refusal, medical reasons for, 10.11.3
solicitor, delay to speak to, 10.11.3
two samples, requirement for, 10.11.3
urine, 10.11.3
warnings of consequences of failure, 10.11.3

spiking drinks, 6.1.1, 6.10, 9.1.5, 10.11.1
spitting, 4.8.1
sport
actual bodily harm, assault occasioning, 2.1.2
assault, 2.3.1
entrance fee, watching sport without paying, 3.9
firearms, 8.1.3

sporting events, 7.18– 7.18.2
alcohol, possession of, 7.18.1
designated event, 7.18.1
designated sports ground, 7.18.1
drunk at, being, 7.18.1
search, 7.18.1

squatters, 7.17, 7.17.1, 7.17.2, 7.17.3
stalking, 7.11, 7.11.1, 7.11.2, 7.11.3, 7.11.4
defences, 7.11.4
examples of acts associated with, 7.11.3
fear of violence/serious alarm or distress, 7.11.4
harassment, definition of, 7.11.3
meaning of, 7.11.3
racially or religiously aggravated offence, 7.10.5
restraining order, 7.11.3, 7.11.4, 7.11.6
stalking prevention orders, 7.11.5
substantial adverse effect, 7.11.4
support agencies, 7.11.3

Statutory Off Road Notification (SORN), 10.20.1
stealth knives, 8.9.4
steering wheels, temporarily grabbing, 10.1.4
stereotyping, stop and search and, 1.3.2
stolen goods, handling *see* **handling stolen goods**
stolen property, stop and search powers, 1.3.2
stop and search powers, 1.3.1
affray, 7.5
articles made or adapted for use in course of or connection with offences, 1.3.2, 1.3.5
behaviour of person, 1.3.2
bladed articles/knives, 7.5, 8.10.1, 8.10.7, 8.12.2
Code of Practice, 1.3.2, 1.3.4, 1.3.5
conduct of a search, 1.3.2, 1.3.3
criminal damage, 1.3.5
detention, 1.3.2, 1.3.3
drugs, 5.4.1
evidence, unfairly obtained, 1.3.5
facts, information and/or intelligence, 1.3.2, 1.3.5
firearms, 8.6.1
fireworks, 1.3.2, 1.3.5, 8.8.2, 8.8.3, 8.8.4
gang membership, indications of, 1.3.2
gardens or yards, restrictions in, 1.3.2
generalisations and stereotyping, 1.3.2
genuine suspicion, 1.3.2
Home Office guidance, 8.12.3
hunch or instinct not reasonable grounds, 1.3.2
information to be provided, 1.3.3
offensive weapons, 1.3.2, 7.5, 8.12.2, 8.12.3
organised protest groups, 1.3.2
PACE and codes, 1.3.2, 1.3.3, 1.3.5
pointed or bladed articles, 1.3.2
previous convictions, 1.3.2
prohibited articles, meaning of, 1.3.2
questions, asking, 1.3.2
race, religion, or appearance, 1.3.2, 1.3.5
reasonable grounds for suspicion, 1.3.2, 1.3.5
behaviour of person, 1.3.2
facts, information and/or intelligence, 1.3.2, 1.3.5
gang membership, indications of, 1.3.2
generalisations and stereotyping, 1.3.2
meaning of, 1.3.2
previous convictions, 1.3.2
public order, 7.17.9
race, religion, or appearance, 1.3.2
stopping to find grounds, 1.3.2
records, 1.3.3, 1.3.5
contents, 1.3.5
copies of, 1.3.3, 1.3.5
written, 1.3.5
riot, 7.4.1
seizure, 1.3.2
stereotyping, 1.3.2
stolen property, 1.3.2
terrorism, 1.3.2, 1.3.4, 1.4.2
vehicles
bladed articles/knives, 8.10.1, 8.10.7, 8.12.2

stop and search powers *(cont.)*
conduct of searches, 1.3.3
fireworks, 8.8.2, 8.8.3, 8.8.4
meaning of, 1.3.2
offensive weapons, 8.12.3
serious violence, 8.12.3
terrorism, 1.3.4
unattended, 1.3.3
violent disorder, 7.4.2
without suspicion, 7.17.9
written records, 1.3.5
strangulation, non-fatal, 2.3.4
streakers and naturists, 6.7.1
street trading, unlicensed
fixed penalty notices, 11.1.2
strict liability, 4.1.2
stun guns, 8.1.1
substance with intent to commit a sexual offence, administering a, 6.10
administer, meaning of, 6.10
causes to be taken, 6.10
consent, 6.10
date rape drugs, 6.10
evidence, 6.10
intention, 6.10
spiking drinks, 6.10
sudden deaths, 2.7– 2.7.6
suffocation, non-fatal, 2.3.4
suffocation of infant *see* **over-laying/ suffocation of infant under 3**
suicide
encouraging or assisting, 2.7.1, 2.7.2
murder, 2.7.1
pacts, 2.7.1
supply
air weapons, 8.7.1
alcohol and children, 9.1.1
ammunition, 8.7.1
butane lighter refills to young people, supply of, 11.5.1
drugs, 5.1, 5.1.1, 5.2.2, 9.3.2
firearms, 8.7.1
fireworks, 8.8.5
fraud, articles used in, 3.8.7
prescription drugs, 5.1.1
psychoactive substance, 5.3.5
pyrotechnic articles, 8.8.5
tobacco, 11.5.1
surgery, 2.1.2
surveys of traffic, 10.2.1, 10.3
suspicious deaths, 2.7– 2.7.6
child destruction, 2.7.6
child or vulnerable adult, death of, 2.7.4
concealment of birth, 2.7.6
corporate manslaughter, 2.7.3
infanticide, 2.7.6
manslaughter, 2.7.2, 2.7.3
murder, 2.7.1
sword with curved blade, 8.9.4
sword sticks, 8.9.1, 8.9.4, 8.10.2
syringes, 5.4.1

table meals, 9.1.4, 9.1.5
taking a conveyance without owner's consent (TWOC), 4.3– 4.3.3
aggravated vehicle-taking, 4.3.2
consent of the owner, 4.3.1
conveyance, meaning of, 4.3.1
defences, 4.3.1
deviation from authorised route, 4.3.1
dinghies on trailers, 4.3.1
going equipped, 3.6
hire or hire purchase, 4.3.1
horses, 4.3.1
interference with vehicles, 4.2.1
owners, meaning of, 4.3.1
pedal cycles, 4.3.1, 4.3.3
prosecution time limits, 4.3.1
pushing vehicles away, 4.3.1
riding, 4.3.1
takes, meaning of, 4.3.1
theft, 4.3.1
tampering with motor vehicles, 4.2.2
target shooting, 8.2.1
taxis, 10.16.3, 10.17.1, 10.17.2
telephone numbers, useful, App 2
telephones
communications causing distress, anxiety, or serious harm, 7.12.1, 7.12.2
harassment, by, 7.11.1
hoax bomb calls, 11.4.1– 11.4.2
mobile phones, 10.4.2
obscene telephone calls, 7.12.2
prostitution, placing of adverts in telephone boxes and, 6.11.1
public nuisance, 7.13.3
silent calls, 7.12.2
telescopic sights, 8.1.1
television decoders, use of, 3.9
terrorism
authorised area, 1.3.3
blackmail, 11.4.2
communications causing distress, anxiety, or serious harm, 7.12.2
consumer terrorism, 11.4.2
directing, criminal lifestyle offences, 5.5
guidance, 1.3.3
hoaxes, 11.4.2
photographs, someone taking, 1.3.4
random, 1.3.3
stop and search, 1.3.2, 1.3.4, 1.4.2
vehicles, 1.3.4
wasting police time, 11.4.2
test certificates for vehicles, 10.16.3
ambulances, meaning of, 10.16.3
exemptions, 10.16.3

failure to produce, 10.16.3
fixed penalty notices, 10.16.3
goods vehicles, 10.16.3
heavy motor cars, 10.16.3
inspection of goods vehicles, directions to proceed for, 10.16.3
road, vehicles left on, 10.16.3
taxis, 10.16.3
types of vehicles, 10.16.3
vehicles left on road, 10.16.3
test purchases
children and alcohol, 9.1.4, 9.1.7
drugs, producing or supplying controlled, 5.1.1
entrapment, 9.3.1
evidence, improperly obtained, 9.3.1
licensed premises, 9.3.1
testing
breath tests, 10.10.2, 10.11.1, 10.11.3
drink or drugs, driving/attempting to drive/in charge of vehicle whilst unfit through, 10.10.2
drugs, 5.2.1, 10.10.2, 10.11.2
eyesight test, refusal to submit to, 10.15
failure to cooperate, 10.10.2
impairment tests, preliminary, 10.10.2
refusal to cooperate, 10.10.2
test certificates, 10.16.3, 10.16.5
test purchases, 5.1.1, 9.1.4, 9.1.7
vehicles for, power to stop, 10.2.3
tethering animals on the footpath, 10.12.4
text messages with intent to cause distress or anxiety, sending, 7.12.1
theft, 3.1– 3.1.2
'appropriates', meaning of, 3.1.1
appropriation, 3.1.1
belonging to another, meaning of, 3.1.1
borrowing, 3.1.1
collection, meaning of, 3.1.2
consent, 3.1.1
control, meaning of, 3.1.1
dishonestly, meaning of, 3.1.1
donated items left outside charity shop, 3.1.1
going equipped, 3.6, 4.2.1, 4.7.1
handling stolen goods, 3.5
holding property on account of another, 3.1.1
innocent purchasers, 3.1.1
intangible property, meaning of, 3.1.1
intellectual property, 3.1.1
intention to permanently deprive, meaning of, 3.1.1
land, 3.1.1
low value shoplifting, 3.1.1
mens rea, 3.1.1
mushrooms, 3.1.1
penalty notices for disorder, 3.1.1, 7.1.2
plants, 3.1.1
possession, meaning of, 3.1.1
postal packages or mail bags, 3.1.1
property, meaning of, 3.1.1
proprietary rights or interests, 3.1.1
public places, removal of articles from, 3.1.2
scrap metal, 3.1.1
spouses or civil partners, 3.1.1
stealing property which is unlawful to possess, 3.1.1
taking a conveyance without owner's consent, 4.3.1
tenancies, meaning of, 3.1.1
things in action, 3.1.1
wild creatures, 3.1.1
wild plants, 3.1.1
thought, conscience, and religion, freedom of, App 1
threatening or abusive words or behaviour, 7.8
actual sight or hearing of person, within, 7.8
alarm, meaning of, 7.8
burden of proof, 7.8
defences, 7.8
disorderly behaviour, definition of, 6.7.1, 7.8
distress, meaning of, 7.8
harassment, alarm, or distress, 7.8
harassment, meaning of, 7.8
intent, 7.8
naturists/nudity, 6.7.1
police officers, against, 7.8
protests, 7.8
public or private places, 7.8
racial hatred offences, 7.9.1– 7.9.2
racially or religiously aggravated, 7.8
religious hatred offences, 7.9.3
threats
affray, 7.5
animals, to, 7.11.2
assault, 2.1.1
communications causing distress, anxiety, or serious harm, 7.12.2
destroy or damage property, threats to, 4.6
fear or provocation of violence, 7.6
food contamination, 11.4.2
kill, to, 2.5
messengers with, 4.8.1
offensive weapons, with, 8.9.1, 8.9.2
paying for sexual services of prostitute subject to exploitation, 6.11.3
witnesses or jurors, intimidation of, 4.8.1

threats (*cont.*)
see also **threatening or abusive words or behaviour**
threats to kill
aggravating circumstances, 2.5
assault, 2.5
defences, 2.5
lawful excuse, 2.5
mens rea, 2.5
miscarriage, causing a, 2.5
self-defence, made in, 2.5
unborn children, 2.5
ticket touting, 7.18.2
tobacco, confiscation of from young people, 11.5.1
torture, App 1
totting up, 10.4.1, 10.13.1
touching, assault by, 2.1.1
touching, sexual assault by, 6.3– 6.3.2
accidental touching, 6.3.1
consent, 6.3.1, 6.3.2
crime scene, management of, 6.3.1, 6.3.2
defences, 6.3.1
evidence of age, 6.3.2
intention, 6.3.1, 6.3.2
intoxication, 6.3.1
person aged 13 or over, 6.3.1
person aged under 13, 6.3.2
reasonable belief, 6.3.1
touching, meaning of, 6.3.1
tractors, 10.14.1
trade plates
display, 10.19
duration of trade licences, 10.19
fixed penalty scheme, 10.19
forge or fraudulently alter, 10.19
improper use of, 10.19
name and address, notification of change in, 10.19
public road, meaning of, 10.19
seat belts, 10.17.1
trade licences, 10.19
vehicle, meaning of, 10.19
traffic
directions, compliance with, 10.2.1
signs, failure to comply with traffic, 10.3
surveys, 10.2.1
traffic data on vehicle categories and minimum ages, App 3
traffic officers, meaning of, 10.2.1
traffic wardens, 10.2.1, 10.2.2, 10.2.3, 10.4.1
see also **driving offences**; **roads**; **vehicles**
Traffic Fixed Penalty Notices, 10.2.1, 10.2.3, 10.4– 10.4.1
crash helmets, not wearing, 10.18
CSOs, 10.12.4
cycles, 10.4.1
declarations, 10.4.1
driving licences, surrender of, 10.4.1
driving motor vehicle of class not authorised, 10.14.1
driving without due care and attention and, 10.6.1
endorsements, 10.4.1
fines, 10.4.1
fixed penalties, 10.4.1
footpath, riding or driving on, 10.12.4
graduated scheme, 10.4.3
hand-held device, control vehicle and and use of, 10.4.2
insurance
registered keeper without, 10.16.2
user of vehicle without, 10.16.1
licences, production of, 10.4.1
meaning, 10.4.1
obscured registration marks on vehicles, 10.20.3
obstruction, 10.21.1, 10.21.4
off-road driving, 10.22
owner, notice to, 10.4.1
receipts for driving licences, 10.4.1
relevant offences, list of, 10.4.1
roadside deposit scheme, 10.4.3
seat belts, 10.17.1, 10.17.2
stopping vehicle on road, 10.2.3
suspended enforcement period, 10.4.1
test certificate for vehicles, 10.16.3
totting up, 10.4.1
trade plates, 10.19
traffic directions, compliance with, 10.2.1
traffic signs, failure to comply with, 10.3
traffic wardens, 10.4.1
trafficking, criminal lifestyle offence, confiscation of cash/assets, 11.3.1
trafficking of people *see* **slavery and human trafficking**
trailers, 4.2.1, 4.3.1, 10.1.3, 10.20.2, 10.21.4
trains
search for alcohol when en route to sporting event, 7.18.1
tramcars and trolley vehicles, 10.8.1, 10.10.1, 10.16.3
transferred malice, doctrine of, 2.3.1, 2.7.1, 2.7.2
transport works, obstruction of major, 7.17.7
travel documents, powers relating to and illegal entry into UK, 11.3.2
trespass on premises/land, 7.17
adverse occupation of residential premises, 7.17.3
aggravated trespass on land, 7.17.4

agricultural buildings, 7.17.1
burglary, 3.3.1
caravans, 7.17.1
failure to leave, 7.17.1
firearms, 8.4– 8.4.2
imitation firearms, 8.4.1
knowledge or recklessness, 8.4.2
land, meaning of, 7.17.4
occupiers, 7.17.1
off-road driving, 10.22
offensive weapons, 8.9.5
prescribed alcohol limit, drive or attempt to drive/in charge of motor vehicle whilst over, 10.11.1
relevant caravan site, meaning of, 7.17.1
residential building, 7.17.1
seizure of property, 7.17.1
sexual offence, intent to commit a, 6.10
squatters, 7.17, 7.17.1, 7.17.2, 7.17.3
temporary residence, 7.17.1
time limits to leave, 7.17.1
trespassers, meaning of, 7.17.4
unauthorised encampments, 7.17.1
vehicles, seizure and removal of, 7.17.1
violent entry, 7.17.1, 7.17.2

trespass with intent to commit a sexual offence, 6.10
Trojan Horse virus defence, indecent photographs/images and, 6.6.1
trolley vehicles, 10.8.1, 10.10.1, 10.16.3
truncheons, 8.9.1, 8.9.4
tunnelling of being present in a tunnel, causing serious disruption by, 7.17.6
burden of proof, 7.17.6
tunnel, meaning of, 7.17.6
TWOC *see* **taking a conveyance without owner's consent (TWOC)**

unaccompanied children, prohibition from certain premises of, 9.1.1
unconscious and sudden illness, driving without due care and attention and, 10.6.1
uniform, possessing or wearing article of police, 2.2.4
university campus, 10.1.2
unlicensed street trading
fixed penalty notices, 11.1.2
unlicensed vehicles, using or keeping, 10.20.1
burden of proof, 10.20.1
exemptions, 10.20.1
Statutory Off Road Notification, 10.20.1
use vehicle, persons who can, 10.20.1
unmanned aircraft (drones), 11.7
permission for certain flights, 11.7.1
unnecessary suffering, animal welfare offences and, 11.6.1
upskirting, 6.7.6
urine samples, 10.11.3
use of force, 1.2
bladed articles/knives, 8.12.2
burglary, 3.3.1
CSOs and CSVs, 11.1.11
drug search powers, 5.4.1
entry, powers of, 1.4.2, 9.3.2, 10.11.1
Human Rights Act 1998, 1.2
licensed premises, powers of entry and, 9.3.2
NHS premises, causing nuisance/disturbance on, removal from, 7.13.5
off-road driving, 10.22
offensive weapons, 8.12.2
prescribed alcohol limit, drive or attempt to drive/in charge of motor vehicle whilst over, 10.11.1
robbery, 3.2.1
search warrants, 8.12.2
seizure, 10.16.6
self-defence, 1.2, 2.1.2
serious violence reduction orders, 8.13
vehicles, seizure of, 10.16.6
useful contacts, App 2

vehicle excise licences
changes of ownership, 10.20.1
keeper details incorrect, 10.20.3
unlicensed vehicles, using or keeping, 10.20.1
vehicle interference, 4.2, 4.2.1
going equipped, 4.2.1
taking a conveyance without consent, 4.2.1
vehicles
abandoned, 7.16.1, 7.16.3
aggravated vehicle-taking, 4.3.2
annoyance, causing, 7.14– 7.14.2
anti-social behaviour, 7.16.3
articulated (bendy) bus, 10.1.3
bladed articles/knives, 8.10.1, 8.10.7, 8.12.2
burden of proof, 10.1.3
City Mantis electric scooter, 10.1.3
community protection notices, 7.16.1
crossbows, 8.9.6
dogs, in, 11.6.5
drunk on a highway, 7.2.2
dumping, 7.16.3
emergency vehicles, 10.6.1
examiners, 10.2.3, 10.16.5
excise licences, 10.20.1
firearms, 8.6.1
fireworks, 8.8.2, 8.8.3, 8.8.4

vehicles (*cont.*)
forfeiture, dangerous driving, 10.7.1
Go-Ped, 10.1.3
going equipped, 3.6
hovercrafts, 10.1.3
illegal entry, 11.3.1
immobilisation
registered keeper without insurance, 10.16.2
roadside deposit scheme, 10.4.3
vehicle left on land, 10.22
Insurance Advisory Letter, 10.16.2
interference with, 4.2.1
invalid carriages, 10.1.3
meaning, 10.1.3
mechanically propelled, 10.1.3
minimum ages to drive, App 3
motor vehicle, meaning of, 10.1.3
mowing machines, 10.1.3
obstruction, 10.21.1, 10.21.4
offensive weapons, 8.12.2, 8.12.3
pedal cycles, electrically assisted, 10.1.3
public place, as, 8.5
reasonable person test, 10.1.3
registration marks, 10.20.2, 10.20.3
removal of, 10.16.2, 10.16.6, 10.22
residing on land without consent, 7.17.1
roads, use on, 10.1.3
searches, 8.6.1
for alcohol en route to sporting event, 7.18.1
for drugs, 5.4.1
seizure, 1.4.4, 10.4.1, 10.16.6
crossbows, 8.9.6
semi-trailers, 10.1.3
shining light or laser towards aircraft or vehicle, 11.8
sidecars, 10.1.3
stop
power to, 10.2– 10.2.3
search, and, 1.3.2– 1.3.5, 8.9.1, 8.9.5, 8.10.1, 8.10.7, 8.12.2, 8.12.3
taking a conveyance, 3.6
tampering with motor vehicles, 4.2.2
taxed but uninsured, 10.16.2
terrorism, 1.3.4
test certificates, 10.16.3
testing, power to stop for, 10.2.3
tractors, 10.14.1
trade plates, improper use of, 10.19
trailers, 10.1.3
trespassers from land, power to remove, 7.17.1
unlicensed vehicles, using or keeping, 10.20.1
vehicle examiners, 10.16.5
see also **driving offences; pedal cycles; taking a conveyance without owner's consent (TWOC)**
vehicles causing annoyance, 7.14– 7.14.2
alarm, distress, and annoyance, 7.14.1
authority, meaning of, 7.14.2
bodies corporate, service of seizure notice on, 7.14.2
charges, 7.14.2
dispersal powers, 7.14.1
disposal of vehicles, 7.14.2
driving, meaning of, 7.14.1
entry, powers of, 7.14.1
motor vehicle, meaning of, 7.14.1
private dwelling house, meaning of, 7.14.1
relevant motor vehicle, meaning of, 7.14.2
retention of seized motor vehicles, 7.14.2
seizure, 7.14.1, 7.14.2
warnings, 7.14.1
vehicles, power to stop, 10.2– 10.2.3
authorised vehicle examiners, 10.2.3
CSOs, 10.2.1, 10.2.3
cycles, 10.2.3
life, protection of, 10.2.1
mechanically propelled vehicles, 10.2.3
notices of intended prosecution, 10.2.1
pedestrians, directions to, 10.2.2
penalty notices, 10.2.1, 10.2.3
road, police powers to stop vehicles on, 10.2.3
terrorism, 1.3.4
testing conditions of vehicles on road, 10.2.3
traffic directions, compliance with, 10.2.1
Traffic Fixed Penalty Notices, 10.2.1, 10.2.3
traffic officers, meaning of, 10.2.1
traffic surveys, for, 10.2.1
traffic wardens, 10.2.1, 10.2.3
vehicles, unauthorised dumping or abandoned, 7.16.3
abandoned, meaning of, 7.16.3
fixed penalty notices, 7.16.3
local authorities, 7.16.3
motor vehicle, meaning of, 7.16.3
verges, 10.1.1
vessels, searches for drugs, 5.4.1
victim support, referrals to, 7.11.4
video recordings
indecent photographs/images, 6.6.1
violent disorder, 7.4.2
defences, 7.4.2
intention, 7.4.2

present together, meaning of, 7.4.2
reasonable firmness, persons of, 7.4.2
stop and search, 7.4.2
see also **riots**
violent entry to premises, 7.17.1, 7.17.2, 7.17.3
access, meaning of, 7.17.2
adverse occupation of residential premises, 7.17.3
arrest, 7.17.2, 7.17.3
defences, 7.17.3
displaced residential occupiers, meaning of, 7.17.2
premises, meaning of, 7.17.2, 7.17.3
protected intending occupier, meaning of, 7.17.2
squatters, 7.17.2, 7.17.3
trespassers, meaning of, 7.17.2
VIPER, 1.4
virus defence, indecent photographs/ images and, 6.6.1
voyeurism, 6.8
consent, 6.7.5
image, meaning of, 6.7.6
operating equipment, 6.7.6
private act, meaning of, 6.7.5
recording beneath clothing, 6.7.6
sexual gratification, for purpose of, 6.7.5
spy-holes or two-way mirrors, 6.7.5
upskirting, 6.7.6
webcams and other recording equipment, 6.7.5
vulnerable adult or child, causing or allowing the death of, 2.7.4

wanton or furious driving
bodily harm, meaning of, 10.7.4
pedal cycles, 10.7.4
wanton, meaning of, 10.7.4
war, murder and, 2.7.1
warnings
annoyance, vehicles causing, 7.14.1
guard dogs, 11.6.6
harassment, 7.11.1
notices of intended prosecution, 10.5
racially or religiously aggravated offences, 7.10.4
seizure, 10.16.6
specimens, 10.11.3
vehicles
annoyance causing, 7.14.1
seizure and removal of, 10.16.6
warrants
arrest without
breach of injunction, 7.13.1
other persons, 1.1.5
commitment, of, 1.4.2
drug search powers, 5.4.1
entry, rights of, 1.4.2, 8.6.3
firearms, 8.6.1, 8.6.3
people, removal without warrant of, 11.2
seizure, 8.6.3
see also **search warrants**
waste *see* **litter**
waste land, off-road driving on, 10.22
wasting police time, 11.4– 11.4.2
articles with intent to make people believe they are bombs, placing or dispatching, 11.4.2
Director of Public Prosecutions, consent to prosecution of, 11.4.1
false reports, making, 11.4.1– 11.4.2
food contamination or threats of food contamination, 11.4.2
hoax bomb calls, 11.4.1– 11.4.2
intention, 11.4.2
penalty notices for disorder, 7.1.2, 11.4.1
substances
meaning, 11.4.2
placing or sending hoax, 11.4.2
terrorist type hoaxes, 11.4.2
weapons
manufacture or distribution of offensive weapons without authority, 8.1.1
see also **bladed articles/knives; firearms; offensive weapons**
wearing or possessing article of police uniform, 2.2.4
websites
useful contacts, App 2
wild plants and creatures, 4.4
witnesses
anonymity, 4.8.1
harassment, 7.11.1
intimidation of *see* **witnesses, victims or jurors intimidation of**
statements, 7.11.1
witnesses, victims or jurors intimidation of, 4.8– 4.8.1
act, meaning of, 4.8.1
financial threats, 4.8.1
intending, meaning of, 4.8.1
investigations into offences, 4.8.1
memory loss, sudden, 4.8.1
messengers, 4.8.1
potential, meaning of, 4.8.1
relevant period, meaning of, 4.8.1
spitting, 4.8.1
threats, 4.8.1
wounding and grievous bodily harm, 2.3– 2.3.2
actual bodily harm, assault occasioning, 2.3.1
arrest, resisting, 2.3.2
cause, meaning, 2.3.2

wounding and grievous bodily harm (*cont.*)
chain of causation test, 2.3.2
corrosive substances, using with intent to cause GBH, 2.3.3
Cunningham malice, 2.3.1
fear, 2.3.1
grievous bodily harm, meaning of, 2.3.1
gunpowder, using with intent to cause GBH, 2.3.3
HIV, infecting through unprotected sexual intercourse, 2.3.1
inflict, meaning of, 2.3.1, 2.3.2
intent, with, 2.3.2, 2.7.1, 2.7.2
maliciously, meaning of, 2.3.1
manslaughter, 2.7.2
minor injuries, 2.3.1
murder, 2.7.1
psychiatric harm, 2.3.1
racial or religious aggravation, 2.3.1, 2.3.2
recklessness, 2.3.1
sadomasochism, 2.3.1
transferred malice, doctrine of, 2.3.1
unlawfully, meaning of, 2.3.1
weapons or instruments, descriptions of, 2.3.1
wound, meaning of, 2.3.1
wounding, meaning of, 2.3.1, 2.3.2

X (formerly known as Twitter)
communications causing distress, anxiety, or serious harm, 7.12.1
XL Bully dogs, 11.6.5

young people *see* **children and young persons**

zombie knives, 8.9.4